America on the Couch

To Vakil,

With love and many blessings,

from Pythia

ALSO FROM LANTERN BOOKS

Pythia Peay
American Icarus
A Memoir of Father and Country
448 pp, 978-1-59056-441-7, hardcover

America on the Couch

Psychological Perspectives on American Politics and Culture

PYTHIA PEAY

When an American says that he loves his country, he means not only that he loves the New England hills, the prairie glistening in the sun, the wide and rising plains, the great mountains, and the sea. He means that he loves an inner air, an inner light in which freedom lives and in which a man can draw the breath of self-respect.—**Adlai Stevenson II**

Lantern Books ● New York
A Division of Booklight Inc.

2015
Lantern Books
128 Second Place
Brooklyn, NY 11231
www.lanternbooks.com

Printed in the United States of America.

Library of Congress Cataloging-in-Publication Data

Peay, Pythia.
America on the couch : psychological perspectives on American politics and culture / Pythia Peay.
    pages cm
  ISBN 978-1-59056-488-2 (alk. paper)—ISBN 978-1-59056-448-6 (ebook)
    1.   United States—Civilization—Psychological aspects. 2.   United States—Politics and government—Psychological aspects. 3.   Psychology—United States. 4.   Psychologists—United States—Interviews. 5.   Psychohistory. I. Title.
  E169.1.P385 2015
  901.9—dc23

                          2014049782

To Terry and Anne Peay

Contents

—Contents—

Introduction

The Force that Is America

IN 1966, WHEN I was fifteen, I read a book called *If the Sun Dies* by Oriana Fallaci (1929–2006), the legendary and fierce Italian journalist. Fallaci's account of her trip to America to explore the U.S. space program, and the extensive interviews she conducted with American astronauts on technology, space travel, and humanity's future, fired my youthful self with idealistic hopes and dreams that streaked across my imagination like rockets aimed at the future. As the oldest daughter of an airman who flew for TWA, I couldn't help but be thrilled by Fallaci's book. The sky and everything in it—the stars, the sun, the moon, and beyond—made up our family myth. The space age was just dawning over the horizon of American life; satellites bobbed through the sky above our Missouri farm; and autographed posters of American astronauts hung on the wall beside my bed. Restless to get off the farm and on with life, I felt stirred to do something similarly daring one day, even to become an astronaut myself and be the first woman on the moon, to reach out to the farthest edges of life and the human condition. Eventually, most of what I remembered reading faded with time, save one vivid, photographic image: that of Fallaci, a tall, striking woman, walking along a sandy white beach in Florida with an astronaut, both immersed in conversation on esoteric and existential matters, such as, for instance, what would happen to humanity when the sun dies.

How and when fate enters our lives is at least as great an enigma as the metaphysics of space travel. As a starry-eyed young dreamer, and as my father's daughter, I found it easy to get caught up in the mystique of the space age as a literal calling to sojourn among the planets. Soon enough, I would discover that being an *actual* astronaut was not a profession I was in any way cut out for. There was, for instance, my fear of heights, my sensitive traveler's stomach, and my complete lack of mathematical skills. But the experience of reading *If the Sun Dies* did contain some hints on the direction I would eventually take in life. Being a writer was one. Being a journalist was another. As for writing about outer space . . . well, I went in the opposite direction, toward inner space, the interior dimension of the human psyche. The fascination astronauts had held for me in my youth was replaced in adulthood by an attraction to the great founding psychologists, especially C. G Jung, but also Sigmund Freud, Wilfred Bion, D. W. Winnicott, John Bowlby, Melanie Klein, and Heinz Kohut—pioneers who had ventured into the darkest recesses of human nature in search of insights into why we are the way we are. The dimension that these thinkers had attempted to map was as unknown, uncharted, and, I might add, as frightening as outer space.

In feature stories and columns, I turned to contemporary psychologists and psychoanalysts for their insights and comments, learning more about the application of psychology to the problems of everyday life. Venturing into individual analysis, I began to get the lay of the land of my own psyche, tracing the headwaters of my emotions and complexes and examining my nightly dreams—an undertaking, as I discovered, that is lifelong and ongoing. And if as a girl my zeal for astronaut heroes and space travel had been sparked by my father's profession, so, too, in the end, had he inadvertently inspired my interest in psychology. For whereas one aspect of my father was an adventuresome aviator, on the ground with his family he was an emotionally wounded man afflicted with depression and alcoholism. The depths my Icarus father plunged into at home, I grew to understand, had something to do with the heights he traversed at work behind the panels of the cockpit. I also came to see that part of my quest to learn more about psychology and the human psyche was a search to understand what ailed him.

I entertained one other bold dream when I was young and imagining a life for myself. I wanted to be the first woman president. Some time after I'd read *If the Sun Dies*, I became involved with a student group organized by a local politician. We took a trip to Jefferson City, the capital of Missouri, where we visited the governor in his spectacular, high-rise office, lined with windows that revealed wide vistas. The governor's enormous, polished desk, the photos taken with presidents and other politicians, the state flag, and all the accoutrements of power were on full display. But the man behind the desk didn't seem as impressive as the trappings of his office. He was obsequious without seeming to really care about any of us; whispering into the ear of the man who'd brought us, he appeared to my admittedly naive younger self as a kind of sly fox.

Politics, I decided then and there, was not my vocation. Still, it would always interest me, and later I would be inspired by Robert F. Kennedy and Eugene McCarthy, and would join in the antiwar marches and activism and protest movements of the late sixties and early seventies. Throughout the years, I maintained an abiding interest in what was going on in the messy and unpredictable world of American politics—whether it was Bill Clinton's impeachment, 9/11, the wars in Iraq and Afghanistan, the election of the first black president, or the BP oil spill. Filling in the blank places in my education, I read histories of the early years of the United States and biographies of the Founders, and began to weave themes on my country throughout my writing.

Over time my fascination for America, politics, and psychology began to coalesce into a distinct form. Psychologists had available to them a body of knowledge on human nature unique to the modern era, one that had been accumulating since Freud published *The Interpretation of Dreams* in 1900. What was more, they were privy to the deepest feelings, secrets, and struggles of individuals. More than anyone, these psychotherapists, psychologists, and psychoanalysts were witnesses to how the American dream played out in the actual day-to-day lives of the country's citizens. And, as I also came to discover during interviews I began to conduct with them on various themes, these "astronauts of inner space" had a strong sense of responsibility toward and keen interest in the external, socioeconomic, and cultural realm of the body politic, and the way that the outer world shaped their clients' emotional and subjective lives. There was even, I discovered to my delight, a unique school of psychology called "psychohistory," which applied the principles of psychology to historical events.

In this manner was born my idea to "put America on the couch," and to ask psychologists to analyze the American psyche. So, too, grew the idea to write about America through the story of my Greatest Generation father, Joe Carroll, and to examine how the historical background of his life had shaped him psychologically. What started out as one book eventually became two: *American Icarus: A Memoir of Father and Country* and now *America on the Couch*, a collection of interviews with psychologists on a range of issues. Each interview, for instance, has been read and reviewed for clarity and accuracy before publication by all the participants.

Indeed, rather than dispassionate interviews, *America on the Couch* is a series of engagements and encounters with thinkers whose work I find opens new angles and perspectives on the American experience. Like every person, I come with certain preoccupations, as do the psychologists with whom I talk. And like many of us in this disputatious country founded on freedom of speech and association, neither they nor I are shy about revealing our political leanings. Because we're involved in a conversation in real time, our thoughts turn to the issues of the day as well as eternal truths. We're no less likely to obsess on something that appears significant at the time, and which later reveals itself to be only a footnote, as we are to miss the momentous event beneath our noses. However, it's my belief that the men and women in this volume have discerned beneath everyday life vital undercurrents and significant themes about our country that hold as true in, say, 1995 as they do two decades later and did two centuries earlier. Indeed, one gift of this collection is the ability to hear the voices of those psychologists who, although no longer with us, speak to us again—full of life and questions, rich with the wisdom of age. That I had the opportunity to speak with the men and women you'll meet in this volume evokes many emotions in me involving the passage of time and what it means to grow old. Even as the book was going to press, I learned of the passing of Robert Langs, M.D., who appears in Part V.

There is one more part to the story of how this book came to be, and it has to do with my Argentine-born mother, who'd come to this country as a young bride of twenty-two. When you're raised by a mother who was a first-generation immigrant, and who was engaged in observing and analyzing the habits and customs of her newly adopted culture, you grow up with a constant awareness of the United States almost as a kind of person, with a force and a will of its own. Those of us born and raised in the United States may be aware of the country's huge political, military, and economic presence in the world. But we may not be as aware of America in its more mythic persona, and the place it occupies in the psyches of other peoples around the world: of how it holds the promise of freedom and possibility; where a better life is always possible and dreams come true. Just as any person in a position of authority has a responsibility to wield their power in as wise, equitable, and just a manner as possible, so America has a responsibility not just as a global superpower economically and militarily, but to live up to its own ideals, to be more conscious of the image it projects, and aware of the influence it has on shaping people's lives and aspirations around the globe.

Do we, for instance, aim *only* to be a military superpower, and a country where guns are liberally brandished as an emblem of individual rights? A place where it is increasingly difficult to earn a living; where the getting and spending of money is life's sole and central aim; and where success is measured by the possessions we own? A place where our consumer-based lifestyle, the largest in the world, is on track to destroy not just the land that we love, within our own borders, but the rest of the global environment of which we are just a small part? Is *that* what the Founders had in mind when they undertook their historic venture, risking their lives to build from the ground up the world's largest experiment in democracy and self-government?

In it origins and in its very nature, America has always aimed, like its spaceships, upward, outward, and onward toward the bright horizon of its dream of freedom, happiness, individuality, independence, and equality. We raise high the red, white, and blue flag of victory, success, and achievement—but keep folded out of sight the worn and tattered flag of defeat, grief, depression, loss, marginalization, and oppression that also signifies its people. If America were a person, he or she could be described as leading a hardworking, successful professional life during the day, but then going home at night to an unhappy marriage and even unhappier children. This America drinks or spends away the disturbing feelings of dissatisfaction that intrude upon his or her well-ordered world, and willfully ignores the less materially successful, poorer, and hungrier people in his or her family.

This scenario is compounded by the fact that the messages this outwardly successful person receives from the culture is to get up each day and, no matter what, keep going, while suppressing this more non-rational, downward-pulling, and more empathic side of life—the part that a psychologist would be well-equipped to deal with. Indeed, that psychologist might warn America that, if ignored, these symptoms could destroy the very life that the country had worked so hard to achieve. Our psychologist might also say that, if listened to and decoded for their messages, these symptoms might lead in the end to a more inwardly meaningful and outwardly ecologically sustainable life.

One of Jung's great contributions to our understanding of psychology was the principle of "the opposites." What is high is linked to the low. Cold moves along a spectrum of temperature to heat. Happiness is inextricably joined to sadness, as failure is the other side of the coin of success. War is at the farthest end of peace, two opposites fatefully bound together. Thus, to Jung, a healthy psychology includes awareness of both poles: including the dark with the light, the great with the ordinary, the healthy with the sick and wounded, the great with the humble.

Using this model, the experiment this book undertakes is to bring America itself as a client into the psychologist's office, to enter a kind of therapy for the distaff side of the American dream. It is to unpack the suffering our country undergoes from the random rampages of violence and high rates of addiction; the failure to protect its land and natural resources; the turning of a blind eye to the meaninglessness of its consumer-based way of life; the ignoring, and, by turn, inflammation of the political and class divisions among its people; and where its original guiding vision is in danger of disappearing.

Many others have made it their task to bring to light America's less visible, less attractive, and destructive side. And although psychologists don't have all the answers to society's problems, they do bring a different set of ideas and perspectives that can prove useful in examining and resolving some of the issues we face as a country. Contrary to the idea that politics is a rational and objective business, psychotherapists by virtue of the work they do bring attention to the dangerous ways unconscious psychological complexes can erupt, roil, and disrupt the best-ordered political career or organization: President Clinton's impeachment that stemmed from his affair with Monica Lewinsky, for example, or New York governor Eliot Spitzer's downfall after his visits to a prostitute. Institutionalized forms of racism and oppression; illegal forms of torture that violate our fundamental principles of human rights; misguided military actions that kill innocents and that worsen, rather than improve, relationships among communities and with other countries, show that state and national governments, too, can be seized by madness and led to do things that later prove to be sins against their better natures.

On this topic, Jung had this to say in an interview:

> "[N]owadays particularly, *the world hangs by a thin thread, and that thread is the psyche of man.* . . . There is no such thing in nature as an H-bomb—that is all man's doing. *We* are the great danger. The psyche is the great danger. What if something goes wrong with the psyche? And so it is demonstrated in our day what the power of the psyche is, how important it is to know something about it. But we know nothing about it. Nobody would give credit to the idea that the psychic processes of the ordinary man have any importance whatsoever. (McGuire and Hull, 1977 [editors' italics])

Although psychology did not exist and was unknown to the Founding Fathers, I like to think that, given their avid curiosity, open-minded and adventure-seeking intellects, and study of Greek and Roman philosophy, they would have taken an interest in this new branch of knowledge. After all, the United States emerged from the European Enlightenment. As the Founders worked to create a new social order, they might have welcomed the insights of a Freud or a Jung into the nature of the individual they'd placed at the centerpiece of their new form of democratic government. As many thinkers make clear throughout this book, growth in material wealth, especially in an era of heightened ecological concerns, can only take humankind so far. Perhaps it is time for a second Enlightenment, a renaissance of ideas applied to the country as a whole. These ideas would power a more environmentally and psychologically sustainable path into the future—one that would guide us to becoming a sager world leader that more truly lived up to its own ideals.

The six parts of *America on the Couch* offer a wealth of perspectives on those symptomatic areas of life in this country where we are faced with continually recurring problems—but also where we may break through to new understandings. Part I, "Violence in America," addresses, among other themes, the psychological and historical reasons for the gun's grip on the American psyche; the violence present in our historical origins; the guilt we bear around Hiroshima and the lingering trauma of 9/11; violence as it exists in *all* our psyches; heartbreak as it drives young men to mass shootings; and war as it lives on to haunt our traumatized veterans. In "Addicted America," psychologists discuss America's moralistic attitudes toward alcoholism and other forms of addiction, and its refusal to address addiction as a disease; the psychological and spiritual drives for altered states of ecstasy and transcendence underlying the use of hallucinogens and other drugs; the archetypal "God" of alcoholism; and the psychological meaning of food disorders.

In Part III, "America's Vanishing Environment," psychologists analyze our deep denial of and dissociation from the environmental disaster unfolding around us, and for which the American way of life is largely responsible, and offer ways to break through our collective numbness. They discuss the "archetypes" of nature and waste, as they appear in our dreams; how nature might be speaking to us through the phenomenon of crop circles; how the disoriented honey bees signal humans' looming "refugee" crisis; and the psychological changes Americans will encounter as they are forced to adjust to the coming "downshift" in their resource-dependent lifestyle—and those parts of our national character that can lead the way forward.

In Part IV, "A Poverty of Meaning: Capitalism and Consumerism," psychologists describe the adverse psychological effects on the American people of our addiction to materialism, not just as it has impacted the environment, but in the unanticipated ways it has robbed us of more genuinely authentic and satisfying ways of living, as well as human connection and creativity. They explore how we have failed to see the "whole package" involved in our economic choices, and how technological forms of consumerism have changed the very shape and definition of the "American self." They include stories of those who have abandoned the corporate world for the less remunerative, but perhaps more meaningful, world of psychological and spiritual growth and development.

Part V, "Presidents, Power, Politics, and Polarization," presents new models for the American presidency, such as the "nurturing father"; the discounted factor of empathy as it operates to bind our fractured body politic and to bring people together across our polarized body politic; how anxiety stresses political organizations, but also how it is an inevitable concomitant of democracy; and childhood trauma as a background force that has shaped all but two of the American presidents. Finally, in Part VI, "The American Soul," psychologists reflect on the deeper meaning of our abiding myths of freedom and independence; the importance of balancing our emphasis on individualism with community and commonality; the unique qualities of the soul of the nation's capital, Washington, D.C.; our enduring myths of "The Promised Land" and the "New World," and how through honoring multiculturalism and through living up to our motto, *E Pluribus Unum*—"out of many, one"—we fulfill our country's highest purpose and our gift to the world.

Readers will find in this book two repeating themes: the need for more connection, relationship, and community to offset what many thinkers see as the culture's exaggerated emphasis on individualism; and, equally as important, the vital necessity to pay less attention to the demands of our outer lives, in order to give more serious reflection to our inner, subjective, feeling, emotional states. I use the word *vital* because without that psychological awareness, we are in danger of falling victim to the different forms of suffering and afflictions addressed in each of these six sections: the violent acting out of historic and personal trauma–related complexes; addictive behaviors driven by genes, disconnection from the deeper side of life, and the need to soothe our fears and anxieties; consumer-driven lifestyles that do damage to our environment and that gloss over the needs of our inner selves; a political system driven by divisiveness, big money, and power for power's sake; and the tarnishing of our beautiful American soul and our original vision of democracy, freedom, liberty, and justice. The kind of psychologically conscious citizenship that strives to be more aware of the way we live, why we make the choices we do, and how we impact the surrounding culture is, I believe, a form of service, just as important as the political, humanitarian, and military kinds.

Readers will also notice what I have *not* included in this project, including most importantly racism, gender issues, immigration, education, religion, and the family, among other things. There is also a gender and racial imbalance, with more white male psychologists interviewed than women and other ethnicities. These are omissions for which I apologize; my only excuse is that the book took on a life of its own, and in the end there simply wasn't room or time enough to include all the themes I wanted to cover. I do, however, plan to compile a second volume that will redress this imbalance. Readers may also note that even each major topic in this volume is not covered to the extent that it could be; countless books and articles have been published on these issues, and the statistics of each issue are always in continual flux. But what readers will find, and that I hope will satisfy, are different ways of seeing the United States—views that will broaden, deepen, and enrich themselves as citizens, and this American life. ■

Part I

Violence in America

There is nothing wrong with a little violence so long as it stands between civilization and savagery.—**Robert Jewett and John Shelton Lawrence**, *The American Monomyth*

The terms of American equality and identity are defined by the arts of the gunfighter.—**Richard Slotkin**, *Gunfighter Nation: The Myth of the Frontier in Twentieth-Century America*

WHY BEGIN THIS BOLD endeavor to explore America's psyche with a chapter on violence? Because from the moment the first settlers landed on the eastern shores of the New World, violence—and its talismanic symbol, the gun—have been fused with nearly every aspect of the American experience. Violence in America, in fact, was never worse than during the colonial period.[1] Faced with the terrors of a vast and—to them—raw and unknown wilderness, the nation's first immigrants buttressed themselves with faith and guns. So fundamental were weapons to America's beginnings that when in 1637 the General Court of Massachusetts put the outspoken Puritan Anne Hutchinson on trial for heresy, her supporters were ordered to surrender "all such guns, pistols, swords, powder, shot, and match as they shall be owners of, or have in their custody, upon pain of ten pounds for every default." On account of the ongoing Pequot War between the natives and the settlers, writes Eve LaPlante in *American Jezebel*, disarming a man at that time was considered a "severe punishment."

For although it might be tempting to think of the Puritans as peaceful, defenseless Christians purified of physical brutality, they proved themselves anything but: at one time killing or leaving homeless "all of the eight hundred inhabitants" of a nearby Indian village. Indeed, one of the ways Anne Hutchinson set herself apart from her community was through her principled opposition to this kind of warlike aggression. Throughout her life she advocated living in peace with neighboring tribes—until that fateful day when her entire family was attacked and scalped alive for being invaders like the rest (LaPlante, 2004). These conflicts revealed that, from the outset, the New World was not the paradise the Puritans had imagined, but an exceedingly dangerous and threatening place.

As noted psychiatrist and psychohistorian Robert Jay Lifton speculates in this part's opening interview, it was the early settlers' anxious and fear-freighted encounters with the wilderness and native peoples that may in fact have laid the psychological foundation for the gun's symbolic place in the developing American identity. In his remarkable work of cultural history, *Gunfighter Nation*, historian Richard Slotkin confirms Lifton's observation, describing the way the myth of the "New Frontier"—another central trope in the American psyche—over time melded into American myths of gunfighting

3

and a kind of renegade lawlessness. Personified by figures like Daniel Boone, Wild Bill Hickok, Annie Oakley, Wyatt Earp, and Jesse James, and fashioned from the simplistic catchphrases of the history of the American West—of six-shooters, sharp shooters, and shoot-outs; good guys and bad guys; outlaws, cattle rustlers, gamblers, and saloons—a uniquely American narrative of violence began to emerge.

As Slotkin emphasizes, this narrative was indeed a mythology—a collection of tales in which guns would become as charged a symbol as the dragon-slaying sword of ancient legends. William F. Cody, for instance, who served briefly as a scout in the Indian Wars, restyled himself for his traveling Wild West shows as "Buffalo Bill," heroic redeemer of civilization against the savages. Wyatt Earp, I learn, traveled to Hollywood to sell his story. Theodore Roosevelt, who had been a frail, asthmatic child, lived for a time as a cattle rancher in the badlands of the Dakotas, dressing in full cowboy regalia. In deliberately fashioning his own "hero persona" writes Slotkin, Roosevelt drew on the exploits of hunter-heroes Daniel Boone and Davy Crockett, even defining history as a series of "great hunts."

These trends culminated in the 1950s when from the pressure-cooker of anxieties heated by the Cold War, a film genre arose of the "gunfighter" Western, in which, says Slotkin, "professionalism in the arts of violence is the hero's defining characteristic." *Shane*, *High Noon*, *Rio Bravo*, and *Gunfight at the O.K. Corral* are all movies, he continues, in which "the role of gunfighting is crucial to the outcome. It is the means by which the oppressed victim gains equality and the immigrant is Americanized. The terms of American equality and identity are defined by the arts of the gunfighter" (Slotkin, 1992).

As Slotkin also points out, the gains of so-called equality won through violence are often made at the expense of democratic ideals. For in a familiar plot twist to these Western legends, the gunfighter hero is all too often forced against his better nature to take the law into his own hands, in order to vanquish the bad guy with predatory intentions. More recently, Harvard psychologist Steven Pinker has likewise attributed America's higher rates of violence to its pioneer origins. Until the twentieth century, Pinker notes, "large parts of the country were in a state of anarchy," and could not count on the government to protect them. When governments finally did arrive, citizens were reluctant to hand over their guns—and because the first government in America was a democracy, he says, "people were able to impose their wishes."[2]

To authors Robert Jewett and John Shelton Lawrence, America's Puritan heritage merged over time with its Western heroic story of guns-horses-and-cowboys frontier violence to produce what they call our fundamental "American monomyth." This is the redemptive narrative, they write in their book of that title, "of an Eden-like society helpless in the face of evil but rescued by an outsider, a superhero, who then disappears again." This powerful theme, the authors continue, has "startling implications for ourselves," with real-world consequences that would carry forward over time—even, as Slotkin points out, shaping the language of the nation's future wars. For so it was, he writes, that American troops would describe Vietnam as "Indian Country," and "search-and-destroy missions as a game of 'Cowboys and Indians'; and Kennedy's ambassador to Vietnam would justify a massive military escalation by citing the necessity of moving the 'Indians' away from the 'fort' so that the 'settlers' could plant 'corn.'"

In America today, these centuries-in-the-making heroic-gunfighter narratives have degenerated into something so pathological as to be rendered beyond human comprehension: the rise of "rampage violence" by lone gunmen opening fire on helpless civilians.[3] Like a sorrowful litany, the names of these mass shootings have now become carved into our collective psyche: Columbine, Tucson, Virginia Tech, Aurora, Fort Hood, Binghamton, and the Washington Navy Yard—a list that will, sadly, be incomplete by the time this book is published.

One of the more recent faces of this tragic American tale belongs to twenty-year-old Adam Lanza. In 2012, Lanza walked into Newtown Elementary School, Connecticut, and turned his Bushmaster rifle not on the "bad guys," but on the most vulnerable innocents of all: twenty six-year-old children seated at their desks, in what would become America's deadliest mass shooting at a school in its history.[4] In Lanza—who was severely isolated and suffered from Asberger's syndrome, and who was obsessed with the Columbine High School shootings, as well as war and violent video games—we see an example of the perfect storm that can occur when serious psychological illness collides with the darker expression of a cultural myth. The deadly wave of young male shooters perpetrating civilian massacres demands not only that we consider new gun regulations and become more psychologically aware, but that we also examine our cultural narratives glorifying violence as an expression of individuality: in our history and in the narratives woven into film, television, video games, and online media. We also need to extend that analysis to those invisible habits and attitudes of violence toward those we live and work with, as well as toward all life and nature.

It is this kind of *sub rosa*, under-the-radar atmosphere of violence that archetypal psychologist James Hillman focused on in an interview I conducted with him nearly twenty years ago (the rest of the interview is included in Part VI). Seated in a television broadcast studio across from the Empire State Building, Hillman reflected on violence in America. "I think we tend to see violence only as somebody shooting everybody up on a train," he said, gazing out the window at the New York skyline.

> But we're making violence too literal: violence has to do with violation. And there's something in our economic structure that is fundamentally violent. Whether we call it take-overs, or talk about corporate raiders, or the abuse of the consumer, a kind of violence is there all the time. Rudeness is violence, and insult is violence, and contempt is violence—and there's a great deal of all that in American culture. There's something about our predatory capitalism that's violent, as is the exploitative vision of production, whether we're exploiting labor, raw materials, or the neighborhood with our pollutants: this is all violence. We've located violence in inner city black men, but that's just part of our old-time racism. So I see violence as happening right in the corporate world, and in what we might call "getting the government off our back" capitalism—the kind of capitalism that doesn't want anyone to tell it what to do. The "this is a free country and I'm going to do any damn thing I want." So I extend the notion of violence.

Statistics add another dimension to our understanding of American violence. Presenting a "big picture" view of the arc of violence throughout history, Harvard psychologist Steven Pinker notes that, from the Middle Ages to the present, there has been a thirty-five-fold decrease in the rate of homicide worldwide. If, Pinker says, we "look at the kind of life that our ancestors presumably lived—a foraging lifestyle, without a government and police force—the rates of death in tribal warfare were really, really high—higher even than in the twentieth century with our world wars."[5] But within that larger historical framework, America occupies a unique place in the world story around violence. Most recently—and perhaps surprisingly—a recent Pew Research Report notes that overall levels of violence in the country have declined. This dramatic drop has been linked to the aging of the Baby Boomers, the waning of the crack cocaine epidemic, and greater incarceration rates—of which America has the highest in the world[6] (and which in my view is yet another expression of violence).

Before we become too complacent, the pace of this decline has begun to slow over the last decade. For although mass shootings account for a relatively small share of shootings overall, half of America's deadliest gun rampages have occurred since 2007.[7] In 2012, levels of violence began once again to tick upward.[8] Compared to other developed countries, violent deaths are more common and occur at a higher rate in the U.S. than in any other wealthy nation.[9] And when it comes to gun ownership and gun deaths, America has no rival, claiming more guns (88 guns per 100 people) and more gun deaths (10 gun-related deaths per 100,000 people) than any other country.[10]

As for that segment of the American population that perishes at higher rates from gunshots, Hillman may have actually been correct when he said that we tend to locate violence in inner city black men: of the 30 Americans on average shot to death each day, half are black males. Making up just six percent of the population, five to six thousand black men are murdered each year.[11] Add to that America's unrivaled military might and pre-eminence[12] as well as our role as the weapons dealer of the world[13] and the revelation of the CIA interrogation and detention programs launched in the wake of the September 11 terror attack[14] and it becomes clear that we are not the exemplars of democracy and protectors of peace we sometimes believe ourselves to be. In a sad postscript to the religious-minded, well-intentioned Puritans who set about four centuries ago to create a heaven on earth on the pristine shores of the New World, the U.S., bristling with weaponry, is now seen as the greatest threat to world peace.[15] It also threatens our own domestic peace. As the ACLU reports, billions of dollars' worth of military equipment from the federal government now flows to state and local police departments for the war on drugs. The use of wartime weapons in everyday policing has turned neighborhoods into war zones, and unfairly targeted people of color.[16]

In the following interviews, seven psychologists go behind the scenes to offer varying angles on the topic of American violence. Robert Jay Lifton discusses the symbolism of the gun and our pioneer origins, America's unaddressed guilt around Hiroshima, and the psychological implications of our role as the first country to use the atomic bomb. New York psychoanalyst and psychohistorian Charles B. Strozier, Lifton's colleague, addresses the lingering trauma of 9/11 on the nation's psyche, how hidden end-of-the-world fears rooted in Biblical beliefs around the apocalypse shaped our response to that event, and the rise of a "new" American violence.

From his perspective living in Milan amid the ruins of the Roman Empire, Jungian psychoanalyst Luigi Zoja speaks about guns as part of a universal archetype (therefore hard to eradicate), America's drone attacks and its "divided soul," or its habit of splitting off uncomfortable feelings around the violence that we do. Jungian psychoanalyst Donald Kalsched, based in New Mexico, places the wave of shootings by troubled young men within the context of underlying trauma, and the possibility for the transformation of violence within a kind of inner and outer democratic process.

New York psychoanalyst Michael Eigen takes us deep into the human psyche, where violence in all its terrors exists in each of us, and offers insights into what to do about that. Santa Barbara–based clinical psychologist Larry Decker shares a lifetime of wisdom from his work with veterans suffering the effects of post-traumatic stress disorder (PTSD) on their wartorn psyches. Finally, clinical psychologist Ginette Paris, also from Santa Barbara, concludes the section with a discussion on the archetypal link between the Greek warrior god Ares and Aphrodite, the goddess of love, and shares her latest research into the neuroscience of heartbreak. She explains how psychologically vulnerable and alienated youth who suffer love's rejection are at risk of becoming deadly mass killers. ∎

Notes

1. Violence in America has been in decline since colonial times: *Crime in the United States*, Wikipedia, online at <http://en.wikipedia.org/wiki/Crime_in_the_United_States>.
2. Quoted in "Why America is More Violent Than Other Democracies," by Ayesha Venkataraman, *U.S. News & World Report*, December 23, 2011.
3. Mass murder, shooting sprees and rampage violence, *Journalist's Resource*, online at <http://www.journalistsresource.org>.
4. Adam Lanza and the Sandy Hook Elementary School Shootings: online at <http://en.wikipedia.org/wiki/Sandy_Hook_Elementary_School_shooting>.
5. "Steven Pinker on Violence," Interview by Indre Viskontas and Chris Mooney, July/August, 2013. *Committee for Skeptical Inquiry* (CSI). Online at <http://www.csicop.org/si/show/steven_pinker_on_violence>. See also Pinker, Steven. *The Better Angels of Our Nature: Why Violence Has Declined*. New York: Penguin Books, 2012.
6. "The United States is the world's leader in incarceration with 2.2 million people currently in the nation's prisons or jails—a 500% increase over the past thirty years." *Incarceration in the U.S.*, The Sentencing Project. Online at <http://www.sentencingproject.org/template/page.cfm?id=107>.
7. "General Homicide Rate Down 49% Since 1993 Peak; Public Unaware." *Pew Research and Demographic Trends*, by D'Vera Cohn, Paul Taylor, Mark Hugo Lopez, Catherine A. Gallagher, Kim Parker and Kevin T. Maass, May 7, 2013.
8. "Violent Crime in U.S. Rises for First Time Since 2006," by Timothy Williams, *New York Times*, June 6, 2013. Also, "Violent Crime Rises for Second Consecutive Year," by Donna Leinwand Leger, *USA Today*, October 24, 2013. Violent crimes rose in 2012 for the first time in six years, led by an increase in major crimes in large cities, according to a report by the FBI after years of steep decline. The last year in which violent crime rose nationally was 2006. Before that, from 1996–2005 violent crime had declined by 17.6 percent. In these statistics, violent crime includes murder, rape, sexual assault, robbery, and assault.
9. *Violent deaths more common in the U.S.:* "U.S. Suffers Far More Violent Deaths Than Any Other Wealthy Nation," by Kevin Freking, *Salon*, January 1, 2013.

10. "U.S. Has More Guns—and More Gun Deaths—That Any Other Country, Study Finds," by Sydney Lupkin, ABCNews.go.com, Medical Unit, September 13, 2013.

11. "The Assault Weapon Myth," by Lois Beckett, *New York Times*, September 14, 2014.

12. "Unrivaled, For Now." *The Economist*, May 3, 2014.

13. "Weapons King: The U.S. is again the world's top arms merchant," with $66.3 billion in sales in 2011, the largest in its history. *The Pittsburgh Post-Gazette*, August 28, 2012.

14. "Rectal Rehydration and Waterboarding: The CIA Torture Report's Grisliest Findings," by Dominic Rushe, Ewen MacAskill, Ian Cobain, Alan Yuhas, and Oliver Laughland, *Guardian,* December 9, 2014. See also "7 Key Points From the CIA Torture Report," by Jeremy Ashkenas, Hannah Fairfield, Josh Keller, and Paul Volpe, *New York Times*, December 9, 2014.

15. "In Gallup Poll, The Biggest Threat to World Peace Is . . . America?" by Eric Brown, *International Business Times*, January 2, 2014.

16. "War Comes Home: The Excessive Militarization of American Policing." Online at <https://www.aclu.org/war-comes-home-excessive-militarization-american-policing>.

—1—

The Gun, the Bomb, and the Wound that Will Not Heal

AN INTERVIEW WITH ROBERT JAY LIFTON, PH.D.

T HERE ARE THOSE WHO make history and those who record history. And then there is Robert Jay Lifton, who in the aftermath of World War II set out to apply the principles of psychology as a way to *understand* the events of history, including such incomprehensible collective traumas as mass genocide. Now eighty-eight, Lifton is widely regarded as a pioneer in the modern discipline of psychohistory: the study of the psychological causes of war and political violence, and how the psychology of individuals shapes historical events.

Lifton began his research in Hong Kong after the Korean War by interviewing former prisoners subjected to Chinese "thought reform," or brainwashing. Next, he dared to delve into the psyches of Nazi doctors, meeting with physicians who'd abandoned the ethics of their profession during World War II to become emotionally detached perpetrators of mass murder at concentration camps—and who suffered no lingering remorse. From his interviews with Japanese survivors traumatized by the dropping of the atom bomb on Hiroshima, Lifton gained insights into the resilience of the human psyche as well as the extreme suffering and psychological consequences of nuclear weapons. And during the war in Vietnam, he organized some of the first veterans' "rap" groups, accompanying them as they shared their emotional agonies around war. He was among the first to recognize the symptoms of PTSD. Lifton is the author of more than twenty books, including most recently *Witness to an Extreme Century: A Memoir.*

The following interview with Lifton took place in the Fall of 1995: after the April 19th Oklahoma City bombing (168 dead, 680 injured), but before the 1999 Columbine School shootings (13 murdered, 27 injured); the 2007 Virginia Tech massacre (32 murdered, 17 wounded); the 2012 Aurora movie theater mass shooting (12 dead, 70 wounded); and the 2012 Sandy Hook elementary slaughter of 20 first graders and six staffers. In the year following that horrific event, gun sales reached record highs, and AR-15s—the firearms used at both the Aurora, Colorado, and Sandy Hook shootings—became the "trendiest" bestselling weapons in history.[1] So it is even more remarkable that, in preparing my interview with Lifton nearly twenty years ago, the topic of guns and the question "Why is America so violent?" should have been uppermost in my mind.

At the time, Lifton had just published a new book marking the fiftieth anniversary of the atomic bombings of Hiroshima and Nagasaki, *Hiroshima in America: Fifty Years of Denial.* Publication of his book, co-authored with Greg Mitchell, came in the aftermath of a firestorm of controversy that had engulfed the nation over a planned Smithsonian exhibit of the atomic bombings at the National Air and Space Museum. In Lifton's view, the fierce debate that arose over how and to what extent the events of August 6, 1945 should be commemorated (such as whether to tell a more complete story, with photos of the decimated city of Hiroshima, numbers of civilian casualties, and photos of and accounts from Japanese victims), exposed America's "raw nerve" over its decision to drop the bomb. Indeed, the topic proved too sensitive to handle, and the museum was forced to cancel the full exhibit they'd originally planned.[2]

In addition to exploring America's "raw nerve" around Hiroshima, Lifton also engages in a discussion around that psychologically loaded national symbol, the gun. How our myths around the gun arose in the vacuum of early America's lack of tradition and acted to shore up its newly developing identity on the frontier of a new world; the psychological consequences to America of being the first to make and use the atomic bomb; and the psychological disruptions of postmodernism as it has shaped contemporary American violence are among the topics of our following conversation.

✳

Pythia Peay: I'd like to ask you a simple question from the point of view of those who, like myself, sometimes wonder about America: "Why are we so violent?"

Robert Jay Lifton: This is a very large question. I find myself a little reluctant to plunge in.

PP: Then let me ask you, having just read your book *Hiroshima in America*, how America's use of the bomb affected us in that regard. Did it alter *how* we are violent, in the sense that violence could now be done from a distance, and thus more easily and frequently?

RJL: I think that American violence starts long before nuclear weapons. Although every nation has its own version of violence, I tend to see us as more violent collectively in certain ways than other peoples—and yet for more general, historical reasons than for reasons of personal badness.

PP: Do you mean that we aren't intrinsically violent as a people, but that historical events influenced us in that direction?

RJL: Yes, I think it has to do with historical and psychological patterns that we've developed over the centuries. I also think a lot of our violent tendencies have to do with American attitudes toward the gun. There's almost a kind of "sacralization" of the gun in our society. As strange as it sounds, I believe that the gun almost replaces tradition. Or to put it another way, America is a culture that lacks a traditional base, and there is a way in which the gun has filled that gap. It has been central to American thinking. And I believe that is a very harmful and self-defeating kind of psychological and historical tendency.

PP: When you say we lack tradition, what do you mean?

RJL: America was built on patterns of movement around the constantly moving frontier and continuous immigration. We also didn't start with a traditional culture in place; maybe no country does, but we had even less of one to begin with. So in America we have all sorts of cultures coming together and forming the concept of "the American." But our identity has always been shaky, and we've always been uneasy about our lack of a longer history and of a traditional culture. Sometimes that uneasiness has made us emphasize what history we do have all the more strongly. So what I'm saying is that as a country we tend to look for ways to compensate for the absence of a traditional cultural base. And in my view the identity we've built around conquering the wilderness, the gun, and our constitutional right to self-defense together form a major compensation for that absence of tradition.

PP: Why the gun in particular? Is it just because, as you were saying, it became prominent for historical reasons?

RJL: The gun is tied up with our American ideal of the heroic and with later commercialization. We saw ourselves as conquering the wilderness and the native peoples. And the gun was key to that. The gun is also called "the great equalizer"— so ironically it was seen as a democratizing device. It was an expression of personal power that gave individuals some sense of control over life and death, perhaps compensating for the terror and fear that many people must have felt in this country in its early decades. So the gun became a symbol on many levels of a kind of organizing principle; as an expression of individualism and individual power; and as a way of dealing with anxieties about death and vulnerability. For all those reasons, the gun became more important to us than perhaps to any other culture

Just before he died, I had a conversation with Richard Hofstadter, the distinguished historian of America. He told me that of all of his discoveries, his most discouraging finding was the inability of Americans to come to terms with the gun. And although I'm the last to diminish the centrality of nuclear weapons in terms of American violence, much begins with the focus on the gun and the near deification of the gun in terms of American violence.

PP: So what would America have to do to come to terms with the gun?

RJL: It's important to see it as a continuing struggle. If you look at the biographical details of Timothy McVeigh, for example, he's an example of someone who had an absolute obsession with guns. But as I've learned from taking part in various political struggles, although it's necessary to take certain actions, our goals can never be fully achieved. For instance, it's necessary to get rid of nuclear weapons. But we will do well if we bungle through and diminish them significantly and gain further control over them. So one has to have large goals and has to see the whole process as a continuing struggle with no end. And I feel that way about the American struggle with guns.

PP: So we will never be a country that doesn't own guns.

RJL: Yes, but much can be achieved short of perfection, or short of eliminating guns in our society, at least in terms of restricting them and restraining their use. That is hard enough to do even in modern ways.

PP: Do you have a concern about how guns are romanticized in this culture? One of my sons, for instance, said that men are told all the time to be nice and to be good, and to not be violent or break any laws. But he said that every time you go to the movies or watch television, that kind of violent behavior is all you see—not to mention all the conquerors in history who are made out to be so exciting.

RJL: That's a very good observation. I'm very concerned about the romanticization of violence and of the gun in particular, especially its presentation in heroic dramatic form in which there is little pain and real suffering. When I worked with antiwar Vietnam veterans we came to refer to it—and it was their term—as "the John Wayne" thing. It was a term that stood for a particular type of American heroic figure with certain good traits: loyalty, bravery, chivalry, and protectiveness toward women. But in this myth there's no real blood, there is essentially only triumph of the good without pain, suffering, or death, and the women have to be quiet and without opinions.

Many of the antiwar veterans that I worked with felt that they had been lured into the Vietnam War out of patriotism, but also in the spirit of that distorted American romanticism around war and violence that plays out in the media. But although I strongly agree with these veterans and your son, I also believe that although the media have a part to play in our American narrative around violence, it's not the central part. The central themes of violence are in the culture itself and in our history. The media exploit these cultural tendencies often and without conscience—but they don't create it.

PP: So then the media are reflecting, and perhaps exaggerating, something already in our historical character?

RJL: That's right. But what is at issue here is the quality of the way in which they reflect it. If you reflect violent tendencies in ways that are serious in their artistic reach, then you're making a critique of that violence, as compared to exploiting those tendencies for momentary appeal with bad art. So the *quality* of what's portrayed on film and on television and in books has a very important moral dimension. For example, there is nothing immoral about Shakespeare's tragedy *Macbeth*. Indeed, one can learn a lot about violence and about the consequences of violence from *Macbeth*.

PP: Do you have examples of contemporary films that might treat violence in the way that *Macbeth* did? For instance, I'm curious what you think about the film *Pulp Fiction*. Many viewers saw it as kind of humorous and edgy, with brilliant dialogue, while others were sickened by the violence.

RJL: I have mixed feelings about *Pulp Fiction*. I think it's an example of evoking almost in caricature the violence in our society. In itself, that would be admirable—except that in the movie there was an element of joyousness in its evocation of violence. So to me the movie was a kind of "two-headed," mixed moral presentation of violence that said something important, yet without being a truly exemplary or responsible take on American violence.

PP: And yet in your book *The Protean Self* you also write about the contemporary self and its sense of mockery and the absurd. *Pulp Fiction* certainly had that postmodern element, and so I wonder how this relatively recent development of postmodernism and moral relativism plays into this discussion around violence?

RJL: If one is sensitive to historical currents, it's in the nature of our time to be an explorer of moral and intellectual issues, as well as other forms of experience. But it's a struggle to combine being exploratory and experimental, while at the same time retaining some moral code of the self. There are many divisions within the postmodern movement; the one position that I take to be irresponsible is the notion that there is no self, no values, and no context. My own work has led me to adopt a more hopeful position shared by others within a division of postmodernism: that of sustaining a sense of self while at the same time living with many-sidedness and flexibility—as opposed to the all-or-none rigidity of fundamentalism.

PP: For most of us going about our daily lives, the subtle realities of postmodernism and moral relativism aren't something we give much thought to. And yet at some deep level, we're all disturbed by these emotionally unsettling cultural trends.

RJL: We're all affected by a widespread sense that something is happening that we're unclear about, and that history is moving in confusing ways. What we once took to be unchanging realities, or clear moral precepts or family arrangements, are no longer fixed in place. And this has led to feelings of stark dislocation—a sense that the rules and symbols that seemed so steady in the past are no longer so clear and unchanging. So what we call postmodernism grew out of that sense of civilization-in-transition that emerged out of the late twentieth century of terrible holocausts and upheavals. Together with the speed and confusion of cultural change, this set of historical circumstances has combined to create a sense of dislocation and of being a survivor—and a confused one at that.

PP: So would you say that one of the causes of violence today is a reaction to the anxieties of the historical moment we're living in?

RJL: Yes, that's right. My argument is that we would do best to recognize that this confusion is inherent in our historical moment. Now that doesn't *solve* the question of violence. But it does help us to understand that a lot of violence stems from the discomfort and anxieties many feel around the postmodern self, with its many-sidedness and moral flexibility, that has been thrust upon us by the times we live in. When you look at the violent expressions of various fundamentalist groups (whether religious, ethnic, or political) they often have a powerful and sometimes violent impulse to assert a monolithic vision of absolute truth and a desire to simplify things into a vision of a past of perfect harmony that never was—and to destroy any who contest it, or who are seen as enemies of their mission.

So really, what we call fundamentalism is a reaction to openness. Even the movement with that name which began in Protestant Christianity in the early twentieth century began in response to liberal Protestantism, and the fear that liberal Christianity would go so far that the "fundamentals" of their faith would be lost.

PP: Is violence a natural impulse in human nature that's "gone wrong" or that is misdirected? It sounds odd, but is there some positive way of looking at violence?

RJL: In my work on violence, and especially in my book *The Broken Connection*, I talk about violence as a misdirected effort to restore or regain vitality. There are studies of individuals who are depressed or withdrawn, but who after committing an act of violence experience a surge of vitality—so in that sense it's a misdirected potential.

Violence is also often bound up with a search for recognition and identity. In studies we did with inner city black youth, we found that for teenagers the acquisition of a gun functioned as a center for identity, or as an object around which an identity could be built. So that when young kids who felt afraid and anxious in their environment got a gun, others were then afraid of them. There are parallel patterns among deracinated white groups who are not only poor, but who are radically dislocated in terms of family and subculture, and who suffer feelings of worthlessness, of being lost and without status—all these factors can give rise to violence.

PP: So where do nuclear weapons and the atomic bombings of Hiroshima and Nagasaki during World War II come into play with the American narrative around violence?

RJL: For one thing, high technology weapons and nuclear weapons can be epitomized as the most extreme model for ultimate violence without feeling, or what I call psychic numbing.

PP: Why?

RJL: Because with nuclear and high-technology weapons, cause and effect are radically removed from one another. But even more important, America's use of nuclear weapons as a legitimate weapon rendered them respectable. This altered our moral standards in a very harmful way, as after that all other weapons became relatively humane in comparison. So in that sense our use of so-called "conventional" weapons, many of which are not too different in their effects from nuclear weapons in their killing power, became more acceptable.

As a result, we became more hardened as a country, especially in our inability to respond to genocides going on before our eyes, such as in Bosnia and Rwanda.[3] The absence of compassion and the scandalous inability of the world to interrupt those genocides was at least partly influenced by the use of nuclear weapons. So our inability to fully come to terms with nuclear weapons with what they really are has affected our relationship to violence across the board.

PP: How would you interpret the furor that erupted around the National Air and Space Museum's proposed exhibit commemorating the fiftieth anniversary of Hiroshima, and their original vision of offering a more complete picture of what happened that August day in 1945?

RJL: It had to do with what my co-author Greg Mitchell and I call the American "raw nerve" in relation to Hiroshima. When you touch a raw nerve it hurts. We have this agitated, anxious feeling about Hiroshima and Nagasaki, and so we don't like to look at it. Above all, we've spent the better part of half a century avoiding coming to terms with its human effects. In saying this, I don't think we are worse than any other people. I say this again and again—but it happens that we were the ones to make the bomb first, and to use it, and this has had its impact on us. The raw nerve exists because we have a need to fend off any kind of guilt or self-condemnation.

The cancellation of the exhibit was also a political act, more or less on orders from leading Republicans in Congress because of their narrow nationalism. People don't often think of American nationalism. We think of third-world nationalism, but we have more than our share. With narrow expressions of nationalism you can only evoke your country's glory and never look critically at its behavior—especially in terms of actions that may be looked upon as profoundly wrong or misguided, or even in some eyes evil. And that narrow nationalism played a large part in the cancellation of the exhibit.

PP: But even though the original exhibit was canceled, leaving only a very pared down display of the *Enola Gay* at a different museum, with a simple plaque, was something gained from the national debate that was stirred up around this event?

RJL: Yes, the reaction against the exhibit didn't represent the whole country by any means; fortunately, there is another side to America. Because it had the effect of raising the issue of our use of nuclear weapons again, we came closer to a national dialogue on Hiroshima and Nagasaki in 1995 than we've ever had before—including admirable statements by some in our main media. The Peter Jennings ABC documentary[4] was a classic in its open-mindedness and its courage in looking at various sides of the issue. So that is the Jeffersonian side of our country that one should never give up on.

PP: Can you say more about America's Jeffersonian side?

RJL: That's the side of our historical character that has to do with true freedom of speech, and the right and even the *obligation* to speak critically about one's government when one considers it wrong. When it comes to Hiroshima, it's not a question of defending Japan, and being blind to its atrocities, or of defending America's right *not* to look at the consequences of Hiroshima or Nagasaki. Everyone is obligated to look at the past and especially at destructive behavior in the past. And I believe that is in keeping with the American Jeffersonian spirit.

PP: So whether we were right or wrong in dropping the bomb, it's a moral act for the country to look back and examine its decisions and ask questions?

RJL: Absolutely. Beyond condemning our use of the weapon, which I do, we can't deny its danger to the human future. Once we have that perspective, the question around nuclear weapons centers on their threat to human existence in general.

PP: Would you say that since Hiroshima, humankind has been psychologically affected in ways that we're not aware of with regard to the future, and how we think of it or look forward to it?

RJL: Yes, I do. I've written in *Hiroshima in America*, and in many other places, about our fear of "futurelessness." We all struggle at some level with the idea of survival: Will we live out our lives, and more importantly will our children and grandchildren fully live out their lives? But nuclear weapons are more bound up with feelings of fear, and even anticipation and expectation, of the end of the world. No one is entirely free of these feelings; it's a worldwide phenomenon, but it's also stronger in those countries that have felt most vulnerable to nuclear weapons—and it's always the possessors of nuclear weapons who feel most vulnerable to them.

PP: Is this fear around whether or not humanity will have a future something new to the human condition?

RJL: What's new is our capacity to eliminate ourselves as a species with our own technology, by our own hand, and to no purpose. That combination is new. It's hard to know how much people in early centuries became adapted to losing siblings or parents or children to disease. But the idea of a sudden mass collective dying by our own hand is what is new.

PP: This takes us into the arena of evil, because it's hard not to think of that kind of mass apocalyptic ending as a triumph of evil.

RJL: Yes. Killing large numbers of people is to me evil. But one unfortunate finding in my work is that ordinary people can be socialized to evil. For instance, Nazi doctors that I studied were for the most part socialized to evil. They might have been ardent Nazis, but they hadn't killed anyone until they got to Auschwitz. I've begun studying the Japanese cult, Aum Shinrikyo, which released poison gas in the Japanese subway [in 1995].[5] Once again, I found that these were ordinary people—including physicists, doctors, and other professionals—who were drawn to that cult for various reasons, and who then became involved in the evil act of manufacturing and releasing sarin gas, as well as plans to do the same with bacteriological weapons and even nuclear weapons.

PP: I find it difficult to take in the fact that people can be so easily socialized to do evil.

RJL: Yes, but although we need a vocabulary of good and evil, we have to be careful not to absolutize these concepts, and to see the good as "us" and the evil as "them." Rather, it's wiser to see good and evil as human potential—as the potential of every newborn, depending upon experiences, directions, and tendencies as opposed to some absolute inborn characteristic.

PP: You mean to say that each one of us could be socialized to do evil, violent acts?

RJL: That's right. Potentially anyone, you or me, could be socialized into an evil project. Of course, it helps to know that this is possible and therefore to look critically at whatever project one is joining, and not hide behind one's own ostensible good or even one's profession as a healer.

PP: Anyone can be socialized to do evil. But at the same time, doesn't culture play a role? A friend just came back from working and living abroad in Egypt, for instance, and he said that compared to the way we do business here, where everyone is so aggressive and competitive, people there were much more polite and kind. Are we an assertive culture by nature, and does this go back to our emphasis on individualism?

RJL: It's possible. There is in American life a "can-do" spirit. We don't want to accept any problem as insoluble. That attitude can have wonderful qualities, and in the best of American minds you see that expressed in a very impressive way, unimpeded by the restraints of traditional thinking. But this same can-do spirit and the sense that anything can be solved can also lead to a kind of aggressiveness. I don't think it's the source of American violence, and I don't know that it makes us more violent—but I do think it can be an extremely aggressive form of expression. And I do think there is an American model of masculinity that allows for less softness and gentleness than in other countries. Of course, one should be careful about romanticizing other cultures because there may be hidden violence underneath that softness. Still, a little bit of softness in the American man wouldn't hurt! ▪

Notes

1. "The American Gun Culture: Stand Your Ground Against the Deadly Use of Popcorn," by Bob Cesca, *The Daily Banter*, January 15, 2014.
2. To celebrate the bombing's fiftieth anniversary in 1995, the cockpit and nose section of the *Enola Gay*, the B-29 used to drop the bomb over Hiroshima, were put on exhibit at the National Air and Space Museum (NASM) in Washington, D.C. After controversy arose over the accompanying description on the plaque (whether to list the number of Japanese casualties), the *Enola Gay* was moved in 2003 to NASM's Steven F. Udvaar-Hazy Center, outside the city, where the entire restored B-29 is on permanent display.
3. From April to July 1994, Hutu rebels murdered between 500,000 and a million Tutsis and moderate Hutus in Rwanda. The United Nations and U.S. President Bill Clinton were widely criticized for their failure to intervene. In 1992, Bosnia and Herzegovina declared independence from Yugoslavia, which led to a war between Bosnian Serbs who wanted to remain in the Yugoslav federation and Bosnian Muslims and Croats who didn't. For four years, the United States, led by President Clinton, took little action against the "ethnic cleansing," concentration camps, and massacres of civilians perpetrated by the Serbs against the Muslims and Croats, leading to criticism of Clinton's indecisiveness. Finally NATO, led by the United States, launched Operation Deliberate Force against Bosnian Serb targets. In November 1995, the parties reached an accord (hosted by Clinton) known as the Dayton Agreement.
4. Peter Jennings ABC News Special: Hiroshima: Why the Bomb Was Dropped. <http://www.filmandhistory.org/documentary/war1/hiroshima-why.php>.
5. On March 20, 1995, members of Aum Shinrikyo, a Japanese cult led by Shoko Asahara, released sarin gas on the Tokyo subway system, killing 13, seriously hurting 54 people, and affecting a further 980.

—2—

The Illness that We Suffer

Why 9/11 Felt Like the End of the World

AN INTERVIEW WITH CHARLES B. STROZIER, PH.D.

O N SEPTEMBER 11, 2001, psychoanalyst Charles B. Strozier stood on the
sidewalks of Greenwich Village and watched in shock and disbelief as the
World Trade Center towers collapsed into rubble. In the aftermath of the
terrorist attack, many traumatized New Yorkers turned to him for treatment and care.
Survivors and family members in search of insight attended the classes he taught on
terrorism at the John Jay College of Criminal Justice in New York City, where he is a
professor of history as well as the director of the Center on Terrorism. This threefold,
intensified experience of the attacks—on a personal level, as a New Yorker impacted
by the shock of that day along with everyone else, and as an American citizen; on a
professional level, as a psychoanalyst helping clients cope with the aftermath of feelings
of trauma and fear; and as a kind of therapist of the American psyche, later attempting
to analyze one of the nation's most significant collective traumas in its history—placed
Strozier in a unique position, allowing him a vantage point that few others shared.

For all these reasons, I was drawn to interview Strozier on the tenth anniversary of
9/11. Recalling an interview I'd conducted with him years earlier on violence and the
American psyche, I was curious to know how 9/11 fit within the broader and continually
unfolding American narrative on war and violence. Like his colleague Robert Jay Lifton,
Strozier is also a psychohistorian, bringing psychological perspectives to the events
of history. Among the earliest practitioners and a noted authority in this field, he has
published books and scholarly articles on genocide, fundamentalism, the apocalypse,

war, trauma, and the psychology of Abraham Lincoln. He has also been nominated twice for a Pulitzer, including for *Until the Fires Stopped Burning: 9/11 and New York City in the Words and Experiences of Survivors and Witnesses*, a psychological examination of the unconscious meanings of the events of 9/11.

In our interview, Strozier is among the first to draw a distinction between the emotional responses of New Yorkers and those in the rest of the country who watched events unfold on television. Why should that matter, I wondered? Because that crucial psychological difference, he answered, was exploited by members of the administration of President George W. Bush to their political advantage. During our discussion, Strozier also makes a compelling case for how the collective trauma suffered by the American people in the wake of 9/11 activated deep-seated complexes in the national psyche around apocalyptic, end-of-world fears, or what he calls "endism"—the location of the self in some future narrative.

Like Lifton in the previous interview, Strozier also traces the rise of a troubling form of "new violence" in the modern era to America's decision to use nuclear weapons to end World War II. He describes nuclear weapons as "the illness that we suffer," and speaks powerfully about the existential crisis this has engendered in the American psyche. As Strozier commented during our conversation, "When things are moving along normally, whether for an individual or a country, the underlying psyche is less apparent, and remains out of sight. But in times of extreme crisis, one gets a clearer insight into the significant forms in the psyche, such as forms of the self and identity structures."

The following conversation combines my first interview with Strozier, which took place in 1995, with additional material from an interview we conducted in 2011 for the tenth anniversary of 9/11 for *The Huffington Post*.[1]

✳

Pythia Peay: You began your career as an historian, and then quickly became drawn to the emerging field of psychohistory, or exploring history from a psychological perspective. You were the founding editor of *The Psychohistory Review*,[2] as well as a prominent student and colleague of the American psychologist Heinz Kohut, the pioneer of Self Psychology. What psychological insights have you drawn from the tragedy that struck America on September 11, 2001?

Charles Strozier: A very important dimension of 9/11 was the contrast between the experiences of those in New York and the rest of the country. This difference has important political meanings.

PP: Before we get into the political implications, can you describe this contrast in more detail?

CS: For those in New York, 9/11 was a visceral, physical, powerful experience. Many saw people die: bodies were raining down and splattering on the ground—it was awful, just awful. There were scenes of chaos, terror, and fear; people were terrified, streaming across the bridges and to the ferries to get out of the city. Then there were the Trade Towers collapsing on the ground, right before everyone's eyes. When did we last have a hundred-and-ten-story building collapse in front of our eyes? Never! So there was no context for what was happening.

All throughout that Fall, New Yorkers continued to live with bomb threats and the lingering trauma. As the ruins continued to burn, a funereal smell filled the air, as we literally breathed the incinerated victims into our lungs. So although there were what I call different "zones of sadness" in relation to each person's physical distance or proximity to the towers, everyone in New York had a visceral, shared experience of immediacy—in an instant we were all survivors.

PP: What do you mean by "zones of sadness"?

CS: Early on, I began reflecting on the difference between the experiences of those who were at Ground Zero, and those who lived further from the epicenter. For example, I work in Greenwich Village. While I watched the disaster unfold, I was a participant-observer: I had my own suffering, but I didn't see anybody hit the ground, and I wasn't caught up in the cloud of debris. So the idea of zones of sadness emerged as a way of appreciating that, during 9/11, there were various topographic and psychological spaces, each with its own kind of suffering, that ordered New Yorkers' survivor experiences.

By contrast, the rest of the country saw it on television. Those in Omaha or Atlanta, for example, didn't have the same physically gut-wrenching experience of terror as those in New York. Not only has there never been a disaster or a terrorist attack like 9/11, it was also the first time in history that a major disaster was watched *live* on television as the event was unfolding before our eyes. But the psychological context of watching 9/11 on television was one of safety—viewers were literally screened from the scenes of death and fear. And all throughout the experience, older, white father figures (television news anchors and reporters) were telling viewers what it meant.

PP: So what were the political implications of this contrast between New Yorkers' up-close experience of 9/11 and the rest of America, who watched from the security of their homes and offices?

CS: People watching the event on television throughout the rest of the country felt horror and anger, which quickly jumped to rage. The key psychological difference between anger and rage is that anger is directed and has a clear target, while rage is diffuse and undifferentiated; it just rails. That's why rage is so easily appropriated in a political context; it doesn't have an object, which is why it can be politically manipulated. And that is the sequence that I would argue occurred in the rest of the country.

As it happened, by an accident of history, we had an authoritarian regime in government that wanted to project American power and make wars in the Middle East. So the Bush administration was able to take advantage of that undirected rage throughout the populace and move quickly on an agenda that had already been defined. This was no hidden agenda: [Paul] Wolfowitz and [Dick] Cheney had been writing papers all through the nineties; they knew what they wanted. In that sense 9/11 fell like manna from heaven into their laps.

PP: I would have thought rage would have been more connected to being in the epicenter of the tragedy, versus having it screened through the media and physical distance.

CS: If you lived in New York there was sadness and fear, as well as a reluctance to see what was very profound suffering turned into war-making abroad. There was a sense of confusion around what was happening and what Bush was doing. Added to that, throughout the country that Fall there was a surge of patriotism, with giant flags flying everywhere. But many New Yorkers felt that the experience was being taken away from them and used for other purposes, while people were still in deep mourning. They didn't even finish cleaning up the pile until May of the following year; the fires burned until December 20, 2001—so it was really a hundred days of disaster.

PP: What has been the fallout from the way Bush handled—or mishandled—the tragedy of 9/11?

CS: The single most important fact of America in the last decade is that we've been a country at war. Within weeks after 9/11 we were at war in Afghanistan, and then we were in another war with Iraq. And those wars have been *huge* wars. The relatively small number of Americans who died in those wars is highly misleading, as tens of thousands of Iraqis and Afghans have been lost. And in another first, Americans, for the first time in military history, implemented a dramatic new procedure—forward operating surgical theaters and trauma centers—within miles of the front. They also perfected the recovery of the injured through Apache helicopters; the injured were stabilized, then flown to a military hospital in Germany.

For these reasons, most of the thousands of injured American soldiers survived. But they survived maimed, without limbs, and suffering brain injuries and filled with PTSD; many of them fell into alcoholism and homelessness. In addition, except for embedded journalists, the administration didn't allow journalists to cover the war; therefore most journalists weren't critical of these two wars the way they were in Vietnam—there were no Seymour Hershes wandering around Baghdad. So, much of the trauma of 9/11 was quickly absorbed into the collective traumas of the wars in Afghanistan and Iraq. But the fact remains we wouldn't have had either of these wars if it weren't for 9/11.

PP: It sounds like a perfect storm of events: the terrorist attacks; an administration with a pre-existing agenda in place, creating the opportunity to go to war, leading to the longest wars the country has ever fought; along with the trauma of the swelling ranks of physically and mentally injured soldiers.

CS: That's a great metaphor. But the crucial ingredient in this perfect storm is the quality of the leadership we had at that moment, and who took advantage of the psychological context of the culture of fear to sell that war. It's difficult to imagine we would have gone into Iraq if Al Gore had been in office. We probably would have had the Afghan war, but not the one in Iraq.

PP: As I listen to you, it's almost as if something very self-destructive to America happened in the way the wars unfolded that worsened the original trauma of 9/11.

Is that how you would see it?

CS: Absolutely. War itself creates a deepening, aggravating trauma that doesn't stop; the wars in Afghanistan and Iraq created an ongoing double trauma on top of 9/11.

PP: In addition to examining these multiple traumas of 9/11 and the two wars we've waged, I'd like to take a longer view, and ask you to talk about the rise of what you've termed the "new violence" in our time. Can you say more about what that means?

CS: Not only have our means of destruction—in which one bomb in one plane can wipe out an entire city—vastly increased with nuclear weapons. Now, with a pull of the trigger, the simplest handgun can get off thirty to forty shots, and with one load a shooter can wipe out an entire store. That's a twentieth- and twenty-first-century phenomenon; one hundred and fifty years ago it took anywhere from twenty seconds to a minute to reload a rifle for just one shot.

So the magnitude of this change in modern-day weapons is phenomenal. Psychologically, this changes the relationship between the perpetrator and the victim. With death by the sword, for instance, the killer and the victim stared into each other's eyes. But now the physical distance between those who carry out violence and their victims has been greatly increased, and this also creates a psychological and emotional distance, a new kind of numbing.

PP: Has the development of this "new violence" filtered through to the wider culture, then, diminishing or even sundering our capacity for empathy and compassion for others? And did that affect our numbed response to 9/11, allowing Bush to tell us to go shopping, while our soldiers went to war?

CS: Yes, I really believe it has. Violence in this dehumanized form is frightening in its capacity to undermine empathy and feeling for others. People's emotions become even more numbed because of the traumatic effects of this new violence that is becoming more widespread.

PP: You also write about the phenomenon of post-nuclear "apocalyptic dread," and how that shaped America's reaction to the events of 9/11. I grew up during the Cold War, I live just fifteen minutes from downtown Washington, D.C., and for a few frightening hours that day I have to admit I thought the world was coming to an end. I'd always been told that D.C. was one of the safest places on earth, because of our secure air space. When that turned out not to be true, and I saw an army tank drive down the suburban street in front of my house, it was like a myth shattered. I thought bombs would begin dropping from the sky.

CS: So you can imagine what it was like being in New York City! But in fact, the culture of fear that emerged out of 9/11 has to be understood in the context of an apocalyptic experience, as much as the actual event itself. Because it was so intense, so awful, such a surprise and so totalistic, our experience of it was apocalyptic. But we have to distinguish between what the event actually was, and our experience of it. Psychologically, the felt experience of the people within the disaster was that it was an apocalyptic event. It was not: it was monumental, but it was not an apocalyptic event.

PP: What caused these apocalyptic fears to surface so quickly?

CS: Apocalyptic concerns have been a part of human culture since the beginning, receding and becoming more acute during times of crisis, like the Black Death in fourteenth-century Europe. That psychological experience, or "endism," as I call it, is the awareness that we could all die, and that the world could end. Until the nuclear age, however, the idea of the world coming to an end took an act of imagination: typically it's been those with powerful imaginations, like artists, mystics, and psychotics, to even be able to take in these kinds of collective death concerns. It also required God. Historically apocalyptic texts have almost all been religious, such as the New Testament's Book of Revelation,[3] because the agent of the apocalypse is the divine. But with nuclear weapons in the world we don't need God anymore.

PP: And we don't need to have an act of imagination?

CS: It's a different kind of an act of imagination. Apocalyptic dread is a new thing in the nuclear age, because we no longer need God to end things. We live in an age of constant, ultimate threats to human existence—*scientific* threats—because we can end the world, and we know it. We don't need to know how a bomb is made to understand that a bomb in human hands has the capacity to end human history. That knowledge changes the meaning of the present, the past, and the whole notion of the human future, even the meaning of life itself. Therefore, nuclear weapons changed us psychologically in ways that we're just beginning to understand.

PP: How has it changed us psychologically?

CS: There's a paradox, at least in the Western hemisphere, of living in relative peace, and of enjoying technological advances and material abundance: all the markers that should bring some degree of happiness. And yet beneath everything there's a profound malaise about life and uncertainty about the future, because now we've opened up a new dimension that reverses the natural sequence of how things have always been. Whereas before it took an act of imagination to think about the end of history, it now takes an act of imagination *not* to think about it. You're a psychologically sophisticated person, and just look at your response that day! It's an example of how those who never think about such "foolishness" as the apocalypse live in a numbed state—because if you're at all aware, this awareness exists just below the surface, and an event like 9/11 immediately brings these apocalyptic fears and fantasies to the surface.

PP: So what you're describing is a deep-seated existential crisis in the American psyche.

CS: Absolutely. What could be more absurd in the true existential sense than the idea of destroying human civilization in the name of defending one's ideology or country? There is no greater collective insanity. Another way of phrasing this is that the illness we suffer is nuclear weapons.

PP: How deep do the roots of this apocalyptic "endism" and nuclear illness go in the American psyche? The early Puritan settlers fled Europe inspired by visions of starting a new life and with the belief they'd been sent on a divine mission to build a New Jerusalem. There's also the idea of Manifest Destiny, and the notion that God chose us to settle the country. Do these historical beliefs factor into our apocalyptic fantasies and fears, unconsciously contributing to a culture of violence?

CS: Yes, I'd say so. The term "Manifest Destiny" was a very imperialistic ideology that arose in the middle of the nineteenth century, and characterized one of the most aggressive, expansive, and violent times in American history. The Puritans, by contrast, were entirely religious—they wanted to create the "city on the hill." They were idealistic people who were trying to create theocratic communities that were fair. But they often slipped into tyranny and authoritarianism, and by the middle of the seventeenth century they were at war with the Indians. The most important example of the apocalyptic strain in the American character, however, is Christopher Columbus.[4]

PP: Christopher Columbus seems like an unlikely avatar of the apocalypse. I thought his goal was the discovery of new sources of wealth in what he thought would be Asia.

CS: There's been a lot of new scholarship around Columbus; his diaries were translated in 1991. As it turns out, he had incredibly wild apocalyptic fantasies, calculating that the world was going to end in 1650. He believed that he was going to discover the Garden of Eden, where he would find gold, as promised in some readings of the Bible, and that he would also liberate the Holy Land. By his third journey in 1495 he was calling himself the "Christ Carrier."

So what really motivated Columbus in his so-called "discovery" of America were these intensely religious apocalyptic images, together with a willingness to set in motion genocide against the Taino Indians. Within a couple of months of landing on Hispaniola, or present-day Santo Domingo and Haiti, for example, all the mountains were dug up; the women were raped, and men's hands were cut off if they didn't produce their daily quantity of gold. Within fifty years, the Indians were gone, every single one killed by the Spanish.

PP: So what you're saying is that our response to the terrorist attacks on September 11 was filtered through this apocalyptic, end-of-the-world strain in our historical character, which dates back to Columbus and extends forward to the atom bombs we dropped over Hiroshima and Nagasaki to end World War II.

CS: Despite our best efforts to forget, these narratives run deep in the American psyche. But these kind of historical memories can never really be eradicated. People I interviewed for my book, for instance, and who saw the towers come down, saw it as a mushroom cloud, and instantly thought that a nuclear weapon had gone off in New York. People caught in the dust and debris also believed that it was the cloud from a nuclear weapon. So apocalyptic dread is a fearsome idea—something powerfully evoked by 9/11, and even mildly suggested by natural threats such as Hurricane Irene in 2011.[5]

Another one of the intriguing but terrifying aspects of 9/11 is that 2,479 people were killed. I hate to even point this out, but there have been events where far more were killed, such as the Battle of Antietam during the Civil War,[6] the 2010 earthquake in Haiti,[7] and so on. So it's not just the numbers of people that were lost that makes 9/11 so huge. It's the apocalyptic dimension that surrounds it, and that locates the event psychologically, as well as when it happened, how it happened and our experience of it, that led to such an incredible psychological and political perfect storm after 9/11.

PP: In your book *When the Fires Stopped Burning,* written for the tenth anniversary of September 11, you describe the psychological significance around anniversaries that mark both private and cultural loss. You say that on the anniversary of a loss, we "re-enter the psychological space of mourning." Can you say more about that?

CS: Technically this is called "anniversary activation," and it happens especially on the first anniversary, which is the most important, and is usually marked by events or rituals. But not all anniversaries are of equal power to evoke trauma. The individual or collective experience of moving forward is unpredictable, and certain things in subsequent years may trigger remembering. It may also be triggered around analogous events that are not necessarily attached to the anniversary—just as Hurricane Katrina, for example, triggered memories of 9/11.[8] But the tenth anniversary moves personal loss into historical memory.

PP: This is a phrase rich with meaning. Say more.

CS: The story of Sally Regenhard,[9] who lost her son Christian, a fireman, during the attacks, is an example. Christian was among the 41 percent of those who died on 9/11 who were never identified. As a result, among the remains of the unidentified dead are thousands of body parts. In the hope that in future years DNA analysis will be advanced enough to make more identifications, these body parts will be stored in a "Remains Repository" seventy feet beneath the 9/11 Memorial. This repository will be located behind a huge wall with a quote from Virgil's *Aeneid* ("No day shall erase you from the memory of time"), and will include a private family room.

This decision has stirred angst and disagreement in families and survivor groups, including Regenhard. She is apoplectic with anger, for example, over the prospect of millions of visitors making noise and eating candy bars while touring the memorial, including this wall of remembrance adjacent to the main exhibit. Basically, tourists will be walking into a gravesite, and they're not going to be prepared.

PP: This is such a poignant story, and as a mother I can empathize with Regenhard's anger. But how does her experience relate to the psychological significance of the tenth anniversary?

CS: Because her memories of her son are being taken from her and put into the memorial. The decision has been made; it's out of her hands. And that's the tenth anniversary: it's now part of history, which absorbs her trauma. You don't necessarily move on when history absorbs your trauma. But it is different.

PP: What do you hope for America after we cross the threshold of the tenth anniversary of 9/11?

CS: We now have some perspective on how stuck we were before and after 9/11 in the superpower syndrome that led us to a misguided attitude that we could control history. We're also beginning to see how 9/11 was appropriated as a moral cover for outrages like torture and as a justification for expansion of control over our privacy and communications. But the tenth anniversary and subsequent anniversaries have the potential to serve as catalysts in interrupting this trajectory of violence, and to define paths toward peace and security.

After we dropped the atomic bomb on Hiroshima, for example, scores of thousands of Japanese survivors took a stand against nuclear weapons that has continued to this day. After Auschwitz, a global movement arose against mass killings. Likewise, 9/11 survivors can help us define "life-enhancing meanings" from this tragedy; they can also take the lead for the culture in acknowledging America's vulnerability and limitations. We don't have to be weak and helpless to be wise.

PP: But America has a hard time facing the idea of limitations. All I hear when we're faced with any kind of setback is that America is the greatest country in the world and it can do anything it sets out to accomplish. Why is that message repeated over and over again?

CS: Thus we doth protest too much, right? Our assertions of strength ring a little hollow. We're highly vulnerable, and in trouble economically. We have this massive inequality in our social and economic system. We've bled ourselves dry by fighting wars we should never have been fighting in the first place. And in the course of one decade we've profoundly damaged the fabric of our freedoms. We've corrupted our soul by embracing torture, here and abroad. We've lost a lot.

PP: Are there any other traits in the American character that could offset these apocalyptic fears and the rise of a new violence?

CS: I do have hope. There are positive strains of idealism, commitment, and compassion within the American character. Those qualities can move us toward greater community and understanding; so the potential is there for healing some of the deepest and most severe problems that we live with. We have tremendous resources and I think we have genuine democracy and genuine free speech—we can get the word out when we want to. And we have great wealth, even though that wealth is distributed inequitably. ■

Notes

1. "The Psychological Meaning of 9/11: Why That Day Felt Like the End of the World," by Pythia Peay, *The Huffington Post*, September 9, 2011.
2. The journal was founded in 1972. In 1986, Strozier turned over his position as editor to a colleague. The journal ceased publication in 1999.
3. The Book of Revelation is the last book in the Christian Bible, and the only apocalyptic document in the New Testament. It is based on the visions of John of Patmos. <http://en.wikipedia.org/wiki/Book_of_Revelation> and <http://www.pbs.org/wgbh/pages/frontline/shows/apocalypse/revelation/white.html>.
4. For further reading on Columbus, see: Sale, Kirkpatrick (1991) and Morrison, Eliot Samuel (1993).
5. Hurricane Irene hit the Caribbean and the United States in August 2011, and was the seventh costliest hurricane in U.S. history.
6. The combined total of dead, wounded, and missing at Antietam was 22,720 <http://www.nps.gov/anti/historyculture/casualties.htm>.
7. The January 12, 2010 earthquake that struck Haiti killed 220,000 people and injured 300,000 <http://www.oxfam.org/en/haitiquake>.
8. Hurricane Katrina struck the Gulf Coast and New Orleans in particular in August 2005, leading to widespread devastation and homelessness, as well 1,833 deaths and $108 billion of damage.
9. Sally Regenhard's story can be read here: <http://en.wikipedia.org/wiki/Sally_Regenhard>.

—3—

America's Divided Soul

An Interview with Luigi Zoja, Ph.D.

THE FIRST THING TO be said about Jungian psychoanalyst Luigi Zoja is that he is not American. Yet as a lifelong citizen of Italy—with its long arc from Republic to Empire, its expressions of Greek and Roman religion and culture, as well as Christianity, and as an elder ancestor of American democracy—Zoja brings valuable cultural and historical perspectives to what he calls the "psychotherapy and analysis" of modern Western culture. Born during World War II to a Catholic, liberal family that ran its own business, he went on to receive a degree in economics. Yet even before he'd finished his degree, said Zoja, he knew he couldn't run a factory like his grandfather (who'd started one of the first factories making medicine in Italy), as he was more interested in "the opposite side." "Studying economics," said Zoja, "I discovered sociology—in studying it, I discovered psychoanalysis." Eventually, he applied to and was, to his surprise, accepted to the Jung Institute in Zürich. In the interest of honesty, says Zoja, he was not "heading *towards* an illuminated destiny" by going to Zürich. Rather, he says, he was simply "*running away from* a dark and coarse one."

Perhaps due to the layers of cultural and political complexity Zoja brings to his work, archetypal psychologist James Hillman described his friend and colleague as an "anthropological psychologist." With his soulful brown eyes, thick shock of gray hair, and somber mien, Zoja to me is more a kind of archaeological psychoanalyst, carefully excavating the layers of the human psyche, beginning with the top stratum of the personal and the private, then descending to the national and cultural, and below that

35

to the universal collective. Though Zoja has been in private practice in Milan for over forty-four years, he tells me that the use of psychoanalysis as a tool to only explore our private lives "reinforces the extreme isolation and loss of connections which brings individuals into therapy in the first place." For this reason, Zoja continues, "I don't want to be psychological as a way to avoid material reality; rather it's my duty to cross-fertilize a psychoanalytic view with historical and political perspectives" as a way to educate people about the deeper collective undercurrents influencing their everyday lives and problems.

A noted writer and the prolific author of over twenty books published in fourteen languages on topics ranging from the father throughout history to addiction, it was Zoja's essay "Violent Hearts: America's Divided Soul," included in the book he edited, *Violence in History, Culture and the Psyche*, that compelled me to interview him for this chapter. The title of his essay seemed to capture the country's conflict around reconciling the angels of our better nature with the less conscious, darker side of our psyche. In addition, Zoja had spent two years living and practicing in New York City—exactly during the period that coincided with the World Trade Center terrorist attacks.

Our interview took place in May 2013, in the heightened atmosphere following the December 2012 massacre at Sandy Hook Elementary School in Newtown, Connecticut. With Zoja as my guide, we entered the labyrinthine topic of American violence, both of us contending with questions around the nation's gun complex, its paralysis around enacting sensible gun-control legislation, and America's deeper relationship to violence as a culture. In our wide-ranging conversation, Zoja builds on Robert Jay Lifton and Charles Strozier's previous contributions, adding an outsider's viewpoint, and elaborating further on the myths and archetypes that surround the gun—we are not the only country, he says, lured by the mystique of guns—even beyond its significance in American frontier history.

Zoja delves as well into the violence embedded in our Puritan roots and how that has shaped us psychologically; how World War II sobered Europe—but not America—and how the hidden effects of our unconscious "religion" influence our secular democracy, among other things. Finally, Zoja discusses his concern over American drone attacks in Africa and the Middle East as a troubling expression of how new computerized technologies of the modern era exacerbate what he describes as the divide in America's soul—the split between our actions and our disavowal of the troubling feelings and emotions that arise as a result.

✳

Pythia Peay: As you know, America has suffered through a succession of horrific mass shootings by mentally imbalanced young men. Despite our cultural soul-searching after each incident, it could be said with some irony that the topic has become so loaded Congress can't even pass a ban on assault weapons. Is this a uniquely American problem?

Luigi Zoja: I don't think this issue is specifically American. If you took away the two World Wars, which left a big scar in the European psyche, and started allowing more gun ownership in Europe, I think we might love guns as much as Americans.

PP: How did Europe's experience during World War II change its relationship to guns?

LZ: Europe has suffered more under the weight of history. In addition to civil wars, foreign invasions, and fascism, Auschwitz and the concentration camps took place on European soil: fifty million people were killed during World War II. Apart from the Civil War 150 years ago, there hasn't been a similar war of occupation or mass destruction on American soil—so your country hasn't had a chance to experience the melancholy that comes with that kind of heavy burden. In addition, America never goes to war with the idea that it might lose—there is no "plan B" so to speak.

So combined with America's optimistic nature as well as its military superiority, this makes a difference. In America there's more tolerance of violence in the culture; sex is censored in the movies but violence is not. Here it's the reverse—violence is censored, but sex is less censored.

PP: Are you saying that Europe is more experienced with the darker side of human nature—warier and thus wiser?

LZ: Yes. In Italy after the war, capital punishment, which had been reintroduced by the fascists, was banned because of its association with totalitarian regimes. In addition, for complex political reasons, everyone was ordered to turn in their guns. Even today, you can be severely punished for possessing weapons, and the topic remains politically charged.

But whether guns are forbidden or allowed, our feelings around them are never neutral—one either loves guns or hates them. My father recently died, and among the things he left behind was an Austrian pistol my grandfather brought back from World War I. I've found myself wondering where it's hidden in his apartment, whether I'll get it, or one of my brothers, or if we should throw it away, because it's forbidden. And because it's forbidden, that makes it even more difficult to throw away!

PP: So you seem to be saying that a gun isn't just a gun, but something much more?

LZ: Right—it would be a mistake to consider a gun as just any ordinary modern object, such as a toaster or a camera. Independent of culture, it has archetypal features because it's connected to the hero myth. And the hero itself is *the* primary archetype: a metaphor for the ego and the development of consciousness, and the nucleus of all other archetypes. However differently the hero appears in each culture, it's an archetype that's inborn in all of us.

PP: So why is the hero connected to guns?

LZ: Most heroes are connected to guns, but not *all* heroes. The Buddha and St. Francis of Assisi, for instance, are mystical heroes who are more complex and psychologically differentiated. But the hero in its most traditional and limited expression, particularly in male-oriented cultures, is somehow always connected with weapons. In humankind's earliest stages, primitive weapons functioned as an extension of the human arm. Greek and Roman mythology is full of Gods represented with weapons. Even the Goddess Athena is shown with a spear. Christ is—un-Christianly—at times pictured with a sword. Both the Crusades and the conquest of the Americas were carried out with the Gospel and the sword, and later, the gun.

So there is something almost religious about guns. This means that you cannot deal with the topic in a logical way, because people feel as if you're taking something sacred away from them. This is even more complicated in America. As James Hillman pointed out, beneath its façade of civil and secular society and separation of church and state, America is full of unconscious, undeclared religion: it's a *religion* of democracy; the gun is a symbol of democracy and therefore it is something very sensitive in the collective American unconscious. So partly because of its history in the country's development, and partly because the gun belongs to a collective archetype around weapons present in every culture, guns in America are imbued with a mythic, religious quality.

PP: And because we're not conscious of the underlying mythological and archetypal symbolism around guns, we expect our debates to proceed reasonably. But wouldn't this awareness that there's a non-rational, deeper side to this issue than even liberals allow change the nature of the debate—wouldn't we treat guns with *more* respect, striving to keep them out of the hands of those who would use them for profane and evil purposes? For example, one of my great-grandfathers, who was born in Argentina and who served in the Argentine Navy, was buried with his sword; it was clearly a sacred symbol to him of his military service.

LZ: Possibly. The task, then, would be to face the problem of guns through a collective, psychologically oriented debate in newspapers, online, and on the radio and television, persuading and educating the public on the history and mythology of the gun—as well as cultivating a sense of shame around the misuse of guns, and encouraging individual soul-searching, whether with a psychoanalyst, a spiritual guide, or in a good conversation with friends and family.

This may sound contradictory to what I've just been saying on the connection between the hero and the gun: but we also have to be equally aware of the pathological, almost pornographic side of America's preoccupation with guns. The commercial, pop side of guns in twenty-first-century American culture has become horrifying. Psychologically, owning guns has become a naïve expression of macho masculinity—a show of sexuality and arrogant power.

When one of those school kids, who's been a nobody, buys a gun and kills defenseless young children, he has the momentary delusion that he has the omnipotent power of a hero, even if he knows that he will be killed by the police, or will even kill himself. So for psychologically weak kids, weapons are a powerful temptation. An automatic assault weapon that can kill dozens in a few seconds offers a dangerous form of over-compensation for weaknesses of character or frustrations with society. And unfortunately, this temptation is constantly fed by the images of guns circulating throughout American culture.

But this is a total degeneration of the archetype of the hero—a kid who kills kids is the total opposite of the hero, no?

PP: So although the targets of these young shooters are innocent children and bystanders, they themselves are powerless on some level. Is there something psychological to be found in that: that these young men, in killing innocent children, are also killing off that innocence within themselves?

LZ: Yes, these shooters don't go out and kill people who are violent or who are potential killers. A school with young children is the archetypal place of innocence, hope, and goodness, a place without much evil. So the paradoxical, horrendous conclusion is that they kill the innocence of the child. If we analyze this behavior, we see totally immature young adults who are unconsciously trying to become the adults they are *not* by radically opposing innocence itself. From a socio-historical perspective, these shootings are also the grossest form of *erostratism*, or the drive to become immortal, as destroying is always much quicker than creating. With modern, cheap machine-guns you can very easily acquire your fifteen minutes of celebrity, because a whole lifetime might not be enough to become an accomplished artist.

And, I must say, there is as well something very American underlying this phenomenon. Postmodern market values emphasize the bipolarity of the "winner–loser," instead of that of "harmony–cooperation." What better way to produce a winner–loser mega-show than to kill, or even better, to *hunt down* little creatures, as animals? In the case of the Aurora, Colorado movie-theater rampage [of July 20, 2012], there may also have been an unconscious attraction on [James Eagan Holmes] the shooter's part to being "seen" and being in a public place where he was in the eyes of other people. So psychologically, we might ask whether putting more cameras in schools or increasing surveillance is really a deterrent—or if, instead, this might attract another exhibitionist with an unconscious need to be on camera. It's at least the duty of a psychoanalyst to wonder about that!

PP: Speaking of deterrents, I was intrigued by a reference you made in your book to a tradition from ancient Roman times, in which the triumphant conqueror in his chariot had a "double" placed beside him whose task was to whisper in his ear that he was a mortal, flawed human being. What meaning might that have for us in this gun debate?

LZ: This is an image of that dialogue between our limited ego, which can fall prey to inflation—like a general coming back from a victorious military campaign—and an inner voice, like Socrates' *daimon*, which we might hear in dreams, and who checks our pride and reminds us of our limitations.

Today, we could use this image to suggest to anyone who is considering buying a gun, particularly a young boy, that they first go within and consult this inner voice accompanying the hero, and ask, "Is it really necessary? Or am I falling prey to pride, inflation, and paranoia as a way to compensate for my human weaknesses?"

PP: These seem like questions America could ask of itself as well, in terms of the gun debate! In going more deeply into the country's psychological background, I'm curious to know more about your assertion in your essay that we were the first country founded on the splitting off of the "shadow"—bringing into being the "first collective soul that would not compromise with the shadow."

For example, you say that the Monroe Doctrine[1] was a "psychological manifesto" that anticipated the Cold War, in which America saw itself as purely democratic, while viewing the rest of the world as more corrupt.

LZ: First I would say that America suffers the problem of a divided soul: the dissociation and projection of evil onto the "other." It began with America's Puritan origins, in which the early settlers projected the primitive side of human nature onto blacks and Indians. George Washington echoed this in his Farewell Address,[2] in which he warned his fellow Americans against the influence of foreign nations, and enmeshment in the English monarchy and Europe's "corrupt" politics. The frontier expansion into the West was certainly a kind of continental "gentrification" line, an early example of a boundary that divides American cities today, much more than in European cities.

This pattern of keeping "America for America" was again perpetuated in the Monroe Doctrine. In its effort to keep the country separate and to prevent "contamination" by other cultures, it was a document that was more a moral exhortation than a political statement. How is it that North America is so developed, for example, while South of the Rio Grande is so underdeveloped—in spite of Mesoamerica being potentially rich in resources and raw materials?

The fact is that North American immigrants were basically religious families made up of a married couple, with children, a gun, and a Bible. The country's founding mythology was based not only on conquering, but cleansing: cleansing the ground to make it prosperous, and cleansing the collective consciousness of contamination by its original inhabitants, because they were thought to lack civilization

41

and were therefore evil. In spite of being a beautiful document, the Declaration of Independence, one of the first expressions of modern democracy, still more or less speaks of the Indians as barbarians to be destroyed.

PP: So this deep split in the American psyche means that we project onto those we view as "outsiders" those qualities we reject within ourselves—then attempt to purify ourselves of these qualities by getting rid of them in others. And in turn this effort to remain uncontaminated contributes to an underlying violence in the culture, in which we kill in others what we reject or hate in ourselves.

LZ: Yes. Even if you're convinced that you're waging war to bring civilization and defeat evil, you will be intoxicated by violence. You might even become evil yourself through an "infection" of violence.

PP: Are you referring to paranoia?

LZ: Yes. Of course we cannot trust everybody—paranoia is normal, archetypal, and even necessary. But one of the aspects of paranoia is that it's contagious; it can spread and even become an historical infection. If I look at you as an enemy, I provoke and activate paranoia in you. An example of this is what happened to gun sales after the school rampage in Newtown. As a reaction to these shootings, the anti-gun initiative gained renewed impetus—but so, too, did sales of guns. More guns were sold, not only among those who were gun fanatics and who belonged to the NRA, but even in the most liberal, democratic, anti-gun sectors.[3] This shows how the slightest paranoia can influence even the person who is *for* more regulations, but who then goes out and buys a new gun anyway.

PP: So our laws aren't really going to address this problem because we remain ignorant of the psychological factors at work. You write in your essay, for instance, that our only alternative to catastrophe is psychology, and the study of the unconscious and the evil within. I wonder what you think about the release of a bipartisan report[4] that found that American forces engaged in torture as part of the War on Terror after 9/11.

LZ: This report reveals a form of collective denial that American military actions could have fostered criminal practices. In the U.S. you tend to assume that these kinds of things don't happen; it's another example of how you diminish the darker side of human nature. Psychologically you could say you are less wise and more naive than older cultures like Europe.

On the other hand, you are less cynical, and there is an optimistic side of American culture. If it is proven that evil has been committed in the name of America, then the average citizen is ready to act, to enter politics, and to repair that evil, which is more difficult in Europe. Because of America's democratic tradition, one is allowed to express one's opinion, and so it's still the best place in the world in that sense.

PP: The lack of transparency around America's unmanned, weaponized drone attacks against suspected terrorists overseas seems to me another example of how America can turn a blind eye to its split-off, violent side. It also seems to take violence into even stranger territory, turning killing into a form of extermination, which many find troubling. What is your psychological perspective on these remote-control strikes executed by what many call "flying killer robots"?

LZ: The psychological risk is that these drone pilots will become dissociated. So in addition to innocent civilian casualties, we should also be concerned about what happens to the psyche of the drone pilot sitting behind the screen who kills his target, then gets in his car, drives home, has dinner, plays with his children, and then makes love to his wife. It's almost inhuman.

PP: Still, it's difficult to make the argument that a soldier should be placed in direct combat. Is that more moral?

LZ: I'm not a philosopher or a minister who can say whether these drone strikes are definitely wrong. Yet the danger is that precisely because of the geographical distance created by technology between the pilot and the target, drone pilots are being conditioned to kill without suffering ambivalence or inner conflicts; they may even lack the perception of having actually killed someone. And, as they belong to a younger generation, these attacks might be unconsciously experienced as a continuation of the video games they played as youths.

In every war there are casualties and collateral damage; still, the point is that even the loss of one life will mark the soul of the American pilot. So although we should continue to keep the debate open on the use of weaponized drones, we should remain aware that among the casualties should be included the psyche of the virtual pilot.

PP: Despite the fact that innocent civilians are killed in these targeted killings abroad, a majority of Americans support the use of drones,[5] because unlike in war, the casualties are limited. So drones are seen as an advance. Is the ease with which the public has accepted drone warfare part of a larger shift around the way technology is reshaping our inner emotional lives?

LZ: In my book *la morte del prossimo* [*The Death of the Neighbor*], I discuss how technology has killed the second Judaeo-Christian commandment: To love God above everything else, and thy neighbor like thyself. Because in this technological, mass civilization, we don't care about our neighbors: we don't even know if our neighbor is sick or depressed or even dying.

PP: So you're describing a creeping dissociation throughout all of our lives brought about by technology.

LZ: Right. I'm not a nostalgic who believes that past ages were better. But the new forms of technology present enormous psychological challenges that did not exist before. It's not that we lack feelings. But our emotional responses and natural instincts are being distorted and disrupted through technology, and we're becoming increasingly removed from the moral consequences of our actions.

PP: Even modern-day guns are influenced by technology. The Western Six Shooter is nothing like the automatic assault weapons used in recent mass murders.

LZ: Absolutely. Because they can kill at a distance, these kinds of weapons enable the aggressor to feel omnipotent and magical. With technology we become more and more dissociated from our moral reactions. It keeps us clean emotionally—and even literally. As long as war was conducted with a sword, there was horror. If a warrior plunged his sword into his enemy's belly, he was automatically soaked in blood; something inside a person instinctively reacts to that. Confronted by the agony of the dying person, ancient warriors felt a natural guilt.

But today we lack the sense of limits that arise naturally when too much blood is spilled, and we fail to suffer the moral consequences of our actions. The pilot who drops an atomic bomb, but doesn't see that he's killed thousands of civilians, or the drone pilot in America dropping a bomb on a target in Yemen, is less likely to feel guilt.

PP: I can see how technology distances us from our feelings and our conscience, but how does it affect our sense of limits?

LZ: Technology gives us the illusion that we can break through limits; it reinforces omnipotence, arrogance, and endless growth and affluence. We've lost this necessary balance between growth and guilt, or between wanting more and finding a natural limit.

PP: It strikes me that this limitlessness is intrinsically American.

LZ: I think so. Because American history was based on the conquest of the enormous and underpopulated West, an underlying historical attitude remains that the country can continue to expand. There's still a lot of territory at your disposal, so there are too few reasons to feel the necessity of limits.

PP: In that regard, could modern-day America be said to resemble the Roman Empire?

LZ: America is like the Roman Empire in the sense that Rome was big and based on continuous expansion. It produced philosophers and artists, but it was imperialistic, not just militarily, but economically—it was the first step toward mass civilization. So Rome anticipated America with its mass consumerism and mass entertainment, and even the whole modern world, with its mass civilization. It was the opposite of ancient Greece.

PP: If the Roman Empire was the opposite of Greece, what are those classical Greek virtues that we're missing in our own culture?

LZ: Greek culture was based on the importance of limits. As I explored in *Growth and Guilt*, the myth of Icarus[6] was a warning against the "sin" of hubris, or pride and inflation, the one "true sin" in their moral code. Whoever desired or possessed too much was punished by *nemesis*. So the idea of continuous growth is relatively recent. The history of the West is a rejection of this paradigm, relegating it to more primitive peoples and supplanting it with aspirations to unlimited expansion.

The ancient Greeks also had more of a sense of tragedy. In America, there is less emphasis on tragic tales, because the commercial side of the culture and Hollywood tend to simplify life by splitting good and evil, and providing a happy ending—some stories end that way, but not all of them.

PP: Indeed, you write that the Greek theater aimed at moving the public to think about good and evil. By contrast, Rome with its Circus of public games and chariot races didn't want the public to think at all.

LZ: The essence of tragedy is more psychological; it poses the problems of ambivalence and complexity. For instance, there are no simple solutions to the tragic problems of drones, torture, guns, and terrorism. These issues take time; in the modern world, we have to examine these issues in complex cultural terms. Real morality lies in not knowing what is black and what is white, or good and evil; it's about having a moral discussion and dialogue, as we are doing in this interview. ■

Notes

1. In his 1823 annual message to Congress, President Monroe warned European powers not to interfere in the affairs of the Western Hemisphere. This became known as the Monroe Doctrine <http://www.ourdocuments.gov/doc.php?flash=true&doc=23>.

2. In his farewell address, Washington advised American citizens to view themselves as a cohesive unit and avoid political parties and issued a special warning to be wary of attachments to and entanglements with other nations <http://www.ourdocuments.gov/doc.php?doc=154>.

3. "One Year After Newtown Killings, Gun Makers Stronger Than Ever," by Alan Farnham, ABC News, December 9, 2013 <http://abcnews.go.com/Business/gun-makers-thriving-year-newtown/story?id=21150188>. The NRA is the National Rifle Association.

4. "U.S. Engaged in Torture After 9/11, Review Concludes," by Scott Shane, New York Times, April 13, 2013. "A nonpartisan, independent review of interrogation and detention programs in the years after the Sept. 11, 2001, terrorist attacks concludes that 'it is indisputable that the United States engaged in the practice of torture' and that the nation's highest officials bore ultimate responsibility for it.

5. Brown, Alyssa and Frank Newport. "In U.S., 65% Support Drone Attacks on Terrorists Abroad." Gallup Politics, March 2013. "Nearly two-thirds of Americans (65%) think the U.S. government should use drones to launch airstrikes in other countries against suspected terrorists. Americans are, however, much less likely to say the U.S. should use drones to launch airstrikes in other countries against U.S. citizens living abroad who are suspected terrorists (41%); to launch

airstrikes in the U.S. against suspected terrorists living here (25%); and to launch airstrikes in the U.S. against U.S. citizens living here who are suspected terrorists (13%)" <http://www.gallup.com/poll/161474/support-drone-attacks-terrorists-abroad.aspx>.

6. Icarus ignored the warnings of his father, Daedalus, not to fly too close to the sun, and fell into the sea after the sun melted the wax in his wings, which Daedalus had made for him.

—4—

Confronting the Violence Within

ADNESS AND MURDER. TOXIC Nourishment. Coming Through the Whirlwind. Lust. Rage. Damaged Bonds. Feeling Matters. Psychic Deadness. The titles of these books penned by the legendary New York psychoanalyst Michael Eigen provide a glimpse into the nature of his work, and reveal his lifelong, fearless quest into the uncharted depths of the human psyche. As if descending into a volcano, Eigen has spent over half a century confronting in his patients the boiling lava and fiery agonies of humankind's darkest side: its evil, madness, terror, and sheer, psychotic craziness. How to make sense of the raging torrents of emotion that sweep through us like tsunamis, or the frozen tundra of *un*feeling that deadens our hearts, freezing our relationships and the lives around us, has been his vocation. Revered by many of his contemporaries as a "psychoanalyst's psychoanalyst," Eigen has been called a "national treasure of psychoanalysis" and a "psychoanalytic visionary." In Eigen, writes British psychoanalyst Adam Phillips, "psychoanalysis acquires a new kind of moral seriousness. . . . Michael Eigen has gone on trying to fathom the terrors of aliveness by asking the disarming question: 'What is normal about being alive?'"[1]

Despite Eigen's Shakespearean panorama as a psychoanalyst, he was unassuming when we spoke, with little pretense to authority over the complex mysteries of human nature. "Even when he conveys the struggle of analyst and patient to overcome the deadness of not feeling," writes psychoanalyst Jessica Benjamin, "he offers no facile rhetoric of authenticity, no sense of having the answer."[2] And yet as I explore with

Eigen in our interview below, probably no more urgent task faces humankind than coming to terms with the intractably violent part of all our natures. Failure to find ways to understand and contain the destructive forces within the human psyche—or, as he explains below, to create better internal "sewer systems"—can lead to the dangerous explosion of our internal furies, unleashing environmental havoc, war, sexual abuse, political torture and repression, unjust economic systems, unhappy families riddled with the fault lines of child abuse and cruelty—and even to the American epidemic of random, senseless shootings.

What better guide to explore the psychological dimensions of these American tragedies, then, than Michael Eigen—that rare thinker who doesn't shy away from the raw and even inhuman aspects of the human psyche. As he points out to me during our interview, what we see happening outside in human affairs has a single, common source—it comes from within ourselves: "An inherently stressed, pressured psyche trying to maintain good feeling in [the] face of bad. Great tension. Great struggle. A war psyche. Every capacity potentially defending against and attacking every other. A psyche constantly trying to keep up with its own destructiveness."

✳

Pythia Peay: Since the 2012 Sandy Hook Elementary School shootings by Adam Lanza there have been forty-four school shootings, and twenty-eight deaths.[3]

Michael Eigen: What do you think it's all about?

PP: What do *I* think? That's why I'm interviewing you!

ME: Oh right, I'm a therapist; this is my normal topic of conversation!

PP: Well, on a serious note, for the most part our public debate on violence focuses on gun control and mental health. So what I want to ask you is this: Where are we *not* looking, and what are the questions we're *not* asking?

ME: The subject of human violence is so complex we can only pick out certain threads. But the two dimensions that you mentioned—which fundamentally have to do with control and madness—have been around for a long time. The human race has been trying to control its madness and destruction for thousands of years: so madness and control are twins. Whether in religion, politics, or literature, these two counterparts have been part of the discourse about who we are and why we do what we do. So couching these random shootings in America in terms of gun control and mental health are just variations on ancient themes.

PP: Psychology is a relatively new development, just a little more than a century old, so what does it add to our understanding of madness, control, and violence?

ME: From a psychological perspective, the topic of gun control parallels what Freud called "ego control." But Freud was too smart to think that the ego could really be controlled. He understood that the ego was not master in its own house, and that the ego was repeatedly humiliated by parts of the self it had no mastery over whatsoever, and that could overturn a person at any moment. Yet Freud also looked for a way to address human destructiveness; it was a great concern of his, something he explored in a correspondence with Einstein on the question, "Why war?"[4]

Eventually, Freud began to realize that when it came to handling its violent and destructive impulses, humankind had to look for something else in addition to control—because control doesn't do the trick. Take, for example, a group of people who decide to do something really good and constructive: like the story in Genesis [11:1–9] about the people who came together to build the Tower of Babel reaching up into heaven. We all know what happened to that—POW! It was knocked down, just like the kid who knocked down all the other kids' blocks and his own. We can take that Biblical story as a partial model of how humankind keeps trying to build something good together—but then a destructive force comes along and overturns it.

PP: Then what do we do with that? How in the world do we begin to live with these violent forces inside of ourselves?

ME: No individual or group, in any part of the Earth or at any time in history, has ever figured out what to do with the destructive side of human nature. But we *can* realize that from the Big Bang to cataclysms, earthquakes, hurricanes, and tsunamis, this destructive force is part of nature itself. And since humans are part of the universe, it's not a big surprise that this is part of *our* nature. For example, we have sunny days and stormy days. We have benevolent and peaceful moments, and we have emotionally turbulent and uncontrollable moments.

Since we seem to be part of a universe that has both ends of the spectrum of violence and aggression and peace and equanimity, the question then becomes: How do we live with this destructive part of ourselves? Are we just passive subjects to these forces? Or, like those who live in an environment with tornadoes and hurricanes, can we build stronger buildings, so to speak? Can we move out of the tornado's path? That's the evolutionary challenge: What do we do with ourselves so that we can become better partners to the different capacities that make up our human nature?

PP: It seems to me that one of the biggest problems America has with the topic of human violence is that we don't even recognize or acknowledge such a thing as "inner weather." We're so focused on the outer world, and very little attention is paid to the unseen things going on inside of us. Even psychologists—or "inner weathermen"—don't occupy a big place in the culture.

ME: Psychology and psychologists are marginal in our society. Feelings are not sufficiently part of the public discourse in any kind of mainstream way. They're expressed in film and theater, but make little appearance in public and political discourse. As I wrote in *Feeling Matters*, "as long as feelings are second class citizens in public dialogue, people will be second class citizens."

There was once a politician who did good things in government, and who ran for mayor in New York City (he was a well known figure, but I'll leave his name out). He lost the election, but when a journalist asked him how it felt to lose, he replied that he'd been in politics for so many years he'd "severed his nerve endings."

The point is that if it's really true that people in government have to sever their emotional nerve endings, that's very scary. It's yet another example of our society's depreciation of feelings—because what good are they? Can we make money off our feelings? Perhaps poets or filmmakers can, but not generally, and certainly not the big bucks. I had a patient who told me about an interview she had for an important job in the financial sector. The CEO who was interviewing her had a sign on his desk saying, "Beware of pity," or in other words, don't feel sorry for anyone. And if that's a widespread ethic, or non-ethic, it's frightening: because then it means that a person has to cut off their feelings in order to succeed.

51

PP: Now you're describing violence in the culture itself. In fact, you've written that we're living in the age of psychopathy.[5] Could you say more about what you mean by that, and how this relates to these recurrent shootings?

ME: It's strongly related, although the causes around each individual shooter are very complex. But one thing psychopathy means is not having guilt over inflicting pain or hurting others. It means not feeling that we shouldn't do something because it might cause a lot of damage and make people unhappy. Psychopaths do something because they want to win; or they want to solidify their position on top, so that the other person loses. In that scenario, inflicting pain or damage becomes part of winning—a victorious, ambitious push to the top. So the psychopath is someone who doesn't suffer if the other person suffers.

For example, if I hurt one of my children, I feel guilty about it—but I know there are people who don't. Child abusers, for example, don't seem to feel guilty. In fact, many feel righteous: they feel they're on the right side of doing the right thing, and that they're on the side of God. In studies of people who inflicted child abuse, it was an interesting early finding that one of their characteristics was a sense of righteousness, and of "correcting" the child by getting rid of the devil or teaching it how to be good. Even sexual abuse was justified by some abusers as doing something "good" for the child.

PP: Do you feel that the kind of psychopathology you've just described might have been at work in Adam Lanza, the perpetrator of the Sandy Hook massacre?

ME: I think there's a parallel. How else could he have carried out those shootings if he'd felt the pain of those children? In his case, then, we have a failure of nature—the part of our nature that feels the pain and suffering of the other person, and that wants to avoid causing that kind of pain. This failed part of our nature can be so damaged, injured, and wounded that it feels justified in acts of revenge, or doing whatever it takes to feel on top of the pain inside, or to get back at those who've hurt us. The side of us that takes pleasure in another's pain gains too much momentum.

But I think what Adam Lanza and the other shooters did was a combination of both psychopathy *and* madness, or psychosis. The great majority of people who are genuinely psychotic couldn't get it together enough to do something like that; they wouldn't be able to organize actions in such a way as to follow through. They might be able to jump in front of a train, or push someone, but most psychotic people just aren't capable of arming themselves and organizing a systematic plan of action to shoot a group of people. So I also think that behind Lanza's horrific act was some kind of fusion or "wedding" between psychotic anxieties and psychopathic manipulation.

PP: That sounds very esoteric. Can you explain what you mean by "psychopathic manipulation of psychotic anxieties"?

ME: An example of what I'm talking about took place on a large scale after 9/11, when the Bush administration told the American public that it should be scared because Iraq possessed weapons of mass destruction. That's manipulating a psychotic anxiety, because it plays on our basic human fear of dying, or our annihilation anxiety, or some kind of holocaustal smashing of our everyday lives. In reality, it turned out to be a delusional scenario that manipulated our deepest dreads, and that got exploited by psychopathic means.

PP: So if we're living in an "age of psychopathy," is there something in the deep background of the American way of life that facilitates someone like an Adam Lanza to go into a school and carry out a mass killing of kindergartners, or other American gun tragedies?

ME: It's more complex. For each particular shooter there are going to be a variety of possible causes. Perhaps they felt a momentary flash of power over their helplessness and the forces of life that made them feel so impotent; or perhaps they felt no one paid them any attention, or even took note of their existence. They could have felt a kind of self-justified power: "Now I'm someone, I've created a ruckus, I've had an effect." So part of the shooters' motivations might have stemmed from feelings of emotional or psychic impotence; that their existence didn't have an impact, and so they sought a way to be felt and sensed by others. And in having a powerful impact, the pain they caused others was a joy to them.

On another level, I think psychopathy is American, but it's also universal. There's the psychopathy of everyday life, for example, when one has to shut out a lot of pain in existence just to get food and shelter, and to survive. Look at the pain we shut out that we cause animals, because we need the food as fuel to survive. So there's a certain necessary psychopathy that's built into existence. It's one part of our personality, but it can be balanced by other sides of our nature.

PP: Again, we're just not educated that psychopathy is a part of the human condition we all share. We toss off words like madness or crazy, as if they belong to another person, but certainly not to oneself.

ME: We're a very, very long way in our evolution from realizing just how crazy and monstrous we are. In fact, I would make the chapter from the Bhagavad Gita,[6] in which Krishna reveals himself to be a monster, to be basic reading for everybody. I'd like to say: "We're that. We have that monster aspect." Obviously, we're not only that, because if we were only that, we'd disappear in an instant. But we do have that inside us, and it *is* scary.

PP: From reading your books, I know you deal with madness and psychopathy as it comes up in your patients.

ME: I recently had a patient who had a dream that by any standard would be awful: it was like a horror movie, or a scene from a battleground, with people's flesh being flayed. After she told me the dream, I said, "Well, that's what the psyche is made of—you're seeing the truth of the psyche." She agreed that she was seeing the truth of this monstrous, damaged aspect of her psyche. Yet she also said, referring to these figures, "I kind of like them."

What she was really saying was that she wasn't so afraid of the horrible things within herself anymore. Typically, when these things come up in dreams we want to run away from them. But these kinds of nightmares highlight important aspects of our existence: feelings that we can't handle, states that are too hard for us, pains that we don't know what to do with. It's almost as if the psyche is trying to communicate to the dreamer, "Look what's inside you! Wake up, wake up! Look at all this stuff that you make believe isn't there so you can get through the day, just so that you can survive." We can get through a lifetime shutting out those parts of our psyche—but it still has its effects on the environment, on our families, and on groups we come in contact with.

PP: Why does ignoring these nightmares and scary, violent parts of our psyche have an effect on our surroundings?

ME: Because everything that is disavowed appears in some other way. In fact, the reason psychoanalysis has been marginalized is because it keeps reminding us, "Look at all this stuff inside you!"—when what we really want to believe is that we don't need to look at all this stuff inside of us, we just need to learn how to modify our behavior.

PP: But when these disavowed destructive forces and nightmarish images do come up, what *are* we supposed to do?

ME: Yes, inevitably, the question of what to do with the stuff inside us, especially the destructive forces, comes up. But the answer is that there is not any answer right now. So the first thing we're going to have to do is say, "I don't know." I think not knowing opens up a path, because we always have to know, we always have to be on top of it, we're supposed to know what to do, and to be in control. And if we don't know what to do, we're at least supposed to act like we do know what to do.

PP: So this brings us back to the question of control, and Freud's realization that control is an insufficient way to handle these destructive, violent impulses. But what happened next? Surely he came up with some approach to this side of human nature.

ME: After he realized that control was insufficient, Freud began to experiment with free association: thinking, feeling, or just sitting or lying down and seeing what comes up. Freud felt that in this way we might begin to fill in the gaps of what we don't know about ourselves, and that we might even begin to learn what we're made of. Like religion and literature at its best, this kind of "mindful" awareness adds a rich network of imagery and associations describing our "inner weather," including the upwelling of destructive urges that threaten to overturn the self.

So the thing to do is to sit with ourselves, be with ourselves, and feel the state we're in and our feelings to the extent we can. In *Rage*, I write that if a person can masticate and chew the cud, little by little a tolerance for those states that one didn't have before gradually builds up.

PP: You do talk and write a lot about the importance of digesting and tasting as a way of working with these difficult, darker states.

ME: That's something I strongly propose and would like to get across. I don't expect this will solve all our problems; it won't. But if we can build up a capacity to sit with something—wait on something, tasting, feeling, and smelling these states—it will help strengthen our endurance for these states. For example, there's an old story about a Talmud scholar. One day, he became furious with his wife and kids. He was just about to blow and let them have it when suddenly he wondered what the Talmud had to say about aggression. So he started studying these different tracts and before he knew it, hours and days had passed and he didn't feel angry anymore.

This story teaches us that when these violent states come up inside, it's a matter of "playing for time" in order to give ourselves a chance to begin to absorb them. In another example, I once read a case study of a prisoner who was in prison for a violent crime. He went to see the prison psychologist, and the psychologist suddenly got the idea from talking with this prisoner that his problem with aggression came from the fact that all his "shitty" feelings immediately got acted out. The therapist realized that what the prisoner really needed was a kind of "sewer system" to flush them out.

So for some months the prisoner and his psychologist worked to build up an internal sewer system. They had setbacks, the pipes broke, and they had to patch up the pipes, or put in new ones. Gradually, over the course of the year they built up an internal sewer system for his anger and dangerous, lascivious feelings. The psychologist felt that the man's life was better off for it, and that he was less damaging, both to himself and to others. So the metaphor of the sewer is important in this kind of work with these psychopathic parts of our human nature.

PP: It's a very powerful metaphor because it's one that everybody can understand. It instantly makes sense.

ME: Right. Instead of shitting on everyone else, it's wiser to make a system in our own being that can somehow process that.

PP: The frightening thing is that most of us are walking around without that sewer system.

ME: Or not a very good one.

PP: Part of the wisdom behind studying, or building an internal sewer system, involves the idea of waiting, and not being impulsive. In *Madness and Murder* you write that if only [President George W.] Bush had been able to wait to see what might have unfolded, we might not have gone to war with Iraq. You say that he wasn't able to do that, because waiting would have been seen as weakness, or that he didn't know what he was doing: "Better to kill and be a bully and act strong," you write, "than to say 'I don't know, I'm waiting on it awhile.'" I love that passage, especially for its political relevance.

ME: Bush couldn't wait, because it wouldn't have been very macho! But the ability to wait is so important. I recall how [President Bill] Clinton was criticized in his first term because he vacillated too much. But I saw that as a breakthrough in politics. Here was someone who could entertain multiple positions at once and be indecisive until something more developed began to emerge. We need much more of that ability to entertain different viewpoints, and over a longer period of time. [President] Obama has had to suffer some of that same criticism. If he's not decisive enough, he's seen as weak, rather than possessing the ability to reflect, and to wait because all the information hasn't come in yet, or we don't know what new developments might come from life itself.

PP: Waiting seems like such a simple thing. And yet in reality it proves one of the most difficult things to do, especially when we're flooded with gusting emotions, from inside and from outside, pushing us to act on this or that impulse.

ME: One of our overarching problems is that we have uneven capacities. In evolution, some capacities are ahead of others. The problem is that there's an evolutionary asymmetry between our psychological and emotional modes of production and our modes of assimilation, or the ability to process and digest what we produce. How that ability could ever gain credibility in the larger public sphere, I don't know. But it's very important to realize that we're unevenly evolved, and that our ability to digest our feelings in such a way that we can talk about them or express them creatively instead of acting them out destructively lags far behind our ability to produce and act on these emotions and impulses.

PP: Is this simply part of the human condition at this point in time?

ME: Yes, it's a human thing. But it's exaggerated in our capitalistic system in which democracy has degenerated into the pursuit of money, and the way money has become elevated over the importance of feelings. It doesn't matter what you feel, in other words, as long as you make money.

PP: So then the fault lies in our economic system?

ME: The fault lies in us; it's in our human nature to produce economies like this. So it's back to the fact that we don't know what to do: we have a problem with ourselves. It may put us in an impotent position to say we don't know what to do. And it doesn't mean that we shouldn't keep trying things: but we need to bear in mind that they're just provisional. Whenever I hear someone say they've found something that's going to work, it makes me scared.

PP: It's almost as if the problem of violence is exacerbated by our pragmatic, solution-seeking culture.

ME: Right. We can do all kinds of marvelous things. We can turn a switch and the light goes on; we can build buildings and knock them down; we're an amazing group. But actually working with our emotional life in a way that would be helpful to society is still far in the future. The Dalai Lama says to be compassionate; and that's not a bad idea. Jesus said on the cross, "Father forgive them for they don't know what they're doing" [Luke 23:34] and that was pretty cool. These are good things to absorb. But the important question still remains: How can we go about evolving a new relationship to our feeling nature, so that our emotional selves become part of the public discourse, and aren't looked down on in a way that causes us to feel shame and humiliation? ■

Notes

1. Quoted in *Toxic Nourishment* (Eigen, 1999).
2. Quoted in *The Electrified Tightrope* (Eigen, 2004).
3. "At Least 44 School Shootings Since Newtown—New Analysis," by Valerie Strauss, *Washington Post*, February 13, 2014 <http://www.washingtonpost.com/blogs/answer-sheet/wp/2014/02/13/at-least-44-school-shootings-since-newtown-new-analysis/>.

4. Albert Einstein and Sigmund Freud, "Why War?" (1932) <http://germanhistorydocs.ghi-dc.org/sub_document.cfm?document_id=3864>.

5. "Age of Psychopathy," by Michael Eigen, c. 2006. Online at Psychoanalysis and Psychotherapy: <http://www.psychoanalysis-and-therapy.com/human_nature/eigen/pref.html>.

6. The Bhagavad Gita is a sacred text of the Hindus, and part of the Hindu epic, The Mahabharata <http://en.wikipedia.org/wiki/Bhagavad_Gita>. Krishna's revelation to Arjuna of his divine nature is in Chapter XI.

—5—

Transforming Violence through the Democratic Process —Within and Without

---

AN INTERVIEW WITH DONALD KALSCHED, PH.D.

RAISED AMID THE LAKES and forests of central Wisconsin in a "gun toting, hunting, and fishing, outdoor-worshiping family," Albuquerque-based psychoanalyst and Jungian analyst Donald Kalsched experienced a classic, 1950s American boyhood. "Long, languid summers" and hiking and canoeing, he told me, allowed him to find his own relationship to the natural world. In old-fashioned cops-and-robbers games with close friends, he recalled, he played out mythic "good and evil scenarios." Yet everything he did growing up, said Kalsched, was always "in the context of relationships. They're so precious, relationships—and they're becoming more and more difficult to maintain in our increasingly fragmented, fast-paced, and impersonal world."

During his nearly fifty-year career in the field of psychology, Kalsched has spent decades in the crucible of the relationship between analyst and patient. His current work as a Jungian analyst is built on a foundation of studies in philosophy, religion, psychiatry, and clinical psychology, as well as a period of time working at a Veterans Administration Hospital in New York City. It was in trying to figure out why many of his clients got stuck in the process of therapy—even sabotaging their own healing—that Kalsched's work began to coalesce around childhood trauma: those whose psyches had sustained severe emotional wounds, misshaping their lives, and hindering their capacity for relationships long into adulthood.

In two major works that have earned him a widespread reputation—*The Inner World of Trauma: Archetypal Defenses of the Personal Spirit* and *Trauma and the Soul: A Psycho-Spiritual Approach to Human Development and Its Interruption*—Kalsched has elaborated his own unique theory of the traumatized psyche and its "self care system," creatively bringing together emerging trauma paradigms in modern psychoanalysis with depth psychology and Jungian archetypes and ideas.

Like other thinkers in the field of contemporary psychology, Kalsched began to apply his psychological insights to the greater American body politic. Trauma didn't just exist in his individual patients, he realized, but in the wider culture as well. In the following interview, Kalsched and I explore the complex interrelationships between the traumatic effects of 9/11 on the American psyche and our polarized politics. We also examine his unique insights into the parallels that exist between the separation of church and state upon which American democracy is built—and between the individual's ego and unconscious. As I discovered in my conversation with Kalsched, America's failure to maintain this firewall, both in the country as well as in the individual threatened from within by destructive urges, combined with a kind of cultural innocence around violence and the human condition, are underlying factors in such American tragedies as the "slaughter of innocents" that took place at Sandy Hook Elementary in Newtown, Connecticut.

✴

Pythia Peay: You've said that the separation of church and state written into the American Constitution was a psychologically wise decision on the part of the founders. Can you say more about what you mean by that?

Donald Kalsched: Separation of church and state is foundational to American democracy and to the U.S. Constitution. This "wall" of separation promotes a diversity of religious expression free of control by the state, giving people freedom to worship as they please. It also means that issues of justice will be decided within a system of secular laws and courts—not by religious authorities such as popes, rabbis, or imams. This separation between the sacred and the secular represents a huge step in the evolution of a civil society. Only a few hundred years ago in the West there were inquisitions, holy wars, and persecutions of heretics, like Galileo and Copernicus, whose discovery that the Earth orbited the sun threatened medieval Christianity.

So this was a wise decision on the part of the founders because it kept religion out of the secular laws that governed people's lives. Religious beliefs were seen as an individual's personal prerogative—but those beliefs were not to become part of the way businesses were run, or the way citizens conducted themselves in public, especially when it came to discriminating against people whose beliefs they didn't agree with, or as a reason to deny individuals basic human rights and privileges. So religion became a private right to believe whatever we want, but not something that leaders could use to control or dictate others' behavior.

PP: You've also made a very unusual and interesting parallel between America's separation of church and state and the "necessary and healthy separation between the ego and the unconscious realm of the psyche." Can you explain more of what you mean by that?

DK: Carl Jung, if you remember, added the collective layer of the unconscious to Freud's model of the psyche. He discovered that in addition to our personal unconscious, there is in each of us a much deeper layer that he called by various names: the "collective unconscious," or the "ground plan," or the "objective psyche." This deeper stratum is where archetypal emotions, images, and mythical motifs and themes reside. These "primitive" emotions and spiritual forces are structured in antinomies. They tend to be experienced as opposites—love vs. aggression, blissful vs. horrific feelings, "all good" vs. "all bad" powers, etc. The collective unconscious is also the stratum of the psyche that mediates spiritual experience. So it's easy for religious categories and attitudes to get wired up with primitive emotions—an incendiary combination.

So on an individual level our psychological health and wellbeing depend on a flexible boundary that separates this deeper layer of the collective unconscious within, from the more limited, human ego that relates these energies to the world. This boundary in the individual is analogous to the separation of church and state as a prerequisite for healthy democracy in our civic life.

PP: I can understand the importance of separation of church and state to democracy. But can you tell me why it's necessary for us as individuals to maintain this boundary between our individual ego and this deeper world of the collective unconscious?

DK: Because whenever our strong emotions are triggered by something, the risk is that powerful energies can come rushing up from the volcanic depths of the collective layer of the unconscious and these energies are hard for us to "hold." They tend to overwhelm us, terrify us, and we defend ourselves against this fear by a defense called dissociation. We don't *metabolize* the archaic energies or *humanize* them or *consider* them as we would in a healthy democracy of the psyche. We get overwhelmed by them and usually end up enacting them, rather than reflecting on them or debating them as we might if we were less threatened. This is especially true if we have suffered a traumatic history, which weakens our capacities to hold and relate to powerful emotional energies.

PP: So if a democracy depends upon a system of laws to maintain the boundary between church and state, how does an individual develop a strong enough ego to handle these powerful forces from within?

DK: Let me give you an example. Say I'm working with a woman who has been severely abused as a child and has therefore never learned to handle strong emotions in relationships. Let's imagine that this person is very lovingly attached to me in the therapeutic alliance, but has been hurt by something I did or said. Instead of telling me about this and working it through to a better understanding, the person doesn't show up for her next appointment. When I call, she doesn't answer the phone and finally informs me via e-mail that she's ending therapy altogether. What is going on here? Well, powerful emotions have erupted. These emotions are dual. On the one hand, vulnerable hurt and overwhelming disappointment; on the other, anger and a wish to hurt me back. On the one hand, a sense of innocence; on the other, a sense of outrage and a wish for revenge.

Here emotional extremes have taken over and the weak ego is further weakened. An inner "democracy" of her psyche has been subverted by totalistic forces. She cannot talk about her hurt feelings. She can only act out her fury, thereby threatening to destroy something she loves. In a case like this, everything depends on whether we can re-establish our connection and explore the human misunderstanding that led to this impasse. If we can do this, her ego will be strengthened and the overwhelming emotional forces flooding her psyche will be humanized. We will have moved her process from a totalitarian solution to a democratic process.

This process is sort of like transforming high voltage electricity—from 880 volts, for example, to 220 and then 110. Such transformations always occur through the medium of relationships. In early childhood, the "transformer" is primarily the parental relationship: the mother and/or the father absorb and survive the child's volcanic rages, as well as the child's blissful idealizations. If this process goes well and is mostly positive, without too much trauma, then a "democracy of the psyche" can come about in which all the parts of the self are integrated into a whole.

PP: So what might happen in such a case? How might the 880 voltage that's taken over in her be transformed?

DK: Well, I might reach out to her and say something like, "Look it seems clear that I've done something or said something that's terribly upset you and I'm very sorry if that's occurred, and I'd like to make it right. Can we get together and explore it?" In the subsequent conversation my patient will have a chance to express her previously unbearable hurt, her fear of what it meant, and her outrage at what I had done. These will be parts of her that she could not witness and express before. They were not part of an inner democracy where they could co-exist and maybe even understand each other. The dialogue between us will strengthen her ego and lead to a clearer boundary between powerful unconscious forces and their imagery (innocent child/monstrous therapist) and her ego. The archetypal forces will be humanized and the world will be a place she can live in more easily and more "democratically."

PP: Are you referring to a kind of inner democracy?

DK: Yes. Inner and outer democracies seem to go together. The inner tolerance for the different parts of ourselves seems to parallel how tolerant we can be to the "otherness" of different people or different lifestyles. In a healthy, resilient psyche, this means that all the different parts of a person, from the weakest to the strongest, are equal and have a place at the table. This fulfills what Jung believed was the psyche's strongest striving: wholeness.

Just as the healthy psyche welcomes all the parts of itself at the table, so a healthy democracy includes all the different groups, organizations, ethnicities, and political points of view at the banquet table: a democracy that's of the people, by the people, and for the people. This imagery of wholeness is part of our national seal on the back of the dollar bill—a banner in the beak of the Eagle that says: *E Pluribus Unum*, or "From the many, one." At some level, I think we all feel this longing for inclusion and wholeness in the culture, and how moving it is when the disenfranchised are included in the political process. The election of our first black president for example was tremendously exciting in that regard.

In the traumatized, fear-ridden psyche, however, democracy is compromised and we get totalitarianism. In a trauma psychology, the vulnerable parts of the self are exiled, and a survivor self is installed. This means that one part of the psyche takes over in the interest of survival, rather than in the interest of relationship and wholeness—just as in my clinical example. On a political level you can see this operating in third-world countries, where there's a trauma history and a trauma psychology, leading to a takeover of the people by tyrannical forces.

PP: So if I understand you, developing tolerance is key to democracy—both in accepting all the parts of oneself and as it functions in a democracy to respect and tolerate the beliefs of others.

DK: Right. But this form of secular democracy can't happen unless people are willing to sacrifice their egos for the rule of a larger reality, which is called the rule of law, fashioned and agreed to by the people. Psychologically and developmentally speaking, this subordination of the ego to the rule of consensually established laws is a *huge* sacrifice of the self-appointed "superiority" or "divine prerogatives" once claimed by kings and emperors. Recall that as recently as 1945 the emperor of Japan was understood to be divine. We see the same effort to enshrine religious rule and rulers in the caliphate that ISIS[1] wants to establish in Iraq and Syria.

In other words, the descent from "on high" into democracy (*demos* meaning the people and *kratos* meaning power—power to the people) requires a dis-identification from spiritual powers. Once we're in a democracy, we're free to *relate* to divine energies. But we're no longer allowed to identify with them or arrogate their power to our ego in a way that gives us power over others. Naturally, many resist giving up their superiority: before the [American] Civil War white men thought themselves to be "superior" to blacks and to women. Tolerance of others is a difficult achievement psychologically. And democracy is slow and painful, too. And we need to remind ourselves how much sacrifice of our "godly superiority" is necessary to fully embrace it.

PP: So what happens on a psychological level to a secular democracy when the boundary between church and state breaks down? What would be some examples of that breakdown, and where are we today with that struggle?

DK: Throughout America's history that separation between church and state has been threatened at every turn. One of the most well-known examples was the 1925 Scopes trial on whether to allow the scientific theory of evolution to be taught in public schools,[2] because it threatened Biblical beliefs.

Some states are *still* having that debate around whether evolution should be taught. I think that we're witnessing a creeping loss of that separation between church and state: a kind of politicization of religious beliefs, where we find religious fervor and terminology leaking into our common language and public debates. Recently the state of Arizona barely defeated a law that was going to allow businesses and shopkeepers to refuse service to gay people, because they felt it violated their religious beliefs condemning homosexuality.[3]

Extremist opponents of abortion, for example, feel that they know what's right and what's wrong, and where innocence and guilt lies—which they feel gives them the "right" to murder abortion doctors to protect the innocence of unborn babies. But the people who protect the innocence of unborn babies don't seem to realize that there's innocence in the doctors who have been vilified, and in the women who are struggling with the horrific decision to end their pregnancies as well. Instead, they see abortion as split into black-and-white categories of good and evil, right and wrong. In fact, it is a terribly complicated issue, made all the more so by how much more we know today about intra-uterine life. I understand and have sympathy with why people are concerned about protecting life growing *in utero*. I also have great sympathy for the women who have decided to end their pregnancies. There are no easy answers here. But we can't explore these complexities because of the polarizing categories and language in which the debate is framed.

PP: So does religion spilling over into our public debates exacerbate political polarization?

DK: I think so. Psychologically, this is because these emotional/spiritual powers and collective archetypes that I've been describing are each made up of two opposing poles: binary extremes, totalistic categories. When they take over the conversation, human dialogue ends. Feelings and opinions are all screened through the lens of right vs. wrong, good vs. evil, believer vs. infidel. Otherwise reasonable people turn into extremists. We see dramatic examples of this in the Middle East today (journalists who defend the right to different opinions are being beheaded!), but lesser examples are apparent in our American Congress where we almost never hear someone admit that the other side has a point of view or an idea that's worth listening to.

PP: So with the erosion of the boundary between church and state comes the danger of intolerance for "the other" and other points of view and ways of being. Then we're left with a split, angry, polarized country instead of a healthy democracy.

DK: Right. The capacity to hold conflict is a *huge* accomplishment by democratic cultures. That's why I believe in them so much. A democracy enshrines conflict as the very source of its energy.

PP: What a profoundly American idea to welcome back into political life! The Constitutional Convention was an exemplification of what you said: all the founders coming together with their opposing religious beliefs and philosophical principles, yet somehow finding a way to transcend those differences to create the Constitution. What's happened to America that we can't sustain conflicting viewpoints anymore?

DK: I'll begin to answer that by describing how psychologists work with individuals who can't sustain conflict in a healthy way. In psychology, for example, we talk about a "dissociation psychology," which is part of a larger trauma psychology: dissociation is a splitting off from an experience that a person can't bear to feel, and the installing of a defensive structure in order to survive.

The example I gave earlier is a case in point. Just as in that example, in my clinical work I'm always trying to help a person who's suffered a trauma move from the defensive posture of a dissociative psychology to a conflict psychology. In this work, the traumatized person learns how to feel the feelings that they don't want to feel, including the hatred that they have for their own vulnerability. We teach them how to witness their vulnerability with an "observing ego," a part of them that can say to someone they're in conflict with, "I felt hurt when you said that," rather than hitting the offending person in the face, or insulting them back, or putting the shame they feel inside that person, because they can't bear to feel it in themselves. In other words, we're trying to help those who've been traumatized to become big enough to tolerate difficult emotions, and provide enough capacity to hold conflicting feelings, so that they can relate to another person even in the storm of emotion without dissociating.

PP: So are you saying that the American psyche is suffering from trauma? I have to wonder if 9/11 damaged the American psyche, wounding this whole democratic experiment and genius around being able to hold conflict.

DK: I think the American psyche is indeed suffering from the effects of trauma, and 9/11 is certainly part of that—even though the full story is more complicated. With respect to that fateful day, if you'll remember, we went through a process. In the first three weeks, there was an incredible outpouring of compassion toward America from around the world. Initially, even President Bush took the courageous stand that the terrorist attacks had nothing to do with the Muslim religion, but with radicals who were misusing the Muslim religion in the service of terrorism: this was a statement that helped to hold a healthy conflict atmosphere. Bush even said that we were "hurting" as a country. Unfortunately, he rapidly shifted from that to "shock and awe" and the invasion of Iraq.

And as soon as that retributive justice came into play—"We're going to hunt you down and get even with you!"—America entered into a dissociative, trauma psychology. Then we split into opposites in which "we" were the righteous victims and "they" were the evil perpetrators. At that point, we stopped asking questions like, "Why did they do this? Who was behind this, and what must have been going on in the psyches of these people? What kind of distorted psychology and way of thinking led to this act?" Those kinds of questions were rarely asked. Our only remaining concern was how to wipe out our enemies most efficiently.

PP: Twelve years later, where do you feel we are as a country in handling the trauma we sustained from 9/11? From what you're saying, it sounds like we've regressed as a democracy.

DK: The acute trauma has come off the American psyche; I don't think we feel as imperiled now by fear. Some of that is due to the fact that we've instituted enough defensive procedures that we've made ourselves more secure. But this security has been gained at the huge price of our personal privacy; this puts us in danger of regressing back to an archaic, primitive, fundamentalist mindset. If that happens, democracy withers and is replaced by totalistic rhetoric.

One of the things that 9/11 brought home to us was how vulnerable we are in the modern world to individual evildoers who can cause us harm from a distance because their power is amplified by modern technology. In today's digitally "wired" world, one hacker can bring down a whole computer system; one suicide bomber can blow up a whole city. This is unprecedented in human history and it justifiably fills us with fear. But if the power to harm is amplified by technology so it is further amplified by religious fanaticism. The binding power of human community fails, and sheer "anarchy is loosed upon the world."[4]

So I believe that what used to be an acute trauma in the American psyche following 9/11 has now become chronic, and has found its way into a traumatized mindset in the American people. We're living in a post-traumatic world, with real threats from extremists, we're suffering from chronic PTSD—and we get triggered very easily.

PP: You mean like a hypersensitive, hypervigilant person would be to any kind of perceived slight or threat?

DK: An example of individual hypersensitivity is what happened in Jacksonville, Florida, where Michael Dunn had an altercation with a group of black kids in a car—then "thought he saw" a shotgun pointed at him. So he emptied ten rounds into their SUV, killing the unarmed, nineteen year-old Jordan Davis.[5] Or like the National Rifle Association (NRA) following the Newtown massacre, suggesting that "an armed society is a polite society" and that "for every bad guy with a gun there should be a good guy with a gun."[6]

This form of absolutist, totalistic thinking that eliminates the middle ground is an example of a regression in our political life to a more primitive psychology—a primitive psychology, by the way, which is extremely seductive and addictive—and that pulls us all into it. The fact that nobody has identified the fear element at the core of the NRA is a sign of how a psychological perspective on current events has failed to help us in our understanding.

PP: Identifying fear as motivating the NRA isn't something I've heard talked much about, or would even associate with that organization.

DK: Let's face it. After Newtown we were all terrified. And we were all grasping for ways to defend ourselves against such a horrific threat. The whole *raison d'être* of the NRA is defense (against real or imagined dangers) so one can readily see how much fear lives at the core of their organization. A fear-psychology (and its totalistic mindset) is at the heart of the NRA, for example, when they say things like, "They're going to take our guns away from us." This makes any reasonable discussion of gun control impossible because the NRA has already vilified those who oppose its policies—out of fear. It is hard to reach a realistic understanding of danger from within such a polarizing mindset.

PP: This brings us to Adam Lanza, and to the horrific, 2012 massacre at Newtown Elementary School. Lanza seems a clear example of someone who lost his conscious footing, so to speak, and was overtaken by those primitive and archaic "titanic powers" of the collective unconscious you've been describing. Like all the other young men involved in mass shootings, he was described as a psychopathic killer.

DK: What united us all after this tragedy was our shared horror. The slaughter of the innocents, to use a Biblical phrase [Matt. 2:13–23], is a terrible thing to behold; it mobilized our deep compassion for the victims and our outrage that something like that could have happened. Although this outrage is understandable, it needs to be channeled into constructive action. But then the conversation quickly broke down into a polarized split between innocence and evil; someone like Adam Lanza was seen as a psychotic killer, who should be killed if necessary. So then the solution is that if someone like Adam Lanza has arms, all citizens should be armed.

Now a gun is archetypal energy put into the hands of humans. It gives a person the power to kill in an instant and at a distance. And if we arm everybody, then we've now put archetypal powers in the hands of everybody. In a democracy these archetypal powers are supposed to be vested in a police force under civilian control. Again, I think it comes back to the question of human relatedness, and its civilizing power. How do we bring those moderating forces into a situation that terrorizes and polarizes us? For example, do we have the courage to look at the complexity of Lanza's situation? He was more than a psychotic predator.

PP: Then what was he?

DK: He was a confused, lost, and very disturbed kid. He had a story of his own trauma, neglect, and marginalization, but he was so alienated and mentally ill that he couldn't tell it. He could only act it out.

PP: Well, the mother was very present, and the father was concerned, although it sounds like both parents didn't know what to do with him.

DK: Right—I'm sure the parents didn't know how to reach their son. Sometimes we're unprepared for the amount of violence that comes up in our children. They thought getting their troubled son a gun and taking him to a shooting range would help. Obviously it didn't.

PP: What you say makes me think that as a culture we don't know the first thing about handling violence.

DK: I think that's right. It's a terribly difficult thing to learn how to handle violence in a related way. It's really hard, because violence frightens us and heightens our defenses, so it's very easy to dissociate from the violence in our kids, in ourselves, and in our parents—consequently, it doesn't get transformed. It stays at 880 volts instead of being transformed to a more usable 220 or 110 volts.

PP: So it's as if we have this high-voltage power floating around in the cultural atmosphere: a very dangerous psychic energy that affects everybody.

DK: Very dangerous, especially when it gets hooked up to innocence.

PP: What do you mean by that?

DK: Well, we all like to think of ourselves as "good" and relatively "innocent." It seems to me that this tendency is especially strong in the American character. We like to think of ourselves as the "good guys." We vanquished the bad guys many times in our history. And look at the violent power we have developed and used over our history! We almost extinguished the aboriginal peoples on this continent, justifying our actions because they were "savages." In World War II, we "rescued" Europe, and became the "shining city on the hill." We don't think we have much badness in us. It's in our

American soul that we will defend ourselves with guns or whatever we need (atomic weapons?) because we tend to be pretty identified with our innocence and goodness.

PP: Well, we do have badness in us, but we just don't think we do.

DK: We don't like to think about it, but of course we do. It's part of human nature. As individual persons, we all struggle with our own darkness and destructiveness but this inner battle is harder to admit on a collective, national level. And the ones who do think about it (or point it out) are often branded traitors and betrayers of the American ideal.

The idea that good can be found within one's antagonist is really hard to maintain psychologically, but it's part and parcel with the developmental achievement of democracy. When we lose this awareness we lose democracy. Look at the people across history who have held the idea that good can be found within one's antagonist. They are the peacemakers—people like Nelson Mandela, Martin Luther King Jr., Anwar Sadat, and Abraham Lincoln. All but Mandela were assassinated by extremists who were threatened by the idea of getting so close to the "enemy." Abraham Lincoln is my paradigmatic and quintessential "democrat." Lincoln didn't claim that the North was innocent, and that the South was evil because they had slavery; he didn't make the South pay for the North's victory. Lincoln was amazing in his ability to hold the opposites together both outwardly and in his own inner world—and yet he suffered terribly. So to me Lincoln was the quintessential American who held together the opposites in his own life, and for that he was assassinated.

PP: So conceivably the inner work we could aim to do as individuals around a kind of inner inclusiveness—knowing and accepting all sides of ourselves (good, bad, weak, strong, and in-between)—could be a model for the psychological work we do on an outer level in politics. In that way the inner and outer work of democracy could conceivably nurture each other.

DK: Absolutely. In today's politics, what we see are politicians and citizens taking the path of least resistance toward bridging these polarized extremes—it's really a form of psychological laziness, because democracy takes hard work, sacrifice, energy, and time to understand the other person's point of view. Instead, we see people reverting to sloganeering and demagoguery; we rarely hear any kind of nuanced discussion of issues because it's so apparently hard to listen to each other. It's easier to slip into a polarized argument. And the media love it. A good fight is always "sensational" and increases ratings. But this is a function of a dissociative psyche, which in itself is a function of a traumatized psychology in the culture.

So at a political level, the inner work we do around accepting the uncomfortable, shadow sides of our own psyches would correspond to something like public conversations, planned debates, and open dialogues that involve real listening between Republicans and Democrats. As I said earlier, what we as psychologists see is that the healthy psyche tolerates differences within the self, and makes room at the table for its full range of feelings. That's not only at the core of a healthy psyche, it's at the core of a healthy democracy: "I don't agree with you, but you're at the table, and you have as much right here as I do. So we're going to debate and hash out our differences and try to find some common ground, if only the common ground of our humanity."

The human realities that bond us and pull us together as people have to be cultivated. We've all suffered the slings and arrows of outrageous fortune. We're all mortal, and life is fleeting, fragile, and impermanent. Why can't we continue to suffer the human condition together? *E Pluribus Unum*—"Out of many, one." That's the precious legacy of democracy—within and without. It seems especially endangered in our time, but well worth fighting for. ■

Notes

1. ISIS, or Islamic State, is an Islamist terrorist group that grew out of the sectarian chaos of the Syrian civil war and collapse of the Iraqi army in 2013–2014 to control swathes of Syria and Iraq. IS's leader, Abu Bakr al-Baghdadi, proclaimed himself caliph (or leader of all Islam) on June 29, 2014.

2. The Scopes Trial famously pitted Clarence Darrow against William Jennings Bryan, arguing for and against the allowance of the teaching of evolution in state-funded schools. More at <http://en.wikipedia.org/wiki/Scopes_Trial>.

3. "Arizona Vetoes Bill on Denying Services to Gays," by Aaron Blake, *Washington Post*, February 26, 2014.

4. Adapted from "The Second Coming," by W. B. Yeats <http://www.poetryfoundation.org/poem/172062>.

5. "Dunn Convicted of Attempted Murder; Hung Jury on Murder in 'Loud Music' Trial," by Greg Botelho, Steve Almasy, and Sunny Hostin, CNN.com, February 17, 2014 <http://www.cnn.com/2014/02/15/justice/florida-loud-music-trial/>.

6. "N.R.A. Envisions 'a Good Guy With a Gun' in Every School," Eric Lichtblau and Motoko Rich, *New York Times*, December 21, 2012.

6

On the Battlefield of the Psyche
War and Trauma

AN INTERVIEW WITH LARRY DECKER, PH.D.

ALL WARS ARE LIKE Greek tragedies: a phenomenon so all-encompassing it's as if the totality of human experience—life, death, love, hate, victory, defeat, tragedy, and hope—has been condensed into one colossal event. Given war's immense archetypal scale, it's hardly a surprise that soldiers returning home not only bear on their bodies the physical scars of battle, but carry within them the emotional traumas of war as well. Abandoned by those they served and fought for, soldiers have been forced to suffer their invisible wounds alone and in silence, lacking even the words to name their affliction, or a healer to ease their soul's pain.

And so it is one of history's more interesting turns that it was in the immediate aftermath of Vietnam—the war that humbled America in its role as a global military power, and that bitterly divided the nation—that a link was officially made between the horrors of war and the psychological harm it can inflict on the human psyche. Finally and at last, soldiers were given a diagnosis for the nightmares, sleeplessness, paranoia, outbursts of temper, alcoholism, addiction, and their inability to return to civilian life that they suffered from and that they blamed themselves for: PTSD, or Post-traumatic Stress Disorder.[1]

Yet even despite this advance, soldiers continue to be seen by society as invulnerable on the inside as they appeared on the outside, with all their weapons and armor. This has meant that combatants of the recent wars in Iraq and Afghanistan, as well as aging veterans of the war in Vietnam and World War II, can still go wanting for the kind of empathic care necessary to bind up the psychological wounds of war. How these undressed wounds affect veterans and their loved ones, how they change our understanding of war, and how PTSD can contribute to more violence in the culture are the subjects of my interview with psychologist Larry Decker.

Decker first began working with veterans in the aftermath of Vietnam, when he was asked to help set up some of the early rap groups in Santa Barbara. The work, he told me, "hooked him" immediately. From the first group he led, said Decker, "the men's stories, and the degree to which they needed and accepted me—even though I was a civilian—was a powerful experience." A clinical psychologist in private practice, Decker has worked for over twenty-five years for the Department of Veterans Affairs, where he is currently a federal contractor counseling veterans of World War II, the Korean War, the Vietnam War, and the wars in Iraq and Afghanistan. He is the author of *The Alchemy of Combat*, and in our dialogue he reveals some of the attitudes and approaches he adopts in working with vets in therapy, as well as what civilians and loved ones can do—and also must *not* do—for those friends, spouses, and family members wounded by war. Our first interview took place in 1994; I followed up with him in 2014.

✳

Pythia Peay: Can you tell me how the psychological work around healing the inner wounds of war—if that's even possible—first arose?

Larry Decker: Soldiers have been suffering the trauma of war for centuries. In his book *Achilles in Vietnam*, the author Jonathan Shay points out all the different instances in Homer's *Iliad* that the warrior Achilles describes his own symptoms. During the Civil War a surgeon named Da Costa started seeing soldiers who exhibited depression, anxiety, nightmares, and intrusive thoughts. He originally thought it had something to do with heart problems, and so he called it "irritable heart," or "soldier's heart." During World War I, these same symptoms were attributed to shell shock.[2]

So it's only recently that we've given this phenomenon a name: PTSD, or Post-traumatic Stress Disorder. Sigmund Freud was among the first to form some of our basic thinking about trauma. The French psychiatrist Pierre Janet also began to research how trauma affected psychic life. He described the human response to trauma as forming a membrane around the core of who we think we are, as a way of protecting ourselves from the horrible thing that's happened. As a result, a part of us becomes lost, unconscious, and relegated to some place deep down inside ourselves. Nonetheless, according to Janet, these repressed emotions tend to come out in all sorts of odd ways, creating problems.

PP: So to sum up, when a soldier is traumatized by war, he seals off the part of himself that's been psychically wounded?

LD: Particularly when he's in battle, he doesn't have a choice—because if he doesn't, he risks getting everybody, including himself, killed. But sometimes the opposite happens, and soldiers deal with trauma by going berserk. They just go crazy and try to kill everybody, sometimes even somebody on the same side if he happens to get in the way.

One man told me about a soldier who had been a berserker in combat. When he returned stateside to base camp, he asked some people to be quiet. When they wouldn't obey him, he tossed a grenade into the group and killed them. Then he was sent to prison at Leavenworth. So this is an example of how some veterans continue to see violence as an option to try to solve problems. To varying degrees, they learn how to resist that option once they return to civilian life. At other times, they don't really re-incorporate the relatively normal parts, and they stay repressed or split off, or they numb themselves through drinking.

PP: So although symptoms of war-related trauma have been recorded all throughout history, do different wars result in different symptoms?

LD: Yes. For example, one of the big differences between World War II and Vietnam was DEROS: the date of expected return from overseas. In Vietnam, everyone was given a tour of duty of one year, except for Marines, who were given thirteen months. In World War II, however, enlistment was for the duration of the war; this made for a very different experience. At one point during World War II there were actually more psychiatric breakdowns on the battlefield than there were people being drafted—soldiers fell apart because they didn't know when they were going to get out and come home.

In Vietnam, a soldier knew when he was going to get out, and basically had to keep it together until then. But then when they got back to America, Vietnam vets suffered "sanctuary trauma": they arrived home with the expectation that home would be a safe place, which turned out to be almost as dangerous as the place they left.

PP: I understand that Vietnam veterans suffered more coming home than World War II vets, because World War II was more accepted and honored in American culture.

LD: I think that's part of the mythology around World War II: that it was a good war, and that they were all praised when they got home. But World War II vets suffered just as much; there was just as high an incidence of suicide after World War II among combat vets; and just as high an incidence of alcoholism, homelessness, unemployment, and domestic violence as among Vietnam vets.

It's just that the effects of war began to be more talked about among Vietnam vets, and that didn't go over well with the veterans of World War II. For example, one Vietnam vet told me about his experience getting up and speaking to a veterans' group. After he'd finished speaking, an older World War II vet stood up and said, "You know, sonny, what you went through was real tough. But it was nothing compared to what we went through and we never talked about it." That was a very common rejection by those men of the Greatest Generation: they didn't think anybody was supposed to talk about what happened during war, and anybody who did was a crybaby, drug abuser, and loser.

PP: Is this difference between the two generations due to the fact that Vietnam vets were more sensitive to feelings and psychology, simply because of the times they were born into?

LD: I think so. At the time, there was much more openness in our culture to express what was real, truthful, and honest about who and what we are; that's what our generation was supposed to be about.

PP: Were there other differences between the two generations of soldiers?

LD: During World War II, soldiers stayed with the unit they were assigned to throughout the war, so there was more of a sense of a cohesive fighting unit. But in Vietnam, men went to boot camp with one group of people, then transferred to advanced infantry with a different group of men, and then went to Vietnam with yet another group. If they formed a relationship with someone in their unit, that soldier might get killed. So they learned *not* to form relationships; they learned how to exist on their own, how not to trust, and to be hyper-vigilant.

Many soldiers left Vietnam without knowing what happened to the unit or platoon they'd been assigned to; some were even pulled out of action in the middle of a firefight—suddenly a helicopter descended, and off they'd go. Then one or two days later, they were in San Francisco, perhaps in uniform, and people were yelling at them and calling them "baby killers."

PP: So it's veterans' sudden and abrupt transition from war to civilian life, with no chance to integrate or understand what they've been through, that can exacerbate the traumas of war.

LD: That's it exactly. Even today, Vietnam veterans still wonder what happened to their platoon. During the seventies, returning vets in VA Hospitals were told to just forget about it all. Many of them bought into that myth that if they just held down their memories of war they'd go away—so they didn't even try to contact anyone from their units, and they didn't want to talk about it.

But back then, PTSD didn't even exist: it was called combat fatigue. The idea behind that was simply to give the soldier a bit of rest and treatment in order to make him a competent soldier again and get him back to the front line. The military didn't want men using this as a way to get out of combat.

PP: So there was no opportunity provided by the military to help soldiers retrieve those buried parts of themselves, or the feelings that they shoved down way inside of them.

LD: No, not at all. That would have been detrimental to the war machine: people wouldn't go to war anymore because they would start feeling that tender, nurturing part of themselves—and then how could they go back out and kill someone?

PP: What are some of the differences that you've seen between Vietnam vets and younger vets returning from the Iraq and Afghanistan wars?

LD: Vietnam vets are now an aging population; they're all in their sixties or older.

Their PTSD is chronic and has become a way of life. Whereas for younger veterans, regardless of whether they were warned in advance about PTSD, they're still unprepared for the kind of difficulties they experience when they come back.

Getting along with civilians is also challenging for many of these younger vets. They see us as being asleep; they feel that if we just woke up, we'd begin to understand what life is really about. They also deplore our individualism and lack of being united around a common mission, which was what they experienced during combat, and which meant an enormous amount to them. To this day, every single vet I see wants to go back to Iraq and Afghanistan.

PP: I confess I'm completely taken aback by what you just said. Why would these vets want to return to a place where their lives are in constant danger?

LD: It's important to understand how meaningful their work was over there. And what do they do when they come home? They stock shelves in a grocery store, or something similarly banal. It's a telling statement about the meaninglessness of our culture: that we can't provide something better than being in a war zone!

But another way of understanding the Iraq veteran's wish to return to the theater of operations is the fact that war requires you to be completely present. Without this sense of urgency that being in a war zone necessitates, soldiers find their attention wandering to the comparative emptiness of their lives. As a result, they feel a desire a return to what engrossed them. Veterans' sense of a lack of meaning on coming home is reflected in the many suicides after each war, including our current ones. These feelings of meaninglessness combine in the combat veteran with the traumas of friends dying, killing the enemy, and believing that in the killing a line (with God) has been crossed, which is irrevocable.

PP: Someone I know who's a Vietnam vet confided that he was petrified of dying, because of the immense guilt he felt around those he'd had to kill during the war, including, by accident, civilians. I felt strongly that his heavy cross of guilt shouldn't be his alone to bear, but that it belonged to me, and to all those Americans he'd gone to war for.

LD: That's very true; we sent them there. At the time, your friend was doing the best he could with what he had. If he'd hesitated, his whole squad might have been killed. Soldiers at war can't hesitate; they have to shoot. That's war, and that's what happens.

I once had an interview with the Tibetan Buddhist leader, His Holiness the Dalai Lama, about my work. When I asked him for his advice on how to work with veterans he said that two things were important: first, they had to have some kind of spirituality. It didn't matter what kind, as long as they had some kind of connection. And secondly, they had to know that it was their job—their duty—to kill people. He also made a distinction between having to kill during war, and committing murder.

PP: So did Vietnam vets want to go back to Vietnam, like Iraq vets wanted to return to Iraq, for the same reasons you listed above?

LD: The vets that I saw didn't give voice to that; most guys just wanted out of the military. But they did report feeling aimless, with no clue what to do with themselves. In his book *Escape from Freedom*, the German psychologist Eric Fromm wrote about the paradox of those who escape repressive regimes—yet who, once they've escaped, can't bear the amount of choices they have to make, because they're used to having their choices made for them. Most returning vets face that dilemma; Vietnam vets especially. And then there was the very negative reception they got when they came home, with the name-calling and harassment.

PP: That was a shameful period in our history.

LD: I believe it was an actual crime. But as a result, Vietnam vets hid; they rarely talked to anybody about the war, and they were very secretive, because it wasn't acceptable to let their experiences be known. But for *all* vets, the reason they don't want to talk about what they did during the war is because they're afraid that people are going to hate them, or that someone might say, "God! How could you have done that?" That's the *worst* possible thing they could hear, besides "What did it feel like to kill somebody?" It's surprisingly common how many people ask returning vets those kinds of thoughtless questions.

PP: As we're talking, it sounds to me as if America hasn't changed that much with regard to its wounded veterans. Have you seen any kind of shift toward our veterans returning from the Iraq and Afghanistan wars?

LD: We didn't spit on them, and we didn't throw things at them when they came back. Now it's more a matter that nobody really cares. As one Iraq war veteran said, "Yeah, it's better than being spit on. But all these people that want to buy me a drink, and tell me what a good job I did—they don't know what I did. If they knew what I did, they wouldn't be buying me these things." So vets returning from the wars in Iraq and Afghanistan still have that sense that civilians just don't get it, and that they will *never* get it. As a result, they're very isolated and stuck in a kind of "Never Never" land: they're no longer in the military, but they're not civilians either.

PP: Because they're never going to be the same person they were before they went to war?

LD: Right. While they're away they suffer horribly from homesickness—but when they finally return, they've changed so much it isn't home anymore. But home hasn't changed: *they've* changed. All veterans returning from war go through this. But nobody has a clue how to help them, and nobody cares anyway, except for those who are very close to them, and who are affected by all the problems around anger, alcoholism, and violence.

PP: So how do you, as a psychologist, work with vets with PTSD?

LD: The work is primarily about integrating what happened. Basically, veterans are struggling with how to handle a hugely significant and new experience that won't fit into their old system—so they have to form a new system. For the majority of people, things change incrementally, in very slow, linear ways that are basically safe. But trauma isn't like that. Trauma is a huge, violent, abrupt change.

Most of the vets I work with say that their first understanding of what they'd gotten themselves into was when they first came under fire: it was only then that they realized people were trying to kill them. Prior to that, war had been just a concept, so they didn't really grasp it. But trauma is like that: until something enormously horrible happens to us, it's just a fantasy.

So in my work with veterans, I've found that healing trauma comes out of connecting to an "innate self" that goes much deeper, and that has nothing to do with the interactive senses that connect us to the external world. This innate self could be called an essence, or our spirit or soul; it's something within us that was present when we were born. In order for veterans to begin living in the world again, there also has to be a kind of purpose to the trauma they suffered. So it's very important in recovery to develop a theory of meaning around what happened to them: "What was the purpose?" "Why did it happen to me?" and "What does it have to do with who I am?" In this sense, it's possible that trauma prepares us for more broadened concepts around life; the knowledge that we're all going to die, and that, as the Buddhists believe, the things of this life are temporary.

PP: So if handled by a wise and skilled counselor, veterans can be guided out of the hellish kind of limbo they find themselves in after war. They might even discover the potential contained in their suffering to widen their consciousness.

LD: Yes, but it's also important to remember that there are certain things we *can't* do in working with survivors of trauma, such as blaming the victim, or seeing them as psychologically deficient if they show any emotional difficulties. There are also different forms of "spiritual blame": the concept of original sin, karmic payback, or telling veterans that they went through trauma in order to become emotionally stronger.

A key factor in working with vets who are in treatment is to give them an anchor—one person that they can feel safe with in talking about their experiences. Talking about things that they never thought they'd be able to say gives vets back their power. It's also an enormous relief to discover that they're not alone.

I also help vets I work with to rediscover and reconnect with a sense of innocence, nurturing, and safety that they'd experienced at some point in their lives. Then, once they're anchored in this firm foundation, they can go back into the trauma.

PP: So before the trauma can heal, there has to be this initial strengthening, then reenactment and reintegration.

LD: Right. I also encourage them to look toward the future, and to see the future as a stronger pull than the past—because how they are now determines what's going to happen next. And so I ask them, "How do you want your future to look? What do you want to have happen next in your life?" This allows for a new self to emerge, with new beliefs, capabilities, and a sense of identity. A sense of relatedness and camaraderie comes back, and they take huge steps forward. This can also be very scary; there's a tendency to relapse at that point, and to go back into the symptoms. A lot of vets will drop out at that point.

So it's a very tricky process that has to be gone through very slowly and carefully, and by giving people the time they need. Some vets who've been with me for years will still have to go back into the trauma again to find lost memories that are still influencing them in some way.

PP: Turning from our vets to the wider culture, where does America come in to all this? For example, as you've just described, one way that vets can begin to heal from war's trauma is to turn toward the future. And although that part of America that is very future- and horizon-oriented might aid their recovery, I also wonder if our resistance to the past might also contribute to our cultural inability to really take in and accept the trauma and suffering that these vets have endured. There's that attitude in American culture toward anyone who is suffering that basically says, "What's your problem? Just get over it, go on, and move forward."

LD: Right; we just don't want to know about it. We're all so tired from our everyday jobs and responsibilities, we just want to numb out—and then get up and do it all over again. We don't want to hear about somebody else's stuff. If people think about what our veterans are going through at all—which I'm sure ninety percent of the population doesn't—they think about it in a surface way, like "Can I buy you a drink?" or "You went over and kicked some butt—you really showed 'em!" Like war was some kind of a football game.

PP: So what *do* our vets want from us?

LD: One of my patients for three or four years was Karl Marlantes, the author of *Matterhorn* and *What It's Like To Go To War*. During his appearance on "Moyers & Company," he told Moyers that veterans don't want a cheering section, with people yelling "Yeah America!"[3] What they really want, he said, is meaningful work. They also, he said, don't want to be forgotten or ignored. And they want to taste some of life's wonderful beauty and gorgeousness. Those are a few key things we could do to help our vets when they come home; it's not about glorifying war, but simply appreciating what our soldiers went through.

PP: So I'm assuming that, even after all the wars of the twentieth and twenty-first century, there's still no real psychological or spiritual preparation before soldiers are sent off to war, and no preparation when they return to help them assimilate back into culture?

LD: It's gotten a *little* better. Soldiers are told about PTSD before they leave. When they return, they're read a cursory checklist of symptoms. One marine returning from Iraq told me that, after hearing the list of symptoms read out loud, he raised his hand. The sergeant then took him into a back room and yelled at him, calling him a "dumb shit" because now his discharge was going to be delayed. The marine apologized, the sergeant had him sign off on a piece of paper, and off they went. And that's what happens. It's just a very masculine, military approach.

PP: After the war in Vietnam, I recall that a discussion arose around providing some kind of a coming home ceremony or ritual for our returning warriors—something to help purify them from what they'd been through, so that they could re-enter society once again.

LD: To have a returning home ceremony would be relatively meaningless because there's nothing in the culture to back it up with. There is no true warrior culture in America—no preparation or training for soldiers. There's none of that.

PP: Given our bloated defense budget, I think the statement that we're not a true "warrior culture" would come as a surprise to a lot of Americans.

LD: We have a warlike culture—but we don't have a *warrior* culture. If we're going to go to war, we should know something about warriors, and we don't know *anything* about them. It's very secretive. The Department of Defense has an annual budget of approximately $550 billion, a budget so huge it dwarfs all of the other departments in the Federal Government.[4] The Veterans Administration has the second biggest budget, approximately $150 billion.[5] But there's nothing of a genuine warrior culture in any of these military institutions.

Millions of dollars *are* spent, however, on programs that train soldiers to become psychologically resilient, so that they don't have emotional responses to killing. Basically, this just removes their conscience, as well as a sense of empathy for the enemy. Instead, soldiers are taught that in order to kill they have to dehumanize their enemy. Thus in Vietnam, they were called "gooks," and in Iraq they became "Hajis" or "sand niggers." By contrast, the Greeks and other ancient warrior cultures understood the concept of the "honorable enemy," or "honorable foes."

PP: What's the psychological difference between killing an "honorable foe" and killing a "gook" or a "Haji"?

LD: As has been well known in the field of psychology, and as I've seen in my own clinical experience, the effects of dehumanizing the enemy can lead to serious problems when soldiers return from war; their PTSD symptoms can become very, very severe. Essentially, when veterans attempt to re-enter the civilian world they eventually have to come to grips with the fact that their enemies, whether Vietnamese or Japanese, are human beings—not just "nips" or "gooks." This realization creates enormous grief over the killing, torture, and mutilation the soldier may have been involved in. He was able to do those things in the war because he had convinced himself that the enemy was not really human. Now how can he forgive himself?

PP: So it's as if we send our soldiers to war with all the weapons they need, but nothing of the kind of psychological and spiritual training that you're describing. On some level, do you think that the vets who are returning from the battlefields with PTSD, and who are suffering this terrible disconnect between themselves and their psyches, and between themselves and the country, are like the proverbial canary in the coal mine, alerting us to something that's missing from our culture?

LD: I like that question. Yes, of course they are. But we're not paying any attention to them, because nobody really gets it. Whenever I tell people that every Iraq veteran I've ever seen wants to go back to war, they're shocked, just as you were.

But think about it: they're twenty years old, armed to the teeth with sophisticated weapons and equipment, alongside an enormous amount of men who are armed the same way, and who are all looking out for each other. Everyone has been incredibly well trained, they all have a mission, and they're all in agreement about how to do things. These young soldiers have the power to go out into the population and kill people if they don't do what they want: if someone comes too close to them, they can kill them. If they argue with them, they can kill them.

PP: It's like being given the power of the Gods.

LD: That's what the Vietnam veteran Karl Marlantes said. He said that these sorts of activities should be left to the Gods, but instead we give them to nineteen-year-olds.

PP: You must get very angry sometimes.

LD: No. More than anything, I can become overwhelmed by grief. That's when I know I'm burnt out, and have to get away for a while. ■

Notes

1. More information on PTSD can be found at the Veterans Association <http://www.ptsd.va.gov>.
2. According to Decker, one of the explanations of shell shock was that it "was caused by the inhalation of carbon monoxide that was produced by the explosions. So the term is *shell shock* and one of the explanations was that it was the inhalation of carbon monoxide that created the symptoms of a lack of self control, an unwillingness to continue to fight, and a general muscle weakness or neurasthenia."
3. You can read about Karl Marlantes on "Moyers & Company," with host Bill Moyers, at <http://billmoyers.com/guest/karl-marlantes/>.
4. Department of Defense annual budget for 2012: 553.Billion. The DOD's budget comprises 45 percent of *all* global military spending, and is more than the seventeen largest militaries combined <http://www.whitehouse.gov/omb/factsheet_department_defense>.
5. Department of Veterans Affairs annual budget for 2014: 152.7 Billion <http://www.va.gov/budget/products.asp>.

7

Heartbreak and the Gods
of Love and War

AN INTERVIEW WITH GINETTE PARIS, PH.D.

INFUSED WITH A UNIQUE combination of sparkling sensibility and philosophical intellect, Ginette Paris trained as a clinical psychologist in her native Montreal, Canada, where she also taught as a tenured professor at the University of Quebec. Influenced by her friendship with post-Jungian American psychologist James Hillman, and drawn to the myths of the ancient Greeks and how their wisdom applied to modern-day psychological dilemmas, Paris eventually became a depth psychologist. Inspired by the creative conjunction of clinical psychology with Jungian perspectives on archetypes and classical mythology, Paris published several books, including *Pagan Meditations: Aphrodite, Hestia, Artemis*. In 1995, drawn by the idyllic weather and the quality of its students, Paris underwent a second life shift, moving to Santa Barbara, California, where she became a permanent U.S. resident and began teaching courses in depth psychology and archetypal psychology at the Pacifica Graduate Institute.

As fate would have it, Dr. Paris would undergo yet another personal transformation. While at a wedding party in 2005, she stumbled and fell backward into an empty, concrete pool, sustaining a near-fatal cerebral hemorrhage. This dangerous accident was followed by a months-long recovery; as her body and mind healed, Paris began to experience a radical shift in her perspectives on love, life, and her ideas of the human psyche. Having literally been "hit on the head," she embarked on an intrepid new area of research: neuroscience, and its applications to depth psychology, eventually publishing her findings in *The Wisdom of the Psyche: Depth Psychology after Neuroscience*.

The following interview captures Paris's intellectual and spiritual shifts across two decades. In our first interview conducted in 1995, she discusses two of mythology's most compelling figures: Ares and Aphrodite, the Greek God and Goddess that represent the archetypal energies of war and love. In 2014, we spoke again; this time the focus was on Paris's most recent book, *Heartbreak*, and her fascinating research into how neuroscience reveals the physical evidence linking grief, heartbreak, and violence—discoveries that have major implications for the epidemic of shootings by young men.

Many of Paris's insights, in fact, challenge some of society's current preconceptions around how to handle boys' physical aggression. Rather than quash adolescent boys as they grow into adulthood, making them more like girls, Paris asserts that they should be better educated by the culture in how to handle the strong urges surging through them—channeling, rather than repressing, "bully energies" in service-related, chivalric activities that protect the fragile and the weak. To facilitate a more nuanced, psychologically based awareness around heartbreak and masculine and feminine psychology, Paris calls for the development of a "wisdom culture": a society built on greater intelligence around human emotions, suffering, and self-knowledge.

✳

Pythia Peay: You've written several books about Greek mythology and its pantheon of Gods and Goddesses, among them Aphrodite, the Goddess of love and beauty, and Ares, the God of aggression and war, or the Roman Venus and Mars. What do these two mythic figures have to do with modern-day violence in America?

Ginette Paris: Aphrodite is the incarnation of beauty—the kind of beauty that is usually fragile and that needs protection, like a garden of flowers that needs tending, or any great work of art. Ares, who was one of her lovers, is the exact opposite. He is the God of aggression, what some might call a "brute," but also an archetype of courage, the "Braveheart" of mythology.

In the Greek mind there was an understanding that you cannot have Aphrodite without Ares. This means that you can't have beauty, sensuality, and the finer arts of civilization without a strong martial figure, so to speak, to protect it and guard it. There is another connection between Ares and Aphrodite and it is the archetypal link between aggression and sexuality, one that is so obvious in pornography and comes from the will to control the source of pleasure.

PP: How fascinating! Which of this pair of archetypes do you feel is most repressed in our culture?

GP: The way I see it is there is more of a problem with Ares than there is with Aphrodite. Although the USA is an empire and one of the most militaristic cultures in the advanced world, there is a denial and a split in our educational values, where young boys are asked to be "nice" in a way that serves girls more than boys. They compensate for this by being bullies and delinquents, initiated by gang leaders because the male elders won't do the job of initiating them as boys.

One way to understand Ares would be to call him "Mr. Testosterone." He is what you might call the "Rambo" of mythology, and can be found in Hollywood movies, where he has found his place. This kind of raw aggression comes out in boys during puberty, when they have this incredible explosion of testosterone in their bodies, and they feel like hitting, fighting, and destroying. Instead of talking and being "nice," like Aphrodite, they'd rather grunt—raw, brute Ares energy!

Parents, teachers, and Western society too quickly judge that kind of behavior as improper or threatening. Any aggressiveness on the part of an adolescent boy is treated as an indication that something is wrong, rather than a value to be cultivated—both in them personally and also in the culture. It isn't Ares' business to be "nice," but to be brave. We don't provide many opportunities for these young boys to take risks and to be physically brave in defense of a cause. Delinquent violence has no structure, no form, they are all "rebels without a cause"—so, of course they want to steal to have a pair of expensive Nike shoes, a status symbol that says they are a "brave guy." Ares is the archetype of *physical* courage. Otherwise, this figure of mythology would just be a bad character and not a God. So why would this God win the most beautiful Goddess of all?

PP: Some might react strongly to this point of view, because what you're saying seems to reinforce sexist stereotypes that encourage men to be misogynistic or abusive toward women. On the other hand, I raised three sons—and I saw what it was like for them growing up to be punished by school teachers and other authority figures for what often seemed to me like natural, boyish, masculine behavior.

GP: To make them be more like women?

PP: Yes. I consider myself a feminist, and yet I saw something disturbing happening that wasn't talked about a lot.

GP: I consider myself a feminist, too, and my books are all written from a feminist perspective. But this doesn't mean that there can't be intellectual debates among feminists. Let's examine some of the clichés and stereotypes that surround Aphrodite, the feminine Goddess of beauty. Aphrodite was imaged as a woman, for instance, because culturally and as an archetype, women have always signified beauty—just as babies and flowers do, as well.

Of course, this stereotype had the potential to become very limiting, repressing women's assertiveness and aggression because it doesn't look "nice." The cultural belief that *all* women should be beautiful and soft is a problem that still afflicts and inhibits women. Women have to push those narrow stereotypes aside, and incorporate other feminine archetypes, like Athena, the warrior, or Hecate, a witch-like Goddess who is a very frightening image of the Feminine. But for women to rediscover these other aspects of femininity does not mean that they have to negate Aphrodite, or deny the fact that some women like to dress up, design clothes, or fuss with their hair. It can be just as repressive to stop a little girl from being charming or from painting her nails red, as it is to repress male aggression in boys, as you saw with your sons.

One should not forget that archetypes, once imagined as divinities, are never gender based. Even Aphrodite isn't just the Goddess of women—she is the embodiment of beauty for men, as well as for women. Men as well as women appreciate beauty, elegance, landscaping, and gardening, and have their own "call to beauty."

PP: Some studies have shown that compared to neglected landscapes of vacant lots and abandoned buildings, natural landscapes of trees, plants, and vegetation actually contribute to lower crime rates.[1]

GP: A group of my students who were trying to help improve a violent district in their area had the following idea: using a piece of land designated as a collective garden, they planted some extremely delicate, beautiful flowers and plants that needed protection. Their idea was to take the most troubled, aggressive boys in that area, and organize them to set up a kind of guard duty around these more fragile plants to make sure that nobody harmed or stole the fruit, vegetables, and flowers. The aggressive "bully energy" was transformed, making them soldiers in the service of something that needed to be guarded. I realized that all by themselves, my students had discovered the link between Aphrodite and Ares: in other words, these young boys could be tough in the service of beauty, which had more of a socializing effect on them than trying to make them "nice" or feminine. Do you see what I mean?

PP: Yes, I think you're making a link that hasn't been made before. As aggressive as we are as a culture, part of our problem is that we have no idea how to handle these energies in our boys, or how to school people in it. But that aggression is there, all over the place, and we act as if it isn't.

GP: There's no recognition of the natural instinct for aggression in adolescent boys, and the waste of occasions where they can channel that energy. Take the ritual of getting one's driver's license. An automobile is an instrument that is so powerful it can kill you and it can kill others. But we're more likely to understand the importance of a girl losing her virginity than when a boy gets his driver's license, although it is an obvious symbol of adulthood.

Nobody I know has organized a ceremony around a boy getting his driver's license. Rarely do you hear of an older, wiser man taking a young boy aside and delivering this message that, in a nutshell, says this: "Yes, as men we all want to go fast, and push the pedal to the metal—it's in our bones. So I understand what you feel when you've been given this enormous, powerful instrument: you want to speed, to risk your life, and to push this machine to the limit." But without an older man acknowledging this aggression as a biological *fact* in boys, they aren't taught that this violent energy in them is also something *good* that when used rightly can be a source of courage: something that will make a boy jump into an icy lake to save someone who's drowning, or that will make him a good fireman, or serve his country as a soldier or general.

PP: But what about that part of America that's often criticized as too violent and aggressive: that cultural role model symbolized by the macho, Western male hero who lacks emotional connection. What I'm trying to say is that we seem to have a conflicted attitude toward violence and aggression as something bad that should be eradicated, but also as a quality that we admire and need to get ahead in our competitive culture. So on the one hand, we have a fascination with violence, and our movies and television shows are saturated with crime and violence. On the other hand, in our daily lives we're supposed to be nice and polite and not lose our temper, and this goes for boys, too.

GP: Aggression can't be eradicated—it will only come back in a more vicious way. I don't want to make a judgment on the whole culture. But sometimes I have the feeling that we're caught in wrong thinking and a religious system that for two thousand years has put the Kingdom of Christ and God all on the side of goodness, love, and perfection, and the devil on the side of all that is bad and evil. Some New Age traditions and beliefs are just these same Christian values given a new twist; a spirituality that identifies with being angelic and that denies aggression and evil.

By comparison, in the classical world of the ancient Greeks, and of Aphrodite and Ares, peace was seen as an *equilibrium* between love and aggression. In the pagan view, each one of the Greek Gods and Goddesses had a dark side, as well as some attribute of perfection. Demeter, for example, was both the Goddess of nourishment and also rage when the child is threatened. So even the mother Goddesses had the capacity and the power to kill: because if you have the power to give life, with it comes the power to destroy life. But we don't like to think that way; women especially should be all giving and compassionate.

This awareness of both the light and dark sides of human nature in the ancient world was a different kind of moral thinking, and it can be uncomfortable. I'm not comparing and saying that the Greek way was better—that's not at all my point. There are historical movements and perhaps we moved toward Christian monotheism because that is what was needed. But now I have the feeling that we're morally stuck with the Christian concept of what is good and what is evil, and that's not working anymore. This results in a lot of hypocritical political correctness that hides what is really going on.

PP: Ares and Aphrodite also have to do with matters of love and the heart. In your latest book, *Heartbreak*, you write about un-mourned grief as a cause of violence, and even link it to the recent wave of shootings by young men. How does a broken heart lead to violence?

GP: Neuropsychology and neuroscience have a lot to teach us in this area. Current research shows that whenever a person goes through heartbreak, it's similar in the brain to being submitted to torture. Young people are especially at risk, as their brains don't fully evolve until early adulthood. So I think it's important to know more about the three levels of the brain, and how they affect us.

The most primitive aspect is the reptilian brain, which is responsible for reflexes and aggression. So if somebody tries to attack us with a hammer, we feel a sudden jolt—that's a good thing, as we need that response for survival. But this same primitive part of the brain that's activated when we're attacked also gets activated when we experience heartbreak. This is why so many young men, and some women, spend their lives in prison: because when someone tries to take their object of love away from them, they react with what I call "crocodile psychology" and take revenge. Or, for example, someone makes fun of a young boy, calling him ugly and fat—making that teenager so angry he wants to get a gun and kill someone. So although we need this reptilian part of the brain for survival, it cannot be controlled, precisely because it's a reflex.

PP: But haven't we evolved ways to deal with this reptilian part of the brain?

GP: I like to use the example of the Buddhist monk: although like everyone else they can't control their basic reflexes of anger or other strong emotions, what they can do is *relate* to their instinctive reactions. And that kind of vocabulary is very important: we cannot control the brain, but we can relate to it with a different response.

Psychologists call this "affect regulation," which is a good but fancy name for learning to think before we act. But what is important to understand is that this capacity is missing in young people, so they lack the capacity to regulate their affects or their emotions, because for the most part their negative emotions are not acknowledged, since they are expected to be nice. It's a kind of psychological correctness that prevents them from developing affect regulation.

PP: Is that because the frontal cortex, which rules logic and reason, doesn't mature until the early twenties?

GP: That's part of the problem. But beginning from a very young age the mind also needs to be trained. In the famous "marshmallow" test, kids three, four, and five years old are put in a room and given one marshmallow. They're told that if they can wait ten minutes before they eat that marshmallow, they'll get two instead of one. Some children are able to wait; others can't control their impulse to grab the marshmallow and eat it.[2] So our capacity to control or fail to control our impulses is already evident from an early age.

PP: Tell me about the second level of the brain.

GP: The second level belongs to the emotional, limbic brain, which we share with mammals. This part of the brain is also activated in heartbreak. When this happens, we regress to the level of a child. If a loved one leaves us, for example, we experience with overwhelming conviction and certitude the emotion that "abandonment means death and I'm going to die!"

I call this level of heartbreak "the puppy level." We all have a little abandoned puppy inside us who will cry for rescue if it's abandoned. We can also hear these feelings expressed in popular songs with lyrics like "don't leave me, or I'll die." The limbic level of the brain, however, is usually treated with medication, with the known risks of addiction.

PP: And what is the third level of the brain, and its role in heartbreak and violence?

GP: This is the level that only humans have and governs what is usually called the arts and humanities, and the ability to tell stories and reflect on our lives: what's traditionally called wisdom. Typically, we're so focused on treating our problems with medication that we rarely talk about what helps people to become wiser. But in order to avoid spending the rest of our lives trying to sue the person who hurt us, or to make him or her go bankrupt, or to indulge in fantasies of retaliation—which can kill us psychically—then we need to develop the capacity for wisdom. But the problem is that our culture doesn't provide the best of conditions for developing wisdom!

The sad thing is that in schools today heartbreak among the young is never taken seriously, or considered of any importance. The usual response is "Oh, you'll get over it!" But one hundred percent of all violent gun attacks in schools are carried out by adolescents who have been rejected, humiliated, isolated, or bullied. So whether for young people or for adults, most of our cultural responses and theories around love and heartbreak are dangerously inadequate, and don't take into account that we can kill or die from a broken heart.

PP: So why do you think these recent shootings have all been perpetrated by young men?

GP: Isolation, rejection, and heartbreak! And heartbreak could be your mom and dad calling you a loser. That's the first heartbreak—"Mom and Dad don't love me!" Or they could suffer from heartbreak because the girls in school don't find you cool, so you don't have a date to go to a dance; you are not invited and nobody seems to love you.

PP: I'm sure girls experience this kind of rejection at home and in school. But they're not the ones who pick up a gun.

GP: Sociology has studied how girls "go bad," and one way is sexual promiscuity. So girls who experience heartbreak can get pregnant and have a child at sixteen just to piss off their parents, or they can become addicted to drugs. So girls turn against themselves.

PP: What would it look like at an educational level to develop more of a wisdom culture?

GP: There should be more character training in schools: zero tolerance for bad manners, being mean and manipulative, hitting, and humiliating or calling other kids names. One thing I'm optimistic about is the fact that more people are gaining awareness around the epidemic of narcissism in our youth: these are the kids who cannot understand that when they attack somebody, either physically or with words, it actually hurts the victim.

But one of the factors responsible for the rise of bullying, I believe, is the culture of consumerism. If a person has money, they can be absolutely detestable—and still have status. It would also help if we could pay teachers more than we do—we pay them roughly the same salary as a parking attendant! So the culture needs to completely change, with no tolerance for the kind of behavior that provokes rage and that creates murderers. Look at all these killers—without exception they've all been rejected. And yet nobody talks to them, and so nobody sees it coming.

PP: So social isolation can be very dangerous?

GP: Rejection combined with isolation *is* very, very dangerous.

PP: I have a close friend who worked for many years as a school psychologist, and who worked very hard to introduce some of these ideas to kids around wisdom, self-knowledge, and emotional awareness. But she found little support among the rest of the faculty: it was as if she spoke a language they didn't understand. The focus was all about learning in order to get a job to get ahead to earn money. So there's little to no "wisdom culture" at an educational level, which it sounds like you're saying would be critical to develop to avert more of these mass shootings by young people.

GP: Well, I'm a bit cynical about that. It seems that we need a bit more killing before we will really get it. Once things are really bad, with more adolescents killing others and killing themselves, and shooting all around, then perhaps the culture will change. You live by the value you live by, and you die by that. It's very, very sad.

PP: That's a very sad statement.

GP: Yes, it is. But what your friend was experiencing is a reflection of the dominant culture of consumerism and competition, and getting on top and becoming a winner—because if you're not a winner then you're a loser. So it's as if there are only two options: either you win or you lose. There's no middle. A person can't just be a decent human being who is happy with work well done.

The culture will also have to discover that drugs for depression, ADHD, and anxiety don't cure these disorders at all: they just sedate people. So number one, you can get addicted to antidepressants; and number two, it won't really do anything to help you! We also use drugs to treat children for symptoms that are cultural in origin, like attention deficit hyperactivity disorder (ADHD). How come there is no ADHD in children who are raised in ashrams? The brain of a child who is hyperactive is different from the brain of a child who is peaceful. But we now know that culture and the brain are in a loop.

PP: So you mean the over-stimulation of our hyper, over-stimulated culture . . .

GP: Yes, culture can change the brain: that's a new recognition by neuroscience. So if the culture changes the brain, there are just two options: medicate the brain, or change the culture.

PP: So what would it look like at a broader societal level to develop more of a wisdom culture, in terms of dealing with matters of the heart?

GP: We could examine some of our beliefs around loss and love. It's not true, for instance, that heartbreak can be healed in a year. The theory of stages of grief (put forth by Elisabeth Kübler-Ross) was disproven.

PP: I'm familiar with the four stages of grief, but not the idea that heartbreak can be healed in a year.

GP: It was thought that after the bereaved person went through a one-year cycle of mourning—one Christmas, one birthday, and one summer—that then they would be okay. But the theory was never tested, and has been proven wrong. Some people never get over the death of the person they lost.

PP: So what kinds of rites or cultural attitudes would help in this?

GP: Let me give you one example. It used to be that when someone was widowed, they would wear a black armband. That would signify to others that they had recently lost a dear person, and were in mourning. People around them would then treat them with more affection; if they went to the café, they'd be encouraged to join friends and have a drink, and to talk about how they were doing. And it was like this for three months. Nowadays, we give the bereaved two or three days off, or money to go to a grief counselor, and the attitude is "get over it." But the person doesn't just get over it: they have to go into their pain, and do their mourning. ■

Notes

1. "Penn Study Finds With Vacant Lots Greened, Residents Feel Safer. New Evidence Supports Earlier Studies Suggesting Greening Vacant Lots May Reduce Violent Crime," by Carolyn C. Cannuscio, ScD, August 7, 2012: News Release, Penn Medicine, University of Pennsylvania <http://www.uphs.upenn.edu/news/News_Releases/2012/08/vacant/>.
2. The Stanford marshmallow experiment was a series of studies on delayed gratification in the late 1960s and early 1970s led by psychologist Walter Mischel, then a professor at Stanford University <http://en.wikipedia.org/wiki/Stanford_marshmallow_experiment>.

Part II

Addicted America

There is a yearning that is as spiritual as it is sensual. Even when it degenerates into addiction, there is something salvageable from the original impulse that can only be described as sacred. Something in the person (dare we call it a soul?) wants to be free, and it seeks its freedom any way it can. . . . There is a drive for transcendence that is implicit in even the most sensual of desires.—**Mark Epstein**, *Open to Desire: Embracing a Lust for Life—Insights from Buddhism and Psychotherapy*

THERE HAS ALWAYS BEEN, write historians Lender and Martin in their book of the same name, "drinking in America." Spirits were brought over by the barrel on the first ships to set sail from England. One of the first crises to erupt in the New World occurred in 1621 when, just after the *Mayflower* landed off the coast of Massachusetts, the settlers began to run out of beer. In an age when liquor was safer than water and when alcohol was considered good for one's health, warding off chills and fever and making hard labor easier to bear, write Lender and Martin, the settlers grew anxious over their diminishing stores of alcohol. After discovering that the ship's crew still had beer and gin—which they were keeping hidden for their return voyage to England—the settlers begged the captain of the boat to leave them with enough alcohol to get them through what they knew would be a brutal winter. Finally, the captain relented, sending word that there would be "beer for them that need it." Even so, there was still not enough of what the colonists called the "good creature of God" to go around during that first winter, and efforts to "secure a reliable flow of alcohol" became a "growing concern shared by all the early colonies." When the *Arabella* set sail for Boston in 1630, it carried three times as much beer as water, along with distilled spirits and 10,000 gallons of wine.

As more settlers arrived and as the colonies continued to grow, they relied less on imports of alcohol from England and began producing their own. Wives brewed beer in their kitchens. Governor John Winthrop Jr. of the Massachusetts Bay Colony brewed his own beer from Indian corn. Thomas Jefferson did a "bit of brewing" at Monticello; Benjamin Franklin created his own "spruce beer"; and, as Lender and Martin note, George Washington drank a "molasses based home brew." The first president also ran a brisk whiskey business out of his estate at Mt. Vernon; at his death in 1799 it was the largest brewery in America, and continues to produce whiskey to this day.

Hard liquor abounded in colonial America: gin or "aqua vitae," "strong" and "hot" waters like grain whiskeys, and peach brandies and potent hard ciders like "Jersey Lightning." America's first laborers, some might be surprised to know, were typically paid their wages in distilled beverages, of which they received a steady supply throughout the day. Simply stated, say Lender and Martin, our first settlers were "serious drinkers" who drank "often and abundantly," whether at the family table or the local tavern; or while clearing fields, raising churches and buildings; or at weddings, baptisms, funerals, town meetings, and militia drills. Even polling places were "wet," with office seekers "treating" the electorate with libations.

Drinking in early America, say the authors, was overwhelmingly a social and communal activity. Taverns and inns were not just for eating and drinking, but gathering places to exchange local gossip, news, and politics. The presence of wives and children acted as a natural restraint on drinking, as did Old World social customs and Puritan beliefs that stressed orderliness and good conduct and that shamed public inebriation (drunkenness was a crime in the new colonies). Though the colonists drank double the amount of alcohol consumed today, note Lender and Martin, they were not "problem drinkers."

With the American Revolution, however, Americans' drinking habits began to change—and not for the better. As settlers moved further west, and as old customs began to break down in independent America, the protective fabric of communal life began to fray. The ethos of individualism spread and to some, drunkenness became a right of individual self-expression, leading Lender and Martin to link alcoholism with the freedoms that came with democracy. Consumption of hard liquor increased, as did displays of public drunkenness. Concern arose, most prominently in the figure of Dr. Benjamin Rush of Philadelphia—a Founding Father who had served as surgeon general for the Continental Army, whose signature was on the Declaration of Independence, and who would become famous as colonial America's first physician.

Although Rush believed moderate consumption of alcohol was healthful, he began to speak out on the dangers of hard liquor that, if unrestrained, could cause death, and in 1794 he published a tract, *An Inquiry into the Effect of Ardent Spirits on the Human Mind and Body*. Remarkably ahead of his time, Rush correctly diagnosed alcoholism as a disease, rather than a lack of morals or a failure of will. Once a person became addicted to alcohol, he said famously, "even a saint would have a hard time controlling himself." Though not a strict prohibitionist, Rush began to petition hard for fewer taverns, heavier taxes on "spirits," and especially for stricter social sanctions against "drunkards," which he had come to view as a threat to citizens' safety—and to the cohesion of the new American republic.[1]

Rush was a progressive and observant thinker in the Enlightenment tradition; future generations would honor him as America's "First Psychiatrist" for his writings on mental illness. He was also a student of dreams, both those of his patients and his own. At his suggestion, Rush and his revolutionary brother and close friend John

Adams shared their nightly dreams in the letters they exchanged after Adams retired from the presidency. It is from this source that a dream of Rush's comes down to us, reflecting his mounting concern for the effects of hard alcohol, and his wish to rid the country of its use. As he recounted in his letter to Adams, Rush dreamed that he had been elected president of the United States. Recognizing the power the office would give him to act on his "long cherished hostility to ardent spirits," Rush decided to go to Washington to accept this position, in order to persuade Congress to pass a law "to prohibit not only the importation and distilling but the Consumption of ardent spirits." At this juncture in the dream, "great opposition" to his idea arose from the public, and Rush received many petitions to repeal this law, which in the dream he refused to do. At that instant, a man appeared in his office: a "venerable but plain-looking" citizen who explained that as reasonable as this law might have seemed to Rush, it was simply not working. The dream ended with the man suggesting that Rush retire from the presidency and go back to his professor's chair to amuse his students with his "idle and impracticable speculations."[2]

Dreams often function to compensate dreamers' extreme, one-sided attitudes in waking life. In this case, Rush's dream seems to suggest he would be better off adopting a more moderate approach—for as the Temperance movement would discover more than a century later, prohibition does not stop people from drinking. Although we cannot know for sure, the dream may have even influenced the doctor's decision to treat alcoholism as a medical issue. Still, Rush remained naively optimistic that one day America would be rid of alcohol. "In the year 1915," he told a friend, "a drunkard I hope will be as infamous in society as a liar or a thief, and the use of spirits as uncommon in families as a drink made of a solution of arsenic or a decoction of hemlock."[3] Today, a statistical picture of addiction in twenty-first-century America reveals that not only does alcohol continue to top the list as the nation's leading substance for abuse, but a roster of drugs Rush could hardly have imagined has flourished in the nearly three centuries since the Puritans first landed.

In a development that would likely make the good Dr. Rush turn over in his grave, opiates legally prescribed by physicians are now the country's fastest growing drug epidemic.[4] As Long Island pharmacist Howard Levine—whose pharmacy has been twice robbed by an addict—asks: How did America come to be "the most painful nation" on the globe, using *80 percent* of opiate painkiller drugs worldwide? Overprescribed and overmedicated as a country, the United States contains more people who are overdosing from prescription drugs than from heroin and cocaine.[5] Other concerned citizens might also ask how we came to be a country that spends $600 billion annually on the abuse of tobacco ($193 billion), alcohol ($235 billion), and illicit drugs like marijuana ($193 billion) in crime, lost work productivity, and healthcare.[6] Americans might wonder as well how, with only five percent of the world's population, we consume two-thirds of the illegal drugs, and pause over the fact that half of American adults have a close family member who is or was an alcoholic.

America might reflect, too, on how its "war on drugs" has led to its distinction as the world's biggest jailer, and the troubling statistic that 80 percent of those incarcerated in adult and juvenile penal institutions are there directly or indirectly as a result of addiction, and that those inmates are disproportionately men of color. They might consider how drug overdose is the number-one killer of offenders released from prison; and that more than 29 percent of teens in treatment are dependent on some form of prescription medication.[7] And though drug use is highest among people in their teens and twenties (led by marijuana and prescription drugs), Baby Boomers, who brought psychedelics and pot into cultural awareness, are catching up. On America's scale of substance abuse, alcohol leads the list (17.7 million, or 6.8 percent of the population), followed by marijuana (4.3 million), and then prescription drugs (2.1 million). Indeed, if America were to attend a global Twelve Step meeting with other countries, it would have to stand and admit that "My name is America, and I am an addict." Some encouraging trends, however, offer hope. Fewer Americans are smoking, with teens experiencing the most dramatic drop in use. And where alcohol is concerned, there has been a decline in underage drinking, binge drinking, and driving under the influence of alcohol. A large and troubling "treatment gap," however, continues to widen: whereas in 2012, 23.1 million needed treatment in dealing with an addiction, only 2.5 million received the help they needed.[8]

In the following interviews, I enlist the help of psychologists in an attempt to bring more depth and wisdom to a subject that has remained mired in judgmental moralism, disapproval, and misperceptions. It is a subject for me that, as for many, is close to home: my father suffered, and died from, smoking and the disease of alcoholism.

It is this personal perspective that opens my first interview with A. Thomas McLellan, one of America's leading addiction specialists, and who has also suffered the loss of family members to alcoholism. McLellan fiercely challenges outdated attitudes that persist toward alcoholism as a moral failure, rather than a disease that should be treated with the same seriousness of purpose as cancer or diabetes.[9] But he finds signs of hope in the new research and treatment models that have been pioneered over the past decade—and which have been shown to work, if only they could be made more available to the culture. Dr. Charles Grob, Director of the Division of Child and Adolescent Psychiatry at Harbor UCLA Medical Center, discusses addiction from the perspective of having treated thousands of young people over his thirty-year career. We also delve into his unconventional, but FDA-approved, research into the use of hallucinogens to treat depression and addiction, and how one of the causes underlying addiction is the need for altered states of consciousness.

In my interview with depth psychologist Ginette Paris, we follow up on the connection between ecstasy and addiction, as she taps the wisdom of the ancient Greeks with a discussion of what she calls "Dionysos, the God of alcohol," and explore what European traditions and the Eleusinian mysteries can teach modern cultures about how the use of alcohol and drugs taken within a social and sacred context can help protect against addiction. Jungian analyst Marion Woodman, revered for her lifelong work on eating disorders and for bringing the more related feeling values of the "Feminine" and the body into therapy, interprets messages from the unconscious that are made visible through eating disorders such as obesity, bulimia, and anorexia. Jungian analyst and existential philosopher Linda Leonard, daughter of an alcoholic father and a recovering alcoholic herself, describes addiction as a reflection of America's "Icarus complex": that part of our nature that seeks the heights and the quick fix.

Karen B. Walant, a psychotherapist specializing in attachment disorders, speaks compellingly about "dependency": how those who struggle with addiction often have unmet needs for intimacy, and how our cultural emphasis on self-reliance and independence fosters addiction by devaluing dependency and social connection. Jungian analyst Ernest Rossi, a former pharmacist, describes the grip of America's powerful "Empire Plantation Complex" on all our lives, and how our tendency to overwork—which overrides the body's need for rest, relaxation, and more rhythmic lifestyles—can drive some to drink and drugs. Finally, depth psychologist and founder of Pacifica Graduate Institute Stephen Aizenstat takes an unusual and unexpected look at addiction by examining how an ancestor's unfulfilled creative genius can be passed down through the generations: a drive that if misinterpreted or ignored can be misdirected into drugs or alcohol. ∎

Notes

1. See Lender and Martin. *Drinking in America* (1987). Also see <http://www.mtvernon.org>.
2. Quoted in "Public Health Then and Now: Benjamin Rush's Educational Campaign against Hard

Drinking," by Brian S. Katcher, PharmD, *The American Journal of Public Health*, February, 1993, Vol. 83, No. 2.

3. *Ibid.*

4. *Epidemic: Responding to America's Prescription Drug Abuse Crisis,* The White House, 2011 <http://www.whitehouse.gov/sites/default/files/ondcp/policy-and-research/rx_abuse_plan.pdf>. "Prescription drug abuse is the Nation's fastest-growing drug problem. While there has been a marked decrease in the use of some illegal drugs like cocaine, data from the National Survey on Drug Use and Health (NSDUH) show that nearly one-third of people aged 12 and over who used drugs for the first time in 2009 began by using a prescription drug non-medically. . . . Additionally . . . the Nation's largest survey of drug use among young people . . . showed that prescription drugs are the second most-abused category of drugs after marijuana. In our military, illicit drug use increased from 5 percent to 12 percent among active duty service members over a three-year period from 2005 to 2008, primarily attributed to prescription drug abuse."

5. "Why Do Americans Consume 80% of World's Painkiller Drugs?" BBC Newsmagazine, May 8, 2013 <http://www.bbc.com/news/magazine-17963222>.

6. National Institute of Drug Abuse <http://www.drugabuse.gov/relatedtopics/trends-statistics>.

7. Intercept Interventions, Facts and Statistics About Addiction: <http://www.interceptinterventions.com/resources/facts-and-statistics-about-addiction/>.

8. National Institute of Drug Abuse: Drug Facts: Nationwide Trends <http://www.drugabuse.gov/publications/drugfacts/nationwide-trends>.

9. In 1956 the American Medical Association classified alcohol abuse as an illness. Ten years later, in 1966, alcohol abuse was classified as a disease. In 1974, the American Medical Association classified drug abuse as a disease.

—8—

Dispelling the Myths of Addiction

AN INTERVIEW WITH A. THOMAS MCLELLAN, PH.D.

A BOLD-SPOKEN MAN OF strong opinions and Irish descent with flashing eyes and a thick white mustache, A. Thomas McLellan is among the fiercest pioneers of the addiction movement. When speaking of his research into the causes and treatment of drug and alcohol abuse—and from enumerating the overall cost of addiction to the economy to describing the percentage of Americans addicted to opioids, he commands an impressive knowledge of this social problem—he reverberates with compassion for the suffering of addicts and their loved ones. This is because for McLellan, finding the holy grail of addiction treatment is not solely a matter of research, but the axis of his life, a deeply personal mission forged out of his own family's tragedies around alcohol and drugs.

"No stranger to addiction," as he describes himself, McLellan is the son of an alcoholic father. In 1990, as he has recounted,[1] he was an emerging national authority in the field of addiction when his own son became addicted to cocaine. Despite his standing as an expert in the field, he didn't know what to do, nor did any of his colleagues. All his research, he realized at the time, wasn't impacting the "real world" lives of addicts and their families. It was to address this issue that in 1992 McLellan co-founded The Treatment Research Institute (TRI),[2] with the goal of translating practical, applied research into tools and policies that would actually be used, and that would serve places where addiction problems are most prevalent—such as schools, businesses, and healthcare settings like hospitals.

Since that time McLellan has won numerous honors for his work, including the Life Achievement Awards of the American and British Societies of Addiction Medicine (2001 and 2003). President Obama appointed him the science advisor and deputy director of the White House Office of National Drug Control Policy (ONDCP) to help shape the nation's public policy approach to illicit drug use (2009–2010). During his tenure, McLellan worked on a broad range of drug issues, including the formulation and implementation of the President's National Drug Control Strategy and the promotion of drug treatment through the broader revamping of the national healthcare system. Today, after more than thirty-five years of addiction treatment research, McLellan's greatest source of pride—and frustration—is that solutions are now at hand to help addicts and their families. "We are," he says, "ready to go." However, as new discoveries and treatments clash with long-held taboos, feelings of shame, outdated cultural prejudices, and even outright ignorance, he says, it has proved difficult for society to begin to accommodate the newer evidence-based practices that are available.

It wasn't until my interview with McLellan, in fact, that I realized the extent of my own unexamined opinions, assumptions, and prejudices around addiction. I was stunned at the moralistic, almost medieval attitudes I held. McLellan's one wish, he tells me, is to be able to get the public to understand substance-abuse problems, not as a character fault or as a moral failing, but in the same way they have come to understand depression, AIDS, and other healthcare problems—in other words, as a *medical* issue. Having made available all the background information necessary for a more complete understanding of addiction as illness, McLellan continues to call for the public to demand more progressive, long-term treatments for their own family and friends. As this kind of demand increases, he says, it will be "the start of market forces, regulatory reforms, and the creation of new tools and services that the country really needs."

Part one of my interview took place with Dr. McLellan in 1995; part two, which reflects changes that have occurred in the field of addiction since that time, as well as in McLellan's own life, took place in 2014.

——Part One——

Pythia Peay: I'm the oldest daughter of a lifelong, chronic alcoholic. My father came from a large Irish-German family of nine children—seven boys and two girls. According to family lore, each one of them was a drinker.

A. Thomas McLellan: And I'm the grandson, son, brother, husband, father, and probably grandfather of alcohol- and drug-dependent people. So I am no stranger to this topic. Was your father a loving guy when he was sober?

PP: He was quiet and subdued when he was sober, and loving and expansive when he was drunk on beer. But when he drank vodka, he could turn mean and controlling. He flew for the Air Transport Command during World War II. After the war he got married, bought a farm in Missouri, flew for TWA, and raised four kids. His routine at home was to drink on his days off, and then sober up for his trips. Eventually, my mother left him, he remarried a young woman from Mexico, and then moved to Mexico, where he bought a boat. He got prostate cancer; he was in hospice at the end of his life, when he tried to make things right with his family. He even reconciled with the Catholic Church, which he'd hated all his life.

ATM: I never knew an Irish guy who drank vodka. My father was also of Irish descent. And I'm sorry to tell you this, but that is not your family story—that is *my* family story. My father was also a pilot during World War II; he became a successful architect and bought a farm in Pennsylvania. He loathed the Catholic Church. But you could put him in a bar and within an hour twenty people would be around him, offering to buy him a drink. Toward the end of his life he got prostate cancer as well, which he survived. Then *he* bought a boat and moved with his new wife to the Chesapeake Bay. Eventually, he reconciled with the Catholic Church and died in hospice, trying to make amends to all the people he'd pissed off and estranged.

PP: What amazing parallels! Maybe it's this shared legacy that's driven us both to study alcoholism, in different ways. I also wonder whether the reason families and loved ones feel such bitterness toward the addict is because they're jealous of their "affair" with the bottle, or cigarettes, or pills. When I was a girl I simply couldn't understand why my father wouldn't stop drinking for my sake.

ATM: How I felt that, too! So many loved ones feel that the addict's addiction matters more to them than they do. And, sadly, it does.

PP: I certainly can see the psychological causes of my dad's drinking in his early childhood; he suffered some terrible tragedies. But often when he was drunk it felt like his addiction to alcohol was physical, as if he had leprosy or some other disease. I've just finished reading Harvard psychiatrist George Vaillant's study on alcoholism, in which he indicates that psychological disorders do not cause alcoholism—genes do (Vaillant: 1995).

ATM: I agree with Vaillant. Remember that it wasn't just your father who was an alcoholic; every single one of his siblings also had a problem with drinking. That awful but amusing saying "Show me four Irish and I'll show you a fifth" is born of truth. If you draw a line above the equator and look at the prevalence of alcoholism, it's significantly higher in any set of people north of the equator, than south of the equator.

So the genetics of alcoholism are very similar to the genetics of diabetes or hypertension or asthma; it's traceable to the genetic differences in the way alcohol is metabolized. You don't find alcoholism in Asians, for example, to the extent that you find it in these other cultures. So it's a fact that genetics is the number-one cause of alcoholism; that accounts for about fifty percent of all cases.

But then comes culture. For example, the male culture of World War II certainly didn't do anything to prohibit alcohol use. Men drank: it was a role expectation. I'm sure your mother saw that and would have agreed.

PP: Yes, she told me stories of how my dad used to sit around and drink with his flying buddies after a flight. Some thinkers have said that drugs and alcohol have always been part of human culture, but that many of the older cultures had containers and rituals to handle these substances: the Irish had drinking ceremonies, and certain Native American tribes had rituals involving peyote. Do you see these kinds of rituals as helpful in handling addiction?

ATM: Sure. There are cultural activities that can contain biology. There's certainly alcoholism in Muslim societies, but nothing like there is in non-Muslim societies. Prohibition is part of their culture. In Italy, however, you're expected to drink wine, but you are taught how to drink from childhood. So social prohibitions can help to contain substance abuse. Even though prohibition against alcohol in this country was widely thought to be a terrible failure because of the way it led to organized crime, never since has the country had lower accident rates, or a lower proportion of liver disease.

PP: So where do psychological causes enter the picture with alcoholism?

ATM: It's not the case that alcoholism and mental illnesses aren't related: they are. But it's a complicated set of relationships. Depression and anxiety do produce situations that set the stage for solitary, medicinal use of alcohol. If a person gets drunk when they feel depressed, they'll feel better. But here's the other side of the picture: alcohol, especially in combination with other drugs like cigarettes, depletes the very enzymes and neurotransmitters that are associated with alleviating depression. So in seeking to medicate their depression by drinking, alcoholics do the very thing that hastens the onset of depression. So it's truly a vicious circle. If they stop drinking, however, their neurotransmitters will regenerate.

PP: So that saying, "first the man takes a drink, and then the drink takes a man," has some truth in it.

ATM: Absolutely. If you're an Asian man who doesn't like to drink, it has little to do with his moral upbringing, his constitution, or his character—it's his biology.

PP: Biology doesn't seem to be widely thought of as one of the causes of alcoholism. How would you describe the public's general mindset toward alcoholism?

ATM: For the most part, alcoholism and addiction haven't been treated as illnesses, but as a result of weak character. Addiction has been variously considered as a sin, a bad habit, or a sign of moral decay or weak will. The treatment then is to "get thee to a nunnery" or put addicts in jail to teach them a lesson or dry them out. We probably wouldn't do that with someone who has diabetes; we wouldn't send them to a priest, or a thirty-day treatment program. Instead, we'd consider diabetes a chronic illness that should be managed through changes in lifestyle, medications, and observant self-management.

As it happens, this is also the right formula for the treatment of addiction, but it's not readily available. Addicts are still sent to the Betty Ford Clinic or some other clinic to "learn their lesson" until they have an epiphany and dry out. We believe that after that they ought to be okay—except that they're not. Relapse rates are fifty percent because there is no follow-up. So it's the wrong treatment model for addiction. If people with hypertension were sent away to a clinic, for example, where they were stabilized and taught to stay away from fatty foods and alcohol, they would relapse very quickly after they were discharged: because they would have received an acute form of care for what is really a chronic illness.

PP: Can you say more about what kind of treatment programs actually do work for addiction and alcoholism?

ATM: There's an interesting study on the kind of treatment physicians receive for addiction that shows us the right path to take. Physicians, for example, have as high as or higher a rate of drug or alcohol dependence than the rest of society. But they don't get the same length or kind of treatment that the rest of society gets. Instead, they get *five years* of treatment. First, they start with thirty days at the Betty Ford Clinic—but that's just the beginning. After that, the family gets involved, as well as their employer, their primary care doctor, and clergy. Information is shared on a weekly basis on how well they're doing, and whether they've missed a meeting or have started using again. Whenever there's a relapse, everyone involved intervenes right away to help them get back on track. This kind of long-term, intensive treatment has an 82 percent favorable outcome, out to six years.

PP: So is that the kind of treatment model you'd like to see used?

ATM: Yes, that's exactly what I'd like to see. Imagine if I told you that there was a very effective treatment for diabetes, but that only physicians were allowed to have it. The public wouldn't stand for it! But that's the situation with drug and alcohol abuse.

PP: It makes me sad to hear what might have been available to my father, if things had been different. In my case, I completely dissociated myself from him; I just wanted to get away and get on with my life. The little scraps of things I was given to cope with around his alcoholism never really seemed to help: "don't be an enabler," or "don't be codependent." So the message was always to distance myself.

ATM: I completely understand the chaos of alcoholism. We can make all these analogies between addiction and diabetes and hypertension. But diabetics don't pass out or knock all the silverware and glasses off the table; they don't lie and cheat and steal. Those are the characteristics of that disease that present huge public health and safety concerns. It's very difficult to feel compassion toward somebody when their illness makes them violent, harmful, and unpredictable. It's much easier to feel pity and concern for people with other illnesses, and who are therefore *entitled*—and I use that word pointedly—to the very best in healthcare.

But a "drunk"—no sirree! "He brought it on himself, look what he's done: he ought to be punished." Those are the emotions that get stirred up when we confront alcoholism. So it's very, very difficult to make what I still think is the right case: we can hate alcoholics, we can despise what they do, but we're just kidding ourselves if we think we're going to punish it out of them. I'd be happy to call alcoholism a sin if going to church made an alcoholic sober, or to call it a crime if putting someone in jail cured their drinking. But those things don't work, and the best treatment is still medical care and long-term treatment.

PP: You certainly make a powerful case that, when it comes to curing addiction, the moralistic approach simply doesn't work.

ATM: Temporarily it feels great. But there is one element of truth to the moral judgments society makes around addiction, although it's not what you might expect. From a moralistic, religious perspective, all these concoctions—marijuana, alcohol, opiates, methamphetamines, and cocaine—produce pleasure. And, of course, in our culture, the dark side of pleasure is the stuff of which good moral tales and Grimm's fairy tales are all woven. Take the old Aesop's tale of the ant and the grasshopper. The grasshopper fritters his time away during the summer partying and singing, while the ant studiously works away storing food for the winter. To teach the grasshopper his lesson, he's made to freeze and die when the cold comes, while the ant has done the right thing.

One of the analogies that I like the best is that addiction to alcohol and drugs is as much a love affair as anything else. From a purely scientific perspective, addiction lights up the same set of structures in the brain that love does. It also produces the same feelings of abandonment as when your lover leaves you; and feelings of fulfillment when your needs have all been satiated by your lover. So ultimately, the cigarette, alcohol, and pharmaceutical industry will always do a brisk business, because it produces pleasure.

PP: So what you're saying is that part of the intense power a substance holds over a person comes from this pleasure principle. And this is also partly linked to the fact that we're such a driven, puritanical, work-oriented culture. America is also a meritocracy: a person is only as good as the job they have and the money that they earn.

ATM: Right now I'm looking out my window at Constitution Hall and the Liberty Bell. To this day, the richest man in the United States was Benjamin Franklin. Not in terms of dollars, but more because of the amount of money that was available to him, more than to any other man at that time. And Franklin thanked alcohol for his wealth, because at that time the rest of society had an alcohol-based payment system. People were paid for showing up at work in the morning with a pint of very strong beer. They got two pints at ten, three pints at noon, two or three more at two in the afternoon, and a meager amount of money at the end of the day, which they used to buy more beer. They were drunk all the time.

So Benjamin Franklin said that he would pay his employees money, but in exchange they couldn't drink on the job. And that was the basis for his printing company and for every one of the institutions that he started. As a result, he had far greater productivity and profits than anybody else. A very significant part of that came from his Puritan, Quaker views.

PP: That's a very fascinating piece of American history—and of our psychological history, as well.

ATM: Every morning I walk past the first treatment facility for alcohol inebriation in America: the Pennsylvania Hospital. Benjamin Franklin and his friend the physician Benjamin Rush founded it because they discovered that people simply could not stop drinking. So they reasoned that it had to be some kind of an illness. They developed this hospital so that they could produce better workers. It was quite self-serving, and very much in the Quaker tradition to do good to do well, and to produce more.

——Part Two——

PP: So here we are, nearly eighteen years later, picking up the thread of our original conversation. Since we last spoke, you've suffered the tragic loss of your own son and wife to the disease of alcoholism, making this an intensely personal issue. My heart broke for you, and I'm deeply sorry for your loss.

ATM: Thank you. I wasn't going to say anything about it publicly, but then I received over five thousand emails from people I'd never met, and who had all lost their kids to addiction. I discovered this *sub rosa* network of people who'd lost their children or loved ones, and who'd had a piece of their lives taken out of them. They're like the walking dead—and they don't know what to do about it.

When I spoke to the newspaper copywriter for the simple announcement of my son's death, for example, and I cited "alcohol overdose" as the cause of death, he replied, "We get that all the time. But what are you going to say in the piece?" When I asked him what he meant by that, he said, "Nobody puts that down. They say 'unknown causes' or 'died in his sleep,' or something like that." And I replied, "No. I'm not going to do that, because that's not the real truth."

And that's when I decided I was going to speak out. Because not only have parents lost their children, they're too goddamned ashamed to even tell people *why* they died. Not only do they walk around feeling negligent as a parent, they feel like they've sinned, and that the one they've lost has sinned. So it's a special kind of hell. It's like those poor people in the eighties whose relatives died of AIDS, and who suffered shame from the stigma that their loved one was gay. What was worse: that they were gay, or that they were dead? And did they die because they'd sinned, or because they'd had a disease?

But the good news is that things are finally beginning to turn around.

PP: So you're actually beginning to see some breakthroughs in this field and in public attitudes?

ATM: Yes. There are a few things that have contributed to a major shift. Number one is the recent epidemic of opioid addiction and overdose.[3] There's no town or state that hasn't been affected by this. It now kills more people than car accidents. So it's just too big and too broad a drug problem for mainstream society to relegate to those "dirty minority people" who inject themselves with that "stuff."

And the second thing has to do with veterans returning from war. In fact, it was during the return of vets from Vietnam during the sixties and seventies that addiction first began to enter the mainstream. Previously, there had been this popular view that people who were addicts were basically scum. But now America's own heroes were suffering from addiction. Attitudes have changed even more with returning Iraq and Afghanistan vets. But the problems were different for these two sets of veterans.

PP: What was the difference?

ATM: In Vietnam, opiate addiction was a problem because smoking or injecting heroin was available to vets locally, from the surrounding cities and villages. In the Iraq and Afghanistan theaters, opiate addiction comes from opioid medications that were given by corpsmen to other members of the army.

PP: To help them through battle?

ATM: Yes. These were terrible circumstances, with extreme heat and extreme cold. Sometimes soldiers had to carry seventy-five-pound packs on their backs for long hours, which caused back pain, battle fatigue, an inability to sleep, and so on and on. In the short run, opioids will help every one of those things, but if taken for everything, they acquire a life of their own.

PP: So how did opioids move from being a problem for veterans, to being a problem for mainstream society?

ATM: In my opinion, it began in 1997. That was when the two major pain societies[4] in the U.S. jointly concluded that pain was undermedicated, and that fears of addiction were unfounded, or at least very minor, and that it was cruel to undermedicate pain. They issued new guidelines for pain management, and made opioids a first-tier medication—meaning that's what doctors should administer first for pain. The record shows that these meetings were sponsored by pharmaceutical firms.

This development had a huge effect on primary physicians, who now had a ready supply of opioids, as well as the imprimatur of pain specialists to administer them for lower back pain, cervical pain, and sleep disorders: sleep and pain are the two biggest symptoms in American medicine. From 1997 to today there has been a *hundredfold* increase in prescriptions for opioids. The U.S. uses opioids by a factor of ten more than any other country in the world. They are the major class of medications prescribed, even more than statins for cholesterol. So, with availability comes use, and with use comes addiction.

PP: Can you give me a well-educated opinion about *why* America takes so many opioids?

ATM: First of all, opioids work: they take away pain and they make you feel good. Two, the population is getting older and they're suffering more from bad backs and other kinds of pain. Third, physicians are reimbursed for providing them. And fourth, that's what patients want. It's a quick, easy, and fairly safe way of satisfying patients' major complaints.

There's one state that stands out for having the fewest opioid problems, and that's New York. Why? I'm pretty sure, and others agree, that it's because doctors must provide triplicate prescriptions: one to the patient and the pharmacy; one for the physician's own records; and one for a state registry. And that one small check has reduced the number of opioids prescribed in that state, because the doctors know someone is watching them.

PP: The last time we spoke you were very passionate about encouraging society to see addiction as a disease. Have we seen any progress on that front?

ATM: Yes, we have. And the reason for that is the passage of The Parity Act,[5] in which benefits for mental-health or substance-abuse disorders had to be equal to care provided for other physical illnesses, and The Affordable Care Act,[6] in which substance-use disorders and mental illnesses are now considered one of ten essential services. In fact, these two acts have been a game changer. A person can't have a health plan without these two services being provided.

PP: And what was the reason for this revolution?

ATM: Well, it wasn't because of political pressure or because it was the right thing to do! It was because of money. The Office of Management and Budget found that the major driver of total health costs was mental health and substance abuse—over $125 billion a year. So it's my opinion that there is no illness that will be more positively affected by Obamacare than addiction. And that's because for the first time addiction will be treated like a chronic illness.

So now anything that might be said about diabetes can also be said about addiction. For instance, the important thing in diabetes is early detection, proper family education, dietary consultation, and lifestyle changes to control it before it escalates into a more serious condition. Even serious cases of chronic diabetes are provided continuous, community-based care, and a full range of FDA-approved medications—all practices that are shown to be effective.

Now, that is a totally banal statement about diabetes. But imagine taking the word *diabetes* out of what I just said, and replacing it with *addiction*, whether to opioids, alcohol, marijuana, or cocaine: that's the significance of the change that has occurred. Most of us would never imagine saying, for example, that diabetes is just a lifestyle of "self-indulgent" overweight people who eat their way into this illness, so why should society pay for it? Or that diabetics don't belong in hospitals along with everyone else, so let's put them in special centers, somewhere outside of town, down by the railroad tracks. Or, let's not teach doctors about diabetes in medical school either, because it's not a "real" disease; instead let's have some small programs for diabetics, and perhaps the states will provide some funding for that.

Everything I've just said about diabetes is exactly what happened to addiction. From the beginning, addiction was ostracized, rejected by the medical community, and uncovered by insurance, or only covered minimally.

PP: So what you're saying is that in segregating addiction from the mainstream healthcare system, it also segregated addicts and the people who love them.

ATM: *And* the people who treated addiction. It was an instant recipe for stigma. Another way to measure the status of the addiction field is to compare it to the treatment of tuberculosis in this country. Initially, nobody knew how to treat TB, or what caused it; it was considered a lifestyle condition, typically of "dirty Irish people." So the medical establishment did two things: they removed tuberculosis patients away from everyone, and created special centers where they were treated with fresh air, sunshine, good food, and a generally healthy environment, which was thought to provide a cure. There was a substantial workforce, journals dedicated to the topic, and at one point there were over eight thousand sanitaria.

Then in the early 1900s, researchers discovered that tuberculosis was caused by a strain of bacteria. So now doctors realized that this disease wasn't just a "lifestyle" issue, it was caused by exposure to a pathogen. For the next nineteen years a battle unfolded between "science" and the "tuberculosis treatment." It was very difficult to get people to see that what they'd thought was a lifestyle condition was actually a public health problem. So they had to turn to a new group of experts who weren't all that keen on taking in a bunch of infectious individuals.

PP: You're talking about the medical establishment, which had to begin taking in tuberculosis patients.

ATM: Exactly right. But then they had to find something to do with the empty sanitaria. Because they were so conveniently located outside of town, fifty percent of them were turned into mental health facilities. And the other fifty percent? They were turned into drug and alcohol treatment centers. I don't really fault anybody for this. In 1965, it would have been very hard to treat a heroin addict who lies, cheats, steals, and is untrustworthy. The best they could do then was to treat the addict as having a character problem, and to teach them honesty, integrity, hard work, and all that kind of stuff that was thought to be at the core of addiction.

But, as we now know, that's not true! In 2014, with genetics and brain science, we see that substance abuse actually erodes parts of the brain that have to do with motivation, inhibition, and the ability to wait and work for longer term reward. It doesn't exactly excuse personal responsibility, but it sure informs us that the addict didn't start out with that kind of lack of character. It's also still unclear whether their brains are ever going to change back.

And what that means is that, like every other chronic illness, if addiction can't be cured, it will have to be managed for a very long time, hopefully with a minimum of intrusion. So that's basically where we are now: the scientific and financial underpinnings are available, but now we need to build a new treatment system.

PP: And from what you've been saying, a treatment system that isn't on the fringes, removed from mainstream medicine, and also at a distance geographically.

ATM: AIDS is one of the best examples of the importance of bringing addiction into the medical establishment. Initially, the AIDS community was offered special congressional funding for AIDS centers that would be developed around the country. And they rejected that. Instead, the AIDS community fought to be right in the middle of medicine and part of infectious diseases. And they were so right to do that.

PP: Because if they hadn't done that, the gay community would have remained on the outside, reinforcing their separateness from society?

ATM: I have never in my life seen separate but equal work; it's yet another pervasive way to reinforce prejudice. It's always the slogan, and yet it's never true. It's only when AIDS became part of the mainstream medical establishment—when people had to work together, and when it was seen as part of a broader category of infectious diseases—that education about how to treat AIDS began to spread. And look at the progress since then.

PP: In 2006, an incident occurred in one of the nicer suburbs of Washington, D.C., that I think speaks to the point you're making.[7] A *New York Times* reporter had gone out for an evening walk and was beaten and robbed and left in the street. Neighbors called for help and a fire truck arrived on the scene. The emergency medical technicians told hospital workers that the victim, who was disoriented, was intoxicated—a misdiagnosis that delayed his treatment. After waiting on a stretcher in the hallway of the hospital for an hour, he died later of severe head injuries. It isn't known whether the delay caused his death, but the incident was very revealing of ingrained cultural prejudices around alcoholism.

ATM: Not only that, but because he was categorized as one of "them" he was treated as if didn't belong in the healthcare system—he should have been in some "other" system. And that's an example of the pernicious and pervasive effects of segregation: it screws with your mind. We are all subject to it. I also don't think that, initially, this kind of segregation around addiction began as an intentional scheme to hurt or exclude people. I truly believe that people were trying to do their best. But it turns out to have been a mistake.

PP: And it was a mistake because . . . ?

ATM: Because the segregation from mainstream healthcare was a setback: it hurt progress. They had to do the best they could do at the time. But we're really foolish if, knowing as much as we do now about the nature of the illness of addiction, and the kind of care that's really required, we keep on doing that. We've tried punishing it and segregating it, and now we know that doesn't work! But with these new advances, the rest of healthcare is going to reap major benefits. Because untreated, undiagnosed substance use is squirreling up the treatment of virtually every chronic illness in this country. And that is not an opinion; that's a fact, as found by the Congressional Budget Office.

PP: Can you give me an example of how alcoholism triggers other diseases?

ATM: I'll give you an example of someone well known to the public: Angelina Jolie, who famously had a radical mastectomy because she has the BRCA2 gene that is very virulent.[8] She smartly never smoked, because she knew that cigarettes trigger that gene, and that it promotes cancer. But here's what most doctors don't know: for Miss Jolie and for anybody else who has that gene the amount, frequency, and duration of alcohol use is a better predictor of whether that gene gets triggered than cigarettes. Not only that, if a woman has breast cancer, any amount of alcohol increases tumor growth; it also works against radiation and chemotherapy. And do you know why most doctors don't know that? Because they were never taught about addiction or alcoholism in medical school.

The amount of alcohol a woman drinks in her pregnancy is also one of the direct determinants of cognitive capacity and brain damage, or fetal alcohol spectrum disorder. However, it's also true that alcohol at less than three drinks a day for men, or two drinks a day for women, is good for the heart and for diabetes. But three or more drinks in a day, or fourteen or more in a week, impedes the treatment of diabetes and most cardiovascular illness. So there's a wealth of information about this.

PP: For the sake of everyone suffering addiction, I'm glad that, overall, the field is moving in a new direction, and that we are on the cusp of a new age of treatment.

ATM: In my life, I've seen the end of segregated education, segregated housing, and now, with regard to addiction, I'm finally seeing the end of segregated healthcare. I predict that there will be bumps along the road. Just as it wasn't easy to desegregate schools, so it won't be easy to desegregate healthcare. But we're going to see healthcare reabsorbing, however reluctantly, responsibility for substance-abuse disorders: preventing them, intervening early, and treating them in a chronic fashion when they become severe. So it's an exciting time. I think we've finally gotten it right!

Remember what Winston Churchill said about the Americans in World War II? When asked if he thought the Americans would enter the war and help fight the scourge of Nazism, he said the Americans could always be counted on to do the right thing—after they've tried everything else. So put me down as hopeful, and put addiction down as having made significant scientific, clinical, and public health advances in the past twenty years. And let's keep our fingers crossed. ◾

Notes

1. Quotes in this section are taken from our interview, as well as Dr. McLellan's personal "impact story," as featured on TRI's official website. More online at <http://www.tresearch.org/>.

2. Located in Philadelphia, Pennsylvania, TRI is an independent, nonprofit research and development organization dedicated to science-driven reform of treatment and policy in substance use, and to translating research into improved policies and programs to address the effects of substance abuse on families, schools, businesses, criminal justice and healthcare. It also helped develop the Addiction Severity Index (ASI), one of the most widely used assessment instruments in the field of addiction. More at <http://www.tresearch.org/>.

3. Opioids are medications that relieve pain. They reduce the intensity of pain signals reaching the brain and affect those brain areas controlling emotion, which diminishes the effects of a painful stimulus. Medications that fall within this class include hydrocodone (e.g., Vicodin), oxycodone (e.g., OxyContin, Percocet), morphine (e.g., Kadian, Avinza), codeine, and related drugs. More information at the National Institute on Drug Abuse (NIDA) at <http://www.drugabuse.gov/>.

4. The American Pain Society (APS) <http://www.americanpainsociety.org>; and the American Chronic Pain Association (ACPA) <http://theacpa.org/>.

5. The Mental Health Parity and Addiction Equity Act of 2008 (MHPAEA) requires group health plans and health insurance issuers to ensure that financial requirements (such as co-pays, deductibles) and treatment limitations (such as visit limits) applicable to mental health or substance-use disorder (MH/SUD) benefits are no more restrictive than the predominant requirements or limitations applied to substantially all medical/surgical benefits. More at <http://www.dol.gov/ebsa/mentalhealthparity/>.

6. The Patient Protection and Affordable Care Act was a statute signed into law by President Barack Obama in 2010, and given the moniker "Obamacare." It represents the most significant overhaul of the U.S. healthcare system since the passage of Medicare and Medicaid in 1965. More online at <http://www.dol.gov/ebsa/healthreform/>.

7. "Sources Cite Delay in Aid to Reporter, EMTs Thought Rosenbaum Was Drunk," by Del Quentin Wilbert, *Washington Post*, January 11, 2006.

8. A woman's risk of developing breast and/or ovarian cancer is greatly increased if she inherits a deleterious (harmful) mutation in the BRCA1 gene or the BRCA2 gene. Men with these mutations also have an increased risk of breast cancer, and both men and women who have harmful BRCA1 or BRCA2 mutations may be at increased risk of additional types of cancer. The National Cancer Institute at the National Institutes of Health, Bethesda, Md., and online at <http://www.cancer.gov/cancertopics/factsheet/Risk/BRCA>.

That Which Hurts Can Also Heal

F
OR MOST ADULTS, THE youth culture of drinking and drug use exists as a kind of shadow realm—a netherworld of wild raves and drunken after-game parties where other people's kids hang out, but not their own. Although many young people emerge from their adolescent and teenage years unscathed, others are not so lucky, killed in car accidents or permanently scarred by addiction. Recently, the father of a high school freshman horrified me with his son's accounts of teens as young as thirteen injecting heroin, drinking, getting stoned, and popping a Molly—during school hours. And this was in a highly ranked public school in a well-off middle-class neighborhood.

Where, I've often wondered, is the wise authority who could speak wisdom to America's young people, offering more than the stereotypical jeremiads against drug and alcohol use? What if someone were available to them who could explain, in a sober and sensible manner, the chemical properties of various drugs, warn them about the dangers of drug interactions, and, most importantly, encourage them to open up about their reasons for *why* they're using these substances in the first place? What if, instead of an expert or a parent intoning "Just say no," they instead counseled "Just say *know*"?

For those adolescents fortunate enough to live in Los Angeles, that authority exists: psychiatrist Dr. Charles Grob, director of the Division of Child and Adolescent Psychiatry at Harbor-UCLA Medical Center. Since 1993, Grob, whose clinical interests include mood and anxiety disorders and the self-medication theory of substance abuse, has overseen the treatment of thousands of young people in the Harbor-UCLA Medical Center psychiatric emergency room and outpatient clinic. When it comes to adolescent drug and alcohol abuse, it could be said that he has seen and heard it all.

What really makes Grob a stand-out in the field of addiction and substance abuse is his decades-long, paradigm-breaking investigation into the use of hallucinogens to actually *treat* depression and addiction, when used within a carefully controlled therapeutic context. His psychiatric research has included the first FDA approved Phase 1 study of the physiological and psychological effects of MDMA, more popularly known as Molly, or ecstasy.[1] In addition, Grob has conducted a multinational study of the Amazonian plant hallucinogen ayahuasca, on behalf of the government of Brazil, and a pilot investigation at Harbor-UCLA Medical Center of the safety and efficacy of Psilocybin in the treatment of anxiety in adult patients with advanced-stage cancer. In 2001, Grob testified as an expert medical witness on behalf of the União do Vegetal (UDV), a Christian Spiritist religion that originated in Brazil, and that incorporates the plant hallucinogen decoction ayahuasca as part of its rituals.[2] When DEA and U.S. customs agents raided a branch of UDV's temple in 1999 in Santa Fe, New Mexico, confiscating their ayahuasca, the UDV filed suit, complaining that their rights to practice freedom of religion had been denied. The case was heard in federal court in New Mexico, and eventually appealed all the way to the U.S. Supreme Court where, in 2006 in an opinion written by Chief Justice Roberts, the court ruled unanimously to defend the right of the UDV to use ayahuasca as a psychoactive sacrament in their religious ceremonies. Grob has also testified before Congress on the effects of MDMA, and has published widely on these topics within psychiatric journals. He is the editor of *Hallucinogens: A Reader,* and co-editor with Dr. Roger Walsh of *Higher Wisdom: Eminent Elders Explore the Continuing Impact of Psychedelics.*

In the following interview, first conducted in 1995 and updated in 2014, Dr. Grob shares stories from his practice of young people's experiences around substance abuse, and speaks frankly about the universal human need for transcendence and ecstasy as one of the root causes of addiction. We discuss his ongoing efforts to conduct more controlled studies in which, under optimal circumstances, hallucinogens that facilitate mystical experiences with potentially powerful healing effects could be administered to those suffering from depression and addiction, as well as the phenomenon of Westerners traveling to the Amazon rainforest to take ayahuasca and how drug prohibition in America has failed. Our interview concludes as Grob bemoans society's suspicion of altered states of consciousness, and we radically imagine a future in which plant medicines, or hallucinogens like ayahuasca, could be safely and legally used in a sacred and ritualistic way to treat the suffering of the human soul.

✳

Pythia Peay: Your work is interesting on two counts: you work with adolescents and addiction; and you also explore psychedelic substances and their relevance to psychological issues and altered states of consciousness. I'd like to start with your views on alcohol, which is a more culturally sanctioned substance.

Charles Grob: I think that where alcohol is concerned, a lot of people are trying to self-medicate underlying psychiatric problems, especially depression and bipolar disorder. Anytime there is chronic, repetitive use of any substance, self-medication may be taking place: the person is in a lot of psychological pain, and they've had experiences of alleviating that pain with their substance of choice. The problem is that ultimately these substances often exacerbate the pain.

I also see this with young people who are chronic marijuana smokers. When I ask them about their first experiences getting high, they frequently say that it was the first time they felt healthy, whole, and cohesive. So they continued smoking marijuana, looking for that original experience—but it becomes more and more elusive over time. So the pattern of taking alcohol or drugs moves from self-medicating as a way to mask underlying pathology, and then to ultimately exacerbating psychological pain. In addition, they become less and less productive; problems in their lives are compounded, and ultimately this feeds into whatever had been going on to begin with.

PP: So how can parents more deeply understand the motivations of their children when they turn to drugs?

CG: First, society has to be more honest in recognizing that there is an inborn proclivity to explore certain altered states of consciousness—and that this proclivity shouldn't be looked on solely as a form of psychopathology. So, in addition to self-medicating underlying psychological problems, it's also often the case that kids who are experimenting with drugs are searching for spiritual transcendence—but they're going about it in dangerous ways.

The second issue is that the "war on drugs" mentality has led to a situation that makes it increasingly difficult to be open and honest about what the problems really are. By assigning drug use and abuse to the criminal justice system, drug use is increasingly looked at as an issue of morality and punishment. This has been the main reason why the situation has deteriorated so drastically over the last decades: prohibition doesn't work.

PP: So our efforts to prohibit people from using drugs are only contributing to the problem?

CG: Absolutely. Our approach and our complete inability to examine alternative perspectives is further exacerbating the problem. The harm reduction approach should be placed at center stage of our policy directives; efforts should be made to minimize the degree to which people harm themselves with their misguided use of substances. This would include clean needle programs, increased access to methadone or other drug substitution models, and providing treatment to individuals who've been incarcerated because they have severe drug dependence problems. The percentage of people who are in jail on drug-related charges is unbelievable. Who has the largest prison population in the world? We do; it's appalling.[3]

PP: So where are we in terms of developing more evolved drug treatment programs?

CG: The medical establishment has failed the public in regards to developing effective treatment modalities. One reason is that for years the psychiatry profession has insisted on maintaining an aloofness from this problem. That's why psychiatrists are often not part of conventional drug treatment. When I first began my psychiatric training in the early 1980s, I asked why those patients who were chronic drug users were never admitted for outpatient treatment—I was told that treatment for chronic drugs users could not be provided until they stopped taking drugs. That's amazing, because it's the psychiatric condition *underlying* their drug abuse that is often driving their need to take drugs recklessly and repeatedly.

PP: Can you say more about what kinds of psychiatric conditions might contribute to drug abuse?

CG: Trauma in childhood; lack of nurturing, connected parenting; and severe psychiatric disorders that have gone unrecognized and untreated. At one point, there was a very interesting (albeit brief) period when the self-medication hypothesis was given serious examination. For instance, it was thought that individuals who had a predilection for using opiates or heroin had tremendous rage, and were taking those opiates to contain their rages, which often reached psychotic proportions.

So what drives one person to opiates, or another to stimulants like cocaine, or yet another to marijuana, has a lot to do with their underlying psychopathology. Stimulants, for example, might be used by people who are depressed. Cocaine, as some clinical reports have revealed, might be used to treat an undiagnosed attention deficit disorder: so the drug wasn't being used for recreational purposes, but as a way to function. A lot of adolescents and adults who get hooked on smoking pot all the time have underlying depression and social anxiety issues. So the issue isn't as clear cut or straightforward as one would like. But because the whole issue is framed within a moral, crime-and-punishment model, we tend to forget to look at the underlying driving forces.

PP: Do you see any troubling new trends in drug use among young people?

CG: They're more likely to get involved in polysubstance-abuse patterns: taking multiple drugs, for instance, and washing it all down with alcohol. Kids are also experimenting with drugs at younger and younger ages. For the age cohort born in 1950 and who graduated in 1968, the average age of experimenting with illicit substances was around nineteen or twenty. Today, the average age of experimentation is thirteen—that's much more risky because their judgment at that age hasn't fully developed, they're more impulsive, and they're more likely to get into dangerous behaviors.

Another trend that started in the early 2000s is rampant drug substitution. For example, Molly, the new term for MDMA (what used to be called ecstasy) continues to remain popular with young people. Enterprising drug dealers who did not have access to real MDMA, however, began marketing other drugs under the name of ecstasy: more than half of analyzed samples consist of drugs other than MDMA. Sometimes it would be mixed with caffeine, Benadryl, or more risky drugs like PCP (Phencyclidine) and even sometimes extremely dangerous and potentially lethal drugs like PMA (para-Methoxyamphetamine)—the most potent amphetamine known, and that has been implicated in deaths through overheating. When the forensic toxicology reports were released for some of these so-called "ecstasy deaths" many of them were attributable to PMA, and not MDMA. So this has been a very serious problem.

And then there is prescription-drug abuse, which has become the largest growing substance-abuse problem in the U.S.; rates are skyrocketing. Many of the prescription opiates, like OxyContin or Vicodin, induce a far more difficult withdrawal than heroin. OxyContin is so notoriously hard to get off of that they've developed a new drug, buprenorphine, to block its effects—but then people have a hard time getting off that as well![4]

PP: So where does heroin fit in?

CG: Heroin is an opiate, so it goes together with the prescription opiates, like OxyContin or Vicodin. Some people begin with prescription opiates and then, if they have access to it, turn to heroin. Although heroin is in the same class as prescription drug abuse, it has a different route of administration. Prescription opiates are taken by mouth, and heroin is usually injected, sometimes snorted.

PP: So the war on drugs has done little to help or protect kids from substance abuse.

CG: The war on drugs is really a war on people. When you look at the fact that almost half of all kids by the time they're in their late teens have experimented with illicit drugs, we've "criminalized" virtually half the youth population. So we've been locked into a very restrictive viewpoint that has led to a refusal to examine what's really going on, and an inability to address this issue in a healthy way.

The first casualty in the war on drugs is the truth: but you cannot lie to kids. They know you're lying and they can sense your dishonesty. If you look at some of the drug education programs, they're full of distortions and mistruths to the point where the kids refuse to acknowledge those parts of the program that are actually truthful and factual. When kids know they're being lied to about the dangers of marijuana, for example, they naturally think they're also being lied to about the dangers of cocaine. As a result, they don't adequately appreciate how dangerous cocaine can be, especially in its more potent forms, like free-base and crack. So marijuana, which we now know is not nearly as physiologically dangerous as other drugs, and with no known fatalities, gets lumped in with heroin and cocaine.

PP: Marijuana is becomingly increasingly accepted. It's now legal in Washington and Colorado, and currently twenty states permit sales of marijuana for medicinal purposes. Do you have any reservations about it becoming more available?

CG: I'm glad to see some of the excessive and oppressive drug war laws easing up. But with any positive change, there is always a downside: and the downside with more availability of marijuana is ready access to edible marijuana products. Consequently, we're seeing more and more people getting into trouble when they take cannabis baked into brownies or cookies.

PP: And these problems would be . . . ?

CG: One problem is that the potency of marijuana-brownies, or cookies or other edible products, varies from batch to batch. So people don't know how to dose themselves properly. For instance, those who smoke marijuana are used to getting an instantaneous effect. But an oral dose of marijuana can take a long time to have an effect, ranging from one hour or, if you've had a meal, a couple of hours. People think it isn't working, and so they take another bite or eat another brownie. Then when the drug starts to kick in it can be overwhelming, because they have unwittingly ingested too much, and they may experience nausea and vomiting, anxiety and panic attacks.

For example, we frequently evaluate people coming into our emergency room thinking that the brownie they ate was spiked with PCP—but in reality, they just ate too much! So with marijuana gaining greater acceptance, more people are taking it into their kitchens and baking it into cookies, cakes, candies, and lollipops—and that's a risky thing, too, as these sweets might appeal to small children. And when a little child eats a candy with marijuana in it, that child might be in for a very psychologically traumatic experience.

Another risk is the availability of synthetic alkaloids of marijuana, particularly THC, which is sometimes marketed under the name of "spice." People who smoke it can have intensely powerful psychic experiences; but the danger here is that people who have vulnerability for manic depression or bipolar disorder could flip into a manic, psychotic state if they smoke too much marijuana in that highly potent form.

PP: Can you give me some examples of kids you've treated, and the different ways drugs have affected them?

CG: Let me give you an example of two kids I saw on the same day. One was a college student coming in because he was in conflict with his father. He'd started out as a pre-engineering student; his father was also an engineer. Then when he was a junior in college he began experimenting with psychedelics. As a result, he switched his major to art, which caused great distress in his father, who had assumed his son would join him in the family engineering firm. Later on that day, I saw another young man, about eighteen years old, who told me that what he and his buddies liked to do every weekend was take some acid, smoke a bunch of joints, wash it all down with Southern Comfort—and then go driving. He reported that everything was fine until the double lines on the highway turned into snakes and attacked the windshield of his car.

So these are different ways that kids are using substances. You could make a case that in the first case the young man was using drugs in a reasonably safe, healthy, and even constructive manner; the second kid, however, was using drugs in a self-destructive way that was potentially dangerous to himself and to others he might come into contact with.

PP: What both these examples underscore is the need for a more complex approach to kids and drugs and alcohol use than the conventional and simplistic "Just say no" approach.

CG: Right. Instead of "Just say no" it should be "Just say *know*." This would require a massive paradigm shift, as well as the recognition that past methods of dealing with drug prevention have been shallow, ineffectual, and ultimately failed models. It would also require parents to engage with their children in a very honest way that explores different perspectives on drug abuse.

PP: I've raised three sons, and what I recall is that there were kids drinking and using drugs from intact, stable, nurturing families as well as kids who came from more troubled or difficult backgrounds. So is there a deeper problem in our collective society that's exacerbating drug use in young people?

CG: These young people are a marker for what's going on in society. Something is way off. They're waving a red flag to get our attention: not necessarily in regards to what we're doing to them, but at what we're doing to *ourselves*. Just look at what we're doing to the world around us, and the way we continue to abuse and defile the environment.

If you look at indigenous people, for example, everything they do is for the welfare of future generations. They're very observant about their impact on the environment because they know they need the environment in order to survive. And what do we do? Among other things we've been stockpiling nuclear waste that will be active for the next 250,000 years. It's incredible.

PP: Indigenous peoples also use psychoactive drugs in a ritual, sacred way. I know you've been involved in research in this area. Can you say more about what you've learned, and how it might apply to America's problems around drug addiction?

CG: I'm very interested in the whole issue of psychedelic substances and their relevance to psychiatry, as well as their potential for use in addiction treatment. In the early 2000s I was part of an interdisciplinary biomedical research team looking at the effects of ayahuasca on adolescent members of a church in the Brazilian Amazon, the União do Vegetal (UDV). During the eighties, the Brazilian judiciary had given the church permission to use ayahuasca as a psychoactive sacrament in their ritual ceremonies. But the government had become concerned about teenagers who were participating in these ceremonies, and so they requested this study.[5]

PP: First, what is ayahuasca, and second, can you tell me more about your study and your findings?

CG: Ayahuasca is a decoction of two plants from the Amazon, which when brewed into a tea and ingested creates a very powerful visionary state lasting about four hours. It's important to keep in mind that the Brazilian church's use of ayahuasca occurs within the controlled context of a religious ceremony, and within the wider context of a religious community.

So for our study, we traveled to Brazil, where we recruited a large subject group of teenagers who'd been introduced to ayahuasca while accompanying their parents to a UDV religious ceremony. Then we recruited a control group of adolescents who were matched for socioeconomic and educational levels—except that they had never taken ayahuasca. We did a variety of studies, and what we found was that the young people who had taken ayahuasca were psychologically quite healthy. The only difference that showed up was that they were less prone to abusing alcohol and other substances. In fact, their experience with ayahuasca appeared to function as a kind of preventive in that regard.

PP: What are the implications of these findings?

CG: Hallucinogens in general induce hypersuggestible states. And when you're in that state and are provided with very positive messages, you're more likely to take them to heart in a very substantive way, and so it's likely to transform you. For instance, during their rituals, UDV ministers would present sermons that would encourage virtues like handling work in a responsible manner, not abusing others, and cultivating a respectful attitude toward all living things. When religious structures provide positive messages, the outcomes are likely that someone can experience positive changes in their conduct and outlook on life. The flip side would be if a person in a hypersuggestible state receives negative, antisocial messages. An example of that would be Charles Manson, who got his followers high on LSD, and then brainwashed them with his crazy worldview, and told them to go out into the world and commit murder and mayhem—which they did.

So I was very impressed during the time I spent in Brazil with the people of the UDV. For their culture, they had created a remarkable phenomenon with their ayahuasca church that had transformed the lives of many people. Many of those I interviewed had been seriously dysfunctional prior to their introduction to ayahuasca and entry into the church. But once again, it's important to bear in mind that the members of the UDV *only* take ayahuasca in religious ceremonies. They would never even consider taking it in a recreational setting.

PP: Can you say more about ayahuasca as a drug that triggers powerful sacred experiences in those who take it?

CG: It's important to stress that whether this is a safe and successful experience depends on what's in the ayahuasca brew, which is made up of plants, as well as the skill of the facilitator; the safety and appropriateness of the setting; and the mental set of the individual: who they are, what their intentions are, and what their underlying vulnerabilities are. If all these things are in order, then there is the potential for someone to have a powerful psychospiritual experience. Among other things participants may view themselves from a different perspective, get insight into personal problems, and often have intense feelings of awe, reverence, a sense of a higher power, and receive messages conveying to them the need to conduct themselves in an ethical manner, and above all, to do no harm.

PP: So this brings us back to where we started our interview, and the link between altered states of consciousness as part of the underlying drive to take drugs. What you're describing in this Brazilian tribe is actually a conscious recognition through sanctioned ritual use of the basic human need to get "high."

CG: Right. In addition to drug use as a form of self-medication, there's another dimension where individuals are turning to drugs in their search for transcendence, spiritual truths, and self-knowledge. Indigenous groups have utilized psychoactive plants in this regard for millennia.

PP: I know that indigenous people often call these psychoactive plants "plant medicine." Can you explain why they use that term? It's radically different from how we typically think of hallucinogens.

CG: The original role of these plants among indigenous peoples was that they were agents of healing. Not that they were without their dangers; some could even be toxic, so a lot of knowledge and caution was recognized as necessary. Currently, people from this country are traveling to the Peruvian Amazon to retreat centers where they take ayahuasca under the guidance of shamans—but the results are mixed. Some report having had positive transformational experiences, while a small number of people have had very negative experiences, and became very anxious, confused, and even psychotic.[6] So it's hard to recommend at this point.

PP: You've also been involved in studies of Psilocybin, popularly known as "magic mushrooms," to treat people with advanced cancer. What have been the results of those studies?

CG: We did a study in the early 2000s, and got very good results in treating terminal cancer patients' anxiety; New York University and Johns Hopkins are replicating what we did, so a new field is being established. At the University of New Mexico they're conducting a research study using a Psilocybin treatment model to treat chronic alcoholism. Similarly at Johns Hopkins, they're using Psilocybin to treat cigarette-smoking cessation.[7]

PP: So how does Psilocybin cure people of alcoholism and smoking, and how did it come to be studied in this way?

CG: In the early fifties, researchers found that in a clinical setting hallucinogens had a positive effect on chronic alcohol or drug abuse. It began with a Canadian psychiatrist named Humphrey Osmond, who started using mescaline at a large institute in Saskatchewan, Canada, to treat chronic alcoholics. Osmond found that the patients who were the subjects in this trial most likely to establish and maintain sobriety over the several-year follow-up period were those who not only had beautiful aesthetic experiences and powerful autobiographical insights, but also intense psychospiritual epiphanies. This seemed to be what propelled people into sobriety, and often it was the result of just a one-session treatment.

Osmond's research brings to mind what the early American psychologist William James said: that the best treatment for *dypsomania* (the old term for alcoholism) is *religiomania*. So if safe and controlled structures are provided for these kinds of hallucinogen treatment models, we may have found a reliable way of facilitating powerful mystical experiences, which may also be extraordinarily healing.

PP: I know that Bill Wilson, the founder of Alcoholics Anonymous,[8] and who suffered horribly from alcoholism before he became sober and founded his organization, had a very profound transcendent experience with LSD.

CG: He did. In the fifties and early sixties, Wilson volunteered to be a subject in some LSD studies to explore the potential of a new treatment for alcoholism. He revealed that his own carefully supervised experiences with LSD had not only been highly valuable personal experiences, but also fully compatible with the tenets of the movement that he had started. But at the time, when public figures like Timothy Leary had just begun experimenting with LSD, it was starting to become very controversial. Consequently, Wilson's extraordinary admission was met with strong resistance from the Board of Trustees of AA, which felt compelled to reject his endorsement of hallucinogens as a treatment for alcoholism.

PP: That certainly would have opened up a radical new direction in the treatment of alcoholism.

CG: Years ago this treatment model was completely rejected; people ran from it in terror. Yet I think that if there are any answers to the problem of alcoholism, that's the area where they may lie.

PP: People just weren't ready for it, then and maybe even now—although I can see that hallucinogens would be something to handle very carefully. But what does it say about us as a country that there's something about a mystical experience curing addiction that's hard for us to wrap our rational minds around? And does that resistance itself have something to do with addiction?

CG: One way to look at addiction is as a failed effort at transcendence, or to experience the sacred. Perhaps that is because the substances people get addicted to are not the ones that facilitate genuine spiritual transcendence, *or* that have become taboo for that very reason. Look at what happened when the Spanish conquistadors came to the New World in the sixteenth and seventeenth centuries. They encountered indigenous peoples utilizing a vast array of plants for their religious rituals. These plants were immediately outlawed, and those who consumed the proscribed plants or participated in the ceremonies were accused of committing heresy and were punished with the worst atrocities of the Inquisition. In South America, the use of these plants was either eliminated, or went deeply underground for centuries.

PP: But is it the plant that's really the taboo—or is it the mystical experience?

CG: Good question. The plants' main property was to facilitate psychospiritual states. And in fact the Spaniards felt that this kind of indigenous religious model was in direct conflict with the Catholic and Christian traditions that they had brought with them across the Atlantic, and that they had imposed on the local inhabitants.

PP: So then both the plants and the experiences threatened established belief systems.

CG: The compounds became identified as catalysts for change. It's no random happenstance, for example, that the rise of the sixties' vibrant counterculture coincided with these substances, either in plant or in synthetic chemical form, being taken by large numbers of people. These hallucinogens were at the core of galvanizing individual change, which in turn created a collective phenomenon. I don't think the role these substances played in the antiwar movement has ever been fully appreciated. Young people then were having these very powerful experiences, making them less susceptible to what elder authority figures were forcing on them, and preventing them from marching docilely off to war.

Another phenomenon that came out of the use of psychedelics during the sixties is that it sensitized people to their environment. The realization began to dawn that nature was alive. People became aware of what they were doing to the environment; this helped spark the environmental movement, which also came out of the sixties. Likewise, many of the leading meditation teachers of our generation came out of the sixties; many had had very intense spiritual experiences taking psychedelics—so intense that they needed to work on getting grounded. Most of them stopped taking psychedelics, and evolved into working with different meditation models.

So all of this was threatening to the status quo, and authority figures recoiled. Once they realized what was going on, they moved rapidly to impose restrictions on the use and dissemination of these hallucinogens. Legitimate medical research was shut down for decades, and they never let a religious model get off the ground. But in regard to controlling illicit use of these drugs they were less effective, and consequently recreational use of drugs blossomed.

PP: And this recreational model might even be what lies at the root of America's problems with drug abuse. So what would be your vision for how these psychedelics and hallucinogens might be legally and socially integrated back into the culture in a safe and sacred way?

CG: From my point of view as a physician, I look at the salutary effects of these drugs to facilitate healing—so ideally, I think that's exactly what's needed. At the same time, we certainly don't want to create a situation where a doctor writes a prescription for one of these hallucinogenic drugs, then says to the patient, "Next time you see me, tell me what it did for you." That would be irresponsible and reckless!

So I think we need a lot more research. However, with certain precautions in place, I'd envision retreat centers that were optimally structured with all the necessary safeguards and procedures, and where people were treated for specific conditions by trained facilitators who'd been through a certification process. Wise elders would be available to help create a sacred context, to inform and educate, and to ensure that psychoactive substances were treated with respect. This is a very different set of circumstances for taking substances than saying, "Let's go out and get stoned or high tonight."

I don't think I'll be around to see anything like this in my lifetime. In the sixties there was the whole notion of revolution, but that didn't work out. There was too much pushback. But an *evolution* with healthier values, lifestyles, and mindsets could really facilitate a profound shift in consciousness.

So as I see it, the greatest job our generation has is to facilitate a healthy world for those who are coming behind us. In a lot of respects, things aren't looking too good for that; there may not be enough time for everyone to wake up. It will require a huge paradigm shift. But if we don't undergo that paradigm shift, things will continue to deteriorate and conditions will become even more pathological and destructive. However, when used under optimal conditions, I do think these compounds could help people wake up and realize what's truly important, and can heighten their awareness of what we're doing to the environment before it's too late.

PP: In regard to the positive influence of "elders," what is your perspective on parents who are open with their teenagers about their own experimentation with drugs and alcohol? I was very open with my own sons about my experimentation with marijuana and LSD when I was in college—not to encourage them in any way to take these drugs, but so that they could feel comfortable coming to me if they had any questions. I was never sure if what I did was the right thing, although I saw the consequences to kids for whom talking about drugs and alcohol with their parents was a huge taboo.

CG: You mean, what do I think about parents saying to their kids, "I'm going to be honest with you about the experiences I went through when I was young, and if you do become interested in this I want you to come and talk to me?" I think that's being a caring, loving, and responsible parent. When that kind of open and honest discussion breaks down, and there's no trust in the home, there are problems. So I think it's recognizing that part of kids' growing up is their need to assert some autonomy, separation, and individuation. Those parents who are able to maintain an open relationship with their child through adolescence can encourage them to use good judgment, and to not do anything that will cause them harm. Personally, I've found that the best policy is to tell the truth.[9]

But the kind of relationship where kids can go to their parents and have this kind of talk doesn't exist in a lot of families. Too many parents have a knee-jerk approach and react out of fear and anger. Then their children don't sense that there's an open channel, and they feel closed off and shut out, which is very unfortunate. In traditional societies, elders would show the way. But in our society that's unlikely to happen, so each new generation of young people is forced to walk down that road ignorant of the experience and knowledge accrued by those who've gone before them. When kids cannot access this wisdom of their elders, they turn to their peers for guidance, and that's like the blind leading the blind: and when the blind lead the blind a certain number of them are going to fall off the cliff. This increases the probability that kids will get into very serious trouble, exposing them to very dangerous experiences that might lead to serious injury and even death.

PP: When you work with adolescents who are experimenting with drugs as a way to change their consciousness, do you suggest alternatives for satisfying their need for intensity, ecstasy, or vision?

CG: Personally, I've always been interested in working with dream reports, but a lot of people are just not tapped into that level of introspection. But I do encourage young people to have experiences in nature, whether hiking, camping, or, if they can, visiting other parts of the world, and becoming aware of the world around them. It's a good way to pull their head out of the sand, and look at the larger picture around them. I also think yoga and meditation would be very helpful for young people who have had trouble with chronic dependence issues with pot, or who have done a lot of psychedelics and have come from those experiences disoriented and confused. Meditation can help them to get grounded and reoriented, and to move on. I also still think it might potentially be helpful for young people to try to work constructively with psychedelics within an optimal and sanctioned ritual setting guided by knowledgeable adults, who could help them to integrate their experiences.

PP: Well, I'm reminded of the ancient Greek Eleusinian mysteries,[10] in which they used a natural psychedelic substance as part of their sacred rituals. These mysteries interest me because it was something you were actually required to do as a citizen, at least once in a lifetime.

CG: During their ceremonies the Greeks used a compound derived from a fungus growing on rye, which had a chemical compound similar to LSD called "ergot." And citizens who participated were not allowed to divulge the great secrets revealed during these ceremonies. They were especially prohibited from taking the "sacrament," or the hallucinogen, outside of Eleusis, and if anyone did they would be punished by death.

PP: But the mysteries of Eleusis are an example of a society that came together in a ritual way to experience the sacred and to have a vision.

CG: And it was a *collective* vision. People would by and large have the same visionary experience. They were conditioned by the setting, by the structures, and by the messages and expectations they were provided.

PP: So there was a protected cultural container for that kind of visionary experience. But strong, Puritan moralistic powers are at play in America's psyche, which may have something to do with our fear and suspicion of these altered states of consciousness, and that might prevent a modern version of the Eleusinian mysteries, or the retreat centers you envision, from happening.

CG: Absolutely. Delving into the unconscious and the great beyond may lead us to see that things aren't necessarily what we thought they were. These experiences alter the way we perceive the world around us, and can be catalysts for change and transformation. That's what happened during the sixties. But the strong catalysts for change at that time led to a repressive counter reaction—to the point where those cultural changes inspired by transformations in consciousness became disparaged. Even today in academic psychiatry there's been a backlash against the insights into consciousness that emerged during that time; they've been completely ignored. Now psychiatrists are supposed to be drug-dispensing agents of Eli Lilly and the rest of the pharmaceutical industry. There's got to be more to psychiatry than that—that's not why I became a psychiatrist! ■

Notes

1. MDMA (3,4-methlyenedioxymethamphetamine) is an illegal drug that acts as both a stimulant and psychedelic, producing an energizing effect, as well as distortions in time and perception and enhanced enjoyment from tactile experiences. Typically, MDMA is taken orally, usually in a tablet or capsule, and its effects last approximately three to six hours. More information on MDMA can be found at The National Institute of Drug Abuse, online at <http://www.drugabuse.gov/publications/drugfacts/mdma-ecstasy-or-molly>.

2. The União do Vegetal (UDV) is now practiced by over 17,000 people in six countries. It is recognized as a church in the United States. União do Vegetal means "the union of the plants" and adherents drink a tea made from two indigenous plants within their religious services. Called "*huasca*" the tea is considered a sacrament that heightens spiritual understanding and brings practitioners closer to God. More online at <http://www.udvusa.org>.

3. "With only 5% of the world's population, the U.S. has 25% of the world's prison population." The American Civil Liberties Association <https://www.aclu.org/safe-communities-fair-sentences/prison-crisis>.

4. More information on PCP, PMA, and other drugs mentioned in this interview can be found at The National Institute for Drug Abuse (NIDA), online at <http:www//drugabuse.gov>.

5. More information on Dr. Grob's Brazil research study can be found in *The Journal of Psychoactive Drugs* 37(2):119–144, 2005, and in the 1997 BBC Psychedelic Science documentary <https://www.youtube.com/watch?v=mEdxrHud5tE>.

6. "The Dark Side of Ayahuasca," by Kelly Hearn, *Men's Journal*, March 2003. Online at <http://www.mensjournal.com/magazine/the-dark-side-of-ayahuasca-20130215>.

7. "Kick Your Smoking Habit With . . . Magic Mushrooms?" by Paula Mejia, *Newsweek*, September 11, 2014. Online at <http://www.newsweek.com/kick-your-smoking-habit-magic-mushrooms-270012>.

8. See "LSD Could Help Alcoholics Stop Drinking, AA Founder Believed," by Amelia Hill, *Guardian*, August 23, 2013. For more on Bill Wilson, see Cheever (2005).

9. For an alternative view on conventional school anti-drug programs by Grob's daughter, read "If Not D.A.R.E., Then What?" by Stephanie Grob Plante, *The Atlantic*, August 28, 2014.

10. The Eleusinian Mysteries were the most famous of the secret religious rites of ancient Greece, and were performed annually in the month of September. They celebrated the story of Demeter and the search for her daughter Persephone. It was believed that those who participated in the rituals were forever changed for the better and that they no longer feared death.

—10—

Dionysos
God of Alcohol

AN INTERVIEW WITH GINETTE PARIS, PH.D.

FROM THE PERSPECTIVE OF the ancient Greeks, we might say that through our teenagers, our drug addicts and our alcoholics, we suffer the vengeance of a God to whom we refuse true Dionysia and whose mysteries, once celebrated at Eleusis, no longer have any equivalent."

When I first read these words by depth psychologist Ginette Paris relating the Greek God Dionysos to addiction,[1] doors blew open in my mind as if the stone had been lifted from Aladdin's shuttered cave, revealing at once hidden treasures of meaning into the mystery of addiction. Alcohol as a divine gift? I had thought our biblical God had long ago exiled that pagan "God of the grape," stripping him of his ancient rites and powers to enchant and lure his devotees into states of ecstasy. Why did the Greeks see a divinity in something so many in my own time had come to see as the very devil that must be cast out?

In fact, it just might take the return of a supernatural force like an ancient Greek God to liberate the topic of addiction from the worn and repetitive tropes of some cultural stereotypes and theories about addiction. As I learned from Paris during our first interview on violence, and now again in our conversation on addiction, one of the great contributions of the classical world is the way the ancient Gods and Goddesses symbolized the sacred within the ordinary. "Abstract terms like communication, desire, power, reason, passion, and the majority of concepts found in psychology textbooks," writes Paris, "describe invisible realities that the ancient Greeks evoked by giving them a personality and a name with a capital letter."

141

The Greeks, for example, did not use abstract concepts to discuss the damaging effects of drugs, she continues, but talked about "the madness that Dionysos sends to anyone who refuses to honor him." This more mythically oriented idea of looking upon the sipping of wine or the inhalation of marijuana as a non-ordinary *ritual* that relates us to another order of reality automatically requires an adjustment of attitude and naturally imposes a set of limits and boundaries—just the same as participating in any Catholic, Jewish, or Buddhist ritual. Paris's perspective picks up on and amplifies Dr. Charles Grob's emphasis in the previous interview on the need to find sanctioned ways to access ecstatic states—a need made increasingly evident through the youth culture's ongoing passion for Molly (MDMA, or ecstasy) and, more recently, ketamine (Known as Special K or Vitamin K, used as an injectable anesthetic by veterinarians and which can cause hallucinations in people). And like Grob, Paris studied the rites of ancient Eleusis, to re-imagine new pathways to altered states of consciousness.

In the following interview, which took place in 1995, Paris begins by stating simply that alcohol and drugs are a fact of the human condition and are part of every culture. From there, she analyzes the way individuals' and different cultures' need for specific substances indicates where they are repressed. During our conversation, she discusses how the Greeks imagined their Dionysos as the great "loosener." With their heightened perception about altered states, they recognized the need for a double consciousness, calling it the "day world" and the "night world." Paradoxically, it is through giving our due to the night world of Dionysos—found in festivals, funerals, social gatherings, and other occasions marked by emotional intensity where we can give vent to other parts of ourselves—that we are able to drink more deeply of life's ecstasy.

Pythia Peay: In your book *Pagan Grace* you make a connection between addiction and the loss of Dionysian revelries in our culture. Can you say more about what you mean by that?

Ginette Paris: This came up during a class I was teaching to students who were working in clinics with people who suffered from different addictions. One of the students asked me why the Greeks had a God that represented addiction: Dionysos. I explained to them that this meant that, with Dionysos, the Greeks acknowledged that all cultures since the beginning of humanity have had some kind of substance that will alter the mind: it's simply a fact of human history. There's no way to have a vision of a world that is completely sober and drug-free. It's never existed, and never will.

Of course, there's a very broad definition for what is considered a drug, including chocolate, tobacco, coffee, hormones, marijuana, and so on. In some cultures, meat is viewed as addictive, because if you eat meat it makes you more of a warrior; so it's the equivalent of taking steroids. We are a nation of addicts: antidepressants, anxiolytics (drugs used to treat anxiety), and painkillers. The dominant ritual is pill popping for every ailment of the soul.

PP: So the Greeks were wise about human nature in a way that America is not?

GP: The Greeks had a God for alcohol because mythology is not about what should be, but about what *is*. And because the need to alter our consciousness exists in human nature, they had a figure representing that instinct.

PP: The Greeks took a very different approach to life than the more moralistic Christian approach.

GP: Myths aren't moralistic; they give us a map that says if a person or a culture takes a certain route, they can expect a certain outcome. So myths give us a sense of direction: if you go there, this is what you get. For instance, at the ancient temple of Eleusis, where Greek citizens celebrated the Mysteries of the Mother Goddess Demeter, participants would first undergo a period of seclusion and fasting. This was to prepare them for the rites that involved ingesting a hallucinogenic substance that was the equivalent to modern-day LSD. Very strong stuff, but the preparation of the initiates was a long and well-defined one.

PP: So why is it important to the topic of addiction to know that the Greeks fasted before taking a hallucinogen, as part of their holiest ritual?

GP: Because cultures need to have a discipline and a guiding spirit that goes with a drug. Think about the place that alcohol has in Western culture. New research shows that taken in the right amount, with the social ritual of a communal meal, some alcohol is even good for your health.[2] The other end of that spectrum is alcoholism.

With an addiction, we always think that there's too much "Dionysos." But in fact, addiction often means that there's not *enough* of the Dionysian element and by this I mean not enough ritual, not enough cultural development.

This is true of every symptom of "too muchness" that becomes destructive. In the past, the concept of nymphomania used to be reserved for women who were promiscuous and who slept with a lot of men. The clinical definition of a nymphomaniac, in fact, is that of a woman who is frigid and who uses sex to get attention, affection, and domination, but who fails at real intimacy and can't experience sexual ecstasy. So an addict is not someone who likes sex so much, it is someone who literally "can't get enough" from it and so keeps looking for it.

PP: And likewise, with drug and alcohol addiction, it's as if we don't get enough of the Dionysian consciousness, ecstasy, and expression of strong emotions, so that the addict keeps ingesting the substance?

GP: Right. And because the Greeks recognized that need, each citizen went once or twice during their lifetime to Eleusis, and took the hallucinogenic drugs: once initiated into that mode of consciousness, they didn't need to ingest it again.

The unwritten cultural rituals that protect against alcoholism were usually given with the way we were raised. In a nonalcoholic family, for example, the unwritten rules are something like this: 1) Don't drink when you're alone. 2) Drink while you're eating with other people, not when you cook yourself an egg on the stove. 3) Take days off from drinking each month and do a "liver cleanse" (no alcohol). 4) Enjoy your wine because it helps to relax and eat slowly—and know and accept that it *loosens the tongue.* "The loosener" was actually one of the names of Dionysos, so when that "loosening" happened, there was a real meeting with the God. But with the alcoholic, there is a failure to really get what is needed from alcohol.

PP: And what is it that the alcoholic is looking for?

GP: I believe it's the deepest experience of the God Dionysos, which is to be taken out of our ego consciousness, the rational day world consciousness that we all need to hold a job. "Getting out of oneself" is what the Greeks understood the word "ecstasy" to mean: to experience the absence of one's ego.

PP: Broadly speaking, I think that this kind of ecstasy is something we fear very much in this culture.

GP: Yes, there's a fear of ecstasy in our culture. Perhaps the last Dionysian period was the counterculture movement during the sixties, and with it came both the gifts and the dangers of letting loose the God of ecstasy. Nevertheless, many of those who went through that period didn't get addicted; they experienced "ecstasy" and then translated the experience into their productive lives. Others, lacking guidance and cultural containers, were stuck in the addiction and destroyed themselves.

PP: So then when it comes to addiction we need to learn the art of . . .

GP: Getting into that state, and getting out of it.

PP: Many experts now view alcoholism as a genetic problem and as a physical disease. What is your view on that?

GP: If you look at addiction from that point of view, every God or Goddess could be a disease, a genetic predisposition, or a possible problem. Each archetype (God or Goddess of the ancient Greeks) was imagined as containing within them a seed of madness, and a gift. Dionysos can bring ecstasy, but also, if you don't do it right, destruction. Zeus symbolized law and order, but authority can also become oppressive and tyrannical. Aphrodite represented sweet love, honey, and roses, but also the torture of heartbreak and jealousy. Demeter is maternal love and also maternal passiveness and smothering—and so on with the Greek pantheon. No power is without its shadow.

PP: Several experts have also told me that Alcoholics Anonymous, although not one hundred percent effective, is the only program out there that offers the potential for treating alcoholism. But for many, AA doesn't work because it becomes a kind of religious conversion experience that they can't relate to. So many addicts are looking for other ways to control their drinking or drug taking, including young teens. What are your insights into other things that might heal addiction?

GP: A Dionysian encounter is one where there is emotional intensity, where one takes the risk of being outside of one's ego. It is that same instinct in young people that will push them to drive a car at a hundred miles per hour: they're looking for strong emotion; risk; something really, really intense and that involves danger. Unfortunately, there's not much of an outlet for that in our legitimate culture; teens have to become delinquents to get it, to carry guns, to practice extreme sports, to take stupid risks. And even that's often not enough to satisfy their desire for intensity. So I believe that whatever will give young people the real intensity they're looking for will also help them with their problems around addiction.

PP: So when we're talking about altered states, and getting out of the narrow confines of ourselves, what do we really mean?

GP: When we're in an altered state, what gets "altered" is our vision of the world, of relationships, of what counts, and what does not. We may have a vision of the world that's killing us when we're sober, and so we need to escape it. For example, for many people, their vision of the world is work, money, competition, and consumerism— and that's what life is all about: to be a winner. So the real need is for something that hints at different values, whatever fits our deepest need. This would be the "night world."

PP: I love the sound of the "night world." Say more about what you mean by that.

GP: The balance between these two worlds is essential for any culture. For example, a culture solely devoted to the rational and logical "Apollonian" brightness of the "day world" will dry up and die; conversely, if it receives too much of the Dionysian element, or "night world," it rots and becomes crazy. A hyper-technological, hyper-rationalized society is as unbalanced as the anti-intellectual, Dionysian-intoxicated, intensely emotional states that are typical of alcohol intoxication. We need *both* Dionysos and Apollo. The Greeks imagined mental health as a balancing act, harmony as between two notes—or as Jung would say, a tension between the opposites.

When a culture is addicted to a certain kind of drug it reveals something about that culture's repression. For example, when I traveled to Morocco thirty-five years ago, they thought that smoking pot was totally insignificant, almost like chewing gum! What some Moroccans wanted instead was to trade hash for a pack of American cigarettes, and to be "high on cigarettes." For them, this was the real drug. They loved it! Whereas being stoned wasn't very different from the rest of the culture they lived in, so they didn't really need it. But they did need tobacco!

PP: So what do you mean when you say that, for Moroccans, being stoned wasn't very different from the culture they lived in? And why did they crave tobacco?

GP: When I was in Morocco, the whole mood of the country felt stoned. The streets, the architecture, and the whole city was like being in a maze, or living in a completely different world. So what they were looking for was something completely different from the atmosphere they lived in every day—and for them that was cigarettes and alcohol. When I asked them what they saw in tobacco, they felt it gave them a sense of individuality. In contrast to their more communal culture, cigarettes provided the experience of feeling like a willful, heroic, separate individual—the archetype of the cigarette-smoking hero of the American movies of the sixties.

PP: Can you say more about the cultural need that different drugs fulfill?

GP: Cocaine, for example, gives a sense of power and being on top. It gives a person the feeling that they can work twenty-four hours a day nonstop, without the need for sleep. So it imbues a person with audacity, and makes them feel that they have the ego that goes with being an entrepreneurial go-getter: until they have a heart attack.

Addiction to alcohol gets us *out* of the ego and the drive for success, which also means that in a culture that stresses ego and success so much, the addiction to alcohol will make someone a loser, an outcast. Alcoholics are all losers in the sense that they would go down, down, down until they've lost everything: relationships, professional status, their home. . . .

PP: So then an alcoholic is somebody who is trying to escape something in the culture that is destroying them, but they do it in a destructive way?

GP: Yes. What's interesting is that the one thing alcoholics are always told by those who reject them is that when they're drunk, they're not really being themselves. So the loved one or friend will say to the alcoholic, "I'm not going to talk to you, because you aren't yourself." But then the question becomes, "Who is that person when they're drunk?"

I've worked with alcoholics, and I believe one of the strangest things in the culture is that no therapist will treat a patient who is drunk, and they won't let the patient drink during the session. As a consequence, there's a total disconnection between these two sides of the alcoholic: there's the life and the person they are while they're drunk, and the life and the person that they are when they're sober and in therapy. It's as if there is no place where the alcoholic can be contained in that drunken, inebriated state; there's not much exploration of this other person, and who they really are. It's just one indication of a split that we have around alcoholism. Sometimes there's a frightening difference between the two personalities.

PP: I had an alcoholic father, and I know that firsthand. He was like Jekyll and Hyde, two completely different personalities when he was sober and when he was drunk.

GP: So then you agree the split should be studied?

PP: Yes, I think you're making a good point.

GP: This "other person" who comes out under the influence of alcohol doesn't receive any attention. Not all alcoholics are the same when they are drunk. This other person may be a crying, vulnerable softy, an abandoned child; or he/she is an angry bully or a mean miser. . . . But to get out of addiction, one has to get acquainted with that Mr. Hyde.

PP: Are you saying that this "other person" needs to be brought out of the alcoholic?

GP: To come to awareness. When we say to someone, "You're not being yourself," it also postulates that we have only one self. So then there is no place where a person can bring out these other parts of themselves and be seen. If there was a place, there would be no need for alcohol to bring out these hidden sides.

PP: There's so much that we miss in addiction when we only take a moralistic or scientific approach.

GP: Science has its place. But I believe that even if we took a pill that would cause us to physically reject alcohol, the underlying problem would remain. The need of the expression of the *other self*, or should I say other *selves*, would still be there.

PP: This brings us back to the balance that's needed between the Apollonian day world and the Dionysian night world. It seems to me that America places much more of an emphasis on living a well-ordered, pragmatic life. Does boredom play a part in problems around alcoholism and addiction?

GP: I think so. It's impossible to be proper all the time. Dionysian festivals in ancient Greece were a time when people could go absolutely crazy, and all the madness inside could come out. Then after the festival was over, the city would return to its normal routine. For example, the Renaissance carnival wasn't just a party where people got dressed up in costumes with masks and gloves. It was also a time of year when the population could spend a week being someone else and being completely unrecognized, doing all kinds of things with different people. A man could dress as a woman, and vice versa. Halloween pales in comparison! It has become a candy orgy.

No one had to feel guilty, for example, for taking on the identity of a different gender, class, or age. A seventy-year-old man could dress as a young girl, and in doing so could act out another part of his soul. Or a lady could be a boy for a few days—whatever someone's fantasy might be! Even during the Christian Middle Ages, cities were periodically allowed to go mad, and then order would be restored. Being proper 365 days a year will drive everyone crazy in very dangerous and unpredictable ways, because some element in society just cannot take it. When societies don't have these outlets, they'll pay in other ways.

PP: So would you encourage more festivals and carnivals as a way to bring the Dionysian element into modern culture?

GP: I think Dionysos can be found in any occasion that stirs up intense emotions. Funerals, for example, used to be a very important Dionysian moment because it was a time when a whole clan would come together for several days and there would be twenty-four hours of eating and drinking: the bereaved could sleep, wake up, cry, eat, get drunk, get crazy, and shout. Now everything is very, very organized. The funeral parlor is one place where excessive emotion around the tragedy of death is being repressed. It is all so proper and good mannered. Bland! If death isn't tragic, then what is? How come I cannot wail and cry, and go berserk over the loss? The same goes for the birth of a child. Births used to be intense moments when we could be exuberant with joy; but the ritual is now overly medicalized. Not that medicine should not play its role, but there is a lack of attention to the huge emotional event happening to the parents. ∎

Notes

1. Dionysos was considered by the Greeks as the God of wine, fertility, and the vine, as well as madness and ecstasy. See <http://www.greekmythology.com/Other_Gods/Dionysus/dionysus.html>.
2. "Alcohol: Balancing Risks and Benefits," *The Nutrition Source, Harvard School of Public Health.* Online at <http://www.hsph.harvard.edu/nutritionsource/alcohol-full-story/>.

—11—

Eating Disorders and America's Neglected Body

AN INTERVIEW WITH MARION WOODMAN, PH.D.

S PIRITUAL OR PSYCHOLOGICAL EPIPHANIES, we are used to thinking, commonly descend upon us through sudden flashes of illumination and insight. But for Canadian-born Jungian analyst Marion Woodman, this classic process was reversed when through the medium of her ill and starved body she became awakened—not to God as Patriarch, but to the Goddess as the Feminine.

At age forty-five, Woodman had taken a sabbatical from the position she'd held as a high-school English teacher for twenty-one years, and had traveled to India in search of a spiritual teacher. Suffering from severe anorexia, she collapsed and fainted in the street. A kind American stranger picked up her "bag of bones," as she recalls, and took her back to her hotel. There, lying on her bed, alone and ill with fever, she lapsed in and out of consciousness, wrestling with whether to live or die. The thing that finally saved her, she said later, was her dog. "I perceived my body as a dog. . . . And I saw this patient, loyal thing lying on the ground. . . . And I thought, 'I wouldn't betray him, but I would betray my own body.' Suddenly I realized what that betrayal meant—to have been given a life and then decide it's not worth living. That seemed to be an ultimate betrayal."[1]

Woodman's revelation put her on a path of healing and led to the dramatic transformation of her life and her purpose in it. Quitting her job, she went into Jungian analysis and then moved to Zürich, where she trained at the Jung Institute to become an analyst. Her thesis, *The Owl Was A Baker's Daughter*—a groundbreaking clinical study

151

of the psychology of obesity, bulimia, and anorexia—would become a classic, putting her in the front guard of Jungian analysts addressing the growing epidemic of eating disorders and addiction so rampant in the modern era. As she continued to publish more books, it was said of Woodman that she effectively "brought the body" into the therapy room, endearing her to thousands of women and men suffering from potentially life-destroying food and substance addictions. In turn, the Jungian perspective she brought to eating disorders allowed her to understand the complexes underlying each one metaphorically, as messages from the unconscious. Weight disturbances such as being too fat or too thin weren't just the result of bad diet choices, for example, but the psyche itself made *visible* in the body. Thus as Woodman reasoned, these symptoms must also have meaning and purpose—if only they could be read correctly.

Taking her research a step deeper, Woodman ultimately came to see that anorexia, bulimia, and obesity pointed to a disorder within Western culture itself. This was the repression of the feminine principle—the body's intuitive wisdom grounded within the cycles of nature; and the need for rest, creativity, and depth relationships—by society's power-driven values of productivity, achievement, domination, and success. In Woodman's estimation, this repressed "Feminine side of God" was attempting to make its way back into the culture through the back door of eating disorders.

Although I had interviewed Woodman before, in 1994, I was pleased to conduct another in-depth interview with her solely on the topic of addiction. The following conversation builds on the foundation of her unique insights into the various psychological patterns underlying different eating disorders and addictions, and shows the way to healing paths out of the trap of the addictive complex. True to Woodman's commitment to the Feminine, and the circular, "meandering" ways of the psyche, we wandered down odd paths in search of the "metaphor" at the root of various addictions. In the process, we discuss things far off the grid of mainstream American life (imagination, communion, creativity, the "positive" mother archetype, play, nature, and love)—all things that enliven, nurture, and feed the needs of the soul within, and that also inoculate the body, and the psyche, against addiction.

✳

Pythia Peay: What I'm interested in exploring with you is a classic Jungian "teleological" approach to addiction: an attitude that seeks to understand the unconscious purpose or drive behind an uncontrollable need for a substance or activity.

Marion Woodman: Let me start by talking about the link between addiction and the imagination. In modern Western culture, our capacity for imagination, myths, and archetypes has become significantly weakened. Take the religious ritual of Holy Communion that is part of a church service. For the person who has no imaginative understanding of what communion is on a deeper level, for example, nothing happens. But the archetypal need for spiritual communion still remains; when unfulfilled, it could be transferred to an eating disorder. In that case, an addict then projects a God or Goddess onto food and, as with the ritual of communion in the church, "eats" the divine being in the hope of having an ecstatic experience.

If an addictive activity or substance—whether sexuality, alcohol, food, or drugs—carries the projection of a God or Goddess, it will initially bring about some kind of ecstatic experience. But because these are concrete substances and not authentic spiritual essences, the addict ends up in an unconscious stupor instead of conscious ecstasy. Even though they try again and again, it can never work, because addicts confuse material existence for the imaginal realm. And that's why many of our church rituals don't work anymore: in ritual there has to be a "crossing over" at an imaginary level, and if a person is using a concrete object to make that crossing, their imagination is cut off.

PP: So then how do we learn to use imagination as a way to redirect an addiction?

MW: The vehicle would be metaphor. My sense is that if a person can get at the metaphorical meaning of what substance they're craving, they can then move into the state it's connected to. For instance, if the addict can understand food as mother, alcohol as spirit, or sexuality as divine union, that enables them to shift away from the concrete object to the spiritual dimension.

PP: So the metaphor of "mother" underlying a food addiction, for example, would have to do with an unfulfilled need for nurturing and caretaking?

MW: Yes, as well as sweetness and comfort. Many food addicts naturally go for sweet things, like milk, honey, chocolate, and grains: all the foods that symbolize the positive mother. In fact, the biggest thing lacking in our culture is the positive mother.

PP: And because it's lacking in the wider culture—in teachers, bosses, relatives, co-workers, and friends—this makes it difficult for a mother to give it to her children herself. So it's not just an individual mother's "fault?"

MW: Right: because she hasn't received it. In order to give something to someone else, a person has to bring it to consciousness. A man or woman could be the best possible parent, but still not give their child the comfort of living in its own body happily, because they didn't get that from their parents, and so on back. Indeed, in spite of the fact that everyone is talking about good food, health, and exercise, the body is hated in our culture. If you look at what's on television, mostly what you see are abused bodies. The society is totally schizophrenic. Pick up a magazine and on one side is an article on how to be thin while the other side has recipes so rich they're killers.

PP: Can you say more about what "positive mothering" really means?

MW: As I understand positive mothering, it's a person who loves their body, loves matter, and does not put spiritual ideals ahead of the body's needs. Most people think it's more important to have a thin, beautiful, sexy, fit body than a healthy one. Many women and men are running and starving themselves into unhealthiness. Or they're poisoning their bodies with alcohol or nicotine. So when parents act this way, why should they be surprised when their children follow in their footsteps? The positive parent is the one who makes the child feel at home in his or her own body; then these children grow up to love being in their bodies, love to nurture their body and to give it the exercise that it needs, and will not poison or abuse it.

PP: So does withdrawing a projection from a substance, like food or alcohol, lead to a kind of painful comedown and sense of betrayal: that a person could be so blind, misled, and deceived?

MW: Betrayal is exactly what a person feels after an eating binge. If they eat twelve chocolate bars and then go into a stupor, they wake up feeling bitterly betrayed. They might have had a moment of ecstasy while they wolfed them down, but then they wake up wanting to commit suicide. Or they feel betrayed because they're eating chocolate all the time; and not only are they not finding the sweetness they craved, they're gaining weight as well. That dynamic can also occur after sexual union. Some people feel betrayed because they projected the perfection of the divine onto the person they slept with. Then they blame their partner, and how crazy is that? It's the same with people looking for a high with alcohol; they give into a drinking binge, then end up in a hideous depression, and that comes from a feeling of betrayal.

PP: At a certain level, there must be a way that a need for sweetness can also be filled by food in a healthy way. I know from your work that you have a genuine reverence for food; so it's not as if one has to renounce the pleasures of food.

MW: No, not at all. It has to do with how the food is made. People who eat frozen TV dinners or fast food all the time may be missing some of the love that goes into the hand-cooked meal. Or if they're eating alone, and just gulping food down as fast as they can, they're not communing with anyone around a meal—so there's no real feeling being taken in with the food. Another place where someone might find sweetness other than food is in dancing. There the person can find the sweetness of ecstasy and music, and the spirit and soul can play.

PP: You've said that the metaphor behind an addiction to alcohol is the yearning for spirit. How would you translate that?

MW: So many parents project a kind of perfection onto their child—so bright, so athletic, so musical, or so witty. They see this very, very special child, so to speak, as carrying "the light of the sun and the music of the wind." Inevitably, the child begins to think he or she is a little prince or princess who will one day come into their kingdom. Many children are brought up with that kind of impossible hope projected onto them. Then when they can't achieve what their parents hoped for, even when they're trying their best, there's a yearning to escape from everyday reality into the transcendence of spirit. They don't really want to know who they are on a human level.

PP: Because they may fail, or because they may not be who their parents think they are?

MW: They *will* fail. Many young men and women are idealized children who have tremendous rage against their parents for putting the burden of such idealistic expectations on them. Of course, even the parents can't live up to those ideals, and

155

then the child feels doubly betrayed. And so to overcome that fear and rage, and to escape from the idealism that's projected onto them, they escape out of the realities of their bodies and into what they imagine is spirit. But they don't realize that they can't get that spiritual high out of a concrete substance like alcohol, and so they end up in obliteration. I don't know that much about drugs. But I do see cocaine, like alcohol, as having to do with the yearning for spirit and light.

Typically, an addiction has to do with a hole in the psyche. What's missing will become a drive for wholeness.

PP: So then finding and filling the "hole" correctly is the key to healing addiction?

MW: Right. You look for what the need or lack is, and then look for how you're "concretizing" it in the wrong way.

PP: So what would be the underlying metaphor in compulsive, addictive sexuality?

MW: It's about divine union with God. In India, you see that expressed in images of the Goddess Shiva and the God Shakti locked in an eternal divine embrace. This couple exemplifies the polarities of the masculine and feminine, as these energies are always at play during intercourse.

PP: So it's not enough to say that what we seek is union with God; more specifically, we seek the union of the opposites within us.

MW: And the *ecstasy* of that union. People accept sexuality much more than they did a century or even fifty years ago, but for many people it's still compulsive. Real eroticism, however, has to do with all the senses and the imagination coming together. When we go outside, for example, we can see the constant intermingling of these two energies in nature: the glorious sun shining on the green grass, for instance; or, if it's an autumn day, we might become aware of the mellowing sun bringing the apples to maturity. We might even feel it penetrating our skin, if we give the sun a chance to come in. Or we might feel the wind making love to our body, like someone on a surfboard riding the waves. That's magnificently erotic.

In other words, I'm describing a mystical experience. Most people don't realize how precious life is; they go running past everything and they don't see the cardinals or the blue jays, or the yellow tulips or the redness of the zinnia. But there may come a moment when they will see, hear, smell, and touch. And that's where the real erotic ecstasy of life lies: when you feel the unity with God, and with all living things.

Unfortunately, a big piece of the problem with sexual addiction is that we tend to separate sexuality and spirituality, and to think that spirituality is better than sexuality. But those two opposites are really one. In fact, what we call the opposites aren't really opposites—they're complements of one another, and together they form a unity. But one of our difficulties as a culture is that we break everything down into contradictions, and fail to see how they're linked. We're a very adolescent culture, and we have not grown up. We've still got ideals that are totally deceiving us.

PP: Can you say more about how these things are linked together: addiction, our "deceptive" ideals, our adolescence as a culture, and how we lack knowledge of "the opposites" in life?

MW: We all carry a heavy load of false idealism. In other words, we don't want to accept our humanity or our imperfections. We're blind to the opposites in human nature; we try to pretend that we're not jealous, or greedy, or that we're not the most greedy nation in the world. And because we can't accept the opposites of the light and the dark that exist in our own nature, and our culture's nature, we fall into addictions. So we have to escape.

PP: What's the difference between genuine idealism and false idealism? As a country, America was founded on ideals.

MW: A false ideal is something that goes far beyond the reach of ordinary human limitations—so much that it denies what it is to be human. But living in integrity with our ideals means that they have to be obtainable, and that we have to be able to live up to them, to fulfill them, and to stand by them. But people who live by false ideals fall by the wayside, because those ideals are unobtainable. A false ideal prevents us from dealing with a problem that's right in front of us: like the husband or wife who has an ideal of a monogamous marriage, and then has to deal with betrayal or infidelity. People in older cultures accepted the limitations of human behavior, and that this is the way we are; people are a combination of opposites, and those opposites are going to manifest.

PP: What does wisdom around the opposites, and the limitations of human nature, have to do with addiction?

MW: Take greed, for example. If we accept, rather than repress or deny, the fact that greed is part of human nature, then we can ask the question, "What am I greedy for? Maybe it's greed for God; the drive that is driving me is the yearning for God." The tragedy is that when we don't ask that question and become conscious of this greed, then our greed for spirituality ends up in a concretized object, like alcohol.

This brings me to something else concerning addiction: many people's energy is so muted that they have no idea how great they actually *could* be. They continually cut off their real desires until they don't have any desire left, and neither do their kids. Then you see children growing up who are afraid to express their real desires, and then that repressed desire comes out in compulsion or brutality.

PP: So what you're saying is that behind an addiction lies a powerful life force.

MW: Right. Often an addiction is expressing a life force that has no purpose or goal. Then that magnificent energy is squandered, forcing the person toward annihilation. The two go together; a powerful life drive can easily flip into death and destruction. In other words, if we allow our life drive—which is a yearning to create, or for union with God, or to dance—to turn into a craving for alcohol, we can end up killing ourselves.

PP: So desire, creativity, and imagination are important in healing addiction. We as a culture neglect that in favor of the practical and the pragmatic.

MW: Yet at the same time, people who struggle with an addiction are also failing to take responsibility for their creativity. They're trying to escape responsibility to their gift; they don't want to grow up. And the addiction will keep them infantile.

PP: I've noticed that in your writing you use the word *play* a lot.

MW: There is a time to work, but there is a time for both children and the inner child in adults to work imaginatively, and to play. So I love that word; play is focused concentration. And I don't think there's anything in life without concentration. Concentration means moving with the center. But there has to be a center.

PP: Most people wouldn't link play and concentration.

MW: No. But for example, if someone is painting or writing, they can forget time and become completely involved. They become what they're doing, and that's concentration. That's when a person is *really* playing, and the soul is just singing. That's where the ecstasy is for me, where the spirit and soul can play, traveling into the depths of the imagination as far as possible.

PP: I wonder if addiction is increasingly a problem because both for adults and kids there's less and less time to play and to be creative—which in turn, keeps us adolescent because we haven't taken responsibility for our creative gift or calling.

MW: Again, it comes back to imagination: we don't have time to imagine. I believe strongly that there has to be time in every day without structure, to make time for the unconscious, because that's what we're really talking about. If the unconscious doesn't have time to come out and play, it will eventually burst out in some compulsive, addictive behavior, because it's got to have room to be recognized. ■

Notes

1. "An Interview with Marion Woodman," by Pythia Peay, *The San Francisco Jung Institute Library Journal*, Volume 11, Number 1; San Francisco, 1992.

—12—

America's Icarus Complex

AN INTERVIEW WITH LINDA SCHIERSE LEONARD, PH.D.

OVER THE YEARS, THERE have been many authors, analysts, and psychotherapists whose work has helped to deepen my understanding of my father's alcoholism, and the ways my girlhood was shaped by that particular journey of suffering. But when I read Linda Schierse Leonard's unsparing account of her own childhood growing up with an alcoholic father in *The Wounded Woman: Healing the Father Daughter Relationship*, a classic that has now been translated into fifteen languages, I felt that here was someone who had traveled a similar road, and who knew well that treacherous terrain.

It was not just the personal stories Leonard shared—which included an account of how, when she was in her thirties and away from home, her father set their house on fire by accident—but the gentleness and compassion she brought to her father's suffering as an addict that opened up in me a new way of being with my own troubled paternal legacy. In telling the poignant story of how she sought to transform her relationship with her alcoholic father through analysis and study, and in stressing the importance of the father–daughter relationship in women's development, Leonard led me to an important juncture, orienting me toward the open-ended direction of healing rather than staying mired in resentment and bitterness.

I was also interested in interviewing Leonard for yet another important reason: her *own* experience as an alcoholic, and her eventual recovery and discovery of the path to the sweetness of sobriety. Today, she is a prolific author, existential philosopher, and well-known Jungian analyst who has been in practice for over forty years. Valued for the spectrum of ideas, insights, and firsthand knowledge she brings to the twin topics of addiction and creativity, Leonard lectures and presents workshops worldwide, helping others recognize and contend with the deceptive guises in which the demons of their particular addictions can appear.

In another classic work, *Witness to the Fire: Creativity and the Veil of Addiction*, she took up the exploration of the dangerous borderland between creativity and addiction. In describing how to free the "daemon" of creativity from the "demon" of addiction, Leonard drew on her own experience as a writer and philosopher, as well as examples from the lives of authors such as Jack London, Fyodor Dostoevsky, and Eugene O'Neill—revealing how addiction, despite its gloss and glamour, ultimately subverts the creative process and thwarts psychological wholeness. As an existential philosopher and authority on the works of Søren Kierkegaard and Martin Heidegger, among others, Leonard brings an unusual depth of thoughtfulness and reasoned reflection to the turbulent topic of alcoholism and addiction.

During our interview, Leonard shone a light on the larger cultural backdrop of American myths, naming beliefs that both inspire *and* that can foster an atmosphere in which addiction can flourish. She points to America's "big dreamer" "Icarus complex," and its tendency to go for the "quick fix" and the ecstasy of the heights as contributing to the country's problems around addiction. Together, we delve further into the relationship between creativity and addiction, and her innovative work synchronizing Alcoholic Anonymous's Twelve Step program[1] with the creative process. Like both Paris and Woodman in the preceding interviews, but in her own way, Leonard, too, interprets the archetypal energies operating behind specific addictions. In the inspiring conclusion to our conversation, which took place in 1995, she encourages more Americans to take up the study of philosophy and to align with psyche's depths and nature's cycles as paths that lead away from the heights of addiction and downward to lives grounded in joy and authenticity.

Pythia Peay: As the daughter of a father who suffered terribly from a serious drinking problem, I found that your work on addiction, which draws on your own background with an alcoholic father, hit close to home. I would imagine there's hardly an American family untouched by some form of addiction: it's one of those perennial problems that we struggle with as a country, though never very well.

Linda Schierse Leonard: The tendency toward addiction is part of the human condition. But certain societies by their nature seem to facilitate addiction more than others. Western culture, for example, is overwhelmed by all kinds of addictions, stemming primarily from our habit of seeking quick-and-easy solutions to life's problems.

PP: So then would you say that the root of the Western problem with addiction has something do with our imbalanced relationship to time, and that we're out of rhythm, so to speak?

LSL: Yes. But on a deeper level, our dysfunctional relationship to time stems from our disconnection from nature. Just like the changing seasons and the phases of the moon, everything in life, from physical, spiritual, and creative growth, is cyclical. By contrast, the Western linear, rational approach is aimed at the "end-point," or the idea that when we reach a certain goal, we'll have arrived at some kind of final destination. But that's an illusion: nature shows us that things keep cycling around and around again. There is a natural up-and-down rhythm to life—but we always want to be up. We don't want to go through the "down cycle," or the "dark night of the soul" stage of growth. And that prevents us from accessing our inner natures at greater depth.

PP: In *Witness to the Fire*, you write more specifically about the alternating rhythms of inflation and deflation, and how drugs and alcohol focus on one end of that polarity, giving us the highs of flight, inflation, and elation.

LSL: Yes, as do euphoria, romance, and power—all those things give us a quick high. Everyone likes to fly, that's natural. The problem is in wanting to prolong flying or being high unnaturally. But in the end, what happens to most of us is what happened to Icarus, who according to the Greek myth got possessed by the ability to fly high and touch the sun, and who then wasn't able to come down until he fell down, into the sea. What consciousness requires of us is that when we do rise up to touch the heights, we have enough wisdom to recognize that there will come a time when we have to descend back down. It's important to see the rhythmic cycle, instead of just blindly falling down.

PP: You also describe the characters in Eugene O'Neill's play *The Iceman Cometh* as hopeless pipe dreamers ungrounded in reality. You quote the drunken character Larry, "The lie of a pipe dream is what gives life to the whole misbegotten mad lot of us, drunk or sober." Is there something of the American psyche reflected in this play—that we're a nation of dreamers always reaching for the sky, always seeking out the endless horizon? I guess I wonder if there's something in the nature of our country itself that predisposes us to be restless seekers after the next high.

LSL: Yes, it's that adventurer aspect of the American character. I see that as a positive part of America, but at the same time our age and history are still so recent. We just don't have that many years of wisdom to ground us, and that's probably what we need. That's why it's important to go back to the classics and learn how other cultures lived. The problem is that our education tends to focus on achieving goals, instead of the process and journey of life itself.

PP: And part of that journey of life includes honoring the wisdom of the cycles, the ups and downs of life that we cycle through along the way?

LSL: For a period of time, my soul-mate partner and I lived with the Reindeer People, traveling with them through Lapland, Siberia, and Alaska: simply to survive, they had to follow the cycles of nature [see Leonard: 2005]. But modern Westerners don't see their survival as so directly related to nature. It's not included as part of childhood education, or honored in the culture; in fact, we've been cut off from nature. So I think the "get there as fast as you can" is part of our addiction complex; we try to take the short cut, to skip as many steps as we can, so that we can get wherever we're going faster.

As a result of living this way, our experience of time is very diminished; it's primarily linear clock-time. When you're in any kind of meaningful experience, like being with someone you love, or creating, there's a kind of timelessness to the experience; it doesn't move forward in a straightforward way. We need ordinary clock-time, too, but that needs to be based in the greater mystery of the rhythms of time. So we need to be able to learn how to dip in and out of different kinds of time.

PP: Can you give me an example of how addiction interferes with our natural rhythms and cycles?

LSL: There's a phase of drinking where a person experiences euphoria and vitality; the drinker is lifted outside of ordinary time. Then as the disease progresses, that quickly shifts to the time of "the living dead" and everything becomes part of a Dracula story, where taking the first drink is like offering your neck to Dracula!

PP: My father flew for TWA for many years, and often he would describe literally "following the sun," or going from one day into the next with no night. His rhythms were so off-kilter that the only way he could relax was to drink. Growing up, it was like watching someone become physically consumed and disfigured by a disease, like leprosy. At the end of his life, he even admitted that he'd never thought he'd make it to old age, which in fact he didn't. That was as close as he came to admitting he had a problem with alcohol; even then, he didn't ask for forgiveness or say he was sorry.

LSL: Addiction is a great tragedy in life. But because our cultural tendency has always been to avoid going into the depths to seek meaning, it contributes to this tragedy. So much of our education diverts us from that deep search for the nature of things. We tend to get caught up in appearances and involvements in the outer world. When that way of life completely takes over, we lose our soul.

And I believe that anytime we lose touch with our souls, there's an addictive process going on, as staying on the surface level of life can be addicting. In that case, it becomes easy to get pulled along by the crowd; a person doesn't even know what their life is really about. Philosophy is supposed to be about the love of wisdom and the search for meaning, but not very many people take up that search. America needs to support and make more of an accommodation for inquiring into the meaning of life, and exploring how the great mystics, artists, philosophers, and ancient cultures sought to answer those perennial questions.

PP: I agree with what you say. But there are plenty of spiritual teachers and thinkers who, despite all their inner work and knowledge, have struggled with addiction.

LSL: That's true; it just shows that the tendency to addiction is *always* there. It's part of all of our challenge as human beings to constantly be aware of not going in those extreme directions.

Sometimes, the worst forms of addiction aren't substance related, but have to do with issues around power, control, food, sex, and shopping and the acquisition of possessions. The Russian author Dostoevsky, for example, wasn't an alcoholic, but he was a compulsive gambler, which can take over a person's life to the point that it can destroy everything. When an addiction reaches that point, that's when a person has to make a choice. Some addicts aren't able to do that, so they die early in life. Author Jack London, for instance, realized at the end of his life that he was an alcoholic, but by then it was too late. The playwright Eugene O'Neill, on the other hand, was able to stop drinking at the age of thirty-eight.

PP: It's interesting to me that so many artists and writers were addicts; paradoxically, creativity is sometimes seen as the solution to addiction.

LSL: Creativity is not the solution to addiction. But it can help in the recovery process. In the beginning of recovery there's a two-year period (at least) when addicts are getting rid of the poison in their bodies and getting their energy back. So it's especially crucial during that time that addicts find something constructive to do with all that energy—because if they don't, the energy will go in a destructive direction.

   Often, for example, there's what I call a "demon lover" behind an addiction— an inner figure that can totally possess and take over a person's life. By contrast, Jung speaks about the "creative daemon," or a powerful, inspired energy of the psyche that a person has to learn how to direct and channel. These two forces are connected, because if you're unconscious of your creative energy—and our culture tends to ignore that—then it's easy for that positive creative energy to turn in a demonic direction. People in recovery are very fragile for a long period of time; and a twenty-one-day program is just a start. Beyond that, most people in recovery have a tremendous amount of unexplored energy, and lack a place to really explore that. And if they can't find that outlet, then they're at risk for a relapse.

PP: In other words, it's important to turn the "demon" into a "daemon." Just like Socrates, whose "voice" spoke to and through him, and guided him. How can a person differentiate between these two forces, especially in creative or spiritual work that can lead to altered states, such as flights of imagination or fantasy?

LSL: Many philosophers and artists describe this voice as a strong inner "calling," or an inner guide or mentor who's asking us to move in a certain direction that has to do with one's fate and destiny. But the demon is always there, and trying to find the creative "daemon" is always the challenge.

The way I differentiate between the two is that an addictive possession drains a person of their energy and lifeblood; they can even drain others. But the kind of possession that happens in the creative process is cyclical; it's also regenerating. If you're familiar with the creative process, you know that there are periods where you have to go down into some unknown parts of yourself, which is scary for everyone. The creative person might also be frightened that there's nothing there, and that they won't have something to create from. This is where faith, hope, and trust come in.

PP: In fact, you make a parallel between the creative process and the Twelve Step process of recovery from addiction.

LSL: Right. The first three steps are part of surrendering: in any creative work, you're surrendering to the unknown, and to the possibility that something greater than yourself can help you bring that new creation into fruition. In Jungian terms, the phase of surrendering corresponds with going into the unconscious.

Then, once you've surrendered and you're "down there" in the unconscious, and something starts to come up, you have to work and struggle with forming and creating it. This corresponds with steps four through ten in AA; that stage is all about looking at your life and the negative energies that have led to fear and resentment that have kept you locked in an addictive cycle—then letting go of those negative emotions. If you're writing and editing a book, this phase corresponds with editing, what to keep in and what to cut, and dealing with other people's opinions.

The last stage in the creative process has to do with rest and regeneration. I see that as parallel to the eleventh step, which is the stage of committing to a daily practice of meditation and prayer, and connecting with the divine. Often in that stage something new breaks through, as though on a creative level the psyche just has to rest, and then emerge renewed, like flowers popping up in the spring. There's a certain amount of gardening you can do, but then you have to let go, and wait for the plants to come up on their own.

An additional stage in the recovery process is that of giving. Through their struggles, addicts have won some spiritual awareness and knowledge, and they want to share it. This sharing helps a person incorporate and integrate their hard-won knowledge. The same thing happens in the creative process, when the artist or writer stops short of sharing because they're afraid they'll be rejected. But it's really important to share their creative work, because it encourages and inspires other people.

So that's a creative cycle. Yet even if we know these creative cycles, and the Twelve Steps in the recovery process, we have to keep reminding ourselves of them again and again, because it's so experiential. It's dealing with states of consciousness. This is why the linear approach is very dangerous, because it promotes the idea that once a person has done something, they're finished—but that's not what this is all about.

PP: Some addiction experts have said that America might do well to adopt a more balanced attitude toward alcohol. In Europe, for instance, children grow up taking sips of watered down table wine; here that's a real taboo, so some say as a consequence kids crave what's forbidden by the culture. Do you believe that if alcohol were less taboo for younger children there would be less of a problem with it in the culture?

LSL: I think we'd still have problems with alcohol. I myself didn't start drinking until I went to Europe, where it was a way of life. If you have the genetic disposition to alcoholism, and you live in a place where drinking is a way of life, you're going to get hooked. So I think it's a fallacy to think that all our problems with alcoholism could be handled with that approach. In his book *John Barleycorn*, Jack London writes that if only there had been prohibition, he wouldn't have been an alcoholic. So there he's putting responsibility on society, not on the individual.

Still, the most important issue to me is the realization that drug and alcohol addictions are symptomatic of deeper problems. The mistake we make is literalizing and concretizing substances like alcohol or cigarettes; we mistake the external, physical thing for the energy behind it. So the lesson is to get at the root of the energy in an addiction, and then learn how to redirect it. Jung for example said that alcohol was really spirit; and in fact alcohol is even sometimes called "spirits" because it can "inspirit" a person. We can do the same thing with romance, money, and power. For instance, we might associate power with how much control a person wields over others, as opposed to a person with good energy. The Dalai Lama radiates incredible power, but he uses it in the most gentle, kind way, whereas Hitler used his power in a very destructive way.

PP: In speaking of the Dalai Lama, I'm reminded of the way you write about the root word of addiction, *addictus*, as "devotion," or surrendering and consecrating oneself to something greater and more all-encompassing than one's individual self.

LSL: Yes, addiction had that original, good meaning of devotion to something regenerative, as opposed to something destructive. That's the basic choice. To the Reindeer People I lived among, for example, their individual lives were less important than the greater force of nature surrounding them. They just radiated gentleness and good will. Jung, for example, spoke about being guided by what he called the "Transcendent Function."

So the practice of devotion is a kind of rhythmic relationship to a greater transcendent force, like riding a horse or a reindeer. We have the opportunity to do that all the time, whether being in nature with animals, or walking outside in nature. But our culture makes even the idea of relating to something greater than our individual selves difficult: it isn't fostered, and it's even scoffed at.

PP: And so we end our interview by returning to the place where we began—that our problems with addiction have much to do with America's neglect of the invisible, deeper side of life.

LSL: As the philosopher Heidegger explains, our Western culture continually faces the dilemma of living out the paradox of two ways of being: "calculative thinking," which is about the survival of everyday life; and "meditative thinking," which is about the mystery of being. When we stay focused only on the calculative way of being, we're in danger of getting on the addictive track, like the alcoholic who calculates every move they make, or the smoker with smoking, or the romantic with romance. We have to learn that this way of being is *manipulative*.

PP: But it's very tough to go against the "calculative" way of being in this culture. It's like trying to go against the very grain of who we are as Americans, and that's hard to do and still feel part of the country we were born into.

LSL: Well, we can't be effective agents for changing a culture without entering into it in some way. As a society we need to try and develop various cultural rituals and rites that help us, especially in our recovery from addiction. Many Native Americans, for example, use the Twelve Step process in conjunction with the Medicine Wheel and the Sweat Lodge as part of their recovery process. So I would just hope that we could all work together to develop more open, reverential ways of being. Each person who does that is an important part of weaving a different kind of culture together. ■

Notes

1. The Twelve Steps were originally used by Alcoholics Anonymous as a method of recovery from alcoholism and other forms of addiction. Online at <http://www.aa.org/pages/en_US/twelve-steps-and-twelve-traditions>.

—13—

America's Empire-Plantation Complex
Workaholism and Addiction

AN INTERVIEW WITH ERNEST ROSSI, PH.D.

ORN IN 1933 IN Shelton, Connecticut, psychoanalyst, psychologist, and Jungian analyst Ernest Rossi at the age of eighty-one is as lively and productive as I imagine him to have been at the age of eighteen. His secret, I believe, lies in the research he himself pioneered in the field of mind–body healing: the concept of ultradian rhythms, or biological cycles of rest and activity that regulate physical and mental health. He first published his findings in 1991 in *The 20 Minute Break*. It was this book that stirred my interest in Rossi's work, for what could be more radical in workaholic America than pausing for rhythmic, regular breaks throughout the day?

Rossi first began his career as a pharmacist, foretelling his later work along the twin tracks of body and mind. He soon became interested in psychology and after receiving his doctorate from Temple University in Philadelphia he trained to become a Freudian psychoanalyst, and then a Jungian psychoanalyst. In 1972, Dr. Rossi began working with Milton H. Erickson. He became Erickson's close disciple, and for his efforts publishing Erickson's complete works he received several lifetime achievement awards from the Milton H. Erickson Foundation.

In the 1980s, Rossi began melding Ericksonian hypnotherapy with his knowledge of the biochemical processes of the body as well as Jungian approaches to the psyche and archetypes. Eventually, he developed his own Mind-Body Therapy techniques, pioneering the new field of Psycho-Social Genomics therapy.[1] Today, he is a teacher and the prolific author of over a hundred articles and twenty-one books, and has received several other lifetime achievement awards from the American Society of Clinical Hypnosis and the American Association for Psychotherapy.

Rossi's work has taken him to Israel, Germany, England, Switzerland, and other countries. Many people, he told me, have asked him what the difference was between their country and America. He responds, he says, by saying that "underneath outer appearances and cultural differences, we're all human beings. There are different blind spots among the different nationalities—but we're all the same people with the same insecurities." That said, in the following interview, Rossi elaborates with powerful conviction on the destructive effects of what he calls America's "empire-plantation"–based, exploitative way of life on our bodies and psyches, and how this way of life, through disrupting our natural rhythms, can lead to addiction. Because of our Judaeo-Christian background, Rossi explains, "we can't relax, or we'd feel guilty, and as a result the country is suffering from stress, addiction, and psychosomatic-related illnesses." Western culture's ingrained habit of overriding humankind's biological and mental needs for rest, he continues, is "the most tragic story of our modern society. When we do not get adequate rest, we try to stimulate ourselves artificially with both legal and illegal drugs. It's not just America who has these problems. But we have to see our own dark side—our shadow—that contributes to our suffering around addiction."

One final note: this interview was conducted in 1995, years before the surge of new technology that keeps us "wired" and connected day and night, and making Rossi's insights as relevant and applicable now, if not more so, than when we first spoke twenty years ago.

Pythia Peay: I'm curious to learn more about your research into the complexes underlying drug and alcohol addiction.

Ernest Rossi: My research is more about the psychobiology *behind* the emotional complex. In my view, the complexes involved in addiction have to do with our lack of understanding of what our mind and body are telling us. Every hour and a half, for example, we need to take a break because we feel a bit tired. Our hunger rhythm also runs every hour and a half, when we need to pause and get something to eat. We have to take a bathroom break every hour and a half or so; our nightly dreams also occur on the same hour-and-a-half rhythm. So that 15–20 minute break is very important, because during that time the body produces protein, enzymes, and energy supplies for the next hour and a half.

PP: So the body's continuous hour-and-a-half cycle throughout the day signals the body's need for a break—and that pause helps to regulate our energy?

ER: Exactly. All drugs have one thing in common: they either turn on or turn off the body's energy-generating systems. Caffeine, nicotine, amphetamines, and cocaine, for example, will turn on the system that makes energy available, because we're tired and we want help. The problem is that these drugs give us a temporary high that lifts and pushes the body's ultradian peak. But then that peak will be followed by a corresponding low, and then we crash.

All the "lowering" drugs—like sleeping pills, tranquilizers, barbiturates, and marijuana—put us toward the lower end of the ultradian rhythm. So all drugs are either giving us a kick up, or they're winding us down.

PP: Can you explain what "ultradian" means?

ER: *Ultradian* basically means more than once a day; *circadian* means once a day. The basic rest–activity rhythm every hour and a half, for example, is a very important ultradian rhythm. The most amazing thing we've learned about all addictive substances is that they imitate the natural hormones and messengers that turn us on and off. In fact, any addictive drug replaces the very same hormones and messengers that are naturally turned off and on during our ultradian peak performance and rest periods.

For example, epinephrine[2] turns us on and gives us a boost of energy for about twenty minutes. Then twenty minutes after epinephrine peaks, beta-endorphin[3] automatically kicks in, lowering our energy and bringing us down to an ultradian rest cycle for about twenty minutes. We turn to addictive drugs because we've forgotten how to listen to our natural mind and body signals for maximizing top performance, as well as rest. So you see how nature works: She knows that she's going to have to lift up a person, and that she's going to have to drop them down again.

PP: I'm fascinated to learn about these innate bodily rhythms. How does your research into the biochemistry of these alternating rhythms, and the effects of different drugs on these rhythms, fit into your work as a Jungian analyst?

ER: Both Freud and Jung were very interested in biology, but the biology of their time wasn't very current with what we know today. So they created these metaphors from religion, mysticism, fairy tales, and alchemy to describe what was happening in the psyche.

Today we know that these archetypes and myths are the phenomenological correlates of deep electro-biology. For example, in mythology there are the "sons of light" and the "sons of darkness." Or there are the heavenly angels on high who bring consciousness, and there is Lucifer, who fell from heaven and became the devil, or the opposite of God. So what I'm providing is the biochemistry behind the mythology: your heart beats and then it stops for a second or two, beats again, and then stops again. We breathe in, pause, and then breathe out. I've found that a disturbance in this rhythm of "relax, recover, work" lies behind emotional conflict and distress, which can lead to addiction.

PP: One of the most visible places we see addiction played out in American culture is with celebrities. Can you give me an example of a famous star that "fell" into addiction, and how their descent into hell, so to speak, mirrors your theory of the link between addiction and our disrupted biological rhythms?

ER: In fact, addiction first broke into American consciousness during the fifties and sixties, when a new phenomenon burst onto the scene: rock groups. One of the biggest rock stars of all was Elvis Presley. He was a beautiful young man who charmed all of us. But as you might expect, life on the road for young musicians is tough. Typically, a gig begins around nine or ten in the evening. For the rest of the night the musicians play like hell, with great fervor and energy, until around two or three in the morning.

Then there they are at three in the morning, high from all the sheer exuberance and effort, and they're supposed to go to the hotel and fall sleep. Naturally, they have a hard time falling asleep. So the doctor gives them some sleeping pills, and they get a few hours of sleep before they have to get on the bus and drive three hundred miles to their next gig. That night, they have to perform again. But they really didn't get enough sleep the night before, and so now they need something to give them a lift before the performance. So they take amphetamines, or maybe alcohol. Alcohol is unique because it gives an immediate lift, and then a drop—so it gives both an up and a down, and that's why it's so popular. So now you see how this cycle starts: the musicians take some drugs to give them a lift so they can work like hell, and then they take more drugs to help them go to sleep.

This happened to the extreme in Elvis Presley's life. He became rich and famous, with a retinue of people attending all his needs. He had one special person just to give him what he called his "attack pills," or downers, at night. Even when he'd stopped touring and wasn't on the road anymore, his attendant still had to bring him a handful of downers at night just so he could fall asleep. But an hour and a half later—one classical ultradian period—he'd wake up, and couldn't fall back asleep. So he'd bang on the wall of his attendant's room until he woke up and gave Elvis another handful of "attack" pills. That same rhythm repeated itself three or four times every night until it finally ended with Elvis's death.

I believe that, in a capsule form, is what's happening to all of America, and to our "addicted society."

PP: But not all of us live like rock stars, so where do you see this extreme kind of out-of-balance way of life leading to addiction?

ER: There are such pressures for excellence in our daily lives. But what happens when people have so many demands from the outside world they can't pay attention to their inner signals and kick back and take a break? Say, for example, a person wakes up at seven in the morning, has breakfast, and gets to the office by nine or nine thirty. Already they're a little bushed, and so they have some coffee and maybe a cigarette to get started working. By eleven o'clock they need to take another break, so they have some more coffee. It would be better if they could have a little snack, some yogurt or a piece of fruit, and then lie down for twenty minutes, because food and rest go together. But most people don't do this. Instead, they find some way to hype themselves up.

This rhythm continues throughout the day until three or four o'clock in the afternoon. This is what researchers call "the breaking point," or that time of day when errors are more likely to happen. This is the point at which the circadian sleep cycle is starting to calm us down so that we can go to sleep later on that evening. In many Mediterranean cultures, people actually take a nap after lunch. But we don't do that in America, and so we go into stress states. It's no accident that the ritual of "happy hour," or getting a drink after work, arose in our culture to help get us through the rest of the evening. So now you see the picture.

PP: So what you're saying is that part of the treatment for someone with an alcohol, drug, or any other kind of addiction would be learning to live more rhythmically according to these natural cycles?

ER: Absolutely. There are natural rhythms behind our daily activities, but to tune into them we have to become more sensitive to ourselves, and learn how to take a break when we feel tired or hungry. But most of us don't do that; instead, if we feel exhausted we feel like a failure, or that there's something wrong with us: and that is often the path that leads to addiction. But this is so far from American consciousness that I've almost given up talking about it.

PP: As a child, I remember being scolded and even yelled at by teachers for daydreaming out the window during class. Was this tuning out and not paying attention a way of taking a mental break during the school day?

ER: When children daydream, they're in a natural rest period of quiet. But instead of just allowing the child to daydream for fifteen or twenty minutes, parents or schoolteachers break into the child's reverie, intruding into this period of healing and comfort by making them take out the garbage or get back to their lessons. Naturally, the child, or even the adult at work, who's been interrupted this way feels instant, reactive resentment. Whenever we're continually assaulted by the demands of the outside world—when someone calls us on the phone when we don't feel like talking, or our boss is talking to us while what we really want to do is just rest—it can be agonizing; time seems to be eternal. Anger can build up. I really believe that this is what is behind a lot of the anger and frustration that build up in personal relationships.

The child or person who likes to daydream may also be more naturally inclined toward the "lower" and slower end of the ultradian rhythm. This tendency is often mislabeled as laziness or even as a learning disability. Instead, it could mean that that person has a greater need to be introverted, and to go inside and imagine and be alone. If people like that are allowed to have that quiet time, they'll naturally emerge with the energy to work or create something.

PP: And what are the problems or misperceptions around the more extroverted and busier end of the ultradian scale?

ER: These are the obsessive-compulsive people who can't rest, and who have a lot of energy. They're more on the peak "up" side of the ultradian rhythm and they want to do something—but they don't know what that is. Maybe they don't have a job; or maybe they don't have any interests or passions. So all the energy that needs to be expressed turns instead into grief; it also becomes very frustrating, and this makes people suffer from anxiety. This feeling of having a lot of energy, and not knowing what to do with it, can be a source of delinquency among young people, and addictions in both young people and adults.

PP: Listening to you describe the way people have their own uniquely personal rhythms makes me realize how our nine-to-five school- and work-days are so outdated.

ER: One of the most difficult problems for people in this country is how to find a job or an organization that takes these ultradian rhythms into account: a job where a person can work for an hour and a half, and then kick back rather than have their employer "crack the whip." That's why people resent work so much; it's also why they don't want any bosses. The need to work according to one's own rhythm is also the reason why there's been such a big movement toward working at home, and having one's own business.

Institutions that don't recognize these natural ultradian rhythms are just cutting off their noses to spite their face. Because it's only if an employee has these rest periods that they're going to have enough energy to do truly great performances and creative work. By not allowing employees to take natural breaks companies are not getting the best of their intelligence.

PP: Well, it goes back to that word *laziness*: we simply don't like it. It's one of the worst things an American can be accused of. To be busy is one of the greatest virtues.

ER: Exactly. It ties into the whole moral fabric of our society.

PP: Can you say more about how laziness and busyness have become so tied into our cultural ideas of what's morally right and wrong?

ER: Our society is so misguided with its religious fervor around work; we've mixed up morals with basic biology. I personally have a strong work ethic, and when I feel the energy coming up I work like hell. Right now, as I'm talking to you, I'm putting out a lot of effort. But I also respect the fact that if I continue to talk to you for more than an hour and a half, I'm going to start getting tired. But instead of rejecting that feeling as "the devil," I say to myself "here is God coming to tell me that I need to rest for fifteen to twenty minutes so I can prepare for the next work cycle." So being tired doesn't have to mean I'm a moral failure. It means I'm human.

PP: So where does America's fixation with busyness and productivity, and its aversion to rest and relaxation, come from?

ER: We're still reeling from the abuses of living in a highly industrialized society. The American psyche is hypnotized by performance demands from the outside world, with little or no awareness of the body's needs, or feelings and emotions. It puts a premium value on productivity, not on how well a person feels. As a result, most of us are hyped up; we evaluate ourselves as a function of how well we've performed a task. Nobody values the recovery or the healing part of the day's cycle: in fact, we have a profound prejudice against healing.

Take corporate America today. They operate on the "empire-plantation" complex. They don't exist for the sake of their employees or the public: they exist simply for the purpose of exploitation. Corporate executives are making millions and millions of dollars a year, while their employees are insecure and stressed. I've worked with a lot of people in corporate America, and there is a lot of suffering in these corporations, from the executives all the way down through middle management—because they're treated as products or slaves, not human beings.

This exploitative system goes all the way back to slavery, and before that, the British Empire. We think we're such a wonderful, humanistic country, but we're power-driven and possessed by an authoritarian complex. We're really imitating old, imperialistic England from centuries ago—but we don't see this side of ourselves. Our kids are committing suicide at higher rates; we're a more addicted society than ever before; we have more guns than we've ever had. So our symptoms are really dire.

PP: Is this why there have always been these recurring cycles in American culture, like the sixties, of wanting to escape "mainstream" culture, with its demands and pressures, into alternative lifestyles, and also, in a more negative sense, escape into addiction?

ER: Yes, I think that there has periodically been a desperate effort to escape from a materialistic, industrialized society where products are valued rather than the human experience. Behind it lies resentment toward science, technology, business, and industry, because they don't respect our *beingness.*

PP: So is this also behind our longing to escape to a Mediterranean country where we can bask in the sun and take naps in the afternoon?

ER: Exactly so. We long to go to the sunny climates where we can experience deep relaxation. That appeal to escape is part of what's operating behind the travel industries, and their beautiful images of sandy beaches and blue skies. It's also why we look forward to our "golden retirement" years. But getting more power, which is what most Americans want, is not the right way to go.

PP: Why? Everybody wants to have more power.

ER: Because a power orientation is just imitating imperialistic England. We think power is so wonderful: we want control over our bodies; drug companies want control over patients' medicine; companies want control over their employees; government wants control over nature. But the whole idea of power is sick and needs to be replaced by the idea of relationship. The key path to healing is to have a deeper connection to the humanity within us. It's the way of the heart, the way of empathy and understanding what's going on inside of ourselves, so that we can understand what's going on in our neighbors. The idea of people-to-people contact is a very grassroots, populist way of saving ourselves. It's one of the best of the American traditions, like the old Town Hall or church meetings, or the grocery store where people sat around on barrels talking to each other, or groups where we can share what our hearts are telling us.

Americans need to recognize that when they want to take a break, that's God talking. That's sacred time. It isn't just that they're being lazy, or that they can't take a break because it's not convenient. They desperately need to stop and rest, and this is the way to heal their symptoms. Even nature wants us to slow down. So we'd better take that break, or our symptoms will become really dire. It's no mysterious process: just stop every hour and a half throughout the day. ■

Notes

1. More information on Dr. Rossi's research can be found on his website <http://www.ernestrossi.com>.
2. Epinephrine (also known as adrenaline) is a hormone and a neurotransmitter. Epinephrine and norepinephrine are two separate but related hormones secreted by the medulla of the adrenal glands.
3. Beta-endorphin is an endogenous opioid neuropeptide found in the neurons of both the central and peripheral nervous system. It is one of five endorphins found in humans.

—14—

What's Love Got to Do with It?
How America's Independent, Self-Reliant Culture
Fosters Addiction

AN INTERVIEW WITH KAREN B. WALANT, PH.D.

DEPENDENCY—LIKE BEING POOR, outcast, or homeless—is a word most Americans instinctively shun. It is a term that induces a slight shiver of discomfort, if not outright repugnance, in that it represents what the culture works against, rather than what it works toward. Because dependency goes against our vaunted ideal of independence, some might even say that it is a word whose proper place belongs in a chapter on addiction, as addicts are those who cannot control their dependency on substances like alcohol or heroin, and so have sinned against the cultural code of honor. In order to break free of those addictions, addicts are taught that they must break free from the chains of codependency, just as the Patriots broke free of England. Or that is how America's deeply held narrative around freedom and independence has unconsciously shaped many of our notions around addiction.

Like other cultural observers, however, I've always retained a certain suspicion around America's "attachment" to independence. What might appear to work well in a political sense doesn't always translate so easily into the more intimate, personal sphere of everyday life. So when I picked up psychotherapist Karen Walant's book *Creating the Capacity for Attachment: Treating Addictions and the Alienated Self*, I was instantly interested. Having grown up with a father who lived (and died) by the American code of independence, and who was a loner and a drinker all his life, Walant's exploration of the link between attachment disorders and addiction immediately touched a chord of recognition.

To Walant, the word *dependency* is itself a clue that reveals addiction's intent and desire for connection and closeness. In her view, the premium America places on autonomy and self-sufficiency, while pathologizing neediness as infantile and regressive, only serves to exacerbate addiction—thrusting fundamental, natural human needs for love and the support of others into the shadow of the American psyche. Drug and alcohol dependencies are not the moral wrongs we've made them out to be. Rather, they are symptomatic of the misdirected, all-too-human yearnings for love, warmth, and containment in a powerful "other"—the kind of "immersive" connections, Walant believes, that bathe the heart and that fill emotional vacancies within the psyche of the addict. And in fact, as she says in our interview, to oppress this need actually constitutes a kind of widespread cultural "abuse":

> Our society's longstanding denial and devaluation of merger phenomenon throughout the life cycle have actually increased the likelihood of personality disorders and addiction, precisely because autonomy and independence have been encouraged *at the expense of* attachment needs. These disorders, which are so pervasive in our current world, illustrate that beneath the veneer of self-reliance lies the core of powerlessness, alienation, and detachment.

A psychotherapist with a doctorate in social work, Walant began her career in a hospital in a "dual diagnosis" unit, working with patients who suffered from both addiction and mental disorders. After setting up her own private practice, she continued to work with many of these patients. As she said at the outset of our interview, "I tend to have a large number of patients who are recovering or who are trying to recover from alcoholism, drug abuse, and eating disorders. In addition, a lot of my patients either come from alcoholic families, or are married to an alcoholic. So in my experience it's uncommon to find anyone who hasn't been touched in some way by an addiction."

Over the two decades since we conducted our initial interview, Walant has continued her psychotherapy practice and, in addition to helping recovering people and families, she treats others with a wider range of issues—including interpersonal struggles, emotional distress such as anxiety and/or depression, and efforts at self-improvement. Still, with the majority of people she sees, the underlying struggles around debilitating feelings of shame, and the difficulty of balancing intimacy with autonomy, remain prominent. She is a frequent lecturer to other clinicians, parents, and educators in the field of attachment research and is a popular speaker at Harvard's Treating the Addictions Conference.

Dr. Walant's insights into the psychology of addiction are an indication of how addiction remains one of life's eternally recurring themes and that, as the old saying goes, the more things change, the more they stay the same. But with breakthroughs in science and the integration of "mindfulness-based" techniques to treat addiction, the field has undergone encouraging changes since we last spoke. Descriptions of these current developments have been added to our interview, updating where we left off. "The wonderful part of my field," commented Walant, is that "we are open to adjusting and shifting, should the science and the society in which we live demand that we do."

✳

Pythia Peay: I'm very intrigued by the link you make between attachment disorders and addiction. Can you explain more about the role you feel the larger culture plays in this dynamic?

Karen Walant: One of the major problems in American culture is something that I call "normative abuse."[1] It has to do with the way our society focuses on children becoming self-sufficient, beginning at an incredibly early age. In fact, I think that the idea of self-sufficiency is a misnomer: the only person who is totally self sufficient or independent is someone who is so detached, self-absorbed, and isolated, or else painfully afraid of attaching, that he or she might be labeled with a psychiatric diagnosis of schizoid disorder or narcissism. I think even Freud would agree that we've focused too much on independence and self-sufficiency as a model of psychological health, to the point that we don't need anybody.

PP: Are you talking about the classic Freudian model of separation from the parents and autonomy as an adult as the centerpiece of psychological development?

KW: Right. I don't think it ever really worked; what happened is that this model of development served the purposes of adults. It was what was done to them, and then what was done to us as children, and so we think it's the right thing to do.

I recently had lunch with a young mother. During the whole lunch she never once picked up her baby; because the baby didn't cry, she kept saying "very good, very good." Unfortunately, that's the norm of what a "good" baby should be like, which is not uncommon: a good baby doesn't cry. A good child doesn't act out, and doesn't need much. But that's not the way it really is; it's not what babies, children, or human beings are really like.

PP: So you're saying that there's a convergence between a psychological *and* cultural emphasis on independence and self-sufficiency, and that has a powerful effect on how children are raised?

KW: Yes. The way we raise our children to basically be gone by the time they're in high school, let alone college, is a terrible thing to do to everyone in the family, children and parents included. It's also very different from other cultures, such as the Japanese or the Filipino, for example, where families stay together and even live together all their lives. In our society, a twenty-year-old living at home is considered dependent, in a negative way. This is beginning to change; but the basic idea in this culture is still predominantly that we should raise our children to leave us. To me, the bond we build with our children is a bond that we will always have, a bond that is internalized inside of them, and a bond that actually becomes internalized into neural structures in the brain.

PP: Can you say more about the changes you're seeing in the culture around young people and issues of dependency versus independence?

KW: A recent Pew report[2] shows that we're in a very different period right now—especially with the Millennial generation (18–33). Whether due to the explosion of connectedness due to the Internet, social media, and cell phones (which they use for social causes); the advent of parenting more focused on forging empathic bonds of connection; more children in daycare, and who are socializing together earlier and more often than previous generations; the stress of 9/11 and the resulting wars; or the 2008 recession that forced many young people to live with their parents, the changes are real and striking. For example, the report found that the Millennial generation is less narcissistic and more empathic, not "an entitled generation but a complex and introspective one," who care more about doing a job they love than making a higher salary, and who get along well with their parents. One in eight Millennials twenty-two and older have moved back home with their parents.

PP: So how does an emphasis on fostering independence and separation in childhood play a role in addiction?

KW: Because with such an emphasis on independence, it naturally follows that a child or adolescent would feel awkward turning to their mother or father for comfort. And so instead, they might turn to a peer group, or to alcohol. Because if a person isn't supposed to have loved ones to comfort them, then they have to find that comfort somewhere else, whether in food, drugs, or alcohol.

In my field, this is what we call "self-medicating" depression or other mood disorders. Whatever the substance, the point is that addicts are trying to take care of how badly they're feeling. When clients with addiction problems come to see me, they talk about how alienated and disconnected they feel. They also blame themselves for feeling weak because they haven't been able to fix these problems on their own.

PP: I think it would be helpful if you could say more about the dynamics of addiction itself, and how it intersects with our need for human connection and attachment.

KW: The way I see it, addiction is a "mal-attachment" to something other than a person. It's saying "I need you"—but to a drug, which is constant and always there, and often more reliable than the people in the addict's life. And more powerful, as it gives the person just what they want when they need it.

PP: So if I understand you, children who are raised in an environment where they're constantly coaxed and pressured into separating from a very young age are at possible risk of growing up with an unfulfilled need, like an emotional emptiness, which could then be filled up by food or some other addictive substance.

KW: We all need what I call a "powerful protective other." We need to have the feeling of someone holding us, comforting us, and soothing us. But even this is something our culture discourages. The classic image of the mother holding the baby is a metaphor for the fact that even into adulthood we need each other; we need to feel that we can sink into the arms of the other or we'll fall apart. Everybody needs that. But when a person can't do that, they build walls and defenses around their vulnerability. Rather than express their needs, they tell others, "I'm strong. I'm fine." But this is only a mask over the inner true self that is scared and terrified, doesn't feel connected, and needs to feel soothed—if not with people, then with something else. It could be work, television, or the computer.

PP: Dependency seems to be so misunderstood; it's even kind of a mystery in our culture. Not many of us know how to be emotionally dependent on someone else to the degree that you're describing. As a society, it's where we're awkward and undeveloped.

KW: We've been so conditioned against intimacy that we've become "dependent-phobic." I can't tell you how many patients I have who value the intense, loving connection we share together, but who then fear their dependency on me as if it's something horrible.

PP: Say more about that fear.

KW: In the word *dependence* we hear "no self." Underlying that fear of "no self" is a sense of shame. Shame begins as a two-person dynamic, with tentacles reaching back into early childhood that become internalized into a dynamic called "negative self-talk." This is the sense that "I am bad"—not "I have *done* something bad." No matter its origins, whether trauma or family interactions, shame can lead to insecure attachment styles, such as "avoidant" (no need for relationships) or "anxious" (the self is unworthy). And if a person doesn't have secure attachments that are attuned, receptive, and responsive, then substances like alcohol or heroin provide the missing security and soothing. From my observation, most alcoholics and addicts fall into an insecure attachment style that is high in at least one of these two dynamics.

The psychologist John Bowlby believed, as do I, that we continue to need our bonds of attachment throughout our lives. The goal of optimal mental health is to be comfortable in our "interdependence" with one another—a word that better describes what I'm talking about: two beings that are connecting, separate but together, but who are not "either/or." I sometimes like to use the image of a hammock, made from the ropes that signify the most crucial relationships in our lives, to describe the kind of support provided by healthy attachments. As we age, this hammock becomes more like a safety net under a trapeze that is there to cushion us from any falls and missteps throughout our lives—that, truly, is secure attachment. It's my thought that addicts "rest" in the hammock of their substance, which gives the illusion of security without the painfulness of relationships.

Unfortunately, although we are much further along than when I was a young mother, and despite recent changes with the Millennial generation, our society continues to dismiss attachment needs. To add to that, we are also a society that on top of saying "Don't ask for help," says "Be perfect." This is very worrisome for young teens and adults, who are getting these messages just at the time they're separating from their parents, and also at a time when they're being exposed to substances for the first time. Then there are the pressures from the educational system to be "perfect" and to get into the "right" colleges. To the young person, the "normative abuse" of society's demands to achieve and to be independent can seem untenable, making the pull toward alcohol, marijuana, and other substances much stronger—as substance use is one way to ameliorate the painfulness of this situation.

PP: So how does this need for attachment and dependency enter into treatment and recovery for those struggling with addiction?

KW: It's easy to see. When someone tries to stop drinking, for example, they immediately feel how needy they are. Then they realize that they're either going to drink to feel self-sufficient again, or they're going to reach out to other people so that they don't drink. This is the whole crux of Alcoholics Anonymous: don't drink—go to meetings instead.

But why go to meetings? Because in these groups addicts are going to find someone else talking about their life that is similar to theirs, and they're going to be in a room filled with other people who understand them, who empathize with them, and who won't judge them. AA is a wonderful place for people to learn how to make strong attachments and feel okay about it.

Today, we have scientific research that shows how strong attachments help to heal addiction. In the last two decades, for example, there has been an explosion of information about the brain, including evidence that shows how critical early attachment is in the growth of an infant's brain. This development has also led to important shifts in the field of psychology. With the help of research in the field of neuroscience, psychotherapists now have burgeoning proof that shows the curative effects of a strong, therapeutic bond. Because it turns out that in close, emotional moments, our brains release biochemicals of "attachment": opioids, endorphins, and oxytocin. So when disconnection disappears, and "belonging" appears, we naturally feel soothed and comforted. So it's no wonder that the therapeutic relationship itself accounts for up to forty percent of patients' most effective cure in psychotherapy. No matter what techniques or insights the therapist offers, it is his or her interpersonal warmth, empathy, and compassion that is most remembered by the patient.

PP: So do you feel that this emphasis on connection and emotional support is part of the reason why AA has been so successful and has endured for so long?

KW: Absolutely. The other thing that AA does, and that psychotherapy has been slow to look at, is the idea of God. There again, addicts can switch their attachment from a drug to God, whatever that may mean to them, who can always be there for them.

PP: Like a "divine mother."

KW: Yes, a divine mother who is continually there to hold and comfort someone when they're in distress. This is expressed in the third step in AA, which is to make a decision to turn our will over to the care of God. The way that third step is worded is exactly as if one is turning to a mother; it's beautifully written.[3]

So in a sense, AA understood even better than psychotherapists the power that comes from becoming totally immersed in a powerful protective "other" that will take care of us.

PP: So being able to surrender is also connected to being dependent. Two words with such negative connotations in our society! Just look at the way we call someone a "baby" for being needy or failing to become wholly self-sufficient in some way.

KW: Exactly. It's like when a baby is crying. They *need* to be able to cry, to disintegrate and lose their whole being inside the mother or father; to be held within a parent's arms and to feel infused by comfort. This need for surrender and dependency is part of the "oceanic feeling" that Freud wrote about over a century ago. That sense that there's an indissoluble bond that cannot be broken—where you feel a sense of eternity, oneness, and empathic connection—can happen anywhere, including in temples and churches. But Freud didn't like that. He felt that places of worship exploited that feeling.

PP: And yet, unlike Freud, you would encourage your patients to find healing from their addiction through connecting to the divine or some larger transpersonal force, in whatever way they might choose?

KW: Absolutely. I strongly encourage people to talk about their need for and use of God. For many of the people I work with, spirituality or religion functions as a kind of "immersion aid" to help them feel connected. For example, when I can't physically be there for that patient, which is how that is between sessions, I can be there in their minds, or they can call and leave a message, or email or write me. But at the same time, if they're at all religious, I encourage them to keep God around to rely on as well. Certainly, it's also important that individuals in recovery develop other skills in order to be able to rely on themselves in the absence of the therapist.

PP: And what would some of those skills be?

KW: One of the most significant developments in recent years has been teaching those in treatment cognitive behavioral therapies, such as Dialectical Behavioral Therapy (DBT) and Acceptance and Commitment Therapy (ACT). These "mindfulness" based therapies, which have taken psychology by storm and which I utilize in my own work, teach specific strategies to people coming into treatment—such as breathing techniques or skills to communicate their needs and emotions—that help them in their daily lives. Among other benefits, the mindfulness techniques[4] that are the basis of DBT and ACT are a *huge* help in showing people how to reduce their reactivity and impulsivity. "Wise Mind," a term used in DBT by Marsha Linehan, the creator of this approach, defined this as "that part of each person that can know and experience truth. It is where the person knows something to be true or valid. It is almost always quiet. It has a certain peace. It is where the person knows something in a centered way."

PP: Can you give me a glimpse of what it's like to be one of the addicts in treatment with you?

KW: Treatment begins with commitment, and commitment means agreeing to come regularly to sessions, to join support groups like AA and get a sponsor (if using AA), or attending other substance-abuse recovery groups (such as Smart Recovery),[5] and to give random urine samples if necessary. If medication is needed, an assessment is made and the regimen is then started. One of the first skills learned in treatment-based psychotherapy is how to "press pause" to delay impulse gratification and how to access "Wise Mind" as a way to fortify their commitment to recovery. Gaining self-compassion and finding empathic support from others, including from me, are also crucial components of recovery. I see myself as being a member of their "recovery team," which includes other treatment professionals, their family and friends (if supportive), their support group, their spirituality, and their inner wisdom. From the beginning, I hope to be seen as "on the side of their recovery," and I make sure that I am available for coaching via phone, email, or texts, as needed. Generally, as people become more embedded in their support systems, the need for coaching from me lessens—again showing the interplay between attachment and autonomy.

For those who don't suffer from addiction, it's difficult to imagine what an addict's life is really like. From my perspective, it's remarkable if they're able to maintain even one day of sobriety. Every minute they're thinking about when they're going to have their next drink. Or they're feeling how frightened and unfortified they are without it. Instead, if they're in therapy, they can think "I'm going to see Karen today." Or, "I think I'll call my sponsor instead," or "I'm going to read a book," or "I'm going to pray to God." Learning how to act on and incorporate those other ways of thinking is a good thing. But that doesn't take just a minute: in fact, it can take years.

PP: From everything you've said and described so far, you could say that the shadow side of our cultural emphasis on autonomy and individualism is this neglected emotional dependency—needs that are human, natural, and common to everyone.

KW: That's a good way to put it. What's very clearly said in our culture is, "Don't need anyone. Don't be dependent and weak." So many of us have started off with this message and this idea about separateness beginning at birth. But the danger is that it can lead us down the road of addiction. Indeed, it doesn't surprise me where we are as a culture, with all our problems around addiction. ∎

Notes

1. As Walant explains, every society has expectations and rules for its members, which are put into effect by parents, teachers, government, and other social and cultural institutions. However, when seen by a future generation, these same customs can be judged as strange, wrong, harsh, or even abusive. As new information, societal demands, or social protest becomes too loud to

ignore, customary norms begin to shift. This paradox—between what is viewed as right thinking and correct behavior in a particular time period, but later viewed as wrong—is a hallmark of the fluidity of social change. Knowing about this dynamic can enable us to have empathy for our parents, because even some of the norms in our own era will be seen as abuse by future generations.

2. *Millennials: A Portrait of Generation Next.* Executive Summary, The Pew Research Center, February 2, 2010 <http://www.pewresearch.org/millennials/>.

3. "Like all remaining Steps, Step Three calls for affirmative action, for it is only by action that we can cut away the self-will which has always blocked the entry of God—or, if you like, a Higher Power—into our lives."

4. "Mindfulness is a state of active, open attention on the present. When you're mindful, you observe your thoughts and feelings from a distance, without judging them good or bad. Instead of letting your life pass you by, mindfulness means living in the moment and awakening to experience." Psychology Today: Psych Basics, "What is Mindfulness?" Online at <http://www.psychologytoday.com/basics/mindfulness>.

5. *Smart Recovery*: The SMART Recovery 4-Point Program is different from Alcoholics Anonymous and other Twelve Step programs, and offers tools and techniques that help to build and maintain motivation; cope with urges; manage thoughts, feelings, and behaviors; and live a balanced life <http://www.smartrecovery.org>.

—15—

Ancestors

The "Spirit in the Bottle"

AN INTERVIEW WITH STEPHEN AIZENSTAT, PH.D.

ANYONE WHO IS AN addict or who is close to one is all too familiar with addiction's mythic emotional proportions: the tempestuous highs of mania, the hurricanes of anger and rage, bitterness and regret; the downpours of tears and the arid desert winds of aloneness and abandonment; and the more paradisal states of bliss and vision, love and wholeness. Often it seems that something more than human, something transpersonal operating from behind the scenes, is at work behind this possession-like aspect of addiction. A genie, perhaps, or a demon, or even the restless spirit of some long-ago ancestor who, as new genetic research reveals, has the power to influence our fate as much as our immediate family of origin.[1]

Finding the ancestor within an addiction is the topic of my interview with clinical psychologist, marriage and family therapist, and dream expert Stephen Aizenstat, chancellor and founding president of Pacifica Graduate Institute.[2] Set beside the sapphire-blue waters of the Santa Barbara coastline, the Institute, led by Aizenstat, is one of the earliest pioneers of depth psychological and physical healing. Home to the archives of Joseph Campbell and James Hillman, the Institute's faculty and curriculum are constructed on an exploration of the interplay between the human psyche, symbols, myth, imagination, and the outer world.

In his guiding role at Pacifica, as a friend and colleague of both Campbell and Hillman during their lifetimes, and as an authority on the realm of our nightly dreams, which he has studied for more than thirty-five years, Aizenstat is eminently qualified as a guide into the less visible, more mythic dimensions of addiction. In his book *Dream Tending: Awakening to the Healing Power in Your Dreams*, he describes multiple new techniques that extend traditional dream work to include that animated realm of the collective unconscious psyche of nature where, he writes, "we encounter living, embodied images in the dream world as beings who exist in their own right, and who offer valuable wisdom and navigational guidance to the struggles of the day world—as well as inspiring inner sources of generativity and creativity in the dreamer."

The "creative, animated" realm of myth and psyche that we access in our dreams is also, Aizenstat believes, that place where the souls of our departed relatives dwell. It is there, too, that our personal ancestors continue to work through unfinished business left over from their lifetimes, and which can sometimes fall to living descendants to resolve in their stead. Indeed, as Aizenstat warns below, if ignored and left untended these inherited dilemmas and conflicts, especially around creativity, can manifest as a kind of possession state through the symptoms of addiction.

I first interviewed Dr. Aizenstat in 1996, seeking to learn what vantage points his depth psychological approach to healing and the night world of dreams might bring to the human problem of substance abuse and addiction. Like the paths that wind from the Institute to the shores of the Pacific Ocean, our conversation led to unexpected revelations into the nature of addiction I'd not heard anywhere else. Although Aizenstat's method of working with addicts builds upon foundational, traditional approaches such as Alcoholics Anonymous and psychotherapy, it expands to include such unconventional methods as learning to identify "the spirit in the bottle" trapped in a family lineage—a long departed ancestor with a gift or talent that over the generations became "too hot to handle"—and how he or she can be a contributing factor in addiction; the importance of identifying the archetypal spirit behind an addiction; and how, through these techniques, adults and adolescents can learn to relate to and integrate these ancestral forces, archetypal images and instincts, and creative talents, rather than succumb to addiction.

✳

Pythia Peay: Given your work with the imaginal world and "dream tending," I'm very interested to hear more about how you integrate this deeper, mythological background into your work with patients struggling with addiction.

Stephen Aizenstat: When I work with people trapped in addictive patterns, I begin by putting into place basic interventions such as Alcoholics Anonymous, as well as behavioral and preventive therapies that squarely face the problem. It's always important to start with an immediate behavioral interruption of the addiction. Otherwise, the syndrome itself takes on its own life and momentum.

After those practical and essential interventions are in place, I begin to reflect on what hidden force in the individual's family lineage of parents, grandparents, great-grandparents, and on back was so powerful and difficult to handle that it fell into some kind of addictive pathology. So I start searching for the "spirit in the bottle"—like an inner figure or muse of some kind—that's at work in the addict's family history.

PP: So how might that "trapped spirit" trigger an addiction?

SA: Let's take a family where the great-grandparent was a remarkable artist, musician, teacher, or religious figure. When the next generation comes along, the son or daughter doesn't feel up to working with the creative spark that marked that lineage. As a result, there's something in that person that becomes "too hot to handle," and they may lapse into some kind of drug or alcohol pattern that limits their expression of that inborn talent. So when a person caught in an addiction comes to me, I want to also know what God or Goddess, or archetypal image or creative potential, lives *behind* the addiction—something that was anchored in the lineage but that they were never able to express.

PP: I would imagine that a creative cut-off in a family line might also happen because, as a culture, we're cut off from our ancestry. In accord with the American dream, each generation has to start anew all over again.

SA: Exactly. And when we're cut off from our ancestry, we're cut off from those invisible figures that carry those creative capabilities. These talents also get cut off because we live in a culture that doesn't value the expressive arts—whether music, art, literature, invention, or all the humanities.

In addition, real life can also intervene in a family history. There can be an economic depression, or some kind of political upheaval, or natural or family catastrophe that represses or limits these creative instincts. When that happens, this potential gets submerged and ignored. But the trapped spirits always come back, either as a creative talent or in an addiction.

PP: So how does your dream work with your clients figure into this kind of ancestral work around addiction and creativity?

SA: In dreams we see these cut-off figures at work in the imagination. When someone seeks my help about drugs, alcohol, or even workaholism, those hidden figures behind the addiction might show themselves in dreams. Sometimes, these images are grotesque and compulsive, with a nightmarish quality—one wouldn't think that they were healing or constructive. But as I've discovered, images in dreams can also reflect the obsessive tendencies of the addiction itself.

Instead of interpreting these frightening images solely as an addiction or a psychological complex, however, I help my clients to develop sustained relationships to the images themselves. That way, they can begin to develop a sense of the separate autonomy of those images, so that they reveal themselves more clearly for what they really are, rather than what we make them out to be. What first looked like a nightmarish image, for example, when allowed to exist in its own right, begins to take the shape of something altogether different, embodying these inner ancestral callings around blocked creativity. That way, these frightening images become less destructive, and more constructive as a helpful ally in a person's life. That's very different, because whereas a destructive image or force can make a person feel caught and possessed by a demon, a constructive image can be very inspiring. So it's a question of getting to the creative spark that lives in the dream image, and that's the kind of dream work I do.

PP: Besides our ancestors, what else has modern culture split us off from, and that might also exacerbate addiction?

SA: Underneath the ancestral level that's been forgotten, there's a deeper level we've also lost contact with: the natural world. We're the children of technology and television; increasingly, we live an industrialized, high-tech way of life. So part of what gets split off is our natural affinity for the rhythms of nature. And as a result of this separation from the organic ground that we've been born out of, pathologies erupt and our species begins to act in peculiar ways. Often reconnecting to the original pulse or breath of nature is in direct contradistinction to being caught in an addictive syndrome.

PP: So are you saying that one of the underlying causes of alcoholism and addiction might be our disconnection from nature? And that dream work might also reconnect us to the healthier rhythms of nature?

SA: Yes, because dreams are an expression of nature. The same rhythm in nature is present in the rhythm of our dreams.

PP: But what about images like cars or computers that show up in our dreams?

SA: It's not the individual image itself that mirrors the natural world: it's the process of dreaming itself that parallels a process in nature. We know that dreaming is one of the essentials to being alive, like eating and sleeping. So since we know that dreaming is grounded in something organic, the nature of the psyche is similar to the nature of nature.

PP: Also, I would imagine, because nature is full of images, just as our dreams are filled with imagery.

SA: From my point of view, nature is always dreaming. So animals, trees, and humans are all images in her dream. To reconnect to dreams through that wider perspective of psyche in nature allows us to reconnect to the pulses and rhythms of nature.

PP: So is connecting to nature through our dreams similar in technique to the "dreamtime" of the Australian Aborigines?

SA: The difference is that the Aborigines don't distinguish between a compartmentalized "awake" state of mind that is separate from dreaming. Rather than our Western view that we're awake and conscious during the day, and then we go to sleep at night and dream, they simply experience themselves as always in a dream. So they're in a continuous realm of dreaming that's inseparable from nature.

PP: But what about the whole thrust of the human potential movement toward greater and greater "consciousness": that humankind is evolving by becoming more self-conscious and self-aware?

SA: My direct experience working with native peoples in Hawaii and Australia is that their quality of consciousness when working in the psychic realm of dreamtime is so sophisticated it puts us to shame—it's almost as if *we* are primitive in that regard. So I have to question what we mean when we talk about becoming "more conscious."

What we in the West are most gifted with in regard to the dream is developing second-generation explanatory systems around dream systems. We have elaborate, intricate, elegant systems of interpretation and explanation. We've developed all kinds of detailed maps that explain different phenomena. But the difference is that we mistake the map for the territory, and that's a distinction that Aborigines don't make. The dream gives them navigational abilities; they don't have a need to interpret the image into something else. Instead, they develop a relationship to an image as a living presence. So their work is to name that image and that relationship. *Our* need is to identify the image and offer an explanation.

PP: So relating this back to drug and alcohol addiction, it's almost as if we in the contemporary American world have severed ourselves from these ancient sources of healing and guidance. For example, to return to the influence of our ancestors, I recall a story from a friend of mine, whose daughter was sent to a court-ordered session with a social worker for an underage drinking violation. When the social worker found out that she had alcoholic grandfathers on both sides of the family, he said flat out that her daughter was an alcoholic. My friend was very angry at the time, because from her perspective, although she was aware of the risks that came from having alcoholics in the family background, it was also difficult to know if her daughter's drinking was a typical teen problem or something more lasting.

SA: That's very sad. Because drinking or taking drugs is not just a "behavior." It's also not just about family history. It's about soul. So what that social worker missed is that for your friend's daughter, a window or a portal opened the moment that she got caught. And what she lost was the opportunity to discover *who*—not *what*—was at work in her soul asking for attention, and that was too hot for her, or her dad or her granddad, to handle. Until you name that presence, the addictive pattern will just be passed down because these ancestors are very intense and hungry figures. Then the addiction becomes compulsory.

From my point of view, in fact, it's these figures from our deep ancestral past that are, in large part, responsible for the psychological issues thought to start in early childhood and adolescence. This turns developmental psychology on its head, because these figures in the psyche exist *a priori*, and our existence is created out of their influence.

PP: So if you'd been working with that young adolescent girl who'd gotten in trouble for underage drinking, how would you have handled that situation?

SA: We'd work on naming that figure, and then we'd work on developing a relationship with that figure by learning its identity, depth, breadth, and potential nature and quality. This gives the figure an opportunity to express itself. We get to know it and befriend it and then it becomes a figure that individuates; as this figure individuates then that young person finds separation from the possession and compulsion. She's not trapped anymore. And often the very thing that's at the root of a drinking problem is the very muse that is a person's genius or talent. The seeds of our destiny, passion, desire, and uniqueness always lie in our pathologies and wounds.

PP: That's very interesting to hear. My father was a serious, lifelong alcoholic, and it used to seem to me that he was possessed by a demon, or what we used to call his "drinking devil." But what you're saying is that this demon was actually the embodiment of some kind of creative angel-turned-devil?

SA: Once an addictive syndrome has been interrupted through intervention, and if the person has some capability to face what's possessing or demonizing them, then the question becomes: Who is that demon in its arrested, possessed state that is so troublesome, horrific, powerful, and intense that it appears as something out of control and scary? What I have found in my experience is that when we develop a relationship to this troubled spirit and are able to look this demon in the eyes, then this "evil spirit" and presence begins to lose its power and settle down.

Its grip on a person is no longer so tenacious, because it's been given attention. Because when we try to eradicate or get rid of a complex like that through medication or repression, it only fights back more strongly, intensifying its claim on a person—

because its fear is that you will threaten its survival. And when those figures feel threatened, when they feel they are going to be made extinct, they fight back. So all my work says: don't eradicate it.

It's like what happens with weeds in a garden. If you use more and more insecticides, they just get more resistant and come back threefold. So what I've found that works is to give this figure a name, and in no uncertain terms let it know that you know that I am present and capable of looking you straight in the eye and breathing fire in the same way that you're breathing fire. When you get to that place, the image begins to show its other side. Nine times out of ten what lives in that image is not only demonic and pathological, but an intense religious, creative, artistic, or passionate flame.

PP: Like Socrates' "daemon" that whispered in his ear?

SA: Exactly! We're looking for the "daemon" in the "demon." And people who do this work feel really good; working with a "disease" model just makes them feel sick.

PP: Can you give me a more specific example of someone you've worked with who had an addiction, and who was possessed by a grandfather or some other ancestral spirit?

SA: One of my male patients was a workaholic who began to develop a drinking problem. The image that kept coming up in his dreams was of a ferocious grizzly bear that snarled and showed him his teeth and kept chasing him. This was a very frightening image; in fact, I don't advise people to confront images like that on their own, as a lot of threat and fear can get constellated. At any rate, this man was exceptional at his job; he was a professor who gave training seminars around the country. His problem was that he felt very frightened about taking time to stop and rest and smell the flowers. So he was always on the go, and very overworked; eventually, he became extremely ill. Even his doctor told him to slow down, or he'd burn out. As a result, he developed a pattern of working very hard, then drinking as a way to relax.

He could have labeled the grizzly bear in his dream as a representation of his obsessive self, or of an intrusive family complex overtaking him, or the deadlines he was up against, or as an image of his ambition—all of which may have been true. But what good was yet another explanatory structure going to do? Perhaps this interpretation would have taken him to a deeper level of understanding about his problem. What was missing in that kind of interpretation, however, was the living presence of the creature at work in the psyche and soul of the person. The extent to which we try to explain this presence is the extent to which we separate from the living reality of its influence.

What my client and I did instead was to listen more to the dream, and to pay attention to what else was in the dream. We realized that in this dream there was another figure that he'd dismissed as a passer-by: a person that was in the dreamscape simply walking by, and that looked rather like a hitchhiker-type figure, but who also seemed like someone who knew a lot. What we did first was befriend that figure. Eventually, he became more or less of a teacher to my client, a being in his dream psyche who was a resource and an ally. The psyche is forever providing us with allies and resources! So we began to develop a relationship with this protective ally: not to get something from him, but to find out what gave him a voice of his own.

Then we began to relate to the grizzly bear, not as a psychologically explanatory complex only, but as a unique grizzly bear with specific characteristics. Gradually, the bear became less fierce and more present in his own right. We found out that what the bear needed and wanted was to be in the world in a very different way than the dreamer: more animalistic, more instinctual. One way to be fierce is to be intellectually competitive, but another way to be fierce is by being present to the immediacy of life the way an animal is. This bear knew how to have two feet on the ground, and to feel a sense of bodily strength in a way that was different from intellectual strength.

Those were its first teachings. After that, it was as if the bear had been alive for a long, long time. So when we asked the bear what ancestor in my client's lineage he had an affinity with, we came to see that he was associated with a great-grandparent he had spent a year or two with when he was young, and had heard lots of stories about, but who had been marginalized. The client felt that the bear was his great-grandfather, and that it was time for this man to do a little research and to get to know about his life's work, and where he got caught and had trouble. It also became very clear that there was something in this man's lineage that hadn't been fully expressed, but that this would come forth after he developed more of a relationship with his ancestor.

PP: So we partly have it right when we say that if we're the child of an alcoholic, we're more at risk for alcoholism. But you're talking about addiction from a more elongated, spiritual vantage point, as the ancestors or spirits that we've neglected and that need to be honored, and also to learn more about the effects of their unfinished business and unlived life on our present-day lives.

SA: Right, and when we are out of connection with that realm of the ancestors we lose connection to our sense of lineage and belonging. We're not just the products of our lives—we're the products of a whole clan, and there is a whole background behind us and in front of us.

PP: So as part of our work connecting to these ancestral backgrounds, and as something that helps to heal addiction and that contributes to psychological health, would you encourage people to go back into their family histories?

SA: Yes, but not just family history as literal, concrete history—I mean more in terms of a family's imaginal development. Each of our parents, grandparents, and great-grandparents had psyches filled with their own muses, demons, and daemons. And these ancestors are here with us now; our own behavior and relationships are the very expressions of these invisibles. In fact, I train people to look at these "invisibles" that are always at work around us.

PP: So if you were going to envision a treatment program that was based on everything you've just been describing to me, what would it look like?

SA: The first plank in that kind of platform would be education. Over the last decades the field of addiction has gained much more information about how chemicals interact in the body. We also know more about genetic predisposition. Second, we have to look more closely at family dynamics to see if something abusive or disruptive is going on at home. And third, it's important to look at the influence of peer groups on people's behavior.

After those three things have been dealt with, I'd be interested in the addict's dream life: What images are showing up in their dreams? I might ask if anything unusual had happened in the past several weeks, and how the person's psyche expresses itself when faced with something out of the ordinary. I'd want to ask them what desires they have that haven't been explored or given voice to. And what about relationships? Often, we tend to project the invisibles or psychic entities in our psyches onto other people. For example, a certain teacher will stand out, or a character in a movie will come forward, who will hold for us the energy of these inner figures. I'd want to establish art programs, so that the person could express what's in their dreams and psyches in clay, drawing, music, or dance. This would give these inner figures a medium to hear what they have to say to us, and a way to name them and develop an ongoing relationship with them. All this would be a way to gather information from the psychic realm in terms of how these figures are active in the soul of the person wrestling with an addiction.

PP: So the treatment program would function as a guide to these other realms of the soul.

SA: And I'll tell you, I've done this work before with teenagers, and it's awesome to watch them come together and talk about this. Suddenly, they're given permission to talk about things they've been experiencing in their dreams since they were three years old, but have been cut off from because their dreams were scary, or their parents said, "Oh honey, it's just a dream. Don't think about it." To allow teens to talk about all this opens them up to their imagination in a creative way, but that's also protected and supported.

And if you're alive and active in your imagination, you're not depressed or addicted: these two things don't live together. When I get kids to become active in their imaginations in a creative, constructive way they become much more interested in that than in self-destructive kinds of behavior like drinking or taking drugs. Children are doing that anyway when they play games that involve myths and mythic creatures; they're absolutely fascinated with the intricacies of the imagination. So it's a question of giving young people and adults more access to the source of their imagination within, because that in turn connects them to their integrity and to their sense of capability.

PP: So is the realm of the imagination more active during adolescence and youth?

SA: Yes, absolutely—imagination is wide open in kids. But then there's a period when they start to get socialized into becoming citizens of a capitalistic, economic, consumer society. Their imaginations become manipulated through mass advertising. Because what society wants is for young people to buy products; they're not supported to become originators of imaginative ideas. So this inborn, generative, and creative spark is diminished to a compulsive predisposition toward buying products, or consuming more alcohol or drugs. And when they're at school, it's all about learning for the sake of quantifying information, and moving ahead at the expense of paradox, poetics, creative tension, or humanity.

When that happens, their imaginations go into a kind of dormancy. Then during adolescence, everything that's been repressed in them erupts. They feel pushed to find a sense of autonomy and identity. When there's no way for that eruption to be channeled creatively, it becomes rebellious and reactive. But if you give these kids a chance to come together and to speak out of their own dreams, myths, and psyches rather than adapting to what they see on television or the Internet or the wider culture, they love it—because throughout time people have yearned for ways of being together in ritual. When we share dreams in groups, we're in ritual time.

PP: So what young people and all people are missing is access to these mythic realms of imagination and creativity.

SA: We're all increasingly separate from the realm of the inner life. As we become increasingly alienated from those inner influences, and from the figures of our ancestry and our lineage, we all experience a lot of trouble. That's what the native peoples say: When we don't pay attention to our elders or to the ancestors, there's trouble in the realm of the ancestors. They haven't been transitioned appropriately to the other side, or listened to. That kind of old knowledge isn't passed on anymore; it's discounted in service to what's modern. But when those realms are troubled, it's not only the adults who will have difficulties, it's the children who will suffer a tremendous amount of upheaval and despair.

So to sum up, separation from our ancestors combined with alienation from the natural world are what add to the troubles in our present world, such as addiction. If ignored, the images in our dreams will show up in demonic form, and looking for attention; rather than in the service of the creative daemon and imagination. To the extent that we can help kids learn to look through the demon into the creative daemon trapped in addiction, it will keep them psychically healthy and alive. Then we'll contribute not just to their lives, but also to the generations that will come, and to the cultivation of a wiser culture. ■

Notes
1. "Your Ancestors, Your Fate," by Gregory Clark, *New York Times*, February 21, 2014.
2. Pacifica Graduate Institute <www.pacifica.edu>.

Part III

America's Vanishing Environment

But when the buffalo went away the hearts of my people fell to the ground, and they could not lift them up again. After this nothing happened. There was little singing anywhere.—**Plenty Coups**, last chief of the Crow nation

SOMETIME IN THE LATE nineteenth century in Montana, a white man named Frank B. Linderman—a trapper, hunter, and cowboy—was befriended by the last great chief of the Crow nation, Plenty Coups. In a moving exchange between the two men, Plenty Coups recounted the exploits of the Crow nation—a warrior tribe of nomadic hunters—in the time before their vast tribal lands had been seized by the American government. As Linderman noted later, he was unable to get Plenty Coups to talk about anything that had happened to the Crow *after* they'd been confined to their reservation. It was as if following the loss of their way of life, writes psychoanalyst Jonathan Lear in describing this exchange in *Radical Hope: Ethics in the Face of Cultural Devastation*, history for the Crows literally "came to an end."

Life for the Crow tribe did go on, however, just not in the way it had in centuries past. Instead of leading his warriors into battle against the invasion of the white man, Lear notes, Plenty Coups peacefully, and unexpectedly, submitted to their takeover. In doing so, he kept his tribe together and helped them adapt to a wholly new future and way of life on the reservation. The Indian chief even took up farming, proudly displaying his crops at agricultural shows. He encouraged young tribal members to adopt the white man's education and religion.

As the leader of his nation, Plenty Coups traveled several times to Washington, D.C., and in 1921, at the ceremony establishing the Tomb of the Unknown Soldier in Arlington National Cemetery, Chief Plenty Coups represented Indian-Americans who had fought in World War I. In what must have been a poignant and elegiac scene, with its backdrop of white crosses on rolling green lawns, Plenty Coups, dressed in beaded buckskin and an eagle-feather headdress and standing among military generals in "polished boots and gold braid," removed his war bonnet and laid it in the sarcophagus alongside his coup-stick—used by Crow warriors to mark a boundary during battle. This gesture of "burying" one of the tribe's most sacred cultural symbols, Lear suggests, marked the end of a way of life for the Crow. "They have reached the end of their traditional lives, and it is time to locate them in a new ritual," he writes, "that of remembering and mourning the valiant deeds of Indians past."

In helping his tribe to make this enormous shift—one that ensured their survival, but that meant acceptance of the loss of the very cultural habits and points of view that had defined them as a people—Plenty Coups was guided by a dream he'd had as a young boy. In this vision, a "Man-person" wearing a buffalo robe revealed to him a great plain thick with buffalo that, with a shake of his rattle, suddenly disappear. Following a tremendous storm that knocks down all the trees, young Plenty Coups is then shown in the dream an old man sitting beneath the one remaining tree, the "lodge of the Chickadee." He is advised in the dream that the fallen trees represent all the other Indian lodges; that the old man is himself, and that the chickadee (a bird sacred to the Crow) is a "good listener" who gains success and avoids failure by learning from others. As the dream ends the Man-Person tells Plenty Coups that, "The mind leads a man to power, not strength of body." Later, after he shares this dream with the elders of his tribe, they interpret the dream's message as a warning that those tribes who went to war against the white man would be wiped out. By listening "as the Chickadee listens," however, the Crow might avoid that fate and keep their lands by learning the white man's ways.

From this dream, the Crows fashioned a foreign policy that, Lear writes, guided them over the next century. Recognizing that their buffalo-hunting way of life was coming to an end, "they decided to ally with the white man," hoping to "weather the coming storm and hold onto their land." And in fact, although they lost millions of acres of their original lands, and although the Crow people suffered tremendous disorientation and depression resulting from the violent uprooting of their cultural traditions, the Crow nation remains intact to this day. Lear concludes his philosophical reflection on Chief Plenty Coups' enigmatic remark, "After this, nothing happened," by admiring the gifted way the Crow chief led the way into the future by linking the past with the new. By drawing on the traditional Crow icon of the chickadee in his dream-vision, Lear says, Plenty Coups "was able to take a valued and honored spiritual force and put it to creative use in facing up to new challenges. Thus, although Plenty Coups was advocating a new way of life for the Crow, he was drawing upon the past in vibrant ways. And thus I think a case can be made that Plenty Coups offered the Crow a *traditional* way of going forward."

The story of Plenty Coups and the wise way he guided his people through the genocide perpetrated against the Indian nations by American settlers takes on ironic significance in our own time. As extreme climate change wreaks it slow but inevitable changes to the planet, we are now confronting the same loss of our American ways of life that the nation's original inhabitants once faced at our own hands. Should a wise person like Plenty Coups come forth with a dream foretelling destruction and offering a way forward that might save us all before it's too late, would anyone, I wonder, even listen? It's as if, with the encroachment of urban sprawl, high rises, shopping centers, factories, housing developments, freeways, and cell phone towers, we've paved right over our own natural resources and animal instincts that long ago would have alerted us to the danger we've put ourselves—and the rest of the planet—in the way of. Just as the Crow people's fate was impossible to avert so, now, our own future of confronting radical changes more drastic than anything we've known before appears certain.

The current facts of climate change triggering these changes are frightening and—if we can even allow ourselves to take them in—overwhelming in their psychological impact. Just in the last decade, global sea levels rose at a rate nearly double that of the last century. Since 1880, global surface temperatures show that Earth has warmed—with all ten of the warmest years occurring in the past twelve years. Warming oceans caused by humans emitting more carbon dioxide into the atmosphere have led to shrinking ice sheets in Greenland, the Antarctic, and the Arctic, and to retreating glaciers around the world—including in the Alps, Himalayas, Andes, Rockies, Alaska, and Africa. Since the beginning of the Industrial Revolution, the acidity of surface ocean waters has increased by thirty percent.

In the United States, record high temperatures and intense superstorms and rainfalls are on the rise.[1] Though it barely registered on the evening news and talk shows, a NASA-funded national climate assessment report predicted that "the utter collapse of civilization will be difficult to avoid." In its most recent report the Intergovernmental Panel on Climate Change (IPCC) stated that climate change has now hit all regions of the world, that "no one on this planet" will be untouched by climate change, and that failure to reduce emissions could threaten society with food shortages, refugee crises, the flooding of major cities and island nations, mass extinction of plants and animals, and a climate so drastically altered it might become dangerous for people in some places to be outside during the hottest times of the year.[2] Even former Defense Secretary Chuck Hagel warned that climate change poses an imminent threat to global security, and announced plans for climate change risks across all U.S. military operations.[3]

Even more dispiriting, and though we don't like to talk about it much, it is our American carbon-based lifestyle that has led us to this cliff's edge of extinction. Although China has now edged past us as the world's leading polluter, it attained this dubious distinction by aspiring to live life the American way. If we in our blindness got ourselves into this calamitous mess, is it possible we could assume responsibility and, like Chief Plenty Coups, lead the way forward to a more sustainable and survivable way of life?

For that to happen, I believe, we would first need to become aware of the split that cleaves our American psyche. On one side, there is our profound identification with "America the beautiful"—that land that we love, once leaping with wild animals amid thick, emerald forests and with fish arcing above sparkling rivers; and once lush with meadows and plains extending from sea to shining sea: where people could fish, swim, hunt, hike, sun, and heal from the stresses of modern life. Opposing that real and genuine love of the American landscape is the nation's addictive impulse to conflate a successful life with material wealth, such as big cars and big houses, urban sprawl and tall buildings, and a diet based on the products of industrial agriculture and environmentally hazardous meat and animal products.[4] If we are to preserve our stunning portion of the North American continent and do our part to become an environmental leader for the world, we will need to follow in the footsteps of Chief Plenty Coups and the Crow nation, and ritually and faithfully once and for all lay down our outmoded materialistic customs and habits in favor of a new way of life—one that *might* save the lives of future generations.

Just as the seeds for the Crow nation's survival and revival lay within its heritage and traditions, so might our own salvation lie in going forward by going backward to the more materially spare lifestyles of our American ancestors. As psychologist Mary Pipher points out in my first interview, our parents, grandparents, and great-grandparents on back all had considerably simpler lifestyles than the American middle- and upper-class of today. Our ancestors' lives, she says, centered more on neighborhood potlucks and family dinners than on the latest smartphone, or shopping sprees and dinners out—thus offering a different model by which to live. In our interview Pipher, who is also an ardent activist against the Keystone XL Pipeline,[5] speaks to America as if to a patient in her therapy room, offering clinical insights into how citizens can begin to break through their collective defenses on climate change. Environmental psychologist Raymond de Young also makes food and simpler lifestyles the centerpiece of our interview. Warning that we must prepare for the inevitable "coming downshift" of resource depletion, he advocates that people begin to live *now* as they will have to live in the near future, whether they want to or not. Although this way of life may leave us less materially well off and circumstances will be hard, de Young believes that these more challenging, locally based lifestyles oriented around food—growing, harvesting, canning, and sharing—will be psychologically restorative.

Jungian analyst and scientist Stephen Foster, who has consulted on cleaning up Superfund sites, discusses the "archetype of waste" and the psychology of recycling, and how nature's distress reveals itself in the nightly dreams of his clients. Bonnie Bright, also a Jungian analyst, turns her attention to the plight of the disoriented honeybees who, contaminated by insecticides, are unable to make their way back to their hives, and links their suffering to how we humans, too, are facing similar dislocation from our homelands as a result of environmental destruction. And in my concluding interview, psychologist Gary S. Bobroff discusses his research into the mysterious phenomenon of crop circles: both as an expression of Earth "speaking" to us at this moment of climate upheaval, but also as a kind of collective dream or vision to which individuals can bring their own interpretations and meanings, helping to orient them in the coming environmental era. ■

Notes

1. Global Climate Change: Vital Signs of the Planet. National Aeronautics and Space Administration (NASA) <http://climate.nasa.gov/>.

2. "The Utter Collapse of Civilization Will Be 'Difficult to Avoid' NASA Funded Study Says," *Guardian*, March 14, 2014. "IPCC Says Climate Change Is Here, World Needs to Adapt," by Andrea Thompson. Climate Central, March 30, 2014. "UN Panel Issues Its Starkest Warning Yet on Global Warming," by Justin Gillis, *New York Times*, November 2, 2014.

3. "Pentagon Signals Security Risks of Climate Change," by Coral Davenport, *New York Times*, October 13, 2014.

4. Animal Agriculture One of the Largest Contributors to Global Warming, UN Body Reaffirms. Humane Society International, September 27, 2013 <http://www.hsi.org/news/press_releases/2013/09/fao_report_climate_change_092713.html>.

5. The Keystone Pipeline System is an oil pipeline system that runs from the oil sands of Alberta, Canada, to refineries in the United States in Nebraska, Illinois, and Texas. In addition to the synthetic crude oil (syncrude) and diluted bitumen (dilbit), the pipeline carries light crude oil from Montana and North Dakota. Three phases of the project are in operation, and at this time the fourth is awaiting U.S. government approval. The Keystone XL proposal has faced strong criticism from environmentalists and some members of the United States Congress for the pipeline's impact on Nebraska's environmentally sensitive Sand Hills region. As of December 2014, the construction permit has not been issued. More information on environmental opposition to the Keystone XL Pipeline can be found at Bold Nebraska <http://www.boldnebraska.org>.

We Are America—and We Are the Earth, Too

AN INTERVIEW WITH MARY PIPHER, PH.D.

CALL CLINICAL PSYCHOLOGIST MARY Pipher, if you will, an apostle for America's most enduring values. Whether guarding adolescent girls in *Reviving Ophelia* or upholding our immigrant ideals in *The Middle of Everywhere*, Pipher draws out the nation's better self. In her book *The Green Boat: Reviving Ourselves in Our Capsized Culture*, Pipher takes up the challenge of global climate change—melting polar ice caps, rising sea levels, and warmer seawater temperatures—from a psychological perspective. Unflinchingly, she writes of the "suicidal behavior" our species is engaged in; and how our collective denial and disconnection from reality puts us at risk for "what could be called a psychotic state." Limited by our basic "*homo sapiens* minds and bodies" that have not changed since the Neolithic era, she writes, "we're in over our heads, and at some level, all of us are looking for a life buoy."

But Pipher doesn't just diagnose our cultural paralysis in the face of looming environmental catastrophe. Instead, through narrating her own courageous struggle as part of a grassroots organization fighting TransCanada's proposed Keystone XL pipeline through her beloved prairie state of Nebraska,[1] she describes how she drew on both psychological insight and "Nebraskan plain talk" to mobilize action. In sharing her own awakening as an activist for the fate of the planet, Pipher reveals a life-affirming process that can help us to stay "present and focused . . . calm and balanced," while attending to the painful realities of global climate change.

Whereas Pipher may be addressing each of us as individuals, and all of us collectively, it is the United States—the world's second largest polluter, just beneath China—who sits across from her in the client's chair. A third-generation Nebraskan, Pipher spoke nostalgically during our interview of the environmental values her grandparents lived by, and didn't even know they had: the humble houses and gardens, for instance, that gave them happiness and contentment. "I never heard anybody talk about having money or wanting a bigger car," says Pipher of those times gone by. "There was a lot of discussion around good food, and getting together with the neighbors to play cards on Sunday."

Before 1950, says Pipher, most people, like her grandparents, "were farmers living in farm communities where they knew everyone's name. The changes in America are relatively recent. They stem from a value system and business model imposed on us by corporate America and advertising that pushed big new cars and all kinds of luxury appliances." This "United States of Advertising," says Pipher, led to "sixty years of mis-education of the American public about the true nature of happiness. And so one of the ways to think of our role in making the world a better place is that we're trying to re-educate people about what's important. Today, I still believe in what my grandmothers believed: getting together with my friends, eating good food, taking walks, watching birds and swimming. The same things that made me happy when I was ten years old make me happy now."

A daughter of the Midwest like Pipher, I appreciated the psychologically grounded yet fiercely engaged approach she brought to the charged topic of climate change. If more of us recognized the cumulative effect of our individual actions on caring for the environment, she points out, America might break through its defenses—and help trigger a global transformation. During our interview, Pipher was also keen to point out that we were both "also America. I never talk in a condescending way on these issues," she told me, "because we are America, and we are the Earth, too. We are all the same lowly beings trying to grapple with the truth."

∗

Pythia Peay: America and China are the world's biggest polluters; together, the two nations are responsible for half the world's pollution. This global rise in carbon emissions is contributing to record droughts, heat, and rising sea levels. So if America were on your couch presenting this problem on climate change, how would you begin to work with such a client?

Mary Pipher: First, I'd be respectful of America as a patient, just as I am of clients in therapy. But one thing I'd assume about my client is something I generally assume about clients who are behaving in a dysfunctional manner: at some level, they know what's going on.

So I'd take it as a given that by now most people have been exposed to issues around climate change. At this point to focus on information would be like telling an alcoholic, "Did you know that it's harmful for you to drink ten beers?" Of course that person knows that! Instead, I'd immediately turn my attention to defenses and resistance.

Dealing with people who are struggling with denial is what therapists do for a living. That's not cause to be judgmental; in fact I have an enormous amount of sympathy for the country as it faces this situation because it's unbearably painful to deal with head on.

PP: Do you feel that an alarmist approach isn't useful in generating more action on environmental issues?

MP: There's been a scolding tone: *Why don't people just wake up and deal with the facts?* But people don't respond to guilt and scolding. What people do tend to respond to, whether they're therapy clients or consumers of media, is a deep belief that they're loved by the messenger. So as a therapist, speaker, or writer, my first goal is to love that person, and my country, and to hold them in my heart as I try to help them cope with upsetting information.

PP: And to America, what you would say?

MP: To America, my patient, I would start by saying this: "I deeply want to understand this place you're in at this moment. Why, from your point of view, is this issue so painful? Is it thinking about your grandchildren's endangered future, or the disappearance of a nearby forest you love? Or is it thinking about how hard it would be for you to imagine changing your life, and how painful it would be to feel like a victim—whatever it is that keeps you from being able to accept this information, let's try to understand that first?"

Because humans naturally resist difficult information, I'd expect people to be angry, and to say things like, "I feel badly about it, but what can I do?" In listening very carefully to what "America" is saying about its collective anguish and inability to deal with this situation, I'd respond with using the client's own language and the metaphors.

PP: And some examples of that would be . . . ?

MP: One thing Americans like to believe is that we're in control; we like to think of ourselves as heroes, and that we're basically good. And so one way to speak to Americans is to say, "If you think you have no power, you have no power. But if you believe you have the power to act in a way that's good for the planet, then you have an opportunity to have control over your fate, and to have the possibility of being a hero." That would be one example of using American language to talk to Americans about this.

PP: This was exemplified in your book in the figure of Randy Thompson, a "political conservative who looked like John Wayne and dressed in jeans . . . and a cowboy hat and boots," and a Keystone XL activist who became the image of Nebraskans' fight against TransCanada.

MP: A lot of the language in my book and in our struggle references iconic American symbols like Randy: "We will not be bullied," or "I stand with Randy," or "I'm fighting TransCanada." One reason Randy has been such a powerful symbol is because he uses wonderful John Wayne American language.

PP: In addition to using classic American symbols and language to awaken "America on your couch" to the urgency of climate change, what other therapeutic techniques would you draw on?

MP: A good therapeutic tool is the "crossroads technique." Say a client was struggling with a problem with alcohol. I might say, "Do you realize you're at a crossroads, and that the decision you make today can take you down one road toward more despair and guilt—or it can take you down another road toward a healthy new life?"

So to America I might say, "I wonder if you're aware that you're poised on the brink of enormous change? Do you understand that you're at a crossroads, where every decision about how we behave in the world can make a significant difference?"

Or, "Do you understand that all Americans are community educators, whether we know it or not—and that every action we undertake is a lesson to everyone we know?"

PP: Can you say more about what it means to be a "community educator"?

MP: One thing I don't do anymore is carry a plastic bottle. Because I want to be the change we need in the world, I want people to see me carrying the metal bottle. A year ago, my husband and I bought solar panels; now our house is on a solar tour for the city. This was an expensive investment that may take about twenty years to recoup—and I'm sixty-five, so I may not be alive in twenty years—but we did it because we saw it as an opportunity to be community educators.

All of us have the chance to be community educators, even if it's little things like bringing a cloth bag to the grocery store so you can tell the clerk, "I prefer not to use plastic."

PP: In discussing how you as a therapist would work with America as a patient on the issue of climate change, it sounds as if you might be describing issues around addiction.

MP: Addiction is a very problematic word, and I don't want to present America as pathological. Most people, if they allow themselves to think about these issues, want their children to grow up on a sustainable planet with clean waters and green spaces. They don't really want more nuclear and coal-fired power plants. So in that sense they want progress toward a sustainable planet.

But there's an axiom in psychotherapy that everyone wants progress, but no one wants change. So the hard part around this topic are the changes we have to make to have that sustainable planet we all want. "What does this mean for me?" for example, is a big question. "Does this mean that I can't use air conditioning when it's a hundred and five degrees?"

These hard questions are made even scarier by the fact that we don't even talk about them. So one of the places we could use an addiction model in this discussion on climate change is around the question of forbidden topics, and the secret that everyone knows. Because one of the biggest problems is that the frightening changes happening to our planet are not being discussed in any kind of meaningful way.

PP: In fact, you describe it in your book as a social taboo.

MP: Absolutely. If you've ever raised this issue with people, you can just feel how they respond. For me as a therapist, it reminds me of when I have to bring up uncomfortable things in a session, such as whether there's any physical abuse in a family. Before asking these questions, I can feel my throat tense up. And in fact that sense that my throat is tensing up is a cue to me that I'm getting near something dangerous for this client.

It's the same with this issue on climate change. It has a *verboten* quality; you know when you bring it up you're likely to encounter immediate resistance. People will basically say, "I don't want to talk about this now."

But when is it that they *do* want to talk about it? They don't want to talk about it at parties; they don't want to talk about it in schools, because it's too traumatic for children. They don't want to talk about it with friends, when they just want to relax. They don't want to talk about it in the workplace because it's too controversial. Essentially, there really is no appropriate time to talk about it—which is what a secret is, as there's no appropriate time to talk about it.

PP: Indeed, these days we can more easily speak about sex or money than our overfished oceans and vanishing species. But just like social conventions once prohibited us from discussing sex, what are the cultural reasons that reinforce this repression around climate change?

MP: One reason Americans don't talk about this is because we don't get good information. For twenty years now the culture has been mired in the least productive of all topics, which is "Do you believe in climate change?" It's as if we were talking about whether or not we believe in extraterrestrials! Climate change is no more a matter of belief than microbes are a matter of belief. It's an empirical fact based on evidence provided by international scientists.

But there are also leadership issues. The last good leader we had on the environment was [Jimmy] Carter: he showed up in the White House wearing a sweater, had solar panels put on the roof of the white house, and talked about the fact that we should ration gas. He was on his way to being a very good leader, but he was clobbered in the re-election. And one reason was for his leadership role on the environment.

PP: He was made fun of and ridiculed; it was humiliating just to watch.

MP: That was an example of how strong cultural resistance can be to a leader who tries to deal with climate change. This gives me some sympathy with leaders and politicians, because it isn't as if they can just stand up and lead on this issue. They run into the same wall of resistance that the rest of us run into, only on a much bigger scale. But certainly if the media covered "parts per million of CO_2,"[2] in the atmosphere the same way they covered the Dow Jones, putting it on the front page or on the evening news every day, we'd be having a very different conversation, wouldn't we?

PP: Which brings us back again to the issue of our collective defenses around the perilous state of the planet.

MP: Well, one thing I'd say to America as a client on the couch is that the amount of psychic energy it spends in denial around this urgent and terrifying issue is enormous. This resistance to facing climate change isn't a passive process. It's a very active process that requires us to continually disconnect from our senses, our emotions, our bodies, our friends, our neighbors, and even reality.

PP: Does this resistance actually feed our symptoms of over-consumption? In other words, rather than face the painful issue of what's happening to the animals, the oceans, and the forests, we say, "To hell with it!" and go shopping or buy a new car?

MP: I recently read a statistic that over six in ten Americans don't believe climate change is a serious threat.[3] That same day I read another statistic that almost seventy percent of Americans are disengaged from their work.[4] I believe these two things are tied together. You can't disengage from one part of reality without disengaging from other parts of reality.

PP: Could you say more about the connection between these two sets of statistics?

MP: Let's return to the example of a family where the father is an alcoholic. All these things happen: Dad's grumpy most mornings, he misses work, and the kids are afraid to anger him—and yet nobody ever talks about alcohol. What that family also isn't doing is feeling safe and vibrant, because there's a big thing they can't talk about. The amount of energy it takes to do all that filtering keeps the family from being loving and engaged in the ways families ideally want to be.

It's the same thing with our denial of climate change. If you use a lot of energy to tamp down despair, you tamp down everything, such as your capacity for joy and love. In writing about Germans during the Holocaust in *States of Denial*, the author Stanley Cohen described the phenomenon of "willful ignorance" in which the Germans both knew and didn't know what was going on at the same time [see Cohen: 2001]. That state of "willful ignorance" he described is not a happy state, and that's the state that Americans are in right now.

PP: In your book you describe certain American characteristics that prevent us from recognizing the urgency of environmental devastation. One is our geography—I'd never heard that mentioned before.

MP: America has certainly begun to experience the effects of climate change. But geographically we're a huge country that's far removed from typhoons and melting icecaps. So it's easier for Americans to feel lulled by their geography into thinking they're safe.

Another belief that hampers us is the distortion of American exceptionalism[5] into the notion that the country can do anything it wants, whenever it feels like it. This in turn feeds an underlying attitude that climate change isn't that big a problem—but if it ever is, somebody smart will fix it for us, whether by sending everyone to outer space, or coming up with some technological fix. Or, at the other extreme, we can also think climate change is a terrible problem, but there's nothing we can do about it.

But, as a country, the place we aren't *ever* in, is that climate change is an urgent problem, and that every one of us needs to do something about it: and that we *can* do something about it.

PP: So what steps can citizens as individuals take to break through America's current state of denial on these life-and-death environmental issues?

MP: In our coalition, we're fans of "actionable intelligence," or giving people assignments. If a person really wants to move from Point A to Point B, we assign them one step they can immediately take to advance toward that goal. For instance, with the apple-pie brigade, I often say, "One pie, one person, one plan—and you've got an event."

Starting an environmental group isn't a complicated thing. A group could be you and one friend sitting at a coffee shop planning an action. Groups also alleviate that feeling of being alone and powerless. You have people to share your burdens and to make plans with.

PP: In fact, you organized the "Grandmothers Apple Pie Brigade," rewarding policymakers working for the environment with virtual or real apple pies—about as American an endeavor as I could imagine!

MP: This is a country that values individualism and it is not a country that recognizes its own tradition of community activism. Starting with the early Revolutionaries, America was built by community organizers! All of the great movements—the civil rights movement, the labor movement, the women's movement, and the environmental movement—began with community organizing.

Most of us probably don't see ourselves as the next Martin Luther King or Gandhi. But almost all of us could see ourselves as part of a potluck group that's making a significant impact in our hometown. Even though community organizing has been the engine for change in this country since the beginning, it's not a model that we teach or talk about.

PP: What would be another example of how citizens can mobilize against climate change?

MP: One thing I'd try to do is to catch America, the client, being good. To use a clinical example, a common intervention I have as a therapist is to ask people to go outside and take a walk. If they're depressed, it generates endorphins. It also connects them to something larger than their depressed brain.

So, perhaps I've had a client for a year that I've tried to encourage to go outside and take a walk. She has a running mental tape about how unpleasant her life is, how she doesn't like her job, or how her family is difficult, etc. But one day in a session she remarks, "I noticed that when I walked to the mailbox my neighbors' roses were out."

Now I would jump on that and say, "Do you have any idea how significant this is? For over a year I've been wishing you could smell those roses. And this week you

219

saw them." So when you witness a positive change, it's like sparking a fire. You grab the bellows and start stoking that fire to make a flame bigger and bigger.

PP: I love the idea of telling America to go outside and take a walk!

MP: Often people are afraid to talk about the environment because they're worried they're going to be made to feel guilty. So just as I built on my client's positive behavior, what I also try to do in my environmental work is emphasize the ways people are already helping the Earth. I might ask individuals to start writing down everything they're already doing—whether planting trees; riding their bike instead of driving; composting; or encouraging neighbors to pick up litter. When people begin making those lists, they start to feel proud of the ways they're already acknowledging this problem.

PP: It seems to me that you're describing how, in therapy, a cumulative effect over time can build in someone's psyche, bringing about transformation. If this same kind of dynamic occurred on a collective level, in America and around the world, couldn't it lead to a breakthrough on the environment at some point?

MP: As a therapist, I know that I can work with someone for a year and not get very far. Then I can have one session where the language and the moment come together to create a "snap of insight" that causes change. In the same way, if certain conditions appear, we could have a worldwide "snap of insight" around our imperiled planet. In a way, that's already happening.

PP: Certainly Nebraska's fight against TransCanada and its proposed Keystone XL Pipeline has triggered a quantum leap in the rare alliance that's formed between liberal progressives and conservative Republican farmers.

MP: All around the world more people are waking up and realizing they want to take responsibility for the environment. In 2008, the environmentalist Paul Hawken documented two million groups working to avert global climate change [see Hawken: 2008]. If these groups all knew about each other, and if what they were doing was front page news all over the world, people would begin to believe that we could avert these crises. The problem is we're not connected to each other.

But imagine if we had an alternate Internet called something like "Motherearthnet" to link all the people working to change the world to each other. Then we'd see this enormous force that's gathering! I'm hopeful we'll make that happen. And when it does, consciousness could change in a matter of weeks. And should our global consciousness change, we would have a new future.

PP: So by each person being aware of what others are doing—as well as how each person's individual action, no matter how small, really does matter—we could "flip the switch of consciousness" where climate change is concerned?

MP: One of the lines I often include on my email correspondence, is "We're all doing the same work now." Whether we're sixty-five or two, we're all in the generation that has a very short window of time to act if we want life on the planet to continue in a more sustainable, vibrant way. ■

Notes

1. See the introduction to this section, n. 5.
2. Many scientists report that 350 ppm (parts per million) of CO_2 in the atmosphere is the safe limit for humanity. We're now at 400 ppm of CO_2.
3. "How Americans See Global Warming—in 8 Charts," by Scott Clement, *Washington Post*, April 22, 2013. Available online at <http://www.washingtonpost.com/blogs/the-fix/wp/2013/04/22/how-americans-see-global-warming-in-8-charts/>.
4. "Most Workers Hate Their Jobs or Have 'Checked Out,' Gallup Says," by Ricardo Lopez, *Los Angeles Times*, June 17, 2013.
5. Dating back to nineteenth-century French historian Alexis de Tocqueville's description of America as "exceptional," the term "American exceptionalism" has come to signify the nation's unique values, as well as its difference from other nations.

—17—

That Which May Destroy Us May Also Save Us

Adapting to the Coming Downshift—Now!

AN INTERVIEW WITH RAYMOND DE YOUNG, PH.D.

WHETHER THEY ARE SCENES of an asteroid hurtling toward the Earth or an alien invasion, we've all seen those movies where life on Earth as we know it is instantly and radically changed, if not outright destroyed. Most of us have also seen the news clips of icebergs shrinking; polar bears on ice floes; and China's hazy, smog-filled air. We've read or heard the ominous reports predicting imminent climate change that, if not averted by some unlikely *deus ex machina*, will end civilization as we know it, leading to widespread death, disease, starvation, and chaos. Those cinematic horror scenes of the Statue of Liberty or the Lincoln Memorial partly submerged in the ocean? Well, if sea levels continue to rise as predicted, swamping the east coast, even that bleak scenario may come to pass. If we were being really honest with ourselves, we'd also admit to the numbness that fogs our minds as we try, but fail, to take in this information.

Very few of us, in fact, have been able to *really* put these two scenarios of world-ending disaster and climate change together. Not so Raymond De Young, associate professor of Environmental Psychology and Planning at the School of Natural Resources and Environment at the University of Michigan. Realizing that the effects of climate change and resource constraints are only going to increase, forcing civilizations to respond, De Young has devoted his professional and personal life to what he calls "the coming downshift." No longer a question of "if" but "when," this period of "resource descent," De Young has written, will be marked by the inevitable decline of resource availability, the plateauing of crude-oil production rates, and the draw-down of fossil aquifers. These are not problems that can be solved, he maintains, but predicaments that will play out over the next century.[1]

It would be a mistake, however, to label De Young's message as solely gloom-and-doom predictions of the death of modern industrial civilization. A little like the Old Testament Moses, his teaching, writing, and research focuses on guiding people out of decaying, industrial-based lifestyles to a kind of promised land of more sustainable—and survivable—habits of everyday living. De Young also explores the psychological resistances and mental ideas that keep citizens trapped in outmoded attitudes and behaviors that are in effect deepening their own graves. If only we could stop "buffering" ourselves from the reality that we're not going to be able to solve problems by applying lots of energy and resources to them, he says, we might be able to rise to the urgent demands these times require of us and learn to become more resourceful. Building simple, place-based lives while there are still options and surplus resources and social capital, he believes, may enable us to thrive through the hard times ahead.

The way to move forward and survive the coming environmental challenges, as De Young outlines in our interview, is through "behavioral entrepreneurship": developing innovative ways of dealing with the practical demands of everyday life in a way that prepares for the coming downshift—*now.* The benefits of living like this now, rather than only later, don't just ensure our own individual survival and that of our loved ones. The more people who begin to model these kinds of environmentally adaptive behaviors, he hopes, the more it might trigger a chain reaction of cultural change. De Young, co-editor of *The Localization Reader: Adapting to the Coming Downshift* and a married grandfather, says he tries to live his own life as a model for how to manage during the coming downshift. A "big part of my socializing," he tells me, "is around food, farmers markets, farms, and gardens. We grow all kinds of vegetables, we can and dry food, and have food parties." But as he is quick to point out, this ecological way of life doesn't just result in increased levels of physical security. Learning from our grandparents' simpler way of life to help us to go forward into the future may also be just what our wounded, disoriented, dissociated, overstimulated modern psyches need to psychologically and spiritually thrive.

✳

Pythia Peay: Recently, there have been reports that climate change has reached such levels there's no turning back: it now threatens our future as a species.[2] This is such a huge piece of information to absorb, and I can imagine that resistance to it will be strong. Aren't we going to have to address climate change psychologically, as well as scientifically and practically?

Raymond De Young: I think that's exactly right. The difference between where we are now and where we've been is stark. For a number of years, I imagined that what was needed to meet environmental crises was to help people make the transition to a more ecofriendly lifestyle—an approach that assumed there was a fully voluntary choice involved. But the "energy-resource descent" model I've been working on over the past fifteen years says that we'll be consuming fewer resources because there *will be* fewer resources to consume. And we *will be* transitioning because there are going to be problems in the resource systems and in the way we provision ourselves, transport ourselves, and feed ourselves. So it's not up to educators and practitioners to decide how to motivate or educate people: *we will be* changing and if we don't, we're going to end up in all kinds of trouble.

So then the question becomes how can we help motivate, inspire, and educate people in new skills in order to make the transition to a simpler life pattern more quickly and easily—and in a way that maintains civility, and that leaves them with a sense of wellbeing. That's a huge psychological and sociological challenge. But if we don't confront that challenge while we have a surplus of time and resources then the transition that will occur will be much harsher and closer to those gloom-and-doom scenarios. The way I see it, the task we face is how to make these ecologically hard times psychologically flourishing times. How do we bring out the kinds of innate capacities necessary to meet challenges well, to cooperate, to innovate?

PP: And what kinds of answers or solutions have you come up with?

RDY: One thing I've talked about with my students is the idea of behavioral entrepreneurship. This is the notion that there aren't only business, technological, or social entrepreneurs; there are also "behavioral entrepreneurs." These are people actively crafting their lives as a work of art, and learning how to step back and say, "That was a good day, or a good week. That worked well."

PP: But according to current mainstream American ideas of happiness or the well-lived life, some might say a really good week was winning the lottery, or taking a Lear jet to Paris, or getting a good deal on a new car.

RDY: There will always be that one percent or five percent who, in one way or another, will have more resources and will judge the good life in material ways. And although that's a larger percentage of America today, that will soon change. But I'm thinking of a good life where we step back and say, "That was meaningful." Or, "That was purposeful. I gave something back, and that feels better than anything I could have taken." At an even deeper level, the non-consumptive version of a good life is to learn just to be in the world now. To not always strive mindlessly for more, but to be grateful for whatever we have.

PP: Can you give me an example of your version of a good day or weekend?

RDY: My version of a day that you look back on is to get up and go to the farmers market. But rather than just being a green consumer and buying stuff at the farmers market, you develop a relationship with one of the farmers, go around to the other side of the table, and volunteer for half an hour to sell some of their goods. This way you're no longer just a consumer: you're a citizen. You're working with that person, giving them a break to go and get a cup of coffee. And then perhaps after that you go and meet someone and talk about what food is in season, or what's going on with regard to events occurring in the town, or catching up with people. Then, in my own version of an ideal weekend, we'd go home and figure out how to prepare the food we brought home. Then I'd spend some time with my grandson, working with him on some project, and have more conversations. I'd try to do something that's not about my work but about our neighborhood and involves working with other people.

PP: As a professor, how do you teach this kind of ecological "behavioral entrepreneurship" to your students?

RDY: I try to get my students to think of the day or the weekend ahead as a canvas. I teach them that what they put on that canvas can endure, or it can be fleeting. I suggest that the more their efforts involve working with other people the more likely it is that the positive feelings will endure. I tell them to do many small experiments and try new things, and to keep a journal and periodically assess the week or weekend. This isn't so different from finding new ways to get up early to go to the gym, or any number of different ways we try to change our habits.

PP: So this would be one way of teaching people how to adapt and live now, in preparation for this coming environmental age?

RDY: And how to live well, on a lot less, with a lot fewer resources coming in, and a lot more wellbeing going out. The "resource descent" scenario that my colleagues and I are working on assumes that we're inevitably going to be consuming a lot less of everything. So it's a good idea to pre-familiarize ourselves with how to do that, and that living with less can even be fulfilling!

PP: Your approach, with its emphasis on the pleasures of the material, everyday world, contrasts with what some perceive as the more ascetic approach of the environmental movement. I wonder if you think that in some ways the Puritan strain in the American character has become woven into the environmental movement?

RDY: I think that's a great question, and it's one that I struggle with. There are two parts to this problem around materialism. One part is that we're always going to consume, because that's what life requires. But what we in the environmental movement did early on was make consumption an evil, and say that there are things you are allowed to do and things that you aren't allowed to do. It was very restrictive—an extreme conservation ethic—and I never liked that because if you frame things negatively, it doesn't get you very far. People don't warm up to what your message is. The adaptive response to a fear-laden and overly restrictive message is to avoid it, because on a day-to-day basis people have to get on with the demands of life.

So I think it's a matter of emphasis. Timothy Miller wrote a fascinating book, *How to Want What You Have.* And in it he said that wanting more is not a bad thing; but it becomes bad when your entire life pattern and expectations are about ever more material growth. It becomes psychologically harmful when the pursuit of ever more becomes your sole reason for living. When wanting more out of life takes that kind of extreme form, particularly when it has material or energy consequences, it becomes destructive to the environment, social relations, and personal wellbeing.

But I also think that extreme frugality, asceticism, and the idea that all consumption is evil are not likely to work any better than an extreme focus on ever-greater material growth and more wealth. In the future, we are going to have to be very clever, resourceful, and mindful about how we use energy, materials, and water, simply because there are going to be fewer resources to go around. But we're still going to have to use those things, because they're essential for life.

PP: So then the right place is somewhere in the middle?

RDY: Right. It's to make sure that we make a shift from a society that has primarily focused on material growth to one that's also focused on nonmaterial growth. At the same time, we would want to accomplish this shift in a way that people can actually find joy in reducing their ecological footprint, so that psychological wellbeing comes directly from mindful ways of being resourceful.

PP: In other words, we can derive emotional and spiritual satisfaction by being more deliberative and forward thinking in our use of material resources?

RDY: Yes, because life seems more meaningful when our purchases support our local community. Such choices may be a drop in the national economic bucket, but they could be very important in supporting local agriculture, local provisioning, and local craftspeople. My purchase of a bag of lettuce at my local farmers market, or in my CSA share (community supported agriculture), may not have a major economic effect—but it may make all the difference to that particular farmer. In this way, little changes in material choices may make my own nonmaterial world much richer; the choice that I make may actually matter again.

I also like to describe this as a "reality-based" lifestyle. To live this way means doing more than just buying local. It involves being more appreciative of quality by buying materials or products that can be repaired or repurposed, even if they don't have the flash of newness. So reality-based lifestyles are a way of being in the middle between the extremes of frugality and conspicuous material consumption.

PP: What you seem to also be saying is that there's an artistic and creative element in this kind of lifestyle that's been overlooked, and that would also seem to be more psychologically nourishing.

RDY: There's a classic book in the environmental field called *A Sand County Almanac*, by Aldo Leopold. Most of his writing in that book was about developing a land ethic comprising a series of rules and regulations that restrict our behavior in order to live sustainably on a finite planet. But in Leopold's last chapter, called "A Conservation Esthetic," he talked about the psychological experience of being out in nature, hunting, fishing, and working the land. I've tried to take that idea and expand it to the notion that life is a creative "work of art." The behaviors we choose and the relationships we invest our time in can all be part of an aesthetic process. Spirituality and how we explain existence are also a part of this behavioral aesthetic. If we can get people to live more reflectively, to mindfully paint the tapestry of their everyday lives, then we might learn how to live sustainably on this finite planet we inhabit.

I like to think of this work of behavioral entrepreneurship as unfolding in a series of small, innovative, but very personal experiments. It becomes a work in progress that may need continual adjusting, and as most artists know, this kind of work is rarely ever finished, but ongoing.

PP: So part of the shift we're making is away from a perfectionistic way of looking at our material lives toward something that is more flawed and messy, but also more fulfilling.

RDY: I think messy is nice. In environmental studies there are different ways of describing the situation we face. One way to think of it is as a puzzle. A puzzle is where we agree on what the outcome should look like; we also agree on the pieces in front of us, and so the task becomes putting the pieces together into the finished picture. Another way to think of it is as a problem where we agree where we want to be, but we don't quite know how to get there, and we might have some disagreement on the next steps to take. So, for example, although we all agree we've got to solve this problem of having disrupted the climate, somebody might argue that the problem has to be achieved through a national policy–level approach. Others might say the solution to the problem lies on a local level, although still others believe it should be through an international coalition. In my area of research the disagreement is often between economic solutions versus non-economic behavioral approaches.

But more and more environmental analysts think of the issues we face as messy. We don't all agree on what the problem is, and we don't all agree on what the proximate solution or ultimate goal should look like, so it's messy. This is very frustrating to anyone coming from a policy or engineering perspective (as I once did), because they like problems, but they don't like messes.

I tend to think that because the situation is messy, perhaps the solution is messy: and so maybe we have to learn to tolerate messiness. It's like gardening: anybody who gardens seriously knows that you can only create a manicured garden with major fossil-fuel inputs and lots of time and money. If you're a "normal" gardener, you certainly can influence what grows in your garden, but you can't control it. The outcome isn't in your hands; it's an interaction among your efforts, nature, chance, genetics, local animals, and diseases. It's a mess, and you're fortunate to get anything out of it at all!

PP: In turning to the larger question of America, what is it in our collective psyche that may resist making the kind of messy transitions and creative adaptations to the coming downshift that you're describing?

RDY: I'm reminded of Mary Midgley, a philosopher who wrote an article on the limits of individualism.[3] Midgley's central theme was that what was going wrong in modern society could be traced to our overemphasis on individualism. This emphasis has come at a great expense to the environment, because a hyper-individual society is made possible by huge amounts of surplus, high-concentration resources. It can be argued that where resources are scarce society has developed more of a communitarian focus.

And so America's hyper-individualism is going to make it difficult to respond well to the impending limits to growth and scarcer resources. Over time, the declining availability of energy or resources will have a negative impact on individualism itself. This is going to further complicate our transition because over the past two hundred years of our history most of our metaphors, shared stories, and measures of success, as well as our legal system and our founding documents, have privileged and protected the individual. That focus on the individual has served us very well during an energy and resource ascent, but I don't think it will continue to serve us as well as we go forward into the future.

PP: If our hyper-individualism is what will work against us in the coming environmental era, what in our American psyche might help us?

RDY: I think it would be those parts of the American spirit and psyche that are about working together. I love hearing old folks talk about the hard times in their lives—a flood, a fire, or the depression, for example—when neighborhoods and friends worked together to solve problems or survive disasters. Even older Americans who lived through the last century of incredible resource growth and the explosion of affluence tell stories that have a community focus. And when these stories are told, the people listening usually smile; they don't make fun of the "old fogies." Sometimes, young people are even envious, and say that's the kind of life they'd like to have. This means that this side of the country's character is at the very least still present within the American psyche.

PP: What's lacking in many people's lives these days is that lack of joining together around a larger purpose. It's a hollow way to live when it's only for one's own self, or even one's own family.

RDY: It also reduces our sense of security and stability. In studying the conditions under which people will change their behavior, the principle of self-efficacy (belief in one's ability to complete and achieve a goal) is always emphasized. But as I always tell my students, that's "individualizing" problems. Take backyard composting, for example, and the idea that every neighbor has to develop skills in backyard composting. But why? I don't know everything my neighbors know. What I *do* want to know is that I can get access to someone in the neighborhood who is a really good composter. Then if my compost heap starts to smell, I can get help. So instead of self-efficacy, I promote *group* efficacy. I want the group to be able to effectively respond to problems. But I don't want to personally replicate everything each neighbor knows or can do.

On a material level, this shows up in a sharing economy. Not everybody has to have a wood saw, a car, or a canning pot: we can share these things. But at the nonmaterial level, skills, insights, knowledge, and abilities can also be shared and that creates a sense of group efficacy. That in turn will increase people's sense of wellbeing, safety, and security.

PP: So in this dawning era you're imagining, people will need to have skills that they can contribute to the group. Will it also mean that some of the skills and talents valued in modern Western culture—like those that make the capitalist go-getter—might become obsolete?

230

RDY: Certainly there still will be those individuals with specialized skills in finance or legal skills or management that they can sell to those who need them. But for the vast majority of people, I think that the future is going to look very different. One of the things we've done over the last two hundred years is to "de-skill society" by encouraging individuals and households to specialize. We each become very effective but at a narrow range of tasks. We then need to earn enough money to buy the services of someone else to do the things that, once, everyone knew how to do. Specialization has served most citizens of modern society very well during a period of industrial growth.

But if we're entering a de-industrialization, resource-descent period, it's likely we're going to have to reskill ourselves. And if specialization emphasizes efficiency, then reskilling, essentially becoming a generalist, emphasizes proficiency: a large number of things a person can do well, maybe not up to world-class performance, but enough to meet the challenges of daily life.

PP: Give me some examples of what you mean by "reskilling."

RDY: Reskilling fairs are popping up across the country, where people are learning how to save seeds for their own gardening, farming, and seed banks. Or they're learning how to grow food or crops when the weather is unpredictable; or how to create a natural watering scheme, rather than just turning the tap on, because in some places access to water is going to be difficult. There's a huge explosion in the food-fermenting and food-preservation industry—and not just for beer or wine, but for food preservation. CSA and farmer-incubator programs are attracting students who want to become farmers. I'm giving mainly food examples but in fact reskilling involves a large range of household, neighborhood, and community tasks.

PP: Can you say more about how the "reskilling" of Americans will draw out our more community-oriented side?

RDY: Take local CSAs, in which individuals buy a share from farmers for a portion of their production. Jointly, these CSA members provide the upfront capital needed in the spring to buy the seeds and other farming inputs. They also assume some of the risk of farming. So if there's a drought, it's not only the farmer who suffers, everyone involved will get a little less in their weekly share. This way, the farmers are more secure and their life is more predictable. This in turn contributes to a more stable and vibrant local economy. CSA also gets people thinking about their investments, not just in terms of how they will benefit personally, but how others around them might also benefit.

In teaching about this, I like to use the notion of "the well-fed neighbor." It's in my best interest, for example, that my neighbors are well fed. If they're not hungry, they're not likely to become desperate. And if they're not desperate there may be less suffering and fear. But this notion is about more than just food. It's also in my best interest to live in a community surrounded by people who are not only physically well fed and secure, but also emotionally and spiritually well fed.

This is a very different way of life from the way we live now. It challenges the simple notion of "self-interest." What's in my own self-interest could be understood to be just about what I have. This narrow form of self-interest is very personal and internal, and perhaps borders on being self-indulgent or selfish. But self-interest can also be directed to another, or to the environment, or the community. This separates selfishness from self-interest.

PP: You almost seem to be saying that this coming "energy descent" and collapse of the industrial era has the potential to not only be more emotionally satisfying and fulfilling, it might even deepen our original democratic values.

RDY: Indeed, I am arguing *for* the end of an industrial lifestyle *and* I think it will collapse of its own weight. Industrial civilization is synonymous (to me) with a growth-based, consumption-focused, resource-intensive civilization, and that's simply not sustainable on a finite planet. This is what sustainability at its core is about—behaviors that are or become unsustainable will end.

At the same time, there is no guarantee that as industrial civilization ends, the transition to a post-industrial society will happen seamlessly. We may have so de-skilled ourselves in providing and handling the basic necessities of life, and remain so mentally embedded in an industrial lifestyle, that the transition will be harder than it needs to be.

But if we are able to make it through these hard times, we may be the happier for it. As psychologists and researchers are becoming more aware, the human mind may not have evolved to deal with affluence very well. Just look at the levels of inequity and angst, the lack of clarity, and the rampant anxiety. A lot of the diseases that we catalog might not be as prevalent in a society that's living much more simply.

PP: Are you also talking about the psychological effects of affluence, like depression?

RDY: Certainly, not all depression is attributable to affluence. But hyper-growth, hyper-materialism, and hyper-individualism are not healthy for the human spirit: our minds did not evolve to deal with these things well. William James famously said that thinking is designed for doing. The need to become more involved in everyday provisioning—in all the many definitions of that word—may actually be what the human mind is prepared for. So the coming resource and energy descent, and the eventuality of hard, lean times, may bring out the very best in people.

However, in order to avoid what could be a painful transition, I'd like to help people to become more aware of what's coming. The idea of pre-familiarization is to help people to pre-adapt their lifestyles, thinking, expectations, language, stories, and metaphors to a leaner life, so when that leaner life does inevitably arise they might not even notice it. It might seem like nothing much has really changed.

PP: People who have "pre-adapted" would also be in a position to serve others.

RDY: Right: they could be both models during the learning process and mentors during the actual transition. And they would be accomplishing this while knowing that it's bringing out the best in themselves as individuals, and bringing out the best in those they're working with. Very little empirical research is being done on the psychological aspects of this, but what work is being done suggests that people's sense of mental wellbeing increases as they reskill themselves and become broadly proficient. The problem is that the effect is very subtle; it's not something you can take to the bank, so to speak.

PP: What are the ways that you model this kind of "pre-adaptive" behavior in your personal life?

RDY: People at a party are more likely to talk about a stock purchase they made, or the big screen television they bought. If they're a professor like I am, they might mention the latest grant they got from NIH. They're less likely to talk about the blueberry jam they made last weekend, or what vegetable is in season this week. So when people ask me what I've been up to at a party, I talk about the Brussels sprouts we found at the farmers market, the tomato jam we made, or the garden bed my grandson helped me plant.

PP: So in a metaphorical sense you're like a Johnny Appleseed, seeding the population with these new ideas around a new way of living. There's a scarcity of imagination on this topic, and the old ways we've lived by have exhausted themselves.

RDY: I like this comparison, because Johnny Appleseed is an old American story. A "Wall Street" or "Goldman Sachs" version of this story would have had Johnny planting his own field behind a fence, and collecting his apples and selling them at the market. But he didn't. He shared his life with neighbors and with people he didn't even know. That's a story we celebrate as part of the American spirit.

Another American myth is the struggle of the underdog. For this reason, one of the stories I like to tell is about the rise of the local food movement, which is only about twenty years old. In the beginning, it was a grassroots, underfunded, underdog phenomenon, and received no help from corporations or governments. Until recently, the U.S. Department of Agriculture provided no support for local food production. Local industries got their county health departments to shut down the sale of certain products at farmers markets because of health regulations, even when the same products could be sold in the supermarket. The new Transatlantic Trade and Investment Partnership (TTIP) contains anti-local elements.[4] So there is an actual fight against the localization trend, and yet the local food movement is continuing to grow.

I also think the green citizen in America is the underdog. Nobody advocates for us; we have no rights. But if industrial civilization is at risk, then we'd better start developing more green citizens.

PP: I would also think that the "can do" spirit that is so quintessentially American would also come into play as we make the leap to a new kind of environmental lifestyle.

RDY: Yes, and there's also that American "against-all-the-odds" attitude. It comes out during natural disasters when people don't stand around waiting for the government to come and repair the destruction, but immediately get to work helping each other.

This against-all-the-odds attitude also goes against the conventional standpoint that we're supposed to accept the role we've been given, and to sit and wait to be told what to do. We're supposed to be consumers, and others will decide for us how the system is to work. By contrast, the underdog, self-reliant stance says, "No, *we* get to decide that. *We* get to choose who produces what we consume and to demand the features we want." Being a green citizen also means choosing *not* to consume: the "no action" alternative. So it's an underdog spirit of self-reliance, and a can-do American attitude that will help us pre-adapt to this coming resource descent.

PP: So in closing, say you have America on your therapist's couch, and you're getting ready to wind up your session on this issue. What would be some parting words?

RDY: One of the mistakes we make in confronting environmental and resource crises is that we try to help people through it by easing their transition. All too often, we try to soothe everyone's pain, maintain their comfort level, and keep things convenient. The advice I give is to not let experts and leaders do that to you, and to not do that to other people. Because in fact, I think life is more satisfying when we face the reality of how hard it is to live well on this finite and often fragile planet. The difficulties and the pain and the confusion aren't something to avoid: they're things to get help in dealing with.

PP: Because as you've been saying, although the transition may be hard, a more pleasurable and meaningful new way of life may be awaiting us.

RDY: Yes. Life is going to be extremely meaningful *because* it will be hard, not in spite of that fact. It's going to be psychologically rewarding not because it will be easy, but because our day-to-day choices will have consequences. So it will be in the challenges that we will reap the rewards. Satisfaction and contentment won't come from avoiding the problem of diminishing resources, but will be derived from successfully confronting and embracing these limitations.

We must accept that our future will be attained through resourcefulness and humility, not by the consumptive growth and boosterism that gave us our fling with material affluence. ∎

Notes

1. Localization Papers: Some Psychological Aspects of Responsibility to Emerging Biophysical Limits by Raymond De Young, Ph.D., personal website <http://www-personal.umich.edu/~rdeyoung/>.

2. See introduction to this chapter, n. 2. And also "IPCC Climate Change Report: Averting Catastrophe Is Eminently Affordable," by Damian Carrington, *Guardian*, April 13, 2014.

3. Midgley, Mary "Toward a New Understanding of Human Nature: The Limits of Individualism." How Humans Adapt: A Biocultural Odyssey (pp. 1–24), Seventh International Smithsonian Symposium. Smithsonian Institution: Washington, D.C., 1981.

4. The Anti-Localization Agenda in TTIP," by Karen Hansen-Kuhn. Published by the Institute for Agriculture and Trade Policy. See <http://www.resilience.org/stories/2014-05-05/the-anti-localization-agenda-in-ttip>.

—18—

The Archetype of Waste

AN INTERVIEW WITH STEPHEN J. FOSTER, PH.D., M.A.

S TEPHEN J. FOSTER'S WORK as a Jungian analyst healing the wounded psyches of modern-day individuals is uniquely paralleled by his position as a trained scientist. For more than thirty years, Foster has been employed in the field of environmental human health and risk assessment, evaluating cleanup levels for Superfund and hazardous waste sites in the U.S. and around the world. In addition to his private practice as an analyst, Foster continues to maintain an environmental consulting firm in Boulder, Colorado. The parallel between the havoc wreaked by unconscious psychic waste on individuals' lives with the destructive effects of toxic industrial waste on the planet was not lost on me, and after reading Foster's book *Risky Business: A Jungian View of Environmental Disasters and the Nature Archetype*, I was eager to interview him for both his technical expertise and his depth psychological perspective on the ongoing environmental crisis.

Foster's personal connection to nature was forged as a young boy growing up in the small village of Bodiam in rural East Sussex, England. Though most people aren't familiar with the name of his village, he told me, they are familiar with its famous Norman castle, with its "traditional four round turrets, four square turrets, and a moat." A small river flows through Bodiam, and it was on its banks that Foster spent solitary time as a child. This early exposure outdoors, he said, "imprinted the value of the natural experience in my psyche and led to a desire to be connected to nature throughout my life." Foster's pattern of combining career interests also began at an early age. After getting his Ph.D. in organic chemistry, he shifted to post-doctoral work in toxicology, followed by a second post-doctoral study in cancer research at the Harvard School of Public Health. Simultaneously, he worked at the Harvard School of Law, examining the resolution of scientific and technical disputes using the risk assessment process.

In the late 1980s, inspired by his wife, who is a Jungian analyst, Foster became interested in the work of Jung and how his "depth psychology could add so much perspective in so many areas." So valuable did Jung's work become to Foster that eventually he decided to become an analyst himself. A resident of the U.S. for more than thirty-three years and a citizen, Foster feels that America, with its talent for innovation and new ideas, has greater potential to address environmental problems than many other countries. Although our awareness around the environment hasn't yet reached a critical point, once that happens, he believes, "things will really start to change. As people start to make the connection between climate change and human behavior, light bulbs go on, and they make shifts to a different psychological level, and a different way of life. So it's an exciting time to live, because, hopefully, I don't think we're too far away from that point. But with climate change, that awareness about our impact on the planet needs to happen very soon."

In the following interview, conducted in August 2014, Foster describes nature's power to cleanse and heal our psyches; the archetype of "waste" within and without; how we suffer the effects of environmental destruction in our dreams; and how learning to hold the "tensions of the opposites" between nature and civilization might offer humankind a new path forward.

✳

Pythia Peay: One of the things that really leapt off the page for me while reading your book was the idea of how simply being in nature can have a cleansing and restorative effect on the human psyche. Can you say more about that?

Stephen J. Foster: Even the most ordinary ways of being in nature can be very restorative to the human psyche. As a child, I used to love to sit on a riverbank and watch the kingfisher birds fish among the bulrushes. It was such a simple moment, but it was an example of how we can become so engaged with nature that we lose ourselves; we dissolve into nature. Many people have experienced the effect of that kind of dissolution; it's almost as if it cleans and heals our psyches. It's an experience that lies at the core of our living connection to nature.

PP: Your insight about how nature cleans our psyches has an added dimension, given the work you've done over the years cleaning up Superfund sites.

SJF: Looking back, I don't think I realized at the time the unconscious psychological drive behind my work. Since becoming an analyst, it's become much more apparent to me that I was driven by a desire to restore nature—just as nature had helped to restore my psyche.

PP: In what ways did your work on those Superfund sites change your relationship to the environment?

SJF: I became very interested in the idea of how we as humans value the environment. At its core, risk assessment is the process whereby we not only calculate what kinds of chemical risks we're exposed to, we're also required to communicate those risks to the public. So in a way it's a tool by which we measure and value the environment. And how we make these risk assessments is essentially how we in modern society balance industrial costs against human health and the health of the environment, or the needs of industry versus the needs of the public.

PP: I was also interested to learn from your book about the psychological and archetypal dimensions of pollution and dumping. You make the intriguing parallel between the environmental waste that we unconsciously dump into the earth, and the "waste" in our psyches, or the shadow material that people process in therapy and other kinds of inner work. You even write that waste is an archetype, which you've devoted your life to exploring.

I don't think I've ever considered the fact that humans have always been dumping waste into Earth—and that the Earth has taken that on as her role—but that now because the waste is so poisonous, and there are so many of us, it's endangering life itself.

SJF: Yes, it's fascinating to realize that as human beings we've always "externalized," or made visible in the outer world, our waste. As we've become more civilized over the centuries, we've developed processes for managing those wastes. For example, it's only in recent history that we've been able to develop waste-water treatment plants that will actually remove the toxic elements before we reintroduce water back into the natural environment.

But the problem is that as humanity has progressed, we've failed to develop the corresponding psychological awareness that we can't dump plastic into the ocean and expect the ocean to take care of it. We've now reached the point where we've produced so many material goods the environment simply cannot destroy them in the period of one or two or even many lifetimes. And because we haven't developed our psychological awareness around how to deal with our waste, we're creating an environment where our children and grandchildren will now have to deal with the problems that we're unconsciously creating for them.

PP: Does seeing waste as an archetype, and as part of the natural processes of life, help us to cultivate more environmental awareness?

SJF: Whether it's in the outer world, where we recycle material goods or food scraps and yard waste back into composts that can be used as fertilizer; or whether it's inside our minds, where we're constantly engaged in reprocessing psychological "waste material" into new ideas and re-imagining ways of seeing things; or as a physiological process in our bodies, recycling proteins and amino acids, we're constantly engaged in some form of reusing and recycling.

PP: That's very inspiring in the way it vastly expands our ideas of waste. So often we think of waste and recycling as something unnatural and distasteful, rather than a part of nature and all life.

SJF: Humans have always found ways to recycle those things that are important. Because, at its core, recycling is a way of taking back part of the energy we've put into things. A practical example of that is the use of pure aluminum for computer parts. It's expensive to process aluminum from ore, but it's much cheaper to use pure waste aluminum from cans and other industrial processes and recycle that back into computer parts. So obviously, the more we can do that, not only will we use less energy as a society, the more we will break waste products down into components that can be reused. And if we can begin to help the country realize that there's value to recycling in saved energy, saved processing time, and saved hydrocarbons, we may in fact be able to save the environment.

Recycling may also help us psychologically in addressing the widespread sense of malaise we're seeing now around our direction as a society.

PP: How would it address that malaise?

SJF: Ultimately, humans like to live in environments that are pleasing to the eye and to the soul. It just doesn't feel good to see plastic bottles or pop cans littering the natural landscape. But we're not really that aware of the impact environmental destruction can have on the psyche.

PP: Have you seen that impact appear in the dreams of your clients? And if so, is nature speaking to us through our dreams?

SJF: That's a good question. It's through our dreams that the unconscious is trying to bring something to our attention, as something for us to explore: What are we not aware of? What is the ego unconsciously avoiding, or trying to not see or look at? What is the unconscious trying to get across to us? And although there are many kinds of dreams, it's interesting to me that all dreams take place in some kind of environment. So I think we're always dreaming within the nature archetype, but especially so when we have these "outside" nature dreams.

Often it's the case that people who dream about nature are connected to it in a very deep way. So if they have a dream where there is some form of environmental waste or damage, it can be interpreted collectively, in terms of how that problem in the outer world is actually affecting them psychologically in the inner world of their psyche. These kinds of nature dreams are also a good place to start exploring people's unconscious, shadow relationships with the environment. For example, many of us are blind to the ongoing destruction in the natural world. So in dreams this might be represented as waste material that is polluting their psyches. And what is that trying to represent? Their own denied or repressed complexes around what we as humans are doing to the environment—a realization that we're unable to accept on a conscious level.

At the same time, images in dreams of uncontained waste, dumping, or contamination may also represent personal psychological issues or problems.

PP: So what kind of psychological issue might show up in dreams as images of waste or pollution? Say, for example, that I had a dream of an oil spill. How would you make that link between the personal and the outer world of nature?

SJF: That's a good example, because during the BP Gulf oil spill in 2010,[1] many of my clients had oil-spill dreams that they related to the images on television. So obviously, as Jung hypothesized, these kinds of dreams reveal the way we're all connected to nature through the collective unconscious. But in boring down and asking clients about their personal connections to the oil spill, they made associations to feeling as if they themselves were also covered in an oily substance that they couldn't remove, no matter what they did. So they related the imagery of the oil spill to some personal issue they were struggling with.

Another theme that was quite common around that time was the issue of fouling. This was brought up by images of pelicans and cormorants fouled and covered in oil. Psychologically, this corresponded to ways they felt that they had been fouled or contaminated in their personal lives or in their surroundings.

PP: So do these kinds of dreams reveal a kind of reciprocity between what's going on in the environment and what's going on within our psyches—and how we're also being affected by climate change? We see ourselves as separate from nature, but really we're nature, too, and so our ways of living show how we're disconnected from nature and suffering from this environmental problem as well.

SJF: I would agree with that, but I would take that even one step further. The core theme these nature dreams bring up is the idea that we are part of nature. But the ego doesn't necessarily see things that way. There are many people who see themselves in a much more concrete way, and as more separate from nature. And it's that very separation from nature that can cause unconscious psychological discomfort.

PP: In fact, I had an interesting dream last night that I thought I might share with you, and that I thought might be my psyche trying to instruct me in advance of this interview. In the dream, I was in a psychology clinic. People were dressed in white coats, busily running around with files in their hands. In the very center of this building was a cage that held a very large tiger. It was very distressed, and was raging and roaring against the bars, trying to break out.

In working with the dream, I could see how it related to me personally. As I try to finish this book, I've been working very hard, sitting at my desk all day in front of my computer and sometimes not even getting outside. So I could see how my own physical, animal nature was in an uproar. But I also saw the dream as the way we as modern humans look at nature as something apart from us, something that we've imprisoned. But what are your thoughts on this dream?

SJF: I think that the dream the way you described it was a great source of insight into your personal connection to your own "nature" at this moment. But if we were to look at this dream from a larger perspective, with the idea that you were having that dream for all of us, it reveals the clinical, scientific attitude we all have toward nature. We have a fear of untamed nature, and so we want to keep it behind bars where we can study it and keep it contained, just the way we have zoos for wild animals—another frequent image in dreams.

But just as the tiger in the cage is roaring against its captivity, so nature is roaring at us. It's angry, and it doesn't want to be caged any longer. So I think the tiger in your dream could be interpreted as nature roaring back at us through changing patterns of weather, and through the ferocity of the storms in winter and summer. If you've ever been close to a hurricane or a tornado, the sound they make could be described as a loud roar. And although it might be necessary to continue to study nature, it's important not to forget its living strength and incredible ferocity.

PP: So beautifully said. How do you work with clients to allow their own "tiger out of the cage"?

SJF: We've been talking back and forth on two levels here. There's that level where we personally connect with nature within ourselves, and then there is the collective level where we are all trying to break through that schism between our inner selves and the outer world of nature.

And I think it's the same problem. If we work to connect more with nature within, my hope is that would in turn transform how we deal with nature in a practical sense. We can experience nature everywhere, even in a city. I just returned from New York, where I visited Central Park, and I was stunned at how—if we set aside our ego—we can in fact connect to nature very easily. It's really a question of turning the ego away from that constant stream of internal thoughts around what's going on with our day, or with our family, or our work, and of being present with nature itself, allowing it to wash into us, and of respecting the value of what we're seeing and experiencing.

PP: What I find interesting about your work is the way you bring together science with a depth psychological perspective. In fact, you write about uniting the opposites of science and myth. Most of us don't think of these two things as having anything to do with each other. Could you say more about the links between science and myth?

SJF: Actually, science and myth are not so different. They are each ways of trying to understand and explain the human experience. It is important, however, to separate science from technology—because technology is a way of taking science and using it for the benefit of society. But science is about learning how things work; and that is much more consistent with the idea of myth.

To explain further, scientific theory starts out as a story constructed from basic thoughts and ideas in order to explain what scientists are seeing. And in fact, science is wrong most of the time. Scientists put out a hypothesis, and then they have these fantasies and ideas—essentially a myth—about what is actually going on. Then when they actually get results back that either deny or confirm their hypothesis, they have to go back and revise their hypothesis, or "myth." So the idea that science is correct and knows what it's doing is not really the case. Because when science is being done at a core level, people are wrong and incorrect most of the time, and are constantly revising their theories and thoughts around the way that things work.

That process is no different than looking at a myth about how the world was formed, and then comparing that to a geological structure and gauging whether the myth got it right or not. So science is disproving itself all the time. In fact, if it's any good, that's what it *should* be doing. So at that core level, I don't see much of a discrepancy between science and myth.

PP: Science also provides a source of mythic narrative. I know that you were inspired by J. R. R. Tolkien's book *The Silmarillion*. Could you say more about why that book was so important to you, from an environmental perspective?

SJF: Tolkien's love of nature was quite profound. His books came out of his own personal background in World War I and the horror he saw there. But they also came out of the destruction of the English countryside as rural England was consumed by industrialization. So I was fascinated by the way Tolkien interpreted that material into *The Hobbit* and *The Lord of the Rings*, but in particular *The Silmarillion*, a collection of stories that describes the lands within which his other books take place.

My own interpretation of this work is that when a particular culture or society possesses something of high value and great beauty that is very important to it, and then experiences the loss of that possession, it will then try to go back and recapture those things of high value and preserve them.

PP: Obviously, through the work you've done on Superfund sites, you've assisted in the restoration and preservation of places that have been blighted by toxic waste. Can you describe how going out to these sites felt personally, on an emotional level?

SJF: There's such an irony to this work. Some of the most beautiful places I have ever seen are in fact Superfund sites, in this country and abroad. Let me explain what I mean. Many of these Superfund sites have been sealed off for many years; people can't go there because they can be quite hazardous. But the fact that they've been sealed off, un-impacted by human activity, often for many years, has allowed nature to come back into those locations. One of the largest stands of blackberries I've ever seen was actually at a Superfund site, because there was no one to pick them and nothing to impact them. All the birds and mammals had moved back in, so nature was really doing its thing. As a result, many of these sites have been turned into parks, nature preserves, or wildlife viewing areas. Inadvertently, we've gone back and created these environments that are quite well preserved.

So the idea that every hazardous waste site is dangerous is not true, and that's where the risk assessment process comes in. On the other side of the coin, I've witnessed some of the most extreme devastation. I've visited mine sites where there's no vegetation, and that look as barren as moonscapes. It can have quite an impact.

PP: Can you say what the impact was?

SJF: Well, it's like how you'd imagine Mordor[2] when you read about it in Tolkien's trilogy, or when you see it in the movies. The taste of sulfur dioxide left over from smelting activities is in the air. There are no plants, there's no water; it's just a completely dry, arid, barren landscape, in reality and in the psyche.

PP: I've explored this topic from various angles with other psychologists, but I'd like to get your Jungian perspective on how we defend against these kinds of feelings in response to environmental degradation. In your book you write about Jung's concept of the "tension of the opposites" as a helpful framework in integrating and dealing with climate change.

SJF: I've thought about this quite a lot. If we look at things using Freudian language, it's easy to see that we develop defenses, denial, or resistances against seeing the damage that we're causing. Climate change in this country is still resisted. But even if we refuse to accept the idea of climate change, the reality is that our environment is changing, and that is changing our lives.

A good example that brings climate change home to America is French Fries. The potatoes used to make French Fries grow best at cooler temperatures. But because of climate change, growers are being forced to move further and further north in order to satisfy the ever-increasing need for French Fries in this country and in other countries. So whether people believe in climate change or not, the reality is that industry, and particularly the agricultural industry, is being forced to respond to an environment that's changing.

From a psychological perspective, the Jungian approach of the "tension of the opposites" can be useful, because it allows us to come to a reconciliation point. Jung's idea was that rather than repress one side or the other (whether of a personal problem or a political issue) it's important to learn to hold that tension between the two opposites. This can be very difficult to do, and often that's where our systems shut down. And when we can't hold the tension, we side, as Jung said, with one pole or the other. But that's when nothing happens. So we go back to living a life that is quite one-sided, because it's extremely painful to deal with the feeling of being overwhelmed.

So when we apply this "tension of the opposites" to our cultural complex around the environment, on one side we all like and value nature, and some of us are trying our best to preserve nature. But on the other end of this pole, most of us live in towns and cities that have requirements for progress, in the form of material goods. So if we could find a way to hold that tension between nature and industrialization, if we could try to recognize in a conscious way that we live in this world where this tension exists, then perhaps, as Jungian theory suggests, a third or a new element could emerge, and we could find a way to move forward.

PP: What would be an example of a "third way" that could show us the direction to take through this maze of an environmental problem?

SJF: For example, every year the Earth gets a year's worth of sunlight. At the moment we're supplementing all of that unconverted solar energy with energy that was around on the Earth back in the time of the dinosaur. But if we could open to this idea as a collective group, and convert to solar energy—and thus convert a year's worth of energy to a year of usable energy on the planet—then we could in fact sustain life without having to go back and use energy that was stored up in the dinosaur era.

PP: I don't think I've ever heard solar energy explained in that way: that we have a year's worth of energy from the sun. It's a very vivid image.

SJF: What you've said is interesting, as it brings up the importance of the image. Jung was very big on working with images as they come up in dreams and in other kinds of inner work. It might be useful, for instance, for individuals to come up with their own images of the environment; it would be one way of cutting through a lot of the denial. Then we could in fact begin to relate on a very personal level on how to hold this tension between nature and civilization, and to imagine some third way forward. For many people, for example, the image of the polar bear floating on an ice floe in the Arctic was an image of something extremely valuable that we will be losing at some point soon.

PP: One of the things you wrote about was the idea of the environmental hero, and the incredible acts of courage on the part of many activists who've challenged what you call the "wolf of industry."

SJF: Yes, there have been many extraordinary examples of activist heroes. But as I've also learned, industry itself is not always necessarily bad. There are companies, in fact, that are environmentally responsible. I've worked with some, and they've been very amenable to taking responsibility for whatever needs to be done in order to take care of whatever damage they've caused. So there are some industries that are very good at this—and then of course there are some that are not so good.

So I think it could also be said that the unsung heroes of environmental change are the heroes *within* those industries that are changing. We don't hear, for instance, about the people inside the boardroom calling for environmental concerns to be brought to the board level and integrated into the way their industry operates. These are the CEOs who are advocating for recycling at source; that is, reusing raw or partially processed materials, preventing them from ever becoming wastes. Not only would their companies save money because they wouldn't have to dump as much, they would in fact be saving more materials that they could reuse. So the people who are thinking this way within industry are also playing a very important role.

PP: As you've described it, these industries are making changes as a way to save costs. Is the way to the American soul on the environment through money?

SJF: I'm not sure it's strictly a money issue, although it is very important in America. If it can be shown that there is an economic reason to do something, then it's much more likely to gain traction, than if it's simply the right thing to do. But the right thing to do does in fact influence a lot of people. It's just easier sometimes to respond to shareholders on the level of money. The way corporations are structured, they have mechanisms for responding to financial concerns, but they don't necessarily have a mechanism for responding to doing the right thing. They cannot account for the moral value of taking action versus inaction. Many CEOs might feel that if it were up to them personally, they would take a more environmental course of action— because it would improve the quality of life for their children and grandchildren. But again, that's an example of how holding this "tension of the opposites" on the environment on a personal level can be very, very difficult.

However, as a psychologist who works with individuals in therapy, I think that if people could deal more consciously with that inner split between industry and the environment by making recommendations that are not strictly based on financial outcome, but on the right thing to do in both a financial and a moral sense, they might begin to heal that split—within themselves, and so within the culture.

PP: Even as we were talking, I suddenly felt a twinge of guilt, because on a daily level all of us, like corporations, are faced with that conflict. For example, I know what it's like to go to the store and not always be able to afford to buy an organic product, even though I want to. Or I don't make it to the farmers market in time to buy my weekly vegetables. So is this an example on an individual level of that "tension between the opposites"?

SJF: Yes, that's exactly right. You've stated exactly what I think we all feel. And in fact, if we can all consciously feel that, then we can gain insight into how we experience the environmental problem for ourselves. Many people have no choice but to drive to work, which is not good for the environment. But not everyone can afford a car that doesn't burn gas. So you've exactly identified the split that I think we all face on this issue. And if we can face that split and hold that tension without siding one way or the other, then it brings the problem *inside*, as opposed to projecting it outside onto politicians or industries who we think ought to do this, or do that— that's essentially maintaining the split.

PP: So by doing this inner work of holding the tensions of the opposites, it really brings environmental issues home to the individual—to *me*. And so local is not even my local city, it's the localized, individual way in which I make my daily choices.

SJF: Local is as simple as where I put my garbage. And the idea that we can act locally is really where I think the environmental movement needs to go or is already going. And that will actually have a much bigger impact, not only locally where a person lives, but globally. It will also force corporate organizations to think locally, generate energy locally, and break everything down to a point where they can be composted or recycled locally. ■

Notes

1. The Deep Water Oil Spill, or BP Oil Spill, of April 20, 2010 is to date the largest accidental marine oil spill in the history of the petroleum industry. It caused extensive damage to marine and wildlife habitats, and fishing and tourism industries.
2. In Tolkien's fictional universe of the *Lord of the Rings*, Mordor was the desolate volcanic landscape ruled by the evil Sauron.

—19—

Hungry and Homeless—Like the Bees

An Interview with Bonnie Bright, Ph.D.

APPLES, BROCCOLI, BRAZIL NUTS, lemons, kidney beans, tomatoes, grapes, plums, peaches: pollinated by the honeybee, all these foods and more flow to us from Earth's cornucopia. Without nature's amber-striped, gold-winged provider, the human species would be faced with spare pickings, as one out of three bites of food comes from a crop pollinated by honeybees. So in 2006, when reports began to trickle in about a mysterious decline in honeybee populations around the world, alarm rippled throughout the environmental community. Many scientific studies have since linked bee declines to pesticide use, specifically a group of insecticides called neonicotinoids.[1] As honeybees and other pollinators make their regular rounds collecting pollen and nectar from plants—a rite of nature rendered into art and myth over the centuries as sweet and hallowed as honey itself—they are exposed to toxic chemicals that damage their immune systems, and to parasites that impair their memory and navigation systems.[2] Disoriented, the honeybees lose their way back to their hives, abandoning their communities and giving rise to the phenomenon now called "Colony Collapse Disorder" or CCD. The ongoing massive die-off of the honeybee is a part of climate change that literally hits us in the gut: for there can be no human species without food.

To Bonnie Bright, who earned her Ph.D. in depth psychology at Pacifica Graduate Institute in Santa Barbara, and who is the founder of the Depth Psychology Alliance,[3] the bee disaster strikes humanity in yet another personal way: that place, and that idea, we call *home*. In her dissertation, she linked the honeybees' CCD to the wider, ongoing "Culture Collapse Disorder": the loss of human connection to nature, evidenced in part by the disappearance of the natural habitat that has sustained humans and animals over time, resulting in a "wounded relationship between culture and nature that has affected our modern mindset," and that in turn has weakened humanity's ancient and archetypal sense of 'home.'" Her research, Bright says, "examines our own relationship as a culture to home, and draws some interesting and even frightening parallels to what's happening to the bees—and what could potentially happen to our culture if we're unable to make some profound changes." Even since our interview in late 2013, in fact, new studies have emerged identifying those American cities that might provide safe haven from the ravages of climate change, and those areas that will either dry up from desertification, or be flooded by superstorms and rising seas.[4]

Raised on a farm in southern Idaho, where she grew up among bee-filled alfalfa fields, Bright came to psychology as a second career. Employed in the corporate world for many years, she enjoyed her work. But in 2005, Bright began to feel that something was missing. Taking time off, she quickly discovered depth psychology, where she felt "immediately at home," and began a master's program at Sonoma State University in Northern California. After earning her degree, she pursued her doctorate at Pacifica Graduate Institute. Since she launched into depth psychology, she told me, her life "has not been the same. It was a baptism by fire: I went from having just briefly heard of Jung to jumping in and embarking on a deep personal search and a new career."

In the following interview we range from the scientific underpinnings of the honeybee die-off to Bright's empathic imaginings of the suffering felt by the honeybee that can't find its way back to the hive before dark. We explore the parallels between the contamination of the bees and the contamination of our own psyches by our environmentally polluted ways of life. We examine psychological behaviors she calls "eco-apathy" and "eco-psychopathy," which blunt us to our own species' looming dislocation and possible extinction; and the representation of the bee in mythology as a symbol of the soul.

✳

Pythia Peay: What was it that first drew you to research bees from a Jungian and depth psychological perspective: was it Colony Collapse Disorder (CCD), or was there something more, something archetypal about the bee itself?

Bonnie Bright: It was through Colony Collapse Disorder, and the sheer unnaturalness of the situation of the bees just vanishing. There are a lot of exotic species going extinct, and I feel deeply about that. But bees are so common, and whether we see them or not, they touch our lives one way or another every single day. So the mystery of their disappearance was a very powerful event for me, as it has been for a lot of people.

We know now that the bees aren't vanishing: they're dying—and they're dying away from the hives. At the end of 2006 when Colony Collapse Disorder was first noted, beekeepers were checking their hives only to find that there were no bees except for the queen and a handful of her attendants. The stores of honey were still there, completely untouched, as well as the brood that was still developing. But the rest of the bees were gone. Strangely, in Colony Collapse Disorder, the worker bees not only abandon the hive, but the queen herself, who is the lifeblood of the hive, laying thousands of eggs a day. Even the other insects and animals that would normally take advantage of the opportunity to raid these abandoned hives won't touch the honey.

PP: According to your research, what's behind this massive die off of bees?

BB: In addition to mites and poor nutrition, pesticides that are commonly used on gardens, crops, and public parks—particularly neonicotinoids, which are *10,000 times* stronger than DDT[5]—are considered a strong factor. You'd think that after Rachel Carson's exposure of the dangers of DDT in the 1950s, we'd have learned something about the dangers of pesticides. But it seems that history still repeats itself.

PP: And behind these dangerous pesticides are big corporations, most of which have little to no concern for the honeybee that feeds humanity.

BB: Right. We live in a culture where corporations are king and where the most important thing is to keep consuming in order to keep the economy going. Globalization is also a challenge. Over the last few decades we've become so dependent on each other as a global economy that what happens here affects China, and what happens in China affects what happens in the European Union, and so on. One of the companies producing neonicotinoids, for example, is Bayer. But they can't afford to take responsibility, because if they did, their entire product line would collapse. At the same time, the power of globalization and technology has allowed people to become more informed about the environment and the dangers of pesticides in ways they've never been exposed to before. And this can help us begin to make our own decisions about pesticides. But although we can become more informed about the decisions we make, the bees have no choice!

There are at least two potential consequences to the bees due to these toxic pesticides. On one hand, honeybees are becoming disoriented due to the influence of toxins on their brains or nervous systems, affecting their ability to navigate. In addition, when they go out and forage for pollen as they have always done, and, if they *are* able to make it back, they bring pollen into the hives that's been contaminated by these powerful pesticides. As a result, the hives themselves are becoming contaminated, and then the bees instinctively can't or won't go home, leaving the hives virtually empty and abandoned. So it's a vicious cycle. More than likely there are other consequences, but one thing is certain: the honeybees usually can't survive if they don't return home to their hive by nightfall because when the temperatures drop at night, their wings can't work in the cold. And if the bees aren't returning, there's no way hives can survive.

PP: What happens to the bees when they're unable to go back to the hives? Where do they go? Do they just wander about? Do they die or find refuge somewhere?

BB: I don't honestly know. When bees die naturally, their bodies often pile up just outside the hives. The reason Colony Collapse Disorder is so often referred to as the "vanishing of the bees" is because although we know the bees are dying, many of them are dying dispersed and far removed from their hives. Even if there were thousands of bee bodies in a big field we'd probably never know they were there, because we couldn't see them.

But over time, since I began studying bees, I've seen hundreds of individual bees struggling and writhing around on the ground. The bee can't take off or fly, so she stumbles in circles and it's obvious she's in trouble; perhaps her navigation system has been destroyed by neonicotinoids. Also, it's virtually impossible for a bee to survive alone for more than a few short hours. She needs the community of her sister bees for food, shelter, protection, and warmth. Among other things, bees in hives fulfill a number of supporting roles for the ongoing wellbeing of the hive, including working together to make the hive warmer or cooler as needed.

This raises the idea of consciousness. Does the bee know what's happening? Bees are such intelligent and animated beings, I can't imagine they aren't aware of their own suffering. So in my own very visual and emotional fantasy, this lost bee quietly passes away during the night, by herself, alone. Unable to return to the hive, she dies completely disoriented, far away from her home and the warmth and companionship of other bees.

PP: The first thing that came to my mind as you were describing the exodus of homeless bees was the image of the refugees fleeing wartorn Syria.[6] Was it the suffering of refugees who've lost their homelands that led you to explore the connection between the bees' CCD and what you're calling "Cultural Collapse Disorder"?

BB: Yes. As I did my research, I began to reflect more deeply on states of isolation, and those feelings of being cut off and unable to return to one's home place—that sacred place where all life is sustained and renewed. So in addition to studying CCD from the perspective of the bees, and from an environmental perspective, I began to think that we also needed to look at this issue from an inner psychological and spiritual level. Jung said that when an inner situation is not made conscious, it happens outside as an event. There's a constant cycling of interaction between our inner world of emotion, ethos, and meaning, and the outer world around us.

PP: So are you saying that just as the honeybees and their hives are being contaminated by pesticides, our psyches are being damaged by the effects of environmental destruction?

BB: What's happening to the planet is affecting all of us. Some of us may be more consciously aware of this than others. But even if what's happening to the oceans, the rivers, the animals, and the forests is unconscious and under the surface of our awareness, it's still having a massive psychological effect. For the first time in our history we're starting to see data that we may actually face collapse as a human race.[7] And how can that not affect us?

I recently read an interview with James Hillman in which he said that when a person passes a place where ground is being cleared for new development, their body registers the loss of the trees and plants at a somatic level. So just as the bees are unknowingly taking these harmful neurotoxins back home to their hives—just doing what they're meant to do in the process of foraging for nectar and pollen—we are all unwittingly contaminating our psyches by living culturally condoned lifestyles that are largely destructive and for which we lack conscious recognition or responsibility for what we're doing to the planet.

PP: I experienced that recently when I was out for a walk in my neighborhood. I passed by a house being torn down, along with all the old, tall trees that had surrounded it. I felt a physical pain that these majestic trees had been so brutally ripped from the ground. So I can see that if more of us were talking about these kinds of feelings, it might lead to more environmental sensitivity. But you seem to also be saying that when I walk by a lot where the trees have been cut down, or a park that's been built over by a shopping mall, it's also an indication of our own "Colony Collapse" or "Culture Collapse Disorder."

BB: I would say yes. There's a profound psychological displacement occurring around the destruction of our home places. It's like the correlation you made between the disoriented, homeless bees and the Syrian refugees. Whether one is a refugee because of war and violence; or whether it's through the destruction of our physical home environment; or through other effects of global climate change like desertification, where herders are no longer able to stay in the same place because they can't find water or grow food—our entire culture is being physically and psychologically displaced.

It's been a long process, but we just don't have the same kind of roots that we once had in days gone by. But without that grounding and that sense of home and place, how can we begin to orient ourselves to the world? Again, it's like the bees: if the bees can't go home to their hives, the hive cannot exist. But if the hive doesn't exist, then the bees will die.

PP: So just as the bees are oriented to their natural environment through their hives, humans are grounded to the earth through their homes?

BB: From an archetypal standpoint, home is very powerful. On a psychological and spiritual level a home place centers us around a sense of identity, safety, and wellbeing. Home is not only a place where we can find respite, it's also a place where we can be renewed and reconnect with whatever it is that sustains us in our lives. For some people, that means a physical home. Those who are wanderers have found a way to carry that sense of home or a sense of the sacred with them wherever they go.

PP: But there also seems to be a connection between home and a specific sense of place, a particular spot or geographical location.

BB: The psychological impact on refugees who've been displaced from their homes and homeland is very profound. For centuries, many people have lived their entire lives in the same place: their ancestors are buried there and they know the landmarks. In the Navajo culture, among others, an individual's umbilical cord is buried near the hogan where they are born, literally and symbolically establishing a connection to place.[8] Without a similar grounding, and that sense of home and place, how can we begin to orient ourselves to the world we live in? We know from indigenous peoples that their stories are all based on landmarks such as trees, boulders, and valleys. The songlines of the [Australian] Aborigines were based on landmarks; they would walk thousands of miles following the same paths that their ancestors had traversed and so knew exactly where to go because of their knowledge of the landscape. When the Native Americans were forcibly removed from their lands, it was absolutely devastating. Some of them never recovered from being removed from the land they'd lived on for centuries, because it was so fundamentally connected to their identity and history.

So without that connection to the land, and that sense of home, the Native Americans had no connection to themselves. The philosopher Edward S. Casey has written about how some Navajos simply disappeared after being displaced from their tribal lands. They just went away and were never seen or heard from again. Personally, I think a lot about my "home base": the house I live in, the land it's on, the community around me, and those things that are anchoring me on the planet.

PP: For all of America's emphasis on home and family, I don't think our modern culture gives much value to being rooted in a particular geographical place over time.

BB: Unfortunately, we've tried to find a sense of home by looking outside ourselves. And a big part of that is consuming. We're consuming products, services, and media at a rate that is unprecedented. Everything is about growth, and everything is compared to where we were last year, and how much more we can do this year. I feel strongly this is because we're not connected to nature and the Earth. If we had that sense of centeredness that comes from being in a home place, and an understanding that the Earth takes care of us in the same way we need to take care of the Earth, we might not be so addicted to things and driven to consume.

PP: This may be a stretch, but I wonder if you think there's a link between our culture's transiency and disconnection from being grounded in home and nature—and the rise of these random mass shootings?

BB: Absolutely. In my research I've found a spectrum of behaviors. On one end of the spectrum, there's what I call "eco-apathy," or the incapacity to look at what is happening to our planet. This has caused us to become split off and fragmented, because our psyches just don't have a way of dealing with this: our capacity to numb ourselves is quite profound. A part of this eco-apathy stems from the fact that there's no cultural framework with which to deal with these kinds of mass die-offs of species—including our own. A trauma scholar named Diana Taylor uses the word "percepticide"[9] to describe how some things are so horrible we can't bear to see them—or we would die. So we have to cut off our seeing, or it would literally mean the death of us.

Then in the middle of this spectrum, there's what can be referred to as being a passive bystander. We see what's going on, but we don't do anything about it; we might even treat it from a distance as entertainment. We see this every day on the media in all the stories about what's happening to the planet, but it's so overwhelming that all we can do is watch it. James Hillman once said that "the eye and the wound are the same." Often there's no differentiation between the "wound" of what's happening around the destruction of the environment and the person who is looking at this without an emotional response.

I see the periodic outbreaks of gun violence by young men as part of the spectrum that I call "eco-psychopathy." Part of eco-psychopathy is the fact that the tragedy of environmental destruction has been repressed to the point that eventually it's got to come out somewhere. Therefore, feelings of loss and a profound sense of isolation and fear can suddenly bubble up, causing these young people to enact the same kind of violent, destructive behavior humankind is perpetrating against nature. What is the future for these young men? The way they're being raised in our society, they often have almost no connection to the Earth or to natural life outside. They are out of balance with a larger, more meaningful context. But I feel that *all* young people—not just the ones who are going to extremes and committing violence—are finding ways to act out their loss of connection to something bigger than themselves.

PP: So you could say that many of our youth who are adrift are like the lost and disoriented bees, psychologically "infected" by the environmental tragedy unfolding around them, and unable to find their way back to a deeper sense of home and place.

BB: Exactly. They lack a connection to a bigger sense of home. Where is the sense of meaning for them, of belonging to and participating in a greater whole? Where is there a sense of the sacred? With no ground to stand on or people to talk to, youth can become so isolated they have nowhere to turn. And so what else can they do except lash out at the very culture and society which are responsible? I know, for example, that if I look into the eyes of an animal I'm going to glimpse something bigger than myself. This experience teaches me that humans are not at the top of a hierarchy where everything is subordinate to us. From that moment of connection to an animal we become but another animal in the web of life. And if young people and in fact all of us had that deep sense of knowing and connection, I truly believe we'd be in a very different place in the world. But the problem is that we don't have a shared framework of cultural understanding to help us connect to the planet in that sacred way.

PP: Perhaps this is too extremist a thing to say, but when it comes to the vanishing of the honeybees, the abuse of animals in industrial agriculture, and the poisoning of the environment, I often wonder why we don't use words like the *Holocaust* or *slavery*.

BB: This is the question of the day. I think it's important that we talk about it, and also why we *aren't* talking about it. Recent research into the brain validates what we've suspected for a long time: human beings are very self-centered. Our instinct for self-preservation comes from the oldest part of the brain that has to do with survival; all animals have it. So whether we're conscious or unconscious of this, things typically revolve around "me, me, me."[10] There are scientific studies that show that even the sight of the polar bears on melting polar ice doesn't have the effect required to instigate change. Sure, we might have a moment of emotion about it—including fear or regret—but these images just aren't enough to make most people actually care![11]

On the other hand, as Jungian analyst Jerome Bernstein has documented [see Bernstein: 2005], there are increasing numbers of people who are profoundly sensitive to what's going on in the environment. It's my dream that at some point each one of us will develop the same ability to feel that deep and instinctive connection. So the psychological work ahead lies in creating frameworks and tools with which to hold the pain of what's happening to the animals and the trees, the oceans and the forests, without splitting apart or fragmenting.

PP: How has your work with the bees changed you, and are there ways that you live differently?

BB: Like everyone else, I find myself guilty every single day of doing the things I know that I should not be doing. Every time I forget to bring my bags with me to the store and come out with two plastic bags, I feel horrible. And yet, as Bernstein has written, simply feeling guilt isn't helping. The Earth doesn't need us to feel guilty; it needs us to meet it in a reciprocal relationship. So feeling guilty is one thing, but opening to that greater sense of connection is where I've felt the most impact.

For example, not long ago I was in the process of selling my house. In my backyard I had a beautiful, long row of roses, and for whatever reason they picked that moment to start dying: they were becoming blighted from aphids. So I rationalized to myself that because the roses needed to look good to sell the house, I needed to spray them with one of those garden products that contained some pretty strong substances, the very kind that are not good for the bees. I felt guilty, but I also knew that the spray would make the roses look considerably better. But just as I was walking back from the garden after spraying the roses, I passed a huge bush with big purple flowers I'd planted just for the bees. And as I walked past that bush, a bee came up to me and buzzed around my face. I had a strong sense of her communicating to me, "What were you thinking?!"

PP: I think that's a very human, relatable story to share. Most of us know that guilty feeling of "sinning" against the environment we're trying to protect.

BB: It was such a profound awakening. I knew with my rational brain that what I was doing was wrong and that it was bad for the environment. But it was only through this personal encounter with the bee that I was emotionally and spiritually touched by the consequences of my actions.

PP: As you were telling the story, it occurred to me that even the roses, in beginning to die, were sad that you were leaving your home.

BB: It's interesting that you picked up on that. I was leaving my home, a place where I'd been very happy and was not ready to give up. But rather than engaging with my feelings of disconnection and loss, rather than dealing with it upfront, I found myself tempted to repress the troublesome emotions by distracting myself through all the usual channels we humans have developed for just such occasions: through the use of technology, entertainment, food, shopping, etc. All this is just another example of how we have to start paying more attention to our interactions with the natural world, and with each other. And from there something can open up that will help us enter into a more reciprocal relationship with the planet.

PP: In your research have you come across symbols and representations of bees in ancient cultures?

BB: As I began studying bees, I discovered layer upon layer of metaphorical and archetypal symbolism. Bees create new life through pollination, so throughout history they've been associated with the life-giving powers of the Great Mother Goddess. In the ancient Minoan and Greek civilizations, for instance, the Goddess is often depicted with bees, or with the head or the wings of a bee. The attendants of the rites at the temples of the Greek Goddess Artemis were called the "Melissa," which is the Greek word for *honeybee*. One of Egypt's origin myths states that after the Goddess Neith emerged from the water after giving birth to the Sun, Ra, she flew away in the form of a bee. As part of my research, I visited Egypt, and there were symbols of bees everywhere etched into temples. They even have temples that are dedicated to the Goddess of the bee.

Because they can go between heaven and earth as messengers to the Gods, bees have also been considered a symbol of the soul. For that reason they were associated with the Greek messenger God Hermes, who traveled between the underworld and the heavens. So I've also come to see the disappearance of the bees as a very profound symbol for soul loss throughout our entire culture. Just as we have to ask why the bees are disappearing, so we have to ask where those lost parts of our souls have gone: how can we re-establish a relationship with that part of our soul that's been missing?

PP: How would you imagine individuals, as well as the culture, should go about reclaiming this lost soul dimension of life? And how would this connect to saving the bees?

BB: I would say that slowing down and reconnecting with our capacity for reflection is critical to finding our lost souls. The pace at which we're living is just not conducive to reconnecting with that part of ourselves that's connected with nature, and with that part of us that would not be able to do harm to a little bee. There are plenty of practices that allow us to reflect in that way, whether meditation, yoga, therapy, or simply sitting in nature. These same practices can also help us to slow down enough to feel the pain of what's happening to the planet and really contemplate what it means.

As difficult as that might be, I think the ability to more deeply feel that suffering around the disappearance of nature would be a real gift. Because that way we can begin to retrain ourselves to tolerate some of the disorientation we suffer as a result of the artificial lives we lead and not further repress it or distract ourselves. Then perhaps we can all return home—just like the bee who while out gathering pollen turns and makes a "beeline" back to the hive. ∎

Notes

1. For more, visit the Center For Food Safety <http://www.centerforfoodsafety.org/issues/304/pollinators-and-pesticides>. Even though the European Union has taken action and implemented a ban on the use of certain pesticides detrimental to pollinator species, our environment and our future food security, the U.S. still allows for their use.
2. See the story on Beyond Pesticides <http://www.beyondpesticides.org/pollinators/chemicals.php>.
3. The Depth Psychology Alliance is the world's largest online depth psychology community <http://www.depthpsychologyalliance.com/>.
4. "Portland Will Still Be Cool, but Anchorage May Be the Place to Be," by Jennifer A. Kingson, *New York Times*, September 22, 2014.
5. DDT ("dichlorodiphenyltrichloroethane") is a colorless, crystalline, tasteless, and almost odorless organochloride known for its insecticidal properties. It was banned for agricultural use in the U.S. in 1972.
6. In Spring 2011, populations across the Middle East rose up to demand greater accountability from their leaders. Known as the Arab Spring, this movement spread to Syria, where it was met with brutal suppression by President Bashar al-Assad. The conflict rapidly descended into sectarian warfare and ultimately civil war. So far, over 200,000 have died and more than 6.3 million people have been displaced.
7. See introduction to this section, n. 2.

8. Hathalie, Jack. *Navajo Madonna.* Online at <http://www.trinitystores.com/store/read-more/navajo-madonna>.

9. "Percepticide," by Diana Taylor, as cited in Watkins and Shulman: 2008.

10. For more on the self-centeredness of human beings and the brain, see Dawkins: 2006.

11. See Saffron O'Neil and Sophie Nicholson-Cole. "'Fear Won't Do It': Promoting Positive Engagement With Climate Change Through Visual and Iconic Representations." *Science Communication* 30, March 2009, pp. 355–379.

—20—

Crop Circles

Revelations of a New Planetary Myth

An Interview with Gary S. Bobroff, M.A.

IT HAS OFTEN SEEMED to me that the only way humankind will change in time to avert its headlong course toward environmental destruction will be through the emergence of a new myth. One with the potential to unite humankind in a wholly different relationship to the planet than it's had in the past; one that is equal in magnitude to the sudden appearance of Gods in our midst, with the power to part the curtains of our consensual reality, revealing existence in all its numinous glory.

Gary S. Bobroff, a Jungian-oriented psychologist, has devoted his life to studying and serving the emergence of just such a history-changing myth that, to him and to others, is transpiring at this very moment. This myth is the appearance of the Divine Feminine,[1] as it appears to be revealed in the phenomenon of crop circles. Inscribed in fields of grain by what some say are human design and what others say are unknown forces, crop circles are mandala-like spheres of richly varied patterns and symbols that have appeared throughout the world, including in the U.S. It is a phenomenon, writes Bobroff in his book *Jung, Crop Circles, and the Re-Emergence of the Archetypal Feminine*, that can be traced back to the seventeenth century through its explosion of frequency in the last thirty years. Too sophisticated and too intricately and precisely "drawn" through cross-woven plant stems to be the work solely of human beings, and with no sign of human intervention, crop circles at this critical juncture in human history signal the possibility of a genuine revelation before our eyes—if only we could read its message.

Although many have focused on crop circles as riddles that require answers or solutions, or have written them off as pranks or "merely" artistic expressions, Bobroff eschews that approach in favor of a more reflective, Jungian perspective. Like our nightly dreams that trace symbols and scenes on our psyches, prompting us to consider the origins of these nocturnal messages, crop circles, he believes, also "invite" us to look more deeply, contemplating the source of their creation. Whether we respond to these ciphers written in grain with a skeptical brow or "wide-eyed enthusiasm," says Bobroff, "[i]t is in how we engage with our own first responses to this phenomenon that the burden of our work in response to it lies. . . . I have yet to meet two people who feel exactly the same way about crop circles." By following the path laid down by our responses this way, he believes, we are led to a more profound engagement and creative participation with the mysterious phenomenon of crop circles—and to nature.

Bobroff was born and raised in Saskatchewan, Canada, in the city of Saskatoon, known as the "Paris of the Prairies." He studied philosophy at the University of British Columbia, and then moved to Santa Barbara, California, where he began studying Jungian psychology at Pacifica Graduate Institute. It was then that, about fourteen years ago, Bobroff found himself reading Jungian analyst Edward Edinger's *Creation of Consciousness*—a book that examines the implications of Jung's master-work *Answer to Job*, and humankind's relationship to God's "dark side" (evil)—when he had a sudden insight. Crop circles, he thought, might be another evolution in the "relationship that we have psychologically with whatever the background of reality is: whether that's God, or whatever we want to call it."

So it was that, to Bobroff, crop circles came to represent a new kind of metaphor for the human–divine relationship: not just as a symbol, but as a living expression of a worldwide phenomenon that was less "abstract and distant," and much closer in physical proximity. That first spark of insight, he said, turned into a well-received essay that became his master's thesis, and then ultimately his book. Bobroff's research has taken him to crop circles throughout the world, including Europe and North America, and he also lectures and presents workshops on the topic.

In addition, Bobroff teaches about the Jungian idea of synchronicity, which he links to the phenomenon of crop circles, as well as the archetypes of the feminine and the masculine. As he explained the connection during our interview, synchronicity emerges out of feeling, and "calls upon us to understand that there's this mystery alive in us that values our heart, that values our feelings, and that values our authentic emotional relationship to the world." Through feeling and synchronicity, he explains, crop circles become "tangible. They're real; they're close to us. We can't say where they're coming from. But there's a relationship to them through feeling." The following interview was conducted in 2014.

✳

Pythia Peay: When you talk about the appearances of crop circles as an expression of something more mysterious drawing closer to us, here on Earth, are you saying that God is speaking to us through them?

Gary S. Bobroff: I'm very careful not to deify the makers of crop circles. But one of the things I ask people to do during my presentations is to ask themselves those traditional "big" questions, which is what crop circles can lead us to do. A lot of people respond by saying it's the aliens who are causing crop circles, while others say it's all just a hoax. Those kinds of answers put an abrupt end to the process, so they don't leave much room for psychological development. They also don't leave room for expanding the box we've put around whatever is on "the other side"—whether that's God, or whatever a person might call that larger presence or energy.

These kinds of answers also reflect the culture we live in, and that has us going "up, up, up" in our heads, and out of our bodies. It's this mindset that has led to illusions of endless economic growth and all kinds of inflated masculine paradigms of success. And as Jung said, the biggest problem afflicting our age is our preference for masculine archetypes and ideas over feminine ones.

So my invitation to people around the issue of crop circles is to ask them to wrestle with their preconceptions. What do they think of, for instance, when they think of extraterrestrials? Most of us just use words like God or alien or whatever as bottle caps: categorizations that limit our participation with those big ideas. And that keeps us from feeling the anxiety and other things we would have to feel to participate in this mysterious occurrence.

PP: So you're saying that the very form our answers take in response to crop circles reflects the crumbling masculine paradigm that the crop circles themselves are trying to break us out of?

GSB: If we are facing the mystery of crop circles, and the extent of our response is to just apply a category to it, and to say, "Oh yeah, we've got it all figured it out," that's a masculine response. It's also completely cutting off a person's process of psychological engagement. So how much work has been done there? Virtually none. I've been working on this process for fifteen years, and I am still engaged with the mystery—I'm not even looking for answers. Here you have a beautiful, creative phenomenon that is created out of sacred geometry, and that is trying to *speak* to us. To me, crop circles are also very similar psychologically to synchronicity.

PP: When you say crop circles are similar to the phenomenon of synchronicity, is that because they're relevant to our time, and are in fact being called forth by the needs of our time?

GSB: To me the calling of our time is to consciously come home to the reality of the feminine in our world—and that means the reality of a living, breathing mystery flowing through us, through phenomena like synchronicity. And when we talk about synchronicity, it's the same principle exemplified in the *I Ching* and the *Tao Te Ching*[2]: our personal emotions and the physical universe are a-causally related. For example, it's not the dream that heals and impacts the dreamer; it's the way the dream fits with the dreamer's real life that's important.

So right now we're living in a time that is suffering from a suicidal overbalance of masculine approaches to life, and a lack of the feminine. To correct this imbalance, our culture desperately needs to make contact with those kinds of phenomena—like synchronicity and crop circles—that can help us to reconnect to the mystery of the universe in its feminine form. At the same time, all the tsunamis, wildfires, and superstorms are also calling us to see the horror of the destruction that we're causing to the planet. Both these phenomena are pulling us closer to nature, bringing us down from the fantasies of the masculine that are all upward and outward: for example, like the idea that the answer to climate change is more technology. But technology *is* the problem.

God willing, we may come up with technologies that will help us get over the effects of global warming. But more likely it's our trust in masculine approaches such as science, technology, and organization that will only worsen the situation we're in. We're crucifying all life on this planet and all future generations through our faith in "economic necessity." That's the word we're using to put the whole planet in the Holocaust oven.

PP: That's a pretty intense way to frame things.

GSB: But that's the reality.

PP: So, the Earth is speaking through the crop circles, trying to get our attention. I don't know if you would use this analogy, but it's as if aliens landed on the planet and yet we can't speak their language, or understand what's being said to us.

GSB: I think that's a good jumping off point. But crop circles also communicate through art, so on a feeling level there's a way that we do understand what's being transmitted.

PP: Can you say more about what you mean by that?

GSB: Crop circles are a visual, aesthetic form of expression. Certainly, there is a way that they communicate symbolically, but the danger again is that interpreting them symbolically can exacerbate the way our culture tends to intellectualize everything. Jung was always warning, for example, not to confuse things with our ideas about them. So with the crop circles, we have a chance to develop a genuine relationship to the mysterious in this world. Most of our culture is very backward in that regard: we've put God in a box, and once a week we go and visit God in that box.

But crop circles are offering us more of a kind of "adult to adult relationship" to God. That means we bring our whole selves to that mystery, while also seeing that each particular crop circle, too, wants *us* to be with *it*. The metaphor that comes to mind for me is the sacred wedding. The masculine, which has lost its way, has to come home, and see all the beautiful things that it hasn't been seeing, as well as the shadow of the damage that's been done through that way of living on the Earth.

PP: Tell me about your personal experiences seeing, and being with, crop circles.

GSB: I've been in many crop circles, and it's a wonderful thing. As a man I come to it first from my rational, skeptical place, so I'm always looking for physical evidence and other kinds of proof. But once I get past that, some really nice things begin to happen, and I start to have a feeling of the energy that's present there. I've had experiences in which I've felt very powerful electromagnetic energies. So it's very exciting. But for many people it can also be a challenge; we're so programmed to be rational and skeptical that we've lost that ancient way of feeling the energy of the place we're moving through. And with the crop circles, that's really what's being asked of us: to be present, and to just be.

PP: Do you feel that crop circles are connected to what's going on with the environmental crisis?

GSB: Absolutely. I do believe that. They're not in metal, they're not in wood, they're not in sand—they're a phenomena that are ingrained in the earth, and the plants are still alive. But at the same time I would want readers to make up their own mind. What I'm trying to do with my own work is to build a framework for individuals to take their own process around their responses and reactions to crop circles more deeply.

PP: How long does a crop circle stay in existence?

GSB: Until it's harvested by a farmer.

PP: What have the farmers' responses been to crop circles appearing on their land?

GSB: It's extremely varied. A lot of farmers live in a very grounded kind of reality. There's a certain percentage that are one hundred percent certain that they're made by people, that it's all a hoax, and that it's causing damage to their crops, so they want people punished and jailed. Then there's another group that doesn't believe it's all a hoax, and there are even some that say crop circles have been appearing on their land since they were children.

In my research, I've discovered archival documents showing that crop circles go as far back as the seventeenth century, including references in *Nature* magazine in 1880, and in 1686, when an Oxford professor documented crop circles that he discovered. But I think it's a phenomenon that goes back thousands of years, and I believe it's the reason that the stone circle culture exists in England, and that the stones were placed to hold the energy of the circles.[3] That's my speculation. But because there's no cultural leadership on this issue, and because governments encourage the notion that it's all a hoax, the farmers don't have a container by which to relate to these crop circles in a more sacred way.

PP: All of this brings to mind the Greek mysteries of the Goddess Demeter, held at Eleusis, that were so connected to the cycles of nature.[4]

GSB: That's predominantly what my work and my book is all about. Symbolically, crop circles show the connection between grain, the miracle of life, and the archetypal feminine. It's very obvious and clear and direct.

But at the same time, it's important to look at the context within which they're appearing. And that context is that the world is utterly removed from the archetypal feminine, and what that stands for. Take our American Thanksgiving feast. Whatever meaning it has is trumped by the day after, which is an orgy of consumerism. But where does the word materialism come from? The word *matter* is derived from the Latin *mater*, which in turn means "mother." So materialism is a shadow compulsion expressing our desire for and lack of connection to the archetypal feminine.

PP: So materialism is symptomatic of . . .

GSB: It's a direct expression of our disconnection from the Feminine.

PP: What has the response been to your presentations on crop circles?

GSB: Surprisingly, very good. So it's very vivifying and enlivening to give that talk and to have that kind of favorable response. What I'm trying to get through to most people is a feeling and a story that makes sense for our time. Because nowhere are we being given that.

PP: I've heard it said that religions arise in response to the needs of our time. Is that what you think is happening here?

GSB: Well, there's a beautiful tradition where participants take the final sheaves of wheat from a harvest and weave it into a corn dolly or human figure to celebrate the end of the harvest.[5] Then it's placed on a mantel or a hearth and venerated; or in

European traditions it gets paraded around. We don't do that anymore. But now, with the crop circles, something else is doing that for us.

PP: How are crop circles functioning like these figures that were used in agricultural rites?

GSB: A basic feature of the ground lay of a genuine crop circle is wheat set down in multi-directional fanned layers. However, what we find in some of the best formations is three-dimensional woven grain, for example the Magic Basket,[6] which is actually woven from the ground up. We also see some weaving occurring throughout some of the authentic crop circle formations today. So just as we creatively honored grain (and its source as the miracle of life) at the end of each harvest in generations past through the creation of woven corn dollies and similar figures, the same sacred ritual is taking place through the medium of the woven grain in the crop circles.

PP: So do you hope that people will have a deeper connection, not just to the crop circles, but also to the idea of synchronicity?

GSB: One of the things I think we're coming to realize is that we live in a heart-shaped world. For example, in Rupert Sheldrake's work with the "extended mind,"[7] tens of thousands of university studies have shown that things like card-guessing and telepathy are statistically proven to happen. But when they looked closely at the results, they discovered that what was at work behind these experiments was feeling. Whether conscious or unconscious, there is no synchronicity without feeling. So for example, Rupert found that family members are best at card-guessing. And what family members were the best? Twins. In addition, Rupert found that people who don't believe in the possibility of the extended mind do significantly poorly on card-guessing techniques and score below average to the point that it's statistically significant. So these studies actually prove that it is our feeling relationship to these things that matters.

Another example of synchronicity in nature is a murmuration of birds, where they all fly together in a pattern, or of fish in schools moving around in that beautiful form they have. But what scientists have discovered is that it is not possible for those movements to be coordinated biochemically. So the only logical explanation for the coordination of those movements is as "emotion in motion." Those are psychic fields. We are coming to understand that, objectively, we live in a world that is heart-shaped. For example, how many times has a family member been visited by a loved one at the moment of death? Or known suddenly that a loved one was gone at the moment they died? There is a web of feeling that surrounds the world, and for which we have many words.

PP: Such as . . . ?

GSB: Well, *grace*, for example. But it's that kind of understanding that might help us break free of this monster culture that we live in right now—and that sees everyone as meat, and as consumers, and as cogs in a wheel, and as utilitarian. But as we're coming to see through phenomena like synchronicity, and extended mind, and crop circles, there's this whole other reality. And this whole other reality is the real world that's a very profound place to live in. So that reality is there, but we're the ones who are lost.

PP: So it's as if we're living within a guidance system, or an invisible GPS system, but we're not plugged into it.

GSB: Again, it comes back to the fact that we're living at a time when we are profoundly imbalanced in favor of a masculine approach to life: that's what Jung said was our primary sickness. We're so hooked on our inventiveness, for example, that we actually think that we invented the world. We actually think we're God. Look at the metaphors we use: artificial intelligence, biological robots, clockwork universe. Those are all things made by human beings. It's that kind of grandiosity and inflation—and sickness—that allow us to destroy the world. So this grandiosity needs to be defeated so that there can be a return to balance and health.

PP: So it's as if the crop circles are a rebuke to that brutal way of seeing and living life, because they're so gentle, even as they point to that other reality.

GSB: An invitation, a wink.

PP: Do you see the crop circles as a sign of something hopeful?

GSB: Absolutely.

PP: Even in the face of predictions that the human race may not make it, or that at least life will be significantly altered from how we know it today?

GSB: The Jungian analyst Ann Ulanov has spoken about the prevalence of visions of the Virgin Mary just prior to the horror of death camps and the Holocaust during World War II. So there is a way in which we might see these crop circles as a beautiful vision before a very dark time. Having said that, I have no idea about the future, except to say that we're certainly entering a transitional time.

In my book, however, I discuss Jungian analyst Toni Wolff's memoir, by one of her patients, Irene Champernowne, an English art therapist. Included in it are a series of remarkable paintings of powerful visions Champernowne had while living in the English countryside during the late forties and fifties. In one of her paintings of these visions, two women are standing on a hill, with the moon and the sun in the background, and UFOs hovering around them. In her descriptions of another one of the visions she painted, Champernowne writes that "suddenly a raging wind and a storm blew up and the sea blew all around me. Thunder and lightning followed each other in close succession. All was dark; one could not see. Equally suddenly a tremendous clap of thunder and all was hushed and the sky cleared. The woman in the sky had fallen from the heights, and all I could see was a great black 5 sticking up like a rock from the water and I knew this rock was She." At the end, she writes that "I saw below me in the clear water fields of waving corn, with the wind passing over them, and I knew that was the future."

In their correspondence about these visions, Champernowne's analyst Toni Wolff spoke about the coming change in era, and how we're shifting to a different eon. And what I found interesting was that some of the images in these visions take us back down to that deep, dark, feminine quality that we've lost and that we need to reconnect with, and that might help to guide us during this transition.

PP: And that may involve fields of waving grain, an enduring American symbol, but that in a new way might lead us forward to a better place. ∎

Notes

1. *Divine Feminine* is a term that arose with the rediscovery of ancient images of the Goddess, and is used to describe a set of values typically devalued by mainstream Western culture, such as interconnectedness, intuition, empathy, process, feeling, and the idea that all created life is imbued with sacred energy.

2. The *I Ching* (Pinyin: *Yijing*) and *Tao Te Ching* (Pinyin: *Daodejing*) are classic Chinese texts of philosophy: the former, a divination manual known as the Book of Changes, and the latter, a work of metaphysics, meditation, and politics attributed to Lao-Tse (Pinyin: Laozi).

3. For a list of ancient stone circles worldwide, see <http://en.wikipedia.org/wiki/List_of_stone_circles>.

4. See Ch. 9, n. 9.

5. A corn dolly is a form of straw-work fashioned from the last sheaf of wheat or other cereal crops and used as part of harvest customs of pagan Europe. See also Frazer: 2002.

6. See North: 2000, p. 71.

7. The term "extended mind," coined by biologist and author Rupert Sheldrake, refers to the mind's perceptive, telepathic abilities that extend beyond its immediate environment.

Part IV

A Poverty of Meaning
Capitalism and Consumerism

Even if we act to erase material poverty, there is another great task. It is to confront the poverty of satisfaction—a lack of purpose and dignity—that inflicts us all. Too much and too long, we seem to have surrendered community excellence and community values in the mere accumulation of material things . . . the gross national product measures neither our wit nor our courage; neither our wisdom nor our learning; neither our compassion nor our devotion to our country; it measures everything, in short, except that which makes life worthwhile. And it can tell us everything about America except why we are proud that we are Americans.—**Robert F. Kennedy**, from "Recapturing America's Moral Vision," University of Kansas, March 18, 1968 (Quoted in Liu and Hanauer: 2007)

THE AMERICAN REVOLUTION AND the forces that led the Thirteen Colonies to break their bonds with Great Britain was, writes historian Gordon S. Wood, "a complicated and often ironic story that needs to be explained and understood, not celebrated or condemned." Reading further in Wood's gem of a book, *The American Revolution: A History*,[1] I was taken aback at what an *economic* story it also was.

So often in narrating our origins we extol the military genius of George Washington, or the sheer grit of the Revolutionary soldiers who battled for the cause of liberty. But there was also a decidedly financial *and* cerebral backstory to the country's founding. Were it not for the intellectual ferment and creative expressions of dissent and protest that arose among the early colonists when faced with a series of oppressive tax and trade restrictions imposed on them by the British in the decade before the Revolution, there would have been no encampment for Washington's troops at Valley Forge, no Declaration of Independence or Constitutional Convention. "Unlike the French Revolution, which had been caused by actual tyranny," writes Wood, "the American Revolution was seen as a peculiarly intellectual and conservative affair, as something brought about not by actual oppression but by the anticipation of oppression, by reasoning and devotion to principle, such as 'no taxation without representation.'"

As Wood tells the story, the North American colonies in the mid-eighteenth century were enterprising, restive, bold, and acquisitive—traits that remain ingrained in our character. With Scots, Irish, and English immigrants pouring across the Atlantic in a steady stream in search of land, the number of inhabitants in the New World exploded, multiplying "more rapidly than any other people in the Western world." The population of New England quickly spilled over, and people set out, moving in all directions. Roads and strings of towns sprung up along the eastern coastline, writes Wood, as way stations to service travelers, but also to distribute produce to other markets. Land fever began to spread "through all levels of society"; even Benjamin Franklin concocted speculative land deals. Local British authorities, Wood recounts, had never seen anything like it before. Astounded, they noted the "avidity and restlessness" of such large groups of people on the move, observing that "they acquire no attachment to place; but wandering about seems engrafted in their nature; and it is a weakness

277

incident in it that they should forever imagine the lands further off are still better than those upon which they are already settled."

When Great Britain's economy expanded during the early years of the Industrial Revolution, trade between the mainland and its new colonial outpost boomed. Unable to produce enough food for its population, England began importing grain and foodstuffs from the colonies. This in turn contributed to a rise in standards of living for many Americans, initiating the country's first "consumer revolution." With few goods produced locally, Wood notes, Americans began to crave imported items such as Irish linen, lace, and Wedgwood dishes. Benjamin Franklin's wife, Deborah, surprised him with the luxury gift of a silver spoon and china bowl to replace his pewter spoon and earthen bowl. George Washington regularly ordered from abroad a new suit of clothes for himself from his London tailor, or toys for his stepson.

But the enterprising colonists knew an opportunity when they saw one. Moving quickly to take advantage of "the rising levels of taste and consumption" they began manufacturing their own American-made goods, such as homespun textiles and shoes. Discontent with the growing trade imbalance due to Americans importing more goods than they exported, and ambitious to corner the market, a movement spread among colonial artisans and manufacturers to boycott English imports.

For the most part, Great Britain had ruled over the North American colonies with a kind of benign neglect. But after the end of the Seven Years War in 1763,[2] interest resumed in the affairs of the new territories. Land claims had to be sorted out, writes Wood, new governments had to be organized, and conflicts between the "land-hungry" settlers and the Native Americans were nearing outright war. To address these problems—and to re-assert their authority—Parliament decided to post a standing army in the colonies. But the British government was broke; there were no funds for this overseas deployment. The United Kingdom could, however, make the colonies themselves pay for the privilege of Redcoats hovering over their affairs, and perhaps, through some creative financing, the mother country might even be able to extract additional revenue from its prospering offspring.

To that end, the British government began to enact new colonial trade policies. The Sugar Act of 1764 imposed new and tighter regulations on America's navigation systems, and granted the British navy power to inspect American ships. It also imposed duties on foreign cloth, sugar, indigo, coffee, and wine imported into the colonies, and lowered the duty on imported molasses (which they hoped, writes Wood, would stop American smuggling and lead to the legal importation of foreign molasses and earn money for the crown). The Sugar Act, sweet as it sounds, did not go over well with the colonies, and they reacted angrily to this intervention in their economic affairs. To mighty Great Britain, the distant, barely civilized colonies hardly posed a threat. Unperturbed, Parliament went forward with the Stamp Act, levying a tax on newspapers, almanacs, legal documents, and all kinds of papers used in the colonies—exactly at a time when the colonies had just entered an economic slump.

It was not a wise move. "This single stroke," declared William Smith, Jr. of New York, "has lost Great Britain the affection of all her Colonies." Emboldened, eight of the colonies came together and issued a formal petition against the Sugar Act, sending it to the royal authorities in England. Not only did British officials once again completely ignore this complaint, along with the mounting unrest, they even passed another Stamp Act. Reaction in the colonies, writes Wood, was immediate. Simmering resentments boiled over into outright activism and rebellion; merchants formed protest associations; in the Virginia House of Burgesses Patrick Henry introduced a series of resolves "asserting the colonists' right to be taxed only by their elected representatives"; and in Massachusetts a mob attacked the home of the local stamp distributor. A resistance movement called Sons of Liberty made up of shopkeepers, mechanics, merchants, and printers, Wood's narrative continues, organized anti-stamp activities throughout the colonies, and enforced nonimportation of British goods.

In 1766, the British were finally forced to repeal the Stamp Act. But it was too late; relations between the two countries had fatally deteriorated. Weakened ties with the mother country, however, only served to strengthen bonds among the Thirteen Colonies—and to forge the destinies of a rare group of thinkers and leaders whose acts of bravery and creative political artistry would live on in world history. "The crisis over the Stamp Act aroused and unified Americans as no previous political event ever had," writes Wood. "It stimulated bold political and constitutional writings throughout the colonies, deepened the colonists' political consciousness and participation, and produced new forms of organized popular resistance."

Still, the United Kingdom under King George III pressed on, imposing new levies on American imports of glass, paint, paper, and tea. Withdrawing British soldiers from the western frontier of their colonies, they concentrated troops along the Atlantic seaboard, and, as planned, charged the colonists for their upkeep. The American resistance movement continued to swell. Its center was Boston, Massachusetts. During animated town meetings, the British violations of American rights were openly debated, and by the end of 1773, writes Wood, "independence was being discussed freely in colonial newspapers."

The "final series of explosions" leading to the American Revolution was triggered by the Tea Act, which granted a monopoly to the East India Company to sell tea in America. On December 16, 1773, as every American child is taught, a group of patriots dressed as Indians dumped tea worth about 10,000 British pounds into Boston Harbor. What is celebrated in colorful, costumed re-enactments today was at the time an extremist insurgent act. "This destruction of the tea is so bold, so daring, so firm, intrepid, and inflexible, and it must have so important consequences, and so lasting, that I can't but consider it an epocha in history," exclaimed Bostonian John Adams.

For its part, the British Parliament passed the Coercive Acts, a series of laws clamping down on Boston's freedoms, and establishing the commander in chief of the British army as the governor of Massachusetts. For the colonists this was the "last straw," writes Wood, that convinced them once and for all "that Parliament had no more right to make laws for them than to tax them." As it was declared during the Stamp Act Congress, the entire stand-off between the colonists and the mighty British Empire came down to one unequivocal principle from which the colonies would never back down: "It is inseparably essential to the freedom of a people . . . that no taxes should be imposed on them, but with their own consent, given personally, or by their representatives." Thus it followed that since the people of America were not represented in the House of Commons in Great Britain, writes Wood, "the colonists would be represented and taxed only by persons who were known and chosen by themselves and who served in their respective legislatures." And the rest, as they say, is history.

So why do I present this brief sketch around the build-up to the American Revolution? Because it was a time, as Wood emphasizes, when American *intellectual* resistance was "raised to the highest plane of principle." Indeed, it should not be forgotten that the tensions between the American colonies and Great Britain around practical economic issues like taxes, duties, currency, imports, exports, and trade imbalances were played out against the larger backdrop of the European Enlightenment, a philosophical movement around the nature and rights of man that greatly influenced the Founders. The first shot fired in 1776 was in fact the end point of a long and considered debate that had taken place in taverns, before fireplaces, and in town meetings and state legislatures around the nuances and finer points of liberty, individual rights, and the relationship between the governed and those governing. This debate focalized around economic principles of fairness and justice so that the unchecked power of monarchy and aristocracy against those less blessed with wealth and property would not be repeated in the new world.

Our Founding Fathers, writes Jacob Needleman in *The American Soul*, "were artists and masters of building a social order. This was their milieu, their instrument, their art form." As they hammered out the specifics of this new social order during the Constitutional Convention that followed the Revolution, special attention was given to the idea of "property," which at the time was extended not only to actual property as we think of it in today's terms, but that also included, explains Needleman, "the general results of the functioning of man in the world," or in other words a person's skills and capacities given to them by nature. (Of course, the Founders' notion of property also extended to human beings, as well, in the form of slavery: a grave oversight with severe economic and personal repercussions for African Americans, and which has triggered a debate over reparations that continues to this day.)

Because people were born with varying degrees of skills and talents, the Founders also understood that a social order must be created, continues Needleman, "that allows every human being to manifest his given . . . functions," while at the same time being protected from the "bestial, egoistic forces" that dominated human nature, and that if unchecked could lead to inequality and oppression. James Madison, who was remarkably prescient concerning the ease with which class divisions can arise between those who hold actual physical property and those who don't, or other kinds of economic distinctions, warned against the "unequal distribution of property." The regulation of these different classes, he wrote, "forms the principle task of modern legislation, and involves the spirit of party and faction in the necessary and ordinary operations of government."[3]

There are many narratives in the epic unfolding of America. But the one I've just outlined—the way the spirited, entrepreneurially gifted, physically hard-working aspects of the American character combined with its intellectual and philosophical side to produce our most valuable asset: the protection of individuals' natural rights in the marketplace of the real world—is perhaps most central to who we are. Today, it seems that we have kept the more practical part of this equation, while allowing the other, more thoughtful side to lapse. Especially when it comes to our deepening class divisions, the mindless consumerism that drives our country, and the encroaching power of corporations over the democratic process, original thinking that could stir peoples' conscience and imagination awake seems impoverished.

This was neatly and wittily portrayed on The Daily Show with Jon Stewart in the aftermath of the 2014 midterm elections (which cost a record $3.67 billion). In a skit, comedian Jason Jones is portrayed with his head in a giant dollar bill as "big money" gloating over its victory over "ideas," as played by comedian Samantha Bee.[4] Like a pendulum, the culture has swung over to a one-sided emphasis on material and financial success as the sole measure of its worth, while taking its eye off the inequities threatening our never-before-seen, one-of-a-kind, self-built economic democracy.

Failing to close the gap between the ninety-nine percent—the vast majority at the lower end of the spectrum who have played by the rules of capitalism, and yet who find themselves barely able to subsist—and, at the tiptop, that fraction of the populace that holds most of the country's wealth,[5] we have abandoned that sense of fairness that was so central to the Founders' apparatus of ideas. And how would the hardy but poor immigrants who settled this country, I wonder, have felt about the demise in our time of that quintessential American Horatio Alger myth, when no matter one's background, a person could always make it in America?[6]

I imagine that not only would our earliest settlers be shocked by modern America's class divisions and its shrinking opportunity, but they'd be just as taken aback by the incongruity of our well-stocked material lives, which they could scarcely have imagined. Never before, in fact, has humanity been presented with such a vast and tempting array of goods for everyday living. Benjamin Franklin's wife's "impulse" purchase of a silver spoon and China bowl seems quaint when measured against Pottery Barn or Macy's displays of dishes in various colors and styles. The grocery store of the 1950s hardly compares to the Safeway and Whole Foods stores of today. Though we are only five percent of the world's population, we Americans account for about a third of global consumption. On average, one American consumes as much total energy output as two Japanese, six Mexicans, 13 Chinese, 31 Indians, 128 Bangladeshis, 307 Tanzanians, or 370 Ethiopians. The average American uses three hundred shopping bags' worth of raw materials every *week*, an amount that weighs as much as a large car—while we throw out 200,000 tons of edible food daily. We use a third of the world's paper, a quarter of the oil, almost that amount of the coal, 27 percent of the aluminum, and 19 percent of the copper. In fact, it has been estimated that we would need the resources of three planets for everyone on Earth to live an "American" lifestyle.[7]

How did we get to this place? Perhaps we are a spent force, too busy working to make ends meet or to keep up with the neighbors or our own expectations of the good life to have much time to think. Or perhaps it's a fault written into the stars of the American character. As far back as 1899, the economist Thorstein Veblen coined the phrase "conspicuous consumption" in his criticism of American society, which he believed to value "*homo consumens*" (consumer human) over "*homo faber*" (maker human). Carl Jung may have analyzed the nation's exaggerated emphasis on material consumption as a kind of *enantiodromia*, in which everything eventually turns into its opposite.

In this case, America, which began poor and humble but strong in ideals and aspirations, has turned into the kind of wealthy, imperial country it once despised and resisted, oppressed from within by our own bureaucracies, corporations, and addictions to consumption, and riven with class divisions. No longer is the American Dream a measure of the quality of one's character or sacrifices made to the larger society, it seems, but a measure of the value of the material goods one has accumulated. As Jimmy Carter said in his 1979 address more than thirty years ago, "Too many of us now tend to worship self-indulgence and consumption. Human identity is no longer defined by what one does, but by what one owns" (quoted in Kazin, Edwards, Rothman: 2011). We are all in this state of affairs together, and together we can ask: Is the materially driven, economically polarized, and socially stratified country that is America today what the Founders had in mind, and what the first patriots fought and died for? And what of our land, and what our materially driven ways of life are doing to the planet? Big money, it could be said, is in politics because it is in all our lives as a major, driving force.

But if a well-considered, moral approach to economics was the fertile ground of democracy, why can't it be again? It is in this spirit that I endeavor in the following interviews to reflect on those pervasive twin forces of capitalism and consumerism. Six psychologists bring their own unique vantage points and insights to bear on questions of materialism, financial inequities, and economic polarization, and the psychological effects of our materially driven way of life on citizens' inner lives.

Psychoanalyst Paul Wachtel, author of the classic *The Poverty of Affluence*, discusses the rising influx of "stuff" into all our lives, including even those lowest on the income level, and the gap between material wealth and happiness. Clinical psychologist Philip Cushman, author of *Constructing the Self, Constructing America*, shares his insights into how consumerism over the past decades has actually changed the structure of the American self—and not always for the better—and the changes it has wrought on the profession of psychology, to the extent that it may soon no longer exist. Psychiatrist Thomas Singer brings a Jungian perspective to what he calls America's "money complex,' illustrating with cultural examples how this potent unconscious collective force operates in all citizen's psyches.

Psychoanalyst A. Chris Heath, who is studying the application of psychoanalytic theories to economics, looks at America's money complex as it ties into narcissism, and discusses gender issues and concerns around finances his clients bring with them into the therapy room. Finally, in two companion pieces, Jungian analysts Lawrence Staples and Bud Harris share their traditional "haul yourself up by the bootstraps" stories of how they became successful business entrepreneurs, then threw it all over to become Jungian analysts. They also offer their insights into money, the human condition, the Great Depression, and the American dream that the next generation should always be better off than the one before. ■

Notes

1. All quotes in this introductory section are from Wood: 2003, and Needleman: 2003.
2. The Seven Years War (1754–1763) involved most of the great powers of the time and affected Europe, North and Central America, the West African coast, India, and the Philippines.
3. The Center for Responsible Politics, October 29, 2014 <http://www.opensecrets.org>.
4. The Daily Show with Jon Stewart (Comedy Central), November 4, 2014 <http://thedailyshow. cc.com/videos/rmyxh7/democalypse-2014---america-remembers-it-forgot-to-vote--money-vs--ideas>.
5. "Who Are the 99 Percent?" by Ezra Klein, *Washington Post*, October 4, 2011.
6. "The American Dream is Now A Myth," by Henry Blodgett, *The Business Insider*, June 10, 2012.
7. Statistics on American consumerism available at "American Consumerism and the Global Environment," Mt. Holyoke <http://www.mtholyoke.edu/~kelle20m/classweb/wp/>

—21—

Too Much Stuff, Too Little Happiness

AN INTERVIEW WITH PAUL L. WACHTEL, PH.D.

WHEN I FIRST CAME across clinical psychologist Paul Wachtel's classic book *The Poverty of Affluence: A Psychological Portrait of the American Way of Life*, I was instantly curious. As a writer and cultural observer, and as someone who respected the wisdom of psychology, I appreciated how, with the turn of one well-worded phrase, the author had neatly portrayed one of modern America's basic conflicts.

I was not the only one to take notice. "Wachtel," wrote *The New Yorker* in its enthusiastic review, "traces much of [our] quiet discontent to the necessary sadness of lives centered on accumulation." In my own reflections, the title brought to mind associations like "poor little rich girl," and those classic tales in which the wealthy protagonist, although lavishly provided for in material ways, had been abandoned to uninterested caretakers, growing up into an adult psychologically malformed by the deprivations of love and family. In Wachtel's book, however, the subject he writes about is not the pitiful child of well-off, inattentive parents, but a nation that in his analysis has neglected essential nonmaterial parts of its character in favor of an obsession with accumulating more and more things, from bigger TVs to more clothes and cars, and ever-larger homes.

As Wachtel makes the case, America has since the mid-1950s increasingly narrowed its definition of what constitutes success and the good life to mean how much stuff its populace is able to produce, sell, buy, and own. Growth, he argues, has come to be measured not in terms of psychological inner states of happiness and wellbeing, or in the value of life experiences (such as taking a walk, conversing with a friend, or playing with a child), but in ever-higher rates of material consumption. "The consumer way of life is deeply flawed," writes Wachtel, "both psychologically and ecologically. It fails to bring the satisfactions promised and its side effects are lethal." Wachtel judges our consumer way of life as unsatisfactory on ethical grounds, as well, as "those fruits it does provide are distributed unevenly and unjustly."

In re-reading *The Poverty of Affluence* to prepare for my interview with him, it became evident to me that Wachtel's insights into our exaggeratedly materialistic American lifestyle remained as topical as when his book was first published in 1989. And yet, as he made the point then, and as he makes it once more during our interview, America's surfeit of material goods has not led to a corresponding rise in happiness and other interior good feelings. After the initial euphoria has worn off, it seems, human beings have a kind of set point beyond which the latest smartphone or bump in salary has little measurable effect on their sense of contentment and satisfaction.[1] Then there is the unassailable fact that our indulgence in material goods and more luxurious lifestyles is directly responsible for the planet's rapidly failing environmental health,[2] as well as the fact that when placed on justice's scales, wealth distribution in America is heavily weighted toward the rich.[3]

A clinical psychologist and psychotherapist as well as an academic, Wachtel, now seventy-four, began practicing in the late sixties. Except for when he was in graduate school, he has lived in New York all of his life and, as he brings to my attention during our interview, although not rich, he lives a comfortable, well-off life. The author of many books, he is a CUNY distinguished professor in the doctoral program in clinical psychology at City College and the Graduate Center of the City University of New York and Visiting Clinical Professor of Psychology (Adjunct) at the NYU Postdoctoral Program in Psychotherapy and Psychoanalysis. Among the themes of his writings, lectures, and workshops are the theory and practice of psychotherapy and the applications of psychological theory to the major social issues of our time.

During the following interview, Wachtel discusses among other things the sharp rise in material possessions, even among those who are not wealthy or middle class; how these things fail to satisfy us or make us feel good in the ways we think they should; and how in fact they may rob us of what really matters. He also describes why we fail to see the whole "package," or consequences, of our purchases. In addition, he looks at the way market forces adroitly play upon our sense of deprivation, our persistent lack of "enoughness," and the unexamined myths of capitalism, like the "invisible hand" of the market.

＊

Pythia Peay: I'd like to start by asking you how you think things have—or haven't—changed since the publication of your book in 1989.

Paul Wachtel: Having this interview reminds me of how I *wish* my book was outmoded. But unfortunately, it doesn't seem to be. For example, most economists still don't take into account how inequality affects people's emotional, subjective experience. They assume that if a person simply has more stuff they feel better, and that our sense of "utility"—as economists, with pseudo-objectivity, refer to simple human satisfaction—is more or less independent of what other people have. In other words, according to this theory, if I have "more," then it doesn't matter if everyone around me has *much* more, leaving me at the bottom of the barrel. I've got more than I had before, so why am I bellyaching?

Actually, it's even worse (or more absurd) than that. They don't even think I *would* bellyache, since after all I have "more." But if everyone is living in a thousand-square-foot home (the average in the 1950s), and then, a few years later, I'm living in a home that is 1200 square feet and everyone I know is living in two thousand square feet, my home is going to feel *smaller* to me, not bigger, because my *standard* is going to change. Our human experience is not geared to absolute numbers but to expectations (there's even a psychological theory about this property of perception called "adaptation-level theory"). And a growth-oriented society keeps *raising* expectations, producing lots of dissatisfaction even when people have "more."

So it's complicated comparing how well off we are now compared to when I first wrote *The Poverty of Affluence*. In some ways, we are worse off economically than we were when I wrote the book. There are more people who are under-employed or unemployed, and there are many, many more people who are either falling behind, or having to work extremely hard not to fall behind. But at the same time—and this is where a lot of confusion enters the picture—if you just look at the sheer quantity of "stuff" that people have, they have a lot more now than when I wrote the book, which was already about how much stuff we had! But although people have a lot more materially, there hasn't been an accompanying growth of good feelings, satisfaction, and sense of "enoughness." So those two things, having things and feeling good, can be very different.

PP: So how does what you just described fit with people who are earning money, but only enough to pay their bills, and who may also be threatened with job loss and insecurity?

PW: One of the factors behind the housing crisis in 2008 was that more people had begun borrowing money on their houses. But *why* were they borrowing money on their houses? Because they were experiencing needs greater than their actual incomes. People kept borrowing with the hope that the value of their house would continue to increase, which created the housing bubble. So underlying that phenomenon was the feeling of "I need more." But if we examine what people actually possessed while they were feeling that they needed more, they actually had a lot more stuff than they'd even had just a few decades ago, when people were actually feeling affluent. At that time, it was easier to feel affluent with less, because our needs were not as amped up as they are now, and our expectations were more reasonable.

Not so long ago, it used to be a commonplace that in a married couple or family just one person had to work. Typically, it was the man who worked, while the woman was a homemaker taking care of the children and the house. Despite the problems that arrangement created around women's equality and lack of fulfillment and potential, there was still the sense that a couple or a family could manage economically with just one wage earner. Now the commonplace is that both partners need to work in order to make ends meet. This development would make it seem like we're doing a lot worse economically. But if you look at what it is that making ends meet actually *means* then you understand why both people have to work!

To understand how this works, let's go back again to the size of people's homes. The average house in America in the late 1950s, when John Kenneth Galbraith wrote his classic book *The Affluent Society*, was a thousand square feet; so one person could easily purchase a house that size. Now people think they need two thousand square feet for a comfortable home. So if it takes two people working to buy a house that size, is that an economic or a psychological change? One person today could *still* support a thousand-square-foot house, but now that seems too small, and everyone wonders why it now requires two people working to support a "modest" house.

PP: And for some, even a two-thousand-square-foot house seems small.

PW: Right, and instead of feeling as if a family or a couple is doing well with one car, people feel they need two or more cars. They also need the latest flat-screen television and computer, and the newest I-pad and I-phone. I'm not denying that there are huge problems around economic justice and how income is distributed in our society. But a very critical aspect of our problems with capitalism today is the way material desires keep getting generated in ways that leave people much more aware of what they *don't* have, than what they *do* have. When that's the sea you're swimming in, it's very hard to have a full and satisfying life.

PP: So what you're describing are two interlocking forces: a flourishing market of consumer goods and "stuff" that is able to play upon people's sense of deprivation and lack. When these two things come together, they create our market-based, material-growth-oriented way of life.

PW: Right. And I'm not an ascetic, so it's not that I think we should be living a subsistence way of life. In fact, I enjoy many of the same consumer luxuries most people possess. But at the same time, I'm one of the relatively few people I know, including most people who are at my income level, who feels that I have more than I need, and pretty much everything that I want. For most people, there's always the feeling that they need more, and then that often leads them to work too hard. We keep hearing that productivity isn't high enough, but one of the biggest problems in our society, really, is that people are working too hard—at least those who are lucky enough to have a job. For example, it used to be considered a sign of human progress if, over the centuries, a work week went from eighty, to sixty, to forty hours. But now it's bouncing up in the other direction, so that when people can get work, they're working more and more.

PP: So where does this cycle begin? And what is it all for?

PW: Economists assume that our desires are completely internal, and that the market is simply supplying what people want. But psychologically, it doesn't work that way. What we want is shaped by the assumptions of people around us, which is what leads to other complications. So say, for example, a couple decides that they want to buy a two-thousand or twenty-five-hundred-square-foot house. They can't afford one that's close to where they work, so they buy a house that's the right size, but it's an hour-and-a-half commute from where they work.

Every day, they struggle through rush-hour traffic, and arrive home at the end of the day exhausted. Their kids are cranky because they haven't seen their parents all day, and the parents are also cranky and feeling lousy. The only compensation for this way of life is the stuff they have that represents their success. So as they feel more and more stressed, they need more and more stuff to feel better; and as a consequence, they work even harder, and feel even lousier, and so need *even* more stuff to compensate and show their life is a success. And it becomes a vicious circle. Once you get caught in that way of life, it becomes very hard to sort out what's the chicken and what's the egg; it's the circle itself that's the reality.

PP: I graduated from high school in 1969, and was part of the sixties/seventies movement toward living simpler, alternative lifestyles. I remember criticizing my parents as being excessively materialistic and consumerist. Now I look back at the way they lived, and it was actually very simple compared to today's standards! And even though I live a fairly simple life, I probably have more stuff in my house than my parents did.

PW: That's certainly also true of me as well. Again, I'm not an ascetic who rejects the pleasures of materialism. But the problem is the way that things can get so out of hand, and how we so easily forget to take into account the costs to us in life satisfaction—and the costs to the environment, which are enormous—of this way of life.

PP: Can you be more specific about the kinds of costs to the environment you're talking about?

PW: Take, for example, taxes on gasoline. People don't want higher gas taxes, because they'd have to pay more for gas. There's lots of evidence that this would lead to people driving less, but most people don't make the link between paying more for gas and having a world that survives and air that we can breathe. It's also true that with higher gas taxes, we'd all have a little less money to spend on stuff. So instead of buying the latest I-phone every two years, perhaps we'd buy one every three years. So what people are not doing when they're faced with these kinds of decisions is looking at which is a better package: the I-phone every three years and more breathable air and more stable climate; or the I-phone every two years and air that's killing me? That's the complete package, so to speak. But despite economists telling us that nobody ever makes an unwise choice, and that we're all hyper-rational about what's good for us, people typically make the unwise choice.

PP: Why do we have such a difficult time with making personal economic choices that are better for the environment, and for our quality of life?

PW: Once we've gotten onto a certain course, it becomes self-perpetuating, and it becomes very difficult to step back from it, and to see the consequences of what we've chosen. I think if most people could see the whole chain from higher gas taxes, to less spending on I-phones, to cleaner, more breathable air and a more stable climate, I think most people would choose to hold onto their I-phone for another year. (Obviously, it's not just about I-Phones; this is just an example of one small piece of the equation.) But people don't think that way. And of course we have whole industries developed to try to make sure that people *don't* think of it that way.

PP: There's certainly nothing much in the popular culture that would phrase a choice the way you just have. So people are left to come up with their own epiphanies.

PW: Exactly. Another big part of the problem is the way the metrics of business and economic thinking are applied to all aspects of life these days. Take the way we talk about the costs of healthcare, which we treat as if it's the last thing we should be spending money on. The way it's typically framed is around how many lives can be saved at what cost through making certain changes, and if, say, having more nurses in hospitals doesn't save lives, we say it's inefficient to have them and is a place to "cut costs."

Obviously, it's important to know how many lives can be saved. When we're sick, we realize there's nothing better our money could be spent on than good medical care. But in addition to providing good treatment, we should also be including costs that aim to make hospitals more comfortable places. When a person is in the most desperate state they might be in for their entire life, having more nurses on call so that when you need something a nurse comes in five minutes instead of twenty minutes can make a huge difference to that patient—*even if* it doesn't influence the survival rate. We tend not to think of these kinds of things when we're healthy, so when it happens to us, it catches us by surprise. And once we're out of the hospital, the forces of denial set in. So we end up ignoring our neediest selves for our greediest selves.

PP: What a great phrase! So, in following the thread of this conversation around the idea that we all have more and more stuff, are you actually saying that those in the ninety-nine percent are not as bad off economically as we're being led to believe?

PW: Stating it that boldly seems insensitive to the very real deprivations lots of people are experiencing. There are certainly many people living in poverty. What I am trying to say is that where it gets complicated is that in a wealthy country like the U.S., today's poor have things that middle class people didn't have fifty years ago. For instance, there are people in housing projects with possessions that nobody had fifty years ago.

PP: You mean like flat screen TVs—

PW: Right, and smart phones, and computers and so on. But at the same time, people in these housing projects also have to bolt the door because there's crime in their neighborhood. And the crime is both itself a tremendous *cost* of poverty, because poor people are forced to live where there's crime; and it's also a *product* of poverty, because it's the despair that generates the crime. So I don't want to minimize the real suffering and injustice that goes on. And in that sense the polarization between the ninety-nine and the one percent means a lot.

But part of what we have to recognize is that the problem isn't just *material* deprivation; it's deprivation of respect and lack of feeling of equal worth. This kind of deprivation can never be solved while the positions and circumstances of people at the bottom and the top of the society are so radically different and unequal, *even if* the people at the bottom have more "stuff" than people at the bottom used to have.

PP: If you were advising politicians who make these passionate proclamations on how to change our economy so that it's more fair and compassionate, what would you say, from your psychological perspective?

PW: What I would hope to highlight, and then find the best possible way to communicate to the public, is this notion of "packages" that we were talking about earlier. I would try to emphasize the fact that the economic problem we're facing is not just one of "Do I have to have more or do I have less?" Rather, it's "What is the 'overall package' I'm getting?"

This comes up whenever we have to make choices around paying higher taxes, which in our country at this point is a very hard sell. The more clear politicians can become in comparing what the country would look like with fewer resources for public projects, and what it would look like with more resources, the more they can help to dispel this myth that anything spent by the government is wasted. Compare the difference, for example, between parks that are created and preserved by the government, and new cars that are provided by the private sector: Which is really providing more satisfaction in people's lives?

So in my view, politicians should begin to highlight the way the choices citizens make often include things that if they knew they were getting, they wouldn't really want. Terms like "side effects" or "packages" or "unintended consequences" that could help us begin to see beyond the tunnel vision we're caught in would be very useful.

PP: One of the more compelling things in your book is the way you examine some of the economic myths that get tossed around in debates without being fully examined. One of them is the phrase "get the economy moving again."

PW: We tend to treat the economy as this single thing that we measure by how much is happening. But what we don't really ask ourselves is *what* is happening. For example, with regard to the one percent/ninety-nine percent: think about all the human labor that goes into making one yacht for a billionaire. Then consider how that same labor could be employed toward housing for people who are either homeless or living in very crowded and uncomfortable conditions. Wouldn't that be a better employment of society's resources? If you're just measuring the number of people working, and the number of dollars moving around, and so on, both get the economy "moving." But the economy is more than just numbers. It's about contributing to how we live, while keeping in mind the subjective and social reality of *how human beings are actually living*, rather than just asking is economic activity *per se* going on—which is all that "getting the economy moving" looks at.

PP: You also write about another pervasive myth, "the invisible hand of the market."

PW: That's a really interesting one. It comes from Adam Smith, who is viewed in certain circles as sort of the patron saint of standard economic thinking, and even of conservatism, since his philosophy seems to be so pro-market. Basically, "the invisible hand of the market" means that if you just let the market's self-interest reign, then invariably it will produce the best results. But I think several things are important to keep in mind about that well-worn phrase. One is that Adam Smith himself didn't limit his thinking to that dictum. And he himself was reacting to political and economic circumstances that were rigidly restrictive, often with the deck stacked against most people. So in advocating a market economy as a means of liberation from the particular economic restrictions of his day, he wasn't dealing with the same kind of market economy we're talking about today. In addition, Smith wrote another book that people don't pay much attention to called *The Theory of Moral Sentiments*, in which he warned that if an economy just runs on self-interest, then there has to also be some counterforce of social feeling, conscience, and sense of limits. Otherwise, that invisible hand doesn't work so well.

The other thing that we can ask ourselves with regard to this idea of the "invisible hand," is how well it works when we measure it against the problem of rising carbon emissions, or when we look at the increasing inequalities in income and opportunities. If we decide that we want to conserve that concept of the invisible hand and the free market, for instance, then we should also begin to include the fact that the market doesn't take everything into account, because it leaves out a wide range of side effects.

If two parties make a commercial exchange with each other, what's often omitted, for instance, is the impact on other people not directly involved. That's a *huge* extra factor, both materially and psychologically, that's left out of standard market thinking. Economists do talk of this phenomenon in terms of "externalities" in their jargon, but it is largely treated as a small inconvenience to an otherwise neat theory of the wonders of the market, rather than as so powerful and pervasive in many cases that it invalidates their basic worldview and threatens both social justice and the planet. So as simple and appealing as the idea of the wondrous invisible hand sounds, we can see what it actually yields by *looking* at what it's yielded. And we can say it does certain things pretty well, but we can also say that there are lots of things it doesn't do so well. So I believe that we need to at least guide that hand.

PP: You write that this idea of the invisible hand "perpetuates an illusion that it somehow moves apart from our own will," so that it has almost achieved a kind of mythic force or presence.

PW: Right—and there's this additional idea that this invisible hand is a *benign* hand. To be clear, there are certain good things that come from this. I wouldn't want to totally eliminate market forces. I remember visiting the Soviet Union when it was still the Soviet Union, and it was a very gray and uncreative place. I remember particularly how the stores and restaurants were just so unappealing. And it made me think, yes, there is something very nice about small, individual enterprises where people put in their own creative efforts, and something distinctive is coming up from below.

So it's not that I'd want to eliminate that altogether, by any means. But I think especially in the current era we have lost sight of the rest of the picture. We only look at one thing that is important, while forgetting that there's so much else to take into account beyond the quantitative and business rubrics we use for assessing everything. And this narrow vision has caused us to lose the larger interconnections, and the *real, felt,* subjective experience of what it's like to be in the midst of this kind of free-market economy.

PP: And that subjective understanding, of how people feel, is what psychology adds to our understanding of democracy and our economic infrastructure. Is that how you would see it?

PW: Yes, I do see it that way. I think it's interesting in this regard to contemplate the Declaration of Independence, and the idea of "life, liberty, and the pursuit of happiness." But happiness is not just measurable by dollars and cents, or whether the economy is moving. It is true that if the economy isn't moving, and if large numbers of people are unemployed and so on, we're not so happy as a country. But it's also true that if we really paid attention to the pursuit of happiness, we would have a very different way of evaluating it and organizing our society.

PP: In fact, there have been studies that examine the links between states of happiness and income levels. The most interesting statistic is that beyond $75,000 a year, there's not a measurable increase in happiness along with income.[4]

PW: Yes, a lot of studies do seem to suggest that. If you just speak to people, it also seems very consistent with their subjective experience. However, the director of the American Enterprise Institute, Arthur C. Brooks, has had a couple of op-eds in *The New York Times* recently that imply that all of these criticisms around income inequalities are due to envy; this is the new rhetoric from the right.[5] In responding to that claim, and saying that I personally am *not* envious of the wealthy, I should acknowledge that I'm speaking from a vantage point of having a very substantial income. I'm not hugely wealthy—academics don't get hugely wealthy—but I do have a good income and I live very comfortably.

Another *New York Times* columnist, David Brooks, has framed a similar argument. He says progressive critiques of growing inequality do not really reflect concerns about the circumstances of the poor but rather reflect the envy of the educated elites in the ninety-eighth and ninety-ninth percentile in relation to the super-rich in the top one hundredth of one percent.[6] And I just don't agree with that. I think there are many people, and I would include myself, who look at income distribution in this country and say it's wrong, morally and psychologically, and it isn't working well. And I don't think those views are coming from a place of envy. I like my life, and I *would not want* the life of an investment banker. I look at some kids right out of college who are making huge incomes, but who are leading lives that are the very opposite of enviable, because they have no real life other than the money that they're earning and the "getting ahead" that they're doing.

PP: But isn't part of the fact that we're even having this discussion due to the fact that there's a prevailing value system in the country that is more driven to becoming successful economically, versus what you write about in your book, psychological or inner development?

PW: Yes, I think in one sense that's true. But I think another psychological phenomenon that I've witnessed throughout my professional career, and that plays an important role psychologically around how the economy is affecting us, is captured by the concept of dissociation. As I've become increasingly aware of this fact, I've come to think that people aren't simply materialistic. In fact, I think it's more the case that people simultaneously have really strong wishes and preferences for a life that has more breadth, more relatedness, more time, and more being with friends and family even while they ceaselessly—and at the expense of those very wishes—strive for material wealth and security. These two aims, and their contradictions, are dissociated. That is, when we don't make the connections, we fail in still another way to see the total package. And numbers and statistics are so seductive, because they help us to not notice the contradictions and tensions by laying out everything along a single axis of "more and less." And if the question is only "Do you want more materially?" or "Do you want *less*?" the answer is almost always that everybody wants more.

But the thing about money is that it lends itself too easily to "more and less." It's much harder for people to know, for example, if their relationship with their partner is better now than it was five years ago, or if it's worse, or the same, or better than their next door neighbors' relationship. Those are difficult things to evaluate; it's very complex and subjective. So it becomes much easier to evaluate if I have more *money* than I had five years ago, or if I have more money than my neighbors. These are the areas where we measure ourselves, and in doing so, we end up forgetting a lot of other things that are truly important to us. In other words, I don't think it's just that we're materialistic. I think it's that we're drawn to that more materialistic side of ourselves by a lot of forces that make us forget the rest of ourselves.

PP: That is very well said, and bears repeating! Can you explain more about what you really mean by the fact that people want more connection and community, but they're dissociated?

PW: What it means is that when they're thinking of one thing, they have a hard time keeping in mind at the same time the other thing. So, for example, when a person is thinking about whether they should take a new job that's been offered to them in another city that pays $30,000 more annually, which will be measurably "better," they may not think about what it will be like for their kids to be pulled out of their schools and have to make friends in a new school, or that they're going off and leaving their own network of friends, and that they'll only be in touch with them over Facebook, but not face to face.

Those things may matter. But if they're thinking about their income, and how can they turn down "x" amount of dollars more, the rest of the possible consequences are shunted aside. Then later, after they've taken the job, and they're feeling lonely because they don't have any friends, and they don't have as much time to be with their kids because they're having to commute too much, they may not be thinking to themselves, "Well, I did that to earn more money."

So that's an example of how we separate the different parts of our thinking, rather than putting them together so that we take all sides of ourselves into account. Again, my point isn't that our material standard doesn't matter; I'm not taking that kind of view at all. But I *am* saying that it tends to become the predominant thing not because it matters to us most, but because it's the most easily accessible choice. And then later, when we feel let down and dissatisfied, we don't see the connections between our choices, and why we're in the rut that we're in.

PP: It's very hard to live that way. What you're describing is living according to a different set of values. I kind of live by those values, and consequently have a less materially successful and secure life than many people I know. It's often puts me in a funny place, and some people think I'm a little crazy, which in turn can make me feel bad, or sad.

PW: And it's especially difficult because if everybody else thinks you're crazy, then it becomes hard to swim against the tide. But if everybody were thinking that way, certainly more people who do choose to live like that would feel better. Because then they'd be making decisions without having to feel that they were doing something peculiar. And they would be able to make choices that paid more attention to what actually makes their lives *feel* better, rather than what *looks* better, or that gives a bigger number financially.

PP: Where do you see examples of hopeful changes in the direction you've been describing?

PW: Even despite some excesses and public relations problems, the Occupy Wall Street movement was very significant.[7] At the very least it introduced the idea of the one percent and the ninety-nine percent, and that made people more aware of the country's economic divide. Another thing is that even as news networks are gaining advertising dollars through their extreme weather segments, which seem to be very popular, they're also sending the message that something is actually happening to the climate. There have also been some encouraging reports about the Millennial generation, who seem to be less materialistic. This trend may have originated in the limited economic opportunities available to them. But according to some reports it's led to a re-thinking of values around how to live their lives. So maybe a new generation is beginning to introduce new ideas. Perhaps these things are cyclical, and the plates are starting to shift again, as they did during the sixties.[8]

PP: The Millennials seem to want more meaningful lives, and how they live is as important to them as the money that they earn.

PW: Ownership seems less important; fewer Millennials own cars, and even fewer drive. This reflects a shift toward urban living, as opposed to suburban houses and lifestyles. So these are some positive potential shifts. But in coming to a close, I'd like to go back to one of the most important things we talked about. To the degree that people can begin to see the "packages" that they're choosing, rather than just the individual choice of "Do I want it?" or "Don't I?" and the more that politicians can also begin to frame things that way, then the more we can all begin to see more clearly, and things can begin to shift in a different direction. I wouldn't say I'm a wild-eyed optimist, but I'd say I see possibilities for that happening. ■

Notes

1. "Materialism: A System that Eats Us from the Inside Out: Buying More Stuff Is Associated with Depression, Anxiety, and Broken Relationships," by George Monbiot, *Guardian*, December 9, 2013. "Why More Things Don't Make Us Happier," by Amanda L. Chen, *Huffington Post*, April 7, 2014.
2. "Who Are the World's Largest Polluters?" by Lucy Nicholson, *Reuters* <http://www.reuters.com/news/pictures/slideshow?articleId=USRTXRKSI#a=2>. The United States is a close second with 5,903 tons of greenhouse gases released each year.
3. "Wealth Gap: A Guide to What It Is, Why It Matters," by Christopher S. Rugaber and Josh Boak, *AP News*, January 27, 2014. "What's new is the widening gap between the wealthiest and everyone else. Three decades ago, Americans' income tended to grow at roughly similar rates, no matter how much you made. But since roughly 1980, income has grown most for the top earners. For the poorest 20 percent of families, it's dropped. Incomes for the highest-earning 1 percent of Americans soared 31 percent from 2009 through 2012, after adjusting for inflation, according to data compiled by Emmanuel Saez, an economist at University of California, Berkeley. For the rest of us, it inched up an average of 0.4 percent. In 17 of 22 developed countries, income disparity widened in the past two decades, according to the Organization for Economic Cooperation and Development."
4. "The Perfect Salary for Happiness: $75,000," by Robert Frank, *Wall Street Journal*, September 7, 2010.
5. Arthur C. Brooks. "The Downside of Inciting Envy," *New York Times*, March 1, 2014. "Capitalism and the Dalai Lama," *New York Times*, April 17, 2014.

6. "The Piketty Phenomenon," by David Brooks, *New York Times*, April 24, 2014.

7. Occupy Wall Street is a leaderless resistance movement founded September 17, 2011, to address the inequities between the one percent and the ninety-nine percent and the corrosive power of major banks and multinational corporations over the democratic process.

8. "The Cheapest Generation: Why Millennials Aren't Buying Houses or Cars, and What that Means for the Economy," by Derek Thompson and Jordan Weissman, *The Atlantic*, August 8, 2012.

The Changing American Self in an Era of Consumerism

AN INTERVIEW WITH PHILIP CUSHMAN, PH.D.

AMERICA, AS HAS BEEN stated often and by many thinkers, was the first nation intentionally and deliberately founded on certain principles and ideas, chief among them the rights of the individual. Although this marked an historic turning point, and although there were arguments about the varying degrees of man's selfishness or selflessness, little exploration was devoted to just what a "self" really was: its internal structures; what in it is abiding, and what changes; and, most especially, the interaction between the individual self and the larger forces of history and culture.

Perhaps taking up where the Founders left off, these are among the topics that historian and psychotherapist Philip Cushman examines in his book *Constructing the Self, Constructing America: A Cultural History of Psychotherapy.* Published in 1995, this remarkable work addresses the widening chasm between history and psychology, critically observing the way current psychotherapeutic theories fail to "take into consideration the sociohistorical conditions that shaped the illnesses they are responsible for healing." In his book, Dr. Cushman also addresses one of the fundamental conditions of modern times: "[T]he culture of consumerism and individualism, and of the psychotherapies that sustain it." Indeed, contrary to the way most citizens no doubt think of their own separate and autonomous "selves," in Cushman's view neither the self nor its attendant problems that therapists attempt to treat are constant, but are continually shaped and re-shaped within the "rough and tumble of the local values and politics of their respective eras." As he writes in his first chapter,

Each era has a predominant configuration of the self, a particular foundational set of beliefs about what it means to be human. Each particular configuration of the self brings with it characteristic illnesses, local healers, and local healing technologies. These selves and roles are not interchangeable or equivalent. Each embodies a kind of unique and local truth that should not be reduced to a universal law, because such reductions inevitably depend on a particular cultural frame of reference, which in turn inevitably involves an ideological agenda.

When I first interviewed Cushman on the American psyche twenty years ago, our conversation at the time centered on what he termed the "empty self" of the post–World War II era, a self that was starved by the non-nutritious calories of hyper-materialism. When I called to update our initial interview, however, the American self we had initially discussed had changed so much I had to disregard our earlier conversation and start anew. As Cushman describes it, many of the recent changes in the American self can be traced to the seismic cultural shifts brought about by technology: the pervasiveness of I-phones, I-pads, computers, and social media like Facebook, Twitter, and the phenomenon of "selfies." Our modern-day technology, Cushman believes, is yet another extension of our culture of consumerism. But instead of the "empty self" of twenty years ago that yearned to be filled, whether with food or therapy, he now describes the emerging phenomenon of the more shallow "multiple, flattened self."

Cushman is currently semi-retired as a member of the teaching faculty at the School of Applied Psychology at Antioch University in Seattle, Washington. His path to becoming a psychologist began in the traditional American "work your way up the ladder" manner: delivering pizzas and inspecting fire extinguishers. Besides being a clinical psychologist, Cushman also holds degrees in American studies and marriage and family studies. The profession he worked so hard to become a part of, and to which he has remained dedicated over his lifetime, however, may now be endangered by what he bemoans as America's reductive consumerist and "procedural" approaches—a development that may even lead eventually to the death of psychotherapy itself.

Pythia Peay: As a psychologist, you've always emphasized how social and historical forces shape us as individuals. So I wonder if you could speak about the rising tide of consumerism, and how that has affected the practice of therapy.

Philip Cushman: For one thing, I think our country's difficulty in spending money to help others is a terrible phenomenon. It's created a great deal of unnecessary suffering, not only around issues like hunger, or terrible inequities in education, but also in the area of mental health. Because of the lack of creative thoughtfulness around healthcare nationally, we've gotten ourselves into a terrible mess in terms of psychotherapy. I'm extremely concerned that it's not going to get any better. Our ability as psychotherapists to treat emotional suffering has been profoundly changed by the influence of these enormous corporations that control healthcare in our society. To make matters worse, they control healthcare through a kind of authoritarian process that has become increasingly procedural and behavioral, and that has controlled healthcare workers, and especially therapists, more and more as the years have gone by.

PP: So you haven't seen any good changes under the passage of the Affordable Care Act (ACA)?[1]

PC: Well, for the most part, no. Of course, it is extremely important that those who have been uninsured get insured: that has been a huge advance. But the ACA left intact the corporate control of healthcare, which continues the tragedy that is healthcare in this country. And with corporate control comes the biggest danger for psychology, which is that scientism and proceduralism take over and define psychotherapy. So I'm concerned that the ACA is just adding to this trend. In general, when new presidential administrations come into office—and this is generally true in the post–World War II era—they tend to draw from a certain segment of liberal academia, which typically reproduces a kind of modern-era "scientism." I'm not talking about science, which is a wonderful thing, but the belief that the physical science model can solve all human problems.

Because that idea has become so prevalent in our society now, most of psychotherapy has been reduced to a kind of cognitive behavioralism.[2] The problem with that is we get unused to being able to think, work, and cooperate together in relation to moral issues. This approach makes it difficult to work with more nuanced problems in our society, and in my opinion, healthcare falls into that category. So as a result, what we're seeing is a continuation of the control of therapists by corporately pushed behavioral proceduralisms. And I think it's really the death of psychotherapy.

PP: I'm very sorry to hear that. As someone who's benefited greatly from being in therapy, that would be a terrible tragedy in the making.

PC: Well, that's right. It hasn't killed therapy yet. But when corporations control what is the right amount of therapy for a particular personal problem and whether it should be six or eight sessions, and when they demand specific behavioral descriptions from the psychologist of the treatment that's been provided, that's making psychotherapy a tool of the state. The emphasis then becomes providing psychotherapy that puts a Band-Aid on emotional suffering, and that returns patients as quickly as possible to their roles as workers and consumers.

PP: What you're talking about sounds like a continuation of your chapter "Self-liberation Through Consumerism," in which you talk about this new era that arose out of World War II, when our modern concept of the individual "self" was radically reconfigured, leading to what you called the empty self. Can you say more about that?

PC: That chapter was written in the early nineties. At the time, the idea of the "empty self" was at the apex of a phenomenon that had been building in the modern era since the beginning of the twentieth century, starting approximately in 1890.

But things have changed since then. In 2000, my colleague Peter Gilford and I wrote an article in *American Psychologist* that was titled, "Will Managed Care Change Our Way of Being?"[3] The argument we made in that more recent article was that we're now seeing a major shift in the self away from "emptiness" to "multiplicity," or what I have since referred to as the multiple, flattened self. Instead of being deep, this flattened self is shallow and superficial. The way our argument went, and the way it still goes, is that this new self is still profoundly consumerist, and based on consumerism. We don't know yet what this new self is going to look like exactly, and how we're going to embody it; but I think it's different, and I think we're seeing something new. Every understanding of the self has its good parts and its bad parts, so I don't think this new way of being is the end of the world. Undoubtedly, there are some good things about multiplicity, such as flexibility, curiosity, and energy. And of course there were plenty of problems with the empty self.

PP: Can you say more about the difference between the empty self and the multiple, flattened self?

PC: The way I came to understand the empty self was that individuals experienced and were thought to be composed of a kind of deep interior that felt empty, and that they felt compelled to fill up in some way. I listed various ways that we try to fill up the empty self, and that mostly involved some form of consumerism: certain kinds of entertainment; following a cult leader, or a charismatic political leader; and items like food that in one way or another individuals could purchase and consume.

We also saw the phenomenon of the empty self in terms of psychotherapy. The two most prominent psychotherapy theories of the postwar era, Object Relations theory and Self Psychology, both conceived of humans as having some degree of an interior emptiness inside that needed to be filled by someone in order to create an interior self. Child development came to be understood as "internalizing" the parents in order to build a self; and if that didn't work, then one went to therapy, which was thought to provide the opportunity to internalize the therapist—and thereby fill the self. This psychological perspective manifested in many, many ways in our postwar society, with people often describing themselves as feeling empty, and searching desperately for some way to feel filled up and relaxed.

PP: But now you're seeing a shift away from that empty self?

PC: Yes, over the last fifteen years, as Gilford and I wrote in an article called "From Emptiness to Multiplicity,"[4] various forces in society have shaped us to live in such a way that we are coming to understand and experience ourselves as flattened, less deep individuals, with a kind of "cluster" of different selves. This means that we live out a particular facet of our self, depending on the demands of the social situation that we find ourselves in. Where we see this reflected in our society is in the whole online, virtual phenomenon, with people using their computers to get involved in chat rooms or massively multiplayer online role-playing games. In those chat rooms, games, or online dating services, people represent themselves in various ways that sometimes don't correspond to how one would think of them if one met them in person. Right? I'm sure you must be familiar with this.

PP: Yes, I've certainly had experiences online. Like many of my friends and family, I'm on Facebook and Twitter.

PC: The most obvious example of this more multiple way of being is when people go online and create an avatar.[5] In creating this avatar, they're able to present themselves in whatever gender they prefer in the moment. Or they can pretend to be old when in real life they're young, or vice versa. So in effect, they make up a self! And, in fact, the movie *Avatar* from a few years ago was a perfect example of that phenomenon I'm struggling to describe. I say "struggling" because we're still in the early years of learning about this phenomenon of the multiple, flattened self. In another twenty years we'll be able to understand and describe it much more clearly.

Another example of this phenomenon that I'm talking about can be found in those books and studies that have described the effects of reading and doing research online. In a recent book called *The Shallows*, for example, author Nicholas Carr argued that what we do online is jump from topic to topic, so that when we're reading something online, some new link catches our eye, and so we jump from one link to the next. But in doing that, we lose the opportunity to really delve deeply into a subject.

PP: So do you consider this kind of online world of skimming and surfing on the surface of things another manifestation of our consumerist culture?

PC: Absolutely. I think we're developing a way of being that lacks a long attention span, that's not really interested in getting into something deeply, and that *thinks* about or imagines something, rather than actually *doing* something. One of the ways this has affected us is that more and more frequently we see people just wanting to consume and to be entertained. In this sense, jumping from one link to another to whatever catches one's eye next that's violent, colorful, attractive, or frightening is just another form of entertainment. In addition, the cult of celebrity has grown increasingly stronger in the last fifteen years. Something I've given a lot of thought to lately, in fact, is the idea that we're all aspiring to, or think of ourselves as, a kind of minor celebrity. We are, for instance, our "own paparazzi."

PP: You mean the way people are always posting photos of themselves on Facebook, and "selfies" on Instagram and Twitter?

PC: Right, we take pictures of ourselves at all hours of the day and night and then post them online. Celebrities used to actually flee from that—they wanted their privacy—but now we do that to ourselves! There have been a few studies recently that seem to indicate that there are some young people who feel imprisoned by being on Facebook, and who feel like they create an image for themselves online; that they then have to keep proving it online. And, of course, for the vast majority, most of these images online do not disclose any kind of depression or unhappiness.

PP: I think most people who are on Facebook are familiar with visiting friends' pages and seeing all the warm and happy photos of family dinners, weddings, trips, and successes. But then when they actually talk to that friend, they hear about the financial losses, career setbacks, or family feuds. The difference between what's on Facebook and reality can be striking.

PC: It should be! I think this is an enormous problem. Every once in a while you find a young person who announces that they're going to stay offline for a while because they feel it's too much, and there's just too much work involved. What many people don't say, but what they do disclose privately, is that they often feel "false," and that they're presenting an image of themselves online that they have to keep up, even though it doesn't represent the fullness of their lives.

On the other hand, one of the biggest problems are those people who *don't* feel that way, and who live out this way of being online to such an extent that that *is* life for them. It then becomes a way of life of choosing and living out one image, and then another, and then another, depending on what the social situation requires. The problem is that those people who are doing that are in danger of losing the vocabulary to express genuine discomfort, unhappiness, or despair. I also see this in my own practice, when, increasingly, people come into psychotherapy who don't want to delve into their subjective, emotional inner lives. They just want to be fixed, quickly, so they can go back out and function better.

PP: A tendency that then gets reinforced by what people see online, and in other forms of media and entertainment.

PC: Right. For example, television ads for psychotropic medications represent themselves as treating depression or anxiety. So first of all, these commercials are identifying and defining our problems as intrapsychic disorders or illnesses called depression or anxiety. And second, they present their products as treating the disorder the way any medical illness would be treated: take the pill and quickly get healed. So this new, "flattened, multiple" self that I've been describing is a different way of being, with a different set of psychological symptoms. The "empty self," for example, was characterized by a sense of loneliness and alienation, symptoms that were considered part of narcissism. But we don't see much of that these days.

What we see more of, and what we've come to describe and treat when therapists have to present their cases to insurance companies, are symptoms around anxiety, as well as depression, and, increasingly, trauma-related dissociation. But all of these psychological symptoms—whether anxiety, depression, and dissociation— are typically explained by the patient as an inability to function at work, and an inability to make enough money to be a good consumer.

But what my argument has always been, and continues to be, is that by medicalizing emotional suffering, we depoliticize it. As I argued in *Constructing the Self,* and as I continue to argue, the profession of psychology has been pushed by these powerful consumerist forces into becoming more of an ahistorical, apolitical practice: and therefore we don't interpret people's emotional suffering in political terms. So even those symptoms that are acceptable today to insurance companies— like anxiety, depression, or dissociation—aren't framed within larger historical, cultural, and political terms. Instead, they're thought of in behavioral or cognitive ways: that the patient is suffering from a "mistaken" idea, and so therapists have to straighten out their incorrect thinking about themselves, and help them to see how "wrong-headed" they are. But what we are *never* encouraged to do as therapists in this highly controlled, business-oriented mental health framework is to think of people's complaints and problems in broader, more contextual, historical ways. Rarely, for example, are therapists able to take up in any nuanced, thoughtful way people's experiences out in the world of work.

PP: So then how does this kind of psychological consumerism, so to speak, end up influencing people's relationship with the larger historical world?

PC: I think many people have come to think of themselves as a kind of creature who wants to be gratified, who wants to purchase things, who loves consumer items, and who wants to eat—but who then gets scared and needs to exercise and go on a diet—and the kind of critter who also wants to be entertained, and who wants secretly to be entertaining to others, and for others to notice and respect him or her.

PP: That's a pretty bleak, dystopian vision.

PC: To the multiple, flattened self the world is experienced as a dangerous place that cannot be appealed to or reasoned with. Therefore, the only recourse to the danger is for a particular self to be summoned at a particular moment in order to escape that danger. Just think about the recent pop-cultural fascination with vampires and zombies. Or the recent automobile commercial featuring a young child peacefully riding in his family's car; but he imagines all sorts of scary threats from outside the car, like a frightening tree that comes to life and tries to grab hold of the car, and a bear chasing the car, and a ship in a storm about to crash into the car. Understandably, in this world of kidnappings, child abuse, drive-by shootings, American troops in never-ending wars, unexpected economic crashes, terrorist attacks, and the threat of flu epidemics, people are afraid. But a difference is that in the world of the multiple, flattened self, there is no sense that we can come to mutual understandings with one another, reason with one another, and thereby prevent conflict or disaster. The only hope is to shift into a different self that can escape the danger.

That's exactly what the protagonist Jake Sully does in *Avatar*. At the start of the movie, Sully was this crass, malicious guy who was disabled from combat during war. And then through the miracle of science, as it was portrayed in this science fiction movie, he was transported into the body of this avatar. By comparison to the old Jake, the life of this avatar was beautiful, spiritual, and meaningful. He could love, protect, and care for others. The avatar wasn't disabled. So in that sense, entertainment becomes a psychological defense in a dangerous world. But we don't ever talk about that dangerous world, except in highly circumscribed ways in psychotherapy, and in society in general. We also project many of our fears onto the "other," like terrorists or the federal government. But we never get to what is *really* bothering us; we just go from Band-Aid to Band-Aid. And that's where I think proceduralism comes in.

PP: I'm not sure I understand the link to proceduralism in this context of the dangerous world you're describing.

PC: Because if we think of the world as being dangerous, then the only way we can protect ourselves in an exchange with others is by being the kind of person who follows procedural rules during difficult transactions, and by insisting that the other person also strictly follows specific rules. So that's why I think our world today is becoming increasingly proceduralized. When you pick up the phone these days, what do you get? A menu! You never get to speak to a person, unless you ask several times. So we have to fit ourselves into these categories, like the ethics codes of various businesses or mental health professions. When a therapist diagnoses someone they have to fill out forms and check boxes. But there isn't room for what's in between, or completely different. The only way to be considered "controllable" is to fit in.

PP: So, after describing the empty self and the multiple, flattened self, what kind of a self would you describe, or have you seen, that would be a healthier self to want to construct or allow to emerge organically?

PC: I appreciate the question, and I think it's a very important one. It's one of the main things that distinguishes humans from animals: we care about who we are, how we act, and we try to do what's right. But it's not a question that can be answered as if we could just choose. Because the self isn't something we can construct in some kind of rational way.

The philosopher Hans-Georg Gadamer once said that history does not belong to us—we belong to history. We're historical beings, and the way that we comport ourselves and think about what the right way to be is, is not something that we can just choose. It's something that happens to us, over a period of time, and that, for the most part, we don't notice.

So it's important to emphasize that there are huge, historical, cultural forces continually at work that bring a certain way of being to light. Right now, it's the multiple, flattened self I've been describing. So when certain therapists tell their clients to just choose a different self and a different story and a different avatar— that very way of understanding a human being is the "self" we're in today. To believe a person can just "choose a different self" is not a radical political position and it's not an enlightened position. It's compliance with the status quo, with the multiple self. I have lots of ideas about how I *wish* we acted and how I wish we could think about ourselves. But in the short run that's not going to change things.

I do think, however, that we could begin to think more about the idea itself of what it means to "construct" a self, and that we could also think about what kind of *social world* we want to live in, because ultimately it is the social world that is the only thing that can shift a way of being.

PP: Then what is a way to live in the midst of this world we're in right now?

PC: One of our problems is that we've become unused to being able to think and work on and cooperate together on moral issues. We're not good anymore at carrying out respectful, moral discourse—all you have to do is read the paper or watch the evening news. We just attack.

But Gadamer also described a good way of life as being able to work together on understanding one another: to notice when there's differences between us, and try to understand those differences, and be able when encountering difference in another person to allow their idea or way of being to put our own opinion or way of being into question in relation to theirs. By doing so, we come to understand the other person better because we come to get a sense of the social world that brought him or her to light in the way it does. And then, if we are lucky, we come to understand ourselves better by asking, "What is the social world that brings me to light in the way it does?"

I would hope that by carrying on this kind of moral discourse we could begin to develop a better ability to think about the good, and to keep a dialogue going. When we can be with people like that, or help people be like that with us, then we can begin to make a better, safer world. That's also what I see as one aspect of psychotherapy that has potential to help us in our suffering. But sadly, we're less and less able as therapists to do that now because of the procedural rules we labor under, and so one of the few ways that way of being can be nurtured and developed in our society—psychotherapy—is being seriously undermined. ■

Notes

1. See Ch. 8, n. 6.
2. For more on cognitive behavioral therapy (CBT) see the National Alliance of Mental Illness (NAMI) <http://www.nami.org>.
3. Cushman, Philip, and Peter Gilford. "Will Managed Care Change Our Way of Being?" *American Psychologist* 2000 Sep; 55(9): 985–996.
4. Cushman, Philip, and Peter Gilford. "From Emptiness to Multiplicity: The Self at the Year 2000," *Psychohistory Review* Vol 27(2), 1999, 15–31.
5. Avatar is a graphical representation or icon of a user or a user's three-dimensional online alter ego in computer games or virtual worlds.

—23—

Is America's "Money Complex" Bankrupting Its Character?

AN INTERVIEW WITH THOMAS SINGER, M.D.

WHETHER RICH, POOR, OR in between, whether we are in an economic boom or a downturn, Americans are awash in a cultural sea polluted with the excesses of consumerism. No longer is sex quite the temptation it once was. Rather, it's that new car with the latest feature in the storeroom window, or the luxurious cashmere sweater on the Home Shopping Network that lures us to charge it on our credit card. This is hardly an indulgence reserved for the very rich. Cars may not draw my interest, but I can always be attracted by the latest style or color of boots: black or brown? Knee-high, thigh-high, or ankle-length? Shouldn't I have one pair of each, and in each color? What about red?! Like most Americans, I've spent money I didn't really have on things I didn't really need. I've also spent money I *did* have on things I didn't really need, just because I could.

What drives this kind of consumer behavior? Especially when, given all the evidence that our materialism is destroying the very ground that supports us, Americans are consuming far more than their fair share of the planet's resources? According to San Francisco Jungian psychoanalyst and psychiatrist Thomas Singer, my private spending habits aren't just driven by lack of will power, or how much money I have or don't have in the bank (or available on my credit card). Rather, forces much greater than my personal will are also at play, arising from psychic depths that, despite the best of my intentions, can swamp me as easily as a small boat overturned by ocean waves.

Singer has termed this force a "cultural complex," in this case as it specifically relates to money. For the past ten years, Singer has researched and presented lectures on seven different American "cultural complexes," among them racism and the environment. His explanation of just what that phrase "cultural complex" means initiates our interview, in which he discusses the shabbier side of America's bright and shiny persona.

This was not our first interview. For years, I had known Singer's work as an intrepid explorer of that mysterious borderland between politics and psychology. Our paths first crossed in 1997, when I interviewed him for a feature story about political, social, and economic issues as they arise during clients' therapy sessions.[1] At the time, Singer had just finished hosting a conference with New Jersey Senator Bill Bradley entitled "Myth, Politics, and the Psyche." Singer's enduring friendship with Bradley would come to symbolize the link between their respective fields, each sharing an interest in the other's profession and how they were related. Psyche and politics are so unconsciously entwined, Singer told me then, that we might think of them as bound together in an "unholy marriage" of conflicting archetypes.

Singer, who grew up in the heartland of St. Louis, Missouri, learned firsthand about the power of the unconscious as a young man in 1965 enrolled at Yale Medical School. He had just returned from a year of teaching in Greece, a time of "glorious discovery and the awakening of a thirst for life," when he'd felt as if he'd been following in the footsteps of Nikos Kazantzakis and the eponymous hero of his book *Zorba the Greek*. Medical school was, Singer writes, "a brutal way to sober up from the intoxication of Greek adventures." On beginning his clinical rounds with the other medical students, Singer found himself floundering, his meager diagnostic skills deserting him as he became swept by uncertainty and anxiety.

Within six weeks, he found himself meeting a Jungian analyst for the first time. It was an encounter that would profoundly alter his life's direction. He began to remember his dreams and to consider a career in psychology. After graduating from medical school, he began his psychiatric residency, eventually becoming a Jungian analyst. In addition to maintaining his own private practice, Singer specializes in writing about culture, psyche, and complexes from a Jungian perspective. He is the editor of the Spring Journal Books series on Analytical Psychology and Contemporary Culture as well as *The Cultural Complex* and *The Vision Thing: Myth, Politics and Psyche in the World*.

Singer is currently at work on a series of books that explore cultural complexes in different parts of the world. Two of these have been published: *Placing Psyche: Exploring Cultural Complexes in Australia* and *Listening to Latin America: Exploring Cultural Complexes in Brazil, Chile, Colombia, Uruguay, and Venezuela*, while a third book, *European Complexes*, is in the works. During our interview, I learned how to identify patterns and images in the media and popular culture exemplifying materialism's grip on the psyche of America. We also explored our sense of "not enoughness," how symptoms of narcissism play into our compulsion for consumerism, and how the American dream has come to equal money. Finally, we discussed *The Great Gatsby*, and also those better sides of the American character that can lead us out of the wilderness of "stuff" and into a more connected and soul-satisfying way of life. The following interview is an expanded version of an interview that was conducted in 2013, and that originally appeared in *Psychology Today*.

✳

Pythia Peay: What exactly is a "cultural complex"?

Thomas Singer: The cultural complex notion grew out of Jung's original theory of complexes, in which a cluster of charged ideas, memories, images, and feelings in a person's unconscious interferes with normal functioning in a specific area of life.

    Similarly, on a cultural level, a complex is a cluster of strong emotions, histories, behaviors, and primitive assumptions that tends to be repetitive in a group of people over a long period of time. It's the form in which archetypal forces have taken shape at a particular time and place in history; it also tends to be unconscious. The hallmark of a cultural complex is that it's inflammatory and irrational; it seizes the culture in a disruptive way that defies reason. People often aren't even aware that they're "in" a complex, or that there is even such a thing. So a cultural complex influences us deeply without our even being aware of its presence.

PP: So, just to be clear, could you compare a cultural complex to, say, a personal complex like a negative father complex, which would translate to mean that a person has problems or issues with father-related issues, like relationships with men, or power, or traditionally masculine activities?

TS: That's right. We all have complexes; Jung thought of them as part of the normal psychological structures of the psyche. So if a person has a father complex that has been untouched in terms of trying to understand it, it could negatively affect them in the ways you've just mentioned. Or, they could become over-identified with the complex, and become the very thing that they don't like about men. So the more unconscious a complex is, the more disruptive or influential it can be on behavior.

PP: In a recent lecture you listed seven American cultural complexes. Do you want to choose one and explain how you see that operating in the American psyche?

TS: The one that causes me the most distress is our "money complex," around money, consumerism, and materialism. Whether its politics, sports, or healthcare, we've become so consumed by consumerism it's taken over every aspect of our lives. We've become accustomed to commercial interests taking over and interfering with everything, even our pleasure. Like the Old Testament Mammon, the beast of greed, we've become consumed by materialism and money. So that's a pretty potent complex. It's so powerful we don't even think of it as a complex. We're just used to it, and we think this is the way things have always been, and that's just the way things are.

It's become such a madness that currently the Supreme Court is deciding whether a gene can be patented and made into a commodity.[2] Even our genetic inheritance is up for grabs in terms of pieces of nature that can be owned by specific companies. So America has a *huge* money complex. On the one hand, we've had an extraordinary increase of material wellbeing for most people in our country. And yet we've become much more consumers than citizens; we're totally geared toward materialism, of which money is the fundamental currency. We buy, trade, and sell stuff to one another.

PP: I think that one of the most telling examples of America's money complex was after the tragedy of 9/11, when President Bush advised everyone to go shopping.[3]

TS: Right: when we're feeling our most vulnerable, the most patriotic thing to do is to go out and shop. It's very hard for us as a culture to feel our vulnerabilities.

PP: Besides the Supreme Court case and 9/11, what are some other cultural examples of our money complex?

TS: Images are one way of revealing cultural complexes. Two images come to mind around our money complex. One is Andy Warhol's image of dollar signs. In the iconography of Warhol's uncanny pop sensibility, the dollar becomes the symbol of everything for us. Another image that comes to mind is of a cosmetics counter in a department store around Valentine's Day. Hearts are everywhere, and the counter looks like an altar, all lit up and warm, but also gaudy and seductive. This image conveys the almost religious quality to our relationship with money and what it can buy. We're fascinated by it, we worship it, we covet it, we can't get enough of it, and we think that everything good in the world comes of it. But it's also an image of consumerism, because at this point, money and consumerism have become almost identical.

PP: I appreciate money as much as the next American, but this image conveys a kind of emptiness of cultural character.

TS: It's empty and it's sad because we equate full pockets with a full life. Of course, people know this; it's obvious. But even if we know intellectually that money isn't everything, it's still got us by the balls because it's a cultural complex, with a life of its own. It's non-rational and it's autonomous, so it's very hard to separate from it, because it's who we are at a collective, unconscious level.

PP: This makes me think of a friend of mine who recently retired. She'd done everything right over the years, building up a savings account for when she stopped working. During a visit to her financial advisor, she asked him what would happen to her savings if the power grid went down, or the banks failed, or if society fell apart: What would she do then? And her advisor said to her that at that point there's nothing she could do, because we're all going to be in the same boat. And that was so hard for her to accept! So I guess my question is whether as a society we've focused too much on money as the be all and end all for our security needs.

TS: Right. Money has become our collective lifeboat. Somehow, we think if we have enough of it, we're safe on seas that may not always be calm. But it sounds like the financial advisor gave your friend a thoughtful response. If everything stays the same, your money will be a good lifeboat. But if things change dramatically and there's not enough oxygen in the atmosphere, or if the economy takes a serious downturn, money will become much less of a lifeboat, or a source of security.

PP: In fact, even today the consequences of not having or making money can be very harsh, not just materially, but psychologically. If people don't make it on a certain level, they don't just suffer material deprivation; they also suffer socially, and are judged losers and failures.

TS: It makes me think of black people who have been written out of the economic equation for three hundred years; or any of the marginalized groups who, because they lack access to capital, are seen as having no power. They may have a lot more spirit, but they're zero in that equation.

Look at the two Tsarnaev brothers who set off bombs during the Boston Marathon. The older brother wanted to be a boxer, but suffered defeats, failure, and humiliations along the way. Apparently, when he was asked on his Facebook page what he valued the most, he said that the most important thing was to earn money. But how many immigrants just like him want to be successful, but then start to fail and become disillusioned?

PP: I see this myth operating during every presidential campaign, when it's almost a prerequisite that the candidates must be self-made individuals who've overcome impossible odds, rising out of the ashes of poverty or family hardship. So although we venerate wealth, we really only venerate it if a person has not only earned it on their own, but has heroically struggled to get it.

TS: Absolutely. Part of our complex is that we're highly ambivalent about our relationship to money and how one comes to it. Our highest value is that of the individual doing it on his or her own, and we give a negative value to inheriting it. But unfortunately, the American dream in general has become equated with money. There's nothing wrong with making money, or enjoying material wellbeing. But when people fail to attain that material version of the American dream, they can get disillusioned. They can question the value of life and they can lose their moorings.

PP: How does this ambivalence around money play out on a cultural level?

TS: On the one hand, we're an unbelievably wealthy country, while on the other hand, we feel so unbelievably poor. We're always feeling that we don't have enough to do what we want or need to do. So we live with a constant depression mentality.

PP: So we suffer from a sense of "not-enoughness"?

TS: We constantly feel that we never have enough. And if a country feels that it never has enough of everything, it's in constant distress, and in a constant mode of anxiety. Obviously, this is not to deny the reality of deep distress in other parts of the world. The money complex as I'm describing it as part of the American psyche has more to do with being possessed by non-rational, collective fears.

But perhaps the most dramatic example of America's money complex is the way money now drives our whole political system. Our obsession with money has taken over politics completely and any attempt to change it through campaign finance reform gets beaten down.

PP: Does America's money complex conflict with its ideals as a democracy? Is this who we really are?

TS: It's hard to know whether America's obsession with money is consistent with its historical experience over time, or whether it represents a deviation. But somewhere along the way there was a transition from a rural, agrarian society, to an industrial society, to the post-industrial consumerist society of today. That's different from how we began. I don't think consumerism is in the Second, Third, or Fourth amendments!

PP: One of the things I learned recently about George Washington and the founders was their aim to live by the virtue of "disinterestedness" [see Wood: 2006]. They weren't perfect, but they aspired to be impartial and unselfish, motivated more by service and obligation than their own material or professional gain. We don't seem to even come close to that these days.

TS: I think that's true—self-interest is a much more highly valued principle today, as opposed to disinterest.

You can see this reflected in sports. Sports heroes such as Jackie Robinson or Stan Musial were all about self-sacrifice for higher causes. Today, sports are totally dominated by personal enrichment, self-aggrandizement, and displays of power and wealth. Self-interest is also tied into narcissism.

PP: Can you say more about how narcissism is tied into a money complex?

TS: A certain amount of narcissism, or positive self-worth, is essential to one's psychological wellbeing. In its more negative form, narcissism is an exaggerated sense of one's beauty, importance, value, and power. When that's the case, we might look for the opposite in the unconscious: of *not* feeling very beautiful, or powerful, or worthwhile. And when a person lacks a healthy sense of inner self-regard, money and the things money can buy can be one way to alleviate that inner sense of impoverishment. Self-worth becomes equated with status and the belief that if we have a lot of money, we're worth a lot more. People start to believe that who they are is defined by the dollar, and the power and access that it can buy. So money fuels a lot of the kind of narcissism that is driven by an impoverished sense of inner wellbeing. The kind of narcissism we as a culture seem to be possessed by is this constant need to inflate one's sense of self, which feels impoverished.

PP: So what does this kind of negative, inflated narcissism you're describing, applied to America, say about us as a culture in the eyes of the world?

TS: On one hand, other countries want to emulate us, and they want the same things that we have: such as air conditioning, cars, and refrigerators. At the same time, for all our riches as a country, we often appear silly, empty, and spiritually poor to the rest of the world. So we're both idealized and despised because of our relationship to money and power.

PP: If America were a client on your couch, how would you diagnose the source of these symptoms of narcissism and obsession with money and consumerism?

TS: The American identity over the past 250 years has been strong. We've mastered the seas, dominated large parts of the world, and endured the Industrial Revolution and the Great Depression. We've created material comfort for a large number of people, and achieved amazing things in science and technology. These feats have generated a tremendous sense of resilience, self-confidence, and resourcefulness.

But as a psychologist viewing the country as a patient, I think we've become over-identified with the accomplishments of the "cultural ego." We've done so well, we believe that this is *all* of who we are. What we don't identify with is what gets tossed aside into the unconscious: our sense of emotional and spiritual impoverishment; our disconnection from the Earth; our origins in other countries; and our vulnerability, failures, and inadequacies.

So if I were treating the country on the couch, I'd want to ask about these repressed parts of the American self. The problem arises when America's vulnerabilities and failings enter the political arena in the guise of poverty, healthcare, immigration or other debates, because it divides the country and provokes a defensive response: "Go somewhere else if you feel that way!"

PP: Are you saying that money has become a source of security and emotional fulfillment, to the exclusion of everything else?

TS: On a cultural level, money does all sorts of good things, such as increasing trade and communication. But it's not so much the part around money that's healthy and well functioning we're examining. It's the way in which our culture as a whole gets caught by it and over-identified with it, and where money has become a substitute for other things.

PP: And those other things would be . . . ?

TS: Education and curiosity. The value in connectedness between people, friendship and community, appreciation for life as it is, nature, or art: all these things can get swallowed up by our money complex. In fact, part of our complex around money is that it becomes a chase and a game that possesses us. Then we have to spend a lot of money to fly away to some remote place where things are simpler and we can start to feel those essential parts of life again.

PP: And ironically, that simpler kind of life is usually where we started out to begin with! Since money has to do with worth and value, is there something meaningful at the core of America's money complex that has become distorted over time?

TS: At the core of a cultural complex is an archetype, or a universal instinct that is the same across time and place. The cultural complex is the form in which an archetype has taken shape during a particular historical period.

The archetype at the core of America's money complex is the entitlement to wellbeing by all: that's democracy. It came out of a wonderful vision of a better life for many people, which then got corrupted by people eager to make as much money as they could as quickly as they could.

PP: So what would a life of wellbeing look like to you?

TS: We can all think of examples of people whom we admire, not because of the money they have but because of qualities they embody: grace and generosity, not just with money, but of spirit or of deep concern for others; the capacity to enjoy life and to share in that enjoyment; or for their creativity or knowledge. For me, it's often being out on a tennis court on a Saturday morning when the air is crisp, with two or three friends. That's about as rich as it gets. I also think of older people who've lived well and who've learned from their experiences, losses, and failures, as well as accomplishments.

PP: This makes me think of my mother, who, although good with money but not a wealthy woman, likes to say that although she's not rich, she's had a rich life. The example of *Zorba the Greek* also comes to mind.

TS: I wrote my college thesis on *Zorba the Greek*! And what I discovered through this character in Nikos Kazantzakis's book was the sense of exuberance and discovery that can come through a life fully lived. And that's wealth, and that's wellbeing. It doesn't preclude money, but it's a spirit of life that's not identified with money.

PP: And then there's the character from F. Scott Fitzgerald's enduring American classic, *The Great Gatsby*, currently a movie.

TS: Gatsby is a complex character, as he is all about the progress of the individual to the highest levels of wealth and achievement. He grew up very poor, amasses huge wealth through some sketchy connections, and lives in this palace of delights. What's interesting is that although he's totally identified with his wealth, he also stands outside it in some way, and realizes it's just an empty game. His ironic, knowing character is the perfect "carrier" of America's complex around our infatuation with money, allowing us to see it. So Gatsby is an example of America's total infatuation with money and material wellbeing, and yet ultimately how hollow that is.

PP: So does Gatsby exemplify a kind of necessary skepticism towards America's infatuation with money?

TS: A little skepticism or irony is a step towards consciousness. A cultural complex is everywhere; it surrounds you and you swim in it. And so to both be of it and not fully of it is difficult to achieve. This means both appreciating all the good things that money can buy, but also that we're all caught in this complex, we all partake of it, and we need some sort of self-reflection so that we don't become totally identified with it. Too much money is often a tremendous burden and can get in the way of individual development.

PP: Is becoming conscious of America's money complex one of our "psychological tasks" as a citizen?

TS: For me, awareness of our cultural complexes is the beginning of being a good citizen. Because they don't just disappear, it's a psychological task to both identify the complexes that are driving the collective psyche and then try to address them in a thoughtful way, rather than being blindly possessed by them. Whatever the complex is—whether a power complex, or a mother or father complex—we can't eradicate them, so we have to develop a human relationship to our personal complex, as well as with a cultural complex.

PP: So it's about finding the right attitude. A person could even do a personal case history on their family story around money.

TS: When we address money psychologically it's a double task, because it's got both a personal dimension and a cultural layer. So it's a matter of citizens examining their own upbringing and the value of money in their family, whether they were born with too much money or not enough. How did their experience around money compare to what they saw around them? Did it mirror the culture, or was it different? But ultimately, it's important to become aware of what the culture is inundating us with, and then to differentiate our own individual relationship to money. And that's no easy task. ■

Notes

1. "The World at the Door," by Pythia Peay, *Common Boundary*, January/February, 1997.

2. Subsequent to this interview, the U.S. Supreme Court ruled that human genes may not be patented. See "Justices, 9–0, Bar Patenting Genes," by Adam Liptak, *New York Times*, June 13, 2013.

3. See "He Told Us To Go Shopping: Now the Bill is Due," by Andrew J. Bacevich, *Washington Post*, October 5, 2008. Bush's actual comment two weeks after 9/11 was 'Get down to Disney World in Florida. Take your families and enjoy life, the way we want it to be enjoyed," but was widely interpreted to mean encouraging everyone to go shopping as a way to boost the economy.

Still Keeping up with the Joneses

An Interview with A. Chris Heath, M.D.

MONEY, SAYS TEXAS PSYCHOANALYST A. Chris Heath, is "weird." His remark, although offhand, captured for me the essence of a topic that is both real and practical, and yet also slippery and ephemeral. The reason money is weird, Heath went on to say, is because the essence of it is symbolic. Even in our modern, capitalist era, money remains one of society's biggest taboos, shrouded in secrecy. In his practice, Heath says, most clients "have a harder time talking about money than any other topic. They have a much easier time talking with me about sex." Psychologically, money's symbolic qualities, he continues, lends itself as a vehicle for allowing "different parts of our psyches to play out"—more so even than with love or relationships.

Currently faculty member of the Dallas Psychoanalytic Center, and in private practice for seventeen years, Heath was initially drawn to the field of medicine, particularly the study of infectious disease and radiology. Gradually, however, his interests turned to psychiatry for the "different perspectives" it offered on health. The symptoms psychiatrists attend to, he says, differ from those of other kinds of disease: anxiety instead of pain, for instance, or hallucinations instead of fever. As Heath pursued his training, his interest was further engaged by psychiatry and psychoanalysis's attention to symptoms' meanings. Anxiety is not just atypical firing of neurons in the brain, for example, he says, "but also a symbol of something greater, usually unfathomed." Today, Heath is strongly influenced by the Kleinian tradition of psychoanalysis, which for him has the "most useful language" for understanding the deeper, archaic levels of the psyche, where visceral reactions such as love, hate, idealization, and devaluation are "continuously present, running parallel with more conscious, logical lines of thought."[1]

One of the clearest examples of how this interior dimension impacts our outer everyday behaviors—made obvious by the material brought into his consulting room, Heath says—is in the way people deal with money, and in the things they buy. This psychological view is at odds with the field of economics, which has historically assumed that where money is concerned, most people behave in rational ways. Yet when these internal feelings and strong drives combine with the external pressures of our consumer-oriented society to use money and physical objects as symbols of status, Heath says, the result can be personal debt, which can be a dangerous thing.

In studying the intersection between money and psychology, Heath hopes to bring greater awareness to economic principles and to people's motivations for spending as a way to increase their sense of personal meaning, and to help them make clearer decisions about the use of their resources. These topics and more—such as persistent gender issues around money; America's idealized image of itself as the richest, most powerful country in the world (and how our hard work goes to support that image); and ways that the economy are evolving in new directions—are explored in greater detail in the following interview, conducted in 2014.

✳

Pythia Peay: I'm curious to learn from you whether your clinical work with patients over the years has revealed any patterns and beliefs in the American psyche around money.

A. Chris Heath: Part of the process in psychoanalysis is exploring how people function for each other. For example, a part of someone we know can become a part of our psychological make-up, or what is called a "part object." One of the important dynamics of this process as it occurs within relationships is "idealization and devaluation."

So in the case of money, a number of my women patients idealize their husbands, not just as breadwinners and providers but also as the person who handles the money. Some wives don't even feel worthy enough to ask, "Where's the money?" or, "How much money do we have in this account or that account?" or, "What happens if you die?" In one particular case, the wife was terrified of asking, because her husband became defensive whenever she pushed him on this issue. For many of these women, there's an unconscious belief that the way their husbands provide for them is kind of magical.

PP: This tells me something about the magical qualities we assign to money, but also that there's still an undertow of gender issues around money.

ACH: Right. Even though the kind of relationship where the husband was the breadwinner and the wife kept the home together was more overtly typical of the fifties, these gender stereotypes still get played out in many of my patients. From the point of view of the men who've been able to talk with me about money, many feel pushed to earn money by the need to prove something. But the question is: Who is it that they have to prove something to?

PP: So women have a tendency to project their own power around money onto men, while men have to prove something around money to some kind of internal "idealized other," like someone from their childhood?

ACH: Men feel compelled to prove something to whomever they idealized that took care of them in childhood, and whom they feel would disapprove of them if they didn't have an "important appearing" lifestyle. Typically for most men, this was the father, who was distant, but bigger than life when he was around. In one example from my practice, a man portrayed a persona to his wife that was like an artificial painting, providing a lavish lifestyle. In reality, he had huge amounts of debt.

But he wasn't so different from many other people: the average American family who has a credit card has $15,000 worth of debt on that card.[2] This is an example of how these primitive, unconscious ways of functioning get translated to a cultural level.

PP: If that's the average, then there must be people with a lot more in debt.

ACH: Absolutely. But why? For some, this might understandably be a result of unemployment and being desperate and needing to eat. But with the people I've seen, that's not the case. More often, there's the need to buy fancy stuff to show off, either to family members or to neighbors in the community.

PP: So it would seem that many Americans are still driven by "keeping up with the Joneses." It's such a commonly used phrase in American culture, but we don't unpack it psychologically as much as we could.

ACH: If someone has plenty of money and they can afford to buy a Jaguar instead of a Honda, it's fine. People should be able to spend their money however they like. There also might be real advantages. For instance, if someone lives in a nice house, people might assume they're successful, and therefore might be more likely to go to them with financial opportunities.

But I suspect that doesn't happen often enough that it's worth going into debt for. So when there's a perceived need to buy something showy, whether a car or a house in order to maintain an illusion, some kind of primitive need is being activated. And it's often unclear what that need really is. In some cases it just might have to do with "keeping up with the Joneses."

PP: Can you say more specifically what you mean by this "primitive" need underlying a need to "keep up with the Joneses"?

ACH: What I mean is the unconscious drive people have to fulfill a need inside them, with something from the outside world. This might mean they're seeking their own self-approval, or the security of knowing that things are going to be okay. To speak in Jungian archetypes, the need might be for a kind of earth mother that provides for them and fulfills what they should have received from their environment as an infant. Yet as the British psychoanalyst D. W. Winnicott taught, no mother or father is perfect, and no child gets through childhood without suffering a wounded sense of safety and security. This in turn impairs almost everyone's ability to feel that they're going to be okay, that they're lovable, and that they're able to love. It's the solution to these inner feelings of lack and insufficiency that people want when they seek approval from an "other."

And who or what is this "other"? Not necessarily our friends and family that let us know that they like us, and that we're lovable, even if external circumstances aren't perfect. Something much more is at work, as if we're still the baby needing its mother or something bigger than us, like the father, to provide and take care of us. So I think *that's* where the primitive quality in everybody comes from, and what's being played out when people overspend trying to show "the Joneses" that they're good enough.

PP: I grew up in a small, Midwestern town during the fifties. What I remember is that, for the most part, everybody seemed to be on the same middle-class economic level. Now, the body politic is economically polarized into the ninety-nine percent versus the one percent, and I'm sure within that there are even more stratifications. If America were on your couch, how would you interpret that extreme polarization psychologically?

ACH: I think it goes back to the psychological process of devaluation and idealization, in which people are either all good or all bad. It's as if American culture is gradually beginning to reflect that dynamic in its economic structures. We're either part of the "idealized" rich or the "devalued" lower middle class or poor, with no in-between as a balance.

But I wonder if one of the underlying reasons for this extreme imbalance is that society hasn't begun to really integrate the huge social changes that have occurred over the last fifty years, in which there was a shift away from the home and toward the workplace. It's possible that those more stable family structures functioned to hold the middle class together. Now, for various reasons, there's much less family stability, and a corresponding increase and reliance on money and stuff.

PP: So are you saying that as these traditional forms of family and simpler ways of life crumbled, wealth and materialism became more important, as a kind of replacement?

ACH: I think so. Readily available credit, for instance, has increased over the last fifty to eighty years. And I don't think that's just because it wasn't available before. I'm certainly not saying that we should go back to the fifties, or that we should do away with the advances brought about by feminism. But I am saying that we haven't psychologically adjusted to the structural changes of how we live, as well as changes in the family itself.

Where raising children is concerned, I also wonder if the culture is becoming more narcissistic. There's been a loss of parental presence and containment of children—and by this I mean containing their hopes and dreams, playing with them, and giving them space to play. And I'm not only referring to our own children, but the child within ourselves as well.

PP: How else do you see the consequences of these symptoms of narcissism and reliance on "stuff" and materialism playing out?

ACH: I think our emphasis on accumulating material goods has contributed to our current fascination for certain narrow norms of physical beauty. It's contributed to dehumanizing forms of prejudice against people who are obese, or those who don't fit conventional, commercial ideals of model beauty.

PP: From what you're saying, it sounds like America is suffering a reduction and narrowing of values, a kind of psychological disorientation and cultural drift.

ACH: That's a wonderful perspective. Because if being "oriented" is being attentive to love and caring for others, and making sure children are cared for, then materialism, objectification of the other, and prejudice against those that are different, negates love. And if love, where one creates a connection to the other person, is optimally mature, then these others ways of being—where the other is controlled, or seen as a tool or an object, and where we're all working harder and harder to achieve some material goal—are much more archaic. Not that these ways of living wouldn't exist, even in the best of times. But the way we're living now is simply not balanced, and we've lost our way. From the way you're talking about this, I can tell that you sense as well that there's something the matter.

PP: Yes. Something just doesn't feel right in the American psyche. I wonder if you have any examples from your practice of people who came to an awakening on their own around issues of materialism, and if so what triggered that awareness.

ACH: Aside from bankruptcy or a major crisis, I don't think I've ever seen anybody change because of external factors—at least not in the extrinsic ways they see themselves and the way they see money—without in-depth psychotherapy. When people who are in therapy suddenly understand that they don't have to prove their success through money or through buying things, it's usually because they realize the "other" they've been trying to impress isn't who they thought that person was.

So the notion that the neighbors whom they thought would judge them for having less stuff, for example, or their spouse whom they thought would judge them for not being bigger than life, turned out to be just a projection. Instead, it turned out to be a part of the patient *themselves* that they were expecting from the other. And when they realized where that came from in their early childhood development, and saw the illusion in those beliefs, they didn't have to keep up that kind of life anymore, and could stop living on credit.

PP: This drive that some have to "keep up with the Joneses" is surely also shaped by America's all-encompassing identity as the richest country in the world—an identity that is beginning to erode. For example, a recent article in *The New York Times* with the headline "America the Shrunken" opens with an anecdote about a man who worries that his children aren't going to have the same opportunities that he had. It goes on to lament that the American dream is shrinking and no longer attainable; that the Chinese economy will soon overtake ours; and that we lack the social will to fix our crumbling infrastructure.[3]

How do you think this threat to America's identity as a rich and powerful player is going to affect us psychologically on a cultural level?

ACH: I see it as part of an evolution. One of the strengths of the American people has always been their ingenuity and ability to invent new ideas and things. But there is a dark side to capitalism, and that's the reliance on buying things and wishing for more stuff. That might have been okay for the last hundred years, but it's starting to fail us.

I still believe that America is a great nation, and that it will end up coming out of this a great nation. But in what way will we be great? Will we learn that taking care of our kids, expressing love and satisfaction with one another, and being content with being less well off and even poor is another way of being great? That might be the outcome of this economic evolution.

PP: America was founded as a meritocracy, or the idea that each man (and by that I mean a white male) would have his own plot of land and be self-reliant. This translates today to the idea that each person must be self-supporting and self-sufficient. But from what you see in our culture and in our practice, is that ideal beginning to work against us? Is it no longer suitable to the times we live in?

ACH: Part of the problem with meritocracy is that it's elevated material goals, making them too prominent, while devaluing other aspects of social and family life. For me, the canary in the coal mine, so to speak, are the women in my practice who talk over and over and over again about the conflict between being a stay-at-home mother and working. For the mother—as well as the father—who is a stay-at-home parent, things aren't really working: because homemaking is not counted as a career.

The problem is that if material goods are seen as the symbol of success, then a duality arises, and the person making the most money or all the money gets the power and control. So for the women I work with who are struggling between being a stay-at-home mom and wife, either direction they go in feels horrible. In their professional lives they feel guilty that they're abandoning their children. And if they stay at home they feel ashamed for feeling less than a person. There's nothing more rewarding than building a home life and family, but it's really difficult. I think people still discount that struggle.

So not for all women, but for many women, working or staying home comes down to a choice. If it's better for that person to work and have that adult contact, and be a richer parent when they come home, that's terrific. But if the choice to work is made because home life is so culturally devalued, or because cleaning house is just a mundane, unrewarding task, then that reveals underlying cultural attitudes around money, power, and work.

PP: Stay-at-home parents still don't get social security, which certainly reveals something about what the culture values.

ACH: It's also possible that the effects of this bias against the home in favor of the workplace could be self-perpetuating over the generations. If a child isn't seen as a rich, whole person worthy of devoting time and energy to, and if both parents are unable to embrace and contain the child, it sets the child up for potential narcissistic and self-esteem issues as an adult. That same child is then going to be more prone to reliance on external factors to prop them up. They're also going to know less about how to parent their own children.

One way to prevent this continuing rise in narcissistic pathologies and acting out of primitive behaviors might be for America to begin to remember what really matters.

PP: This gives new urgency to the growing idea that it's time to stop striving to be the dominant world power, and start taking care of matters at home.

ACH: If we're seen as the most successful nation in the world because we make more money or have more stuff per person, then I think that's a problem. Then we have an issue, and the world does, too. America's blind spot is that it's unable to see that there are other kinds of success in addition to material success. So changes in the economic world environment might even help us begin to see what's truly important.

PP: You mean we might stop having to be this big, swaggering power with all our glitter and gold as a way to get the world to recognize and love us?

ACH: I believe the world might like us even *more* without our stuff! And also America might do well to realize that whatever entity it's trying to impress is at bottom just a projection. And if we can extrapolate from my patients, most of my patients didn't have to go through a bankruptcy to realize that. So we have two choices as a country: either we go financially bankrupt, or we gain some insight and start doing things differently. And the latter is a lot less painful.

PP: So in your imagination around America and our history, who is it that we're trying to impress?

ACH: Yes, who *is* it we're trying to impress?! I hear a lot of fear in people's voices when they talk about China and India becoming major world powers. Ultimately, what country we're trying to impress, or what country we're devaluing, may be intangible. But what seems clear is that America's identity is bound up with being "on top," and "number one" in the eyes of the world. In this psychological split, "we're" better, and "they're" not.

PP: What a burden for us to carry!

ACH: It's a really stressful dynamic for us as individuals, and as a country. This kind of pressure to live up to our own idealized image of ourselves may be why we're all working so hard. We're all trying to sustain America's persona as the richest country in the world. We work harder and take fewer vacations than most other countries,[4] and most people think they need two incomes in the household just to make ends meet. But what is "making ends meet?" If it involves buying lots of stuff, and having a lifestyle that's beyond what most people really need, then we're on a kind of hamster wheel we can't get off of.

PP: Is this manic overwork a defense against something?

ACH: Perhaps it's a defense against the possibility that America as the best and the greatest country is really just an illusion, and that at some point, this illusion will fall.

PP: Do you see any hopeful signs of a shift in Americans' attitudes toward work and money?

ACH: I believe there has been a gradual shift over the last ten or twenty years. Because of social media and the way people market their businesses or goods through Twitter or YouTube or Facebook, a lot of stuff is being offered for free, such as free software or articles. Part of this is to capture people's attention so they'll ultimately buy something; but I still don't think that's the central factor. A recent study, for instance,[5] showed that employees aren't purely motivated by money. It was found that if employees were offered bonuses of free time one day a month, when they could do any kind of creative work they wanted versus paid work, they were much more productive on the job. So people's optimal motivation, at least as it's begun to change over recent decades, might not just be about money anymore! ■

Notes

1. A. Chris Heath notes that the Kleinian perspective (after psychoanalyst Melanie Klein) has been expanded by the English psychoanalyst Wilfred Bion; Argentine field theorists (such as Willy and Madeleine Baranger); and more recent developments in Italy (such as those undertaken by Giuseppe Civitarese).
2. For 2014, the statistics can be found at NerdWallet.com <http://www.nerdwallet.com/blog/credit-card-data/average-credit-card-debt-household/>.
3. "America the Shrunken," by Frank Bruni, *New York Times*, May 3, 2014.
4. "U.S. The Only Advanced Economy That Does Not Require Employers to Provide Paid Vacation Time, Report Says," by Tanya Mohn, *Forbes*, August 8, 2013. See also "Americans Work More Than Anyone," by Dean Schabner, ABC News, May 1, 2014.
5. "Why Free Time Frees Creativity," by David Burkus, *The Creativity Post*, August 26, 2012.

—25—

An American Awakening

AN INTERVIEW WITH LAWRENCE H. STAPLES, PH.D.

L AWRENCE STAPLES HAD THE kind of classic Horatio Alger success story that reflects one of America's most enduring myths: that of the person from a poor background who, through luck, smarts, hard work, drive, and ambition, overcomes adversity to become rich and successful. Who among us doesn't thrill to this story? Like children with our bedtime fairy tales, we beg to hear it over and over again, in books, movies, and on television. Few are the tales told, however, about the distaff side of this American success story: the toll it can take on personal relationships, and on one's soul and creativity. This is the narrative that Staples shares in our interview: the "awakening" that would descend on him at midlife and that, in a dramatic turn, would lead him to abandon a successful career in the corporate business world and become a Jungian analyst.

Born in 1932 at the height of the Depression, Staples grew up in Ardmore, Oklahoma. At seventeen he was chosen to go to Boys Nation, an American Legion–sponsored organization that mentors youth. There, a visiting professor from Oklahoma University helped the young Staples win a full scholarship to a private preparatory school in St. Louis for his senior year in high school. From there, Staples received another full scholarship to Harvard College. His run of good fortune continued, and after graduation he went on to Harvard Business School; after which he took a position in the corporate world. Hired by the Olin Corporation,[1] a Fortune 500 company at the time, Staples continued his rise up the proverbial ladder, becoming an officer and a corporate vice president. As the general manager of Olin Corporation's paper division, Staples oversaw about three thousand employees at its plants in North Carolina and South Dakota, where they processed flax for the fine papers the company produced.

"It was a big job and I made a lot of money," Staples told me. "And then I went to the Jung Institute in Zürich, where I spent it all." After depleting his savings, Staples moved next to Washington, D.C., where he opened a practice as a Jungian analyst. Among his clients were politicians and other powerbrokers. One thing he learned about powerful people, he said, is that "fantastic appearances of a self-confidence that struts its way across life's stage almost always conceals a mere human who is as frail, vulnerable, and insecure as the rest of us." Staples would also pen several books on guilt and creativity, including *The Creative Soul: Art and the Quest for Wholeness* and *The Guilt Cure*, co-written with his wife, Nancy Pennington. Staples' interest in creativity sparked early in his career as an analyst, when he realized that creative work was one of the most effective means of self-discovery, and that art in all its forms helps us "recover large parts of ourselves that were lost in the process of socialization at the hands of parents and society." His interest in guilt, he says, also arose quickly, as he began to see so many patients suffering deeply from its corrosive effects on their lives. But Staples' research was also stoked by the tremendous guilt he'd suffered as a young boy raised by a "rigidly puritanical" grandmother whose definition of sin was so far reaching, he says, that it was impossible to live a normal life without incurring guilt. To this Calvinist grandmother, Staples recalls, "the only sin greater than sex was idleness. Overwork nearly killed me at midlife."

These days, Staples, who recently retired to Florida, has few qualms about the pleasures of living in a warm and sunny climate. His classic American story of hard-won achievement, first-hand experience with American capitalism, and his knowledge of the human psyche drew me to him in my search for deeper insights into America. Just as Staples shocked his peers in the corporate world by becoming a Jungian analyst, so he surprised me during our interview with his personal revelations about alcoholism and addiction, as well as the deeply religious, moral perspective he brought to issues around wealth and poverty. A tall, lanky man who speaks in an easy Oklahoman drawl, Staples possesses both a refreshing frankness and a plainspoken humility: qualities that underscore his well-deserved reputation as a wise man. Among other things, Staples speaks about money as a "fateful thing," and the role destiny and luck play in success; how capitalism has become a kind of faith in America, taking the place of authentic religion or spirituality; the way money, like alcohol or drugs, can be used in an addictive way to make us feel better; and the wealthy and elite's "delusion of independence."

✳

Pythia Peay: So what drew you to enter the corporate world of America?

Lawrence H. Staples: Money! I grew up poor and I wanted to make money. And I thought I'd be good at it. I had a lot of drive and energy and a reasonably good personality. It wasn't any big earth-shaking decision; it was a practical choice. I also thought it was the quickest way to get "into the fray" of life, so to speak.

PP: What was the first intimation that corporate business wouldn't be your sole pursuit in life?

LHS: I developed a bad drinking problem. Then when I was thirty-seven, I had a spiritual experience, and stopped drinking and smoking at the same time. This gave me an enormous amount of energy, and from that point my business career took off. So the experience with alcohol and addiction opened me to a spiritual life. But it wasn't until I began having really serious midlife problems that my interests turned toward Jung and psychology.

PP: What was the turning point for you?

LHS: The turning point came when I got sick and nearly died. At forty-eight, I developed pericarditis (an infection of the heart), and had a pericardiectomy. Fortunately, the operation went well. But afterward, I began to reflect on the fact that we never know how much time we've got left. This led me to wonder if there was something else I wanted to do with my life. Then I had a big dream, which knocked my socks off. It was *such* a big dream that I had to go and see a therapist about it. This led me to begin studying Jung's writings, and it was at that point that I said to myself, "*This* is what I want to do!"

So I immediately applied to the C. G. Jung Institute in Zürich to enter a Ph.D. program in clinical psychology. Without even waiting for a response from Zürich, I resigned from my company, giving them just nine months notice. With my business background I didn't think the Institute would accept me. But to my surprise, they did. So in 1982 I went to Zürich and ended up staying there for nearly ten years.

PP: Can you share the big dream that changed your life?

LHS: I'd rather not say. But I can tell you that it was a very powerful dream that really set me off on a new path, and that is still present in my life, and in a lot of my creative work and writing.

PP: When you were building your successful career in the corporate world, did you ever feel as if something was missing? Or did it take that illness, and that dream, to put you on a new path?

LHS: Yes, I'd already begun to feel a lot of restlessness and dissatisfaction. At first, that discontent expressed itself as thinking of other businesses I could create on my own. But it took a health and spiritual crisis for me to get interested in doing something other than business.

PP: Were your corporate colleagues surprised at your decision to leave the company?

LHS: Most of my colleagues never thought of doing anything else, and stayed on until they retired with lots of money. When I gave my boss nine months notice, he couldn't believe that somebody would walk away from what I had—so much so that by the eighth month he still had not gotten a replacement for me. He thought I was going kind of crazy, and that eventually I'd come to my senses. He himself never walked away from the corporate planes and money and status, and didn't retire until he was seventy.

So it was a real transformation that occurred for me. I'd gone through one when I'd stopped drinking, and then I went through another one when I had the illness and the dream. The material "fix" had drawn me into business. When I quit, I knew it meant going into a life in which I wouldn't make nearly the amount of money I'd made before. Oftentimes, it's an illness of some kind that causes us to question ourselves, to realize how helpless we really are, and how powerless we are over our fate.

PP: But it would seem to most people that the position you were in gave you quite a lot of power, in a worldly and financial sense. Was it hard to walk away from that kind of power?

LHS: In fact, one of the things I realized was that the power I'd had didn't really belong to me. It belonged to the *position*. And the only way to keep that power was to keep the position. Another realization I had was about the elderly male workers who ran the paper machine at the company where I worked. These men were real artists who made very fine, flax papers. If a few of them got sick, it would have shut the company down; whereas, if I got sick, nothing would have changed. They'd miss me, but only over the short term, as these artists were much more important.

I also remember watching my boss and thinking to myself that I could be just like him, working hard and making more and more money; but did I really want to be like that? And the answer to that was "No." Because when you have a religious experience, as I did, you realize that material stuff can't save you. So all those realizations made it possible for me to just walk away. I've not gone without a meal since then. But my colleagues are really rich!

PP: Do you have any regrets?

LHS: No, not at all. Well, let me say that I wouldn't mind having the money, but I wouldn't have wanted to do what you had to do to have it! If it just dropped in my lap, I'd love to have it, because money gives you a lot of freedom. Ten years in Zürich took most of the money I'd saved, and I had two kids in school. So after I came back, I had a little left, but not much. I was able to make a good enough living for myself, but always figured that I'd die in my chair seeing clients, because I couldn't afford to retire.

So I worked until I was eighty, and then around that time they struck oil and gas on some parcels of land that I'd inherited from my aunt and grandmother out in Oklahoma. I'll probably pass away before I realize any huge profits from it. But it was enough to allow me to leave Washington, D.C., and retire to Florida.

PP: So you've worked hard, and taken chances. But you've also had some lucky turns of fate, or maybe it was an instinct that you followed.

LHS: I realized a long time ago that everything that happens to us is fate. There is nothing that I did to be born white and American, in Oklahoma, with parents, with brains, and to people who had some property that was one day going to end up producing oil. We don't have much influence over the really big stuff that shapes us in life: like where we're going to be born—or even *if* we're going to be born—or our siblings, schoolmates, neighbors, or the time period we're born into. And so life is both a great privilege and a piece of luck; people have different fates, but somehow we work with the cards we've been dealt.

PP: But that kind of worldview that takes fate into account directly contradicts the American trope that if you work hard enough in life you can succeed at anything.

LHS: It's baloney! There are things that it would seem that we choose, but I'm increasingly unsure how much freedom we really have. I suspect that an awful lot of what we *think* are choices in life are made by the unconscious. There's something "back there" that is shaping what we do.

PP: So what kind of insight does this shed on capitalism and America, as the richest country in the world?

LHS: The problem is that the givens in life shape what we believe about things. We believe in capitalism because we were born into it, just like many people are Catholic because they were born into that faith. So most Americans believe in capitalism because that's what they were taught.

But what I've come to know is that capitalism doesn't create happiness or a spiritual life. And the cycles of civilizations teach us that someday America will decline and something else will come along. But that's a natural phenomenon. We're stronger in life at one time, and then we become weaker at other times. So I don't think America is any happier than the poorest country in the world. But I also doubt if we're any more miserable, either. But happiness is episodic. We all have happiness in life, but it's not a constant thing.

PP: Does the point you're trying to make have something to do with the Jungian concept of the opposites, those polarities of light and dark, or feminine and masculine, or sadness and happiness?

LHS: Yes. Wherever we are in the world, the principle of the opposites causes us to move back and forth between happiness and feeling miserable. There's a spectrum, and we move between the two. It has to be that way because as long as there is consciousness, the opposites are present. So there can't be a one-sided experience of anything all the time: like happiness all the time, or misery all the time.

As the American author Robert Penn Warren said, we're not good *or* bad, we're good *and* bad. Out of our goodness comes badness, and vice versa. So there are no one-sided solutions. Capitalism isn't the solution, but neither is communism the solution.

PP: So then what is the way to more consciously relate to capitalism, and the earning, getting, and spending of money?

LHS: I've never read a book, or seen a movie or a play, in which the ending was completely satisfactory. And that's because the story never really ends. A story only ends when we get to the point where we can no longer ask "What's next?" As long as we can say "What's next?" then nothing has ended.

PP: I certainly know that feeling as a writer, because whatever story I'm working on, there's always more to write about. But how does what you're saying apply to this topic of money?

LHS: There's never a satisfactory ending because life is "asymptotic": a curve that approaches the limit, but that doesn't ever get there. An example of what I'm talking about is the story of Moses. After all his wandering in the desert, he got to see the Promised Land, but he didn't get to go there. Just as, mathematically, infinity and zero cannot be calculated—they can only be assumed. So we never really get "there" because there is no *there*. This principle shows up in writing, art, business— and money. No one ever has enough money. I don't care how much money people have; it's never enough.

PP: So is this "never enoughness" just a part of human nature?

LHS: I don't know. But it might stem from what Goethe wrote about as "divine discontent." There's something in life that seems to make us want more. God, for example, doesn't ever stop creating, or simply stop the universe as it is and not have anything change. So if as it's said in the scriptures that we're a reflection of God [Genesis 1:27], then there's something in us that just wants more of everything. So wanting more must be in our wiring.

PP: But in America does this "wanting more" sometimes become conflated with money? In other words, do we think we can get something from money that we could get elsewhere?

LHS: Yes, but money is no different in that regard from sex or drugs, or houses or cars. We're trying to get something from these material things because they make us feel good temporarily—but it's not sustainable, so we have to keep trying to get more. This is why someone becomes an alcoholic. They take a drink and it makes them feel good, but then it takes two before they can feel good, and then suddenly it takes ten. And then there's not enough alcohol to feed an addiction, the same way there's not enough money. So there's an addiction to anything that makes us feel good, because we want to feel better.

    The problem starts when we become dependent on something outside of ourselves in order to feel better or to feel happy inside. And the only way to not become dependent on something outside to feel good is to be in touch with our own feelings. But that's much harder than it sounds! Because anytime we start paying careful attention to our feelings, and give them precedence over other people's feelings, we get accused of being selfish and self-centered. In the end, most of us make compromises, and we do enough to keep other people from getting too mad at us. But to honor and pay attention to our feelings is the only way I know to prevent getting addicted to anything. Because then we've got so much richness of feeling we don't have to have a big house, or a car, or a lavish vacation or anything *outside* that makes us feel good *inside*.

PP: It's not even that we just feel good when we pay attention to what's going on inside. From my experience it's also enlivening and creative.

LHS: Yes, because if a person follows their feelings, it gets expressed as interest. *I love math; I'm interested in math. I love writing, and I'm interested in writing. I love that person, and I'm interested in that person.* So to follow our interest or our feelings, as Jung said, leads us to ourselves.

But people who do that often get crucified, like Jesus, because they don't do what the patriarchy, or the matriarchy, or society, wants them to do. Following our own feelings and interests often gets us into trouble.

PP: Why is that?

LHS: Well, I think it's because we're afraid. We're ultimately dependent beings, and so we're afraid of losing contact with people and losing their love.

PP: But why do other people crucify the person who follows their feelings and their interests?

LHS: Because that person isn't living the way they are, and so that calls into question their way of life. And that feels threatening, so they say things to make that person behave differently. Most of us try to find some midpoint. The way I put it is that if you put others first, you can't stand yourself; and if you put yourself first, others can't stand you. The problem is we're human, and as humans we always have problems to work on, and our most important problems are insoluble—for the obvious reason that they're not solvable.

PP: Money would certainly seem to fall into that category. What insights did you gain into the American psyche about money, and what have you learned as a Jungian analyst working with people around issues of money?

LHS: I don't really know! Money is such an all-pervasive part of life. Even Bach and Beethoven worried about money, and had to have patrons in order to do their work. So to say, for example, that money is more important to businessmen than others isn't right. Everybody needs it: it's just that some find they don't need as much in order to pursue their interests or what they want to do in life.

This may not answer your question directly, but once when I was traveling in Indonesia, I visited a Chinese businessman. He lived in a gated compound, and ran a huge business. We were having coffee when I noticed that he had a watch with perhaps a hundred diamonds on it. So I asked him, "What's the story with that watch?" And he told me that the Chinese made up just three percent of the country, but were always under attack politically because they owned ninety-eight percent of the money. He said that because the Chinese were always worried that they were going to get sent out of the country, he had to have something to live on in the event he suddenly had to leave.

We also talked about the poverty in Indonesia, even though the people there seemed nearly as happy as we are here. He said that the government was trying to take the wealth away from the Chinese and redistribute it to the people. The problem with that, he told me, is that the Chinese would have it all back in ten years. When he made that remark, I suddenly realized that although there are some people who will always know how to make money, most people really don't know a lot about making money.

So this is one reason why we end up having such a concentration of wealth. If you're born into the top twenty percent economically in this country, for example, chances are that you're going to remain there or get better, because you've got capital. And the person who grows up in a household where the parents both know how to make money, handle money, and invest money, has a hugely different fate from the person that grew up in the Bronx dirt poor and with no education. So we can give money to the poor—and there's a lot of merit in that—but because they don't have the wherewithal or knowhow to shop well, they may not handle it well. But whether it actually helps them or not doesn't really matter; because in the end, it helps the person who gives. So, again, money is a fateful thing.

PP: And what kind of insight can we take from that?

LHS: We could ask ourselves, "How did Jesus handle the poor?" Well, Jesus said the poor will always be with us [Matt. 26:11]. But did he try to get the poor to *not* be poor? No! That's not what he tried to do at all. Instead, Jesus tried to remind the rich that it's harder to get into the kingdom of heaven than it is for a camel to get through the eye of a needle [Matt. 19:24]. So in terms of spiritual matters or coming to self-knowledge, Jesus was saying, so to speak, that money is a hindrance. He wasn't trying to get the Romans to distribute the money, right? And he wasn't trying to bring people out of poverty. He was trying to show us that, in fact, being poor might even bring a person closer to God.

And there's a lot of truth to that. If you don't have any money and you're sick, and you don't have any health insurance, you're like the proverbial soldier in a foxhole—and then, man, you pray! Whereas if you've got one million or ten million dollars, prayer is likely to be much more perfunctory. It's usually only when you're in trouble that you really begin to pray. It's how I prayed when I took my last drink. And I hadn't prayed like that in all my life.

PP: What was your prayer?

LHS: "God help me." But that kind of prayer is fervent. It's real. You don't make it up. You really *feel* that prayer. Whereas to pray "God, will you make my stocks do better," doesn't have much passion behind it, because it doesn't come from a deep place of need. And so I think that Jesus was basically saying that being poor puts you closer to God, because you're much more likely to acknowledge your helplessness. But if you're a very wealthy man or woman, you don't think you're helpless. Yet even wealthy people aren't aware of how hugely dependent they are on others, and on the big things like sunshine, water, air, roads, and telephones.

The difference in dependence between a rich person like Bill Gates or Mitt Romney and a poor person, for example, isn't as great as you might think. Someone has to build their cars and grow the green beans they eat. But what do they actually produce themselves that they consume? So although those who are wealthy are in fact hugely dependent, they walk around in a "delusion of independence," unaware that the hand of fate was the thing that gave them the big blessing. But poor people don't suffer from that delusion. They're aware of their dependence, and so they turn to God more. And that's what Jesus did.

PP: Partly this American myth of meritocracy plays a role, because independence is defined through the money we earn and possess, and the kind of lifestyle it provides. American attitudes around money don't include this kind of Christian, spiritual perspective, or even a more developed philosophy around independence and dependence.

LHS: Well, whether we like it or not, we're dependent. We can act as if we're not, but it doesn't mean we aren't. But the poor are *extremely* dependent; so much so that they really know it. But just like they say there are no atheists in foxholes, so there are no atheists in the midst of great suffering. And this is why almost no transformation occurs without suffering.

PP: I wonder if the absence of genuine suffering is itself a kind of suffering.

LHS: It is in the sense that if you don't suffer, you remain unconscious. Suffering brings a lot of consciousness. I would never have stopped drinking if I hadn't suffered. People can't get unhooked from an addiction or an obsession, whether it's money or alcohol, until they start to suffer from it. Why would anybody change if they didn't suffer? This is why they say in Alcoholics Anonymous that if someone has a drinking problem, they have to hit bottom first. I know the day that I stopped drinking, I was in bad, bad pain. At the same time, it seems to take different things to cause people to suffer to the point of transformation. I hit bottom without having run over a child, or getting sent to prison, or put in an asylum. Some people have those kinds of terrible things happen to them, and yet they still haven't suffered enough to unhook themselves from the addiction.

PP: This was the case with my father, who drank himself to death. He didn't kill anyone, but he suffered terribly in other ways from alcoholism, and it never stopped him.

LHS: My father was the same. He died when he was sixty-three. He never stopped drinking. He lost both legs and an arm, and still he never stopped. So then we have to wonder why some people stop drinking and others don't. And I think the answer is that it's just the grace of God. You can't figure it out. In AA, you'll find people who know everything about alcoholism. Then the first thing you know, they're drunk. So it's not knowledge: it's just luck and fate and grace. And if you get it, you get on your hands and knees in gratitude, because you didn't really do anything to earn that grace. You can look at all the right things they tell you to do in AA, and some people do it and get sober, and others don't. There are some things that we just can't solve, and so we've got to let it go and say, "I can't solve this."

PP: So then the problem of addiction and maybe even materialism is further compounded by this "delusion of independence," or that American "fix it" attitude.

LHS: Right. If the power to get sober on my own had belonged to me, I would have stopped drinking ten or fifteen years earlier than I did. But the power simply doesn't belong to us, anymore than the power belonged to us to be born where we were. The Creator—whatever that is—does it his, or her, or its way.

And money and alcoholism are related; they can both become addictions. Money is just something that we need; we just don't need as much of it as we think we need. It's useful to us, but it can blind us to what's important, just as a thousand other things can blind us to what's really important. Look at all the huge houses that are built. People felt they needed them in order to feel a certain way about themselves, although it usually doesn't work. But this same phenomenon of people being obsessed with money, or something else like drugs, or sex, will repeat itself billions of times in life, until they finally get to that place where they can be fed from within. I'm not trying to be judgmental; I've certainly got my obsessions. Most of us struggle along until we suffer enough to give up these obsessions and find out that they're not as important as we thought.

PP: I know from my own experience that creativity is something that has "fed me from within." Can you say more about how creativity works to fulfill us in that deeper way, and that might offer more of us a different path than consumerism?

LHS: Just as we see the unique stamp of all artists in their work, so we discover our own unique identity through our creative projects. Even without seeing the signature, we can see a painting and know if it's a Picasso or a Renoir. Or we can hear a piece of music and know if it's by Beethoven, Bach, or the Beatles. So our art creates our identity, and we begin to know who we are from our own work, just as we know Virginia Woolf or Isak Dinesen from their writing. Every one of us has an identity *just* as unique as these famous people, and that appear as faithfully in our work as theirs do.

I also found that creative work gives meaning to our lives because it connects us to something bigger than ourselves. When we create, we connect with the creator within, and when we do that, we also come in contact with all the vital, creative processes that develop and sustain both our inner and outer worlds. Finding meaning through creativity also helps us to bear the suffering, hardships, and unhappiness that life inevitably brings. Jung once pointed out that we are able to bear almost any suffering and unhappiness if we're doing something meaningful.

PP: You have such insight into the creative process. How does creativity enter into your work as an analyst?

LHS: Therapy is an art form in which therapists can help shattered people piece back together a broken life that has fallen apart. They do this by providing a mirror that helps clients to see within, where they can find the lost pieces of themselves. This process enables them to "paint" these pieces onto the canvas of their lives. In this case, I don't mean literally "painting" with a brush (although it often involves that), but painting as a metaphor for the psychological reconstruction of the self. Such "painting" produces a portrait that includes what patients knew themselves consciously to be, as well as those unconscious, unknown parts of themselves they'd lost. As their canvases begin to fill up with colors and hues brought forth through the mirroring process that takes place between the analyst and the client, their lives get stronger and colorful, and they continue to evolve and change. So the portrait patients "paint" early in therapy is much less complete and very different from the portraits they paint later; just as Frida Kahlo's self-portraits evolved and became fuller and richer as more and more of herself emerged onto her life's canvas.

In this creative therapeutic process, therapists not only witness the portrait of the mirrored patient change and grow, they also see their own portrait transform. It's as if two portraits are simultaneously being painted, formed, and shaped by the reflected images of unconscious material coming out of both the patient and therapist. I always feel very thankful for that process. ∎

Notes
1. Incorporated in 1892, Olin Corporation concentrates in three business segments: Chlor Alkali Products, Chemical Distribution, and Winchester <http://www.olin.com>.

—26—

Analyzing the American Dream

An Interview with Bud Harris, Ph.D.

IN 2008, AS AMERICA was contending with the onset of the Great Recession, I attended a lecture by Jungian analyst Bud Harris in Washington, D.C. During the course of his talk, Harris, a tall, stocky man with a shock of white hair who emanates both grandfatherly wisdom and firmness of conviction, told two stories that stayed with me. One was about how he'd once handled his desire to buy a new Porsche. The other was his commentary in response to a remark his daughter had recently made, lamenting the fact that her children's generation would be unlikely to do better than her own generation—until that point, one of America's most unshakable beliefs.

As I was to learn, the brief but tantalizing insights into American tenets of capitalism Harris shared that evening came directly out of his own experience as a successful entrepreneur. Like Lawrence Staples, with whom he shares a close friendship (the two trained at the Jung Institute in Zürich at the same time), Harris, too, had once been a businessman before undergoing a major transformation and becoming a Jungian analyst. Indeed, as a young man starting out, the life Harris is living now was not even remotely close to the life he'd imagined for himself then.

After graduating from Georgia Tech in Atlanta with a bachelor's degree in management, Harris became a buyer for Macy's Department Store, and then later started his own company. But at midlife, exactly at a time when he was at a peak of success professionally and financially, and as a husband and father with three children, Harris heard the call to change his life's direction. The call, as he describes in more detail below, came in the form of a depression. With everything going so well in his outer life, the depression caught him off guard, and he was compelled to go into therapy to find help.

"One of the most complicated questions we face," he wrote in the book by him and his wife, *Like Gold Through Fire: Understanding the Transforming Power of Suffering*, "is how to know when we are really suffering. If we don't appear to be suffering, can we be suffering? If we have a stable family, a good career, a fine standing in the community, how can we be unhappy? This is often the first question people who show up in analysis must face. They are yearning, restless, and often depressed—and their spouses, friends, and often they themselves can't understand why. For whatever reason, they are losing the struggle to convince themselves they are *happy*."

Today, at age seventy-seven, Harris lives in Asheville, North Carolina, where for over twenty-five years he has maintained a private practice as an analyst. The prolific author of many books, including *Sacred Selfishness: A Guide to Living a Life of Substance*, Harris continues to write, give lectures and seminars with his wife Massimilla Harris, Ph.D., also a Jungian analyst, and to enjoy his children and grandchildren. But as he discusses in the following interview, the road to his new life was not without its own kind of suffering and hardship, including financial insecurity. Who better to reflect on our nation's money complex, then, than someone like Harris, who has lived both sides of the "American coin," so to speak, enjoying both the pleasures and successes of American prosperity, and, on the other side, its shadow of emptiness and discontent, as well as its potential to offer a less materialistic but more enlivening and soulful way of life?

In the following interview, first conducted in 2008 and updated in 2014, Harris shares more details about his personal shift from businessman to analyst; the impact of the Great Depression on the Greatest Generation and how that generation in particular shaped American attitudes toward money and the economy, including his own father's story. We also explore the country's baseline mindset of "scarcity" that we inherited from waves of immigrants fleeing poverty, and how commercialism exploits our Icarus tendency to fly high above unpleasant feelings of sadness. Examining the country's money complex through his trained analytical eye, Harris also supplies an answer to his daughter's plea, offering his vision of what a better life for the next generation might really look like.

✳

Pythia Peay: I've heard it said that money is the soul of America.

Bud Harris: I would disagree. I don't think money is the soul of America. I think money is the "false self" of America, in the way that psychoanalyst Heinz Kohut defined it. It's a false self that's developed because we've lost touch with how to develop our true self. It's compensatory for a lot of wounding stemming from our history, particularly around the Depression.

I remember reading the anthropologist Loren Eiseley's autobiography, *All the Strange Hours,* in which he talked about his father's generation as being "storm driven men." It's a term that I've used in my own writing, because my father was also a "storm driven" man. He had that wounded masculinity that came from scarcity and the loss of his father, who died when he was young. So he was driven by a constant sense of anger. And that constant sense of anger came from his fear. In some way, he was trying to compensate for the insecurity of not having a father. But he achieved a lot, and went from being a small town boy to becoming an athlete, and then the president of a small college.

PP: Do you regard the Great Depression as a psychological trauma for the country?

BH: It definitely was. It left that whole generation of adults, particularly men, very wounded. The men who came out of the Great Depression were trying to become unchained from a prison of their past and a wounding that they were not able to go inside and learn how to heal. So they came back after the war and they wanted to create a culture that was affluent, that was safe, and where you heard nothing about troubles. And they held onto that attitude right through the fifties and into the sixties, which turned into a disaster. And even then they still had trouble giving up the idea that they didn't want to hear about troubles, they just wanted to go forward. It was a compensatory reaction to the Depression, and it still hasn't been worked through.

PP: How were you personally shaped by your father's life experience around tragedy and poverty?

BH: My own personal money complex came from a sense of scarcity that I inherited from my father, but that also stemmed from events in my early life: my mother died when I was fourteen, and after that I never lived at home. What I experienced was very akin to what Kohut wrote about regarding early deprivation and wounding as a source of trauma, and which makes life very insecure. That complex can also create an Icarus type who is always trying to fly high and overcome their personal history. But that never works. Because then everything they achieve is hollow.

PP: Before you became a Jungian analyst, you were a successful businessman. So it seems that, from what you've said, you started out by following in your own father's Icarus footsteps. Can you say more about that part of your life, and what led you to make such a radical career shift?

BH: After I graduated from college, I went to work for the Junior Executive Training Squad for Macy's Department Store. I then became a buyer for Rich's, which became a Federated Store, and began traveling throughout the Far East representing Federated Stores. I rose up that ladder very quickly, and by the time I was thirty, there wasn't much further to go. So I decided to go into business for myself with another buyer, and over a period of time we opened over twelve stores in Atlanta. That was a fun time, and I got to the point where I had built a fairly successful life. At thirty-three, I had achieved the American dream. I was professionally and financially successful; I had a wife and three kids, a nice home, and a membership in a country club; and yet I couldn't understand why I was depressed. So I went into therapy.

PP: And?

BH: And I was fortunate enough to find a good therapist, who was very oriented toward humanistic psychology, and who had developed an interest in Carl Jung. I began to look at life in a deeper way, and to realize that I'd been living a life that wasn't really true to myself. After several years of therapy working with that realization, I decided to sell my share of the business to my partner and go back to school to become a psychologist. Then in the early seventies, there was an economic recession; my partner's stores went out of business, and he couldn't continue to pay me anymore. So I had to go back to work while I was still in school, and that made it a long, hard finish—but I did it. Then, after I'd built up a successful practice as a psychologist, I decided to go to the Jung Institute in Zürich, where I stayed for five and a half years. And that was also a financial struggle.

So most of my adult life has been spent with my back to the wall financially. But although that has been the cause of a lot of anxiety, I'm one who feels very strongly that we have to do what's right for our life, and not let anxiety about money define that.

PP: Your story makes me wonder about the role of money and finances in the individuation process, by which we become more aligned with our truer selves, especially for Americans, where there's such an emphasis on money as the definition of success.

BH: It's an interesting question because America is very pragmatic, and values the practical and the conventional. But valuing money this way means that it's hard for people in the general public to value the psychological process of analysis, and the time and money involved in that process. Because of this, Americans don't typically go into analysis for personal growth and development. Usually, they're forced into it because of personal problems, and sometimes that gradually shifts toward inner development.

PP: It seems to me that something in the American psyche shies away from grappling with suffering, whether around the poor, the sick, the depressed, our veterans traumatized by war, or our own personal suffering. Every commercial essentially has a kind of perky, uplifting theme. It's so ingrained in us that it goes against the culture to be otherwise.

BH: Our commercial culture has discovered that what is compensatory to suffering sells products. We sell the "Icarus dream."

PP: You mean we sell the idea of moving toward a new horizon, of flying onward and upward?

BH: Or of getting more gusto out of life. Or of material things as a source of happiness. But part of America's problem around suffering is that we lack the grounding of an older culture and deeper religious and cultural traditions to support us.

PP: What does that kind of cultural grounding provide?

BH: It provides a stability that makes it easier for us to withstand our suffering. Our country has had such a traumatic life; almost every generation has suffered some form of major trauma. And although that's probably true in most cultures, those other cultures are more grounded in their religious and cultural traditions, and so are better equipped psychologically.

PP: You've also made the point that America was originally settled by Puritans and convicts.

BH: Right. Europe sent all their religious fanatics, prisoners, and poor indentured servants over here. So initially the country was made up of the rejected parts of Europe. America got Europe's shadow.

PP: So has this European shadow that we've inherited also shaped our relationship to money?

BH: It has. The underlying sense of scarcity that the poor and the impoverished criminals brought with them when they emigrated here was exacerbated and brought back to the surface by the Great Depression. We saw this even more recently during the recession in 2008, when that sense of scarcity again rose to the surface so easily. We saw how scared people can get, how grim the news can get, and how everyone starts talking about apocalyptic scenarios. When in fact, the reality is, we're still the most affluent people in the world.

Part of our culture's wounding and trauma is that all our value goes to money. It doesn't go to spiritual things, or to community, or to other nonmaterial interests. I think materialism has replaced spiritual values in our culture; we have certainly made materialism our true religion. So I think one of the answers as we go into the future is that we need to turn from quantity to quality.

PP: And on that theme, I know that you have a very interesting personal story about the time when you were tempted to buy a Porsche.

BH: Buying a Porsche had been a dream of mine for a very long time. At forty-five, I finally got to the point where I could afford one. So I went to the showroom. But when I sat down in the car, I didn't fit: my eyes were looking straight at the top of the windshield! I'm not that tall, but I was too tall for that car. That's when I realized that the Porsche had really been a symbol, and that I didn't need to "concretize" it in a material way. I also knew that I would have been tired of it in sixty days.

PP: So what did the Porsche symbolize for you?

BH: It was an image of how I wanted to get around in the world with a certain kind of persona of empowerment. But it dawned on me that I was projecting onto the car what I needed to get from inside myself, in terms of perspective and energy, and a certain sense of inner liveliness. (I think a Porsche is a lively car!) So then I had to ask myself, if the car meant that much to me, then what was I projecting onto it? And how did I need to develop those qualities within myself?

PP: I think that's such a creative way of working with a material desire: not viewing it in a puritanical, judgmental way as something to feel wrong or guilty about wanting, but engaging with the object itself in a much richer, more meaningful way. We'd probably consume much less, and more consciously, if we followed this example. I wonder if you could bring this same kind of thinking to bear on the American dream that each successive generation has to be better off than the last generation.

BH: There are two aspects to this American belief. As I said, I was born during the Depression, to parents who were struggling during that time to come out of poverty. So I think it can be a natural, loving response for parents who have struggled financially to want their children to do better materially than they did. This was what happened after the Depression and World War II, and it led to a better life materially during the fifties.

But I also think that, after World War II, as a culture we got caught up in a patriarchal dream of successful identity and successful accomplishment materially. We stopped thinking about what success means in terms of courage, love, and transformation. So I think that we need to change this American belief that each generation must have a better life materially, and begin to dream for our children that they should have bigger hearts than we did; to dream for them to have more courage than we did; to dream for them to have more creativity than we did; and to dream for them to care more about life than we did.

And although it makes sense to want our children to go beyond where we are, there is a limit to materialism. And in fact we may be in a time and a place where growth needs to be seen more as a matter of heart and a matter of spirit.

PP: Why is this redefinition of the American dream so important at this particular time?

BH: Because we're reaching the limit of how much better off our children can be than us materially.

PP: Because? I think some of us might need to have that spelled out.

BH: Because there is a limit to how much better materialism can make life in this country compared to the rest of the world; and I think we've reached that limit. We simply can't have more things than we already have, and have a better life because of more things.

So we can hope that our children have financial security. But we can also hope for them that they have bigger hearts than we have, and that they have a greater concern about life in general, which would include the environment, but also the environment of human beings, and people who can barely get by on the minimum wage, like those the author Barbara Ehrenreich wrote about in her book *Nickel and Dimed*.

PP: During the lecture you gave that I attended, you said that one way for the Baby Boomer and younger generations to come to an understanding of the Depression— and what that was like, and how to understand its impact psychologically on us as a country—is to think back over their parents' and grandparents' stories.

BH: And to not just *listen* to the stories, but to actually put themselves in that place. To imagine what it was like to be unable to support one's family, and to be unable to meet even the basic responsibilities and obligations in life—especially for men, as to be a provider is such a part of the masculine identity, going all the way back to the hunter gatherers. Then you can see what a trauma the Depression was for one's mother or father, or grandparents, which was further compounded by what was happening all around them.

PP: One response I come across frequently whenever I talk about the suffering our parents or loved ones endured in the past is that "life happens." So why even bring up these tragedies from the past?

BH: I understand how people might respond in that way. But it's important to understand the value of looking at stories, and the value of trying to feel our wounds and grow from our wounds rather than to just "get beyond" them. And that's because we've discovered that we never really get beyond our wounds. They're part of our beings forever.

PP: Why is it valuable to touch that sore place where it hurts?

BH: Because to me that's the only way to heal, that's the only way to grow, and the only way to find the potential in it. It opens our eyes to a consciousness we haven't had before, which is the consciousness that comes from suffering: it forces us to the ground, to be still, to be dark, and to feel pain. Much of our activity is spent trying to flee from pain, like Icarus—or at least mine and my father's was.

In *A Farewell to Arms*, Hemingway wrote that we have to accept the broken places and acknowledge and learn from them. We have to go into the pain and the emotion of the complex in order to find the other side that can then take us to a much more healing, fulfilling place in life. It broadens our humanity and our compassion to understand these stories.

PP: I know that you left the business world to become a therapist. But I wonder if there are people in business and economics who also go through the same kind of inner awakening to a deeper side of life, and yet remain in their chosen profession. In your imagination, what would that more conscious businessperson be like?

BH: I have worked with a number of businesspeople, over the years, who have been seeking a more meaningful, a more creative, and a more heartfelt life. I don't use words like "awakened." "Awakened" implies a state to be achieved. I prefer the Jungian term "individuating," where, through developing our conscious self-knowledge and trying earnestly to live by this knowledge, we are coming closer to realizing the wholeness of our potentials. This is a life-long process and is more comprehensive than "awakening."

Business can be a very creative and heartfelt field. I'm not sure the corporate world can be. Most of the business people with whom I have worked own their own businesses and, in their own way, are creative, courageous, and are eager to learn about almost everything. Business people like this can enrich their lives, their families, and our culture.

Part V

Politics, Presidents, Power, and Polarization

A letter from you calls up recollections very dear to my mind. It carried me back to the times when, beset with difficulties and dangers, we were fellow laborers in the same cause, struggling for what is most valuable to man, his right of self-government.—**Thomas Jefferson** in a letter to John Adams

THAT AMERICANS REVOLTED TO secure the autonomy and rights of individuals against tyranny is a commonplace so fundamental to our identity that its principles have been engraved in stone and recited during national ceremonies and in school classrooms. Less celebrated, however, are the complex relationships forged among the Founding Fathers, or "brothers," as they have sometimes been called, who worked alongside each other during the Revolution, and who afterward came together across great philosophical and political differences to painstakingly construct the infrastructure of the new republic during the Constitutional Convention in 1788.

Among the most longstanding and extraordinary of these kinships was the bond that formed between John Adams and Thomas Jefferson. Though it was a companionship of equals, these were two very dissimilar men. Tall and lanky with sandy-red hair and tastes for life's aesthetic pleasures, including art and expensive wines, Jefferson was a refined man of great political vision and brilliance. He was also a Virginia plantation slave-owner who, after the death of his wife, had a long-term relationship with one of his slaves, Sally Hemings, as well as a spendthrift who was constantly in debt. Circumspect, well-mannered, and with an aversion to argument, irreligious but philosophical, Jefferson once went through the New Testament with a pair of scissors, cutting out all references to miracles and other supernatural occurrences, and pasting together his own "Jefferson Bible."[1]

By contrast Adams was a short, stocky, opinionated man with a hot temper and a marked sensitivity to slights. He was also, as David McCullough notes in his biography, warm and loquacious with a sense of humor. Equally a genius at political theory as Jefferson, Adams was by nature a stoic and devout Christian, loyal husband, and stern father, who lived a disciplined, hardworking, and thrifty life on his Massachusetts farm—and who never owned a single slave. Both Founders were book lovers and exceptionally gifted writers who helped to craft democracy into words. Both would become presidents, Adams as the second, following George Washington, and Jefferson, who followed Adams as the third.

Whether it was the fire of history they'd passed through, their commitment to liberty's cause, or their common ground of intellect, the two men developed a rare and close bond. Just as the new American government launched into existence, however, their friendship began to fray, as the two Founders found themselves on opposite sides of a partisan divide that has defined American politics since its inception. That divide pitted Adams, a Federalist, who believed in the centrality of the Federal government in binding the states together as one nation, against Jefferson, a Republican, who believed in the more diverse and diffuse power of the states and the people. Tensions came to a head during the presidential campaign of 1801 between Adams, still in office in his first term, and Thomas Jefferson, who was running against him.

So bitterly divided had the two parties of each respective candidate become, notes McCullough, there was even talk of civil war. Perhaps no friendship could have survived those kinds of pressures. When President Adams lost the election to Jefferson, he didn't even stay long enough to witness his Revolutionary brother being sworn in during his inauguration. Boarding a public stage at 4 A.M., Adams fled the capital in a "morning flight" to his farm in Connecticut. Eight hours later, as he addressed the crowd that had assembled to watch him being sworn in, President Jefferson famously proclaimed, "We are all Republicans, we are all Federalists." Even so, although he paid tribute to Washington, notes McCullough, "of Adams he said nothing." The two men would never see each other again.

Eleven years later, however, Benjamin Rush, the Founding Father and physician who'd remained close friends with both men, had a dream that would alter not just Jefferson's and Adams' friendship, but that would add significantly to the historical record of the American Revolution. In his dream, as McCullough recounts it, Rush found himself reading a history of America written in the future, and of a particular page saying that among the "most extraordinary events" of the year 1809 was the renewal of friendship and correspondence between the two former presidents, Mr. John Adams and Mr. Thomas Jefferson. In Rush's dream, it was Adams who rekindled the "old friendship" by sending the first letter.

The physician excitedly shared his nocturnal vision with Adams, who had great respect for Rush's dreams, and who responded that although the dream was "not history" it "may be prophecy." Still, Adams did not immediately act to contact Jefferson. But in 1812, after a series of personal tragedies, and after Rush reminded Adams of a confession he had recently made to a mutual friend ("I always loved Jefferson and I still love him")—words that made their way to Jefferson, and which in turn "revived" his affections for Adams—the two began a correspondence. They exchanged letters about "old friends, and their own friendship . . . common memories, books, politics, education, philosophy, religion, the French, the British, the French Revolution, American Indians, the American navy, their families, their health, slavery," writes McCullough, and "always, repeatedly, the American Revolution." Even in their exchange, notes McCullough, "each proved consistently true to his nature—they were in what they wrote as they had been through life."

Adams' and Jefferson's correspondence lasted well into their old age. Both men became increasingly ill and frail. In 1826, as the fiftieth anniversary of the Declaration of Independence drew near, both men's conditions weakened—though both resolved to live to see one last Fourth of July. As that historic day dawned, both Jefferson and Adams began to die. At one o'clock that afternoon, writes McCullough, Jefferson took his last breath, the bells celebrating the holiday ringing in the background in Charlottesville, Virginia. At his farm in Quincy, Massachusetts, Adams, too, lay on his deathbed. When told that it was the Fourth of July, he replied, "It is a great day. It is a *good* day." He died at 6:20 that evening.

As often as I've read this account, it still stirs me to awe. What forces lay behind this extraordinary confluence of events between two such close friends bound by such an extraordinary shared fate? "That John Adams and Thomas Jefferson died on the same day, and that it was, of all days, the Fourth of July," writes McCullough, "could not be seen as a mere coincidence: it was a 'visible and palpable' manifestation of 'Divine Favor,' wrote John Quincy [Adams] in his diary that night, expressing what was felt and would be said again and again everywhere the news spread."[2]

Adams' and Jefferson's friendship—how it began as part of a great quest, how it split apart under the pressures of translating soaring democratic ideals into the down and dirty theater of politics, and how it came back together again through the intervention of a wise healer—embody the central tensions within our American democracy. In his book *American Creation*, historian Joseph Ellis further describes this tension as the conflict between nationalists such as George Washington and John Adams in favor of a strong central government, and, on the other hand, those like Thomas Jefferson and Patrick Henry who believed that such a government violated the very "spirit of '76."

To Ellis, however, "taking sides in this debate is like choosing between the words and the music of the American Revolution." When the Founders undertook to directly confront this tension during the Constitutional Convention—which Ellis describes as the most "creative moment in all of American history," as well as a process of "painful compromise and elegant improvisation"—the argument that eventually won out, and which emerged from "the messy political process itself" rather than from any single thinker, made *argument itself* the answer to the dilemma. It did this, Ellis concludes, "by creating a framework in which federal and state authority engaged in an ongoing negotiation for supremacy, thereby making the Constitution, like history itself, an *argument without end*" (my italics).

To be a participant in American democracy, then, is to symbolically add our own signatures to the Constitution and to agree, simply put, to disagree. It means not only expressing one's individuality, but, like the members of the Constitutional Convention, being able to engage with each other in a fractious climate of uncertainty in which democracy is a work in process, continually being thrashed out in heated, rude, unsatisfying, and either misinformed or uninformed but oftentimes inspiring and educative debates on issues that have enormous impact on our daily lives: the wars we do or do not fight; the taxes we pay; who we are allowed to marry and the children we choose to have or not to have; the healthcare we do or don't receive; the quality of our children's educations; the food we eat; the roads we drive on . . . and on and on. It would seem that although it's been said before and although it appears obvious, the first step in dealing with polarization would be to accept political conflict as an inevitable condition of democracy.

As the history and the trajectory of Jefferson and Adams' friendship shows, polarization has been a constant throughout the American story. It spiked after the Civil War and Reconstruction, write Jonathan Haidt and Marc J. Hetherington in "Look How Far We've Come Apart,"[3] then dipped after World War I, and remained low throughout the Depression, World War II, and the post-war decades. This lowering of political temperature was due among other reasons, say the authors, to the shared experiences of war and economic hardship. Things began to shift during Vietnam and the rise of the culture wars around the feminist and civil rights movements of the 1960s and 1970s, effectively pushing each party into their respective corner of the boxing ring.

Since then, partisanship and polarization have grown in force and impact. According to a recent Pew Research report, Congressional Republicans and Democrats inhabit different worlds, reflecting an "America that has been growing further and further apart for decades." Bemoaning the disappearance of moderates in Congress, the report concludes grimly that "given that trends in polarization have continued unabated for decades and appear to be related to underlying structural economic and social factors . . . it is unlikely that this deadlock will be broken anytime soon."[4]

The growing divide between conservatives and liberals extends even beyond politics to how and where they live. Conservatives prefer living in large houses farther apart, and at a distance from shops and schools, while liberals prefer urban living in smaller houses closer to amenities. Conservatives value communities with shared religious values; liberals prize diversity. Some similarities exist: both parties attach great importance to living close to family, and both ends of the ideological spectrum engage in intense political conversations—but only with those who share their own views.[5] Finally, there is economic polarization, with U.S. income inequality steadily increasing since the 1970s, reaching levels not seen since 1928.[6]

What is needed in our time is someone who can bridge these great divides, and who can dream for us a way forward: someone like the wise Dr. Benjamin Rush, who was artfully able to repair the friendship between Jefferson and Adams. In healing the rift between the two estranged Revolutionary brothers, and by encouraging them in their correspondence, Rush helped to give future generations of Americans an example of democracy as a form of friendship and dynamic engagement between equals who are able to bear the tension of strong differences. In paying such close attention to his dreams, Rush was also giving value to the unconscious, laying the groundwork for future generations of American psychologists.

Indeed, as I mentioned in the Introduction, I like to think that the Founding Fathers, who were open-minded men of great intellectual curiosity, would have been keenly interested in the findings of psychology, and its insights into human nature. What would they have thought, I wonder, about British Jungian analyst Andrew Samuels, and his theories about the "nurturing father" as a template of leadership that replaces old masculine stereotypes, offering new ways to be a powerful leader of democracy? Or feminist psychologist Judith Jordan, who puts forth the idea, based on decades of research, of empathy as a plank in America's political platform, for its power to ease differences across America's great cultural, racial, and economic divides?

I believe the Founders would have been intrigued by Jungian analyst Murray Stein's comments on how anxiety is a concomitant of federal elections, something ancient Egyptians under the rule of Pharaohs would not have been subjected to. Given the Founders' preoccupation with acting as men of character, I think they would have been fascinated by my conversation with Jungian analyst John Beebe on integrity as a vital and shaping force in the American presidency. They would have been interested, as well, I like to think, in my interview with the noted psychologist James Hillman, published just before his death, in which he takes up the difficulties of accepting dependence in a culture that celebrates independence—from the perspective of his own personal experience as a cancer patient—and his vision of a coming "shift in ages." And the

Founders would surely have learned unexpected things about themselves from New York psychiatrist Robert J. Langs, who in our interview describes his years-long research into the personal lives of American presidents, the traumas they endured, and how trauma shaped them in their policy and decision-making.

In all the following interviews, a common theme can be found: the value of compassion, empathy, nurturing, and an appreciation for the effects of emotions and conditions such as anxiety and depression. Although no doubt known and experienced by our Founders in their psyches and personal families and friendships, these qualities and experiences fell into the shadow of those brighter values of individuality and independence. This section corrects, I hope, these scales of psychological imbalance. ■

Notes

1. "How Thomas Jefferson Created His Own Bible," by Owen Edwards, *Smithsonian*, January 2012.
2. See McCullough: 2002. All references in this section are from this remarkable biography.
3. "Look How Far We've Come Apart," by Jonathan Haidt and Marc J. Hetherington, *New York Times*, September 17, 2012.
4. *Partisan Polarization, in Congress and Among Public, Is Greater than Ever*, by Drew DeSilver, Pew Research Center, July 17, 2013. According to this study, the average difference between the opinions of Republicans and Democrats on issues from foreign policy, government, and social and economic issues stands at eighteen percentage points: twice the gap in surveys conducted from 1987–2002.
5. "Section 3: Political Polarization and Personal Life: Liberals Want Walkable Communities, Conservatives Prefer More Room." *Political Polarization in the American Public*, Pew Research Center, June 12, 2014.
6. *U.S. Income Inequality on Rise for Decades Is Now Highest Since 1928*, by Drew DeSilver, The Pew Research Center Fact Tank, December 12, 2013.

—27—

The Politics of the Father as Leader

H E COULD HAVE BEEN ASSISTANT director at the Royal Shakespeare Company. Instead, British Jungian psychoanalyst Andrew Samuels chose to stay the course he'd already set for himself: working with underprivileged children through the drama and youth counseling project he'd established, and running the radical theater company he'd founded in the late 1960s. But drama of another kind would soon make its claim on Samuels: the Shakespearean tempests and upheavals, conflicts and crises that seize the human psyche, threatening the equilibrium of the sanest among us.

Drawn to the work of Carl Jung, Samuels went on to train at the Society of Analytical Psychology in London. Today he is himself a training analyst and, as Professor of Analytical Psychology at the University of Essex, among the first professors of analytical psychology in the world. But Samuels' passion for politics and his revolutionary, sixties-born instincts to address the social injustices of the world did not fade with time. During the Persian Gulf War of 1991, he began to notice more patients bringing war-inspired dreams, fantasies, and visceral reactions like disgust or fear into therapy sessions. Was the traditional inner-world stuff of therapy, he wondered, masking the attempt to talk about outer-world politics?

Over time, Samuels became increasingly aware of the extent to which large-scale political events have a dramatic impact on our inner lives. Not only were we shaped psychologically by our parents and early-childhood traumas, Samuels came to realize, but by the epic triumphs and tragedies of our particular historical era. Humans' instinctive political energy, as well as their non-rational responses provoked by world traumas, he realized, needed to be both honored and decoded.

Driven to map the links between our inner and outer worlds, and between the "seemingly opposite realms of psychotherapy and politics," Samuels published a trilogy of books: *The Plural Psyche* (1989), *The Political Psyche* (1993), and *Politics on the Couch* (2001). Remaining true to his activist roots, he also cofounded The Foundation of Psychotherapists and Counsellors for Social Responsibility,[1] an organization that applies psychological perspectives to the political discourse, and began leading workshops around the world, using psychological exercises he developed to help people connect to the enlivening power of their political instincts. Conversely, Samuels also became known internationally for applying his brand of "therapy thinking" to political themes. In that capacity, he has worked as a political consultant to activist groups, political organizations, and individual politicians like former Prime Minister Tony Blair and, more recently, American politicians. In 2009, Samuels was elected chair of the United Kingdom Council for Psychotherapy (UKCP), which is the main professional organization for psychotherapists.

As deep and broad as Samuels' work has been over the decades of his career as a psychologist and political activist and commentator, one theme has remained constant: what he calls "the father thing." It is in the mold of the father rather than the mother, maintains Samuels, that politicians in Western culture—whether men or women—cast themselves in their public roles. But, as we explore in our extensive interview on American leadership and the presidency, the question is: What kind of father? The more nurturing, emotionally attuned father that has begun to emerge into prominence over the last few decades? Or the patriarchal, dominating, warlike father that has predominated over the past millennia, and that excites our admiration? The following interview was conducted in the summer of 2014.

✳

Pythia Peay: I'd like to get your observations from "across the pond," as they say, about our American presidency. How did you come to link the archetype of the father with leaders?

Andrew Samuels: When I first began writing and speaking about leadership, I deliberately *didn't* connect leaders and fathers, as it seemed so obvious—and so sexist. But now I see that irrespective of the actual sex of the candidate or the president, there is a very interesting connection between the "father thing" and leaders. Many American politicians I consult with, for instance, often express a desire to be the "father of the nation." This goes back to the early Founding Fathers, who wanted to follow in the tradition of Cicero, the statesman of the Roman Republic.

PP: So is the kind of father they're thinking of suitable to the needs of America today?

AS: That's the question. What I discovered was that the father that politicians have in mind when they talk about being the "father of the nation" is a tremendously out-of-date father. This is the macho father who provides physical and economic security and discipline, and who needs to manufacture a crisis in order to stay in power. But psychology and in fact many other people now know that there are other kinds of fathering. So one of the things I've been doing for some politicians is to introduce them to the "new-fangled" nurturing father, who is about emotional interaction, respect, recognition, and non-possessive admiration of the growing body of the child—but who isn't the Victorian, old-fashioned father focused on discipline, convention, and spiritual morality.

PP: Although all our Founding Fathers were men, Britain has had both Kings and Queens. You've also had Margaret Thatcher as Prime Minister, while America has yet to elect a female president. Has a history with more women in power brought a more nurturing style of leadership to England?

AS: You just have to Google Elizabeth the First (who was known as the Virgin Queen) to realize how annoyed she was to be in a woman's body. England's female leaders were all very macho, male-identified women leaders—what I call "fathers of whatever sex," with Mrs. Thatcher being a prime example. So I don't think you're going to find a softer, more nurturing type of leader over here as a result of our history.

PP: What are some other differences between the Founding Fathers and the modern-day presidency?

AS: Leaders in America today face a totally different set of problems than the original

Founding Fathers. While Thomas Jefferson, George Washington, John Adams, and the others were basically English, and belonged to an ethnically and culturally homogeneous group, the nation today is very diverse and disparate. This makes it very difficult for a leader to authoritatively tell everyone to just be "one big family" and get along.

The complex mix of America today reminds me of those "blended" modern families where the bloodline can't be used in an authoritarian way: like the child who says "You're not really my father: you're my stepfather," for example, or when the mother's partner is another woman. So this could either be a wonderful moment for politicians—or totally confusing.

PP: In what way could this moment of cultural diversity be a wonderful thing for leaders? And in what way is it confusing?

AS: It's wonderful because it offers an opportunity for leaders to still play the father role, while not falling into the model of the outdated "dinosaur father." The confusion comes in when political candidates put these PR spins on their warm and nurturing personal family life, but then when they go to work, they're just as warmongering as traditional leaders. I don't think we've seen a leader yet who has *really* embraced a model of the nurturing father leader based on mutual respect and admiration between parent and child.

PP: So what you're saying is that the presidency hasn't caught up with the rest of the culture?

AS: That's exactly right. And when politicians talk to me about wanting to be father leaders, I tell them that they don't have to be the kind of father they had growing up. It's about being the kind of father *they* are. Former Prime Minister Tony Blair, for example, was a good example of someone who at home was a quite nurturing, hands-on father who had deep relationships with his children. But when he went to work he was a very bloodthirsty guy.

PP: I think you've put your finger on the disconnect many voters have been having, especially around President Bush, who took us into two wars, and now Obama, who's been so hawkish around drone strikes and National Security Agency secrecy and spying. Both are very hands on, compassionate fathers in their personal family lives.

AS: This very issue is something a lot of senior American politicians have been wrestling with. The issue is actually about how to lead from behind, as opposed to leading the charge.

PP: Say more about what you mean about "leading from behind."

AS: In my experience, many politicians are actually seeking a more direct emotional connection with the people. I detect an appetite in America today for a more subtle form of leadership. Indeed, I predict that the country is about to enter a new age of subtlety because so much of the electorate is sick of the rhetoric of threats and promises. Because of your traditions of town meetings, America is better placed to make this shift than Britain. We just don't have that tapestry of informal gatherings where things get thrashed out.

PP: But I wonder how often politicians get caught in a vise between wanting to be a different kind of politician and the public or commentators who try to shoehorn them into old styles of governing. For example, the *New York Times* columnist David Brooks recently said that, with regard to the conflict in Ukraine,[2] President Obama has a "manhood" problem.[3]

AS: I agree; and it is intensified by racial dynamics. But what you're describing is the "right now." I'm saying that I detect something else not yet out there, but bubbling up from underneath, because everybody is sick of the male game. And I think the populace understands, especially in America, the limits of hard power. Over and over again, I hear that what we need to think about is soft power: and I think we're also talking about soft leadership.

PP: I'm still not sure about that. I imagine that on the issue of soft power and soft leadership the electorate falls along party lines. For example, it's often said that liberals fall into the more nurturing "maternal" style, and conservatives fall into the "old world" category of father as strict disciplinarian.[4]

AS: I'm not disputing that plenty of people think Obama should be more aggressive. But plenty of people involved in world politics, whether around Syria, the Middle East, or the Ukraine, are also coming to understand that that aggressive, cowboy style of leadership just isn't always going to work. The rise of China is also forcing the Western powers to think again about the natural supremacy of the West. I may be wrong, but I think this is a very exciting time.

For example, I recently worked with a mayor who wanted to be the "father of the city." But the question is, according to what model of the father? If it's going to be by following a kind of folk psychology that says the role of fathers is to teach you how to shoot, or wring the neck of a chicken, or fight—well, we now know that there's something else that fathers do that we didn't know before. I don't think I invented this. I think many fathers got involved in very direct, nurturing, mutual-recognition, and respect processes with their children. If you look, you can see it in art from the seventeenth or eighteenth century onwards. It's just that these so-called soft men have been suppressed below the cultural radar. This model of leadership is never going to completely *replace* heroic leadership. But it might significantly temper it—and that's a big, big thing.

PP: Why is the more nurturing style of father-as-leader never going to completely replace the heroic leader?

AS: Well, there's always going to be a potential physical risk to a nation or to a community. Then we may need a heroic leader. However, it is not so clear-cut. Good political leaders in our times don't have to know how to lead troops into battle. They just need to know how and where to hire someone who can, and when to fire someone when they can't. So political and military leadership are strikingly different.

PP: How do the two styles of leadership differ?

AS: A military leader is the old style, ram-it-through patriarch. We have an English expression from cricket, "Don't take your eye off the ball." If you take your eye off the ball you're finished, because in cricket the damn thing is coming at you hard and fast. So that's a good slogan for a general. But political leaders need to be neutral about violence. Sometimes, they have to be violent. But it's better for them to organize the military to do it instead. Take those war-room pictures taken during the capture of Osama Bin Laden, with Secretary of State Hillary Clinton looking like she's either shocked or excited or both, and President Obama being very self-contained, as if he was an experienced warrior who had witnessed this kind of thing all the time, and trying to hold it all in.[5] This is a terrible mix-up of the military and the Presidency.

PP: But this goes back to 9/11, and how that had such a dramatic impact on the American psyche. After sending troops to Afghanistan, President Bush made his dramatic landing in a plane on the deck of the aircraft carrier *USS Abraham Lincoln*, emerging in a flight suit. Later he gave a speech, with the now-notorious "Mission Accomplished" banner behind him—though as it turned out we hadn't won the war, we were just beginning it.[6]

AS: Yes, and look at where this mix-up of political leadership and the military got us. I don't know to what extent Bush interfered with his generals, but I do get a sense that Obama has been too involved in military actions abroad, too admiring of what drones can do, and American global reach. But at the same time, with the Internet and social media, many people have lost some respect for outright military power. They may even think it's necessary. But there's still a degree of cynicism.

Again, what I'm trying to say is that there are signs that there is an incipient divorce between the old structures, which are, in father terms, the dinosaur patriarchal father, and some new and interesting structures, which are more about the use of a kinder, nurturing capacity. I call it fathering, because anyone who becomes a leader gets father projections—even a woman.

PP: For many, Obama was initially seen as the more dignified, gentler, smarter, and more conciliatory "father leader," and then almost immediately began to disappoint those who'd helped elect him by taking a more militaristic stance. I was one of those who had high ideals for him as president. Did we completely misread Obama?

AS: Well, I once thought Tony Blair was the "bee's knees." I worked for him, I loved him, and I thought he was the first "modern man" to become prime minister. In the end, I was similarly mistaken. But the idealization of heroic leaders is a very powerful, sexual dynamic: we're all susceptible to it. It's often said, for example, that all pacifists are fascinated by military parades. So the arousal that the heroic leader produces—and she can be a woman—is one of the most dangerous political phenomena we know of.

PP: I'm not sure I understand what you mean.

AS: It's a "head–groin" split. For example, in their heads, most people are suspicious of *generalissimos* and know that military bigwigs cannot always be trusted. But that's with their *head*. In their hearts, in their guts, in their genitals, people are absolutely aroused by heroic leaders. And one of the things heroic leaders do is make crises and problems. But the danger is they can only think of a problem in terms of something they're going to charge at—rather than accepting, as America might have done after 9/11, that some problems cannot be solved quickly. In workshops, I frequently ask the question, "What would have happened if America had done nothing?" after the terrorist attacks.

PP: And what would have happened if we hadn't gone to war in Afghanistan?

AS: I don't really know for sure, obviously. But it is worth thinking about it. Yet people have had trouble even thinking about it. It's as if they had been so encouraged to think like the nation, they *were* the nation, so that the idea of not doing anything wasn't even discussed. But what was it that got everybody so aroused in the first place? It was bloodlust and revenge, and the idea that a good offense is a good form of defense.

PP: So you're saying the heroic leader under these kinds of conditions speaks to our more primitive selves?

AS: No, it's even worse. We're excited; even those who are sophisticated liberals are in some way affected and excited by the *generalissimos*. They turn us on! And that is something that old-style fathers tend to do. They thrill us with their bombast.

PP: So you're saying heroic leadership is very seductive.

AS: Yes, very seductive, very arousing, and it feeds on itself. But the heroic leader is just one end of the spectrum of leadership. At the other end, is what I call "sibling leadership," or non-hierarchical, team forms of leadership. But I think even these two styles of leaderships are now equally old-fashioned.

PP: You mean in addition to the emerging model of the nurturing father, another new kind of leadership is beginning to take shape?

AS: Yes: it has to do with the management of failure. And failure is everywhere in American business discourse, with famous entrepreneurs talking about their failures and what they've learned from them. Leaders who admit that they can't do things, or that they can't make promises: this is something other than the conventional, successful patriarch. I actually think what happened to Obama was that he couldn't see any other way to lead than the heroic model. You can't really blame him. The "Book of Rules" said things had to be done a certain way.

PP: And he was probably under more pressure because he's black.

AS: Of the many pressures Obama is under, one is that he mustn't be angry. As the first black president, he had to show that he wasn't wanting when it came to moral fiber and moral courage. At the same time, he had to prove that he wasn't the primitive, out-of-control black man that stalks the unconscious of Western culture. I've got some sympathy for him. How can you at the same time be the tough guy and the nice guy?

PP: So in your mind, what kind of "father of the nation" has Obama proved to be?

AS: It was Obama who renewed the popularity of the phrase "the father of the nation" and all that goes with it. That's what he said he wanted to be. But I don't know that he really came to grips with what kind of father his own version of the "father of the nation" was going to be.

PP: And then that's complicated by his own father story. I just wrote a memoir about my own father—who was a heroic "old-style father"—and by extension the American father, and my country as father. I think the whole idea of the father is a big issue in this culture, and that we're more "complexed" around the father than we are around the mother, maybe for some of the reasons you've just said. Would you agree?

AS: I don't know. But the debates in psychology around the father and what his absence or presence bring to his children intersect in a very interesting way with discussions of political leadership. It's not that mothers don't lead. It's just that years and years and years of men being in that role have equated political leadership with masculinity, even when the leader in power is a woman. Whether Indira Gandhi, Golda Meir, or Margaret Thatcher, some of the toughest, most macho leaders have been women: because they've got to bridge a gender-credibility gap. And the way they bridge that gap is by becoming tyrannical, patriarchal, father-like leaders.

But the main point I'm trying to make is that people are beginning to have doubts about this old style of leadership. Increasingly, the issue is not really around women or minorities in American politics. It's around manhood, masculinity, and what kind of father the father of the nation is supposed to be. Those sorts of men—the traditional fathers who keep order in the family and give spiritual instruction to their families and who are looked up to by their wives—have made enough of a mess of the world. Do we really want to bring them back? Even most men feel hopelessly inadequate comparing themselves to that old model of masculinity.

PP: Because they can't possibly live up to that rarefied ideal of manhood?

AS: Or men achieved that ideal and then hated it, and may have decided to consciously experiment with other ways of being a man and a father.

PP: Do you think the American people could accept the kind of more nurturing president or political leader who is more open and accepting of failure that you see beginning to emerge?

AS: Yes, I think they would. For example, people loved Obama's autobiography and the story of his personal life; and they loved it when he said he wasn't perfect. His opponents didn't, but I think people chose him over Hillary Clinton with these things in mind.[7] So I think Obama was trying to prepare people for failure. I had a sense that he was struggling towards a kind of "good enoughness" style of leadership.

PP: So you're talking now about what you call the "good enough leader"[8] versus a leader who seeks to maintain the ideal image that people have of him, or her.

AS: Both the development of the "good enough leader" whose expertise is in accepting flaws and managing failure, and the surge of interest in the "nurturing father" point in the same direction: the quest to overcome our infatuation with heroic leaders. The idea that fathers are physically and emotionally available to their children in direct personal relationships isn't that radical; it's something most people are in touch with. So isn't it reasonable that politicians who are looking for the next best thing would be interested in these developments as models of political leadership?

PP: I would think so. Can you tell me what kinds of questions you're asked in your role as a consultant?

AS: The number one thing I'm asked has to do with exploring new images around leadership. The other thing I'm asked about involves the idea of sacrifice. Massive hikes in taxation for healthcare, for example, require a huge sacrifice, because it would take money away from the people. But this is where the Jungian theory on sacrifice is so potent.

PP: And what does Jung say about the idea of sacrifice?

AS: That if you give something up, you get something. But it's not the same as an investment model or an ordinary trade where you give up two jelly beans and you get four back, so to speak. Sacrifice involves the idea that something much more emotional and qualitatively different will happen if you give things up. And that's something that political people are beginning to become interested in.

PP: Are you hopeful for the future of the American presidency evolving in this new direction?

AS: On the whole, the American presidency and Western leadership has remained within the area of the hero—like Clint Eastwood in *The Good, the Bad and the Ugly*. Sadly, I think that's still where we're at. But at the same time, something is bubbling up; it's very unsettling and exciting, and it's modeled on the nurturing father. So I'm optimistic. I think ideas travel; they get around! There are even jokes about nurturing fathers on *The Simpsons* television show, and how Homer just can't do it!

PP: You mean Homer Simpson is a caricature of the old world father?

AS: Yes, but he knows he should be different. And actually that aspirational atmosphere is very present in modern Western politics and culture. The populace isn't stupid: it just isn't offered any other style of doing politics than this macho heroic model.

   Still, there's a shift; and though the idea of the father will be shaping discussions of political leadership for thousands of years to come, the question remains: What kind of father should a president, candidate, senator, or mayor have in their mind when they want to be the father of the people they're thinking about leading? ■

Notes

1.   The Foundation of Psychotherapy and Counsellors for Social Responsibility (PCSR) can be found online <http://pcsr-uk.ning.com/>.

2.   Following a popular, pro-European uprising in Kiev in February 2014 against the corrupt government of President Viktor Yanukovych, who fled to Russia, separatist forces in Crimea and eastern Ukraine, backed by Russian special forces and military, began an armed resistance to efforts by the new Ukrainian government, led by Petro Poroshenko, to pacify that region. At the time of writing, a putative ceasefire, mostly honored in the breach, is holding in eastern Ukraine.

3.   "David Brooks Actually Talked About Obama's Manhood Problem in the Middle East," by Katherine Fung, *Huffington Post*, April 20, 2014.

4.   "The Enduring Mommy-Daddy Political Divide," by David Paul Kuhn, *Real Clear Politics,* March 2, 2010.

5.   The photograph can be seen at <http://en.wikipedia.org/wiki/File:Obama_and_Biden_await_updates_on_bin_Laden.jpg>.

6.   On May 1, 2003, George W. Bush landed on the USS *Abraham Lincoln*. He posed for photographs while wearing a flight suit, and then gave a speech announcing the end of major combat operations in Iraq. Above him, a banner stated "Mission Accomplished."

7.   Hillary Rodham Clinton and Barack Obama fought each other for the Democratic party's nomination for President in 2008.

8.   The " good enough leader" is a phrase coined by Andrew Samuels from the psychologist D. W. Winnicott's term "the good enough mother." As Samuels writes in his essay "The Good Enough Leader," the good enough mother refers to the process by which a kind of "graduated let-down or disappointment of the baby" is carried out by the parents, who cannot help but fail to fulfill the omnipotent demands and idealistic projections of their infant. Through this process the baby is carefully introduced to the realities of life. His essay is included in Singer, ed.: 2000.

—28—

The United States of Empathy

An Interview with Judith Jordan, Ph.D.

FEMINIST PSYCHOLOGIST JUDITH JORDAN grew up in the small town of Stroudsburg, Pennsylvania, in the Pocono Mountains. Her double calling in the field of psychology and as an activist challenging cultural stereotypes that diminish so-called "feminine" values of empathy and compassion in favor of more "masculine" virtues of heroic individualism was handed down to her from her parents. It was a heritage that she accepted with enthusiasm, and that she has carried forward in her profession.

Her grandfather, a pacifist and brilliant chemist, was conscripted to work in a German munitions factory during World War I, and resolved to escape the ongoing militarism at the first opportunity. Because Germany did not want to lose the valuable patents her chemist-grandfather owned—one was for an indigo dye that eventually was used to create blue jeans!—he and his family had to be smuggled out of the country. Throughout his life, he and his family maintained an enormous sense of gratitude to America for facilitating their escape. Jordan's mother was an unapologetic liberal in the predominantly conservative town where the family lived. One of her earliest political memories, recalls Jordan, was as a young girl during the 1956 presidential race between Republican President Dwight D. Eisenhower and his opponent, Democratic candidate Adlai Stevenson II. "I was the only kid who had an Adlai Stevenson scarf. My mother had gotten it for me," she told me. "It was orange and blue, and I wore it to school. But none of the other kids had even heard of Adlai Stevenson; they'd only heard about Eisenhower. I didn't realize how out of sync I was!"

Jordan also didn't realize how "out of sync" she was with some of the fundamental principles of separation and "stand-strong-alone" within her chosen field of psychology. Early in her career, she confided, she found herself feeling judged by her colleagues for the amount of energy and time she was devoting to traveling from Pennsylvania to Boston to care for her ill and dying mother. The prevailing theory suggested the path to maturity involved making a clean break in adolescence with one's parents and childhood past, in order to achieve the autonomy of American adulthood. It was while working with the feminist theorist Jean Baker Miller, author of *Toward a New Psychology of Women*, that Jordan began questioning these unspoken cultural assumptions.

In their groundbreaking research in the field of women's psychology, Miller and her team had noticed that women cared about, and contributed to, relationships as central to their wellbeing—pursuits mainstream psychology negatively labeled as dependency or neediness. "When those old, male-model standards of self-sufficiency and autonomy were applied to women," said Jordan, "[women] constantly looked deficient, needy, too emotional, and irrational. It was an incredibly destructive model, not just for women, but ultimately for all human beings." After Miller's death, Jordan continued to make empathy, belonging, relationships, dependency, mutuality, and connection the centerpiece of her research and work as a psychologist, not just for women, but for men, too.

Today, Jordan is the director of the Jean Baker Miller Training Institute at the Wellesley Centers for Women (WCW). Together with the late Jean Baker Miller and her colleagues Irene Stiver and Jan Surrey, Jordan is one of the creators of the nationally recognized psychological theory known as "Relational-Cultural Theory."[1] In addition to her position at WCW, Dr. Jordan is an assistant professor of psychiatry at Harvard Medical School, and was the director of psychology training as well as the director of the Women's Studies program at McLean Hospital. Among other publications, Dr. Jordan authored the book *Relational-Cultural Therapy*, and has co-authored several books, including the classic *Women's Growth in Connection*. She travels the country as a speaker, and is widely known as a popular lecturer and commentator, appearing on radio and television shows.

In the following interview, Jordan discusses the radical idea of how empathy might one day become an accepted plank in American political platforms. She exposes the flaws in society's ongoing idealization of those "cowboy" virtues of separation and autonomy: especially as it plays out on the political landscape, resulting in real world policies that marginalize those who fail to meet impossible standards for independence, self-sufficiency, and emotional control. We also discuss the harmful psychological effects of our deepening political, social, and economic polarization.

During the course of our interview, I asked Jordan if, during her thirty-five years of research and practice, she'd seen progress throughout the culture in recognizing the importance of this different set of values that she has dedicated her life to serving. "Something is shifting," she replied, "even though the movement is glacial (big, but very, very slow). I see the word *connection* everywhere: in advertising for banks and stockbrokers, or on the Internet and social media. I dislike some of the ways this term is being used as a form of marketing, or the way empathy gets used to manipulate people in negotiations. But the trend does indicate that something is shifting. We are changing from an industrial-machine society, to a service society, to a culture of understanding and communicating—and that has to do with empathy and connection." And although Jordan doesn't expect to see this shift completed in her lifetime, she is undeterred. "I am certainly going to keep working, because I have to bring that kind of intensity and passion toward creating a change I believe in, even though that change is far bigger than anything I'll see in my lifetime." Portions of the following interview were conducted in 1994, and updated in 2014.

✳

Pythia Peay: The country is suffering through some of the worst political and economic polarization it's ever experienced. I'd like to get your vantage point on this phenomenon from the Relational-Cultural psychological theory you've developed, as I think the culture could use some "relationship therapy."

Judith Jordan: One of the factors underlying these splits has to do with our assumptions about human nature. And from Freud on back in history, one of those assumptions has been that human nature is at its core selfish, greedy, self-interested, and aggressive.

If we assume that all people are like this, and that self-interest is a biological imperative, then we will tend to take a pessimistic view toward social intervention. Adopting a defeatist response to these negative characteristics, we shrug our shoulders and say, "What can you expect? It's just human nature." Expecting greed and encouraging self-interest, we fail to support the truly positive aspects of our nature. This unhealthy dynamic contributes to increasing economic disparities. And where we have the largest gaps between rich and poor we also have the least tolerance for differences. Where we segregate around difference (race, class, caste, sex) we have less mutual respect and empathy—the very qualities that help reduce polarization.

But increasingly, the new data from neuroscience and neuropsychology reveal a picture of human nature that is completely at odds with the old view. This research shows that we are relational beings, and that most human beings possess an enormous amount of energy for giving and not just taking; for nurturing and helping others; and for developing mutual empathy and participating in what Jean Baker Miller called "growth-fostering" relationships.

PP: These findings must be very gratifying, because the importance of connection and empathy is what your work has been all about.

JJ: For thirty-five years the Stone Center Relational-Cultural theory has been saying that the brain grows in connection, we are happier when we are in growth-enhancing connection, and we have healthier societies when we are in connection. We need growth-fostering connection to survive and to thrive! In this context, the current crisis of polarization can't be split off from its harmful effects, not just politically, but to human nature and society. Studies have shown that a culture with great disparities of wealth and income inequality, as we have now, is a culture that is less empathic, that is more violent, that has poorer health, and that fails in terms of the education of girls and women.[2] In such a culture it is more likely that certain groups will be actively marginalized. This in turn affects people in negative ways. And as groups become distanced from one another, there is less and less opportunity for empathic bonds to form between them.

These findings are backed up by two neuroscientists from the University of California, Lieberman and Eisenberger, who've examined the impact of exclusion on the brain.[3] And what they've found is that when people are excluded, even in very minimal ways, the pain registers in the same place in the brain as when they are in physical pain. So to the brain, being marginalized is no different than putting your hand on a hot stove. This research on how social exclusion can lead to emotional and physical pain is called "SPOT," or social pain overlap theory.

PP: What does "social pain overlap" theory mean?

JJ: It refers to the fact that social pain signals and physical pain signals travel the same pathways to the same place in the brain. The two kinds of pain, if you will, overlap and are indistinguishable neurologically. This tells us that the alarm system that is activated when our physical safety is threatened or when we need water or air or food is the same alarm that gets activated when we are excluded from relationships, and when we feel isolated. We are wired to experience isolation as endangering us. We need connection like we need air and water.

This research has important political implications. Often, those who complain about the social pain inflicted on them from being pushed out of the mainstream by polarization are judged by the dominant group as wimps who "just can't take it." Or their pain is thought to be fake, or psychosomatic. But we now have the data that say these people's brains are actually being hurt, and their bodies are being injured, by the physiological effects of the stress of exclusion.

PP: But I think that even many of those who recognize that the pain inflicted by social and economic marginalization is physically harmful *still* wouldn't care. They'd still say, "Get over it" and, "Stop being such a wimp."

JJ: I think you're right: the major thrust is to be dismissive and to say, "They're just making excuses for themselves. They're not really handicapped by marginalization and exclusion, and in fact the only people who really care about exclusion are wimps, like women and girls."

Still, part of what we're trying to do is raise awareness that social pain isn't any different from physical pain—*and* that physical *and* social pain exist for a reason. Because if we don't feel pain when we put our hand on the stove, we're in trouble; the same way we're in trouble when we don't feel the pain of being isolated and lonely. The brain is wired to respond to social exclusion with the same degree of alarm that it feels when there's physical wounding or endangerment. Pain is pain. The more we can challenge the myth that social pain is a function of a person's weakness and show how we are *all* wired to feel the pain of social exclusion, the more we can begin to see each other as sharing a kind of vulnerability. Then we can begin to own that vulnerability rather than deny it.

So the broader messages coming through this new research in neuroscience are that, number one, connection is just as important to people as oxygen and food. And number two, those people who are excluded, bullied, or marginalized are actually experiencing something that is harmful to them physiologically and neurologically: and that these findings should not be ignored.

PP: So to be clear, you're saying that it's not only that people suffer when they lack intimate family and social connections. They also suffer when they feel excluded and disenfranchised from the wider culture and body politic?

JJ: Absolutely. But here's the dilemma. Although we have a brain and a body that is wired with signals that go off in our system if we're isolated, and that is geared toward motivating us to connect, all of our acculturation and socialization is directed toward making us into separate, autonomous, invulnerable, and independent individuals—and there ain't no such thing!

 We act as if dependence is a choice. But the fact is we are simply dependent. At the Stone Center we say "interdependent" because that's a more accurate description of the connections between an individual and others, whether family, friends, or wider social connections. But our foundational American myths have to do with our development into strong, separate individuals who stand on their own and haul themselves up by their bootstraps. That's another important polarization in the country: dependence and independence.

PP: But these are the basic myths that were born with America's very origins. So how does all your work, as well as these new findings from neuroscience, square with the underpinnings of our belief system, and what we as Americans hold as our defining myths?

JJ: We do need protection of individual rights. But in our emphasis on the "separate self," we've lost sight of the critical importance of support systems and networks and community. The problem is that living by these myths of the lone hero is simply not a sustainable way of being in the world. We're constantly setting ourselves up for failure and shame, and I think that drains more creative energy from us than it contributes.

 There are so many ways that we put the wrong lens up to the light, and keep seeing things through a distorted perspective. I value differentiation and individuality, but I think we create more pain, violence, and isolation because we only see half the picture. People quote Darwin, for instance, emphasizing that the survival of the fittest is about the survival of the most alpha and aggressive creatures. These theories are seen as validation of the American myth of the independent and lone hero. Yet actually Darwin talked extensively about the importance of cooperation and collaboration. As social creatures we survive *through* our connections, not in spite of them.

But to talk about these opposing ideas and myths comes up against something central to our prevailing social constructions as Americans. I may be over-correcting an imbalance in our understanding of human behavior in the direction of emphasizing cooperation and connection. And I do that partly because the prevailing culture in America has been so imbalanced in the other direction. We need to re-balance, to see connection as a powerful force in humans' lives.

PP: Do you think one way of healing our underlying polarization is to reframe some of our basic democratic ideals around the hero and the individual?

JJ: Yes, like those iconic images of the Lone Ranger[4] or the Marlboro Man,[5] so many of our myths and images of independence picture the solo courageous hero facing the frontier and incredible dangers. But counteracting this hyper-individualism in the story of our country are all the stories and images of community in our history, like the early Puritans who established communities together in the wilderness, or those wagon trains of settlers heading west, not alone, but together.

I also think part of the deeper background work has to do with bringing the supporting cast out of the shadows. Often people take personal credit for great achievements, claiming that they did it all on their own. But that just doesn't represent most experience. I ran across an interesting quote by Einstein that speaks to this point. He noted, "A hundred times every day I tell myself that my inner and outer life are based on the labors of other men, living and dead, and that I must exert myself in order to give in the same measure as I have received and am still receiving."[6] Most achievements are the result of something interactive; a lot of creativity takes place in a dialogic or collaborative mode. It's like you and I talking right now! You're getting sparked listening to some new ideas from me, and I'm getting sparked by your questions.

PP: Courage is another defining American myth. But you've even broadened traditional definitions of courage to include "courage in connection."

JJ: That's right. We typically talk about courage as being characteristic of people who jump out of planes or scale mountains, while forgetting about the courage it takes to encourage or support others—especially those who may be different from us. Yet we all share a common humanity, which is quite humbling when we think about it in terms of our vulnerability. It can be very difficult to dialogue across differences and to stay open and responsive, rather than react in anger or self-protection. But responsiveness, in fact, is allowing ourselves to take in and be changed by the other person. The other point about courage in connection is that we all need to be *en*couraged by others throughout our lives. Courage is created in relationship. It is not a stable, internal trait. We can help one another create more courageous responses to the challenges of life, providing hope in difficult times.

PP: It takes a lot of courage to be responsive in that way to someone we disagree with, or can't relate to.

JJ: It sure does. We have to have the courage to risk being open to being changed. But we also have to be able to assess risk, and to figure out if this is a safe person to be responsive to, or whether we need to protect ourselves. So it's not an easy thing to do.

PP: In listening to your thoughts, I wonder if some of our own history has been lost in the telling. I think of the Constitutional Convention, where all the Founders came together from their different regions and with strong differences of opinion and faith, and yet in spite of those differences were able to craft the Constitution and the government we have today.

JJ: I'm not much of an historian. But I certainly know the broad painting of that time was one of enormous compromise and bartering. The political person who I think epitomizes what needs to happen to heal our polarization is Abraham Lincoln. This was a man who was able to take his ego out of the picture, and to be there for the good of the whole at a time when the good was breaking apart in a frightening and destructive way. He was able to skillfully manage great differences, and instead of excluding and pushing out his opponents, brought them right into the center of his cabinet: it was not only brilliant, it was in the service of the larger good. We have so celebrated the individual hero and individual accomplishment that we forget that one of the greatest sources of wellbeing and happiness is found in serving the greater good. In contributing to the growth of others, both the individual and the larger community benefit.

PP: So, say President Obama and Speaker of the House John Boehner came to your office, seeking advice for their relationship. Where would you start, and what would you say?

JJ: What a crazy idea! (Crazy good, I'd add). Well, first I would try to get my own personal reactivity and feelings about political issues under control. This is actually something that all politicians are fairly good at doing. But what they *don't* do is take the next step, which is to be genuinely responsive to one another's points of view and needs.

So that's the path I'd want to take if I had those two men together in my office. I would try to help them reach places of compromise and responsiveness, to understand one another's point of view, and to let each other see what their experience is like from inside, from an empathic place. But I wouldn't expect to be successful in that effort. One of the obstacles in Obama's presidency, I believe, has been that we are still struggling with the legacy of slavery and racism. We are definitely not living in a post-racial society. I think we're trying, and the fact that we elected an African-American president is a hugely important event in our history. But some of those underlying and ongoing wounds around racism and oppression get exacerbated and played out in the political realm. *We urgently need to pay attention to the harmful oppressions and marginalizations that still plague our culture.* I think it's a much bigger issue than psychologists can get their minds around. But we need to keep trying to make positive social change. As change agents we have a responsibility to tackle the big problems as well as the more personal sources of distress. The status quo is not working for most people.

Some people have said to me jokingly, "We've had the Democratic Party and the Republican Party. Now we need an 'Empathy' party!" I kind of believe that. If we could really support the development of empathy in this country (which of course we don't), it would heighten the spirit of mutuality and I think it would make a difference. In Canada, they're starting to develop programs in training schoolchildren in empathy.

PP: Can you say more about this program on empathy that they're doing in Canada?

JJ: It's a brilliant program called the "Roots of Empathy," started by Ruth Gordon.[7] Once every week or month they have a baby and a mother come into a school classroom. The students all sit on the floor, and observe and talk about how the baby communicates to the mother, or how the mother picks up the information coming from the baby. Outcome studies of this program have shown that it dramatically reduces bullying. Basically, bullying is overriding any empathic response a person might have, and trying to hurt the other person and defeat them, rather than appreciate their experience. And in fact, to get back to politics, there's a lot of bullying going around on the political scene.

PP: It would be an interesting experiment to have a mother and a baby come to the Capitol and be observed by the President and Congress. Some might laugh at the thought, but maybe something that basic has to happen to break the chokehold of bitter partisanship.

JJ: Recently, I saw photos of the leaders of Congress and the Senate celebrating the fiftieth anniversary of Freedom Summer and the passage of the Civil Rights Act. They were gathered in the Capitol Rotunda, and were standing in a circle holding hands, swaying together and singing "We shall overcome."[8] When I saw this I had a moment of crazy hope; I literally got goose bumps, and my eyes teared up.

PP: I saw the same scene and surprised myself by having the very same response! But if a single image of political unity could bypass cynicism and evoke such powerful feelings, it must signal that at a certain level, we're all longing to see more camaraderie, unity, and respect among our leaders.

JJ: Part of that very visceral response you and I experienced was because they were making physical contact, singing together, joining for a moment to honor the cause of social justice—something much bigger than partisan advantage. These two groups are so alienated from one another they literally don't want to even touch or get near each other. I can imagine there were people who looked at that picture and felt disgust; because many of us, especially little boys, are taught to suppress that kind of empathic vulnerability.

One of the differences between Republicans and Democrats is how they manage vulnerability. The Republican stance is to basically say that what we really need is to be invulnerable, to stand on our own two feet; there is a tendency to blame and denigrate those who are vulnerable. There is a notion of "just desserts," built on the myth of meritocracy. On the other hand, the Democrats' position is toward supporting those who are vulnerable. There is more appreciation that the playing field is not level.

To cite another example, when the tragedy of 9/11 happened, instead of admitting that America was just as vulnerable as the rest of the world, we attempted to deny our vulnerability and to reassert our military supremacy. However, attitudes toward vulnerability may be starting to change, particularly in men. I've been very touched recently by the number of men who have started to talk about the costs of masculine socialization. We socialize boys to be tough, independent, and autonomous. But they need love and tenderness and are just as vulnerable as little girls are.

PP: What you're describing seems to be a much deeper division than exists between Republicans and Democrats, or maybe even than between men and women.

JJ: Yes, it's a split between two opposing worldviews. And in order to reconcile these two points of view we have to begin to find ways to connect across differences. I've always stressed the importance of empathy across difference as one of the main growing points for individuals, but I think it's also a cultural growing point.

Our way of dealing with difference at a cultural level has become entwined with competition, ranking, and stratification: this group is better than or worse than others, or society ranks people according to gender, race, or class. What we just don't seem able to do is acknowledge that this or that individual is different from us or that we're different from them—then ask what we can we learn from each other about these differences. Our difficulty with difference may stem in part from waves of immigrants coming in, wanting to feel included and respected, but instead feeling disrespected and rejected.

PP: You've already spoken about the psychological effects on those who are marginalized by whoever is in the current mainstream of society. But what are the effects on those who perpetrate these differences through racism, exclusion, and isolation?

JJ: When we start treating people as "other" and "less than," it's an objectifying, dehumanizing, distancing approach, which allows us to stay in our comfort zone of just being with people who have exactly the same beliefs as we do or who look like us.

And then we don't get people talking about the common good; we get people attacking each other for not doing something right or having the wrong values. This kind of stratification creates a communication gap: people don't connect across differences of economic inequality or racial or cultural difference, which then leads to more negative, caricatured images of the "other" rather than respect for their essential humanity.

PP: So would you say that responsiveness and empathy are democratic skills that should be taught and cultivated as much as the values of independence and autonomy?

JJ: I would say democracy would work a lot better if we had more emphasis on mutuality, empathy, and respect.

PP: Why would it work better?

JJ: Because then we wouldn't get stuck in patterns of "me versus you" or "this is mine; this is for me." Instead, we'd begin to realize that what is good for the larger community is also good for the individual. We'd begin honoring our commonality and not be ashamed of the ways we need each other—because we do need each other.

PP: So what is an image that is both quintessentially American and that would represent these principles of empathy and relatedness—and that would complement those images of the Lone Ranger or the go-it-alone person who hauls him- or herself up by the bootstraps?

JJ: We need to alter our stories of lone achievement. We need to highlight the stories of joining together to effect social change. Bring the supporting players onto center stage. Notice the empathic moments of feeling "with" another person and how empowering these moments can be. Highlight those moments when we join hands, like those senators and representatives, and appreciate the courage we can create with one another. But here's a specific image that someone gave to me recently, and that I pass on to you. I was doing a conference in California when a woman asked, "Do you know what makes the redwood trees so strong and enduring?" I wasn't sure but I replied that maybe it was because they had thick bark and deep roots. She smiled and responded, "Actually, the redwoods have very shallow roots, but their roots intertwine with the roots of nearby trees. They literally hold each other up."

It's a lovely image of mutual enhancement and growth and strength coming from connection, rather than from armored self-reliance. That image counters some of our dominant cultural images of solo strength and "stand-alone" fortitude.

PP: I like it because it's an image of both connection and separateness.

JJ: Yes, the trees are strong and sturdy, but only because of this underlying web of support. There is an African proverb, *ubuntu*: "I am because we are." Or we could say, "Relationships come first." Another saying is, "All of us are smarter than each of us." I might also add, "Together we can create change." These are useful reminders to put relationships, not selves, first. ■

Notes

1. The Jean Baker Miller Training Institute (JBMTI) at the Wellesley Centers for Women is the home of Relational-Cultural Theory (RCT) which posits that people grow through and toward relationships throughout the lifespan, and that culture powerfully impacts relationship. For more information, visit <http://www.jbmti.org/>.
2. "The Question Is: How Does Inequality Matter?" by R. A., *Economist*, January 21, 2011.
3. Eisenberger, Naomi I., and Mathew D. Lieberman. "Why Rejection Hurts: A Common Neural Alarm System for Physical and Social Pain." *Trends in Cognitive Sciences*, Vol. 8 No. 7, 2004.
4. The Lone Ranger was a children's character on radio, television, and in several films. He fought outlaws in the Old West, with Tonto, his Native American friend.
5. The Marlboro Man. The iconic image of a lone cowboy in the American West, smoking the advertised product, Marlboro tobacco, defined American masculinity as white, rugged, solitary, and silent <http://en.wikipedia.org/wiki/Marlboro_Man>.
6. See Miller and Lapham: 2012, p. 52.
7. In 1996, Mary Gordon created Roots of Empathy in Toronto, Canada. Roots of Empathy became a charitable not-for-profit organization in 2000 with the goal of offering empathy-based programming for children. To date, the award-winning program has reached over half a million children worldwide <http://www.rootsofempathy.org>.
8. "Watch Lawmakers Hold Hands, Sway to 'We Shall Overcome,'" by Arlette Saenz, ABC News, June 25, 2014. The Freedom Summer occurred in 1964, when activists—many of them students—traveled to the American South to register disenfranchised African-American voters in Mississippi. The action was met with violence, including the murders of three activists: Andrew Goodman, Michael Schwerner, and James Chaney. On July 2, 1964, Congress passed the Civil Rights Act, which outlawed discrimination based on race, religion, sex, color, or national origin. "We Shall Overcome" was a resistance song that became the unofficial anthem of the civil rights movement.

—29—

On Election Day, the Voice of the People Will Speak

AN INTERVIEW WITH MURRAY STEIN, PH.D.

E VERY FOUR YEARS, THE American body politic convulses with anxiety as it suffers through a presidential election. Buffeted by rich and powerful special interest groups; deluged by wave upon wave of radio, television, and Internet promotional and attack ads; romanced by local and national party loyalists; and skeptical of ever finding a shard of truth amid the media torrent of boasts, mistruths, and glad-handing; the electorate and its candidates are swept along turbulent currents until they wash up on that promised shore—where the President elect emerges to stand before the people. Afterwards, we wonder: Has democracy survived? Or has its original promise eroded just a bit more? And why, we ask, must our elections always be so messily and bitterly fought, as if each time we were fighting the Revolution or the Civil War all over again?

Perhaps only a thinker or philosopher above the fray, someone with insight into the human psyche and the ability to see patterns where others see only random events—someone with a love of America and a sense of wisdom and psychological perspective on the game of politics—could really answer these questions. This was the quest I undertook in 2012 when, in an attempt to understand some of the hidden forces shaping the upcoming presidential election between President Barack Obama and his Republican opponent Mitt Romney, I turned to Jungian psychoanalyst Murray Stein.

Born in Chicago, Stein currently lives in Zürich, where he is president of the

International School of Analytical Psychology. A worldwide lecturer on analytical psychology, Stein is the author of many books, including most recently *The Principle of Individuation*, and the editor of many others, including *Psyche at Work*. With a focus on applying the insights of analytical psychology to the contemporary world, he has consulted internationally with executives and corporations around the globe, offering workshops on psychology and transformational leadership in the workplace.

Well-positioned between the inner world of the psyche and the outer world of business, culture, and politics, Stein is an elegant and thoughtful man who bears a resemblance to an older Jimmy Stewart: a bit sardonic and wry, yet concealing depths of integrity and intellect. Grounded in the American heartland of the Midwest, but with a perspective broadened by his stance as an American living abroad, Stein enlightened me on the psychology of being a voter in America's large and ever-fluctuating democracy. He pointed to things I'd never considered before: the link between anxiety and democracy; sobering truths about our worsening polarization; the necessity of "healing symbols"; America's midlife identity crisis and the tasks of the country's next phase; and the larger archetypal forces and American myths operating behind the chaos and dissension of the election, such as those of the pioneer and the spirit of democracy. After our interview, I felt a curtain had parted on a grander, more soaring vision of America than I'd experienced before. And it gave me faith.

✳

Pythia Peay: In 2003, you left Chicago to live in Switzerland. This vantage point must give you an interesting perspective on the presidential election.

Murray Stein: Yes, I was just thinking about that. The Swiss Constitution was modeled on the American Constitution. But they made some changes that, in light of the polarized American electorate, seem significant. Instead of a single president, the Swiss system has a council of seven leaders elected from their congress every four years. The presidency rotates among this council each year. They also have four strong parties—two are extreme and two are in the middle—as opposed to the two-party system in the United States. Everyone has to compromise; nobody gets everything they want.

Psychologically, this has a moderating effect that disperses the power, rather than focusing it on one leader. This also prevents the severe splitting effect that we see in the States, where the parties are set so strongly against each other. Whenever you have two of anything running against each other you're going to have a splitting process; it's a psychological phenomenon. People side with one against the other, and then those differences become pushed to an extreme.

PP: A "tension of the opposites," or the ability to hold two opposing views at the same time, is considered psychologically healthy. Why isn't this working on the collective level of the American psyche?

MS: Differences are necessary in order to have growth and dynamic movement. Out of the dialectic between two polarities, a new possibility emerges. But if the "opposites," or in this case the two parties, become completely unrelated, then the collective psyche is in danger of splitting. There's no forward movement, there's just mutual aggression, stalemate, and stagnation. The system doesn't evolve, it devolves, and you don't want to see that happen.

PP: Why, what happens to a society that splits into unrelated, opposing factions?

MS: Then you have disintegration and even war in the streets. You can look at history and see where it's happened: Germany after World War I, for example, tried to form a democracy. But the parties couldn't work together, and they broke into opposites, with the communists fighting the fascists in the streets, until one party killed the others off, or put them in prison. So if the public splits without being able to contain this play of opposing party beliefs, then you have a very dangerous situation of one or the other prevailing. And that's a psychological recipe for a neurosis or a psychosis on a collective level.

PP: When an individual person's psyche goes through this process of splitting, what is the therapeutic intervention?

MS: Initially, what a person who is suffering this kind of severe splitting does is blame everything that's gone wrong in their lives on someone else. They're innocent and the other person is guilty.

    For that dynamic to change they have to develop a strong-enough identity and feel safe enough to recognize their own faults. As trust builds slowly between the therapist and patient, a safe container for holding these uncomfortable feelings is created. Then the idea is gradually introduced that perhaps that person bears some responsibilities, too. So overcoming splitting means taking back what you've put out there into the world to protect yourself from feeling threatened from within.

PP: It seems to me America has that tendency to put all that is bad onto the "other." What does this say about our sense of self as a country? Do we have a weak sense of identity?

MS: I think the feeling of security in the United States is quite weak right now. And when you feel insecure in your identity, you don't feel safe, and your defense mechanisms take over, and projection gets going. We saw this after the trauma of 9/11, and the aggressive attitude that developed toward finding the enemy. I'm not saying that that there aren't very real, serious threats to our national security; it's a crazy world. But we have to be careful in distinguishing what we're projecting onto the "other," and what presents a genuine threat.

PP: Do you feel that the increasing polarization of the electorate over the last decade has something to do with the trauma we suffered after 9/11?

MS: Yes. In addition, there's another trauma the country has been suffering through: the financial crisis has also added to people's insecurity.

A really good politician can do a lot to heal these wounds by giving people something to believe in, or a healing symbol that will pull the people out of their fear. [Franklin] Roosevelt was good at this. He had a way of inspiring people and getting things moving. Reagan was skilled at using symbols, such as the image of "the city on the hill," and as a "light to the nations," to unite people. These are classic American symbols, derived from the Bible [Matt. 5:14; Isa. 49:6]. Kennedy, with his various programs and his call to "ask not what your country can do for you, but what you can do for your country," gave Americans a sense of mission.[1]

A strong candidate like Obama in the last election [2008] generated a surplus of symbolism. Because of his character and his multicultural background, he was a reconciling figure who symbolized the coming together of opposites. When he was inaugurated, it was a numinous moment in American history that generated a lot of hope. People were hoping that he could end the nuclear arms race, solve the problems in the economy and the Mideast, and that everything would work out. But the hope was too great. He couldn't do it; nobody could. It was too much.

PP: So, in a way, Obama represents both the benefits and the pitfalls of the enormous power and symbolism the American president carries. Can you say more about that?

MS: The American president is a big, big figurehead who has to make the voters feel proud that they're a part of this people that call themselves Americans. Because the president represents the whole people, a lot of psychological material gets loaded up on the two candidates. There's a lot of fear that somebody will get elected who will make us look bad. And if the individual voter doesn't feel good about the person representing them, they don't feel good about their country; they could even feel ashamed of themselves as an American.

So when an election takes place, what the American people are really deciding is what identity they're going to present to the world as "The American." Do they want the world to see us as a Mitt Romney, or as a Barack Obama? In a sense, the president is a kind of "self-representative" in the world—an archetypal, larger-than-life "American" whose qualities go beyond the capacities of an ordinary human.

PP: How does the rest of the world play into these heightened expectations surrounding the presidential election?

MS: The American president is also a world leader. So in addition to the projections of the American voter onto the presidential candidates, there is the enormous attention paid around the world to an American election. It's on the news every night and in the newspapers every day. And right now the world is watching very closely. Even an unknown congressman from Missouri like Todd Akin[2] can make a controversial comment, and the whole world hears about it.

PP: Speaking of Todd Akin's offensive remarks around "legitimate" rape, it seems that no matter how much we strive to talk about what we think we should be talking about, like the economy, these culture-war issues keep cropping up. What's going on in the American psyche to cause this recurring phenomenon?

MS: The huge wave of consternation generated by this incident is yet another symptom of the in-between state America is in. Things are in a lot of flux. So there's tremendous fear on both sides that the country is losing its identity, and in that climate so-called little things can get blown up out of proportion. As a result you get this tug of war over what we stand for: Who are we? What kind of people are we going to be? And because an election is a turning point when anything can happen, this mood of anxiety is heightened even further. Thus, when Todd Akin makes a statement like that, it sets off bells of alarm on one side that the country is going backward to the days when abortion was illegal.

PP: So you're saying that as much as we want to believe that the election is about policy issues, it's really about who we are as a country, and our identity. Would you say America is in the midst of an identity crisis?

MS: Yes, America is struggling with its sense of itself. And all Americans are a part of this process. If you grow up in America, and you participate in American culture, you're affected by this, because it's a part of your own personal identity.

PP: You gave the example of abortion as an issue that triggers an identity crisis for liberals. What would be an example of how this identity crisis in the American psyche is playing out for conservatives?

MS: For many, the influx of foreign cultures threatens the roots of their American identity; there is the fear that, "We're losing our identity, this isn't who we are." As a result, there's a big push-back to recapture our previous and imagined pristine identity. At the edge of this movement are extremists who are ready to take all kinds of crazy action.

PP: How does the role of big money in this election play into America's identity crisis? Money seems to have become the very face of America itself.

MS: The bottom line is that money has become a fundamental symbol of value: it's power, position, and social status. So when a candidate raises a lot of money, people think, "Wow, he must really have something." This is not only true in America, but on the global stage. A rich country is seen as powerful, and if a country like Greece goes broke, it pays a terrible price.[3] If America goes broke because it's borrowed too much money, it won't be as valuable. And that gets translated into people's personal lives.

PP: So that even if you don't have a lot of money personally, you can still identify with your rich country?

MS: Right. Just look at the symbol of the "rich American." It used to be that Americans could take a lot of pride in the power that was projected onto them when they traveled around the world. They might not have had much in their pockets, but because they were Americans they could catch that projection. It's not like that anymore, because the dollar is weak against the other currencies, and because other countries are now becoming wealthy economic powers.

PP: In terms of the healing symbols that you mentioned earlier, is there anything you can point to that is emerging out of the country's soul-searching on these various issues?

MS: One positive self-image would be that of the "generous American." Bill Gates is one of the wealthiest men in the world, and he's committed to doing good things through his foundation to deal with problems in other countries. It's not often the case that people of great wealth in other countries are willing to share it with the rest of the world; it stays at home more.

And as much as some feel threatened by the foreign "other," the new immigrant has always been central to our American identity. It's what sets America apart; we've done a good job, to a point, of creating a society out of immigrants that can work together. Because America is like a miniature globalized culture in a way that older cultures can't be, other countries struggling with globalization look to us as a model for how to deal with differences. But the country can't see this positive self-image, because from the inside it's suffering all the difficulties around it.

PP: Where do you see the country in its psychological development?

MS: Since the nineteenth century, America has been seen as a great power. So I would say it's reached a point of maturity and is at midlife. For an individual at midlife, part of the crisis is coming to terms with death and decline. For America, this means that it can't go on expanding as a world power indefinitely; it has to come to terms with its limitations. I think it hit that point in its wars in Vietnam, Iraq, Afghanistan, and other places.

PP: What would be the tasks of America in its second half of life?

MS: If the first half of life for an individual is about achievement and expansion, the second half of life is about the richness of maturity, deepening one's spiritual values, cultivating the next generation, and preparing for death.

PP: This brings to mind the soldiers returning from these wars bearing both physical wounds and the invisible wounds of PTSD. As they courageously face their inner struggles in the same way they faced outer battles, would you say they're the harbingers of the healing culture developing in this country around psychotherapy, meditation, yoga, and other kinds of sustainable lifestyles that are part of a wiser, more mature American identity?

MS: Yes, that's part of it, absolutely. America is a very extroverted country; for a young, expanding country, this side of our American character has been an asset. But now that America is mature, it needs to develop its other side: a sense of interiority, and a turn toward contemplation and religion—not in the sense of a missionary drive to convert the world, but a spiritual reflection on the meaning of life. America could also become a nation of culture that doesn't just provide entertainment, but literature, music, and art that nourishes the soul and that sustains people when they go through dark times.

PP: Speaking of dark times, every four years American voters endure a period of anxiety as they wait and see who their next president will be. No one ever talks about this, but is this chaos that we go through just part of the territory that comes with participating in a democracy?

MS: Absolutely. A person living in ancient Egypt wouldn't have had to endure these seasons of anxiety around election time, since the pharaoh decided everything for them. So it does call for emotionally mature people to tolerate the uncertainties of an election.

With all the money that's behind the creation of images and ads, the dilemma that voters face is whether they can believe what they see. But on a personal level, voters have to be aware of other psychological factors influencing their decision—family dynamics, for example, such as "my father is voting for that candidate, so I'm choosing the other candidate." So the demand on voters to educate themselves in order to make a conscious choice when they pull that lever is very high.

PP: I can imagine that for some citizens, the feelings of discomfort could become so pronounced they might even shy away from voting. Could you say more about how to tolerate these feelings of anxiety?

MS: Nobody likes anxiety. Pharmaceutical companies make a lot of money from this type of psychic pain by marketing anti-anxiety drugs. But the desire to be rid of anxiety is really a desire for regression to a childlike state where you don't have to worry about anything, because everything will be taken care of.

Freud said that the ego is the seat of anxiety, because anxiety is linked to becoming a separate individual with choice and responsibilities. So those who are psychologically mature carry around anxiety all the time. If they're living their life fully, they're always taking risks, they know that the people they love are at risk, and politically they know that there are no guarantees that their candidate will win the election.

PP: If the recent debates are any indication,[4] it seems that one of the criteria by which Americans judge their presidents is their ability to be strong and aggressive. To an extent, I think it's important for a leader to possess these traits. But is our over-emphasis on strength part of our discomfort with freedom: we want a powerful leader to compensate for our anxiety?

MS: The desire to have a strong leader comes out of profound anxiety and the wish to get rid of it. People look for somebody to lead them, and to tell them what to do. But as history has shown, the so-called strong leader can sometimes be a dangerous figure. For a democracy like ours, it's better to have someone with common sense and the ability to find a sane balance among competing forces.

What we look for in citizens in a democracy is that *they* are able to be strong individuals who can carry anxiety and accept the responsibility to vote according to the best interests of the country. They also accept the results if an election goes against their wishes. That's a part of maturity; you can't win every game. An election is a contest, and someone will lose, while the other wins.

PP: On the issue of competition, I wonder if some of the anxiety voters experience around the election stems from the combative nature of American politics. For instance, one of my sons said he was excited to watch the debates because they were going to be like good boxing matches. I, on the other hand, experience a lot of anxiety around watching the two candidates go up against each other. In handling my anxiety in a mature way, do I have a duty to watch the debates despite my discomfort?

MS: These political contests are like a blood sport. The two candidates are highly trained political athletes; they know how to accept a victory or a loss. Some people who are watching the debates and the race get a thrill out of seeing whether their guy is winning or not, while others find it agonizing to watch.

That said, there are some anxieties that aren't necessary to take on board. If watching the debates makes you too anxious, I would suggest you stay away from them, and study them afterwards. The most important duty of a citizen is to cast a ballot that is informed. Elections can go awry; people can elect the wrong person and then regret it. But these are the risks of democracy, and I don't see any other system given the stage in the evolution of consciousness that we're in today.

PP: What does democracy have to do with the evolution of our human consciousness?

MS: As I alluded to earlier, people were once satisfied to live under rulers they believed it was their duty to obey. But that isn't the case today. Americans especially don't think like that. Increasingly, we're living in the age of the individual, and individuals demand a voice. If you take that freedom away, a huge pressure builds up; you can see this happening in the Middle East.[5] So despite the inevitable setbacks, I believe that the growing awareness that the individual has rights, dignity, and even a quasi-divine status as a soul is a part of the evolution of human consciousness. And basically, democracy is the only system that respects this kind of awareness. So we have to have democracy and bear the anxiety of these elections.

PP: The force and fury of Hurricane Sandy[6] reminded me that although democracy rests on the shoulders of the individual voter, there are other factors at work in this election that, to some extent, none of us can really control: call it destiny, history, nature, the will of God, or some other transpersonal force.

MS: Thinking of this terrible storm falling upon the country so near to Election Day [November 6], I am reminded of a scene from Richard Wagner's opera cycle, *The Ring*.[7] The chief God, Wotan, goes to consult Erda, the great Goddess who lives underground and who can foretell the future. He asks her what is going to happen to himself and to his kingdom of Valhalla. Erda rises slowly out of the ground and tells him in a deep voice that his hold on power is doomed and that Valhalla will be destroyed. It's a bad moment for Wotan!

Sometimes, democratic elections also feel like this. The people of the nation are asked for their choice, and when the voice of the people speaks, we may fear for our future. It's a moment in the nation's ongoing life when we hear the source of political power speak out. The final decision is in the hands of no single person, but of the whole voting population. It's like a force of nature. This is the difference between democracies and aristocracies or theocracies. On this one day in November, the collective voice of the people declares who will be put forward as the leadership for the next four years.

Listening to the voice of the people is a kind of mystical moment in our secular world. It's like waiting for an oracle to make a pronouncement. Who will the people elect? Where is the collective will going to take us as a nation? The polls predict now this and now that, but there can be surprises, and no one knows ahead of time exactly what the voice will say.

PP: That's a different perspective from anything I've ever read on an American election! So if you had the American electorate—buffeted by attack ads, talking heads fighting it out in the media, and the tension of political differences among family and friends—on your couch, what advice would you give to help relieve some of the anxiety around voting?

MS: I would say it's important to be aware that the decision on Election Day doesn't rest entirely on your shoulders, and to remember that these election results are not the last word. In four years, the people can elect another president, and in two years they can elect another Congress. So it's okay to have anxiety and to put a lot of energy into the candidate that you believe in, but on Election Day lay down your sword and wait and listen and accept the result.

Respect for the voice of the people is essential for this kind of political system to function. This attitude of respect for the transcendent voice of the people is a kind of replica of a theological attitude where you work and pray, but in the final analysis you accept the will of God, no matter what it is. Work as hard as you can, but at the end of the day accept the result that comes from beyond your own personal preference.

I would also say that one may trust that there is a spirit at work behind the scenes of the nation's history. The spirit behind the life of the nation speaks through the voice of the people, so that although the elections may take a turn now and then that looks disastrous at the moment, in the end this guiding spirit will bring things right. It is something you can trust and put your faith in.

PP: Would you say there is a spirit of democracy?

MS: Oh, absolutely. It is the spirit of individual voices sounding loud and free. The American poet Walt Whitman expresses this spirit for us brilliantly in his poetry. The spirit of democracy inhabits America and is well-housed in its mythic narrative. As we go forward into the future, we can build on some of these myths that connect us to our deep history.

PP: Can you give me an example of the evolution of a classic American myth, and can you say why it's relevant to the American citizen grappling with "voter anxiety" during an election?

MS: One important image deeply rooted in American myth is the pioneer. At this time of high anxiety, the pioneer image speaks to us of resilience and steadfastness, of vision and risk-taking, and of the call to a new future. Americans may not be pioneers any longer in the literal sense that our forebears were, but the pioneer image can be elaborated in new versions that continue to speak to Americans today and tomorrow. After the storm and following a contentious election, the pioneer spirit in our people would have us shake off the fear, pick up the pieces, and go to work fashioning a future better than the past.

So one way for individuals to hold in mind the "bigger picture" around Election

Day is to remember the mythic images of our nation's history, and to stay aware that although we each must do our part for our democracy, no one of us is in control of the outcome. We are dependent on the voice of the people as a whole for the outcome, and this voice speaks for a spirit that guides our collective destiny. ■

Notes

1. In his inauguration address on January 20, 1961, President John F. Kennedy stated, "And so, my fellow Americans: ask not what your country can do for you—ask what you can do for your country." For his entire speech, visit <http://www.ushistory.org/documents/ask-not.htm>. Ronald Reagan used the image of the city on the hill several times, most famously in his 1984 speech accepting his party's nomination for a second term as president. The images of America as a city on a hill or a light unto the nations goes back to John Winthrop's sermon in 1630 to new immigrants to the Massachusetts Bay Colony. Franklin Roosevelt's most well-known iteration of American optimism was in his first inaugural address, in which he said, "the only thing we have to fear is . . . fear itself."

2. "Todd Akin Provokes Ire With Legitimate Rape Comment," by John Eligon and Michael Schwirtz, *New York Times*, August 19, 2012.

3. Following the financial and banking crisis of 2008, countries around the world went into recession, particularly Greece, which by 2013 saw the Greek economy shrink by twenty-five percent from its 2007 levels. For more, see <http://www.indexmundi.com/greece/economy_profile.html>.

4. Republican candidate Mitt Romney and President Barack Obama conducted three debates: October 3, 16, and 22, 2012. For more on these, visit <http://en.wikipedia.org/wiki/United_States_presidential_election_debates,_2012>.

5. See Ch. 19, n. 6.

6. Hurricane Sandy ripped through the Caribbean and the Mid-Atlantic states, before barreling into New York and New Jersey on October 29, 2012, causing widespread damage from flooding and nearly 150 direct deaths.

7. *Der Ring des Nibelungen* (*The Ring of the Nibelung*) is a tetralogy of operas by German composer Richard Wagner (1813–1883), loosely based on characters from Norse sagas and the *Nibelungenlied*.

Looking for Integrity in America's Political Leaders

AN INTERVIEW WITH JOHN BEEBE

BORN IN WASHINGTON, D.C., in 1939, Jungian analyst John Beebe grew up in a family that was caught up in the swirl of history, and was raised by parents with a keen interest in national politics and presidents. His father, who joined the Army during World War II, became a career Army officer. The family moved a lot, "most interestingly" recalls Beebe, to China in the last years of Chiang Kai-shek's Kuomintang[1] government, when he was just seven. After his parents divorced in 1949, talking politics with his father, says Beebe, became a "rare point of connection between us. He himself had presidential ambitions, and had hoped his war years would lend credibility to a political career."

Though Beebe's father never attained higher office than president of the local Kiwanis Club, he retained his passion for politics throughout his life and at his death the headline of his obituary read "Government Watchdog Beebe Dies." For her part, Beebe's mother, he remembers, "loved Franklin and Eleanor Roosevelt," casting the lone write-in vote for Eleanor Roosevelt for President in the 1952 New Jersey presidential primary, and later becoming "quite taken with the Kennedys." Reading Morison and Commager's *The Growth of the American Republic* in a high school honors history class further instilled in Beebe a profound and "real love for American history."

Beebe's path to becoming a Jungian analyst began on his nineteenth birthday when, diverging from his father's military career, he made the decision to become a psychiatrist. The first person he told was the mother of a friend of his, who had had

Jungian analysis and who enjoyed discussing it with him. Then, while on scholarship at Harvard, Beebe took a class co-taught by Henry Murray, a prominent psychologist who had been a patient of Jung's. Beebe was assigned Carl Jung's *Modern Man in Search of a Soul*, an unusual choice for 1957, since Jung wasn't widely known at the time or accepted as part of legitimate psychology. At the age of twenty-six, Beebe began therapy with a Jungian psychotherapist. Together, these three influences led to Beebe's decision to become a Jungian analyst.

After graduating from the University of Chicago Medical School in 1965, Beebe moved to do a medical internship in San Francisco, where he has lived ever since. Today, as a senior Jungian analyst, he is a noted lecturer in this country, throughout China, and in many other international venues. He has also published in a number of Jungian and psychoanalytic books and journals. The founding editor of *The San Francisco Jung Institute Library Journal*,[2] Beebe is also an authority on Jung's theory of psychological types, or typologies, and well known as an author and psychological commentator on American cinema, glimpsing in movies myths and archetypes of the American psyche.

My own path crossed with Beebe's in 1994 when I was drawn to interview him about his newly published book *Integrity in Depth*. During our extensive conversation, my understanding of integrity was broadened beyond conventional notions of "doing the right thing," or "staying true to oneself." Instead, Beebe defined integrity as the more complex task of remaining committed to one's own ideals and pursuits, while *at the same time* upholding the wellbeing of the larger "whole." This expanded definition of integrity, I learned from Beebe, was also critical to a healthy democracy, continuously storm-tossed between the rights of the individual and the larger community of citizens and government, and was especially prized in those holding public office.

Just as Beebe's book has proved to be an enduring classic, so our original interview has stood the test of time. Drawing on such classic thinkers as Confucius, Lao-Tse, Cicero, Benjamin Franklin, and presidents Lincoln, Carter, and Clinton, Beebe discusses examples of integrity as it manifests itself on the difficult moral terrain of war and politics. In our follow-up interview in 2014, Beebe talks about President Barack Obama's typology and his "tragically" understated brand of integrity. We also examine America's unique brand of humor that is the key to its genius, how nations are at risk of becoming the countries they conquer, and examples of films that exemplify American integrity.

✳

Pythia Peay: When it comes to politics and presidents, we hear a lot about character and integrity—especially during elections. Can you say something about integrity, and what it means in a political context?

John Beebe: Integrity is more complex than we take it to be. A lot of people assume that integrity means sticking to your guns. But I would call that stubbornness, as almost anyone can take a position and not budge. Integrity to me means more than taking a position and sticking to it. It means taking a position that really does something for the whole situation of which any individual is a part. In any given situation, for example, there's inevitably a larger picture that goes beyond what the individual thinks or needs. And again and again, we find that the people of the greatest integrity have taken stock of the whole situation and have tried to fit themselves into it in such a way that they take care of the needs of the whole. For me, that is the greater integrity.

PP: Can you give me an example of someone in American history that to you possessed integrity?

JB: I think many of us would find integrity in the first Republican president, Abraham Lincoln. He took stock of the whole situation of the United States and decided that slavery was not a good thing nor was breaking up the Union—so that those who believed in slavery could have their way, and those who didn't believe in slavery could have their way. Lincoln realized that was not going to be for the good of the whole continent, and so he had the courage to stand against secession as well as to stand against slavery.

Let us not forget this was an extraordinarily painful decision for him. Many people in Lincoln's time considered him a tyrant. Why, they wondered, in a country that had a tradition of individual liberty, couldn't those states that didn't agree simply secede? People today still accuse him of starting a war, and ask whether we ought to have taken a nonviolent path to ending slavery. But Lincoln had an understanding of what this country was about. He felt that we'd created a government, and that we should stand by that government, because it stood for something. So he took the needs of the whole into account and stood by it even when it wasn't easy to do.

I doubt that very many Americans today would not feel in their bones that Lincoln was right; that's why he remains in our imagination the greatest president.

And whatever else we can say about this country, we were able to banish slavery and hold together as a continent that stood for the idea of freedom for all of its citizens. That's a tremendous moral achievement that required the leadership of a man who had a vision of what was good for the whole. So in my view, Lincoln is the image of integrity. When I see a politician coming into power I ask myself if they're defending the one or the few, or if they're defending the good of the whole.

PP: You seem to also be implying that standing for the good of the whole requires vision.

JB: Integrity always involves maintaining fidelity to the truth of one's vision. In trying to understand this concept, I found myself reading Chinese philosophy, because the Chinese people have a strong tradition of integrity in government. I know there are some people who might smile at that statement, except that's exactly what Confucius the sage was interested in: honorable statecraft. I should say that in his own lifetime Confucius found it as hard to find as we do in America today. But Confucius did create a philosophical ideal of what good statecraft *might* be.

There is also the *Tao Te Ching*,[3] the famous Chinese book of wisdom written by the sage Lao-Tse, and that means the book of integrity and "the way," or the right way of conducting oneself in the world. The ancient Chinese image of *integrity* is an image of a man with an eye looking straight ahead, the heart, and a sign for movement. That seeing eye in the Chinese pictograph not only looks inside to what one feels and thinks, but looks outside at the whole situation to see what is needed.

So one can't say integrity is only public or only private; it's acting with both vision and inner feeling in the face of difficulties. And again, our best personification of this is Lincoln. As a psychiatrist, every so often I see Lincoln come up in a dream. It's always very powerful, and represents a call to courage or a sign that the person has acted in accord with something that reaches beyond the selfish need of the moment.

PP: Why does integrity and character matter so much to the American people, perhaps even more so than in other countries?

JB: The advantage of our country is that we're so alive to this issue. We were born at the time of the Enlightenment;[4] our democratic ideals are extremely idealistic, and we've never lost that sense that we can make a better government. When America broke away from the English monarchy and established the Constitution, it's as if the democracy the Greeks and Romans had briefly sustained for several hundred years, then lost, was fully reborn on our shores. We're carrying the vision that the Roman statesman Cicero had.

PP: Indeed, you write that Cicero is accorded the distinction in Latin dictionaries of being the first to use the term integrity.

JB: I bring Cicero up because he was the first to coin the phrase *integritas* from an old Latin adjective, *integer*, which means "whole" or "entire." It was that ideal that the Roman Republic stood for, and that the Roman Empire ended. Today, it would be similar to a Mafia takeover of the government, with a Mafia Don as Caesar.

But the old Roman value of *integritas* returned once again as a kind of underlying spiritual principle of the representational democracy of American government and institutions. Our great presidents and leaders have been those that understood that, which is why our political discourse always becomes a moral discourse. I personally think there's a dangerous blurring of distinction when we bandy the word *character* about as if it were the solution to the word *integrity*. Character is a set of personal attitudes, traits, and moral habits. But integrity, by contrast, is our willingness to take responsibility for the character of our personality and moral habits.

PP: So by that definition, integrity means to take responsibility for our actions?

JB: And our own effect on people. I have met people who have reasonably good character, but relatively little integrity. And I have met people without very good character, but who have rather remarkable integrity.

PP: For example?

JB: A person with a weakness for alcohol may have a problematic character and be capable of doing a great deal of damage to family and friends. But that same person may go to Alcoholics Anonymous and admit that he or she is powerless over alcohol; to admit to that limitation is a step of great integrity. Often, the person who admits a severe limitation of character ends up displaying a greater integrity than a person who has relatively few major character flaws, but who can never accept responsibility for their failures.

So when I see someone trumpeting his or her moral character with great pride, I think that this is not a person of great integrity. By contrast, when I see someone who has done some dreadful things, but who humbly asks for help, from God and neighbor, to transcend those things to the best of his or her ability—that to me is a person of great integrity. I trust that person more than the moral paragon who's never done anything particularly bad. We all have some character flaws; it's critical not to pretend that we don't. I'm not interested in people who tell me they've never been tempted sexually or falsified their own position for gain, or how wonderful they are. Surely that was Jesus' message: we are all sinners. Whenever anyone started becoming judgmental, Jesus was very clear to say "thou hypocrite."

PP: This description of integrity reminds me of President Carter, a devout Christian who famously confessed in *Playboy*[4] magazine that he had "looked on a lot of women with lust in my heart" and had "committed adultery" in his heart many times.

JB: That's right. Carter, who is a kind of moral saint of our time, also had a remarkable ability to go into a politically charged situation without that righteous indignation that has characterized so much of America's behavior in international situations. It's very easy to be right. But it's much harder to remain in a conflict or a difficult situation until the situation rights itself: and that has integrity. When faced in post-presidency with the crisis in North Korea,[5] for example, Carter didn't respond by condemning the dictatorship. Instead he met with Kim Il-sung, and praised him where he could; and then the situation began to change. First, in a completely unexpected event, the longstanding leader died. Then a peaceful way for North Korea to pull itself out of the nuclear club was negotiated.

In the example of Haiti, Carter had every reason to morally denounce the military leaders who had seized control of the country and been guilty of tremendous human rights abuses.[6] Instead, he praised the parts of their personalities that could be praised, and then showed them that it was in their best interest to leave their country. Of course, behind these negotiations was the physical force of the U.S. government. Carter also didn't make the mistake of allowing anyone to think he was delighted with the way the dictators were treating the people. It just simply wasn't useful to rub their noses in that fact, at the risk of getting their backs up and triggering a bloody confrontation. So by finding a way to help the dictators see that it was no longer in their best interest to remain in power, he made it possible for them to step down, leading to a transition of power with a minimum of bloodshed.

PP: For all his successes, Carter was not a terribly popular president. He was attacked by both liberals and conservatives. Why do we have such an aversion to his more diplomatic approach to solving conflict?

JB: It's a gentler approach that most people don't experience as very "masculine" or serious. To sit with a situation for several years, and to be patient until a way is found that causes on balance the least damage to all concerned, is something many psychotherapists have learned.

But that's a value that's practically disappeared in modern America. So when it surfaces in someone like Carter it immediately becomes suspect. The level of criticism he received was far beyond what he deserved. Similarly, [President Bill] Clinton's willingness to accommodate to different points of view and adjust his position as he tried to let the situation in Bosnia right itself was also seen as moral weakness on his part.[7]

It's true that if one changes one's position too often one can lose the trust of others. But we also need to understand that holding the tension between different viewpoints until one finds a way that is satisfactory to everyone involved often has greater integrity than simply taking a stand. We should also never be afraid to change course having seen more accurately what is right. I think these are psychological lessons our culture ought to learn.

PP: Are you emphasizing these "psychological lessons" because the problems of today's world demand a different response?

JB: We no longer live in a world in which the individual is the single most important thing. The entire political fabric, the environment, and the survival of the whole human race must be considered in relation to the individual. So the more examples we can develop of people who have successfully been able to be true to themselves while at the same time taking care of everyone else, the more we will understand integrity within American democracy.

I believe that if we can develop more of a feeling for that kind of political process, we'll be much further along as a country. Rather than leaders imposing their will, the people will be more likely to come up with solutions together that improve the governing of their country.

PP: But on some level, this might be what we really want: the authoritarian father who tells us what to do. Because then we don't have to take that burden of responsibility onto our own shoulders.

JB: That's an excellent point. The most dangerous thing that we could do is delegate the obligation of managing our national integrity—a terribly difficult thing to do—onto a leader. That would ultimately be American fascism.

PP: So taking up the challenge of our own integrity means having enough courage and psychological strength to go through this excruciating process that Clinton put us all through around Bosnia. It means paying attention to the process, the doubt, and the anxiety, rather than pushing it aside.

JB: It's accepting the difficulty. On a personal level, one way to understand integrity is that we are all in a double bind morally speaking most of the time. We all know the feeling of not being able to do something without violating ourselves, and yet if we don't we might violate someone else. I find myself in this kind of double bind every day of my life. So when it comes to maintaining our integrity, there's always some kind of tension of the opposites that has to be held.

Sooner or later, however, a decision has to be made; action must be taken. But I've noticed that there seems to be a divine grace that's granted to the person who's willing to accept that double bind, and to stay in the field of moral internal struggle. Those who accept the suffering often get unexpected help from the universe. Because it's often at those points of extreme inner conflict that an opportunity comes, and the way is shown: sometimes it's shown inside, through our feelings, a dream, or a hunch; and sometimes it's shown outside in unexpected opportunities: a phone call, or a chance encounter with someone that offers an opportunity to resolve the situation in an unexpected way. And in that struggle lies our integrity, because having lived through that conflict brings the deepest pleasure and a kind of true bliss. One glows with satisfaction and delight long after one has forgotten the conflict that brought us to this point.

PP: We often think of integrity as a kind of burden, but using words like *pleasure* and *delight* gives it a different perspective.

JB: Those with the greatest integrity have always taken a delight in it. Socrates took a great deal of pleasure in integrity. During the vote on whether or not he should be put to death, for example, Socrates knew very well that he was likely to lose, and yet the speech he gave was filled with irony and playfulness. The same was true of Lincoln under pressure: he had a tremendous sense of humor, which to me says that this man somehow enjoyed the fact that he'd taken on the responsibility of trying to make an imperfect world a somewhat morally better place.

But I feel that there's a marvelous sense of self-deprecating, dry humor, mixed with a kind of frontier stoicism and an appreciation for paradox, that runs throughout the whole American character. It's the key to our genius, and we see it in all of our greatest politicians, entertainers, writers, and artists, including Lincoln, Franklin, Emerson, William James, Hemingway, Edward Hopper, Mary Cassatt, and comedians like Lucille Ball, Joan Rivers, or Jay Leno. I know of no other country, in fact, that has a better sense of humor than America: it's something that I deeply, deeply love about this country.

PP: I've always thought that our tradition of comedians who make fun of presidents and other politicians is one of the best parts of our democracy. And one of the most important: critics and comedians often lose their freedom of speech under a dictatorship.

JB: Yes, and I think it's important the way our comedians get together with the politicians they kid, as did Bob Hope with Ronald Reagan and Tina Fey with Sarah Palin. I think this tradition is tied in with the Native American figure of the "Trickster," a mythological figure found on American soil. This is the archetypal figure that makes fun of those in power and makes them look silly. That wonderful way of teasing and mocking ourselves has gotten into the American character through the Trickster figure, and I think that's very healthy.

Benjamin Franklin, for example, had a wonderful sense of humor. Take the famous comment that Franklin made during the American Revolution, when the Founders were trying to put together a government. To that point they'd been working together to win the war against the British, but then they began to disagree.

And during this debate Franklin said, "Assuredly, we must all hang together, or we will certainly hang separately." That was a wonderfully wry way of saying that integrity includes a healthy self-interest.

Franklin was also very direct and honest about himself, and so possessed a great deal of integrity. He kept a diary in which he recorded how he had behaved during the day, and would score himself on how well he'd lived up to the various principles that guided him. He knew, for instance, that it was very important to have a reputation for industry, because he felt that would serve him well in business. So in order that people would think he was very busy working, Franklin made a deliberate point of being seen going to his printing firm very early in the morning, and then being seen leaving late at night.

Yet as he wrote in his autobiography, he was also quite aware that he was obviously manipulating appearances, as in reality he had a lot of free time left to write. But the very fact that Franklin would share that in his autobiography shows that he was able to tell the truth about himself, and that he took integrity seriously.

PP: Currently polarization between the two political parties is tearing at the fabric of the body politic, and making it hard for the government to get anything done. If we apply your concept of integrity to this situation—which you define as not just what's good for the individual, but also what's good for the whole—then is the American government "out of integrity," so to speak?

JB: Well, in the history of any country, polarization is a recurrent process. Certainly polarization during the Civil War was far worse than it is now—the country actually went to war! If you saw Stephen Spielberg's movie *Lincoln*, even the level of insult was worse. But I agree that this is a very difficult time. It's hard to feel that the politicians are looking after the needs of the nation as a whole, or that they can sustain different opinions. But I think one of the conflicts underlying our polarization has to do with how Americans define two concepts central to democracy: integrity and freedom.

For many Americans, for example, freedom means freedom to do business. It means, "I'll take care of myself, and you take care of yourself." But for others, as for myself, freedom gets back to what President Roosevelt described in a speech he gave on January 6, 1941 as the Four Freedoms: the freedom from want, the freedom from fear, the freedom of speech, and the freedom of religion.[8]

So you might say there's a war around what integrity is! Some people think that being on welfare lacks integrity. Some people wonder why, if they don't have children, their tax money should go to the education of other people's children. Or they feel that integrity has to do with the protection of personal boundaries against government intrusion, and the desire to be left alone. We can scarcely talk about integrity without bringing up the concept of boundaries.

PP: How do you explain the link between boundaries and integrity?

JB: A simple example is the statement that President George H. W. Bush made as his rationale for the Gulf War, when he said that we "have to protect the territorial integrity of Kuwait":[9] by which he meant the territorial boundaries that Iraq had breached. So a sense of territoriality and boundaries is very tied up with the idea of integrity: the property lines that surround our house, the borders that create a state or a country, the circle that makes a family, or even one's side of the bed. In other words, we have an instinctive sense of maintaining certain thresholds or boundaries, and we all struggle with how to draw the circle that bounds what is important and what must be protected.

But the other definition of integrity concerns the willing sensitivity to the needs of the whole, and the idea that we're all in this together and need to give each other a leg up. For example, I have no children, but I would gladly pay twice as much in taxes as I currently pay if I it meant that a third of our children in America were not living in poverty. I feel that way because the failure to educate our children properly creates all kinds of social problems, from which I might suffer, and from which the whole country suffers.

In traditional indigenous cultures, for example, there exist sacred sites and sacred ways where the whole tribe comes together. The purpose of the initiation ceremony is to learn submission to a cultural pattern that is larger than the individual, in which the hero bows his head to the group. Now this goes very much against the grain of the democratized American individual, who feels that the point of life is liberty and the pursuit of happiness. Certainly, we should be rightly suspicious of any authoritarian "group think" organizations. But in its best expression, the meaning of groups is that they offer a way to help the hero find his or her place in the cosmos.

So there is a great tension in our culture between two very different models of integrity. And the problem with the more boundaried and separative notion of integrity is that in the political sphere it creates a gridlock where very few people get any power to do anything. And then a lot of good public projects, like high-speed rail or good climate controls, suffer. But we're living in an ecological world, with an atmosphere that is breathed by all, which means the needs of one particular factory, for example, are not as important when measured against the health of many.

PP: And does this tension that plays out in the political sphere also play out in the soul of the individual American?

JB: Yes, we're dealing with one of the most difficult problems in human psychology. It was Jung's great genius to recognize that there are two dimensions to what we call the "I." There is the ego side of the "I," which is our bounded, separate, autonomous sense of agency and identity as an individual—and that is well-tooled for the great American dream of success, achievement, and responsibility.

And then there's the other dimension, which is what Jung called the "Self": an aspect of ourselves that is more instinctive, holistic, more oriented toward being than doing, and more mysterious. It's in the Self that the ego finds meaning, and it's in the ego that the Self finds individual identity and agency, or the ability to carry something out. So the ego needs the Self, but the Self also needs the ego: we are both these things and have to live the paradox. In order to prevent being manipulated or controlled, for example, we need to have a strong, individual sense of our own unique body and mind; in order for life to be meaningful and purposeful, we need to make our own distinct imprint. But the deeper one goes into the mystery of the Self, the more one finds that our individual personhood is connected to an entire ecological web of invisible, but very real, connections to the wider environment, an animated divine nature shared by everything in existence.

I think the healthiest and happiest people I know—and the most truly *American* people I know—are those who are able to live both dimensions of the individual "I" as intensely as possible. I think that's what the greatest Americans, like Franklin, Lincoln, and Emerson, have always asked us to do and to be. But I have to admit that because of the ever-constant risk posed by charismatic groups, or the terrible tendency of oligarchies to impose control over others, we can't dispense with the tradition of democratic individualism. We need to have skeptical individuals with strong egos and a healthy tradition of doubters who are watching the tendencies of nations, groups, cults, and families to act manipulatively and territorially toward other countries, the environment, and individuals.

PP: Turning to President Obama, what is your estimation of him in terms of integrity?

JB: I feel better about Obama than most Americans do. By and large, he keeps his agreements. He's done a tremendous amount for the country with not a whiff of personal scandal; he's shown fine personal behavior. I like his timing and I like the fact that his decisions are nuanced. But I'm also aware that he sends drones out, often endangering innocent people under the blanket excuse that if he doesn't, terrorists are more likely to get us.[10]

America has bombed other countries in most of the years of my life. Recently, an international poll came out that showed that, hands down, the country that is seen as posing the greatest threat to world peace is America.[11] I think Russia, North Korea, Iran, and Pakistan are all far greater threats to world peace. But think of the implications and the sadness of what those poll results mean, and how the rest of the world sees us. And where are we with that? How can we allow these bombings to keep happening? It never seems to change.

PP: I can see how America appears as a greater threat because we're so powerful, and so big, and our reach is so long. But with regard to Obama, what is your point in bringing up these bombings?

JB: The point is that I think we want to add a value to integrity, and that is empathy. We're creatures who are deeply attached to our homes, families, countries, our selves, and each other. So we should have more empathy for the people we feel we have to stand up to. It's important for me, however, to have empathy for what an American president has to be going through when he makes a decision to bomb. For a period of time, I was the president of a small organization, and that small leadership role changed me. I developed empathy for presidents everywhere, because I learned you'll rarely be able to make a decision that won't hurt or seriously disappoint somebody.

PP: What else did you take from that personal experience as the president of an organization, in terms of trying to lead with integrity?

JB: Well, first of all, integrity is not perfection. Second, it's important for leaders to keep themselves available for dialogue and process. I'm very glad, for example, that Obama and Russian President Vladimir Putin are on the phone with each other, and that Obama and German Chancellor Angela Merkel are talking, even though they all get mad at each other.

PP: Obama may be communicating with world leaders, but one of the complaints is that he doesn't communicate well with the American people. He's seen as remote and aloof.

JB: I've never met Obama, or done a professional evaluation of him, so I'm just a citizen like everyone else making observations about his behavior. But I have done some work on his typology, and what we see corresponds to the type of person Jung called the "introverted thinking" type. And the introverted thinking type is famous for having "inferior extroverted feeling."[12] When Obama has defined a situation for himself, he lacks empathy for the fact that many other people are still struggling to understand it.

So, for example, when Obama makes a comment that Paul Ryan's budget is "nothing but thinly veiled Social Darwinism," he may be absolutely right.[13] But obviously ninety percent of the population is not going to understand that he's talking about the cruelty of the survival of the fittest. Compare Obama's statement to Ronald Reagan in the 1980 election, when he said, "Are you any better off than you were four years ago?"[14] Everybody who heard that immediately got what Reagan was saying. So Obama fatally lacks that common feeling touch that made Reagan the "Teflon president." Franklin Roosevelt also had that ability to communicate well with the people. But Obama is tragically understated, and his use of the bully pulpit has been very poor.

PP: I notice your use of the words *tragically* and *fatally*. Why do you put Obama's failure to communicate in that kind of dramatic context?

JB: Well, I think another president or a better politician could have gotten serious gun legislation out of the tragedy of the Newtown shootings.[15] I feel that Obama tried very hard and was quite eloquent, but it didn't work. If anything he was too tasteful. He doesn't seem to know how to get into a fight in the vulgar way that many presidents have been able to do. Theodore Roosevelt, Franklin Roosevelt, Truman, and many other American presidents were very good at being just crude enough to get people to believe that they meant what they said, and to get them to follow them.

Still, Obama has more integrity than almost any of those people. So this is a terribly sad story.

PP: I think the word *tragic* is the right word, because to so many Obama has such potential and vision. Sometimes when I hear him speak, I want to weep at his seeming lack of passion. But I also wonder what this disconnect says about the American people. Is it rare for an American president to be an introverted thinking type?

JB: If he is—and I think the most we can say is that's the style Obama *appears* to be using—then yes, it's extremely rare because America is an "extroverted thinking" country.[16] And so when the country uses extroverted thinking, and Obama uses introverted thinking, then he's a reform president. In other words, he's doing everything in a different way, and talking in a different way, than the American public is used to. And so the temptation is to say that he isn't saying anything, or not to believe him when he speaks. But then it becomes shocking how often he keeps his word!

PP: Can you give me some examples of how to you Obama has kept his word?

JB: His health plan is working. He saved Wall Street. He brought the economy back. People were complaining a few years ago that Obama hadn't done anything about gays in the military or gay marriage, and then suddenly new regulations were in place in the military, and gay marriage is becoming legal in more and more states. So he is amazingly consistent in keeping his agreements, but with a funny kind of timing, and using rhetoric Americans aren't used to. But the public doesn't know what to do with his way of doing things; they almost never believe him, as they're not used to politicians who actually say what they mean.

I'm afraid that it says something about us that we haven't let him lead us more. And for that we have to look to the Republican Party, and how the needs of the country have taken second place to their need to make sure the president doesn't get anything done. And I think there may be racism in that, because there's never been this little respect for an American president.

PP: One of the areas where there has been disillusionment with Obama has been around the NSA warrantless searches of people's private emails and phone calls that, to be fair, began under President Bush. I think the continuation of this violation of our privacy is a *very* big deal.[17]

JB: It is a big deal. It's hard not to feel that Edward Snowden and the whistleblowers[18] did us a favor. There I think what happened is that we didn't dismantle the police state that emerged out of the anxieties after 9/11. And so we became more like the Soviet Union. It would have been better if we'd just used the procedures we already had in place more effectively.

PP: Which is an ironic twist to the end of the Cold War.

JB: But it's often the case that countries become more like the nations they conquer.

PP: Can you expand on this psychological idea that you just touched on: that in our efforts to fight the enemy, we *become* the enemy?

JB: That's the irony. It's an idea that Jung puts forth in *Two Essays in Analytical Psychology*: that whenever one person kills another person, they get the manna, or the psychological energy of the other person. In primitive mythology, for example, if you eat meat, you also get the spirit of the animal that was killed. So in other words, countries should watch what countries they conquer, because they may be conquered from within, as some of the enemy's energy inevitably becomes part of their national psyche.

And I do think that some of how the Soviet Union was during the Cold War has now become part of America. It's a tragic act of life—I don't know what more to say about that. But we have to ask ourselves if, even as individuals, when we beat somebody, we want to absorb that person's way of being.

PP: Can you give me some images or movies that express American ideas of integrity?

JB: We have two. One is the image of Gary Cooper in the Western movie, *High Noon*: that of the man who stands up to the whole town. That same image of integrity is also in Marlon Brando's very touching performance in *On the Waterfront*, where he stands up to the corrupt system. Or we see it in the movie *Norma Rae*, with the character played by Sally Field organizing her workers into a union, or *Erin Brockovich*, the environmental activist played by Julia Roberts. It's the image of the heroic individual who finds it in him- or herself to stand up to a system of oppression.

A more complex American image of integrity, however, is the person who inspires a community to come together. Martin Luther King, Jr., would be an example of that kind of integrity, because he was able to mobilize people to come together around racial equality. Nelson Mandela was also an example of someone who, after he came out of prison, was able through a community process to lead a peaceful transfer of power in South Africa after apartheid.

I think Obama is modeling himself more on Nelson Mandela than Martin Luther King. When Mandela spoke, for instance, he didn't raise his voice above others' voices. And although Mandela wasn't particularly charismatic, he possessed a quiet dignity that fostered consensus. I think Obama is *trying* to do that, but he isn't getting very far. Partly that's because the American people are still looking for "the leader." The problem is that we always want to turn the person of integrity into the "Great Man."

PP: Does that have to do with America's enduring fascination with the hero?

JB: I think so. We can't seem to get past it. We wish we could, but we can't.

PP: Does the American hero have the potential to evolve into the kind of hero with integrity, and who is more community oriented?

JB: Obama has been trying to do that with his idea of "leading from behind."[19] Sometimes that seems appealing, but at other times the people have wished he would just come forward and lead. So it's an issue that we haven't yet resolved.

PP: Is there an American movie that to you is the representation of the more communitarian expression of American integrity?

JB: Most people wouldn't frame this movie as an example of American integrity, but I would recommend the movie *Boyhood* by the director Richard Linklater. It's a complete masterpiece. It portrays a boy growing up over a period of twelve years, from the age of six to eighteen, in unfavorable circumstances, in a semi-unhappy Houston family not unlike many families all over this country. He's one of two children of a divorced mom who has to work and who tries to better herself and form relationships; he also has a father outside the home and two stepfathers to deal with.

As the movie unfolds over time, you see this young boy's individuality develop. But to me the reason the movie has integrity is because of the way it shows individual consciousness emerging from a collective group, rather than an individual consciousness *imposing* itself on a group. The boy develops into a serious photographer, so he's actually a stand-in for Linklater himself. Yet though this boy has a very individual character, and is an introverted thinking type who contemplates everything around him, he never leaves his family group. He goes to school, and not all that much happens: but out of that, consciousness emerges.

So this is a very different image of integrity than one where a strong rebellious stance is taken against an opposing force. The boy in the movie does assert his individuality, but quietly. There are threats of violence, but there's never a moment where violent confrontation defines everything. What prevails instead is a certain willingness to appreciate each individual and their role in the shaping of things. It's a movie that speaks of a new American value.

PP: Of individuation that takes place through relationship?

JB: And through complexity and personal agency emerging from complexity, rather than from the heroic individual's ability to impose himself on others. What's also interesting about *Boyhood* is that this young man, the main character, is not especially charismatic. Traditionally, the heroic character is an imposing and aggressive character that seduces others to submit to his or her power. So that to me is a tremendous step forward. There's heroism in *Boyhood*, but it's a much quieter form. It's a different kind of integrity than we see portrayed in *High Noon*. So I would say that the film indicates we're moving in the direction of a different world than we've been in before as a country.

PP: You've also said that *The African Queen* is your favorite American film. Can you say why, and whether that film also reflects a certain kind of American integrity?

JB: In that film, and in the unlikely hero played by Humphrey Bogart, I see the beginning of a different kind of integrity than we see portrayed in *High Noon*.

The film takes place during World War I. It's about a plan that Katharine

Hepburn hatches, and that she gets Humphrey Bogart to go along with, to blow up the *Louisa*—an enemy ship dominating a major lake in Africa—so the British can make a safe passage. Symbolically, the *Louisa* represents the patriarchal, dominating, and controlling attitude, and the *African Queen*, the little tugboat carrying Hepburn and Bogart, is the African Mother Goddess, or the values of relatedness and community. Somehow, this unlikely combination of two very different people eventually come to love each other, and are able in a tricky way to detonate the enemy ship. I think it's a wonderful metaphor for a different set of values and a different kind of spirit.

PP: A more maverick spirit, would you say?

JB: Maverick, and also more feminine and more related, with less bullying, domination, and competitiveness. These two unlikely actors and characters have to cooperate in order to achieve their goal. It's their ability to unite the opposites that makes the difference.

PP: And coming together across differences, which is a very positive American trait. ■

Notes

1. Chiang Kai-shek (1887–1975) (Pinyin: Jiang Jieshi) was a Chinese nationalist political and military leader whose forces, ultimately, lost to those of Mao Tse-Tung (Pinyin: Maozedong) in 1948. Chiang fled to the island of Formosa (now Taiwan), where he led his Kuomintang (Pinyin: Guomindang) party until his death.
2. Now called *The Jung Journal: A Quarterly Publication of the C. G. Jung Institute of San Francisco* <http://www.jungjournal.info/jungjournal.info/Home.html>.
3. See Ch. 20, n. 2.
4. The interview appeared in the November 1976 edition.
5. In 1994, with the U.S. and South Korea on the brink of war with North Korea over the latter's development of nuclear weapons, President Carter and his wife, Rosalynn, met with Kim Il-sung in Pyongyang. North Korea agreed to hold its nuclear program. Kim Il-sung died in July 1994 and was replaced by his son, Kim Jong-il.
6. In September 1994, Carter assisted the Clinton administration in negotiating an agreement to avert a U.S. invasion of Haiti, then led by General Raoul Cédras. Cédras was replaced by Jean-Bertrand Aristide, whom he had overthrown. See <http://www.cartercenter.org/news/documents/doc218.html>.
7. See Ch. 1, n. 3.
8. The speech can be read in its entirety at AmericanRhetoric.com <http://www.americanrhetoric.com/speeches/fdrthefourfreedoms.htm>.

9. Quoted from "Letter to Congressional Leaders on Additional Economic Measures Taken with Respect to Iraq and Kuwait," by George H. W. Bush, August 9, 1990.

10. See "The Toll of 5 Years of Drone Strikes: 2,400 Dead," by Matt Sledge, *Huffington* Post, January 23, 2014 <http://www.huffingtonpost.com/2014/01/23/obama-drone-program-anniversary_n_4654825.html>.

11. In Gallup Poll, The Biggest Threat to World Peace Is . . . . America?" by Eric Brown *International Business Times*, January 2, 2014.

12. See Jung, *Psychological Types*, 1971: pp. 383–387.

13. See "Obama: Paul Ryan's Budget 'Nothing But Thinly Veiled Social Darwinism," by Amie Parnes, The Hill, April 4, 2012. Paul Ryan was the Republican chairman of the House Budget Committee.

14. You can see Reagan asking that question at <https://www.youtube.com/watch?v=rU6PWT1rVUk>.

15. Following the shootings at The Sandy Hook Elementary School (see the Introduction to this book) attempts to pass gun legislation foundered in Congress.

16. See Giannini: 2004, p. 111–112.

17. "U.S. Confirms Warrantless Search of Americans." *USA Today*, April 2, 2014 <http://www.usatoday.com/story/news/politics/2014/04/01/us-confirms-warrantless-searches-nsa/7176749/>.

18. "Edward Snowden: The Whistleblower behind the NSA Surveillance Revelations: 29 Year-Old Source behind the Biggest Intelligence Leak in NSA's History,"by Glenn Greenwald, Ewen MacAskill, and Laura Poitras, *Guardian*, June 9, 2013. Poitras directed a feature film about Snowden, entitled, *Citizenfour*, in 2014.

19. See "Leading from Behind," by Ryan Lizza, *The New Yorker*, April 26, 2011.

—31—

American Zeitgeist and a Shift in Ages

An Interview with James Hillman, Ph.D.

WORLD-RENOWNED AS A THINKER and post-Jungian psychologist on the human psyche and an array of topics from animals to dreams to cities, James Hillman absolutely loved to talk politics. And I loved to talk politics with him. Because of his lively imagination coupled with a keen intellect, I could always count on Hillman to espy that particular angle on a current issue that no one else saw. It was almost as if he was gifted with a kind of "archetypal second sight." I could also count on Hillman to unsettle whatever comfortable habits of thought or opinion I'd drifted into. An interview with him was something akin to bungee-jumping or skydiving, and I had to prepare myself in advance for an adventure of the mind.

Writers live by ideas; and in that regard, Hillman, a prolific author, possessed an enviable, luxurious excess. But he was no ivory tower thinker. Deeply immersed in the issues of the day, he was profoundly and personally affected by the twists and turns of current events and both fascinated by and concerned about the effects of American culture on citizens' everyday lives. Hillman's keen interest in the interplay of culture and psyche was shaped by early influences: his childhood growing up near the Atlantic City boardwalk in New Jersey in the family-owned Breakers Hotel; his time in the U.S. Navy Hospital Corps during World War II, where he experienced his first call to psychology; as an adult living abroad in Europe, earning his degrees and pursuing his training as a Jungian analyst; and his return from abroad to the states once again,[1] living in Dallas, Texas, and lastly in a small town in Connecticut.

Though I had interviewed Hillman on the American psyche and other topics many times in the 1990s,[2] years would pass before our interview in February 2011 for *The Huffington Post*. As it turned out, that was to be our last conversation. As he approached his eighty-fifth birthday, he was recuperating from two years of illness. "It's a new life," he told me. "A lot of reflection instead of ambition." His wonderful mind was soon engaged, and he spoke compellingly on the American zeitgeist and America's coming "shift in ages." Hillman died on October 21, 2011. Like many others, I continue to miss him greatly, and often find myself wondering what he might think of this or that political issue. What would he see, that everyone else was missing?

I am grateful to be able to share our last interview, and Hillman's typically unconventional vantage points on topics such as polarization, conservatives and liberals, and the Jungian idea of the opposites; as well as his thoughts on gun violence, wealth, President Obama, the failure of American exceptionalism, and his announcement of the death of certain abiding American myths. After I'd transcribed and written up our interview, Hillman reviewed it with me in a phone-editing session with his well-honed writer's eye, changing this word and that phrase—leaving for the reader a kind of last tribute to his eagle mind.

✳

Pythia Peay: The Tucson shootings[3] triggered a debate over the ongoing polarization of the right and the left. What is your psychological perspective on this?

James Hillman: We have to realize that our minds are our enemy. The current debate has become very ideological, with certain fixed ideas dominating the discussion. This is a result of thinking in opposites; it goes back to the Greek philosopher Aristotle, and has to do with an either/or kind of logic: If something is this way, it cannot be that way.

But this isn't how the world really is. For example, most people think that the opposite of white is black. But there are shades of black—from blackberries, to black coal or blackbirds—that have nothing to do with white. The point is to learn how to evaluate each issue on its own merits without having to bring up the opposition's point of view. In therapy, when you have a dream of your mother, for example, you don't necessarily have to talk about your father as a supposed opposite.

PP: In other words, a conservative or liberal will often have a predictable reaction to a specific issue. But in therapy, an important part of the psychological process involves examining how we think. You seem to be saying that we need more of this kind of critical examination in our political process.

JH: I agree, for instance, with some of the extreme propositions from both parties. On the left, I think we should make extreme cuts to the defense budget. On the right, I agree with the extreme proposition that we should close the Department of Education, because it's a total failure. And possibly Agriculture, too, since it's dominated by the agribusiness giants it's supposed to supervise.

PP: So by saying that you have radical views from both the left and the right, how does this address the issue of polarization?

JH: It addresses the issue by saying that a person doesn't have to cling to certain ideas just because they're on the left or the right. There are other ways of putting things together so they're not necessarily opposed; there is the idea of collaboration, or the phrase "coterminous," meaning where one appears, the other has to appear. Chinese culture has the Yin/Yang symbol, with its interwoven extremes. It seems to me that we lack this kind of complex imagery in the media. Television foments this by bringing two people together from opposing positions, as if every situation has just two sides.

PP: There is a growing weariness among the public with this kind of ideological boxing match.

JH: Democrats and Republicans sitting side by side during the recent State of the Union address may have been a psychological breakthrough.[4] Do you remember [broadcast journalist] Fred Friendly? He used to host a television show with Supreme Court Justices, ambassadors, and intellectuals from the left and the right. He'd ask very tough questions that produced true intellectual discussion on current issues. That would be one example of how to handle differences without simplifying into polarities—a word, by the way, that comes straight out of electrical engineering. It's not a psychological term and doesn't help solve a problem for the psyche, as what is psychological isn't as rigid as scientific models of thinking.

PP: When it comes to handling polarized political viewpoints, I wonder what you think about Obama. Many on the left have a problem with Obama's temperament; they see him as weak when he's conciliatory to the Republican right.

JH: Obama's temperament is a tremendous virtue. At last we have somebody who is cool-headed, who tries to think things through, who can take the pressure, and who can even concede having made a mistake. The speech he gave at the Tucson Memorial was a masterpiece. He walked right into the middle of all these conflicts and the problem of America, and he said something that had real content, and was not sentimental. He did not use highly intellectual or rigid ideological language. By referencing the little girl who was shot, and by encouraging us to live up to her expectations of our democracy, he was able to revitalize the American dream and engagement in political life, through her own dream of becoming politically involved. And personally, I think the agreement Obama struck with the Republicans over the tax bill was clever.[5]

PP: But many on the left faulted Obama for caving in on this issue. Was this an example of fixed ideology at play in the political arena?

JH: Yes, it's an ideological fixation for the left: We must not let the rich get richer. I'm all on the side of the ideological left, but on this issue, I think the left is wrong. Let the rich take their jillions—they're going to, anyway! This is just how the situation is until the rich begin to convert on their own, like Warren Buffett and Bill Gates, who are now trying to change the minds of capitalists.[6] And if the rich have more money because of the tax deal, let's appeal to their capacity for citizenship and hope that they find ways to help the country, whose condition affects them, too. There are a lot of things that we don't know about that might be going on in the psyches of the super-rich.

PP: You mean that the rich may themselves be harboring new perspectives on their wealth?

JH: Exactly. I can't imagine that the rich or the conservatives are utterly closed off from the changes going on in the collective psyche. But the ideological left locks us into a fixed view of "the other"; this traps them in having to be worse than they may possibly be.

PP: Are you saying that the liberals' fixed view of the right might actually be helping to create the "enemy" that they're locked in battle with? But isn't the right just as guilty in this as the left?

JH: I'm not saying that there aren't some fanatical activists on the right. But I'm on the left, so I'm trying to bring more psychology to their situation. And the ideological left runs a danger of continually nailing the coffin on the enemy. By fixing the opponent, it puts them in a box and omits the possibility of the kind of transformation exemplified by John Dean, Nixon's lawyer, who then testified against him during the Watergate hearings.[7] But if a political party is seen only this way or that way, then we prevent what else might possibly be going on in their psyches, and we're not bringing any insight to the process.

For example, if I have a wife and I only see how mean-spirited and quick-tempered she is, and I see her that way all the time, then she becomes fixed into that character definition, and nothing else.

PP: In using marriage as an example, you're implying a relationship. Does this mean that both the Democrats and the Republicans are overlooking the fact that they're in an intimate relationship, instead of being unrelated strangers? I admit I feel that way sometimes when I listen to Glenn Beck.

JH: It's clear every day that the left and the right are in a marriage. Fox News' Bill O'Reilly talked obsessively about MSNBC's Keith Olbermann; and Olbermann talked obsessively about O'Reilly; they were locked in a marriage. And for all that the liberals want to mock Glenn Beck, he is talking about American history and political theory that the left neglects.

PP: I agree. But what you seem to be saying is that, just as in therapy, there needs to be more reflection on the country's past.

JH: Even MSNBC is "leaning forward."[8] But I'd like to see it lean backward, which is what the word *reflection* means. What, for instance, is in the shadow of these fixed ideals? One thing that's being ignored is history. In a certain way, the liberal world has been lax about standing for true American history. I think of Howard Zinn and his leadership on this subject.

PP: Besides ignoring the past, what might be some other effects thinking in opposites has on our culture?

JH: It leads to the extreme moralism in our society, which declares one side good, and the other bad, and then the "other" becomes evil. All of which leads to conquest, warfare, victory, and those other destructive Western ideas.

PP: Indeed, one of the ongoing debates after the Tucson shootings was whether the climate of violent political rhetoric contributed to what happened.

JH: My perspective on this is a little different. I think that this kid was made a loner by an American educational system in which there is no room for the weird or the odd. The moment [Jared Lee] Loughner began to become schizoid [isolated from society] in class, he was thrown out; he became lost in the great Tucson mass of people. He wasn't being held by anything.

PP: So instead of political polarization, or the lack of a stronger mental health system, you see this tragedy as related to our educational system?

JH: We need to have an educational system that's able to embrace all sorts of minds, and where a student doesn't have to fit into a certain mold of learning. Our educational system has become so narrowed to a certain formula that if you go through a weird phase, you're dropped out—often at the age of schizophrenia, 19–23—and that's the danger. And in addition to that problem, you've got the availability of guns and the pressure of a society that can't take the peculiar. But I can imagine that this young boy did not have to do this shooting.

PP: If you can imagine that this tragic shooting didn't have to happen, then what do you imagine might have happened instead?

JH: He would not have been thrown out of school; and he would have spent some time with his teacher, who would have made an effort. We also need a kind of counselor who isn't tarred with the brush of making psychological "assessments," and where he wouldn't have been cursed with the idea of insanity. Right there is an insult. Instead, we need a school counselor who is more like a wise man or woman and who would listen to a guy like this without pathologizing his concerns. The problem with the educational system is that it lacks love.

PP: You're talking about bringing back a person's humanity, so that they aren't depersonalized, which only increases their marginalization.

JH: Right. Instead of having that kind of discussion, we have a factual examination of the incident and talk about reducing the gun clips from thirty-one bullets to ten. But the boy himself is left out of the discussion.

PP: Here we are, this great country with all our emphasis on the individual, and yet we fail the individual?

JH: Absolutely. The person becomes an oddball, a kind of isolate, cut off from everything.

PP: So this kind of psychological perspective on America's problems begins with more careful reflection . . .

JH: And a little more curiosity about people and events. And we don't have that. We really don't.

PP: Earlier in our conversation you said that America today has a certain "tragic aspect." Can you say more about that?

JH: Everything that everyone is afraid of has already happened: the fragility of capitalism, which we don't want to admit; the loss of the empire of the United States and American exceptionalism. In fact, American exceptionalism is that we are exceptionally backward in about fifteen different categories, from education to infrastructure. But we're in a stage of denial: we want to re-establish things as they used to be, to put the country back where it was.

PP: For many, those are fighting words. People don't want to question American exceptionalism, because if America isn't exceptional, then what is it, and what am I?

JH: The capacity for people to kid themselves is huge. Living on illusions or delusions, and the re-establishing of these illusions or delusions, require a big effort to keep them from being seen through. But a very old idea is at work behind our current state of affairs: *enantiodromia*, or the Greek notion of things turning into their opposite.

It's said, for instance, that we're in a change of age. And as the ages change, those old things that seemed to be great virtues suddenly become vices. The two thousand years that preceded this was the great expansion of the West, and the age of the great monotheistic religions: Judaism, Christianity, and Islam. Yet these three salvational prophecies with their tremendous aesthetic accomplishments and enormous civilizing effects have turned into monsters in their self-absorption, with their righteousness and orthodoxies. They lack insight; all three claim to be "the one."

PP: What would be another example of something turning into its opposite?

JH: I would point to the great beliefs of secularism and humanism that began in the seventeenth century or even earlier. So as we see today with writers like Christopher Hitchens and Richard Dawkins, the "fourth religion" is throwing out religion. This leaves us with a kind of barren scientism, or what religious people describe as a Godless humanism. These are the great currents that are going on right now. People still want to find something further, but things haven't yet fully disintegrated.

PP: What you're saying is that these powerful myths that have defined America—the monotheistic religions, secularism, and our economic myths—have peaked and are in their decay, but not quite.

JH: Yes, but it doesn't look that way. It looks like they're being powerfully reinforced, which is always a sign of a lack of vitality. If they were vital they wouldn't need to be defended. And the fanaticism we're witnessing goes along with the deterioration of the vitality of these myths.

PP: So when a society is trying to defend something this strongly it's really a symptom of the decay that's going on beneath the surface?

JH: Right. Take, for example, the economic myth, the major myth that we live in this country. Now, economists all declare that the world problem today is the falling off of demand, and that we must stimulate demand, whether by the government or through bank lending. But if you were to look at the problem of demand falling off from an ecological point of view, what could be better? Doesn't that show an extraordinary disruption between the kind of economic thinking that dominates our capitalist world, including China, and the Earth's point of view? But the ecological way of thinking creates a huge panic problem for capitalistic economics.

PP: You mean because these societies sense that an old way of life is dying?

JH: Exactly. Now there are plenty of intelligent people who are working on how to live in an economic no-growth society. And Obama has been very important in trying to bring new structural thought to these questions. But as long as the economists and the bankers rule, the old way will die very slowly.

PP: Still, the death of the old always implies that something new is coming.

JH *(in an exasperated tone)*: This looking for the "new" is an American vice! We always want to see what's coming next—we're addicted to the future! Futurism is another American myth: whether Kennedy, [Lyndon] Johnson, Reagan, or Obama, American presidents all come into office with a new program, and the conviction that the country is going to be better than ever. But I think you have to hasten the decay. The classic view is always to look back, and to watch and help the dying.

PP: As I hear you speak I'm thinking of how my family and I helped my father die, which was a very profound experience. And I'm wondering what a similar experience might mean in a cultural sense.

JH: One would have to think about what needs to die in this culture; what attachments need to slip away, such as white supremacy, male supremacy, and the sense that we are the really "good people." America has a certain hubris about its virtue. Another thing would be our "unanalyzed" understanding of the word *freedom*. Probably one of the striking things in the dying of your father was his dependence on help, like nursing homes and nurses and crutches. Yet out of his lack of freedom arose another kind of freedom.

PP: My father was particularly stubbornly American in that regard. He wouldn't even go into a hospital because then he wouldn't be "free" to smoke or drink. But you seem to be saying that as we lose one kind of freedom, there arises the possibility of another kind of freedom.

JH: I'm saying that we haven't thought about the idea of freedom enough. It needs to be internalized as an inner freedom from "demand" itself: the kind of freedom that comes when you're free from those compulsions to have and to own and to be someone. For example, think of the kind of freedom that Nelson Mandela must have experienced when he was imprisoned. He completely lost his freedom in the outer world, yet he found freedom within. That's an example that broadens our current limited idea of freedom: that I can do any goddamn thing I want on my property; that I am my own boss and don't want government interference; that I don't want anybody telling me what I can and can't do; that we've had too much regulation, and so on. This is the freedom of a teenage boy.

Another strange aspect to this shift of ages is people's fear of getting cancer; it's absolutely endemic throughout the population.[9] The healthcare bill stirred this up, and people began to wonder what would happen to them if they got cancer.

PP: Why do you take note of that?

JH: Because it's more than simply the fear of dying and the fear of disease. It's part of this period of things breaking down, and that it's only going to be a matter of time.

PP: It makes sense that people would have this fear, because you're describing this huge cultural moment in which not just one myth, but also three or four of our most fundamental myths, are all crumbling at once. And because most people don't have these changes put into a broader context, the way you're doing now, they're picking up the changes and feeling the anxiety. . . .

JH: They are feeling it personally only.

PP: So people are feeling this shift, sensing that things aren't going to be the same anymore—and this fear is making this whole process worse?

JH: Definitely. We see this reflected in the fear of immigrants and of our borders being transgressed. We're afraid of running out of all the things we're dependent on: of losing power and our military bases all over the world; of our educational levels falling and of America being the best and the strongest. But the point is: it's already collapsed, it's over with. And that's what's interesting!

PP: And why is this so interesting?

JH: Because once we understand what's really happening, we can see what else can emerge once the structures that are worn out finally crumble. There is a huge amount of stuff going on underneath these old forms. We don't know exactly what it is yet; it's all very different, unorganized, it doesn't coalesce, and it's diverse and dispersed. But it's very important that people take part in some of these emerging projects.

PP: Can you give me some images or ideas of what you're talking about?

JH: At a recent Bioneers[10] conference, the environmentalist and entrepreneur Paul Hawken put up a film on the screen. It was simply a list of names of organizations who are doing inventive things all around the world—whether on trees, fisheries, rivers, different modalities of communities and economic systems, materials that don't use up scarce resources, people harnessing sea waves to escape from oil dependency, and endless other things. Hawken said that he could let this roll for weeks and there would be thousands and thousands of names working on what's happening beneath the surface of society.

PP: But for many the psychic atmosphere is so charged with a kind of floating fear and uncertainty that it's like being at sea in the middle of a terrible storm, with no sense of direction. So the question becomes, How do we live during this shift between ages?

JH: It's important to avoid wanting these innovative structures to conform to the models of the past: and that means unified, organized, and from the top down. What's beginning to emerge is very different from what's gone before. We can't entirely eliminate things like hierarchy, but what's coming may have no tops or bottoms, or even a name. Remember that in the early days of the feminist movement, they refused to have a leader; different women would just stand up and speak. The early feminists were very careful to not put what was spontaneously arising back in the old bottle.

So I think it's a matter of being free-wheeling, and trusting that the emerging cosmos will come out on its own, and shape itself as it comes. That means living in a certain open space—and that's freedom. ∎

Notes

1. See Russell: 2013.
2. More interviews with James Hillman appear in this book in Part VI.
3. On January 8, 2011, U.S. Representative Gabrielle Giffords and eighteen others were shot, including the nine-year-old Christina Taylor, during a constituency meeting held in a supermarket parking lot in Tucson, Arizona. At the memorial ceremony, President Obama gave a widely praised speech, which you can read here <http://www.whitehouse.gov/the-press-office/2011/01/12/remarks-president-barack-obama-memorial-service-victims-shooting-tucson>.
4. "Who Sat Where: The State of the Union Seating Chart," *New York Times,* January 25, 2011. Online at <http://www.nytimes.com/interactive/2011/01/25/us/politics/sotu-closer-look.html>.
5. "Obama Signs Bill to Extend Bush-Era Tax Cuts for Two More Years," by Lori Montgomery, Shailagh Murray, and William Branigan, *Washington Post*, December 17, 2010.
6. "Bill Gates, Melinda Gates, and Warren Buffett are asking the nation's billionaires to pledge to give at least half their net worth to charity, in their lifetimes or at death. If their campaign succeeds, it could change the face of philanthropy." "The $600 Billion Challenge," by Carol J. Loomis, Fortune.com, June 16, 2010 <http://fortune.com/2010/06/16/the-600-billion-challenge/>.
7. The Watergate hearings were convened by the U.S. Senate in 1973 to investigate the 1972 burglaries by Republican party operatives at Democratic National Committee headquarters at the Watergate building in Washington, D.C. It transpired that the plan, and the subsequent cover-up, went to the very top of the Republican administration. The investigation led to the resignation of President Richard Nixon in 1974.
8. "Lean forward" was the slogan adopted in 2010 by MSNBC, a left-of-center cable news channel established in opposition to the right-of-center Fox News.
9. "The EPA's "Cancer Premium' Shows How Fear Overshadows the Greater Risks," by David Ropeik, *Washington Post*, February 2, 2011. The healthcare bill that Hillman refers to is the Affordable Care Act (see Ch. 8 n. 6).
10. Founded in 1990 by social entrepreneurs Kenny Ausubel and Nina Simons, Bioneers has acted as a hub for social and scientific innovators to present visionary solutions to the world's environmental and social challenges <http://www.bioneers.org>.

—32—

The Politics of Anxiety

AN INTERVIEW WITH HARRIET LERNER, PH.D.

A NXIETY: AS INEVITABLE A part of the human condition as this psychological syndrome may be, it can undermine the most confident and courageous of individuals. Yet as analyst Murray Stein pointed out in a previous interview in this section, anxiety is also a natural consequence of democracy, something all citizens living within the conditions of freedom and independence must find a way to bear, as best and as consciously as they can.

From the following interview with clinical psychologist Harriet Lerner, I learned further that anxiety is a characteristic of all human systems, including work organizations and political systems. And although individuals have recourse to the calming effects of religious and spiritual practices, or the insight and support of counseling and therapy—not to mention taking anti-anxiety medications, or the less desirable course of drinking or taking illicit drugs—treating anxiety in an organization or a political system is a different thing altogether. And in the hands of the wrong politician or leader, as psychohistorian Charles Strozier warned in the first section, anxiety can even be exploited as a dangerous tool of manipulation.

But perhaps just *knowing* and being educated about the effects of anxiety on larger institutions and democracies can give citizens an edge in keeping its debilitating effects from subverting the process of government—as well as from creating polarization and political stalemate. It was in the quest of more finely tuned insights into the specific dynamics of how to identify and handle anxiety on a systemic level that I sought out

Lerner, a lifelong expert on family and couple's relationships. Over the past twenty years I have interviewed Lerner on a variety of topics, from raising sons to the philosophical divides within feminist psychology. Her knowledge and calm manner combined with her scholarship and roster of bestselling books on relationship dynamics made her an ideal person to turn to on the issue of political polarization.

Lerner is also remarkable for realizing at an extremely young age just what she wanted to be when she grew up: a psychologist. Her surety of purpose came initially from her Russian-Jewish immigrant parents, who had high hopes for their two daughters to *be* someone at a time when women were only supposed to *find* someone. Also remarkably for her time, Lerner's mother stood out in another way. Unlike others of her day who considered therapy something for the mentally ill, Lerner's mother considered it a learning experience and placed her in weekly therapy sessions—at the age of three. By the end of kindergarten, Lerner had decided to become a clinical psychologist, and eventually set out on a course from which she never wavered.

Lerner was born and raised in Brooklyn, and received her Ph.D. in clinical psychology from the City University of New York, where she met her husband, clinical psychologist Steve Lerner. They headed west to do predoctoral training in San Francisco, and from there established their married and professional life in the American Midwest of Topeka, Kansas, where they did their postdoctoral training program at the Menninger Foundation, and subsequently joined the staff. Although the couple had intended to head back to either coast, they stayed on. Over time, Lerner came to identify herself as a Kansan who "loves the simple life and the big open skies."

In addition to becoming a faculty member and supervisor in the Karl Menninger School of Psychiatry, Dr. Lerner was also among the first pioneers in the formation of feminist psychology theory and therapy, contributing research and scholarly works on the psychology of women and family relationships, feminism, family systems, and revisions of psychoanalytic theory. Not content to keep this kind of valuable knowledge within academia, Lerner wrote many popular, best-selling books, including the classic *The Dance of Anger* and, most recently, *Marriage Rules: A Manual for the Married and the Coupled Up*, and became a commentator and relationship expert in the media. With over thirty-five foreign editions of her books in print, Lerner lectures nationally and internationally, and has received many awards for her work, including Kansan Woman of the Year. She has been a practicing psychologist for over thirty years, and she and her husband currently maintain a private practice in Lawrence, Kansas. The following interview was conducted in 2014.

*

Pythia Peay: As a psychologist, you've made it your life's work to focus on the "dance" of intimate relationships. So I'm very interested to learn, from your relational perspective, what psychological insights you might have into America's polarized body politic.

Harriet Lerner: I'm not an expert on the political system, but anxiety affects all human systems in predictable, patterned ways. Anxiety drives polarities, whether we're talking about a couple, a work system, or two political parties. Humans are wired for dichotomous polarized thinking under stress. The higher the level of chronic anxiety, however, the more difficult it is for an individual or a group to see two sides of an issue, and it's even more difficult to see six or seven sides to an issue.

For example, an anxious couple may come to therapy polarized around how to care for their symptomatic child. Mom stands for law and order and Dad stands for love and understanding. Because they are unable to limber up their brains and find a consensus that both can live with, they stay stuck in downward spirals of anger and blame—while little Johnny gets increasingly symptomatic as they fight about his care.

Ditto for two political parties. It's the same process. You can think of the American citizens as "little Johnny." High levels of chronic anxiety erode the capacity for empathy and cooperation. Anxiety rigidifies thinking, destroys the capacity to tolerate ambiguity and complexity, and leads to a steep decline in civility and cooperation among participants in the system. Anxiety causes a loss of objectivity and balance, pushing people to extremes. Anxious systems do not orient themselves toward the facts. Again, it doesn't matter if we are talking about a marriage, a mother and daughter, or the two political parties.

PP: Are you talking about the same kind of anxiety that individuals suffer from, like panic attacks?

HL: We are all familiar with the individual experience of anxiety. There are also those who suffer from more intense forms of anxiety, which are very real, and that are described in the DSM (The Diagnostic and Statistical Manual of Mental Disorders),[1] and for which they may need professional treatment. However, I'm talking about chronic underground anxiety that operates as an underground force in all human systems. We don't see anxiety as it is because anxiety erodes that most basic human capacity to think about our thinking. We mistake anxiety-driven reactivity for doing our best thinking, for giving people what they need and deserve.

PP: Where does this anxiety spring from, and how does it affect groups?

HL: Anxiety hits us from multiple sources as we move through history and through the life cycle of individuals and political systems. Life is one thing after another. You can make your own list.

But anxiety is not all bad. In fact, anxiety is necessary for the survival of every species and organization. In the right doses, it signals us to act—or to resist the impulse to act—and to make wise choices. An individual, family, or political system that doesn't register anxiety won't survive.

Anxiety can operate as a solicitous friend—a natural survival mechanism that primes us to fight, flee, or freeze when the wolf is at the door or has found his way in. In the face of imminent danger we need to act, not stop and ponder the pros and cons of various options. But in modern times we are not facing a wolf-like threat, though it may feel that way. The stresses we face today require us to calm down, limber up our brain, and do our best problem solving that considers the needs of all. As I mentioned, anxiety blocks the ability of individuals and groups to do this, and locks us into a narrow, rigid, simplistic "good guys vs. bad guys" quick-fix mentality.

PP: What is the dynamic between the individual and the wider system suffering from anxiety? Is it a kind of vicious circle of psychological infection?

HL: When stress hits, anxiety will zoom through the system as everyone tries to get rid of their own anxiety by dumping it on someone else. Depending on the level of calm and maturity of a particular individual, he or she will either calm things down, or further rev things up. Typically, in anxious systems each person's style of managing anxiety will interact with the other person's style of managing anxiety, generating increasingly high levels of tension. It's an automatic process, not anybody's villainous plan. But it's important to understand how anxiety travels, so we can avoid absorbing too much of it ourselves, or passing it along to others. A good leader or political party will always pass on less anxiety and intensity than he or she receives.

PP: What are some other systemic responses to this underground anxiety and intensity?

HL: Like I've said, anxiety leads to polarized thinking, where people very quickly divide into opposite camps, and lose the capacity for creative thinking and problem solving. Each group is over-focused on what the other is doing wrong, and under-focused on their own creative options to act differently, and to de-intensify a situation.

All anxious systems have certain characteristics in common, including a loss of objectivity and balance, and a move toward the extremes. Humans are hard-wired for a fight–flight response, so the greater the underground anxiety, the more you will see individuals stuck in fighting and blaming on one hand, or distancing and cutting off on the other.

PP: In your book *Marriage Rules* you also talk about the importance of listening in defusing conflict and anxiety. The art of true listening seems in short supply in politics and the culture these days. In fact you write that you want to add a new disorder to the DSM manual: Listening Deficit Disorder. What a great idea!

HL: Yes, I would like to see LDD added to the DSM. If only our wish to understand the other person was as great as our passion to be understood. If that were so, we would be living in a very different world.

Obviously, anxiety impedes the capacity to listen to a different point of view. When we feel threatened, our central nervous system overheats and we become tense and guarded, unable to take in new information. We listen defensively: that is, we listen for what we don't agree with, so we can swing into debate mode. This holds for political parties as well. But there's no solving or loosening up polarities without true listening, and by that I mean not just listening defensively. When we listen defensively, we listen for the inaccuracies, distortions, and exaggerations that will inevitably be there. Or, we listen for the correct facts, and then present our own case. But in order not to fall into polarized communication, one has to *really* listen to the other person for the parts that we can understand in order to get what they're saying, and even be able to apologize for one's own part.

PP: You're an expert in family systems. How would you describe an anxious family system? Does it operate in the same way as an anxious political system?

HL: Yes, as I said all systems have certain characteristics in common. In families, anxiety drives people toward polarities, toward fusion or cut-off, toward glorifying or hating differences, toward avoiding a subject entirely or focusing on it incessantly. Anxious families may deny differences in a "group think" mentality that compromises individual autonomy, or that exaggerates differences out of proportion. Chronically anxious families are characterized either by rigid authoritarian rules, or, on the other hand, they might operate like a glob of protoplasm, without clear leadership and hierarchy. Anxious families deny the realities of change and try to hold the clock still, or, on the other hand, family functioning can become so chaotic there's no consistent structures or traditions to be counted on. In sum, anxiety pushes us to one extreme or the other. Anxiety also drives triangles, so as tensions mount, family members take sides, lose objectivity, and join one person's camp at the expense of another. So when the level of underground anxiety or emotional intensity is high, a political system acts just like a dysfunctional family.

PP: So if America were to come to your office for relationship counseling around its polarized political situation, who would walk in the door? Would it be a Democrat and a Republican, for example, President Obama and Republican Speaker of the House John Boehner?

HL: I would hope that whoever walked in my door would possess goodwill and a genuine wish to find solutions that would take into account the needs of all. It would also be important that that person be self-focused, by which I don't mean self-blaming. Without the capacity to focus on the self, and observe and change one's own steps in the patterns that aren't working, nothing will change. I'd also want to see the person or party who had the capacity to widen the lens and view problems through the largest possible historical perspective—because anxiety always leads to a narrowing of perspective, a "who started it" or "who is to blame" mentality. So I would like to work with the person or group who could widen their focus and see patterns rather than blame or diagnose a particular individual or political party.

It would also help to have the person with the most power in my office. If there is a symptomatic child in a family, for example, I want to see the parents because they have the most power to change the emotional climate of the family. From this perspective, I'd want to start with Obama, though I am no longer clear "who has the power to do what" in Washington. Nor do I have the illusion that any of the nation's problems could be solved in my consulting room.

PP: And what would be some techniques that you would recommend for lessening anxiety—both for individuals, and for political systems?

HL: There is endless help and good advice for individuals suffering from anxiety disorders. Far less has been written about lowering anxiety in large organizations and political systems. The solution can't be found in "techniques" but rather in a clear understanding of how anxiety affects organizational systems and how individuals in a system can identify and modify their patterned ways of navigating relationships under stress.

It is not easy to learn to "think systems" because we naturally blame or pathologize a particular person or group. In my book *The Dance of Fear*, there is a chapter on how to stay clear and calm in a crazy workplace, and it illustrates how systems get anxious and develop an anxiety disorder of their very own, separate from the individuals who comprise the group. Anxiety never stays contained within one or two individuals. Rather, it zooms through a system at high speed, gathering steam at every point along the way. I also recommend an excellent book called *The Anxious Organization* by organization consultant Jeffrey Miller. Without having a systems view of anxiety and organizational functioning, we're left with pathologizing and diagnosing particular individuals and groups, which ultimately is a narrow perspective that will not facilitate change. ∎

Notes

1. DSM (The Diagnostic and Statistical Manual of Mental Disorders) is a compendium of standard criteria for the classification of mental disorders. It is published by the American Psychiatric Association. The most recent edition, the DSM-5, was issued in 2013.

—33—

Trauma

The Hidden Power behind the American Presidency

AN INTERVIEW WITH ROBERT J. LANGS, M.D.

A LL BUT TWO OF America's forty-three presidents—Millard Fillmore and Jimmy Carter—suffered major trauma in their lives. Twenty-four presidents lost siblings and half-siblings during their childhood. Thirteen endured this trauma more than once. Eighteen presidents lost siblings as adults, either before or during their presidencies. Fifteen of the twenty-four presidents who lost siblings also lost children of their own in their adult years, adding to the initial death-related traumas they'd already suffered. Three presidents lost fathers before they were born. Twenty presidents suffered the loss of a parent in early childhood through death, abandonment, illness, or divorce. Five presidents lost their wives before they took office; three lost their wives while in the White House. Six presidents had wives who were seriously ill physically while they were in office, and three had wives who were severely depressed by the death of one or more of their children.

So says the classically trained, New York psychotherapist, psychoanalyst, and psychiatrist Dr. Robert Langs, who recently passed away. The prolific author of more than forty books and 175 scholarly articles, Langs has in recent years delved into the treasure trove of presidential papers, speeches, and biographies for insight into the psychological effects of trauma. In addition to deepening his knowledge around the workings of trauma, Langs also found intriguing evidence revealing how the trauma-impacted inner lives of presidents shaped the office of the American presidency. Most political analysis and presidential biographies, says Langs, bypass psychology and present

America's leaders as "fleshless policy-making machines whose personal lives are largely irrelevant to their political careers." This leaves presidential histories without a center, he explains, as most biographers ignore the "red thread that runs from a president's emotional issues and their sources to his favorable and unfavorable decisions as our nation's leader."

In Langs' analysis, American presidents scarred by trauma are either fatefully propelled toward war-making, personal risk-taking, and endangerment—even leading to their assassination—or, as in the unusual case of Barack Obama, the avoidance of conflict and confrontation. As the material for his study accumulated, it became clear to Langs that "the history of the United States was, in significant part, the result of one long, collective, post-traumatic syndrome endured by one president after another." For although America's presidents may appear to be in command and outwardly unaffected by the tragedies they've suffered, as Langs noted in our interview, the lingering after-effects of trauma exert hidden, but powerful, effects on their administrations. Operating at deeply unconscious levels, trauma in general, he maintains, creates an undertow of "existential death anxiety," as well as feelings of guilt around deaths of loved ones, even if we are not at fault. In his experience as a clinician, notes Langs, "so many things that we do in our lives that are self-punishing come from these traumas, including borrowed guilt" for the sins of our parents. And unconscious guilt, he says, "is a powerfully destructive force in human life."

Lest citizens become alarmed at destructive patterns at work in the American psyche and the American presidency, however, it helps to put trauma in perspective. In the same way that Buddha said that all life is suffering, all of life, says Langs "is trauma. Few if any humans go through life trauma-free." Despite trauma's prevalence, however, Langs discovered a statistically higher rate of trauma among American presidents than in the general public. This has led him to theorize that trauma might even be a motivating factor driving presidential ambitions: an insight that has compelled him to call for "trauma profiles" of potential presidential candidates. In the following interview conducted in 2014, Dr. Langs illustrates his theory of how trauma influences presidential decision-making and behavior with examples from the lives of presidents Andrew Jackson, Harry S. Truman, Bill Clinton, George H. W. Bush, George W. Bush, and our current president, Barack Obama.

✳

Pythia Peay: Before we get into a discussion of trauma and the presidency, it would be helpful if you could explain some of the terms that you use to describe how trauma works. For example, what do you mean when you refer to the "frame"?

Robert Langs: The "frame" as I use it refers to the ground rules and boundaries of any relationship. For example, in psychotherapy there exists a specific set of ground rules that provide a secure framework: these include a set fee, a private setting, the anonymity of the therapist, and the privacy of the treatment. In other words, the patient and therapist can be considered a kind of bi-personal field—and fields need boundaries. Boundaries have enormous influence on what takes place within the boundaries themselves. So when I talk about the "frame" in light of traumas, most of it has to do with violation of a set of ground rules.

There's always a natural tendency, however, to "break the frame." The basic reason for that is because secure frames—which are very healthy and holding—also evoke existential death anxiety. And because we are terrified of death anxiety, we are "frame breakers" by nature.

PP: But why does a secure frame trigger death anxiety? I would have thought the opposite would be true.

RL: The reason is that a secure frame also means we're entrapped. And this feeling of entrapment resembles the existential rule of life: which is that we're all trapped in life, of which there is only one exit, and that's through death. The essence of this form of *existential death anxiety* (which we try to keep suppressed most of the time) is that we become aware that in the future we will die, and that we can never defeat death.

So what does this realization drive us to? Denial. To deny death is the only thing we have. If we can do that in a reasonable amount, we're okay. But people don't confine themselves to that; they get too terrified and that can mobilize two other forms of death anxiety. One of these is *predatory death anxiety*, where someone is our enemy and is trying to harm us so we have to mobilize our resources and fight them off. This has been with us since the origin of living beings.

PP: So existential death anxiety is the inborn fear that we all have around dying. Predatory death anxiety is the fear that someone will kill or destroy us. And *predator death anxiety* is the fear . . .

RL: That we've harmed others. We all have a system inside of ourselves saying that if we've harmed someone in some form, it means we're trying to kill them, and so in the unconscious (which always sees things in the extreme) we must suffer the consequences and be executed. This comes up in situations where there's been any harm or destruction on any level, whether physical or psychological, to any human being. This feeling that we must be punished because of the guilt we feel that we've harmed others comes with the human mind.

PP: Even if the suffering or the death of a loved one is through no fault of one's own?

RL: It doesn't matter. A great illustration of this is the Christian theologian St. Augustine. He had only one friend; when his friend got ill and died, Augustine nearly committed suicide—even though he had nothing to do with it. We hold ourselves accountable.

PP: Why?

RL: Because we have an unconscious system that feeds our guilt. But there is a purpose to our guilt: it's to prevent violence, as our violence is our biggest problem. So part of the structure of the human mind is trying to curtail violence, which obviously is not working very well! But it's inescapably true that if someone in our lives gets ill or dies, it's astounding how, unconsciously, we hold ourselves accountable. And unconscious guilt is a very powerful, destructive force in human life.

PP: Can you give me an example in the American presidency of how this kind of unconscious guilt and death anxiety played a role in shaping their lives, as well as their presidency?

RL: With the exception of Millard Fillmore and Jimmy Carter (and they were kind of lackluster presidents) all of the American presidents have suffered traumas around the deaths of siblings, spouses, parents, or children. For example, both Andrew Jackson and Bill Clinton lost their fathers before they were born.

PP: And how would the effects of the death of these presidents' fathers before they were even born have affected them?

RL: Some of the most troublesome consequences of this type of trauma would be a reckless and relentless quest for power, a powerful inclination to break rules and defy laws, and a tendency to unnecessarily risk their lives and seek punishment.

In Jackson's case, for example, his need for power is seen in the risks he took for both his men and himself to win the Battle of New Orleans against the British in the War of 1812. He got into battles where he was very vulnerable to being killed—so there was an unconscious need to find some way of harming himself. He executed two British soldiers without fair trials and ruthlessly slaughtered members of the Seminole Indian tribe. Socially, he lived with and "married" a woman before she had obtained a legal divorce from her first husband. No affront or insult was small enough to be ignored, and as a result Jackson engaged in many frivolous duels, trying to get himself killed. In one of those encounters, he allowed his opponent, who was a marksman, to fire the first shot! He was hit near the heart, and the embedded bullet remained in his chest, leaving a wound that caused him pain until the day he died.

PP: And Clinton?

RL: Clinton obviously did a number of things that were enormously self-destructive. He both sought power and invited punishment through his promiscuity and his handling of the Paula Jones affair, and of course his infamous relationship with Monica Lewinsky while he was president. In the trial that ensued, he testified about his affair with Lewinsky in an evidently perjured way, which led to his impeachment by the House of Representatives and acquittal by the Senate.

At the same time, both Clinton and Jackson were great presidents, because they were expansive and had a certain grandiose flair. But the law really didn't matter much to them at all. They rode roughshod over the law, and just kept going.

PP: You've said that Clinton and Jackson were "frame violators" and "boundary breakers."

RL: Right. Imagine the existential death anxiety Clinton and Jackson felt over the deaths of their fathers before they were born: how long were they going to live? One way to handle this kind of existential death anxiety is denial. And one of the forms of denial is that if I can break a boundary, then I'm the exception to the existential rule that I must die. All of this takes place unconsciously, but it is still driving actual behavior.

PP: Would they have also felt a sense of powerlessness due to the loss of their fathers before they were born?

RL: Jackson's and Clinton's quest for excessive power was a reflection of their need to deny the utter helplessness caused by the premature loss of their fathers. So their need to act in ways that denied these extreme feelings of impotency was enormous. They were out to prove that they were invulnerable in the face of loss and physical threat—that they could take on and defy death. Although their rule breaking was a way of denying their limitations, it was also an effort to prove that they were more powerful than the rules of nature that deprived them of their fathers. Their risk taking, although a power play, also stemmed from their unconscious survivor guilt and from a need for punishment, because they harbored a hidden belief that they themselves caused the tragedy that befell them.

PP: You also mention a need to make up for "the sins of the fathers" as a source of trauma in political families. Can you say more about that?

RL: The fathers of both Joe Kennedy, Jr., who was being groomed to become the first Roman Catholic president, and George H. W. Bush, supported the rise of Hitler. As U.S. Ambassador to Great Britain, Joseph P. Kennedy, Sr. sanctioned the killings of German Jews, and advised against the U.S. sending aid to Great Britain; he also supported efforts to appease Hitler. The late U.S. senator Prescott Bush worked for a company that had ties with a German industrialist who helped fund Hitler in the thirties. And so both Joe Kennedy, Jr. and George H. W. Bush were unconsciously guilt-ridden.[1]

PP: So the guilt these two sons felt on behalf of their fathers is like the Biblical saying that the sins of the father are—

RL: You've got it: it's exactly that: "for I the LORD your God am a jealous God, visiting the iniquity of the fathers on the children to the third and fourth generation of them that hate me" (Exodus 20:5). The Bible foretells this particular psychological mechanism, and that guilt shall be handed down from generation to generation.

PP: So are you saying that both Bush and Kennedy put themselves in harm's way to expiate their fathers' sin of supporting Hitler?

RL: Well, let's take President George H. W. Bush. Just eighteen when he entered World War II and joined the U.S. Navy, he became a torpedo bomber pilot. He volunteered for fifty-eight high-risk missions in the Pacific theater, and repeatedly flew into enemy fire. During an attack on a Japanese installation, a radio tower on the island of Chichi Jima, the plane he was piloting came upon intense enemy anti-aircraft fire. His plane got hit and his engine caught fire. But instead of leaving, Bush basically said, "To hell with it, I'm going down there anyway to drop my bombs," which he did, hitting the enemy target. With his plane still ablaze, he flew away. At that point, his only option was to bail out. He ordered his two co-pilots to bail out. Both died; one fell to his death when his parachute didn't open and the other co-pilot is assumed to have died aboard the plane. Bush himself was injured before he hit the water, where he paddled for several hours before being rescued by an American submarine. He felt responsible for his crewmen's death for the rest of his life, and even stayed in touch with their families.

The Kennedy story is even more incredible. Joe Kennedy, Jr. had completed his tour of duty in the European theater, but volunteered to stay on for an extremely dangerous mission. The Allies had come up with a plan to load planes with explosives and target German sites in France. Once they were over their target, the flight crew was to light the fuse connected to the explosives and then parachute from the plane before it exploded. Kennedy died when his plane exploded prematurely. So whereas Bush survived the expression of his evident unconscious need to pay for the sins of his father, Kennedy did not.

PP: So then unconscious trauma could also be seen as a source of murder and war?

RL: Right. It's an extremely important source of murder and war.

PP: And yet we don't know about this connection.

RL: The best example of that is President George W. Bush's decision to go into Iraq. There was a trauma behind his decision, and that had to do with his drive to finish his father's business. The story behind this takes place when he's seven years old.

His parents, George H. W. Bush and Barbara Bush, had taken their three-year-old daughter Robin, who had leukemia, to Memorial Sloan Kettering Center for Cancer in New York for surgery. His uncle, who worked there, had mentioned there might be new treatments. Tragically, Robin died there. Rather than bring their daughter home for burial and a funeral, George H. W. and Barbara Bush decided to bury her in the Bush family burial plot in Greenwich, Connecticut. Then he and Barbara drove back to Texas. When they arrived, they drove straight to George W. Bush's school, where he happened to be outside. When young George saw his parents drive up, he ran over excitedly to their car; he thought he saw his little sister in the back seat. But she wasn't there, and his parents told him she'd died. He'd known his younger sister Robin had been sick; but had not been told that she was dying.

So then, decades later, George H. W. and Barbara Bush moved his sister's body from Connecticut, and buried her near plots reserved for them at the George H. W. Bush Presidential Library in College Station, Texas. Clearly, this family trauma was a factor influencing Bush's reaction when he heard the news of the World Trade Center buildings being hit, and he visibly panicked: the underlying feeling this triggered in him was that his sister was being killed all over again. And in his unconscious, his parents had killed his sister—and so he was going to be next.

PP: And you surmised that this scenario was behind Bush's reaction on 9/11 because . . .?

RL: Because the unconscious mind has a different set of values and a different way of thinking: and it always takes the worst case scenario. It's pretty rough, but that's why it's unconscious—because we can't bear it. But the trauma around President Bush's younger sister's death was also a critical factor in his decision to go into Iraq. At the time, the decision to invade a country that didn't have anything to do with 9/11 seemed inexplicable. But among the many forces driving Bush's behaviors, one very significant factor that was overlooked was his unconscious drive to complete his father's unfinished business: to find a way to get into Iraq, and to get rid of Saddam Hussein, which his father had failed to do during the first Gulf War.

PP: What about presidents who suffered childhood illnesses? I would imagine that would be a source of trauma that would carry over into adulthood.

RL: President Theodore Roosevelt suffered from severe, death-like asthma as a child.

He became president in 1901 after the assassination of William McKinley. Years earlier, his wife had died two days after giving birth to their first child, and his mother had died in the same house and on the same day. He never mentioned his first wife's name again (he married a second time). Although he was a great conservationist who fought fiercely against corruption, in 1898 during the war against Cuba, he led an unauthorized charge up Kettle Hill that took a huge toll in lost life, as well as wounded soldiers, and he barely survived himself. After his presidency, he led an expedition down an uncharted river in the Brazilian rain forest that was extremely risky; he became gravely ill from a wound, and nearly died.

Whereas his charge up Kettle Hill has been seen by most historians as an act of bravery, the other side of the coin speaks for it as a veiled attempt at suicide; much the same can be said of his trip to Brazil. These actions and giving a speech for ninety minutes with an assassin's bullet in his chest speak for a near-fatal mixture of unconscious causative and survivor guilt, and extremes of existential death anxiety, which evoke needs to "prove" his invulnerability to harm.

A similar pattern, with more dire consequences, can be seen with the helplessness experienced by President Harry S. Truman who had diphtheria when he was ten, and was confined to a baby carriage for several months. He was completely paralyzed and unable to move. I believe that had a major effect on his decision to drop the atom bomb.

PP: How so? I know that serious questions have been raised around whether it was really necessary for the U.S. to drop the bomb at that particular time, as a way to end the war.

RL: Absolutely. I'm totally critical of that decision. Truman could have dropped it offshore; or he could have done something to show the Japanese that we really had nuclear weapons. But the remnants of this early experience of paralysis of inaction haunted Truman all of his life. And so he decided to exert this enormous power, and that led to enormous loss of life. He even dropped bombs on not just one, but *two* cities!

As I read Truman's biography, it just blew me away to see these connections: that if a person is paralyzed, and unable to move, and stuck with existential death anxiety, at some point they're going to prove that they have the power to defy it. There were of course other factors in Truman's decision, but nevertheless his early brush with immobility and death may well have tipped the scales towards his decision to drop the atom bomb on two populated Japanese cities, rather than acting in a less devastating manner. And so the man who had been the victim of helplessness and entrapment caused a most devastating form of helplessness and entrapment in the victims of these bombings.

I need to also mention the deaths of the four presidents who were assassinated: Lincoln, Garfield, McKinley, and Kennedy. Each of them had lost children in the months or a couple of years before they were killed. A short time before his death, Lincoln actually dreamed that he had been assassinated. Each had been warned of severe danger to their lives, and each ignored the warnings. The unconscious causative and survivor guilt from which they suffered undoubtedly played a role in their deaths.

PP: In our own time, President Obama has been unusual in the sense that he's written a memoir of his own life story, and has shared the traumas he suffered during childhood—such as growing up without a father.

RL: Obama's early traumas began with his origins. He was conceived before his parents were married and in all likelihood accidentally. This is hinted at in his 2008 inauguration speech, when Obama spoke of "the accident of our birth." Further complicating his origins, Obama's father, who was from Kenya and who married his eighteen-year-old sweetheart when she was three months pregnant, was a bigamist who was neither an American citizen nor a long-standing resident. So Obama was both foreign-born and American, as well as the child of a mixed-race couple.

Another mixture was that his parents had different religious backgrounds. Although neither practiced their faiths, his mother was Protestant, whereas his father was Muslim. He also experienced a series of abandonments by his father, stepfather, and mother, although these abandonments were compensated for by the caretaking of his maternal grandparents. There was also a set of traumas—"sins of the fathers"—around his father, who after his return to Kenya became a heavy drinker and a reckless driver who had three serious car crashes (he lost both legs in one crash, and the last took his life). Obama's father also came under suspicion for a political assassination, and failed in his attempts to have a successful career in government. But although there was a lot of trauma in Obama's childhood, loss through death did not touch him until he was an adult, when death claimed his father, stepfather, mother, and grandmother.

PP: Many of your insights into Obama have come from interpreting what you call the "encoded narrative" in his personal stories and speeches, such as the phrase "the accident of our birth" you just referred to from one of his speeches. Can you give a brief explanation for what you mean by that?

RL: There are two basic forms of communication. One centers around non-narrative intellectualizations and explanations, and the other form of communication is narrative storytelling. So every story we tell has two levels of meaning. One level is the story as we're telling it. The other level has to do with the way in which the story that we tell is being told in a certain way to encode and disguise trauma, and our reactions to it. To understand this second level within a narrative, we have to know the "trigger" in order to decode it.

PP: So can you give me an example of an encoded narrative within some of President Obama's communications?

RL: Obama is the classic example of this. He's a storyteller. There are two stories he tells that conceal encoded trauma narratives around his mother and father. The first story is when Obama's father, Obama, Sr., visits him when he's ten years old. Obama, his father, his grandfather, and a friend hike up a mountain. The friend borrows a pipe from Obama's father, and then drops the pipe down the ravine. His father grabs the friend by the feet and dangles him over the ravine. Now that's an encoded narrative in which Obama is saying about himself, "my father nearly let me die, he nearly killed me."

The other example is even more revealing: the topic that he picked for a 1990 paper for the *Harvard Law Review*. His topic was whether a child could sue its mother for prenatal injuries caused by negligent driving while the fetus was *in utero*. The tort ends with the idea that prenatal education is the best way to prevent unwanted children from being born into lives of pain and despair.[2] Now we know that Obama was conceived out of wedlock, accidentally, and probably in a car. It's possible he was also subject to an attempt at an abortion while his mother was pregnant with him. So encoded in the topic of his paper is whether he can get revenge on his mother for having tried to harm him when he was still a fetus.

PP: I'm obviously very psychologically oriented, so I don't have any difficulty with reflecting on the trauma of Obama's origins as you interpret it here through these "encoded narratives." But what do you say to those who might dismiss some of your interpretations as a bit far-fetched?

RL: People often ask me how I really know how much of an effect these traumas have had. But I know from story after story that these are archetypes around trauma that are at work, and that they're having an effect. I have identified a large group of universal ways in which all humans respond to traumas and the three forms of death anxiety. Although I do seek evidence in each individual case, the archetype guides my search and is a highly reliable guide.

PP: Given this confusion around Obama's origins, did you read anything into his response to the drama that erupted around whether he had a legitimate birth certificate that proved his American citizenship, and which at first he refused to share publicly?[3]

RL: Yes, I did. Obama spent millions of dollars over several years fighting lawsuits that were trying to force him to make his birth certificate public, when there was no reason to doubt that he'd been born to an American mother in Hawaii. So Obama's defiance on that issue spoke for his hidden, unconscious conflicts regarding his birth and identity. But in a broader sense it also illustrates our natural tendency to deny these traumas, even while they're exerting such powerful effects.

PP: Obama's father, as you've described him, and as I've heard him described by others, appeared to be very aggressive and even violent. Would Obama then have guilt toward his own aggression and violence?

RL: Well, he would certainly try to curtail it in himself. But with Obama it's very difficult to gauge, because the effects of his traumas are hard to nail down. Except for the fact that he tells this astounding narrative of his origins, it's very hard to see the influence. Until now, Obama's strong intellectual and distancing defenses seem to have spared him from any dire consequences of his trauma-related, unconscious conflicts. His main vulnerability seems to be a tendency to back down and not take strong action when challenged. He avoids making powerful statements. He seems unable to make a strong decision until he's absolutely forced to.

Of course, there are other factors at work, but my view on Obama is that he continues to behave as if he feels, on an unconscious level, that he is still the helpless fetus who may be aborted or abandoned at any moment. He's unconsciously convinced that anyone can do him in or kill him, so his childhood traumas seem to have cast a cloud over his presidential thinking. There's also a sense that his traumas are seething beneath the surface, and that he could make a catastrophic error at any moment—especially if he were to suffer a fresh, damaging event.

PP: So in your opinion do you believe President Obama has come to terms with the traumas of his childhood?

RJL: No, I don't think Obama knows any of this. There's so much denial around his early years, including as well the stepfather that he lost, his mother's second husband she married when she was living in Indonesia. Just consider the fact that his mother sent for him as a young boy to be with her in Indonesia, a foreign country with a risk of disease and an unstable political situation.[4] The traumas Obama went through are enormous.

PP: When we first began our interview, you mentioned something about Presidents Jimmy Carter and Millard Fillmore having had lackluster presidencies. Are you saying that was due to the fact that they didn't suffer traumas like the other presidents did?

RL: The implications are that these two presidents weren't working over some kind of acute trauma. With most presidents there are some very defining moments in their personal history—so if you're looking for a link to trauma, it's really quite detectable. But there is a positive side of trauma, in the way that it can also motivate us to take effective action. Everything we do has an unconscious source! Yet it's not always negative; it can also be very creative.

PP: How can trauma be creative?

RL: Because it unconsciously drives a person to show power in a way that's tame, and that's suitable to the situation; so in that way it can be a positive motivation. Our first president, George Washington, for example, lost his father at age eleven, and then became the ward of his older half-brother, Lawrence, who died when Washington was just twenty years old. So with Washington we have a more positive example of a president and a leader who's suffered trauma.

But the problem still remains that most of the time these early traumas can derail our best intentions. For example, had [George W.] Bush been more aware of his own childhood traumas, he could have come up with some more constructive ways of finishing his father's business than going into Iraq. So the goal with this kind of research is to alert presidents and others in power to their vulnerabilities, and to compel the public and historians to examine the trauma history of presidents.

PP: So then what's important is that we begin to cultivate an attitude toward trauma that's educative: to learn about trauma and its effects, for ourselves personally, but just as importantly, how trauma operates *sub rosa*, influencing leaders and presidents on the world stage of politics.

RL: Right. If there had been more awareness around Bush's personal trauma history, we might have said, "Wait a minute George! We think there are some other factors at work here. We think you're going out of your way to do something that doesn't seem justified."

At the very least, we could begin to bring trauma into public awareness, and to factor in how trauma motivates our presidents and leaders, rather than ignoring it. Hopefully, as more experts and political analysts study the stories of American presidents, they'll begin to take note of patterns and themes around trauma. "Finishing father's business," for instance, is something that is very real and powerful in the unconscious.

PP: So would you envision something in the future like an examination and review of presidential candidates' trauma histories?

RL: Oh yes. I think it would be very good to vet presidential candidates around their trauma histories. The goal would be to provide them with a list of their vulnerabilities and to put them on alert about how these unconscious factors might be affecting them. It should be part of every presidential candidate profile.

The aim of my work can be summed up by the wisdom of George Santayana's well-known words: "Those who cannot remember the past are condemned to repeat it."[5] The study of presidential trauma and their effects call for an addendum to these wise words. It tells us that in order to learn and benefit from remembering the past, we must first ferret out the part of the past that we have barred from awareness. We must reclaim that which we have obliterated or not experienced in the first place. For this reason, my work is dedicated to uncovering hidden remembrances in the hope that our current and future presidents may more knowingly move this country and themselves toward a better future. ■

Notes

1. For Joseph P. Kennedy's anti-Semitism, visit <http://en.wikipedia.org/wiki/Joseph_P._Kennedy,_Sr>. For Prescott Bush, Sr., see "How Bush's Grandfather Helped Hitler's Rise to Power," by Ben Aris and Duncan Capital, *Guardian*, September 25, 2004, in which they write, "George Bush's grandfather, the late US senator Prescott Bush, was a director and shareholder of companies that profited from their involvement with the financial backers of Nazi Germany."
2. "Exclusive: Obama's Lost Law Review Article," by Ben Smith and Jeffrey Ressner, *Politico*, August 22, 2008.
3. "CNN Investigates: Obama Born in U.S.," by Gary Tuchman, CNN, April 25, 2011.
4. Indonesia underwent a civil war in 1965–1966 following a failed coup. Some half a million people were killed. Subsequently, the authoritarian regime of President Suharto quashed dissent.
5. Quoted from *The Life of Reason: Reason in Common Sense*. New York: Scribner's, 1905: p. 284.

Part VI

The Soul of America

These Are the Times that Try Men's Souls

Citizens by birth or choice of a common country, that country has a right to concentrate your affections.—The name of AMERICAN, which belongs to you, in your national capacity, must always exalt the just pride of Patriotism, more than any appellation derived from local discriminations. With slight shades of difference, you have the same Religion, Manners, Habits, and Political Principles. You have in a common cause fought and triumphed together; the Independence and Liberty you possess are the work of joint counsels, and joint efforts—of common dangers, sufferings, and successes.—**George Washington**, from his Farewell Address, September 19, 1796

W HEN I WAS IN second grade the Daughters of the American Revolution, in search of potential members, paid a visit to my classroom. As the child of an Argentine mother growing up in a rural Missouri town, I knew, even at that young age, that I'd never make the cut. Even so, my mother, Sheila, reacted strongly when I was passed over. "They should have chosen you," she said, archly. Yet my mother could offer no explanation as to why I—the daughter of an immigrant and an Irish-American father with no known ties to the American Revolution—should have been selected by this patriotic women's organization.

Some fifty years later, while writing *American Icarus: A Memoir of Father and Country*, I came across a file of papers on my mother's ancestry. In it was a family tree tracing her lineage back to one Master Commandant John Cassin who, I discover, had fought alongside George Washington at the Battle of Trenton. Yes, *the* Battle of Trenton, when on Christmas night in 1776 in the midst of a freezing hailstorm General Washington ordered his threadbare soldiers, many barefoot and tracking blood in the snow, to the banks of the Delaware River. There, in a massive undertaking, troops, horses, and artillery were loaded onto open boats for passage across a river made exceedingly dangerous by ice floes swirling among the swift-moving currents.

Landing on the opposite shore just before dawn, Washington led his troops onward through a blizzard, marching five miles inland to Trenton, where they surprised the sleeping enemy troops, scoring a much-needed victory at one of the lowest points of the war. Not just military action and bravery, but words had helped to win this key battle. In the weeks before the attack, the patriot and essayist Thomas Paine, who had been traveling with the troops, had been ordered by senior officers back to Philadelphia because "the country needed him writing more than fighting." As soon as he arrived back in the city, Craig Nelson recounts in *Thomas Paine*, he "frantically" set to work composing a series of thirteen pieces, one for each colony. The finished pamphlet was called *The American Crisis* and it began with these words:

> These are the times that try men's souls. The summer soldier and the
> sunshine patriot will, in this crisis, shrink from the service of their country;

but he that stands it now, deserves the love and thanks of man and woman. Tyranny, like hell, is not easily conquered; yet we have this consolation with us, that the harder the conflict, the more glorious the triumph. What we obtain too cheap, we esteem too lightly; it is dearness only that gives every thing its value.

Two days before the attack, on December 23, 1776, General Washington had ordered Paine's entire pamphlet to be read aloud to his troops. During their raid on Trenton, writes Nelson, shouts of *"These* are the times that try men's souls!" could be heard above the musket shots and shouts of battle. Paine's essay with its charged phrase would live on, helping to swell the thinning ranks of the Continental Army, and infusing the flagging Revolution with renewed momentum.

Paine's words would even make their way into my fifth great-grandfather Cassin's obituary: "He served in the army during that memorable crisis which 'tried men's souls'. . . and his patriotic aid in the defense of the rights of the American Republic was employed at other interesting periods of the Revolutionary War."[1] Pulling at this worn thread in the weave of my family history, I unravel the story of this dimly known ancestral figure. Born to an Irish immigrant dairyman in 1760, Cassin joined the struggle for independence when he was just sixteen. Following the Revolution, Cassin, who was recorded to have been personal friends with Washington, became a merchant seaman, sailing to France. In 1799, he was ordered to Washington City, as the new capital was called then, to help establish the U.S. Navy, serving as second in command in the Washington Navy Yard being built on the shores of the Potomac, and engaging in some swashbuckling pirate-fighting in the war against Tripoli.

When the War of 1812 broke out, Cassin was ordered to command the naval forces in defense of the Delaware. In the last years of his life he became commanding officer of the Navy Yards at Norfolk, Virginia, and then Charleston, South Carolina, where after being promoted to the rank of Captain he died in 1822. He was preceded in death by his wife, Ann, who died at sea, and survived by his son, Master Commandant Stephen Cassin, who earned a gold medal for bravery during the War of 1812, and who was later buried at Arlington National Cemetery. His daughter, Eliza, from whom I am descended, also married a Navy hero, Commodore Joseph Tarbell; both died young, leaving behind two orphaned daughters.

How I came to be the descendant of a Revolutionary patriot through my Argentine mother is recounted in *American Icarus*. Suffice to say, the discovery that I was more deeply rooted in American history than I'd ever thought possible had a powerful impact. Seated in the hushed atmosphere of the DAR Library in Washington, D.C., coming face to face with a portrait of the burly, uniformed "Master Commandant" Cassin in a history of the U.S. Navy, a jolt went through my body. As a student of meditation, I'd had spiritual awakenings. In therapy, I'd had psychological awakenings. But the discovery that I was descended from what in DAR lingo is called a "patriot ancestor" stirred in me an American awakening.

To that point, my knowledge of America's early origins had been almost cartoonish, a montage composed of grade-school images of cherry trees and aloof images of George Washington and, later, liberal tenets around sexist dead white men. Now, delving into histories and biographies, events that had been dry and distant became animated. Cardboard cutout–heroes became three-dimensional figures of complexity. My relationship with my mother country, as with my mother, changed. "If I'd known about that," remarked Sheila after I'd relayed tales of her Patriot forebear, "maybe I would have felt more as if I belonged to this country."

As the loneliness behind my mother's words sank in, I realized that I, too, had never quite felt as if I "belonged" as an American. Since then, it has often seemed to me that my mother and I were not alone in how we felt, and that intrinsic to the American experience is that sense of always arriving, never quite belonging, unsure of where exactly we have come from, our lives like a chapter midway through a book whose first chapter we've never read. Cut off from our histories and stories of how we came to actually *be* American, we never really gain the solid ground of citizenship. Lacking that foundation, we lack connection to the soul of America, in its most authentic, lived, grounded sense.

In reflecting on his own "fateful" ancestral links, the psychologist Carl Jung wrote in *Memories, Dreams, Reflections* that he felt that he "had to answer questions which fate had posed to my forefathers, and which had not yet been answered, or as if I had to complete, or perhaps continue, things which previous ages had left unfinished. . . ." What did it mean, I now wondered, with some irony, that I, a child of the sixties who'd marched against wars from Vietnam to Iraq, was a "daughter of the American Revolution"? The bold John Cassin had risked his life in service to America, so that seven generations later I could write in freedom. His sacrifice seemed to demand something of me—but what?

Many times I have summoned this ancestral father: standing beside him as I imagine him listening to Tom Paine's words, young, cold, and scared; or crossing the Delaware;

or dodging musket balls during battle; or sailing on high seas through sun and storms; or testifying before Congress for more funds for the Navy Yard; or worrying about the son who had followed in his footsteps for a life at sea; or suffering—as I know he did—in his last years, living in a shabby house that leaked and that was damp and cold; or grieving over the death of his wife at sea. I also must imagine him, as I am sure happened, ordering about slaves—at the Navy Yard, on the ships, and in his home. So it was written by history, to be taken in as part of my American story.

For whatever force propelled John Cassin to fight for the American Revolution passed down the chain of my ancestors, arriving in me—even before I knew anything of this fifth great-grandfather's existence—as a drive to understand something of what makes America what it is. The clue to what we are, I think, can be found in Paine's phrase: *These are the times that try men's souls.* The United States, writes historian Gordon S. Wood in *Revolutionary Characters: What Made the Founders Great,* "was founded on a set of beliefs and not, as were other nations, on a common ethnicity, language, or religion." Hence, he continues, "Since we are not a nation in any traditional sense of the term, in order to establish our nationhood, we have to reaffirm and reinforce periodically the values of the men who declared independence from Great Britain and framed the Constitution."

Being an American, then, as Wood suggests, is not something one is automatically born to, but something one enters into a commitment to *become* through a kind of ongoing Revolutionary struggle to protect the cause of liberty, for oneself and for all. This *being* American versus being *born* an American is thus a task that daily tests and tries our very souls, as we strive to honor on the battlefields of our daily lives those principles the revolutionaries fought and died for. This was something the Founders themselves realized, as early on they became preoccupied with being "civic-minded men of character" whose behavior was governed by these enlightened and classically republican ideals, values, and standards. Men like Washington and Adams sought to be, Wood continues, what Jefferson called "natural aristocrats," those who "measured their status not by birth or family that hereditary aristocrats from time immemorial had valued but by enlightened values and benevolent behavior."

As exalted as the ideals they strove to embody, so were the Founders greatly flawed, as I and many other thinkers have pointed out before. The democratic experiment they set in motion was marred from the start by slavery, the omission of women from power, and the oppression and genocide of the First Americans. Thus, part of their legacy was the unfinished business they left behind for future generations to take up and work through. But another, less discussed task they left undone was the *inner* work of democracy. What mattered most to men like Franklin, Adams, Jefferson, Madison, and Washington, writes Wood, were their public personae and not their private lives, which the founders believed should have nothing to do with how they lived on the stage of public life.

Here is where psychology has something to contribute. By shining a light into the darkened terrain of the human psyche, the psychological perspective illuminates those parts of ourselves that remain bonded and indentured to behaviors that prevent us from fully and freely living out the promise of democracy. As those who have been in depth kinds of therapy know, this inner exploration is not easy. It is work, to use Thomas Paine's words again, that, as we go up against the internalization of mindless social conventions, outworn habits, and learned prejudices, *tries men's souls*. But this inner work, I believe, could help to cultivate a more reflective and wiser kind of citizenship.

One of the ways the Founders proved genuinely interesting, in fact, was in their equal pursuit of both political activism and study and reflection. As George Washington came to realize in the later years of his life, outer power in the public world had its place, but in order to be truly democratic, it should be limited. Twice he lived this out through decisions that truly astounded. On December 23, 1783, General Washington resigned as Commander-in-Chief of the American forces, surrendering his sword to Congress and retiring to his farm. It was, he wrote, "his legacy." Washington's decision triggered an avalanche of awe throughout the Western world. Because it had been widely believed that Washington could have become king or dictator, his retirement from power, writes Wood, was "unprecedented in modern times." Washington was similarly reluctant to assume the Presidency. Finally coaxed into office, he resigned after a second term, shocking the world all over again. Indeed, writes Wood, Washington's most important act as president "was his giving up of office."

Washington's actions were influenced in part by the practice of "disinterestedness," a term the founders used for the concept of self-sacrifice, or, Wood writes, "being uninfluenced in one's actions by private profit or advantage." Thomas Jefferson and John Adams, too, as I have written, retired to their respective farms after their presidencies. Ensconced in their book-lined libraries, they studied the works of the Greek, Roman, and Enlightenment philosophers, and wrote and reflected on the historic undertaking they had been part of, and spent a great deal of time outside, in their fields and in nature. As I've written before, and as I write again, the physical courage and bravery that characterized the Revolution was only one half of our story; as remarkable was the Founders' reflective, adventuresome, and risk-taking minds.

In the following interviews, seven psychologists also reflect more broadly on the deeper myths and symbols of our unique democracy. Just as visitors to Washington, D.C., pay a visit to the monuments and memorials as a kind of contemplation of the nation's history and the principles that animate the body politic, so these psychologists, too, circumambulate the nation's myths, symbols, and ideals, examining the ways these principles animate and shape the psyches of America's citizens, and also where they have become tarnished and obscured with time.

In my first interview, Jungian analyst June Singer talks about America as the great "I am," unaware of its power drive, and offers images that inspire a truer vision of what it means to be American. Psychologist Mihaly Csikszentmihalyi elaborates on the idea of the "evolving self," expanding on American ideas of individualism as we prepare to meet the demands of a more environmental future. James Hillman poses the question, "What do you do with tragedy in America?" and talks about our denial of depression and our addiction to innocence. In our second interview, he muses on the soul of Washington, D.C., and the symbolism of the swamp, as well as the depression etched into Lincoln's face and that can be felt at the Vietnam Memorial.

In the next interview, psychotherapist Thomas Moore also reflects on the soul of the nation's capital, envisioning it as a place of religious pilgrimage. Then, in our second interview, Moore addresses America's narcissism, seeing in this symptom an opportunity for the country to deepen and ground its high-flying ideals in reality. Israeli Jungian analyst Erel Shalit contemplates America's core myth of the hero, recasting the hero for our times as one who possesses the courage to take up psychological work and face the shadows within. Finally, "American Jungian" Edward Edinger offers an inspiring meditation on America's great gift of multiculturalism, seeing in its fulfillment America's promise as the last, best hope of the world, and showing a way forward through the times that try men's souls. ■

Notes
1. Obituary of Commodore John Cassin: *Charleston, South Carolina Courier*, April 1, 1822.

—34—

The "Great I Am"

America's Mythic Blueprint

An Interview with June Singer, Ph.D.

JUNE SINGER WAS ONE of America's earliest, pioneer Jungian analysts. Her book *Boundaries of the Soul: The Practice of Jung's Psychology*, originally published in 1972, remains to this day a lasting classic on Jungian principles. The scholar and mythologist Joseph Campbell called it "certainly the very best introduction to Jung around." A founder of the C. G. Jung Institute of Chicago and of the Inter-Regional Society of Jungian Analysts, Singer practiced and taught for more than thirty years.

When I first approached Singer for an interview on the soul of America in 1994, I felt an immediate resonance with her unrushed, contemplative, and penetrating manner. Even as she spoke, she seemed to "see," as if she were directly engaging America as an individual. Our conversation took place at the end of her long career as an analyst, and an American life (her husband was a well-known minister) filled in equal measure with personal suffering and professional fulfillment. As befits a Jungian perspective, Singer's insights into her country's psyche were both analytical—where we were blocked and blind around injustices such as racism and inequality, and our insecurity—as well as inspiring and uplifting, or where we still possessed vision and hope. Her words also had a devotional quality, as if in addressing America this way she was speaking of something sacred.

Singer passed away in 2004 at the age of eighty-four; our interview was never published. But her insights into soul, the American psyche—its power drive and shadow side of greed and insecurity, as well as its better nature as a beacon of hope—and her poignant memories of viewing Jung's body in the hours after he died and the lesson she took from that have remained with me over the years.

✳

Pythia Peay: You are an American Jungian analyst whose work revolves around archetypes, myths, and dreams. I wonder if you could reflect on the soul of America?

June Singer: To begin, I think I should say what soul is, at least in my terms. Soul and psyche mean approximately the same thing; the word *psychology* comes from *psyche*. Soul is that part of us that mediates between the visible world of everyday practicality that is before our eyes, and the invisible world that we know in a deep, inner way, the dimension of mystery. When we neglect the soul, then life loses its meaning and purpose, and we begin to feel isolated and disconnected from the life force. It's as if the noise of the everyday world deafens us, and we can't hear the beautiful music of life, or take in the rewarding quiet and companionability of being with friends and family.

You could also say that soul is a kind of blueprint. So, for example, there is the "house" that is America, and then there is the invisible mythic blueprint upon which America was originally based. Part of that blueprint is the deep belief that those who were unable to express themselves, one way or another, came here in search of freedom and opportunity. At the same time, most of the African Americans came to America because they were forced to. Other immigrants also came to this country because they had nowhere else to go. So along with our idealism, which I like to associate with soul, we have to remember that there is another part of us which works against the soul, and that in Jungian terms is called "the shadow." This is the part of ourselves that is very real, but that we don't like to acknowledge.

PP: Such as the darker side of our origins as a country—including slavery, and the displacement and near-extinction of the American Indians?

JS: Right. If I had America on the couch, for example, I would say that our image of ourselves is that we think we are pretty good. America sees itself as the great "I Am" that thinks it is the best country in the world, that knows what's right for the world, and that is going to be responsible for fixing all the problems in the world. So another aspect of our shadow is that we are caught in a power drive, needing to control our own destiny and that of other nations. Beneath that power drive, however, is insecurity: more deeply than anything, we want security. In order to get security, we pile up wealth, and we use any means to do that. But if we were truly secure we wouldn't need to go to such extremes.

PP: What do you feel is behind America's insecurity?

JS: I think we find it hard to trust that we will be secure. It is a kind of vicious circle where our insecurity creates greedy, ambitious habits, and the feeling that there will never be enough. This is also a part of America's shadow. On one side, we have our ideals of generosity and inclusiveness; and on the other side, we have insecurity, which leads to greed and self-centeredness. Somehow, we have to recognize that giving in to the shadow is a short-term solution that makes things worse in the long run.

If I were speaking to America on my couch, for instance, I'd talk about faith, one of the qualities that Jung related to the soul.

PP: In what way does faith relate to the soul, or psyche, of America?

JS: Part of faith has to do with having trust in the natural process of life: to be able to accept what is, and not always try to improve it. What I mean most specifically is ecology and nature: trusting that it can grow and mature, with some guidance, but not exploitation, and accepting the will of God in nature. This works in psychology, too. There is in each of us a natural process of maturation and development; we have to be careful not to mess this up, and to have faith in the human spirit. We have to be like a good gardener who pulls up the weeds, and cultivates the plants that nourish.

PP: What does it mean to bring this kind of soulful perspective to citizenship?

JS: I think being a citizen implies a very deep and wise awareness of the world around us. I don't just mean our neighborhood, but our sensitivity to the total human community. Jung told us that we are living with something larger than ourselves, and that we need to give to it of our substance: our work, our labor, our awareness, and our sensitivity. An example of this would be the cathedral builders in the Middle Ages who didn't expect to see the results of their work in their lifetime. Yet they had the awareness that they were contributing to something that would survive long after they were gone.

PP: You're talking about linking up our personal lives with something more meaningful—that transpersonal dimension you mentioned earlier that co-exists with our daily lives.

JS: I am an old lady now. Let me share something very personal with you. I have no children; I had one daughter, who died. At first, I was devastated, crushed by this. But somehow I came to the realization that the world is my child, and that the people in prisons because of their political beliefs are my children (I am very devoted to Amnesty International),[1] and that the people that I work with in my practice are my children, though not in a personal sense. Over the years, I've worked with a lot of clients. Some have been successful; some have not. But the interesting thing is that in giving one gets so much back. Just to see people grow and develop, to see them accomplish things, and to know that you had a little part in helping, in turn helps me. Sometimes life deals you some pretty rotten blows. But the best healing is to be able to help others heal.

PP: In your years of experience as an analyst, have you noticed a recurring theme to your clients' issues?

JS: Many of my client's issues have to do with finding one's self, and with finding one's own meaning.

PP: Can you tell me something about your training as a Jungian analyst?

JS: I did my training in the early '60s, and have been an analyst since 1964. I didn't work directly with Jung, but was fortunate enough to have been trained by somebody who had worked with him, Liliane Frey-Rohn. But I was in Zürich when Jung died.

PP: That must have been an extraordinary moment. Can you tell me something of what you experienced?

JS: It was quite an experience. It was a stormy day. My analyst called. She told me that Jung had died, and that if I wanted to, I could go to his house in Küsnacht and spend some time there. And so I did. I recall walking up the long path to the entrance. At the end of the walkway, the front door stood open. I passed through this open door, over which Jung had carved in Latin the words *Vocatus atque non vocatus, Deus aderit*, or

"Called or not called, God will be there." A family member was waiting inside, and told me that I could go upstairs to Jung's bedroom. So I went up the stairs. At the top of the stairs was another open door, and through it I could see the flickering of candles.

I stood in the doorway, and saw Jung laid out in his bed in a white nightshirt. At that moment, something came to me. I saw that the candles were symbolic of Jung's work, and that it was my task, or anyone's task who chose to take it up, to take that candle and use that to light the candles of others. It just came to me as I was there, almost as a message. I've always followed the philosophy that there is plenty of light and that if we pass it on it does not diminish.

PP: As you're speaking, what comes to mind is the image of the Olympic torch that is passed from runner to runner, circling the globe.

JS: Well, the Olympic torch, as I understand it, is carried past the people, yet doesn't light other torches. But what if the runner could stop long enough to pass on the light, and people along the way could light their own candles from that torch?

PP: That's a beautiful image of Jung's legacy. In closing, I'd like to ask you one more question about America, and what you see as its soul potential.

JS: I believe that the best teaching is setting an example. If we are going to survive as a country, we will have to become a beacon. A beacon isn't aggressive, it's a light to be seen, like the Statue of Liberty with her torch. This is a very different image from the cowboy and the conqueror, and yet we need new images like that of the torch or the beacon to take us into the next century. ■

Notes
1. Amnesty International is a global movement of people fighting injustice and promoting human rights <http://www.amnestyusa.org/>.

—35—

New Visions of the American Self

An Interview with Mihaly Csikszentmihalyi, Ph.D.

A TALL, BURLY MAN WITH white hair and a beard, and a wide, engaging, open face, Mihaly Csikszentmihalyi looks exactly the part of a wise psychologist frequently called upon as a source of knowledge on happiness and creativity. The bestselling author of many books, and a lifelong scholar who has spent most of his life in academia, Csikszentmihalyi is most widely known for his work on "flow": that enhanced stream of consciousness people enter into when fully engaged in a complex, demanding project—whether painting, parenting, tinkering, or doing business—a kind of altered state in which the cares and concerns of the world fall away.

As he has noted in his popular TED talk (which at this writing has garnered two-and-a-half million views),[1] Csikszentmihalyi's lifelong immersion in the mysteries of creativity and contentment had its initial origins in suffering. When just a young boy in his native Hungary during World War II, he observed the anguish endured by his parents and other adults, and witnessed their inability to recover from the shock and trauma of war. This intimate, personal, first-hand encounter with the darker side of the human condition fueled in him a desire to discover the elusive substance that sustains humans during difficult times. Embarking on a quest, Csikszentmihalyi began studying art, philosophy, and religion. But it wasn't until a skiing holiday in Switzerland, when, as he recalls, he stumbled by chance into a lecture being given by C. G. Jung that he found the wellspring he'd been seeking: psychology.

After emigrating to the U.S. at the age of twenty-two, Csikszentmihalyi became a psychologist, then professor and chairman of the Department of Psychology at the University of Chicago. Currently, he is the distinguished professor of psychology and management at Claremont Graduate University. A member of the National Academy of Education and the National Academy of Leisure and Sciences, he is also the author of many books that have garnered widespread public attention, including his classic work, *Flow: The Psychology of Optimal Experience*. It was Csikszentmihalyi's book *The Evolving Self: A Psychology for the Third Millennium* that, in 1994, drew me to interview him.

As we explore in our conversation below, he mines that most bedrock of American ideas: the individual. In addressing the question of what exactly constitutes an individual, he reflects on whether our Enlightenment-based, American ideas of self-reliance can continue to sustain us as humanity advances further into the third millennium, with its rapidly emerging global culture and environmental pressures. What in the individual, for instance, will need to change and adapt to meet the greater needs of the planet? And how will this "evolving self" conflict with American ideals of individualism and independence? In his thought-provoking answers to these and other questions, Csikszentmihalyi reframes accepted American ideas around competition; redefines individuation as a process that takes place along a lifelong spiral of differentiation and integration; and revisions individuals more as "transcenders" than as self-encapsulated and self-driven. He also celebrates America's genius at multiculturalism, and finds inspiration in American classics such as *Adventures of Huckleberry Finn*. This interview was reviewed by Csikszentmihalyi in 2014.

Pythia Peay: In your book *The Evolving Self: A Psychology for the Third Millennium*, you write about the need for new ways to image the "self." Since the individual is one of the primary archetypes of America, I wanted to begin by asking you to reflect on American individualism.

Mihaly Csikszentmihalyi: When we look at the composition of America, we find a nation of people who had to break away from family, country, and tradition in order to move to a new place. So this means that there has been a tremendous process of natural selection at work. If you take any Central European or Vietnamese village, for example, the person who will end up in America will be the one who is able to break away with less pain from his roots. There may be other things involved, like chance or opportunity. But since the early Puritans, the people who've ended up in this country are those who are more individualistic to begin with.

PP: And what have been the effects of that process of natural selection?

MC: For one thing it means a more flexible group of people. If you look at individualism in terms of its effects on culture, America was essentially built to have interchangeable parts, whether human or mechanical. So although people are expected to be proud of their community and march in the local Fourth of July Parade, they're also expected to move when their jobs change locations. They're also taught to believe that there's always a better opportunity around the corner. These things encourage individualism, because Americans feel that they can survive anywhere.

PP: Whereas in other countries . . .

MC: Whereas in a highly industrialized country like Germany, for example, it's much harder to get a person to move from one town to another, even though the factory where they work has closed, or if there's an opening somewhere else. So it's not as obvious to the Germans that, in order to move somewhere for a better job, cutting ties with the place where you were born and raised and where your friends and family live is always the best thing to do. But in America, even if people start to think that they want community, they move to a place where they think they can *find* community, rather than looking for community where they are. For example, someone who lives in Chicago may decide that the city is too big and impersonal; so they decide to move to a town in Indiana or Montana, where they try to forge new loyalties or relationships. Whether that works out or not is an interesting question.

PP: Sometimes I think that if Americans could see the downside of our myths of individualism, it would be better for their mental health.

MC: Yes, I think that when self-reliance and self-focus become excessive, they can have negative consequences for the individual, and also at the social level of society. Obviously, there are many cultures where the opposite is true, and where people are so dependent on their social network, or friends and family, that they lack a sense of their own individualism. So the question becomes how to find a balance where, on one hand, you feel that you belong and have cherished social ties, but also have a strong sense of your own individuality. That would be most conducive to the kind of complexity that is potentially there when these two poles are in balance.

PP: On that topic, you also write about *differentiation*—a system, like a family or an individual, composed of different parts—and *integration*, or a system where all the different parts communicate and enhance each other. Would you say that as a country we're more differentiated, and that in order to find balance we need to cultivate the skills of integration?

MC: That's right. There are many ways where this could be implemented on a larger cultural scale, from transportation, to technology, to the legal system. Right now, everything contributes to either exacerbating individualism or helping integration.

For example, in this country we have inheritance laws, which work to protect the material interests that keep families together. But children often don't believe that their parents could even be that much use to them, either in a materialistic sense or in being a source of knowledge and wisdom. The other thing that works against integration is the way families live in single, unattached family dwellings. Neighborhoods and suburbs contribute by either making it harder or easier to feel that we belong to a family, or to a group.

PP: So are you saying that the nuclear family reinforces the individualism that runs through American society?

MC: In one sense it does, because it allows a person to feel that they have a group they belong to. So it satisfies some of the need we have to feel that we aren't alone. At the same time, in most nuclear families, there isn't that much tradition, or even extended family. The important value that comes from belonging to a large social unit is that one has to partly submit oneself to a group or entity, so that life isn't solely about calculated individual decisions. Even if something might not be in a person's best interests—like recycling—it might be in the best interests of the larger group or country.

So the problem that can arise is that, without more integration, society will break down into little enclaves, which isn't connected by anything commonly binding.

PP: You also write about developing a "self" that's a conscious contributor to evolution; or the idea of building one's self around larger, more transcendent themes. That would seem to advance the idea of American individualism, which initially was dedicated to these larger principles of freedom and democracy, but now seems to have degenerated into something much more narrow.

MC: I think it's important for people to begin to see themselves as part of a larger pattern. For example, there's a pond on my property. Every night the beavers keep damming it up, flooding the access road and causing it to wash out. So the question is: Who has precedence? For the beavers, building their dam is a matter of life and death. On the other hand, every morning we have to dismantle the dam. Some neighbors just tell us to shoot the beavers. It seems like the obvious solution, but it's still very difficult to do. This is a very simple example, but it illustrates the need we have to search for ways of handling different needs and competing interests,without literally shooting from the hip to fix problems.

To begin to do this on a larger scale, I think we'll have to change the way we look at history, the making of history, and more importantly, how we shape the consciousness of our children, because the old ways of learning and thinking about life are no longer adequate to our time.

PP: Is this what you mean by the need for self-reflection and the development of an "evolutionary self" or "ecological self"? And how would we begin to train children to develop that way?

MC: I think we have to begin teaching children interdependent, systems thinking. This means showing them more precisely what happens when one part of the system changes, and how it influences the rest of the system. For example, what happens to a family when the father becomes unemployed, or what happens to a seal when it's introduced to chemicals? Or what are the unintended consequences of a certain course of action? Children need to be taught that they can't understand things in isolation from the rest of a system: for instance, how do math, English, biology, geography, and the social sciences all relate to each other? What I'm talking about is the need to educate our children in how to be a living human being related to everything else.

PP: I'm also fascinated by your call for us to develop new images of the self for the future. You say that our traditional image of the self is based on the human body. So our internal "self-image" might be similar to that of a "traffic cop" or a "little human being" directing consciousness. Instead, you say that a better image of the "self" for the future is more of an "overtone" or a "harmonic" of consciousness. Can you say more about that?

MC: That image of the overtone or harmonic is essentially my understanding of how neuroscientists understand the evolution of consciousness. We all need an information processing system to create some kind of order out of the disparate pieces of sensory input coming at us. The bits of incoming information that a person selects to pay the most attention to then becomes the central organizing principle of their own awareness and inner experience. The self-image of some people, for instance, will be focused on those things that are immediately to their own advantage—and everything else will become irrelevant. On the other hand, there are others for whom the self is organized around the notion that to feel good or to have integrity, they need to feel that everybody around them is happy, satisfied, or content. They can't experience inner harmony, in other words, unless there is harmony around them. That person might become a kind of Mother Teresa who struggles to help those who are suffering.

So those are two extremes of self-images, and there are many others. But I believe that in our time, if we don't begin to include the needs of other people and spiritual perspectives into our idea of selfhood, then the country is going to continue along the path of fragmented individualism. Extreme individualism prohibits us from thinking of other things that aren't part of us. That kind of narrow individualism forestalls evolution, because it truncates the development of a more integrated and complex identity.

PP: You also write that "competition is the thread that runs through evolution." But then you go on to say that species survive because they've found ways to improve their chances of survival through cooperation. Competitiveness is certainly an all-American trait and wedded to our idea of individualism. Can you say more about where we fall as a culture on that spectrum between competitiveness and cooperation?

MC: There is no question that a lot of great achievements are accomplished by people who are trying to beat someone else; so I wouldn't want to go so far as to say that all competition is bad. But in fact, the Latin word *competere* means to seek together. The idea behind the Olympic Games was that athletes couldn't really tell how fast they were running unless they matched themselves against someone else. So the feedback we get from trying to match someone else is important in giving us the limits of our performance, and what we can do. That is a very different notion than trying to beat the other guy out.

PP: So even when we're competing with someone, we're still in a relationship with them?

MC: At its best, competition is a kind of synergistic system in which participants learn what they're capable of doing. It sounds ridiculous, because we've gotten so far from the original meaning of competition, but actually there are still situations where the winner and loser are almost equally happy with what happened.

It's a bit like after the Indians killed an animal: they would pray to it, make a ritual offering, and apologize for having to hunt it down. It was understood that the Indians needed to have the meat of the animal to support their family, yet they were still thankful to the animal, and prayed that the spirit of the animal had a better life. Those seemingly "primitive" kinds of relationships had more ecological consciousness than we do today. They may have lacked other kinds of knowledge, but they understood the mutual interdependence of life—and that kind of knowledge will be necessary in the future.

PP: In terms of individual development, you talk about people becoming "transcenders." I know that in some schools of psychology the goal of development is separation and individuation. But this seems to be adding another level of development.

MC: Increasingly, current notions of the life cycle see human development as culminating in individuation. Now development is seen to take place along a spiral: we have to differentiate from our mother as infants, and learn that we are separate organisms. But then almost immediately we have to reintegrate ourselves, understanding that we are dependent, and that there is a bond between us and our caretaker, or mother or father. This is followed by another new spurt of individuation, which is followed by another spurt of reintegration. So it's a dialectic of development that moves in a spiral, alternating between feeling that we have to do things on our own—developing our skills, and finding ways to satisfy our own needs and interests—but also realizing that this development takes place within the context of relationship.

This alternation takes place forever! The question of what comes last is moot. At the end, both differentiation and integration will be together, because the two are so merged in a process that they're inseparable. So when we think of someone who is a "transcender," that person is both absolutely individuated, and at the same time they are part of the web of life. In this kind of complex consciousness, both individuation *and* integration are equally developed.

PP: You describe a stage of development where one's own personal needs are not as important as being devoted to a higher ideal, or giving back to humanity. Is that also part of being a "transcender"?

MC: That's quite common for that type of person, because they identify with something that takes precedence over their own needs. What is sad to me is that the need to feel part of something greater and more enduring than our personal needs gets such short shrift in American culture.

PP: So building a life around helping the world to become a better place—knowing that we're doing something to contribute to evolution—is a way to find meaning in life?

MC: In the past, a person could feel good if they had a family and fulfilled the expectations of their community, or if they were a good member of their particular faith. Those basic things can still make us feel good. But what's needed now in the way of making people feel more deeply satisfied as a human being is finding something that will give them a sense of connection to the larger world.

PP: Given how big, fragmented, and diverse America is, connecting to something larger than one's own individual self and world can be difficult to do.

MC: I'm not sure intellectual reasoning alone will be enough. The only force capable of changing society would be the rise of a new myth, something more emotionally charged. So far, myths have operated in all of humankind's great changes.

PP: For example?

MC: Marxism was the myth of the overthrow of capitalism and the rise of a classless society. Hundreds of millions of people around the world were affected by Karl Marx's vision of a kind of Utopia. Before Marx, other ideologies that influenced cultures had a more spiritual, emotional basis: a supernatural being such as Mohammed or Christ, for instance, who proclaimed the truth. So this gives you an idea of what we might need in our culture to bring about a great transformation.

For a long time I've thought that the best way to achieve some sort of integrated purpose across the whole planet would be to plant some spaceships in a jungle somewhere in Africa, with a message from a civilization warning us of their plans to invade the Earth in twenty years. Maybe that would mobilize people to come together around a common goal!

PP: I think it's a great idea to bring up, because just thinking about another race landing on our planet jolts us awake to the level of intervention that's needed for some kind of planetary awakening.

MC: We don't realize that we're all in this human experience on the planet together, and that we have to find some way of preventing ourselves from destroying the whole thing. But the problem is that we are all so steeped in parochial history that we don't see the need for uniting in a meaningful way around husbanding and developing our resources, which would be such a beautiful outcome.

PP: I wonder if some of our American ideals could be put to work to advance the planetary evolution you're describing. We were the first country to be founded on ideals, rather then ties to land or race. You've said, for example, that we are one of the first countries in history to value the idea of multiculturalism.

MC: Yes, it's always seemed strange to me that there's been so much "beating of breasts" in America about not being sensitive enough or appreciative enough of other cultures. It seems to me that we're so far ahead of other cultures in that respect that it's almost parochial to think badly of ourselves. It doesn't mean that we shouldn't do more, but, on the other hand, it's very difficult to move out of one's own values, morals, habits, and loyalties to appreciate other cultures for what they are.

PP: So, in an historical sense, seeing value in other cultures represents a major paradigm shift?

MC: Yes. The general attitude has always been that one way of doing things is always the right way. We talk about America's melting pot, for example, as a symbol of how we've been put together from so many different sources. So the melting pot assumes that there was no great advantage in being any specific culture. It was assumed that wherever a person came from, they could turn into an American once they'd arrived. At the same time, anthropologists like Margaret Mead at the beginning of the twentieth century developed an ideology of multiculturalism: the notion that every culture is equally valid to that of another culture. So it seems to me that the combination of these two things made it possible for the flowering of America's multicultural society.

PP: So are you saying that we might do well to take more pride in our accomplishments in multiculturalism—seeing it as something that contributes to humanity's evolution in a better direction?

MC: Yes. Rather than realizing that what we have is an immensely difficult but important achievement, we tend to believe that multiculturalism is natural—so if we're not perfect at it, we think we've somehow failed. You know the homey image of the "glass half full, glass half empty"? I have a more pessimistic attitude toward the image (which is actually more optimistic): I don't expect there to be any water anywhere. So when there actually *is* a little bit of water, I'm overjoyed! I think this is a good perspective to have as Americans, because in a way we've been spoiled. The one danger that I see in this culture is that people are born expecting that they have the right not only to freedom and happiness, but also to health and wealth—so any little "fly in the ointment" makes us feel discouraged, as if we're not getting our due.

In reality, however, life never provides a guarantee to anyone, ever. So while the kind of life we have is a tremendous improvement over anything that has come before, it's important to cultivate the feeling of gratefulness for what we do have, instead of feeling that if we don't have everything we expected, of if we haven't perfectly fulfilled our ideals as a democracy, we've somehow been betrayed.

PP: Besides the melting pot and multiculturalism, what other myths or archetypes come to mind that describe or capture America?

MC: I think immediately of the frontier archetypes that literary critics point to: Mark Twain's Huckleberry Finn or James Fenimore Cooper's *Last of the Mohicans*. I think also of the archetype of the immigrant from another country who arrives here and thrives in this kind of climate. It's interesting to reflect on what other cultures see when they look at America: a country where people are not as shackled by traditions and institutions, and where they are free to act on their own initiative and develop their ingenuity. I think those are the reasons why America is really looked up to, and why it has this powerful, positive aura: not because of our wealth or power—in fact, these are the parts of America that are often ridiculed in other countries—but for our respect for personal freedom and the ability to live one's own life. So the archetypes that represent independence and freedom are quite powerful to me.

PP: So the underlying conditions that *create* wealth and power, not those things themselves, are what other peoples respect about our country?

MC: Yes, that's true. Wealth and power are obviously things that people would like to have; other countries are envious of that, but they also see the downside—that when we are wealthy and powerful we can become bloated, despondent, and isolated. So it's the uniqueness of the freedom and independence that is of the most historic importance, and what people appreciate.

PP: In *The Evolving Self*, you write about the "three veils of Maya"—an ancient Hindu term to describe the fact that "what we see, think, and believe" is not always the truth. You say that it's an attitude that must be stripped away before we come to a true sense of self. You also say that our conditions of freedom and democracy make it easier for us to go through that process. Can you say more about that?

MC: Our cultural conditions of freedom and democracy are an important reason why the social sciences have flourished here. It's much easier to examine and to go beyond one's own "cultural veil," or cultural identity, in this country than it is in those countries where habits are more ingrained. In this way, America shares something with the ancient Greeks. Like us, they lived in a culture based on commerce; they were also exposed to many different cultural traditions. Out of that, the Greeks developed the ability to distance themselves from their environment and to cultivate a sense of philosophical detachment and observation. Perhaps hundreds of years from now, civilizations in the future will look back on America, and say that we were able to see beyond these illusory veils of life into what is more permanent and that unites us all. ∎

Notes

1. You can watch his talk at <https://www.ted.com/talks/mihaly_csikszentmihalyi_on_flow>.

—36—

What Do You Do with Tragedy and Depression in America?

An Interview with James Hillman, Ph.D.

J AMES HILLMAN, WHO DIED in 2011 (and who was first introduced in Part V) left behind a rich legacy of his discoveries into the interior world of the human psyche, as well as the "world soul," or the dimension of depth to be found in the outer world. A man of many passions and pursuits, he was also a man of many titles: among them culture critic, founder of Archetypal Psychology, and author of more than twenty books, including the bestselling *The Soul's Code: In Search of Character and Calling.* One of the modern era's most original thinkers, he was hailed by some as the most important psychologist since William James.[1]

As I mentioned earlier in this book, I count myself fortunate to have had the privilege of interviewing Hillman multiple times over two decades. Blunt-spoken and gruff with an electric personality that could both shock and enlighten, Hillman could also be delightfully warm, charming, witty, and funny. A kind of philosopher-psychologist, with a mind that was something to behold, he was deeply preoccupied with the human condition. For most who knew him, Hillman will be primarily remembered for two things: his groundbreaking ideas on the psyche and culture, and the remarkable force of character with which he both lived and delivered those ideas.

Though Hillman's body of work spanned a variety of topics—war, psychology, dreams, the Gods and Goddesses of the classical world, power, suicide, animals, character, and destiny—his opus centered on one thing: that invisible force the ancients called *soul.* In his essay "Peaks and Vales," collected in the edited volume *Puer Papers*, Hillman defined soul as the opposing pole to the transcendent heights of the spirit. Earthly existence, sadness and depression, the pull of memory and the drag of the past, sleep and dreams and the iconography of images and archetypes all fell within the soul's province.

Soul, or psyche, as Hillman pointed out, is also to be found in the material stuff and things of this world, from buildings, to food and nature, as well as our personal "case histories": the joys and tragedies of love, the failures and successes, fears, conflicts, and neuroses that form the basis of therapy. According to Hillman, these case histories also involve us "in history . . . our individual case history, the history of our therapy, our culture as history." In fact, it was from Hillman that I first learned that my psychological complexes had much deeper roots in history and culture than I'd ever imagined— and that in addition to people's inner lives, therapy could also be applied to political problems, countries, and cultures.

Hillman himself was profoundly shaped by America. Though he studied and lived abroad for more than thirty years before returning to the states in the 1960s, he maintained an abiding fascination for politics and the psychology of the American psyche—especially its underbelly of depression. When I first began this project in 1994, Hillman's was among the first interviews I scheduled. Our conversation took place that fall, on a crisp day in New York City, in the offices of the Canadian Broadcasting Corporation (CBC), where Hillman had just finished an interview with a broadcast journalist on the topic of depression.

In the following wide-ranging interview that resulted from that conversation, Hillman addresses America's discomfort with depression and its repression of tragedy, our "hugeness complex," and his strong dislike for the then-current movie *Forrest Gump* and how it represents our "deep, deep, deep addiction to innocence." Conventional therapy, Hillman believed, isolated people's problems within the consulting room, rather than in the wider culture. He even once famously said that people should stop meditating, as it distracted them from attending to the world's problems. The following dialogue bridges the ever-widening gap between the personal and the political, allowing others to cross over into a deeper understanding of the American psyche, and its mythic power and global reach.

✳

Pythia Peay: When I first called to set up this interview, you felt strongly that you'd like to speak about depression. So many people suffer from depression: I'm curious how, or if, you think the larger American culture contributes to this growing epidemic.

James Hillman: Let's start with the fact that we're clearly a manic nation. We wouldn't have to go far to prove that. All we have to do is watch the cars burning up on television, the hyperactive kids, and the pace of everything: everybody flying around! On television now we can have a split screen, so we can watch two things at once. So depression just doesn't fit in. It's a real no-no. The general attitude is that it's got to be stopped.

PP: So what are some of the ways America tries to stop depression from "getting in"?

JH: Right now as a nation—I'm speaking psychologically now—a breakdown is going on. And what usually happens in a breakdown is that a person goes more and more into denial, and more and more into a manic defense. That's why they call it a "manic defense against the breakdown." So as a culture we turn to drugs like Prozac, Zoloft, speed, uppers, amphetamines, or any other drugs we can get, just so we can keep it all going and hold it all together. We stop depression by trying to cheer each other up, or by turning to other defenses like shopping and consumerism, or entertainment that speeds up our manic defense. Or we dedicate ourselves to "high performance" at home and at work, and to aerobics and running in marathons. That's the point of view the culture takes toward depression.

So if depression were a figure, how would he get into the culture? There seems to be no way, except through individual suffering and pain. The major complaint that shows up in the clinician's office today—whether it's a clergyman, physician, or psychotherapist—is depression. The amount of depression is enormous.

PP: So you're actually making the radical point that depression *should* be brought into the culture, which in itself is a statement many would find surprising because, as you point out, the whole idea is to get rid of it.

JH: That's right. And the moment we buy into the notion of getting rid of depression, we've been bought by manic civilization. It means that we've become consumers, and that our fundamental value is to keep going, to not slow down, or to realize, reflect, look back, or sympathize with what's happening to the fish, the trees, and

486

the rivers. All of that goes with depression. And those are not high values in our culture.

PP: In fact, you've been critical of the fact that even within psychology, most therapy focuses on what's going on inside the person, and not in the culture outside them.

JH: But what is going on in the outside world is coming into us anyway through depression. I try to say that if a person isn't depressed, they're sick and mentally ill, because they're out of touch with what's going on in the world. That means destruction, pollution, toxicity, and the homeless and undernourished children in America. But doesn't the soul know all that?

PP: You're saying the soul does in fact know that.

JH: The soul does know that, and it says it through depression.

PP: But I've known people who have been crippled by depression. I've had my own depressed days.

JH: That's not depression, that's just a bad hair day.

PP: I wouldn't say that! I had a period of years where I felt depressed, but they were valuable to me. I'd always been struck by Jung's phrase that depression comes from the Latin *deprimere*, or to press down. So perhaps my depression was a bit easier to handle because I had that orientation and because I'm a writer; but I also know people for whom that would be impossible to do. I was also never bedridden, or so handicapped by depression that I couldn't go out of the house.

JH: Like most people, when we talk about depression, we usually talk about those who are in really terrible shape. But that isn't the general condition: the general depression is your sort, and my sort. We've both had times when we couldn't answer the phone, and hidden it under the laundry so we couldn't hear it ring, or even enjoyed getting "down and dirty." It's a funny thing with depression: letting it all go and beginning to smell; or feeling ugly, or not being up for all the demands of life. These are almost ritual things around depression, which conventional therapy calls self-destructive or a loss of self-esteem. But if you look at it another way, these are also the rituals of what Robert Bly calls "getting into the ashes" or "getting into the shit." In alchemy, those are necessary pieces of inner work.

PP: But this way of thinking about depression is so far from mainstream attitudes, people might not even know what you're talking about.

JH: Our difficulty is that we don't have any rituals for this kind of inner work; we don't have any meaningful background for those states of the soul in our culture. There's no way in which depression is honored or understood in individuals or in collective rites, except for some Catholic rituals like Good Friday, or Jewish rituals on the Day of Atonement.

So there's little place for grieving, or for deep misery in the wider culture. Think of the mourning for the Vietnam War that has yet to be done. All those vets came back and they were invisible. There's been no accountability for all the soldiers who were killed, or the policies that led to Vietnam. No one was ever fired or held accountable for the wrongs that were done.

PP: No day of reckoning for those in power.

JH: Right. No public humiliation; no public figure admitting "I sinned," and who could carry the burden of shame. So all of that is thrown onto ordinary individuals—and that's psychiatrically disastrous. That's why I believe some elements of the recovery movement have been important. It's still limited, because it's all about the individual; but it's important because they're attempts at ritualizing the tragedies that people go through in a society that doesn't really help them.

PP: I've been reading your essay called "Senex and Puer," or the archetypes of the old man and the young boy. Would you say that we're a *puer* or more youthful culture?

JH: No, I think we're a very complicated culture. Or perhaps I'd rather say we're more a "Christian heroic" culture, in the sense of trying to be redemptive, always doing good, and spreading the word of God the missionary way. For example, the way we go to places like Somalia and Haiti in order to do good things.[2] That's the myth of America.

PP: Is that not a good myth to have?

JH: I don't know; I don't want to judge that. But the downside of this Christian heroic culture is depression. The early Christians, for example, were called "athletes of God," so they were out in the world doing good things.

PP: So you're not making a value judgment—just pointing out the side effects of that myth.

JH: Right. It's a myth that contributes to the way we "fight" depression and try to get rid of it.

PP: What do you think of Prozac and other antidepressants in treating depression?

JH: I think that there's a kind of moral dilemma around taking antidepressants: we know that it's producing people who can go on being good shoppers. We know that Prozac helps people adapt to a society that creates extroverted "go get 'em" people. So there are two parts to antidepressants that are troubling: one is that it locates depression in the body, as something that's going on with serotonin and our synapses. Secondly, it makes depression the individual's problem.

PP: Then where is depression really located, and whose problem is it?

JH: I don't think it's located in an individual's body; I think depression is part of the body politic. The individual is just a symptom of the larger body politic, and of our manic culture. So it's not in the body, and it's doesn't belong to the individual: it's social, collective, and psychological, in Jung's sense of the collective unconscious. Again, where can depression go? It's banned from the culture. There are no rites or temples to Saturn, the God of depression.[3]

PP: Trying to make people aware of the collective American culture and how it's impacting them psychologically is just what I'm trying to do with this book. I don't want to look for solutions, but I do want to look for ways we can begin to deepen our understanding around depression.

JH: I understand what you're wrestling with. You don't want to come up with a solution, but you want to come up with *something*. That's our American heroic thing. And if I give you an answer, then I've fallen prey to that way out. And I don't want to do that! I don't want to say there is or there isn't a solution: I don't even want to entertain that kind of question because then we're not sticking to the real question.

PP: Which is?

JH: Which is "What does the depression want?"—not "What do *I* want?" That's basic Jungian thinking: What does the symptom want? What does the dream want? What does the depression want? Now I know what *I* want. *I* don't want to be depressed. *I* want to earn money and run around and have a good time and have lots of libido and energy, and not be constipated, and have light feet: all those things that go with not being depressed. So I know what *I* want, but what does the depression want?

PP: So, what *does* it want?

JH: What is the depression trying to do? That's the big question. Well, it's trying to slow me down. It's trying to opt me out of the pressures of something I can't do, and that raises terrible fears of poverty and loneliness. But what else is it trying to do to me? Does it make me notice beauty? Does it make me feel certain things that I haven't felt? Does it make me feel like an exile? Not just loneliness—but *exile*. Where do I belong, and where am I? So that's a Jungian reading of depression that everything is in a sense purposeful. So the idea is to read the symptom purposefully.

PP: It's interesting that you say depression can make someone feel like an exile. It's like that feeling we all have sometimes of being a stranger in our own land.

JH: Or a stranger in some philosophical way. Part of depression forces us to think philosophically. What am I doing here? Why am I alive? What is life about? Why do I suddenly have so much time, as if I have all the time in the world? In fact, all this time is killing me.

PP: So an elongated, never-ending sense of time is part of depression?

JH: Yes, that's part of it. It's not pleasant. I just did a commentary on a documentary for the BBC called *Kind of Blue*. There were about three or four seriously depressed people in it; I could see it in their eyes. The reason I mention this is because the people in the film were all able to express profound thoughts and feelings. They revealed a dimension of life that I call melancholy. *Depression*, in fact, is the secular word for melancholy; it's melancholy without the Gods.

Melancholy deepens depression towards more profound, impersonal things: Gods, art, music, beauty, religion, spirit, soul—all those deeper things. There's even an aspect of nature that's depressed; we can feel it in the trees in the winter, without leaves. So depression is a season of the year. Japanese poetry expresses that beautifully—brooding, exile, loneliness, and death. All these things give a different angle to depression.

PP: Does depression, I wonder, make us more aware of something else you've spoken about: the "inner community" existing inside each person? And perhaps you could explain more exactly what you mean by that.

JH: We're all living with what I call "the invisibles." The relationship with the invisibles is very important in therapy, because most of us don't know the other people that we live with, or listen to the voices in the other rooms of our psychological house.

When someone is thrown back on their own in extreme cases, for instance, like people who sail around the world alone, or who go to the Arctic to do research, or who climb mountains—again and again, they have invisible companions. So when it's quiet, the people in the other rooms of the house appear. Children have these invisible companions between five and ten years old; but statistics show that they lose touch with these companions as they get older, and when the ego takes over. But I think that when we cohabit with the people of this inner community, we're more like the archaic tribal peoples who live with the invisibles.

PP: Can you give me some guidelines or guidance for dialoging with these invisibles?

JH: For example, there are the warnings we pick up. We go to a party and we meet someone new, but for some reason we don't like them, and we have a feeling that we'd better watch what we say, and we don't want to get too close. Where does that intuition come from?

PP: I don't know. Where does that come from?

JH: Socrates had a *daimon* who told him what to do and what not to do. We still have those guardian angels.

PP: Guardian angels have really come into American culture right now. It's been phenomenal. It's something that everybody can relate to. I've done several stories on it. I can talk to a New Age person, a Fundamentalist, an agnostic, and everybody relates to angels.

JH: That's good. That's better than nothing. But the danger is literalism: that is, the guardian angel told me to jump out the window. Or the guardian angel told me to join this cult and make poison. Literalism is still one of the big problems—and that's American.

PP: Can you say more of what you mean by that?

JH: America is not a place; it's a religious belief. We believe in America, but we don't live in it. We vote for someone because we believe in that person. We buy toothpaste because we believe in the brand. We're a very weird country: so when a voice says something, we believe it!

PP: So there's meaning to the toothpaste we buy?

JH: No, it's just that we trust it, and have faith in it, and it's good, so we can believe in it. But on the other side of belief is this terrible cynicism. Everybody's a fake—

PP: And all our heroes have feet of clay.

JH: It's because we *believe* in them. If we didn't believe in them, we wouldn't get into these dilemmas. If we could get rid of these Christian virtues—belief, hope, salvation, virtue, and redemption—we'd be a lot better off. We don't see the mean, even fascistic, shadow of the person or the politician promoting these virtues.

PP: I was very intrigued by the idea that you have of "reading history backwards" or reading "the image in the heart" as a way of finding one's individual calling. Is that something that we could do with America?

JH: You mean, could we discover the image in the heart of the nation that appears again and again? I do think it's the religious. I really do. America was founded by religious nuts—the Puritans—and all the people who came afterward to escape religious persecution. They came with faith, belief, and hope. These are tremendous American virtues that dominate America.

PP: But you've just been very critical of these virtues.

JH: Yes, because of the naiveté that goes with them. Because they're all wrapped up with Christianisms, or "Forrest Gumpisms."

PP: Tell me about that movie. I haven't seen it, but something tells me I'm not going to like it.

JH: Can we be very modern and talk about a movie that neither of us have seen? I know people who have seen it, and I've read the reviews. I think it's a film that is the epitome of our belief system: the best thing that someone can be is innocent and stupid. And if they can stay innocent and stupid, they can survive. In addition to that, the message goes, your dreams will come true, and you can erase the tragedy of history. This is also going on in *Forrest Gump*: the Holocaust, Vietnam, all the other wars and everything else that has happened over the course of our history is trivialized in this movie. I think this is terribly serious.

PP: I couldn't agree more. Although most people I know view it as a movie that's about overcoming obstacles, and the American dream that no matter what your limitations are you can achieve your goals. But something about it just felt off; maybe you can tell me why.

JH: Because it's about the worship of innocence, which is our deep, deep, deep Christian myth: we don't want to know. We're anti-intellectual. We believe in the natural child who was "born in a shoebox," but who grew up to become the head of General Motors. Nothing really matters, as long as you're good. It's very un-European, un-Chinese, un-everything. We understand that leaders in other countries might have sex with their secretaries, or conduct shady financial dealings on their way up to power. But we expect our presidents to be innocent, because we want Forrest Gump to be president. Really: a man without sin!

PP: And a man without sin is someone who hasn't really lived; he's done nothing.

JH: But he's "been there." That innocence is what I've been fighting for years and years and years. That's what I mean by America being a "religion." We worship innocence. Our problem with cities, for instance, stems from the way we see them as corrupt, bad places. Going all the way back to 1799, the first novels by Americans have the country boy as the hero who goes to the city, where he gets corrupted by money, sin, women, disease, and drinking.

We have a lot of trouble just sitting in the shadow, and so it just piles up. We think the tragedy of Vietnam will go away when all the veterans are dead, or that we won't suffer the burdens of that war anymore, which is absolute nonsense because we're still suffering the Civil War and all the veterans of *that* war are dead. We're still suffering the destruction of the American Indians. Vietnam will fester forever because we haven't done any of the acknowledgments and rituals of sin, of grief, of wrongness, and of tragedy.

So what do you do with tragedy in America, that deep question that was so important to the Greeks and to the Elizabethans, and which was the foundation of their high level of culture? Where does it fit? How do we deal with tragedy?

PP: I can't see that we do. In some ways, we're continuously trying to redeem or mitigate the consequences of tragedy.

JH: That's what I mean about the country being a land of religion, or faith or a belief system. I think we suffer tragedy terribly in our personal lives, and then attempt to take it to Jesus or drink it away.

PP: Is that because people have lost their connection to the greater tragedies unfolding in the world around them?

JH: I never know why anything is. But tragedy is certainly a huge American question.

There's an enormous tragedy in America today with the children that are hungry and badly cared for. It's an overwhelming tragedy that so many children are on welfare relief.

PP: And yet at some level, that's not felt. The Russian culture has many flaws, but one thing that's often said is that the "Russian soul loves to suffer." They've been described as more complex psychologically because of their capacity to suffer, but we seem to lack that.

JH: That's absolutely right.

PP: Is this innocence and naiveté in the American character something that could change with time, over the centuries?

JH: It may not. I don't look at change. We have to work our character for what it can do, and realize that our tragedy is that we are missing certain things. I'm not therapeutic in the sense that all these things are going to get better, or that we can do something about it. I think it's very important to see what is. What you're thinking about what to do is already American. You want to fix it! But I'm not "thinking American."

PP: It's just built in; apparently I can't help it!

JH: In America we think one of two ways. We think either, "How did this happen?" Meaning, what is the cause, what are the origins of something? And the second thing is, "What are you taking for it?" Anybody who walks into a room and says that their ankle is swollen, or that they have a sinus problem, the first sentence is, "What are you taking for it?" or in other words, "How are you fixing it?" Well, there's no Eros, or genuine feeling or connectedness, in that at all.

PP: But if you had a headache and suffered through it without taking anything for it, wouldn't that be masochistic?

JH: It doesn't mean that you have to walk around with unbandaged wounds. But it does mean that the first thought shouldn't be how to fix it. Now, that's an American virtue. But we have to see the shadow of that virtue. It isn't that we should change it, but [recognize] that there's a shadow to it. We can fix all kinds of things; we're an amazing people that way. But we also don't realize that not everything in the world needs to be fixed.

PP: So that things within the psyche . . .

JH: Need to be *felt* first of all. And seen, watched, and noticed. And, the Russians would say, enjoyed.

PP: To return to the image in the soul and America's calling: Is there something deeper at work in the phrase "manifest destiny" that's not about acquiring more territory, but about manifesting a certain purpose?

JH: Well, to the rest of the world America has always held that image of the "city on the hill": the New Jerusalem, Zion, or the Promised Land that immigrants have to cross the water to get to. That is the image of the deep vision in the soul of America. Not just the earthly paradise of finding gold in the streets, but the myths that America still holds around the world for people who set out on a raft from Cuba; or who smuggle themselves into the hold of a Chinese steamer and spend twenty days with rats to get to New York.

At the same time, there is within the American soul this constant feeling of bitterness, of being really pissed off because once immigrants arrive here, they find that it isn't the Promised Land of their dreams. What they don't realize is that this myth is filled with expectancy, and not just of economic success. Why do blue-collar and poor people, for example, vote for legislation and politicians that are unfair to them and that favor the rich?

PP: What is your thinking on that phenomenon?

JH: Because politicians like Reagan, for instance, hold out that vision of the Promised Land—where America isn't just an ordinary garden, but Paradise, and where we can all be redeemed and freed of sin. Still, this image in the heart of America as the "city on the hill" carries great power. It's why we're liberators and it's why we're amazing to other people.

PP: I was in a hotel recently having a drink with a friend. Our waitress was from Ethiopia, and she poured her heart out to us, saying repeatedly that we didn't know what a wonderful country we had. She said, "You have such heart. Your hearts are wonderful." I was deeply touched by her words.

JH: I've heard that so often. And it's true. That's why American foreign policy going back to [Woodrow] Wilson has been driven by two motives: power and morality. Either we go into other countries out of pure self-interest, or we go out of moral concern, which is always half of why we do anything. Americans never really want to do anything unless it has a moral dimension to it.

PP: Is this the Puritan in us?

JH: I don't know if it's just the Puritan; it's the ideal of a creation on this Earth of a religious nation, a City of God.

PP: But we don't consciously think of ourselves that way. No one I know goes around thinking that America is a "City of God."

JH: But I believe it's the unconscious motive behind everything we do, such as urban renewal. I recently read that William O. Douglas wrote the decision of the Supreme Court for urban renewal.[4] He was a tremendous idealist. He loved nature and climbed mountains. When we read his words, we can see that he was an extraordinary man. But he's the one who ruined our cities with his particular idea of urban renewal. It was an idealistic vision of creating the right sort of "Paradise." But Douglas didn't understand cities; he didn't even like alleys.

PP: This brings me to what you've described as America's "hugeness complex." Because doing things on a big scale is certainly American: urban sprawl, pollution, superhighways, super-malls, mega-millions, McMansions, Big Macs, and so on. Do you think our collective depression is a natural compensation to all this continual expansion and hugeness?

JH: America's hugeness complex is part of its dedication to mania as a defense against depression that we were talking about earlier. Psychiatrically, a manic condition is a state in which a person has unbounded energy and a flight of ideas; everything is speeded up. If you try to put limits on someone with mania—if you interrupt them, confine them or try to stop them from what they're doing—they can fly into a manic rage.

The mania in this country is without borders. I lived in Dallas for six years; it's an amazing place; they boost themselves with all kinds of slogans. All the corporations wanted to locate their headquarters in Dallas, so the whole city was one giant billboard. It's known as the "city without limits": now that's a manic phrase.

PP: It seems to me that this mania is also tied into our conviction that things have to continually increase in value. Everything has to keep moving onward, upward, and forward. Where did this idea of constant growth and development come from?

JH: There are many components. But one of them is the historical view of life, especially in the Bible: the idea that everything moves forward in time. When you read the Bible, for instance, you learn about the succeeding generations, and that this follows that, and so on. And then there's the Darwinian idea that things are all growing "up" and improving. Humans are at the top of the tree, and animals are at the bottom of the tree. Then in the nineteenth century, with the Industrial Revolution, there was this incredible expansion, and we just kept improving everything, from railroads to the light bulb. We only saw things through the eyes of improvement: that is, we didn't see the distaff side of improvement.

But if we only see through the eyes of improvement or progress, we don't see the shadow of progress: the toxic waste dumps, the spoiled rivers, the destruction of forests and the loss of animals. Despite all this environmental destruction, we still continue to believe that constant improvement is awesome.

PP: Is there anything in America that acts as a counterforce to our mania, our hugeness, and our forward-moving drive?

JH: I'm encouraged by the growing sense of regionalism in America: I think that's part of our deep roots, too. The local places that were originally settled; the soil of the regions; the recovery of the Indians; the reintroduction of native wildlife to these local regions. There are now many regional writers who are connected to America's different geographies. All of this will become more and more important.

PP: Why? What's important about regionalism to the soul of America?

JH: It goes back again to the fact that America is not a place—it's a faith and a belief system. For that reason we have a lot of problems getting into the "place of America." So because America's the dream—geography is the place. You don't live in America; you live in Nebraska. But the dream is American. So geography is a way out of history.

PP: You mean geography anchors our high-flying American dream?

JH: I don't know how I can say it in a few words; but being in a specific place is what is crucial to stop the rush of time and being driven forward by our history. We've never really gotten ourselves into the geography of our own land. Partly this has been because this was always foreign soil—and our souls just didn't get into this soil. And we oppressed the Indians. So I think it's been a very slow process of getting into the land, and that's part of why we've abused it so much: we were never really into it! This might begin to change now that we've been here over four or five generations.

PP: Did the Puritan myth of America as the "City on the Hill" function as a kind of barrier to putting down deep roots in American soil?

JH: Yes: we have to know our roots, as well as our baggage, and we have to realize that America was settled by unerotic religious fanatics. I suspect that a great deal of the projection of the Puritans upon the American natives had to do with their fear of Eros: I don't mean just sexuality, I mean a whole way of living that includes pleasure, connectedness, and sensuousness. So from its inception, part of the problem of America has been that the natives, as well as the slaves, represented the repressed body.

PP: How does this fear of Eros the Puritans brought with them show up in the culture today?

JH: We constantly have cycles of repression and liberation—for example, prohibition or the repression of blacks or women. At the same time, we have a gigantic pornography industry. All you have to do is turn on television and you can watch pornography disguised in ads, or MTV or on talk shows where people come on and talk about how they slept with their husband or wife's father. I see this as the "revenge of Aphrodite": because how else can this Greek Goddess of Eros get into the culture except that way? Just compare us with other cultures like South East Asia, or Bali or Brazil, where the erotic is much more important and where life is built on the erotic. These cultures see us as gauche, awkward, and productive—but not sensuous or erotic.

So we have to realize that every American's problem with Eros and sexuality is a collective, cultural problem: it's not just that a couple is having trouble, and therefore they should have sex therapy, or relationship therapy or family therapy—all these are aspects of the erotic—but that we should realize that this is an *American* cultural problem. And we have to realize that there are certain foundational myths or structures that continue to run this country—and the Puritan is one of those myths. ■

Notes

1. "James Hillman Obituary: US Psychologist Who Concluded that Therapy Needed to Change the World Rather Than Focus on People's Lives," by Mark Kidel, *Guardian*, December 21, 2011.
2. From December 1992 to May 1993, U.S. forces were engaged in a U.N.–sanctioned mission to provide a protected zone for humanitarian aid in southern Somalia, which was in the throes of civil war. The mission, originally limited in scope, expanded, until eighteen U.S. servicemen were killed, and the U.S. withdrew. The episode was dramatized in the book and film, *Black Hawk Down*. The Haiti mission is described in Ch. 30, n. 6.
3. Saturn was the Roman God of time and agriculture; in Greece he was known as "Kronos," or "Chronus." Typically pictured as an old man, Saturn in astrology represents, among other things, limitation, depression, and melancholy.
4. See the 1954 Supreme Court case *Berman v. Parker* at <http://en.wikipedia.org/wiki/Berman_v._Parker>.

Washington, D.C.

The Political Soul of America

INTERVIEWS WITH JAMES HILLMAN, PH.D.
AND THOMAS MOORE, PH.D.

O NE WARM, BEAUTIFUL SPRING afternoon in 2000, I found myself seated around a conference table in the editorial offices of the *Washingtonian*, D.C.'s city magazine. My editor, William O'Sullivan,[1] had invited me in to explain to the rest of the editors the radical idea I'd pitched: a feature story on the "soul of Washington." The first thing I had to explain to my puzzled listeners was the notion of "soul" itself. Previously I'd written about angels in Washington; now the staff automatically assumed I'd be writing another "spiritual" piece.[2]

Instead, as I explained, I was referring to the definition of soul as it had been used in the classical world of Greece and Rome: *genius loci*, or the particular soul or "genius" of a physical place or person. I'd first learned about the modern relevance of the ancient notion of soul from James Hillman and his colleague, Thomas Moore. Bonded by their shared interests in Greek polytheism, the Renaissance, Jung, and the soul, the two men had developed a profound and deep friendship. Their respective lectures and books on the soul as a force that "ensouls" all aspects of earthly life had recently landed them in the pages of *The New York Times Magazine*.[3]

Moore, I knew, had begun his public career lecturing at the Dallas Institute for the Humanities and Culture, founded by Hillman and other thinkers in 1980,[4] and had participated in the Institute's now thirty-year-old ongoing lecture series, "What Makes a City?" Both had given thought to this idea for a long time, and both had given talks on the souls of cities, traveling across America and around the world, lecturing urban planners on the unique constellation of characteristics—geography, history, legends, landmarks, people, food, and restaurants—that all went into making the "soul" of a place.

It was an idea that immediately stoked the editors' attention and interest, and they shared their own insights and associations with verve. I got the assignment, and began scheduling interviews. Both Hillman's and Moore's quotes were laced throughout the feature story that was published in January 2001. But most of the rich insights the two thinkers provided into Washington remained unpublished—until now. In the first of these two original, complete interviews, Hillman peers into the soul of the city that he called the "political soul of America"—a place, where, as it turned out, he himself had deep family roots, and that would play a role in shaping his own destiny.

In our interview, Hillman also carries forward his theme of America's avoidance of tragedy and depression, noting the capital's relatively unknown history of slavery; the lack of a true memorial for the American Indian; the "downward moving" Vietnam memorial, in contrast to the city's more soaring, triumphal monuments; and the melancholy carved into Abraham Lincoln's face. But Hillman also speaks about the political marches over the decades that live on in the city's memory as powerful symbolic moments, as well as Marian Anderson's inspiring performance on the steps of the Lincoln Memorial.

In my second interview with Thomas Moore—who once described Dallas as a city of "silky materialism," and who appreciates architecture as a "sub-branch" of theology—our conversation turns more toward the sacred and the archetypal aspects of the nation's capital. To my delight, I discovered that Moore also had a long and intimate connection with D.C. As he shares in our complete interview below, he regularly undertakes his own solitary walking pilgrimage of the city's sites and monuments.

Despite his abiding friendship and shared work with Hillman, the two were not always like-minded, and in this interview Moore brings a somewhat different perspective to the soul of Washington than his colleague. Where Hillman saw into the city's underlying archetypal structures and darker underside, Moore glimpsed the religious elements of our democratic ideals embedded in the city's history and architecture, honoring the "rites and rituals" of democracy, and recasting tourists as "pilgrims." Viewing the capital through the lens of his classically trained imagination, Moore also spoke inspiringly of Athena as the Goddess of the city atop the Capitol, describing her role as a "weaver" in the ongoing work of democracy, and the "presences" felt in the Washington, Lincoln, and Jefferson memorials. But Moore also described the "weightiness" of the psychic atmosphere of D.C.—that place where the world comes to lay its burdens—and how it affects its citizens. He ends our interview with a stirring call to politicians to rise to their higher calling as caretakers and even "priests or priestesses" of the country they serve.

✳

1

JAMES HILLMAN

Pythia Peay: I understand your grandfather lived in Washington, D.C. At one time, he owned a restaurant called Harvey's, an old and venerable Washington institution.

James Hillman: My grandfather's name was Joel Hillman; he was a restaurant man, and he was the owner of Harvey's through the 1920s. It was a center for politics, and J. Edgar Hoover used to eat there every day. I was introduced to him when I was about sixteen or seventeen. My grandfather was an extreme *bon vivant*; he saw food aesthetically, and thought of food as a medium for connecting people.

PP: I'd imagine that being part of a restaurant with such a history must have given you a special feeling and connection to D.C.

JH: My goodness, it really did! My grandparents were also married there; my grandmother on my father's side was born and educated there; and my father was born on New Jersey Avenue. My sister also ran a bookstore there and worked in the Library of Congress for many years. During World War II, in 1943 and 1944, I worked for the radio station WTOP as a copy boy. I used to be sent all over the city to pick up news and copy. This was at the time of great reporters, like Eric Sevareid. So I was also imbued with politics through that, in addition to having deep family roots in Washington.

PP: A theme throughout all your work is the topic of calling and destiny. Did having this ancestral connection to America's capital shape your destiny in any way?

JH: When you ask that question, and looking back now, it could have to do with the fact that, ever since my early boyhood, when I was around twelve years old, I've had a tremendous interest in American political history.

PP: You've certainly always seemed to have an abiding passion and curiosity in the American soul.

JH: Yes, and a great deal of the American soul is involved in its political life—and Washington D.C. is at the center of politics. That's why all this talk about "inside the beltway" actually refers to being inside the political soul of the country: it's a crucible or a container of our political energy.

I became a psychologist in my late twenties, so my interest in politics never became a political career. And by living in exile in Europe for nearly thirty years (which I enjoyed) there was no opportunity for its expression. Ever since I've been back in the States, however, I've been involved with cities: I've been brought to Dallas, Buffalo, Pittsburgh, Atlanta, and cities in Italy for consultations on urban questions, by people who are trying to get at the "soul" of their city.

PP: And now I'm asking you to do the same for the nation's capital. As I researched the city's history, I came across accounts of slaves who helped to build our monuments and memorials, even the White House and the Lincoln Memorial.[5] I felt such shame around this ugly part of our past, and somehow it felt important to begin with that emotion.

JH: It's very difficult to take our capital of Washington, D.C., and feel a sense of glory and beauty around its history, because of its racism. Cities in Europe have their poor quarters and foreign-born populations, but racism is embedded in the very structure of our nation's capital, and represents our nation in microcosm. So colonialism exists right in the heart of our capital, and that is *shameful.* Therefore, Washington is symbolic, not just for its monuments, but as a living monument to American racism. I still recall the ninety-year-old woman named Hattie who was the "hat check girl" at my grandfather's restaurant, and who we all greeted with huge awe because of her age, her smile, and [her] having been a slave. That was back in the thirties, when the waiters were all black, or "colored" as they were called then. Even the elegant Willard Hotel was served by an underclass of Southern black workers.

At the same time, some of our greatest moments of anti-racism and protest have also occurred in the heart of the capital: Marian Anderson singing on the steps of the Lincoln Memorial; Martin Luther King, Jr. giving his great "I Have a Dream" speech, also on the steps of the Lincoln Memorial; and the Million Man March.[6]

PP: I interviewed a young black man for my story on the soul of Washington, D.C. He worked as a security guard for the Library of Congress, and his family had a long history in the city going back generations. He recalled marching with Martin Luther King as a young boy, and said that this city was the "nation's conscience." I thought that was beautiful. But some people might also see these kinds of marches or protests as hollow or empty gestures.

JH: The endless symbolic moments in our country's history touch the soul; it's like a mark or an imprint or a landmark. Think of the World War I veterans who came to the capital in the early thirties during the Depression to demonstrate for more benefits,[7] the antiwar demonstrations during the sixties, and so on. These were all great, symbolic moments in our nation's history, like the tossing of the tea chests into the Boston Harbor.[8] People return to these images and memories, like Marian Anderson and Martin Luther King, again and again. These gestures don't necessarily lead to rational political consequences: therefore, some people think they're hollow. But those people have no sense of soul! Nations live on in their symbolic gestures.

PP: Washington is also famously known as the city built on a swamp: a geographical metaphor for the political corruption that has always been wedded to the city's identity. But one of the interesting things I discovered in my research is that there is actually some controversy over this fact: some geologists say it's technically incorrect that the city was built on a swamp, while others disagree, so there are two camps. Historically, the term arose when Northerners first starting coming down to the capital, and they experienced it as "swamp-like."

JH: But the swamp is part of the mythic imagination of Washington. I think that is important. History may show a very different story—meaning the facts, the geology, and the topography of the city may show one thing. But the city's reputation throughout the years has maintained this "swampy" myth.

And so there must be something about the city that reinforces that myth, or it would go away. Even if it's not topographically true, then it's psychologically true. Psychological truths are emotional; they don't necessarily follow the facts, and can't even be corrected by facts. There will always be those who believe that once we get the "facts" everything will change: but it doesn't. So the myth of the swamp still remains, and it's very difficult to change these deeper truths that continue to resonate: the swamp metaphor describes the psychological reality of Washington, D.C., because it fits!

PP: If the swamp is a metaphor for a label that has always stuck to the city, then how would you interpret the fact that the Founders chose this spot as the capital of American democracy?

JH: If we take it as a metaphor, then, as originally laid out by Pierre L'Enfant the capital is a swamp with French rationalism and eighteenth-century right-angled structures built on top of it. This rationalism is carried out further in the streets, which are all named after the states. So it's a kind of conceptual structure on top of a bog, a downward-sucking swamp. The fantasy behind that metaphor is that we're trying to "clean up" the underlying muck with the emphasis on white: white marble, white structures, straight lines, and strong columns. You can feel the weight of those buildings, like the Jefferson Memorial, the Lincoln Memorial, the Supreme Court building, or the Library of Congress. My God, those are fantastically overbuilt structures! It's as if they're trying to hold something down; they're almost like gravestones on the soul of the city.

Washington is also a colony in its own government; it's not a state, so there's a colonial atmosphere in the city. But I also see it partly as a kind of Disneyland, a destination for tourists visiting these monuments that have carved into stone or marble all the grade-school clichés about America. In a way it's like going to a site on a computer, where you can see all those wonderful sentences—"Liberty and Justice for All" and "We the People"—as well as all the heroes of the secular state: Lincoln, Jefferson, and Washington.

PP: It brings to mind something that you've frequently said about America: it's an idea that we believe in, but that we don't really *live* in.

JH: Right. We believe in the country and its ideals. Washington is the symbol, and the monuments and memorials are the images, of that belief system. That's what brings the schoolkids and the people. It's like going on a pilgrimage to be reinforced in our beliefs.

PP: In your essay "Peaks and Vales" in *Puer Papers* you write about the two polarities of spirit, which has more to do with ideals that are upward-lifting and transcendent, and soul, which has more to do with the low-lying vales of feeling, psyche, and suffering. I can see how "spirit" is reflected in places like the Washington Monument or the Capitol, but where are the places that carry soul in the city of Washington?

JH: The soul of a city is in its depths, and the Vietnam Memorial is a place of real soul; of all the monuments, it's the only one that really "gets down." It goes downward, pulled into the center and the earth itself. It honors the dark, the tragic, the defeat, the ruin, and the commons. So with this memorial, there's a very important recognition that with the Vietnam War something changed in the soul of Washington. It's one of the first places where something deeper and more humbling within the American soul was discovered. It's where the throngs come and the tears flow.

PP: So it's where America's relationship to tragedy changed?

JH: There's been a tremendous effort at denial of tragedy in America's history. So we're missing something. We've left out half of our history, and half of the people. So we've only told half of the story, and therefore we only have half of a soul. I sometimes like to think of the city of Washington when Lincoln was President—that man who carried such depression in his face and heart, and who carried this terrible burden. No one today could be visibly depressed like that and still hold a high office. But Lincoln could do that.

I think of Lincoln going out every day for his ride in his carriage through the streets of Washington. And I think of Walt Whitman, who worked in the hospitals during the Civil War. These were two visionaries who had depth and who were able to embrace the tragic, and to be with the people. They had truly democratic feeling; they carried the pain of the people. There's a lovely story that when Lincoln used to go out for his carriage ride, Whitman used to walk down the street. They never met each other, but they passed each other on the street; probably Whitman doffed his hat to Lincoln as he passed by in his carriage. That's a beautiful image of two people being in Washington at an historic time.

Also, when we talk about Washington, it's important to remember that this is also where Lincoln was murdered; that's also part of the tragedy in the soul of the city. One of the greatest people we ever had in the country was murdered in the capital of the country. So murder is in the ground of the city: this is something that we need to take in, and reclaim and meditate on as a way to deepen the whole approach to Washington.

PP: One of the functions of memorials is to honor our history. And isn't history connected to soul, and so therefore isn't soul found in all the city's monuments and memorials?

JH: In America, we only commemorate history as victory. The Vietnam Memorial is the only place where we commemorate loss. There's a Holocaust Memorial in D.C., which is very important, but that was about an event that took place outside the country. What about our own Holocaust? Is there any commemoration to the American Indian? Have we a true memorial to the people who built the city, of whom many were black slaves? Who labored, dug the trenches, drained the swamps, and did the physical building? There is something still to be done there. On the other hand, there is some wisdom reflected in the fact that the Pentagon is located outside the city walls.

PP: What would that wisdom be?

JH: It's a tradition that goes all the way back to Rome, when the God of war, Mars, was not allowed in the city. The people were afraid of Mars, because they recognized that he was a great power. Caesar was the first emperor who marched his troops into the city of Rome: before that, the military wasn't supposed to be in the city. This is also a very important part of American democracy: to preserve democracy, we must have civil rule over the military, and we honor that by keeping the Pentagon on the other side of the river. So Mars in the ancient world was seen as a dangerous power that should not take over the city, as we've learned today from examples in Latin America, Greece, and Argentina, where the military juntas took over democracies.[9]

PP: Speaking of Rome: In talking about the myths and archetypes associated with Washington, the first word that comes up is always *power*.

JH: I don't know whether I would say that. Certainly it's a "house of power" and there are a lot of power brokers in the city. But there is so much more power in Wall Street and the media. Washington is a curious place because it almost cancels its power out. It's a place where there are both sky Gods and earth Gods; the light and the dark;

the Founding Fathers and then the whole other side of the Great Mother, the earthy mother's world. There's the sociology of absent fathers and black single mothers raising their children alone and white men in their suits going off to work for the government agencies. There's the enormous corruption in the white ruling class: criminality, drug abuse, lobbyists, and deals. And there are the people on the street who are afraid of being robbed or even sometimes of getting into taxicabs.

So the city has two different populations: there are all the lobbyists, politicians, media, and representatives of the various national and international organizations that come and go; but they're not really part of the city's soul. Then there are the people who were born here, and who have this tradition of working in the city more than working for the government: so they carry the value of the soul. They care about the city because they're involved with it as an actual place; they have more of a physical, sensory feeling for it, and they suffer with it as a place. So it's almost a tragedy the way the city is set up.

PP: Does this go back to the split between the swamp and those soaring ideals of French rationalism and liberty, justice and equality for all?

JH: Right. The rational enlightenment overlay of the late eighteenth century is susceptible to infiltration from below. Inevitably, therefore, the city is always suffering from corruption, graft, and dirty deals: whether it's Truman who was accused of being corrupt at the end of his administration; or Lyndon Johnson trying to put Abe Fortas onto the Supreme Court; or Monica Lewinsky corrupting Bill Clinton. Washington is known as the "city of scandals" because it tries to be too clean. It tries to go against the human condition. But the human condition comes in anyway, through the back door, or below the stairs. ■

2
THOMAS MOORE

Pythia Peay: When I first broached the idea of writing an article on the soul of Washington, most people thought I'd be writing about the religious life of the city. Can you explain what "soul" means to the layperson?

Thomas Moore: Generally speaking, the spirit is the "upper half," the part of us that is looking for transcendence, or to evolve, grow, or improve. Whether a city or a person, it's an orientation toward the future, the eternal afterlife, or those universal values that are above individual circumstances. But the soul is always particular: it's about family roots, memory, and the past. Spirit is more interested in planning, and the soul is more interested in remembering. The soul works through mood, emotion, reverie, and dreams: all those things are proper to the soul. The mind is not part of the soul: it has to do with facts, measurements, interpretations, and explanations.

The artists, writers, and other thinkers of the Renaissance, for example, saw the world from the point of view of the soul. They were very interested in science, and developing a more scientific view of the world. But they didn't separate their science from magic, or from being in the world in a way that accented the mystery of existence. Renaissance philosophers wanted to conceal and hide meaning; Renaissance paintings are often full of hidden images and levels of understanding that evoke reality like a poem.

So, soul also has a lot to do with those invisible currents that are in the background of everything that's going on. And one thing that's always going on in the background is the history of a place. Usually history is presented literally, as events that happened in the past. But history in a deeper sense is connected to memory: and that is an important part of the soul of a city. When a city loses its memory, that's when things start to fall apart.

PP: Washington, D.C. would be even more significant from a soul perspective, then, because it's the city of our national memory. It's also rich with images around democracy and the story of the country's beginnings.

TM: Exactly. The monuments and memorials are extremely important, not just for the city, but for the nation. When I travel throughout the states—and it doesn't matter what's going on politically—I find that people feel very deeply and strongly about Washington. The people who have power and money will come and go, but the memorials will remain. So to me, Washington is one of our nation's treasures, and its primary job is to act as a guardian for the nation's memory.

PP: I have to admit that sometimes the city feels more like a tourist destination than one of our nation's sacred treasures.

TM: I wouldn't call those visitors "tourists." They're clearly pilgrims. People are not going to D.C. as tourists the way they would visit another city. I understand that people don't get that today, and they think that religion is something that only goes on in church. But what these tourists are doing as they tour the monuments and the city is an aspect of civil religion: it's honest to goodness deep, deep, soul religion. That's different even from the spiritual dimension of religion.

PP: So how would this apply to Washington, D.C., and what would a "soul" and a "spirit" approach to the nation's capital feel like?

TM: The spirit part is to make everything function well, and to be efficient. The hierarchy of the government also belongs to spirit: but soul is not hierarchical at all. With spirit, there's a tendency to be educational and to explain everything, rather than letting people have the simple experience of the images and the memories they evoke.

So experiencing the soul of the city would be to keep and guard those things for the people as a way to keep the past living in the present, not as something that's relevant to the present, but that is actually *present*. A soul approach would be to visit an old building, for example, and go into a room where an old document was signed, without having to listen to someone give a lecture about it. The soul is not found in correctness, but in an experiential feeling, where the imagination plays a role in connecting the present with the past. So when someone is standing in front of a monument, or is in some historic room or building, they need to allow their imagination time and quiet.

PP: D.C. is so rich with statues and images carved into its buildings. Is there a particular figure that to you embodies something of the soul of the city?

TM: The art of weaving things together is a very traditional image of soul. The Goddess Athena, who was the patroness of Athens, and who is the patroness of *all* cities, was a weaver: I see Athena in all of the buildings, and particularly in the Statue of Freedom[10] atop the Capitol. Being able to weave together cultures and personalities and all sorts of peoples and religions—that is the work of Athena, and that is the work of the city and of the government. So she is the patroness of the soul of the city: not the running of it, but the weaving.

I think that's something politicians often get confused about, because they think they have to have the power to control everything—instead of realizing that to serve the soul of the city or the nation, all the disparate elements have to be woven together into a tapestry. Politicians who are more interested in the power aspect of politics may judge that kind of work as too sentimental, or secondary to what's really important. That's a big mistake because the functioning and efficiency of a group should be in service to the soul.

PP: There's more partisanship than "weaving" together going on in the city of Washington these days.

TM: Partisanship is the very opposite of politics. With the political polarities dividing the government and the country, there's been a serious loss of the work of the politician, as well a breakdown of the soul of the city from that divisiveness. So the work of the soul of Washington would be to recover a sense of the caretaker and weaver aspects of governing, as opposed to partisanship. The soulful politician is one who works for the good of our disparate, diverse nation: that's the essence of being a politician.

PP: I think there's some notion now that the way a politician maintains his or her integrity is by sticking to their ideals, without compromising them.

TM: If all the politicians believe very strongly in their ideals, then not much weaving can go on. So if someone is going to be both a believer *and* a politician, then I think we're in trouble: because then it's difficult to compromise and work out deals. There's so much moral preaching going on these days; we've lost the original meaning of the word "moral." But morality is largely about being in community and taking care of people. So morality is subtler than believing in something and then sticking to that belief no matter what: that's old-time religion.

PP: When we think of Dallas, we think of cowboys and Stetson hats and cattle. When we think of Los Angeles, we think of Hollywood. What comes to mind when you think of Washington, D.C.?

TM: When I come to Washington, I feel as if I'm in a whirlpool, or a vortex. In

Washington there's the sense that this is the place where the country and the world holds together. It's a city where you're not just thinking of the place itself, you're thinking of the rest of the country and the world in a way that I don't feel anywhere else. When I'm in D.C. there's that sense that people everywhere are looking to the city for their wellbeing: by that I mean peace, justice, and the democratic ideals. That's what all those institutions, the exalted language carved on the monuments and the great documents that are kept there, are really all about.

So, therefore, Washington is a place where it's appropriate to reflect on what it is that holds this world together. The average person in Nebraska or California doesn't have to think about that kind of life and death stuff as much. But D.C. is where it all happens—or doesn't happen. Even the monuments and memorials are about wars and battles and great figures, so the city raises us to a level of great reflection. Other places don't have the opportunity—or the burden—of having to think about these matters.

PP: It's interesting that you use the word *burden*. Often people living in the Washington area feel it's kind of a heavy place to be, even if they're not in politics. I know I feel physically lighter when I leave the city.

TM: The average person doesn't have to deal with these absolute life-and-death matters, or deal with what it means to be a democracy—just as the Athenians were trying to resolve centuries ago—as directly or self-consciously as D.C. does. But that's also a wonderful opportunity. Look at all the adulation the city gets if it does something right; or the power that comes from it. But the burden is very, very heavy, and I would think that would be a terrible weight.

When Lincoln was president, the weight he felt almost stooped him over physically. And that is true of anybody who is sensitive to what is going on, and not just caught up in power. But the soul is always found in the underworld, among the heavier things like depression and suffering. I think that to be able to carry that burden and not defend against it would be the sign of a mature society in the city of Washington.

PP: I think it would help the ordinary person who lives here to know about this deeper background, or the idea that there's an invisible atmosphere that affects them psychologically.

TM: There is no way to live in Washington without being affected by what goes on there. That city is a place in the dream life of people in cities and capitals around the world: Washington, D.C. has a place in their imagination, more prominently than other places in this country. So I don't think you can be a citizen of that city without carrying the weight of that projection.

PP: "Weightiness" would definitely be a characteristic I'd associate with D.C.

TM: Every time I go there I'm just overwhelmed by the heaviness of the buildings. They're massive. I've even done interviews in some of these places, and there's no other place I go to in the world in which I enter such vast buildings that are so heavy on the ground. And the endless, blind corridors with no windows! It's like being in a labyrinth; not a slim building where you can look out the windows and know where you are.

PP: One of the recurring themes that often comes up around the city's future is the conflict between the old and the new, and the desire to break free of the past. So there's a tension; periodically people talk about changing the image of the city forever, and making it a city of the future, and not the past.

TM: Please save us from that! However, I understand the flight from the past—especially if it's full of painful memories. I lived in Dallas many years ago, and at one time there was a movement to tear down the Texas School Book Depository, because it was such a blight on the image of the city. In fact, the building was a painful burden for the city, because there were so many bad memories associated with it around President Kennedy's assassination. But it was still important to keep it as a landmark.[11]

PP: Why?

TM: Well, imagine if a person came into therapy and said I want to forget about all the bad things that happened to me in the past and start from scratch all over again. Any decent therapist would say that person is headed for trouble because we have to own our own life: it's part of becoming a mature person.

PP: Do you mean in the sense that we can learn from the mistakes of the past?

TM: No. It's that our character is made from the suffering and experiences of the past. To pretend that those experiences are no longer relevant is a repression of the past. So to say, "Let's move on and become a new city" is also a repression of the past. It's not really moving ahead—it's an aggressive thing to do; it's anti-soul, and it's a movement *against* the past. It can lead to nothing but trouble.

PP: Of course, America is founded on leaving the past behind. We left Europe, and then we left the east coast for the Midwest, and the Midwest for California.

TM: That's the country's strength; but it has a big shadow. In everything we do—every country does this, but we do it to absurd lengths—we continue to try to be new and to get rid of the past. But in a part of our national psyche, we're still fighting the Revolution, and we're still trying to shed the old king! So we have to learn to see ourselves as part of a long spectrum. We can demonize the past and all the mistakes that have been made. But that kind of abrupt movement away from the past is an adolescent kind of behavior that doesn't want anything to do with all that "old stuff."

PP: But what's interesting is that our national memory and national history celebrates revolution. It's as if that abrupt break from the "old country" is what our very identity as Americans is based on. So we immediately run into a paradox.

TM: My first thought to what you said is that we have all these cities [and states]—New London, New York, New Boston, New Hampshire—that are both new but that also echo back to the old country. The memory doesn't go away, it gets incorporated, but not very deeply, just superficially. So even though some people rebelled against England in forming the country, at an underlying level the connection remained there anyway. And if we identify with the rebels and romanticize the Revolution, which we tend to do, we're only talking about half of the story. Hardly anyone talks about the violence of the Revolution, or the people who were killed in the process, as if there might have been another way to separate from the Fatherland. That kind of reflection on the Revolution would be more sobering; we wouldn't want to go out and celebrate that all the time.

PP: So you're talking about experiencing the deeper side of the country's founding, the loss and the tragedy in our past that we rarely connect to.

TM: In a way, the celebration of Revolution continues the defense against the loss, and the pain and complexity of that event. That's the same as a person who has to go through a kind of renewal. Yet until they come to grips with their past they're going to be quite immature.

PP: Do you feel that our European past still lives on in the architecture of Washington, D.C.?

TM: Look at all those Greek buildings: Athena is present in those buildings! Lincoln, Jefferson, and all the Founding Fathers were all well educated in Greek philosophy. The reference to the old country can be found not just in the Greek style, but also the Victorian-styled buildings, as well. What is the alternative to that memory? To build characterless boxes made out of glass? Those kinds of buildings are extremely defensive against the past and the soul.

PP: What do you feel about the Vietnam Memorial?

TM: It's very effective, because it's not representational. The names on the wall mean the memorial is about the individual, rather than the group: soul is local and individual, as opposed to universal. It's a place that favors a kind of walking meditation; it invites people in because it doesn't explain or tell them what to do. So it's where visitors can make up their own rituals, which they do daily by placing objects and crying at the wall.

PP: What about the monuments and memorials that are built around Lincoln or Jefferson or George Washington?

TM: These images aren't just representations: they're presences. There's a big difference between representing something and making a presence. When a monument is done well and carefully with some depth to it, a certain spirit of personality comes through and is present. A monument is really "working," for instance, when we see the crowds that are drawn to it, and how the people are behaving. When we see people being quiet in the presence of a place, or crying or talking softly to each other, or coming up with their own rituals, for instance, then we know that there is a real presence there that allows a person to be there with their own soul.

PP: Do you have certain rituals of your own when you visit the capital?

TM: I come with some regularity, and often stay at some older hotel that's right in the center of town. I want to be in a place where there is memory, even in a building. I also go for long walks, and make a circle around the White House. I meditate and go around the Capitol very thoughtfully, feeling the presence of what the place is, where it is in the world. I feel a tremendous sense of responsibility, and an increased sense of my place in the world. I also go to the different neighborhoods in D.C., and walk the streets; a city is in its neighborhoods. As soon as you leave D.C., though, you're in America today!

PP: Being alone with the city that way must stir up very profound feelings.

TM: A friend once took me through the Capitol building after hours. I got a feeling for the place as a monument and as a place of memory, but also where things happen. So I don't want to only glorify the memory aspect of Washington. What is being done there daily, making national and world decisions, is a big part of the dream and the soul of the city. To be in the presence of that can be quite overwhelming and powerful. The mix of history and the present in the Capitol, and the level of attention that was required just to be there filled me with awe. I think back to that visit many times.

PP: People often talk about "power" as part of the myth of D.C. But you seem to describe it as more "power-full."

TM: Right: it's full of power, but not in the way we might say that a person has great power. Again, it goes back to Washington as a place whose focus is on holding society together, and it takes a person with a large sense of self to do that. So in that city there are many people who fulfill that function. It's tricky, because if they appropriate too much power to themselves they can easily get corrupted.

PP: So you're saying that the danger lies in identifying personally with the power that belongs more widely to the city and to the government?

TM: When someone becomes a national leader on that scale, it's fine to give them adulation and money and perks, because their roles and responsibilities are far above what the average person has to deal with. But if someone exploits that personally, they have ruined the agreement. They have destroyed their participation; their part has been ruined and tarnished. Their job is to be in the office, but not to identify with it. If they can't do that, then they should get out of there.

PP: You're differentiating the power of the office as impersonal, rather than personal, and that has a life of its own.

TM: In my view, Washington is the spiritual center of the country. I don't mean that in terms of a church or beliefs. I mean that in the very real sense of a religious way of being. Those who work and serve there could be compared to priests and priestesses. I think politicians get into trouble because they think of themselves as managers, and they view the whole operation as purely secular—but it isn't. To have the role of leader and to be someone who decides these great issues of democracy and government: that is a religious role. They're speaking for the spirit of democracy, which is much greater than themselves or their personal philosophies.

PP: By using the word *religious*, do you mean something different from church-related religiosity?

TM: What I'm suggesting is that what holds our nation together is beyond any individual's power to control. Anyone who is in a position of leadership there has to be open to that influence, and to inspiration far beyond what they are capable of doing themselves—like artists with their muses. At that level of impersonality, we're in the realm of religion, and the eternal issues of how to live together as a society. It's like a marriage: a marriage is by its nature religious, because when two people realize that they're committed to something much bigger than themselves, they've entered into an eternal construction here on Earth.

So the only way democracy is going to work is if politicians realize that they're serving something that's beyond their individual power. It's also important that they accept the "rituals" of politics. The special robes worn by the Supreme Court Justices, and the ceremonies when the President enters the Capitol building: these vestiges of the past in our modern-day society are hints that what government and politicians are doing have profound religious dimensions. If we don't recognize these rites and roles as sacred, then our government and politics will turn into a personal operation, and that's where it falls apart. The monuments and stories of our Founding Fathers and the founding of the country are mythic. These are our heroes, and this is our American mythology. ■

Notes

1. William O'Sullivan is *Washingtonian*'s senior managing editor. From 1999 to 2007, he was features editor, and in another lifetime, assistant managing editor.
2. "Heaven Sent: Angels in Washington," by Pythia Peay, *Washingtonian*, December 1993, and "The Soul of Washington, D.C.," *Washingtonian*, January 2001.
3. "How the Soul is Sold," by Emily Yoffe, *New York Times Magazine*, April 23, 1995.
4. More on the Dallas Institute of the Humanities and Culture at <www.dallasinstitute.org>.
5. See Holland: 2007.
6. On October 16, 1995, between 400,000 and a million African-American men gathered on the Mall to affirm black values and family unity. It was one of the largest gatherings in American history.
7. In 1933, World War I veterans set up a tent city in Washington to protest for more benefits.
8. In 1773, Sam Adams and the self-proclaimed Sons of Liberty protesting British taxation on goods imported to the colonies, boarded three ships and threw forty-five tons of tea into the Boston Harbor.
9. Julius Caesar, who was not an emperor, took his army across the river Rubicon that separated Rome from the rest of its empire—the first general to do this during the Republic. The military dictatorships that Hillman refers to were in Greece, where a group of generals ruled (1967–1974); Argentina, under General Jorge Videla and others (1976–1983); and Chile, under General Augusto Pinochet (1973–1990).
10. The history and images of the Statue of Freedom can be found at <http://www.aoc.gov/capitol-hill/other-statues/statue-freedom>.
11. The Depository is the site from where, on November 22, 1963, Lee Harvey Oswald, fired the bullets that killed President Kennedy as his motorcade drove by.

—38—

America's Narcissism

The Key to the Fulfillment of Our Myths and Ideals

AN INTERVIEW WITH THOMAS MOORE, PH.D.

I N 1992, THOMAS MOORE—a kind of Renaissance figure who had once been a Catholic monk and a university professor, and who in addition to being a writer is also an accomplished musician and practicing psychotherapist—vaulted onto *The New York Times* bestseller list with *Care of the Soul: A Guide for Cultivating Depth and Sacredness in Everyday Life.* It was a turning point for the nation's own soul, as Moore's lyrically composed wisdom, which revealed the deeper meaning in the most ordinary of everyday things, seemed to provide a kind of essential quality many people hadn't even known they were lacking.

Philosophically elegant in its simplicity, his message for many, as for this writer, led to an awakening: God was not only to be found in the rarefied heights of solitary spiritual communion, but in the bustling streets, buildings, and cafés of big cities, suburban neighborhoods, and the main streets of small towns; in bookstores, museums, golf courses, stores, and hospitals; as well as in the joys, messes, and sorrows of friendship and family life, and the mundane stuff of commercial transactions, illness, shopping for groceries, and going to work every day. The merely mundane, was, in fact, sacred. In the succession of books that followed, Moore continued his life's work of grounding "the pure, visionary spirit in the imperfect, intoxicating sensuousness of everyday life." His fidelity to depth combined with his engagement with life in all its various expressions have made him one of my favorite thinkers to interview. This was especially true when it came to politics.

Each of us intersects with the body politic in our own way; most often we come to know our country through the lives of our parents. Of Irish descent, Moore credits many of his gifts to his father, a remarkable individual who lived by a democratic code of respect for others, regardless of their position in life. He has described his father as a "philosophical plumber" (he was indeed a plumber by profession). Once, Moore recalled, his father took him on a plumbing job at their local morgue. Using the occasion to teach his young son a "life lesson" on the mysteries of death, Moore's father arranged for him to take a tour that culminated in viewing bodies in storage.[1]

It is that same kind of uncommon insight found in the unlikeliest of places that Moore imparts to our exploration of the American psyche. Plumbing the country's oft-noted and disliked side of narcissism and callow youthfulness, he instead discovers the gold of meaning to be found within this psychological symptom. Among other things, we discuss America's superpower and hugeness complex; his views on the Horatio Alger myth and ideas around individualism; and the arts as one of the country's greatest strengths and sources of inspiration. Conducted in 1994, my interview with Moore changed how I saw the country that I thought I knew, and it remains for me a classic.

✳

Pythia Peay: You've written that if we were to put America on the couch, narcissism would be its most obvious symptom. Yet you also say that our narcissism holds the promise of fulfilling our American myth of becoming the "new world" of opportunity. Others have also criticized America as being narcissistic, but they haven't seen the potential in this symptom the way you have.

Thomas Moore: What I'm trying to do is to apply the principle from Carl Jung and James Hillman to honor the symptom and to see it as a guide—rather than to take the approach of getting rid of a symptom as some kind of pain or nuisance. Narcissism is undoubtedly a very strong part of the American psyche. We're a very young country, so this could be expected—not literally in terms of years, but because America in its relation to other cultures has always been seen as the "new world" and as a place of progress and starting over.

In the imagination of the world, America has always maintained a certain youthfulness. It participates in the myth of renewal and starting over again. All the old maps show America as *terra incognita,* or an unknown land. This further suggests that America is seen as unexplored and yet to be discovered. It also suggests that the American psyche has what the Jungians would call a *"puer* psychology." Psychologically, America's "symptom" of narcissism is our raw material, or what Jung referred to in alchemical language as the *prima materia*: meaning that the pain and difficulty lies in the rawness of the symptom, not the material itself.

PP: In Jung's alchemical process, the *prima materia* is the raw material of our personal problems and limitations that we work to bring to consciousness through reflection and imagination, and which then (hopefully) turns into the gold of wisdom. What would it mean for America to work with this raw material around our narcissism?

TM: One way to work with our narcissism would be to actually *become* that place of idealism and renewal the rest of the world sees in us. We could elaborate and stand behind our ideals much more than we do, rather than letting our democratic principles be merely empty words or "floaty" things. We could begin to really *live* these ideals and become a people worthy of recognition. All too often Americans publicly profess their democratic ideals, but when they get right down to it, they don't stand behind them.

PP: Can you give me some examples of how we might go about better fulfilling our ideals?

TM: One example would be the Statue of Liberty, and the ideal it stands for of accepting other peoples into this country. There's a great deal of xenophobia in this country: even the people whose families have come here from other lands and done well and lead established lives don't want immigrants to come here, because they're different or threatening in some way. But eventually, we have to stand behind the Statue of Liberty and do what it says. Another example is the way we think of ourselves as peacemakers, when in fact we bring out our guns at the slightest provocation, and we often fail to explore possibilities for international understanding.

PP: So how does not fulfilling our ideals tie in with narcissism? Does it mean there's a split between how we see ourselves and how the rest of the world sees us?

TM: The narcissist tends to close himself off from the real world, living in a bubble of self-appreciation. He doesn't want contamination or complexity. He enjoys it when people are swayed by his posing and respect him for his ideals, but then eventually his shadow appears and people dislike him with unusual intensity. The solution, as I say, is simple: he can really live his ideals, not perfectly but genuinely.

PP: One of the strongest underlying myths in our country is the myth of the heroic individual. By that I mean the Horatio Alger-type, lone cowboy hero who goes off into the sunset conquering new horizons, but who isn't very connected to family or community. Wouldn't that myth somehow work against what you're talking about in terms of really fulfilling the American promise of immigration and peace?

TM: To take a Freudian approach to your question, when individuality becomes something that's strongly insisted upon, it means we don't actually have it. Freud's idea was that when someone displays a thing excessively, it means they don't really have possession of the thing they're displaying. And I think that's the case with our emphasis on individuality—especially in certain parts of the country where they don't want to let in any government interference, and are against welfare, and where there seems to be a strong resistance to any kind of communal decision-making. Lack of empathy is also a characteristic of narcissism, and that outlook lacks empathy and connection.

So I think that suggests another split in the American psyche, and that is the split between the individual and community. The only way to be able to resolve these two things is to be able to live the paradox, or to be at a point where the two come together. I believe that one thing that stands in the way is the intellectual definition of community as a group of people who think alike and who live alike. But that's not a community.

PP: So what would be your definition of community?

TM: In my lectures I frequently quote from Emerson, whose idea of community was the notion of a neighborhood. The people in a neighborhood are there because fate brought them together. No one may think alike or live alike, but it's that kind of variety that makes a real community. So it seems to me that if we can move from the notion of community as based on common compatibility and similarities to the idea that community comes from variety, then we're moving closer to that paradox where people living individual lives together create a community. Because the only *real* way to be an individual is to be communal.

When an individual is comfortable being in a community, it's not a threat to them. People become paranoid when they feel insecure, threatened, and anxious about their individuality. So I think our country's obsessive focus on individuality reveals that we're not very developed in what it actually means to be an individual, and that we also have a hard time knowing how to become part of a community. Both these things are very difficult for us to do. We've had a lot of people telling us how to go about finding community, but without much wisdom. But the wisdom has to come from the recognition of paradox and irony, things that are very much out of vogue today. Everyone wants to come up with a new program or a simplistic philosophy or spell it out in ten steps: but there's no wisdom in that. And until we can bring wisdom to this issue, we're not going to have communities *or* individuals.

PP: Your idea of community is very radical. So many people feel that community is something you choose based on shared ideals or political or religious worldviews or life experiences. But you're talking about something much more complex.

TM: In the history of America, there have been many Utopian communities, especially in the nineteenth century in New England, Ohio, New York, and Indiana. So it's a strong part of the American spirit to say, "Let's get together and form an ideal community where everyone will think alike, and where we can implement our own vision of what human life ought to be." But I don't think that really works. A community that's been chosen along the lines of conformity and compatibility is by its nature defensive and protective, because it keeps challenges out. Secondly, it generates paranoia from people who don't share the same values.

That kind of community is a purely spiritual endeavor, with little soul, because the soul comes in when the individual and variety and multiplicity enter the picture. This kind of defensive community also fosters that brand of patriotism that accounts for so much warfare and which is paranoid and exclusive.

PP: So in terms of helping people connect to others, and living life in more soulful and also genuinely democratic ways, how would we begin to do that?

TM: I think we have to start close to home. This is such a difficult point to get across, because it's so simple. So one way to find community is to start with our own immediate home and family, as well as our own neighborhood. Live as an individual; paint your house the color you want, and if the neighbors complain, then you're going to have to work it out. It's not a place where everything is in balance; it's a place of being on the edge, of always being in dialogue, working out solutions. It's like being in a marriage: How do you stay married and acknowledge the individuality of your partner as well as your marriage? Well, you don't. You keep living both sides, and keep working out ways to hold both things at the same time. The same thing goes for neighborhoods, families, and cities—the whole works. What the soul needs is more conversation, more dialogue, more talk, and less decision-making.

PP: So it's an ongoing process, rather than an unattainable, transcendent ideal we fix our hopes on.

TM: Right; it will never happen fully. This issue of individuality and community is our raw material to work with as a democracy, and it will engage us for a lifetime and for generations. We've already done a lot, but it may be generations and generations before America begins to realize its full potential. But part of our problem is that we don't have the ideas and intellectual life adequate to what we need to work through these issues. Many people in the intellectual world and in higher education have done this kind of research, but they keep themselves at arm's distance. So the "ivory tower" theme is very strong in the American psyche as well.

PP: One major stumbling block on this topic—and that hasn't been explored that much—is embedded in our very founding: the "Declaration of Independence."

TM: In many of my talks, I speak about the need to write a "Declaration of Dependence," because we need to restore the value of the notion of dependency. Recently, for example, I was criticized for speaking out against the word *codependency*. But I was doing that because it's a term that puts a very negative connotation on the notion of dependence, of being mutually related, and of being able to rely on each other.

PP: If you were going to write your own "Declaration of Dependence," what would it sound like? How would it be different?

TM: We the people need to rely upon each other. Our lives are intertwined, every inch of the way. None of us individually knows everything we need to know, or can control everything that needs to be controlled, or can solve everything that needs to be solved: we need each other, and we need to listen to each other. I've even said that we even need to obey each other in a certain way, in the sense that we could listen for guidance for our own lives from each other. We could even hear the voice of the other as the voice of our own destiny. I don't mean that in a masochistic way, where we just do what somebody else tells us, but rather in terms of listening to what other people say—mulling it over for a long period of time, and taking it seriously, especially if it stings or is counter to our own present position. That's being dependent; that's declaring our dependency.

PP: The word *dependency* is so loaded that, even when you say it, I notice I have a reaction. So I can imagine that this aversion to it goes very deep in the American psyche. But what you're offering is a more profound idea of the individual as more complex than we've imagined so far.

TM: In fact, people are going to be individual about how they go about becoming an individual: even individuality itself is going to be individual! Our very notion of what individuality means needs to have a great deal of variety to it, so that a person can be an individual even if someone else feels they don't fit their idea of the "ideal individual." So I don't think there should be some kind of structure or developmental scheme around how to become an individual. Some people may be extremely introverted in their style of life, or pass through periods of introversion. Others may be just the opposite, being way out there in the world; so there are many ways of being an individual. There are infinite possibilities for being an individual.

PP: So far we've focused on those parts of America that need more development. But I'm curious what you see as some of our "soul strengths," so to speak.

TM: If you look at the whole history of America, I think one of the areas where we're in great shape is in the arts. Think of the writers we've produced, for instance, who've grown up out of the American soil: William James, Eudora Welty, William Faulkner, Ralph Waldo Emerson, Emily Dickinson, and Mark Twain, to name just a few. So we have an extraordinary literary tradition and we continue to have excellent writers. In many ways, we've led the way with painting, architecture, and music; we've had, and still have, extraordinary musicians. So I think there's something in the American soul that nurtures the imagination.

PP: That's interesting, because it's more often the image of the cowboy than the artist that we associate with America.

TM: Well, much of our creativity is nurtured by that part of the American spirit that honors place, the way the cowboy is part of the land, and which is also a part of soul. In almost all of the artists and writers I've just mentioned, there's a close relationship between their art and their deep love for a specific place or region. Poets like Gary Snyder of the West Coast and Wendell Berry in Kentucky, for instance, write out of the souls of those places. So even though we still have trouble with our relationship with nature, we still have a strong love for nature. But I don't think we realize what a strong connection there is between nature and the imagination. When we have a close relationship with nature, our imaginations are fostered, and I think that's also something to recognize and celebrate.

So the country isn't to be found only in its narcissism, which is kind of an excessive spirit, but also has a soul dimension to it that's reflected in the arts. Unfortunately, this soulful part of America doesn't seem to touch our political life at all, and that's a big problem. Politicians would do well to listen to our people of vision, like those who write good stories or who make really good movies.

PP: I also wanted to talk to you about America's myth of progress, and what Hillman describes as our "hugeness complex." In *Care of the Soul*, you write about the "god of growth" who is dishonored by our technological and economic fanaticism. What do you mean by that—and is it that we've lost our sense of proportion or aesthetics, and that we're driven by this need to be a big superpower? As a country, we seem to love to do everything on such a grand scale.

TM: Well, let me tell you the story that comes to mind. Some years ago I was living in Dallas, where I used to work at the Dallas Institute for Humanities and Culture sponsoring lectures and conferences. As part of a conference, there was a lecture given on the topic "small is beautiful." So in my typically perverse way, I gave a lecture on the value of bigness. I just couldn't pass it up! I thought that if everyone

527

was going to talk about how wonderful small was, then we were going to create a monster out of bigness. It would become the "repressed opposite" of what we value as small, and criticize as big. So I don't think the way to go with America's "hugeness" is to simply reject "big," even though I do talk and write about the importance of small things, and the idea that small is beautiful.

PP: Then what is the way to understanding our American fascination for bigness and hugeness?

TM: I think we have to ask ourselves what it is that America is searching for when it tries to do everything on such a grand scale. And I think the answer to that question is that we actually do need bigness; the soul needs bigness. It's no accident that in some religions, for example, the Gods are giants: if you want to present the Gods, you present them as big. So I think that's something that is worth reflecting on.

But our preoccupation with hugeness and bigness is problematical because we're not approaching it with enough subtlety. And so the American soul's desire for bigness gets displaced onto building big shopping malls, like the Mall of America, or urban sprawl or huge houses or buildings. The lovely town of Amherst where I live, for instance, is next to the University of Massachusetts; but the skyline is scarred by all these big skyscrapers and high rises. You see the same thing in towns across the country. There's a certain kind of bigness that can destroy the soul of a place.

So while our obsession with bigness and sprawl and making things huge suggest to me that hugeness has value to America, it also means that our vision is not big enough. We've substituted physical size for grandness of vision. I think we have to be much subtler.

PP: And what would a more subtle approach to bigness mean?

TM: What if, instead of building another big shopping mall filled with the same chain stores that are everywhere across the country, we were to build a small shopping market that was one hundredth the size of a shopping mall, and that was remarkable for its architecture, and for the things we could see and buy there? What if the experience there was tremendous, awesome, and overwhelming: aesthetic, but still a market. The soul needs good shopping.

PP: Well, I think of the old bazaars.

TM: Right. Now how is a shopping mall not like a bazaar? That's a good koan[2] to meditate on. This is one way of learning to see how bigness is a symptom of something else that we actually do need. Despite the size of our mega-malls, we have a very small vision of what shopping could actually be. So if we enlarged our vision, we'd have something that's vast in its potential. As it is now, we have buildings that are huge, while the possibilities for shopping are minuscule.

PP: I don't think I've ever heard it said that the soul needs shopping!

TM: The soul needs shopping for the fantasy involved. All the things that you see are a way of relating to the world of things. To go window-shopping is actually a form of contemplation, where we contemplate the particularities, colors, shapes, and individuality of things. We talk about the individualism of people, but we could also talk about the individualism of things. From that point of view, shopping is very valuable. Shopping is also another form of community, a kind of neighborhood with people coming together, but who are not all coming together to talk the same way or be the same way: it's a bazaar-like atmosphere. So good shopping is very nutritious for the soul.

PP: So the soul is fed through shopping that provides a physical experience of variety and richness, rather than sameness and uniformity?

TM: The sameness is what allows these places to be so big physically. If we didn't have the sameness they'd have to be smaller. But correspondingly, they would be larger in imagination.

PP: How would you read America's desire to be a superpower on the world stage?

TM: I think it's something we have a lot of hubris about; it's a posture. We could be a superpower in ourselves: not just through our military or economic clout, but as a people living an incredibly rich kind of life. That would give us a different kind of power. As it is now, our "superpowerness" hides a great deal of shabbiness. People in other countries hear about America, and immediately think of the land of plenty. Then they come over here—and one look behind the façade of the buildings in the streets of New York, or any major city, and they can immediately see that we're not such a rich place. We're not really super; but we could be. And if we were, we could be even more of a light to the world. Then our power would be more grounded, and we wouldn't have to be displaying and protecting it defensively all the time. There are small countries all around us, but we don't even understand what they're doing or what they're saying. We just don't get them, because they're so small, and so we don't pay any attention to them.

PP: So we have a hard time paying attention to any other country unless they're on the same level as we are.

TM: Right, we don't want to relate to another country unless they're another superpower! I would think that if we were to become a bigger, richer, and more interesting country internally, we wouldn't have to use the word *super*. Then we could drop that superpower façade, have some humility, and just let our richness show itself. We're excessive in our ways of acting out, but we're not really excessive in our passion. What the soul of America really needs is a more passionate approach to life.

PP: You also write about the idea of the country taking a "collective vow of poverty." It made me think more broadly in terms of taking a vow of living with more of a sense of proportion and limits, especially in terms of caring for the environment.

TM: I lived for a long time in a monastic community, and lived under a vow of poverty. But the purpose of the vow was to promote community. If everybody had a sense of owning everything together, for example, then that would automatically generate community, because we'd all have mutual responsibility for the things around us. So things might be in better shape environmentally, just as you suggested, if we were all really living the vow of poverty. But without that spirit or vow of poverty, then everyone tries to get the most of what they can get; and that exploitation of resources doesn't foster community. ∎

Notes

1. Quotes and stories of Moore's father from <www.careofthesoul.net>.
2. In Zen Buddhism, a koan is a succinct paradoxical statement or question used as a meditation discipline.

—39—

An Israeli Psychoanalyst Reflects on America's Myth of the Hero

AN INTERVIEW WITH EREL SHALIT, PH.D.

OUR AMERICAN HERO IS a tough guy, whether man or woman. He is lean, taut-faced Gary Cooper in Stetson and boots, gun in holster, in his role as town marshal singlehandedly facing down a gang of killers in *High Noon*. She is Sally Field in *Norma Rae* leaping onto her work table at the local cotton mill, holding up a cardboard sign emblazoned with one word—UNION—silently exhorting her fellow laborers to unionize for better working conditions; and she is also textile worker Crystal Lee Sutton, who heroically played that role in real life.[1] Our American hero is Captain Chuck Yeager, played by Sam Shepard in *The Right Stuff*,[2] piloting the X-1 rocket plane to the edge of the atmosphere, becoming the first man to break the sound barrier— the day after he'd broken his ribs while out riding horseback. More personally, the American hero is my own father during World War II, sent on a secret mission from Los Angeles to Rio de Janeiro, flying with no radar through the steep passes of the Andes Mountains.

The hero archetype, the mythologist Joseph Campbell taught, is common to all cultures. Yet as many psychologists have commented throughout this book, the hero is writ especially large in the American psyche. It animates the telling of our history and operates as a background force in all our lives. But in a telling moment at the end of my father's life, he inadvertently revealed a more humble, human side to our idea of the victorious hero. After recounting his wartime flying feat on his deathbed, my father added these sparse but telling words: "Boy, was I *scared!*"

It was to learn more about these kinds of darker emotions that parallel the hero's journey that I was drawn to read Israeli Jungian psychoanalyst Erel Shalit's book *Enemy, Cripple, & Beggar: Shadows in the Hero's Path*. In his thoughtful reflections, Shalit recasts the modern hero as one who possesses psychological courage, able to venture bravely into the perilous underworld of the psyche. As, Shalit writes, "the Hero-myth is the central myth of Jungian psychoanalysis," because for Jung the hero's "grand opus" concerns the relations with the unconscious. In this Jungian interpretation, the "hero goes forth into the netherworld of the shadow, in spite of being threatened by the monsters that lurk in the darkness of the unconscious, to save an endangered soul . . . or to redeem a dormant myth or mythical motif, which he has to bring into consciousness. The hero thereby creates a new sense of meaning and relatedness."

Shalit himself is something of a hero, having stepped off the beaten path at a young age. As a teenager he became interested in reading Marcuse, Freud, Marx, and other progressive thinkers. Eventually, he became a psychologist; continuing his existential search, he read Jung's autobiography, *Memories, Dreams, Reflections*, intuitively grasping Jung's language of imagery, myth, and imagination.[3] Having struggled with the obsolete laws, commandments, rules, instructions, and particularities of "official Judaism," which tends to "take things in an overly formalistic direction, sometimes even to absurdities," says Shalit, studying Jung served paradoxically to reconnect him more deeply to his own ancestral background and faith. Jung, he says, "spoke about something very different. He spoke much more about the soul of religion—not the dogmatic framework of religion that detracts energy from the individual ego, and from individual will, consciousness, and decision-making."

A practicing psychologist for more than forty years, and a Jungian analyst for over twenty years, Shalit is currently the academic director of the Jungian Psychotherapy Program at Bar Ilan University. He is also a supervising analyst and past president of the Israel Society of Analytical Psychology (ISAP), and the author of many articles and books, including *The Complex: Path of Transformation from Archetype to Ego* and co-editor of *The Dream and Its Amplification*. Dr. Shalit travels widely, presenting lectures throughout the world in Israel, Europe, and the United States.

Not long after our phone interview in 2014, in fact, I had the pleasure of meeting Dr. Shalit in person while he was on a visit to Washington, D.C. to present a workshop on dreams. We discussed the interesting accident of fate that my father had flown the earliest flights for El Al, Israel's national airline, creating in me, like many Americans, a close bond to the country. In our dialogue, Shalit elaborates on the three rejected figures that shadow the hero on his or her quest—the enemy, the cripple, and the beggar—as well as how heroes are those who go in the opposite direction of convention. We also explored the American action heroes, and the nature of the abiding bond between Israel and the United States.

∗

Pythia Peay: I'd like to begin by asking you to describe some basic myths of the Israeli soul, in comparison to the American soul.

Erel Shalit: All cultures have mythical motifs that circle around in the deeper layers of our individual souls. In a society or culture, some motifs become more dominant than others. When the time is ripe, some mythical motifs may be replaced by a new guiding myth that surfaces in a culture's collective consciousness. In Israel, the cultural myth is based on the idea of the collective. It began to take shape around 1860, during the formative years of modern Zionism,[4] and the rise of ventures like the Kibbutz—collective communities which were based on socialist principles such as "from each according to his capacity, to each according to his need." So the myth of the collective has been very strong in Israel. To some degree, this was due to pragmatic reasons: the earth, for example, was too harsh to work alone.

This is in striking contrast to the American myth of individualism, where it's believed that each person can attain their goals through his or her own will, resources, and decisions. And although the United States is often harshly criticized all over the world, it's still the country where most immigrants want to go.

PP: And from your point of view, why is that? Is it because of the perception of abundance and material prosperity, or do people come here because they can have more freedom?

ES: I think that many immigrants see America as a place of great freedom and possibility. The sense of constriction and limitation, which individuals may have felt in other countries, such as Israel, is replaced by a sense of "open space"—like the vast prairie that symbolizes that part of America where, through hope, determination, and hard work, personal aspirations can be fulfilled.

But every guiding myth has a negative shadow side, which often becomes visible, paradoxically, at the very time the myth has become obsolete, and has lost its original ability to inspire. Having lost its meaning and significance, a myth whose "expiration date" has passed can become rigid and even extremist. As an outsider with limited ability to comment on American society and its pioneer mentality, it's possible that in its definition of freedom as the right of each citizen to own a gun, the country is witnessing the expression of a dying myth.

PP: That's a very interesting perspective and a very different take on the country's ongoing problem with gun violence. To go back to your point about America as a pioneer society, however, there is no pioneer or frontier without the hero—and a common representation of the hero in America is that of the cowboy with a gun. Given the recent wave of mass shootings, I wonder if you think that our hero myths need deepening and maturing?

ES: I think you're making an important point here. But often we tend to confuse the "hero" with "hero ideals." For example, the *archetypal energy* behind a gun and war is totally separate from the way these energies get *acted out* in reality. Heraclitus said that war or strife is the father of all things. So the energy of Mars, the classical God of war and aggression, is tremendously important; it's something that we all need. The word *aggression* comes from the Latin *ad gradere*, which means "to move toward." So without aggression, we don't move or take action. While Freud speaks about Eros as the life instinct, Winnicott, in fact, speaks about aggression as the life force.

But in our era the gun has become an archaic representation of this natural life force and sometimes of the hero ideal. In other words, the archetypal energy carried by the gun and the heroic ideal might be fine, but the actual manifestation of that energy may turn out to be quite distorted. Many things that are significant on an archetypal level can become dark and shadowy, or arrogant, tragic, fundamentalist, or pathetic, when they get acted out in actual reality.

PP: Is that because the archetypal energy behind the hero and his or her gun, for example, can get lost in translation?

ES: Yes, that's a good way to put it. In the transition from the archetypal level to actual living reality, much of the grandeur and divinity of the Gods is lost—and it *has* to get lost. Actual, personal, living reality entails archetypal energy at the kernel of our beings, but must not be *dominated* by archetypal energy and images. If that happens, we either become flooded (as in psychosis) or inflated—overly identifying with something that then becomes grotesque or dangerous.

So I think it's important to distinguish between the image of the "hero ideal" and the actual hero on the ground. Psychologically, whether male or female, the hero is an aspect of our conscious ego and identity. More important, it is that faculty in our conscious identity that takes the opposite direction.

PP: How does the hero take us in the opposite direction?

ES: Jung speaks about personal and collective consciousness. The latter is the layer of cultural conventions, norms, and habits, either in society or in our individual psyche. The superego is a manifestation of that collective consciousness. Now, ego consciousness has a tendency toward laziness: it gets into certain habits, prejudices, and ways of thinking. For example, whenever we come to an intersection, we wait for the traffic signal to tell us whether to stop or go. Most of the time we rely on that signal, without critically observing whether it is valid: if someone crosses the road on a red light, for instance, or if someone does not observe the rules. Similarly, many supposedly "personal" decisions are made based on social conventions rather than reflection in depth. The television sitcom character Archie Bunker[5] is a prime example of someone whose personal consciousness has practically stopped functioning. He reclined in his armchair and fell into the slumber of habitual and stereotypic ways of thinking.

The price we pay for this natural laziness is that we stop thinking independently, critically, or self-reflectively. But the hero, as a faculty of ego consciousness, is the one who goes in the opposite direction. That could be venturing out into the world to explore new ground, or undertaking some creative or political task. The hero, as Campbell said, either breaks up or departs from the safety of the familiar. To me as an analyst, the hero is primarily that faculty within the ego that turns toward the shadow and explores psychologically those hidden areas in the unconscious regions of the psyche.

PP: So how well developed do you think America is when it comes to this more inward expression of the hero?

ES: I think that societies in general have a tendency to be undeveloped in this area; they move naturally towards collective consciousness. This certainly pertains to the extroversion of America and much of Western society, which is less inclined toward introspection and soul-oriented reflection, and more focused on goal-oriented external achievements. So I think it is important that a place of respect is provided in society for those that balance this culturally dominant attitude—such as the philosopher, the writer, and the artist—so that their "hero-task" of going against the collective dominant attitude, and of drawing from otherwise neglected sources of wisdom, can be carried out.

PP: You've written about three figures—the enemy, the cripple, and the beggar—that you say are the "shadows in the hero's path." Can you say more about these figures, and how our encounters with them are part of the heroic journey inward into the unknown realms of the psyche?

ES: Enemy, cripple, and beggar are figurative images that I draw on to evoke certain features of the unconscious. The enemy, for instance, carries our projections. And as such it's easy to fight the enemy "out there": because it's a way to delude ourselves that we can get rid of our own shadow, or the unconscious, unacceptable parts of ourselves. When we confront an enemy "out there" for example, it's always an "other." But that enemy inevitably carries our own shortcomings, becoming a detested opponent whom we need to face—as initially we see our own shadow through the image of the enemy.

PP: That's very hard to do. Can you give me an example of how that works?

ES: I think it works on both individual and collective levels. During the Cold War, for example, both America and the Soviet Union demonized and imbued the other side with evil. We easily see this in the conflicts around the world today. But when each country in a conflict can begin to see the individual face of its enemy, there's a greater possibility that the enemy can become humanized, and then respective enemy countries can begin to withdraw some of their mutual projections.

This takes place not only on a national level, but in everyday life as well. The neighbor across the street who screams and shouts can easily become a bad "other" whom we might see as an enemy, and who carries the shadow for us unless we start facing it. When I see my shadow in my neighbor, for example, I might feel "this is not me." And if I feel any doubt, well, that can easily be compensated by anger, rejection, and contempt, which all serve to increase the distance between the other and myself. The alternative is to re-own my shadow and look into those aspects of myself—my weaknesses and my shortcomings—that I don't want to accept.

PP: Can you say something about the cripple as the shadow of the hero?

ES: The cripple is the name I decided to give to that part of the shadow that carries our weaknesses. I'm sensitive to the fact that using the word *cripple* is not politically correct. But the cripple appears frequently in fairy tales and in the dreams of those who aren't physically crippled, carrying those elements within which we experience as crippling—the paradox being that the more we disregard them, the more they cripple us. The hero ventures into the land of shadows in the psyche to encounter these crippled parts of ourselves that we have split off from awareness.

PP: I've certainly had dreams with crippled figures, and it's something I've always wondered about.

ES: I've also had the cripple appear in my dreams, and I think that variations of this wounded figure are among the more common dream motifs. In real life, we often detest encountering a sense of being crippled: for instance, when in old age we become acutely aware of the limitations of our body and the loss of strength, whether mental or physical. However, it is through embracing our complexes, and in this case recognizing an inner sense of crippledness, that we become human. It's also tremendously important in the transference that takes place between the patient and the therapist. A critical juncture has been reached in therapy when a patient starts relating to the therapist or the analyst as being crippled, as that's when the initial idealization begins to break down.

PP: Can you say more about what you mean by the transference in therapy, and how the figure of the cripple enters into the therapeutic process?

ES: When clients come for therapy or analysis, they frequently experience themselves as wounded, crippled, depressed, or anxious. Just the decision to go into therapy is an acknowledgment of those crippled parts of our own psychology, which is important. But while clients may experience themselves as a failure, or incapable, or sick, they often initially idealize the analyst as healthy, clever, and accomplished—and that creates a split. In the beginning, it's an important stage, because the analyst becomes imbued with healing capabilities. But patients cannot be truly healed until they can connect to the healing faculties in their own souls. And in order to do that the split between the patient as sick or crippled, versus the analyst as healthy, whole, and accomplished, needs to break down. And that happens when the patient starts to see that the analyst is not that great!

To use an example from my own practice, one of my female patients idealized me far beyond my personal capabilities, beyond anything that I really am. As her analysis progressed, she had a dream in which she was sitting across from me in the analytical setting: but I was sitting on a broken chair, trembling, as if I was very old, sick, and scared. But to discover that I, the analyst, also had parts of myself that were sick and crippled freed her up; she could now withdraw the projection onto me of her own healing abilities. The projection had initially been important in order to see the archetypal image of "healing," but then it was necessary to bring it back into herself.

So for both the analyst and the analysand it's tremendously important to experience the cripple within, because without that awareness, we remain in a state of projecting these unwanted, shadow sides onto the "other."

PP: That is so very beautifully said. What about the beggar?

ES: There are different cultural and individual attitudes toward the actual beggar in the street. Some say beggars are an expression of a malfunctioning society. Others refuse to give anything to beggars because they think they should go out and get a job. Another person might say they can never pass by a beggar without giving them something.

But the beggar in the psyche is a figurative way of describing the furthest reaches of the soul. In this sense, the beggar is not someone we need to give something to. He or she is someone who holds the whole world in his or her hands. It's an aspect within us that is totally free of the social persona, or the face that we present to the world. The beggar is totally rid of that kind of mask. It is an archetypal image of someone or something who holds in his or her hands the key to the "Self," and to something greater and beyond the world of consciousness.

PP: In modern-day society, the beggar would be the homeless person we see on the street holding out a can for money; and, as you pointed out, that stirs up all kinds of political debate. But you're almost saying that the beggar, in this inner sense, is a holy person.

ES: The idea of being homeless in actual reality is terrible; I wouldn't wish anyone to be homeless. But the beggar in one's soul doesn't need the kind of home that we require in real life. Again, this reflects the contrast between the inner world and the outer, and how important it is for the ego to differentiate between them, so that inner images aren't acted out in the real world. The beggar within is beyond everyday reality. In that sense, the beggar turns toward something holy, and stands at the gateway to the Self.

PP: So there is no coming to wholeness, or holiness, without these shadow figures.

ES: Right: There are no shortcuts to the Self, to an inner sense of wholeness. Claims of holiness by those who haven't walked the shadowy paths of the soul are very dangerous, because then the shadow is projected upon an "other," who becomes an evil to be destroyed. The inner figure of the beggar who faces both the shadow and the Self, like the Roman God Janus, also ensures humbleness.

PP: As an analyst, do you find that's it difficult for people when they encounter these shadow figures in their dreams?

ES: Yes, axiomatically. Because it involves coming face to face with those aspects of one's self that the ego doesn't want to have anything to do with. And that is exactly where we need the hero in this internal sense. Because the hero is the one who responds to a call. Frequently in dreams, the dreamer hears a voice saying something that no one else hears, because the hero's journey is always an individual journey, and it's a journey into the shadow. The hero is that aspect within the ego that undertakes the journey into the shadowland, whether through dreams, or through introspection or reflection. There the hero finds and struggles with the enemy within, and encounters those weaknesses that often take the shape of our complexes.

Do you know where the word *complex* comes from? It comes from the Latin *complectere*, and it means "to embrace." And that's what we need to do with our complexes: we need to embrace them. But that requires courage. It requires not the hero as an ideal, but the true hero function within us that dares to look at our weaknesses, shortcomings, difficulties, and sense of inferiority.

PP: The word *look* in this process seems important to me, because so often we think of the hero as confronting something in the outer world. Speaking personally, whenever I've had a difficult dream or encounter with my shadow, I often don't want to look at it. I want to look away. Is that why looking at the shadow as it comes up in our dreams is a form of heroism that takes courage?

ES: That's a wonderful of putting it! To look inward is also a way of being respectful of our unconscious. *Re-spect* comes from looking again, so it's also important to look—and to look again, and to look again. Therefore, inner work is no quick matter. And if you want to relate that to American society, American society is one of great speed; as if there is no time to look backwards or inwards or to look twice at something. Great speed can sometimes be very important, but like everything else it has a shadow side. Speed, quite naturally, makes it difficult for us to slow down, and to really look at ourselves, and to digest what we take in. Especially when we look into our shadow, we need to look not once, but at least twice.

Think for example of those old photos that we used to have: on the back side of the photo there was usually a date, a place, and sometimes a note. So when we looked at these old photos, we could once again recall and talk about particular memories and experiences in our past. This is in dramatic contrast to the newer digital photos that are numbered into infinity, and that are often without a name and a date. There are so many of them, and they're so easy to access, that we just take a quick glance, and then never really go back to look at them again.

PP: These digital photos also rarely become real photos that you hold in your hand and put in an album, and pass down the generations. I could not have written my memoir about my father without the old photos my parents kept, with their dates and inscriptions on the back, just as you described. But the point you're trying to make with these old photos is . . .

ES: Is that too great speed, and too great quantity, make it difficult to be steeped in memory, introspection, and reflection. These are qualities that are required to look into the less conscious parts of our soul, which is tremendously important, in order to be anchored in soulfulness and not pass through life as if it were a soap opera. Speed inhibits the depth of memory. It takes time to remember, to put together, to look at the old photos, for instance of your father. To write a memoir requires memory be kept, so that we can write (not necessarily literally), and live our life as a narrative worthy of remembering, a life accounted for.

PP: A popular phrase comes to mind that we use in America, called the "action hero." These are the mythic superheroes like Superman and Spider-Man and other figures that are made into movies and toys. I wonder what kind of name you would give to this opposite kind of hero you're describing, which is more of a thinking, reflecting hero.

ES: Well, the action hero is of course very energizing, and we need that aspect as well. There is a reason why children and the young are drawn much more to an action hero than a kind of reflective, introspective hero. So I wouldn't dismiss those young hero figures: they have a place as well, especially during certain stages of life. But if these superhero action heroes are everything, and if all our energy goes in that direction, then we are in great danger.

PP: Because?

ES: Because if we believe in speed, action, and unimpeded progress, then we don't account for the shadow. And the shadow has to be accounted for in order not to create a world in which the shadow gets projected wholesale onto the other, or unconsciously acted out, rather than something reflected upon. The shadow creates depth and volume; without it, we become shallow. Think of still life paintings: without a shadow, the objects are dead; but with a shadow, they come alive.

PP: I think you will have to give me a practical example of what you mean by the shadow getting "unconsciously acted out" in a culture. Are you talking about "unintended consequences" of our actions?

ES: For example, I once read an editorial from a magazine written in 1906 that described how wonderful the new motorized vehicles would be, because they would make cities cleaner, unlike horses that shit in the streets. The article went on to say that there would also be fewer accidents, because it's easier to control a motorized vehicle than a horse. Of course, we know now that cars and their drivers do cause accidents, and that it's not always so easy to control a motorized vehicle. We also know that cars cause pollution that fouls the air. Likewise, today we have brilliant young men and women creating apps for everything. But as brilliant as they are, those who are in the forefront of technological development are lagging behind in their awareness of ethical issues, or the inevitable side effects and shadow sides of some forms of technological progress.

I'm not a Luddite,[6] and I don't want to stop progress. But this tendency to move forward blindly at greater and greater speed has something to do with a cowboy mentality (not necessarily only in America, but wherever there is youthful recklessness). Whether geographically or technologically, this hero is going to speed ahead and conquer new areas. What's critically needed as a counterbalance is something like a "council of elders"—just like in old Roman times, when an old man sat in the cart with the hero returning triumphantly from the battlefield, and whispered in his ear, "You're also mortal, calm down."

The shadow can also sometimes grab a whole country, as for instance during the Nazi era.

PP: You seem to also be saying that, in this way, our inner work confronting the shadow images of the enemy, the cripple, and the beggar changes our relationship to the outer world—maybe even transforming the way we see these actual figures in the outer world.

ES: Essentially you are absolutely right, but I would like to differentiate a bit between these figures, and what happens externally, when we approach them internally.

The enemy, as I mentioned, first appears externally, because we tend to become aware of our shadow by means of projection. So we first see what is detestable and rejected within, when it crystallizes without. Thus, the enemy within represents that which is threatening me from my very own shadow. That encounter with the shadow in its projected form gives rise to the following reactions in the ego:

1. It puts the ego in a fighting mode, infusing the ego with Martian energy in order to fight off the enemy. This may be good or bad: if we are perpetually stuck in fighting a projection of ours, it can lead to a state of constant warfare.

2. It separates the ego from the "other." This is both good *and* bad: the ego needs to separate from the other within the unconscious and the other without in order to grow up and become independent. It does so by drawing a border and a boundary: for example, it builds a bulwark against intruding armies (whether within or without). But if it separates from the other, it loses a sense of connection, and becomes unrelated to itself, and to its own inner resources.

3. The enemy also offers an opportunity to lay down the sword. When I have established the boundaries of my ego and my independence, I may look the enemy (as the one who carries my projections) in the face. Then I have the opportunity to withdraw my projections, and to recognize that the evil that I saw in the other, is, in fact, within myself. I can then free the *actual* other (whether a person, a people, or a race) from my projection, and face the projection within. Thus, the enemy is humanized, and stops carrying my enemy projection (I don't, however, claim that this is always possible).

After I've taken back my projection from the enemy, I have to face what I detest and reject inside myself, which is typically the painful realization that I am also weak and bad, etc. This is when I encounter the cripple within. To accept the cripple within myself requires shifting from Mars to Eros, or to love and relatedness. And if I'm able to do that then, as you rightly say, I will be more compassionate and able to accept weaknesses in the other person. In fact, the more I am in touch with my inner cripple, the more I will be able to respect the person who is visibly crippled, whether physically, psychologically, or otherwise handicapped—seeing them more as a person, and less as a label. So this is the compassion that helps one to become freer from one's phobias and prejudices.

PP: And regarding the beggar?

ES: The internal beggar is similar to the beggar in the outer world in the sense that both lack a social persona. But the internal beggar in the depths of our shadow does not beg. The beggar doesn't ask for anything, and has nothing to offer—unless through reflection I find the treasures hidden in the emptiness of his hand, the emptiness that holds the soul of the world. This is the opposite of the beggar on the street who begs and who asks us to give him something. But if I am reflective about the beggar in my soul, then I will be able to see how in fact the beggar on the street corner holds a fragment of the beggar within. And then I might be able to glimpse the depth and the soul of the world in the beggar's outstretched hand.

PP: This sounds to me like a kind of spiritual practice of democracy. In closing, I'd like to ask you about the special, almost mythic bond shared between Israel and America. How would you describe the archetypal nature of this unique connection between the two countries?

ES: I would try to give two very brief answers to that. The first answer goes beyond the boundaries of America. To most of the Judaeo-Christian world, the land of Israel carries a kind of grand projection of the Heavenly Jerusalem. But just as every charismatic politician who gets into power eventually becomes more of a real, flawed person who fails to live up to those grand archetypal projections, so the same is true with Israel. Terrestrial Jerusalem on the ground, or Israel as an actual political reality, cannot carry the enormous burden of being as holy as the world's projections sometimes make it out to be.

With America, however, there is one additional aspect, and I think that is the pioneer aspect. There is something similar in certain ways about the mentality of the United States and Israel. Even though I spoke about the collective myth, which in Israel at least in the past has been very collective, whereas in America the collective guiding myth is much more individualistic, the two nations share a great pioneer spirit and a strong belief in being able to achieve something beyond the present. Entrepreneurship in Israel and in the States, for example, is considerably greater than in Europe.

Israel, for example, is sometimes called a "start-up nation." There is a lot of innovation and improvisation, plowing new ground, experimentation, and opening up to finding new ways of doing things, and less restriction by presiding collective formalities. So I think that reflects a certain attitude that Israel and America have in common. It does, however, also entail a constant need not to run away from one's shadow. ∎

Notes

1. For more on Crystal Lee Sutton, see <http://www.crystalleesutton.com/>.
2. For more on the life of test pilot and retired Air Force Brigadier General Chuck Yeager, see <http://www.chuckyeager.com>.
3. See Jung: 1989, and Jung: *Archetypes*, 1981: "The Psychology of the Child Archetype," par. 284.
4. Zionism began as a movement for the re-establishment of a Jewish nation in what is now Israel,

and is now about its development and protection. It was established as a political organization in 1897 under Theodor Herzl, and was later led by Chaim Weizmann.

5. Archie Bunker is the central character of the 1970s popular sitcom *All in the Family*, about a bigoted, conservative, blue-collar worker played by the actor Carroll O'Connor.

6. A Luddite actively resists technological innovation. The term comes from those who destroyed textile-making machines in Britain in the early nineteenth century under the banner of "Ned Ludd," a folkloric character who'd done the same.

America

The Last, Best Hope of the World

AN INTERVIEW WITH EDWARD EDINGER, M.D.

JUNGIAN ANALYST EDWARD EDINGER was the first psychologist I interviewed on the American psyche. So it seems fitting that our interview should bring this book to its conclusion. The year was 1994; I was steeped in my own personal Jungian analysis, and I had just begun my years-long journey to understand the American psyche through a psychological lens. Reading Edinger's book, *Ego and Archetype: Individuation and the Religious Function of the Psyche*, I'd become fascinated with how Jung's idea of the individuation process deepened American ideas around individualism.

So often, it seemed to me, the individual in modern-day culture seemed untethered to anything greater than meeting the demands of day-to-day needs. This was not a moral judgment, as like everyone else I was juggling as well as I could the demands of work and family. But was this, I wondered, the fulfillment of the American individual? Or did something more come with that choicest accident of fate and history, of having been born into the "land of the free, and the home of the brave"? Did only soldiers "fight" for America, or were there other ways of serving and defending the country?

These were some of the feelings behind the questions I took to Edinger, and which he answered in the most inspiring, patriotic manner. But before we began our interview, he had a few things to say to me. Was I, he wondered, writing out of my own "individual experience"? Because, he continued, "if you know what I'm talking about from your own experience, you can write out of that. But if you haven't learned it by your individual experience, then you're just playing with ideas, and then I'm afraid that what you have to write won't amount to much." I replied hopefully that the impetus for this project had indeed arisen out of my own inner psychological inner work, dreams, and creative process. "Then," Edinger said, "that's what you must be thinking about all the time as you write. It's difficult to make a bridge, but you have to find some way to translate and to give expression to whatever insights you've gained."

Sometimes referred to as an "American Jungian," Dr. Edinger was born in 1923 in Cedar Rapids, Iowa. He was a medical officer in the U.S. Army in Panama. After practicing as a supervising psychiatrist in a psychiatric hospital, he began studying with Esther Harding, one of Jung's first students. Eventually, Edinger became a Jungian analyst himself. He was also a founding member of the New York Jung Center, a frequent lecturer at the Los Angeles Jung Center, and wrote more than fourteen books expanding upon Jung's ideas. In the following interview, Edinger's ideas about America's archetypal role in world history proved a revelatory experience, as did his ideas about the work of conscious individuality—the work of differentiating who we truly are from the conventions and collective norms of society—as a form of citizenship and a more genuine fulfillment of what it means to be an individual.

During our conversation, Edinger was intent on educating me about America's place along the continuum of history; how its vision of democracy emerged out of the cultural convulsions of the sixteenth century; and how this historical "individuation" process continues to unfold in our struggles around immigration. He brings our interview to a ringing conclusion with his discussion of America's great task of multiculturalism, and how, if the country can hold together despite the tensions of a body politic comprised of citizens of various ethnicities, it might fulfill its purpose of bringing about world unification and peace to the planet. It was a perspective that inspired me anew about being an American, even as I go about my daily tasks shopping for food at the grocery store or chatting with my neighbors. I hope it will inspire others as well.

Pythia Peay: My first question concerns the Jungian principle of "individuation" and how it might deepen our American understanding of the individual. For example, in your book *Ego and Archetype* you say that the basis for almost all psychological problems lies in an unsatisfactory relationship to one's urge toward individuality. So perhaps you could begin by speaking to this issue.

Edward Edinger: I'll be glad to do that. But I think I need to preface my remarks on the individual with my more general picture of how I see America as a phenomenon in history as a whole. Jung has laid the groundwork for this in all of his work, especially in his book *Aion*, for what I call "archetypal psychohistory," a whole new discipline of study. We've had the development of psychohistory in the last few decades, but archetypal psychohistory has more of a personal nature.

PP: Can you say more about what you mean by "archetypal psychohistory"?

EE: I mean the unfolding drama of archetypal processes as they manifest in the collective history of the human race. All viable societies have at their core a central collective religious myth that represents the "God-image" for that civilization. America, for instance, is an offshoot of Western European civilization, which was hatched out of the theological mythology of the early Christian church.

As Western civilization unfolded, critical developments occurred around the beginning of the sixteenth century that led to a change in the Western ego. This began during the Protestant Reformation when, in effect, the traditional God-image in the sky "fell out of heaven" from its centuries-old place in the metaphysical system of the medieval church, and into the human psyche. The energy that was released from this fueled individual initiative, and in turn helped to give rise to the Renaissance, the scientific revolution, and the beginning of the great geographical explorations. The colonization of America was a result of those great geographical explorations.

PP: I'm not sure I understand what you mean by God "falling out of the sky" and into the human psyche, and how that triggered these enormous changes and cultural movements.

EE: The core idea underlying the Protestant Reformation was that every individual should be able to have his or her own direct relationship to God without the intermediaries of the Church or priests. Thus, the Reformation inevitably led to the splitting up of the Church into more and more denominations. Carried to its ultimate conclusion, the Protestant Reformation results in an almost infinite number of denominations, each with a membership of one: that's the very nature of the Reformation. So that's how individualism gets into American society so prominently.

This symbolism of each person's individual relationship to the Deity is also the essence of Jung's individuation process.

The main point I want to make, however, is that North America was largely colonized by the Puritans (who were an outgrowth of the Protestant Reformation), with the underlying conviction—and here is where the archetypal image of our American origins comes in—that they were repeating the journey to the Promised Land. This is the Old Testament narrative of the exodus of the Jews from Egypt; their wandering in the wilderness as they traveled through inhospitable territory; and their arrival in Canaan, where they had to conquer the previous inhabitants in order to be given what Yahweh had promised them.

This archetype of the journey to the Promised Land lived itself out quite specifically with the early colonists, who felt that they were fleeing persecution. It gave them the incentive to fulfill what they felt was their divine mandate to leave Europe and to make the crossing over the "wilderness of the ocean." Eventually, they arrived in the new "Promised Land" (of the New World) where very shortly they had to oust the current occupants—the Indians—and set up a theocracy.

So to follow up on your question concerning the individual, the imagery that lies behind the entire historical, collective phenomenon of the colonization, expansion, and consolidation of America is the imagery of individual development, as it initially arose out of the Protestant Reformation. That's why it makes sense that although the colonization movement started out as a collective undertaking, the archetypal background behind it led to more and more of an emphasis on the individual. So it's certainly true that individual development is a prominent feature of American society, and of our culture and history.

PP: And where are we today with regard to that historical evolution around the rise of the individual?

EE: We emphasize human rights a great deal; that's a big issue with "conscious" America. But what we're noticing in modern times is that although individuality is very consciously America's virtue and our value, there's been a very sizable *unconscious* backlash, so that we're becoming more and more collective. For a long while we had the Soviet Union to project our collective shadow onto. Now that's breaking down, and I think we're going to be more exposed to the realization about how collective we're actually becoming, even while touting our conscious values around individualism.

PP: Can you give me some specific examples of what you mean by that? I think you're saying that the shadow side of our country may be a sameness, or conformity.

EE: Yes, there's unconscious conformity. A clear, modern current example is the phenomenon of political correctness, which is becoming so prominent, and is also true in our general behavior.

PP: Do you mean examples of neighborhoods with their neat lawns all in a row?

EE: That's an obvious example. I'm thinking more in terms of our way of thinking, and what's permitted to be said, and what isn't permitted. The general attitudes and categories that operate in our collective public discourse are all collective. The containers of value that are generally acknowledged are all collective: churches, family, political organizations, ideological factions, or isms of various kinds—what Jung called the "wretched isms." These are the general containers of our psychic and spiritual values, and they're all collective.

PP: So you mean that there's no cultural container for the individual?

EE: The individual *is* the individual container, but he's apt to get pretty short shrift, because everything is governed by statistics. Jung goes into this in *The Undiscovered Self*.

PP: I wonder if you could say more about something you wrote in *Ego and Archetype*, that our era could be called the "Age of Alienation."

EE: Here's the way I see it. As I said, American culture is a branch, bud, or outgrowth of Western civilization as a whole. But it's going through a crisis because it's lost its core religious mythology. That's true for Western society, and it's also true for America. What once held society together is a common God-image that we all shared, and that was embedded in the metaphysical myths of Christianity. But now that's dissolved. I don't care whether church attendance has gone up statistically, or not. So far as the general American psyche is concerned, the effective functioning of that myth is gone. Nietzsche was right a century ago when he announced the fact that "God is dead." And that's been a catastrophe for society.

PP: Are you saying that this loss of our core faith is similar to a natural catastrophe, like a flood or an earthquake, but on a psychological level?

EE: Yes, but on an even greater, universal level, as it affects the civilization as a whole, not just one section of it. And since America is the youngest, living edge of Western civilization, it's going to manifest the phenomenon of the descent into chaos more quickly than the older, longer established, more historically based European aspects of civilization.

We're seeing that now in terms of violence and general disorganization and fragmentation. Part of it is a regression to anachronistic, factional fundamentalisms of various kinds that start warring with one another. We're seeing that in Eastern Europe now as communism breaks down as well. I view what's going on in the former communist country Bosnia[1] as a preview or a coming attraction of what's going to take place in America and eventually in Europe, too. There's an inevitability to the situation, I'm sorry to say, but I think it's better to state it baldly.

PP: That sounds frightening.

EE: Well, it's better to be prepared. Jung has spelled this all out in his book *Answer to Job*: for those that are willing and able to hear, the world is in for a vast "Job experience." Which means having to undergo catastrophic events for the purpose of the discovery and transformation of the God-image. I have written a little book on Jung called *Transformation of the God-Image*. My books all have historical references—because what is history? It is no more than the sum total story of all the individuals that go into making it up. But it's got individual psychology at its core.

PP: Much of this book is about ways people can recognize collective forces influencing their individual lives, and how they can find their own way to relate to these larger forces, and to live as best they can. So what does an individual who is experiencing this sense of loneliness and alienation think or do?

EE: First, realize that it's an individual experience and that it exists in the collective only because a sum total of individuals are feeling it. So just as its origin is in the individual, so healing of this existential crisis is to be found in the individual, one person at a time.

So if a person is feeling alienated, then his or her task is to discover the inner psychic realities of his or her individual existence, and to reconnect with the lost God-image within. To the extent that individuals do that, they are contributing to the redemption of society as a whole.

PP: Is it important in this process to learn the difference between the ego and what Jung called the "Self"? In other words, can individuals learn once again how to relate to that core within them as the Divine Source?

EE: That's the whole point of Jungian psychology, the whole thing in a nutshell! That's what my book is all about.

PP: I don't know if I can recommend everyone go into Jungian analysis, or if that would even be the right thing for everyone. But there is growing receptivity and even a hunger now to relate to something larger and more transpersonal.

EE: There's no point in everyone going into Jungian analysis. But there is a desperate longing, because as Thoreau wrote a century and a half ago, the mass of men lead lives of quiet desperation. That's compounded many times currently. It's very widespread, even while everybody is consciously spending all their time and thoughts on largely material matters.

PP: So if a person wanted to cultivate a relation with the "Self," or God within, and they weren't involved in Jungian psychology, or any other spiritual path, what steps could they take? What advice would you give?

EE: One thing I would tell people right away is to rehabilitate Emerson. He's pretty much gone by the board. I think it's absolutely disgraceful that he doesn't get major attention in all the public high schools. Aside from a few sentences in American lit class, you can go all the way through high school and never hear of him. But he's the wisest man America soil has produced, and he was the prophet of the individual.

Now Emerson can be misunderstood, and he is often criticized for over-emphasizing individualism at the expense of the welfare of society. But that's a misunderstanding, largely because Emerson's great intuitive powers perceived what we now call the Self: the transpersonal center of the individual. But he didn't have the terminology to distinguish that from the ego. Individualism—if it's ego-centered—is selfish, greedy individualism. But individuation is of another order. It's the development of the individual out of an awareness of the transpersonal center of the individual psyche, and that transforms selfishness to a whole new conscious level of a religious order.

PP: So you think Emerson is an important historical and even spiritual figure for America?

EE: Yes, because he was related to the inner life. He had a real living connection to the transpersonal dimension of the psyche.

PP: In a way that was archetypally, or essentially, American?

EE: Well, his work is universal, but he was an American and he arrived out of the American experience, so he's our gateway to the objective psyche.

PP: Which of his essays in particular would you point to?

EE: "The Over-Soul."[2] All of his essays explore this in one way or another, but this one describes it most explicitly.

PP: You've also spoken about the individuation process as it applies to a whole nation. Could you talk more about that in terms of America's "individuation process"?

EE: What I see going on in world history is a process that mirrors what goes on in the process of the individual. One of the features of the individuation process is the way a fragmented psyche that is made up of unconscious complexes—and that work against the conscious ego—can be progressively brought into a state of unification. And world history, I think, also has as its goal unification, and that means political unification and psychological unification. Needless to say we're a long way from that. But through understanding the symbolism of the individuation process, one can see that if the human race survives, world unification will eventually happen.

Now America is a kind of advanced laboratory for the world in that regard. We are the one nation that on principle has turned itself into a microcosm of the world as a whole. We've got the most open borders of any nation in the world, and on principle we are a nation of immigrants from all over the world. We've got little communities all over the United States that represent every major ethnic and national entity in the whole world. So when something goes on in another country, there's a demonstration in front of the White House for that particular community. We are a microcosm of the world, and we're the experimental laboratory for world unification. And that's why our motto is *E Pluribus Unum*. That's an individuation motto.

PP: Can you say more about why *E Pluribus Unum* is an individuation motto?

EE: It means "From the many, one." Just as the psyche starts out as a multiplicity; so the goal of the individuation process is that wholeness can be achieved by the integration of its totality into a unity.

PP: So that we're seeing that acted out in . . .

EE: America is living that historically, in miniature, as a microcosm of the world. And that's why we're the last, best hope of the world. We really are, and if we don't make it the world hasn't got a chance. And if we do make it, then the world has a model that makes it likely that it can make it, too. It's a big deal, as I see it. We're experiencing a lot of pain and distress because of our diversity. Certain nations that have more or less ethnically uniform populations don't have that same problem. Japan, for example, is a good example of ethnic uniformity. And while they can criticize us for all of our problems around diversity, our diversity is part of our historical purpose and the purpose of our existence as a country. It's part of what makes us the hope of the world: because America is diverse, just as the world itself is diverse. Thus, the task is for one national entity to be able to integrate that diversity into a unity—*E Pluribus Unum*—without splitting.

That's what Lincoln realized, and that is what made the Civil War so crucially important psychologically. Together with Emerson, he's the other great historical figure in American history. Lincoln recognized that if the overriding value was the Union, then it had to be union at all costs: and this is because it's our country's historical purpose. I'm not sure if Lincoln perceived that at the level that I'm articulating now, but his sound instincts sensed this, and he gave everything for the Union.

As I said earlier, the U.S. has been living out the same archetype of the Sacred Land that ancient Israel lived out. But ancient Israel failed; not long after it attained its greatest success under King Solomon, it split apart into a northern and a southern kingdom, and then was later destroyed by invaders. And that was the same issue that confronted Lincoln during the Civil War: Were we going to split apart the way ancient Israel did? And in fact we broke that archetypal pattern, and we didn't split. Lincoln was the one that saved us. He could have agreed to secession and there would not have been a civil war. But he didn't do that, and he paid a terrible price for it.

We see minor versions of the Civil War all around us, as the various diverse competing factions that make up our totality as a country deal with one another. The problem is whether or not they will succeed in fragmenting us as a nation, or whether the historical purpose of the "unification of the many" will be able once again to predominate.

PP: On a practical level, the struggle of America to hold together almost always comes down to a boundary issue: How many people should we let in, and should we have more border patrols, and how can we live together despite all of our cultural differences?

EE: We have to be able to control our borders, otherwise we won't be a vessel. If we become too porous, we will lose our containing capacity entirely within our borders, and that will hinder unification.

PP: So how does that work out on an everyday level, for example in schools with large segments of Latino or Asian or Arabic-speaking children all in the same classroom, or other situations of cultural diversity?

EE: I'll tell you exactly what the task is. That task is to provide education in our public schools right down to the elementary level that all individuals need to be taught on principle that identification with ethnic, political, and ideological factions is not permitted. *Conscious relationship* to these various ethnic roots is greatly to be desired. But identification is not permitted.

PP: Why do you warn against this kind of religious-cultural identification?

EE: Because identifications are unconscious phenomena. They generate conflicts because each cultural entity or nation has its own collective God-image that reigns supreme, and who then tends to project the "devil"—the opposite—onto some contrasting collective culture or country.

So psychological understanding of the perversity of unconscious identification and projection needs to be standard teaching everywhere—to the point where overt shadow projection will then be immediately recognized and condemned.

PP: It would seem important for people to find psychologically enlightened ways to renew their sense of idealism around America. You've given us a lot of new perspectives in that regard, but in closing, could you say more about what it means to be a more conscious citizen or patriot?

EE: The collective unconscious has a national layer in it. It's not the deepest layer, but it is a real layer in the collective unconscious, and patriotism is an authentic religious phenomena. It's an authentic relation to the transpersonal psyche on the national level. And for a nation to be healthy, the populace needs to have a living connection to that level of the transpersonal psyche.

If that's a conscious connection, then it's not just mindless jingoism. Not at all! Rather, it's an aspect of the religious function of the psyche that is required for healthy living for the individual. It would be wonderful if some of our political leaders had the psychological vision to be able to communicate and articulate something of that sort for the nation. It would certainly help us as we go through the ordeals that are in store for us as the ethnic and ideological and political factions fragment more and more. It would be a unifying counter position to the fragmentation.

PP: Could you go even further into the question of what it means to be an American citizen?

EE: Yes, what does it mean to be an American citizen? That is the question. It means all the things that I've been talking about. It means my realization that I participate in this historical process that I've been describing, that is America. Because we really are the last, best hope of the world. And if we as individuals and as a nation understand the historical role that we're performing for the ongoing historical process that I just briefly outlined, that gives America, and its citizens, a sense of its transpersonal purpose. And ultimately that process has at its root the individuation of the world.

PP: And by individuation you mean a world that's whole, and unified—like the image of the planet Earth as seen from space?

EE: Yes, that's a good question. What does the individuation of the world mean? It's a kind of symbolic statement in itself, and as soon as you start to define it you lessen it. It's a sizable notion to take all that we mean by the word *individuation*, all that Jung has elaborated in his work as belonging to the individuation process and apply that to the historical process of the world unfolding. Just to make that connection generates reflection. I don't know if I'm capable of defining it more precisely.

PP: Does it have to do with a different state of consciousness or awareness?

EE: Individuation is something that takes place in individuals. Collectivities do not carry consciousness. Individuals do. So the individuation of the world means a conscious wholeness predominating in the world. And that will occur only when a sufficient number of individuals have achieved consciousness of wholeness, and when that has taken place then the world itself becomes whole.

PP: And individuation from the way that you describe it is a very distinct process from individuality. ■

Notes
1. See Ch. 1, n. 3.
2. Emerson's essay can be read online at <http://www.emersoncentral.com/oversoul.htm>.

Acknowledgments

IN THE ACT OF writing their acknowledgments, authors pay tribute to the unassailable truth that while they may have been the ones seated alone at their desks, putting word after word, paragraph after paragraph, page after page, and chapter by chapter together to construct a book, they are all too aware of the fact that they could never have accomplished such a feat without the support, inspiration, and encouragement of others. It is also true that in writing their acknowledgments, writers are keenly sensitive that a linear list of names of family, friends, colleagues, and contributors can never do justice to the special part played by each person on that list. Nowhere are these two things truer than with this book, *America on the Couch*, which, from its inception, has been a collaborative work of ideas dedicated to deepening our ideas and understanding of the United States.

In taking the first step onto what I imagine as a spiral of names, I would like to thank first of all those psychotherapists, psychoanalysts, Jungian analysts, and clinical psychologists who have given generously of their time, the depth of their knowledge and experience as teachers, writers, and practicing therapists, and the best of their thinking on the American psyche. In order of their appearance in the six chapters, those thinkers to whom I would like to give my sincerest and warmest thanks and appreciation are: Robert Jay Lifton, Charles B. Strozier, Luigi Zoja, Michael Eigen, Donald Kalsched, Larry Decker, Ginette Paris, A. Thomas McLellan, Charles Grob, Marion Woodman, Linda Schierse Leonard, Ernest Rossi, Karen B. Walant, Stephen

Aizenstat, Mary Pipher, Raymond De Young, Stephen J. Foster, Bonnie Bright, Gary S. Bobroff, Paul Wachtel, Philip Cushman, Thomas Singer, A. Chris Heath, Lawrence Staples, Bud Harris, Andrew Samuels, Judith Jordan, Murray Stein, John Beebe, James Hillman, Harriet Lerner, Robert J. Langs, June Singer, Mihaly Csikszentmihalyi, Thomas Moore, Erel Shalit, and Edward Edinger. Thank you, thank you all, for your thoughtful and wise perspectives, and for bearing so patiently with the editing and review process involved in each interview. I would also like to thank my friend, journalist, educator, and Jungian analyst Susan Roberts, for her behind-the-scenes insights into the shaping and implementing of this project over the years, and also for her love of country.

To my extraordinary circle of friends who have borne with me as I have vanished from their lives for long periods of time, I cannot thank you enough for your nourishing love and interest. For her lifelong friendship, spiritual guidance, and incredibly generous financial support for this project over the years, I want to thank Taj Inayat; thank you also to Sylvia Seret as well for her financial support, enduring friendship, and for our dreamwork, and a similar share of gratitude to dear friends Lis Akhtarzandi and Elise Wiarda for our long and precious friendship and home-cooked meals; and to Janet Meyerson, Ann Cochran, Sally Craig, Barbara Graham, Harriett Crosby, Yvonne Seng, and Dodie Brady, thank you for our conversations, lunches, dinners, and for always being there; and to my neighbors Jack, Pauline, and Bernie, who bore patiently with my neglected lawn while I worked on this book. I am also grateful to Scott Brickman for his generous financial support of this book.

To my family, my foundation, I want to thank my mother, Sheila, my brothers and sisters-in-law John and Tracy, Steve and Inyeong, and my sister Colleen for their love, patience, and encouragement. It is not an understatement to say that this book would not exist were it not for the truly generous practical, financial, and extremely patient support provided by Terry and Anne Peay, father and stepmother to our three sons: thank you, thank you, many, many times over. Our family dinners, gatherings, and ongoing adventures together are the bread of my life. And to my three sons and daughters-in-law, Kabir and Alison, Amir and Carol, Abe and Vera and to my darling granddaughter, Eslyn: this book is really for all of you, because I love each one of you, but also for the hope of a wiser and more grounded American future. A special thank you goes to my middle son, Amir, for his inspired suggestion to introduce each chapter in this book with a vignette from American history, and to Carol Montoni for her invaluable technological expertise, especially during those moments of "computer crisis" every writer suffers.

I am also very grateful to the creative and dynamic director/producer team of Snapdragon Films for the luminous and evocative book trailer they made for *American Icarus* and *America on the Couch*. And finally, rounding up the circle, I want to thank my editor, publisher, and soul brother, Martin Rowe—I wish all writers could know what it's like to be so fully supported, and to collaborate with someone in possession of such a well-educated intellect and creative and lively imagination. In an era of the vanishing editor, he has held high the standard, offering valuable editorial insights and guidance, patiently allowing me time and space to write and complete this monumental task, painstakingly editing the final manuscript (a Herculean effort) and, together with his lovely wife and also my friend and soul sister, Mia MacDonald, always, always keeping faith. ■

Dramatis Personae
Historical figures who appear in this book

Adams, John (1735–1826). Federalist and second President of the United States (1797–1801) and first Vice President, under George Washington.

Adams, John Quincy (1867–1848). Democratic-Republican and sixth President of the United States (1825–1829) and a longstanding member of the House of Representatives.

Alger, Horatio (1832–1899). American author, best known for his "rags to riches" stories about poor boys rising from humble backgrounds through diligence, bravery, and uprightness.

Anderson, Marian (1897–1993). African-American contralto, and civil rights icon. When, in 1939, the Daughters of the American Revolution refused permission to allow her to perform at Constitution Hall in Washington, DC, First Lady Eleanor Roosevelt invited her to sing on the steps of the Lincoln Memorial on Easter Sunday. 75,000 attended, while millions listened in on the radio.

Aristotle (384–322 BCE). Greek philosopher and teacher, most famously of Alexander of Macedon. Among his writings are his treatises on ethics, poetics, zoology, and metaphysics.

Augustine of Hippo (354–430). Born in Africa, Augustine was a Christian theologian and influential writer and apologist. He is the author of *Confessions* and *City of God*.

Bach, Johann Sebastian (1685–1750). German organist and composer of sacred and secular music. Famed for his *St. Matthew Passion* and *Mass in B-Minor*.

Ball, Lucille (1911–1989). Pioneering film and television comedienne, who became a studio executive. She was known for her slapstick humor.

Baranger, Madeleine (b. 1920) and *Willy* (1920–1994). French-born psychoanalysts who settled in Uruguay and Argentina.

Beatles, The. Quartet of British rock musicians—Paul McCartney, John Lennon, Ringo Starr, and

George Harrison—who achieved unparalleled success in the 1960s, and influenced pop music in numerous and lasting ways.

Beck, Glenn (b. 1964). Controversial conservative American political commentator and television and radio host. His Glenn Beck program ran on Fox News Channel (2009–2011). Since then he has broadcast on his own television network, TheBlaze.

Beethoven, Ludwig van (1770–1827). German composer and pianist, known for his nine symphonies, five piano concerti, and his string quartets.

Berry, Wendell (b. 1934). American novelist, poet, farmer, and environmental activist. He was awarded the National Humanities Medal in 2010.

Bion, Wilfred (1897–1979). British psychoanalyst. He is known for his work on group dynamics.

Blair, Tony (b. 1953). British Labour Prime Minister (1997–2007). He took the United Kingdom into war in Afghanistan and Iraq.

Bly, Robert (b. 1926). Poet, author, and leader in the popular men's movement of the 1990s, where he worked with Michael Meade, James Hillman, and others.

Boehner, John (b. 1949). Republican Speaker of the House of Representatives (2011–).

Bowlby, John (1907–1990). British psychoanalyst who became noted for his interest in child development and for his pioneering work in attachment theory and how separation from caregivers impacted children.

Bradley, Bill (b. 1943). Democratic U.S. Senator from New Jersey (1979–1997) and Hall of Fame basketball player.

Buffett, Warren (b. 1930). American investor and philanthropist. In 2013, *Forbes* magazine estimated his net worth at $63.3 billion. In 2006, Buffett announced his intention of giving billions of dollars worth of his Berkshire Hathaway stock each year to the Bill and Melinda Gates Foundation. The gift for 2014 alone was worth $2.1 billion.

Bush, George Herbert Walker (b. 1920). Republican and forty-first President of the United States (1989–1993). In 1991, Bush led a coalition of forces that forced Saddam Hussein, President of Iraq, out of Kuwait, which he had invaded in 1990. This operation was named "Desert Storm," and is referred to as the (first) Gulf War. He is married to Barbara Bush.

Bush, George W. (b. 1946). Republican and forty-third President of the United States (2001–2009), and son of G. H. W. Bush. He initiated war against Afghanistan (2001–present), following the 9/11 attacks, and overthrew Saddam Hussein following the U.S.–led invasion of Iraq in 2003.

Caesar, Julius (100–44 BCE). Roman general and statesman, whose campaigns in Britain and Gaul won him renown in Rome. When, however, he brought his army to Rome in 49, many leading senators and leading citizens felt he threatened the security of the Republic, and he was assassinated. After a civil war, his nephew and adopted son Octavian ultimately became Augustus, the first emperor.

Campbell, Joseph (1904–1987). American mythologist and scholar of comparative religions. He is the author of the tetralogy *The Masks of God*.

Carson, Rachel (1907–1964). Scientist and author, her classic *Silent Spring* was first serialized in *The New Yorker* in June and then published as a book in September 1962. The outcry that followed its publication forced the banning of DDT and spurred revolutionary changes in the laws affecting our air, land, and water.

Carter, James ("Jimmy") (b. 1924). Democrat and thirty-ninth President of the United States (1976–1980). During his presidency, the United States experienced high gas prices and an energy shortage, as well as high inflation.

Cassat, Mary (1844–1926). American painter who lived most of her life in France, and exhibited her work with the Impressionists.

Cheney, Richard ("Dick") (b. 1941). Forty-sixth Vice President (2001–2009) of the United States and U.S. Secretary of Defense (1989–1993) during the administration of President George H. W. Bush.

Churchill, Sir Winston (1874–1965). A British politician, writer, and historian, Churchill was prime minister of Britain during World War II.

Cicero, Marcus Tullius (106–43 BCE). Acclaimed Roman orator, philosopher, and politician, who tried to uphold the principles of the Roman Republic in its final years.

Civitarese, Giuseppe (b. 1958). Italian analyst, who publishes widely on various subjects including the theory of the analytic field and psychoanalytic criticism.

Clinton, Hillary Rodham (b. 1947). Senator from New York and U.S. Secretary of State (2009–2013). She campaigned for the Democratic nomination for President in 2008.

Clinton, William Jefferson "Bill" (b. 1946). Democrat and forty-second President of the United States (1993–2001).

Columbus, Christopher (1451–1506). Italian explorer (Cristofo Colombo) who, working under the auspices of the Spanish, conquered islands in the Caribbean and the coastal regions of Central and Latin America.

Confucius (Pinyin: Kongfuzi) (551–479 BCE). Chinese philosopher and political theorist, known for the *Analects*.

Da Costa, Jacob Mendes was a surgeon who researched and investigated "soldier's heart" during the American Civil War.

Dalai Lama, H. H. the 14th (b. 1935). Also known as Tenzin Gyatso, the Tibetan spiritual leader has lived in exile in Dharamsala, India, since 1959.

Darwin, Charles (1809–1882). Geologist and naturalist, whose *Origin of Species* (1859) describes his theory of evolution.

Dawkins, Richard (b. 1941). Evolutionary biologist and public intellectual and bestselling author of *The Selfish Gene* and *The God Delusion*. Dawkins has in recent years been associated, along with Christopher Hitchens and philosophers Sam Harris and Daniel Dennett, with the "New Atheists."

Dean, John (b. 1938). White House counsel for Richard Nixon from 1970 to April 1973, when he resigned during the height of the Watergate scandal. Subsequent to Watergate, Dean became critical of authoritarian conservatism, particularly during the presidency of George W. Bush.

Dickinson, Emily (1830–1886). American poet and recluse, who spent virtually her entire life in Amherst, Massachusetts. She was known for her distinctive poetic style and voice.

Dinesen, Isak (1885–1962). The pen name of Danish-born novelist and memoirist Karen Blixen, who lived in Kenya for many years and wrote *Out of Africa*.

Douglas, William O. (1898–1980). Associate Justice of the Supreme Court of the United States (1939–1975), the longest term ever for a Supreme Court Justice. He was known for his commitment to civil liberties.

Dostoevsky, Fyodor (1821–1881). Russian novelist, short story writer, essayist, journalist, and philosopher.

Eisenhower, Dwight D. (1890–1969). Republican and thirty-fourth President of the United States (1953–1961). He was a former five-star general who was Supreme Commander of Allied Forces in Europe during World War II.

Elizabeth I (1533–1603). Queen of England and Ireland (1558–1603), she famously remained unwed.

Emerson, Ralph Waldo (1803–1882). American poet, essayist, educator, and Transcendentalist philosopher.

Erickson, Milton (1901–1980). An American psychiatrist, specializing in medical hypnosis and family therapy. The founding President of the American Society for Clinical Hypnosis, he was noted for his approach to the unconscious mind as creative and solution-generating.

Faulkner, William (1897–1962). American novelist and short story writer, with a special concentration on Mississippi. He is known for his novels *Absolom, Absolom!* and *As I Lay Dying*. He was awarded the Nobel Prize for Literature in 1949.

Fey, Tina (b. 1970). American comedienne and writer, who appeared on NBC's *Saturday Night Live* from 1997 to 2006 and the TV show *30 Rock* (2006–2013). She is known for her satirical impersonation of Sarah Palin.

Fillmore, Millard (1800–1874). Whig and thirteenth President of the United States (1850–1853). He took over when President Zachary Taylor died in office and was the last Whig president. He consistently ranks among the worst ten presidents of the United States.

Fortas, Abe (1910–1982). Associate Justice of the U.S. Supreme Court (1965–1969). He was closely allied with President Lyndon Johnson. However, ethics problems forced him to resign from the court.

Franklin, Benjamin (1706–1790). Ambassador, printer, scientist, philanthropist, and Founding Father.

Frey-Rohn, Liliane. One of Jung's closest collaborators, she was also the author of *Friedrich Nietzsche: A Psychological Interpretation of His Life and Work.*

Friendly, Fred (1915–1988). President of CBS News and the creator, along with journalist Edward R. Murrow, of the documentary program *See It Now.* He originated the concept of public-access television cable TV channels, and in 1988 he hosted a PBS series, *Ethics in America.*

Freud, Sigmund (1856–1939). Born in Austria, and a neurologist by medical training, he is considered the founder of psychoanalysis. Among his many books are *The Interpretation of Dreams* (1900) and *Civilization and Its Discontents* (1930).

Gadamer, Hans-Georg (1900–2002). Leading Continental philosopher of the twentieth century. He rose to prominence with the publication of *Truth and Method* (1960).

Gandhi, Mohandas K. (1869–1948). Known as "Mahatma," or "Great Soul," Gandhi was an Indian civil rights leader who developed the concepts and practice of nonviolent civil disobedience.

Gandhi, Indira (1917–1984). Prime Minister of India (1966–1967, 1980–1984). She declared a State of Emergency (1975–1977) following unrest in the country and was assassinated by her bodyguards.

Garfield, James (1831–1881). Republican and twentieth President of the United States (1881). He was assassinated by Charles J. Guiteau.

Gates, Bill (b. 1955). Co-founder of Microsoft and, in 2013, the richest man in the world, with, according to *Forbes* magazine, a net worth of $81 billion. The Bill and Melinda Gates Foundation, with an endowment of $42 billion, is the largest private foundation in the world.

George III, King (1738–1820). King of Great Britain and Ireland (1760–1820). Under his reign, the American colonies achieved independence as the United States of America.

Giffords, Gabrielle (b. 1970). Democrat who represented Arizona's 8th congressional district in Congress. On January 8, 2011, she was among those shot by Jared Lee Loughner, as she was talking with her constituents in Tucson. She underwent extensive surgery, and resigned from Congress on January 25, 2012.

Goethe, Johann Wolfgang von (1749–1832). The towering figure of German letters, Goethe was the author of plays, novels, and poems, including *Faust* and *The Sorrows of Young Werther.*

Gore, Al (b. 1948). Forty-fifth Vice President of the United States (1993–2001), and Democratic nominee for President in 2000. He was awarded the Nobel Peace Prize in 2007.

Hagel, Charles (b. 1946). U.S. Secretary of Defense (2013–2015) in the Obama administration.

Harding, Mary Esther (1888–1971). British-born American and the first major Jungian analyst in the United States.

Hawken, Paul (b. 1946). American environmentalist, entrepreneur, journalist, and author who writes on sustainability and changing the relationship between business and the environment.

Heidegger, Martin (1889–1976). German philosopher, associated with existentialism, whose main focus was ontology, or the study of being.

Hemings, Sally (c. 1773–1835). Thomas Jefferson's slave and the mother of six of his children.

Hemingway, Ernest (1899–1961). American writer who won the Nobel Prize for Literature in 1954. Among his novels are *The Sun Also Rises* and *The Old Man and the Sea*.

Henry, Patrick (1736–1799). First (and sixth) Governor of Virginia in the United States. He is best remembered for his oratorical skills, especially the famous line, 'Give me liberty, or give me death."

Heraclitus (535–475 BCE). Pre-Socratic Greek philosopher, who argued that the universe was constantly in flux.

Hersh, Seymour (b. 1937). Investigative journalist and author. He first gained worldwide recognition for exposing the My Lai Massacre and its cover-up during the Vietnam War, for which he received the 1970 Pulitzer Prize for International Reporting. His 2004 reports on the U.S. military's mistreatment of detainees at Abu Ghraib prison gained much attention.

Hillman, James (1926–2011). Noted author and American psychologist who studied and became Director of Studies at the C. G. Jung Institute in Zürich. He also founded the new discipline of archetypal psychology.

Hitchens, Christopher (1949–2011). British-born American author, journalist, and provocateur, Hitchens was a virulent critic of religion and popular religious figures, particularly Mother Teresa of Calcutta. Among his books is *God Is Not Great: How Religion Poisons Everything*.

Hitler, Adolf (1889–1945). Nazi leader, who led Germany from 1933 until his death from suicide at the end of World War II. Responsible for many atrocities and for the Holocaust.

Hofstadter, Richard (1916–1970) was an American historian, public intellectual, and professor of American history at Columbia University. He was the author of many books, including *Social Darwinism in American (1860–1915)* and *Anti-Intellectualism in American Life*.

Holmes, James Eagan (b. 1987). Accused shooter of twelve people at a movie theater in Aurora, Colorado, on July 20, 2012.

Hoover, J. Edgar (1895–1972). First director of the Federal Bureau of Investigation, which he led from 1935 to his death. His counter-intelligence program (COINTELPRO) in the 1950s and 1960s tried to undermine the civil rights movement and protest against the Vietnam War.

Hope, Bob (1903–2003). British-born comedian and entertainer, with a wiseacre persona, who for fifty years was a fixture on USO tours to support American troops in combat.

Hopper, Edward (1882–1967). American realist painter, best known for *Nighthawks* (1942), a depiction of a sparsely populated urban diner at night.

Jackson, Andrew (1767–1845). Democrat and seventh President of the United States (1829–

1837). Hero of the 1812 War with the British, where he acquired his nickname of "Old Hickory" because of his toughness, Jackson was also a slave-holder and planter.

James, William (1842–1910) was an original thinker in the fields of physiology, psychology, and philosophy, and the author of the classic work on the phenomenon of religious experience, *The Varieties of Religious Experience* (1902).

Janet, Pierre (1859–1947) was a French psychologist and neurologist influential in bringing about in France and the United States a connection between academic psychology and the clinical treatment of mental illnesses. He stressed psychological factors in hypnosis and contributed to the modern concept of mental and emotional disorders involving anxiety, phobias, and other abnormal behavior.

Jefferson, Thomas (1743–1826). Democratic-Republican and third President of the United States (1801–1809). He helped draft the Declaration of Independence.

Johnson, Lyndon B. (1908–1973). Democrat and thirty-sixth President of the United States (1963–1968). He came to power on the assassination of President Kennedy, and passed the Civil Rights (1964) and Voting Rights (1965) acts, as part of his commitment to what he called "the Great Society." Mired in the expansion of the American involvement in the conflict in Vietnam, he didn't seek renomination.

Jones, Paula (b. 1966). A former Arkansas state employee who sued Bill Clinton for sexual harassment, following an incident in 1991 when the latter was Governor of Arkansas.

Jung, Carl Gustav (1875–1961). Born in Switzerland, Jung was a friend and colleague of Sigmund Freud, before breaking with him and founding the school of analytical psychology. He developed many popular concepts associated with psychotherapy, such as archetypes, the collective unconscious, and introversion and extroversion.

Kahlo, Frida (1907–1954). Mexican painter, best known for her self-portraits.

Kennedy, John F. (1917–1963). Democrat and thirty-fifth President of the United States. His youth and glamor offered a stark contrast to the Eisenhower years. He narrowly avoided a nuclear war with the Soviet Union in 1962, and advocated what he called "the New Frontier." His assassination on November 22, 1963 in Dallas sent shockwaves around the world.

Kennedy, Joseph P. (1888–1969). Former U.S. Ambassador to the Court of St. James in the U.K., as well as businessman, Kennedy was the father of John, Robert, and Edward Kennedy—all who became politicians.

Kennedy, Jr. Joseph P. (1915–1944). Oldest son of Joseph P. Kennedy, he was a naval pilot whose bomber carrying explosives blew up on a mission. He was posthumously awarded the Distinguished Flying Cross.

Kennedy, Robert F. (1925–1968). U.S. senator and former Attorney General in the administration of his brother, President John F. Kennedy (1961–1963), Bobby Kennedy was running for the Democratic nomination for President when he was assassinated.

Kierkegaard, Søren (1813–1855). Danish writer, critic, and theologian widely credited as the first existentialist philosopher.

Kim Il-sung (1912–1994). Dictator and founding President of the Democratic People's Republic of Korea (North Korea).

King, Jr., Martin Luther (1929–1968). American civil rights leader. He is best known for his stirring oratory, including the "I Have a Dream Speech," delivered at the Lincoln Memorial in Washington, DC, on August 28, 1963, and the "I've Been to the Mountaintop" speech, given on April 3, 1968, the night before he was assassinated in Memphis, Tennessee. King was awarded the Nobel Peace Prize in 1964.

Klein, Melanie (1882–1960). Born in Vienna, Klein extended Sigmund Freud's understanding of the unconscious mind. Known for her work on children's play and the mind of the infant, she made original theoretical contributions to psychoanalysis, most notably the "paranoid-schizoid position" and the "depressive position."

Kohut, Heinz (1913–1981). Vienna-born, American psychologist who broke from Freud to establish his own school of Self Psychology.

Kübler-Ross, Elisabeth (1926–2004) was a Swiss-born psychiatrist and a pioneer in near-death studies. The author of *On Death and Dying* (1969), she outlined the five stages of grief: denial, anger, bargaining, depression, and acceptance. See <http://www.ekrfoundation. org/bio/elisabeth-kubler-ross-biography/>.

Laden, Osama bin (1957–2011). Saudi-born jihadist and leader of the Islamist terrorist group Al-Qaeda, who masterminded the 9/11 attacks in the United States from a base in Afghanistan. After escaping from Afghanistan, he went into hiding. He was eventually assassinated by U.S. Navy Seals in Abbottabad, Pakistan, and his body buried at sea.

Lanza, Adam (1992–2012). Shooter of twenty six-year-olds and six adult staff at the Sandy Hook Elementary School, in Newtown, Connecticut, on December 14, 2012. Lanza, who committed suicide at the scene, had previously shot and killed his mother.

Lao-Tse (Pinyin: Laozi) (c. 6th century BCE). Semi-mythic writer of the *Tao Te Ching* (Pinyin: *Daodejing*), which advocated the following of the Tao/Dao or "Way."

Leary, Timothy (1920–1996). U.S. Harvard psychologist and writer, who experimented with LSD in the early 1960s, and became synonymous with the counterculture of the 1960s.

L'Enfant, Pierre Charles (1754–1825). French-born American architect who laid out the streets of Washington, DC.

Leno, Jay (b. 1950). Stand-up comedian who was the host of NBC's *The Tonight Show* from 1992 to 2009, and 2010 to 2014.

Lewinsky, Monica (b. 1973). In 1995, Lewinsky was an intern at the White House when she and President Bill Clinton entered into what he called an "inappropriate relationship." She was the victim of a politicized investigation that would ultimately lead to the president's impeachment.

Lincoln, Abraham (1809–1865). Republican and sixteenth President of the United States (1861–1865), who led the Union during the Civil War, issued the Emancipation Proclamation, which freed the slaves, and was assassinated by John Wilkes Booth.

Linehan, Marsha, Ph.D., is professor of psychology at the University of Washington, director of the Behavioral Research and Therapy Clinics, and founder of the Linehan Institute of Behavioral Technology. She is the creator of DBT (dialectical behavior therapy), a treatment that combines the technology of change derived from behavioral science with the radical acceptance, or "technology of acceptance," derived from both Eastern Zen practices and Western contemplative spirituality. For more information visit, The Linehan Institute <http://www.linehan.org/about-Linehan.php>.

Loughner, Jared Lee (b. 1988). Loughner shot and killed six people (including a nine-year-old girl), and severely wounded Rep. Gabrielle Giffords, in Tucson, Arizona on January 8, 2011. He pleaded guilty to nineteen charges of murder and attempted murder and was sentenced to life in prison without parole.

Madison, James (1751–1836). Democratic-Republican and fourth President of the United States (1809–1817) and one of the framers of the U.S. Constitution.

Mandela, Nelson (1918–2013). South African anti-apartheid revolutionary. He was imprisoned for twenty-seven years by the apartheid regime, after which he was elected as President of South Africa (1994–1999). He was awarded the Nobel Peace Prize in 1992.

Manson, Charles (b. 1934) was a cult leader who led a family commune. In 1971, he was found guilty of the murder of seven people, including the actress Sharon Tate.

Marcuse, Herbert (1898–1979). German-born American philosopher, affiliated with the Frankfurt School of social theorists. His books include *Eros and Civilization* and *One-Dimensional Man.*

Marx, Karl (1818–1883). German philosopher and economist, whose theories on historical and social development, and the inevitable demise of capitalism, birthed communism.

McKinley, William (1843–1901). Republican and twenty-fifth President of the United States (1897–1901). The last president to have served during the Civil War, McKinley was elected to the highest office twice. He was assassinated by anarchist Leon Czolgosz and succeeded by Theodore Roosevelt.

McVeigh, Timothy (1968–2001) was an American who detonated a truck bomb in front of the Alfred P. Murrah Federal Building in Oklahoma City on April 19, 1995, killing 168 people and injuring over 600. It remains the most significant act of domestic terrorism in United States history.

Mead, Margaret (1901–1978). American cultural anthropologist, whose books include *Coming of Age in Samoa* and *Culture and Commitment.*

Meir, Golda (1898–1978). Prime Minister of Israel (1969–1974), during which Israel fought and won the Yom Kippur War (1973).

Merkel, Angela (b. 1954). Leader of the Christian Democratic Union party since 2000 and Chancellor of Germany since 2005. She is the first woman to be Chancellor, and in 2014 was named by *Forbes* magazine as the most powerful woman in the world.

Midgley, Mary (b. 1919) is an English moral philosopher and author of many books. She was a senior lecturer in Philosophy at Newcastle University and is known for her work on science, ethics, and animal rights.

Monroe, James (1758–1831). Democratic-Republican and fifth President of the United States (1817–1825) and U.S. Secretary of State (1811–1817).

Murray, Henry (1893–1988). American psychologist who was director of the Harvard Psychological Clinic in the School of Arts and Sciences at Harvard for over thirty years.

Musial, Stan (1920–2013). Hall of Fame baseball player with the St. Louis Cardinals, and widely considered one of the greatest hitters in the game.

Nietzsche, Friedrich (1844–1900). German philosopher and poet, who first mentioned the death of God in *The Gay Science*. He also wrote *Also Sprach Zarathustra* and *The Birth of Tragedy*.

Nixon, Richard (1913–1994). Republican and thirty-seventh President of the United States (1968–1974). Vice President under Dwight Eisenhower, Nixon lost narrowly to John F. Kennedy in the 1960 election. He was forced to resign as president to avoid impeachment, after he was found to have known about the break in at Democratic National Committee headquarters at the Watergate complex in Washington, DC.

Obama, Barack (b. 1961). Democrat and forty-fourth President of the United States (2009–2016). Born in Hawaii to a Kenyan student and Ann Dunham (Soetoro), he was the junior Senator from Illinois when he ran for the presidency in 2008, and became the first African-American head of state. He passed the Patient Protection and Affordable Care Act (PPACA, known as ACA or "Obamacare) in 2009. Before his election, conservative media demanded he prove he'd been born in the U.S. by producing his birth certificate.

Obama, Sr., Barack Hussein (1936–1982). Kenyan politician. In 1960 he was a student at the University of Hawaii when he met Ann Dunham. Their son, Barack Obama, was born a year later. Obama, who had other wives and children, returned to Kenya, and saw his son for only a few weeks thereafter. An alcoholic, he died in a car accident.

Olbermann, Keith (b. 1959). Left-of-center American political and sports commentator, who hosted Countdown with Keith Olbermann on MSNBC cable channel from 2003 to 2012. He has since returned to hosting sports programs.

O'Neill, Eugene (1888–1953). Irish-American playwright and Nobel laureate in Literature (1936).

O'Reilly, Bill (b. 1949). Conservative American television host, commentator, and author, whose show *The O'Reilly Factor*, has run on the Fox News Channel since 1996.

Osmond, Humphrey (1917–2004) was a British psychiatrist known for inventing the word *psychedelic* and for his research into useful applications for psychedelic drugs.

Palin, Sarah (b. 1964). Former Republican Governor of Alaska who was chosen as the Vice Presidential candidate on the ticket of Republican Presidential nominee John McCain in the 2008 election.

Picasso, Pablo (1881–1973). Spanish painter and sculptor, whose work spans several decades. His most famous painting is, perhaps, *Guernica*.

Presley, Elvis (1935–1977). One of the pioneers of rock 'n' roll, he became addicted to prescription drugs and died of drug misuse.

Putin, Vladimir (b. 1952). President of Russia (2000–2008, and 2012 to the present).

Reagan, Ronald (1911–2004). Republican and fortieth President of the United States (1981–1989). Former Governor of California (1967–1975), he was called the "Great Communicator" and known for his positive and optimistic outlook. His ability to survive scandals led to him being called the "Teflon" President, after the non-stick chemical coating.

Renoir, Pierre-Auguste (1841–1919). French Impressionist painter, known particularly for his painting *Dance at Le Moulin de la Galette*.

Rivers, Joan (1933–2014). Comedienne, writer, producer, and talk-show host, known for her outrageous and often self-deprecating humor.

Robinson, Jack "Jackie" (1919–1972). African-American baseball player who broke the "color barrier" when in 1947 he became the first black man to play Major League Baseball.

Romney, Mitt (b. 1947). Republican nominee for President in 2012, the former Governor of Massachusetts was also a successful businessman, with a net worth in 2012, according to *Forbes* magazine, of $250 million.

Roosevelt, Eleanor (1884–1962). The spouse of Franklin Roosevelt, Eleanor was a political force in her own right, as a columnist, advocate for progressive causes, and, ultimately, as a delegate to the United Nations General Assembly, where she was instrumental in the drafting of the Universal Declaration of Human Rights.

Roosevelt, Franklin Delano (1882–1945). Democrat and thirty-second President of the United States (1933–1945). Elected four times to the office, Roosevelt oversaw the New Deal in the Depression, and was known for his optimism and ability to communicate with ordinary Americans.

Roosevelt, Theodore (1858–1919). Republican and twenty-sixth President of the United States (1901–1909). Adventurer, environmentalist, writer, trust-buster, imperialist, and militarist, he incongruously was awarded the Nobel Peace Prize in 1906, for forging an accord between Russia and Japan at the end of Russo-Japanese war in 1905.

Rush, Benjamin (1746–1813). A U.S. physician, social reformer, public health advocate, educator, and politician, Rush signed the Declaration of Independence and was involved in the Continental Congress.

Sadat, Anwar (1918–1981). Third President of Egypt, who, under the auspices of U.S. President

Jimmy Carter, signed the Camp David Peace Accords in 1978 with Israeli Prime Minister Menachem Begin, with whom we shared the Nobel Peace Prize that same year.

Santayana, George (1863–1952). Spanish-born American philosopher, essayist, and critic.

Sevareid, Eric (1912–1992). American radio and television journalist for CBS. He was the first to report the fall of Paris to the Nazis in 1940 and was a commentator for twelve years on CBS Evening News.

Sheldrake, Rupert (b. 1942). Author and biologist, who has researched parapsychology and coined the terms *morphic field* and *morphic resonance*.

Smith, Adam (1723–1790). Scottish moral philosopher, a pioneer of political economy and cited as the "father of modern economics," Smith is still among the most influential thinkers in the field of economics today. Smith is best known for two classic works: *The Theory of Moral Sentiments* (1759), and *An Inquiry into the Nature and Causes of the Wealth of Nations* (1776).

Smith, Jr. William (1728–1793). A loyalist and chief justice of New York province from 1763 to 1782, who left the U.S. for Canada following the American Revolution.

Snowden, Edward (b. 1983). Computer expert who in 2013 leaked information about how U.S. National Security Agency was spying on Americans and other citizens to the *Guardian* and *Washington Post* newspapers.

Snyder, Gary (b. 1930). American poet and essayist, with a special commitment to the environment. He won the Pulitzer Prize for his poetry collection *Turtle Island.*

Socrates (469–399 BCE). Greek philosopher and provocateur who was immortalized by his student Plato in his writings. The Athenians condemned Socrates to death, by drinking hemlock, for corrupting the minds of the city's youth.

Soetoro, Ann Dunham (1942–1995). The mother of President Barack Obama. After marrying and divorcing Barack Obama Sr., she moved to Indonesia as an anthropologist and social activist. She met Lolo Soetoro, and had a daughter, Maya (b. 1970). She died of cancer.

Stevenson II, Adlai (1900–1965). Twice Democratic nominee for President of the United States (1952 and 1956), he lost twice to Dwight Eisenhower. He also served as United Nations Ambassador (1961–1965) and as Governor of Illinois (1949–1953).

Stewart, James ("Jimmy") (1908–1997). American film actor, who often played ordinary, decent men faced with difficult moral choices, most famously in *The Man Who Shot Liberty Valance* (1962) and *It's a Wonderful Life* (1946).

Teresa, Mother (1910–1997). Roman Catholic nun and ethnic Albanian who dedicated her ministry to assisting the dying of Kolkata (Calcutta) with the Missionaries of Charity, which she founded in 1950. She was awarded the Nobel Peace Prize in 1979, and in 2003 was beatified as "Blessed Teresa of Calcutta."

Thatcher, Margaret (1926–2013). First woman prime minister of Britain (1979–1991), she led the Conservative Party from 1975 to 1991.

Thompson, Randy. Nebraskan rancher who has become the public face of opposition to TransCanada's Keystone XL Pipeline project.

Thoreau, Henry David (1817–1862). American philosopher, social activist, naturalist, and writer. His most famous works are *Walden* and *Civil Disobedience*.

Truman, Harry S. (1884–1972). Democrat and thirty-third President of the United States (1945–1953). Truman became President after Franklin Roosevelt died in office. He approved the decision to drop atomic bombs on Hiroshima and Nagasaki, and had a sign on his desk in the Oval Office stating: "The buck stops here." He is also reported to have said, "If you can't stand the heat, get out of the kitchen."

Tsarnaev, Dzhokar "Jahar" and his older brother Tamerlan are two Chechen brothers, who were suspects in the bombing at the Boston Marathon on April 15, 2013, which killed three and injured as many as 264. Tamerlan was shot and killed by police shortly after the bombing. Dzhokar is, at the time of writing, on trial for murder.

Twain, Mark (1835–1910). The pen-name of Samuel Langhorne Clemens, an American satirist, humorist, publisher, and traveler. He is most well known for *The Adventures of Tom Sawyer* and *Adventures of Huckleberry Finn*.

Ulanov, Ann (b. 1938). The Christiane Brooks Johnson Memorial Professor of Psychiatry and Religion at Union Theological Seminary in New York City. She is also a Jungian psychologist.

Warhol, Andy (1928–1987). Pop artist and impresario. He is perhaps most famous for his silkscreened reproductions of American celebrities, as well as his famous statement that, "in the future, everyone will be world-famous for fifteen minutes."

Washington, George (1732–1799). Commander-in-chief of the Continental Army during the Revolutionary War and first President of the United States (1789–1797).

Warren, Robert Penn (1905–1989). American poet, novelist, and literary critic. His most famous novel is *All the King's Men*.

Wayne, John (1907–1979). American film actor who often represented the archetypal hero of Western movies.

Welty, Eudora (1909–2001). American author of short stories and novels, with a focus on the American South. She won a Pulitzer Prize for her novel *The Optimist's Daughter* in 1973.

Whitman, Walt (1819–1892). Poet, essayist, and American original. Best-known for his compilation *Leaves of Grass* (1855).

Wilson, Bill (1895–1971). Co-founder of Alcoholics Anonymous.

Wilson, Woodrow (1856–1924). Democrat and twenty-eighth President of the United States (1913–1921). A leader of the Progressive movement, although with reactionary views on race, he took the United States into World War I, and then campaigned unsuccessfully for the U.S. to ratify the League of Nations.

Winnicott, D. W. (1896–1971). English psychiatrist and a leading object relations theorist.

Winthrop, John (1587–1649). A major figure in the foundation of the Massachusetts Bay Colony, which was the first substantial and lasting settlement of the Puritans in the New World.

Wolfowitz, Paul (b. 1937). U.S. Deputy Secretary of Defense (2001–2005) during the administration of President George W. Bush.

Woolf, Virginia (1882–1941). British novelist and essayist, perhaps best known for her novels *Mrs. Dalloway* and *To the Lighthouse*.

Zinn, Howard (1922–2010). American radical historian, author, and professor of Political Science at Boston University. He is best known for his book, *A People's History of the United States*.

Psychological Terms

The following definitions have been sourced from professional analysts, the Mayo Clinic (online), the *Penguin Dictionary of Psychology* by Arthur S. Reber, and *Jung's Map of the Soul* by Murray Stein.

Affect Regulation. This term refers to the extent to which an individual's expressions, responses, and feelings are considered appropriate from a "normal" point of view. Inappropriate affect is, in general, a hallmark of all psychological or psychiatric disorders.

Alchemy. Jung adapted the ancient proto-science of alchemy—turning base metals into gold—to describe the psychological stages of transformation and individuation into one's complete or whole self.

Attachment Theory. "Attachment" refers to a child's bond with its primary caregiver(s) in infancy and early childhood, which is thought to set the tone for all future relationship patterns and interactions. There are considered to be three main types of attachment: secure, anxious, and disorganized.

Attachment disorders. Attachment disorders are generally considered the result of disrupted, negative, or abusive childhood experiences with parents or caregivers, and can negatively affect emotional bonds and relationships in childhood and adulthood.

Cognitive Behavioral Therapy (CBT). Unlike psychoanalysis and other psychodynamic forms of therapy that examine unconscious forces driving behavior, CBT encourages patients to examine the thoughts behind their self-destructive actions and beliefs, so that they can modify their thoughts and change their behaviors.

Collective Soul. This refers to a shared sense of transcendent purpose and identity by a large group, whether a country, ethnicity, or the planet as a whole.

Collective Unconscious. Also known as the "Objective Psyche," this term refers to a large grouping of universal concepts, archetypes, symbols, values, morals, dreams, experiences, and images shared by all of humanity: for example war, love, marriage, and childbirth.

Complex. An unconscious, emotionally charged cluster of feelings and fixed ideas, such as a "father complex" or a "victim complex," typically activated by a form of psychic trauma, and that interferes with conscious functioning.

Daemon/Daimon. In the Jungian-oriented, depth psychological approach, a *daemon* derives from the ancient Greek word that refers to a person's unique, inborn creative talent. If the *daemon* or creative talent doesn't find expression in the outer world, it can turn into a demonic, negative force leading to addiction, depression, and even violence.

Dissociation. The defensive process whereby certain of an individual's activities, thoughts, attitudes, or emotions becomes separated and disconnected from the rest of his or her personality. A milder form is seen in *compartmentalization*, in which an individual mentally separates one set of activities from others. It is also used to describe the process by which thoughts or memories that cause anxiety are cut off from consciousness.

Differentiation. This refers to a kind of psychological maturity whereby a person is able to distinguish between various negative emotions (such as shame, guilt, and disgust), thus allowing them to address the problem that caused those emotions. Differentiation may also apply to the process by which members of a family individuate.

Ego. From the Latin for *I*, referring to the sense of one's individual consciousness and sense of agency. In classical psychology, the ego represents a cluster of cognitive and perceptual processes that are in touch with reality. Like an executive that functions to maintain psychic balance, the "ego" also includes defense mechanisms that help mediate between primitive instincts, internalized parental and cultural inhibitions, and reality.

Erostratism. A desire to gain fame and immortality through outrageous behavior, derived from Erostratus (d. 356 BCE), also known as Herostratus, who attempted to become famous by setting fire to the temple of Artemis in Ephesus, and was burned to death as a punishment.

God-Image. A living myth or deity commonly shared by a culture, or as the Self or transpersonal center, within an individual.

Individuation. The process of psychic development that leads to the conscious awareness of one's wholeness, and also of fully becoming the person one is meant to be. It is characterized, according to Jungian analyst Edward Edinger, by a relationship between the ego and the "Self," or the transpersonal center of the psyche; a commitment to the lifelong process of one's individual development; and a search for a meaningful life.

Integration. Generally, the process by which disparate elements—whether of one's individual psyche, personality, and behavior; a family or organization; or of the different segments of a larger city, culture, society, or nation—are brought together into a coordinated whole.

Narcissism. A feature of Narcissistic Personality Disorder (NPD), narcissism is characterized by grandiosity, rage, an overwhelming need for admiration, and a lack of empathy for others. Obsessed with their own power and success, those with NPD can display snobbish and patronizing attitudes and a sense of entitlement; they demand constant attention, have expectations of special treatment, and find it hard to maintain healthy relationships. These behaviors are all compensations for a deficient sense of self at the core of narcissism.

Normative abuse. See my interview with Walant, n. 1 (pp. 189–190).

Objective Psyche. Another term for the collective unconscious, coined by Carl Jung to describe inherited patterns of memories, instincts, and experiences common to all mankind. These patterns, called *archetypes*, influence behavior through dreams and unconscious ways of thinking and behaving.

Object Relations Theory. A school of psychology developed by Donald Winnicott that is centered on the emotional bonds between oneself and another, typically expressed in the sense of one's capacity to love and care for another as balanced against interest in and love for the self. Patterns of early relationships are thought to be internalized and then reenacted in subsequent relationships.

Paranoia. Symptoms of paranoia—a delusion that occurs in Paranoid Personality Disorder, schizophrenia, and other psychotic states—include feelings of persecution and irrational and intense mistrust and suspicion. Those suffering from paranoia may be defensive and argumentative; have difficulty with forgiveness; and be perfectionistic, stubborn, and preoccupied with being taken advantage of.

Prima materia. A phrase used in alchemy to refer to the raw material (such as lead or dirt) that is brought in at the beginning stage of the work to be transformed into gold or a higher metal. Jung adapted this phrase psychologically to refer to the personal problems and limitations an individual brings to analysis, and that are then brought to consciousness through reflection and imagination, with the aim of turning them into the gold of wisdom.

Psyche. The oldest use of the term dates to the early Greeks, who envisioned psyche as the soul or the essence of life. It can also be used to denote the *mind* and is the sense carried in the word *psychology*. In its broadest sense, it refers to the levels of consciousness beyond rational ego consciousness.

Psychopathy. Among the most difficult disorders to diagnose, the psychopath can appear normal, even charming, but underneath lacks conscience and empathy, making them manipulative, volatile, and sometimes (but not always) criminal. Although this condition is largely resistant to treatment, the vast majority of people with antisocial tendencies are *not* psychopaths.

Psychosis. A condition in which the ego is flooded by contents that erupt from the unconscious, resulting in a break with reality, whether through delusions or overwhelming emotions.

Puer. In Jungian psychology, the *puer* is the archetype of the young boy. This represents the possibility of newness, hope, and growth, but can mean, like a "Peter Pan," an individual who doesn't want to grow up and be an adult. The *puer* is opposite to the *senex*, or old man.

Relational-Cultural Theory. As developed by Judith Jordan and her colleagues at the Wellesley Centers for Women, RCT is built on the premise that human beings grow through and toward connection, and need connections to flourish, or even to stay alive.

Schizoid. A term that refers to some of the characteristics of *Schizoid Personality Disorder*, which is a personality disorder characterized by emotional coldness, secretiveness, solitude, withdrawal, an inability to form intimate attachments, and a pattern of detachment from social relationships. A person with schizoid personality disorder often has a restricted range of emotions when communicating with others.

Schizophrenia. Schizophrenia is a general label for a number of psychotic disorders with various cognitive, emotional, and behavioral manifestations, and is characterized by at least two of the following symptoms, for at least one month: delusions, hallucinations, disorganized and/or incoherent speech, and grossly disorganized or catatonic behavior.

Self. In Jungian psychology, the Self is the center of the psyche; the source of all archetypal images; the goal of psychic development; the wholeness of the personality, which cannot tolerate self-deceptions; and the principle and archetype of orientation and meaning.

Self Psychology. Developed by psychoanalyst Heinz Kohut, who stressed empathy in Freudian psychoanalysis. He saw many of the problems modern individuals encounter as stemming from a deficit of self, rather than a conflict of internal drives.

Separation-individuation theory of human development. As developed by the Hungarian psychoanalyst Margaret Mahler, this model posits that healthy human development unfolds as the infant moves away from a state of symbiotic oneness with the mother, gradually becoming a separate and autonomous adult with an individual identity.

Shadow. A term used in Jungian psychology to refer to the rejected and repressed parts of the ego's ideals and the conscious persona.

Synchronicity. A term describing the simultaneous occurrence of two events that have no apparent causal connection—a meaningful coincidence that, in Jungian psychology, can trigger a breakthrough or insight.

Tension of the Opposites. The tension between two opposing forces or viewpoints, within one's psyche or in the outer world. In Jungian psychology, this tension occurs between the conscious and the unconscious, which creates an inner conflict; through "holding" this tension without choosing sides, a third, unexpected solution arises that integrates both perspectives.

Transcendent Function. A term coined by Jung to describe the new attitude that arises out of the link between the conscious and the unconscious brought about by therapy, dream work, and other forms of inner work that provide renewal and open a way forward.

Typologies. A theory originally developed by Jung that identifies four psychological functions: feeling, thinking, sensation, and intuition. All of the above can be directed inwardly (through introversion) or outwardly (through extroversion).

Unconscious. A lack of awareness; and also used to refer to those repressed, internal processes made up of memories, feelings, and images that take place outside of consciousness. It is made up of both the personal unconscious and also the collective unconscious.

Bibliography

Books

Aizenstat, Stephen: *Dream Tending: Awakening to the Healing Power in Dreams*. New Orleans: Spring Journal, Inc., 2011.

Apperson, Virginia and John Beebe. *The Presence of the Feminine in Film*. Newcastle upon Tyne: Cambridge Scholars Publishing, 2009.

Bercovitch, Sacvan. *The Puritan Origins of the American Self*. New Haven: Yale University Press, 2011 [1975].

Beebe, John. *Integrity in Depth*. College Station: Texas A&M University Press, 1992.

Bernstein, Jerome. *Living in the Borderland: The Evolution of Consciousness and the Challenge of Healing Trauma*. New York: Routledge, 2005.

Bobroff, Gary S. *Jung, Crop Circles, and the Re-Emergence of the Archetypal Feminine*. Berkeley: North Atlantic Books, 2014.

Bowlby, John. *Attachment*. New York: Basic Books, 1969.

———. *Loss: Sadness and Depression*. New York: Basic Books, 1980.

———. *The Making and Breaking of Affectional Bonds*. New York: Routledge, 1979.

———. *Separation: Anxiety and Anger*. New York: Basic Books, 1973.

Carr, Nicholas G. *The Shallows: How the Internet Is Changing the Way We Think, Read and Remember*. New York: Atlantic, 2011.

Carson, Rachel. *Silent Spring*. New York: Houghton Mifflin, 2002.

Casey, Edward S. *Getting Back Into Place: Toward a Renewed Understanding of the Place World* (2nd edition). Bloomington: Indiana University Press, 2009.

Champernowne, Irene. *A Memoir of Toni Wolff.* San Francisco: C. G. Jung Institute of San Francisco, 1980.

Cheever, Susan. *My Name is Bill: Bill Wilson: His Life and the Creation of Alcoholics Anonymous.* New York: Washington Square Press, 2005.

Cohen, Stanley. *States of Denial: Knowing about Atrocities and Suffering.* Malden, Mass.: Blackwell Publishing, 2001.

Cooper, James Fenimore. *The Last of the Mohicans.* New York: Bantam Classics, 1982.

Csikszentmihalyi, Mihaly. *The Evolving Self: A Psychology for the Third Millennium.* New York: HarperCollins, 1993.

———. *Flow: The Psychology of Optimal Experience.* New York: HarperPerennial, 1991. Also. *Flow: The Secret to Happiness.* Ted2004; Filmed February 2004. Online at: <http://www.ted.com/talks/mihaly_csikszentmihalyi_on_flow?language=en>.

Cushman, Philip. *Constructing the Self, Constructing America.* New York: Addison-Wesley, 1995.

Dawkins, Richard. *The Selfish Gene* (30th anniversary edition). Oxford: Oxford University Press, 2006.

Decker, Larry. *The Alchemy of Combat.* New Lebanon, N.Y.: Omega Press, 2014.

De Young, Raymond and Thomas Princen, eds. *The Localization Reader: Adapting to the Coming Downshift.* Cambridge: MIT Press, 2012.

Edinger, Edward F. *Creation of Consciousness: Jung's Myth for Modern Man.* Toronto: Inner City Books, 1984.

———. *Ego and Archetype: Individuation and the Religious Function of the Psyche.* Boston: Shambhala, 1992.

———. *Transformation of the God-Image: An Elucidation of Jung's Answer to Job.* Toronto: Inner City Books, 1992.

Eigen, Michael. *Coming Through the Whirlwind: Case Studies in Psychotherapy.* Wilmette, Ill.: Chiron Publications, 1992.

———. *Damaged Bonds.* London: Karnac, 2001.

———. *The Electrified Tightrope.* London: Karnac, 2004.

———. *Feeling Matters: From the Yosemite God to the Annihilated Self.* London: Karnac, 2007.

———. *Lust.* Middletown, Ct.: Wesleyan University Press, 2006.

———. *Madness and Murder: Eigen in Soul, Volume One.* London: Karnac, 2010.

———. *Psychic Deadness.* London: Karnac, 2004.

———. *Rage.* Middletown, Ct.: Wesleyan University Press, 2002.

———. *Toxic Nourishment.* London: Karnac, 1999.

Eiseley, Loren. *All the Strange Hours: The Excavation of a Life.* Lincoln, Nebr.: Bison Books, 2000.

Ehrenreich, Barbara. *Nickel and Dimed: On (Not) Getting By in America* (10th anniversary edition). New York: Picador, 2011.

Ellis, Joseph J. *American Creation.* New York: Vintage Books, 2007.

Emerson, Ralph Waldo. *Self-Reliance, The Over-Soul, and Other Essays*. Claremont, Calif.: Coyote Canyon Press, 2010.

Fallaci, Oriana. *If the Sun Dies*. New York: Atheneum Books, 1966.

Fischer, David Hackett. *Washington's Crossing*. New York: Oxford University Press, 2004.

Fitzgerald, F. Scott. *The Great Gatsby*. New York: Scribner, 2004.

Foster, Stephen J. *Risky Business: A Jungian View of Environmental Disasters and the Nature Archetype*. Toronto: Inner City Books, 2011.

Frazer, Sir James. *The Golden Bough: A Study in Comparative Religion*. Mineola, N.Y.: Dover Publications, 2002 [1922].

Fromm, Eric. *Escape From Freedom*. New York: Holt Publishing, 1994.

Galbraith, John Kenneth. *The Affluent Society* (40th anniversary edition). New York: Mariner Books, 1998.

Giannini, John. *Compass of the Soul: Archetypal Guides to a Fuller Life*. Gainesville, Fla.: Center for Applications of Psychological Type, 2004.

Grob, Charles, ed. *Hallucinogens: A Reader*. New York: Tarcher, 2002.

Grob, Charles, and Roger Walsh, eds. *Higher Wisdom: Eminent Elders Explore the Continuing Impact of Psychedelics*. Albany, N.Y.: SUNY Press, 2005.

Harris, Bud. *Sacred Selfishness: A Guide to Living a Life of Substance*. Makawao, Hawaii: Inner Ocean Publishing, 2002.

Harris, Massimilla and Bud Harris. *Like Gold Through Fire: Understanding the Transforming Power of Suffering*. Carmel, Calif.: Fisher King Press, 1996, 2002.

Hawken, Paul. *Blessed Unrest: How the Largest Movement in the World Came Into Being and Why No One Saw It Coming*. Penguin Books: New York, 2008.

Hemingway, Ernest. *A Farewell to Arms*. New York: Scribner, 1995.

Hillman, James. *The Soul's Code: In Search of Character and Calling*. New York: Grand Central Publishing, 1997.

——. ed., *Puer Papers*. Dallas: Spring Publications, 1979.

Holland, Jesse. *Black Men Built the Capitol: Discovering African-American History In and Around Washington, D.C.* Guilford, Ct.: Globe Pequot Press, 2007.

Jewett, Robert and John Shelton Lawrence. *The American Monomyth*. New York: Anchor Press/ Doubleday, 1977.

Jordan, Judith. *The Power of Connection: Recent Developments in Relational-Cultural Theory*. New York: Routledge, 2013.

——. *Relational-Cultural Theory*. Washington, D.C.: American Psychological Association, 2009.

Jordan, Judith V., Alexandra G. Kaplan, Jean Baker Miller, Irene P. Stiver, and Janet L. Surrey. *Women's Growth in Connection: Writings from the Stone Center*. New York and London: Guilford Press, 1991.

Jung, Carl G. *Aion: Researches Into the Phenomenology of the Self* (2nd edition). Princeton: Princeton University Press, 1952.

———. *Answer to Job* (Collected Works of C. G. Jung, Vol. 11). Princeton: Princeton University Press, 2010.

———. *The Archetypes and the Collective Unconscious* (Collected Works of C. G. Jung, Vol. 9: Part 1, second edition). Princeton: Princeton University Press, 1981.

———. *Memories, Dreams, Reflections* (edited by Aniela Jaffé and translated by Clara Winston). New York: Vintage Books, 1989.

———. *Psychological Types* (Collected Works of C. G. Jung, Vol. 6). Princeton: Princeton University Press, 1971.

———. *The Portable Jung* (edited by Joseph Campbell and translated by R. F. C. Hull). New York: Penguin, 1976.

———. *Two Essays on Analytical Psychology* (Collected Works of C. G. Jung Vol. 7). Princeton: Princeton University Press, 1972.

———. *The Undiscovered Self.* New York: Signet, 2006.

Kalsched. Donald E. *The Inner World of Trauma: Archetypal Defenses of the Personal Spirit.* New York: Routledge, 1996.

———. *Trauma and the Soul: A Psycho-Spiritual Approach to Human Development and Its Interruption.* New York: Routledge, 2013.

Kazantzakis, Nikos. *Zorba the Greek* (3rd edition). New York: Touchstone, 1996.

Kazin, Michael, Rebecca Edwards, Adam Rothman, associate editors. *The Concise Princeton Encyclopedia of American Political History.* Princeton: Princeton University Press, 2011.

Langs, Robert. *Fundamentals of Adaptive Psychotherapy and Counselling.* New York: Palgrave MacMillan, 2004.

———. *Unconscious Communication in Everyday Life.* New York: Jason Aronson, 1983.

LaPlante, Eve. *American Jezebel: the Uncommon Life of Anne Hutchinson, the Woman Who Defied the Puritans.* New York: HarperCollins, 2004.

Lear, Jonathan. *Radical Hope in the Face of Cultural Devastation.* Cambridge, Mass. and London: Harvard University Press, 2006. All quotes and references in Part III are from this book.

Lender, Mark Edward and James Kirby Martin. *Drinking in America: A History* (rev. & expanded). New York: The Free Press, 1987.

Leonard, Linda Schierse. *Following the Path of the Reindeer Woman: Path of Peace and Harmony.* New Orleans: Spring Journal Books, 2005.

———. *Witness to the Fire: Creativity and the Veil of Addiction.* Boston: Shambhala, 1989.

———. *The Wounded Woman: Healing the Father-Daughter Relationship.* Boston: Shambhala, 1998.

Leopold, Aldo. *A Sand County Almanac: Outdoor Essays and Reflections.* Ballantine: New York, 1986.

Lerner, Harriet B. *The Dance of Anger; A Woman's Guide to Changing the Patterns of Intimate Relationships.* New York: HarperCollins, 1985.

——. *The Dance of Fear: Rising Above Anxiety, Fear, and Shame to be Your Best and Bravest Self.* New York: Perennial Currents, 2005

——. *Marriage Rules: A Woman's Guide to Changing the Patterns of Intimate Relationships.* New York: William Morris Paperbacks, 2014.

Lifton, Robert Jay: *The Broken Connection: On Death and the Continuity of Life.* Arlington, Va.: American Psychiatric Publishing, 1996.

——. *The Protean Self: Human Resilience in an Age of Fragmentation.* New York: Basic Books, 1993. A discussion of postmodernism and moral relativism is included in this book.

——. *Witness to an Extreme Century: A Memoir.* New York: Free Press, 2011.

Lifton, Robert Jay and Greg Mitchell: *Hiroshima in America: Fifty Years of Denial.* Part III, Chapter 5: "Commemorating Hiroshima: The Smithsonian Controversy." New York: Grosset, 1995.

Liu, Eric, and Nick Hanauer. *The True Patriot.* Seattle: Sasquatch Books, 2007.

London, Jack. *John Barleycorn: Alcoholic Memoirs.* New York: Oxford University Press, 2009.

Marlantes, Karl. *Matterhorn: A Novel of the Vietnam War.* New York: Atlantic Monthly Press, 2011.

——. *What It Is Like to Go to War.* New York: Atlantic Monthly Press, 2012.

McCullough, David. *John Adams.* New York: Simon & Schuster, 2001.

McGuire, William and R. F. C. Hull, eds. *C. G. Jung Speaking: Interviews and Encounters*—"The Houston Films" [1957], conducted by Richard I. Evans. Bollingen Series XCVII, Princeton: Princeton University Press, 1977.

McKee, Christopher. *A Gentlemanly and Honorable Profession: The Creation of the U.S. Naval Officer Corps 1794–1815* (first edition). Annapolis, Md.: Naval Institute Press, 1991. The profile of John Cassin is by C. E. J. Févret de Saint-Mémin.

Miller, Jean Baker. *Toward a New Psychology of Women.* Boston: Beacon, 1987.

Miller, Brian, and Mike Lapham. *The Self-Made Myth: And the Truth about How Government Helps Individuals and Businesses Succeed.* San Francisco: Berrett-Koehler Publishers, 2012, p. 52.

Miller, Jeffrey. *The Anxious Organization: Why Smart Companies Do Dumb Things* (2nd edition). Tempe, Ari.: Facts on Demand Press, 2008.

Miller, Timothy. *How to Want What You Have: Discovering the Magic and Grandeur of Everyday Existence.* New York: Henry Holt, 1994.

Moore, Thomas. *Care of the Soul: A Guide For Cultivating Depth and Sacredness in Everyday Life.* New York: HarperCollins, 1992.

Morison, Samuel Eliot. *Journals and Other Documents on the Life and Voyages of Christopher Columbus.* New York: Heritage Press, 1993.

Morison, Samuel Eliot, and Henry Steele Commager. *The Growth of the American Republic, Volumes I and II*. Oxford: Oxford University Press, 1942.

Needleman, Jacob. The American Soul: Rediscovering the Wisdom of the Founders. New York: Tarcher/Putnam, 2003.

Nelson, Craig. *Thomas Paine: Enlightenment, Revolution, and the Birth of Modern Nations*. New York: Penguin Books, 2006.

North, Carolyn. *Crop Circles*. Berkeley: Ronin Publishing, 2000.

Obama, Barack. *Dreams from My Father: A Story of Race and Inheritance*. New York: Broadway Books, 2004.

Paris, Ginette. *Dionysos, Hermes, and Goddess Memory in Daily Life*. Woodstock, Ct.: Spring Publications, 1990.

———. *Heartbreak: New Approaches to Healing—Recovering from Lost Love and Mourning*. Minneapolis: Mill City Press, 2011.

———. *Pagan Meditations: The Worlds of Aphrodite, Artemis, and Hestia*. Dallas: Spring Publications, 1986.

———.*Wisdom of the Psyche: Depth Psychology after Neuroscience*. New York: Routledge, 2007.

Peay, Pythia. *American Icarus: A Memoir of Father and Country*. New York: Lantern Books, 2015.

Pinker, Steven. *The Better Angels of Our Nature: Why Violence Has Declined*. New York: Penguin Books, 2012.

Pipher, Mary. *The Green Boat: Reviving Ourselves in Our Capsized Culture*. New York: Riverhead, 2013.

———. *The Middle of Everywhere: Helping Refugees Enter the American Community*. Boston: Mariner Books, 2003.

———.*Reviving Ophelia: Saving the Selves of Adolescent Girls*. New York: Riverhead, 2005.

Reber, Arthur S . *The Penguin Dictionary of Psychology*. New York: Penguin, 1985.

Rossi, Ernest. *The 20 Minute Break: Reduce Stress, Maximize Performance, Improve Health, and Enjoy Well Being Using the New Science of Ultradian Rhythms*. New York: Tarcher, 1991.

Rossi, Ernest, and Kathryn Lane Rossi. *Creating New Consciousness in Everyday Life: The Psycho-Social Genomics of Self Creation*. Pacific Palisades, Calif.: Palisades Gateway Publishing, 2012.

Russell, Dick. *The Life and Ideas of James Hillman: Volume I: The Making of a Psychologist*. New York: Skyhorse Publishing, 2013.

Sale, Kirkpatrick. *The Conquest of Paradise: Christopher Columbus and the Columbian Legacy*. New York: Plume, 1991.

Samuels, Andrew. *The Plural Psyche: Personality, Morality and the Father*. New York: Routledge, 1990.

———. *The Political Psyche*. New York: Routledge, 1993.

———. *Politics on the Couch: Citizenship and the Internal Life*. New York: Other Press, 2001. This book was awarded the Gradiva Prize in 2001 by National Association for the Advancement of Psychoanalysis.

Scott, Janny. *A Singular Woman: The Untold Story of Barack Obama's Mother.* New York: Riverhead, 2012.

Shalit, Erel. *The Complex: Path of Transformation from Archetype to Ego.* Toronto: Inner City Books, 2002.

———. *Enemy, Cripple, & Beggar: Shadows in the Hero's Path.* Skiatook, Okla.: Fisher King Press, 2008.

Shalit, Erel, and Nancy Swift Furlotti, eds. *The Dream and Its Amplification.* Skiatook, Okla.: Fisher King Press, 2013.

Shay, Jonathan. *Achilles in Vietnam: Combat Trauma and the Undoing of Character.* New York: Simon & Schuster, 1995.

Singer, June. *Boundaries of the Soul: The Practice of Jung's Psychology.* New York: Anchor/Doubleday Dell, 1972, 1994.

Singer, Thomas. *Listening to Latin America: Exploring Cultural Complexes in Brazil, Chile, Colombia, Uruguay, and Venezuela.* New Orleans: Spring Journal Books, 2012.

———. *Placing Psyche: Exploring Cultural Complexes in Australia.* New Orleans: Spring Journal Books; 2011.

———., ed. *The Vision Thing: Myth, Politics and Psyche in the World.* London and New York: Routledge, 2000.

Singer, Thomas, and Samuel L. Kimbles, eds. *The Cultural Complex: Contemporary Jungian Perspectives on Psyche and Society.* London and New York: Routledge, 2004.

Slotkin, Richard. *Gunfighter Nation: The Myth of the Frontier in Twentieth-Century America.* New York: Atheneum, 1992.

Smith, Adam. *The Theory of Moral Sentiment.* Economics Classics (EMP), New York: Barnes and Noble, 2013.

Staples, Lawrence S. *The Creative Soul: Art and the Quest for Wholeness.* Carmel, Calif.: Fisher King Press, 2009.

———. *Guilt with a Twist: The Promethean Way.* Carmel, Calif.: Fisher King Press, 2008.

Staples, Lawrence S, and Nancy Pennington Staples. *The Guilt Cure.* Carmel, Calif.: Fisher King Press, 2011.

Stein, Murray. *The Principle of Individuation: Toward the Development of Human Consciousness.* Wilmette, Ill.: Chiron Publications, 2006.

Stein, Murray, and John Hollwitz, eds. *Psyche at Work: Workplace Applications of Jungian Analytical Psychology.* Wilmette, Ill.: Chiron Publications, 1992.

Strozier, Charles B. *Heinz Kohut: The Making of a Psychoanalyst.* New York: Other Press, 2004.

———. *Until the Fires Stopped Burning: 9/11 and New York City in the Words and Experiences of Survivors and Witnesses.* New York: Columbia University Press, 2011.

Tolkien, J. R. R. *The Silmarillion* (edited by Christopher Tolkien). New York: Del Rey, 1985. A collection of stories that describe the "pre-world" background to *The Hobbit* and *The Lord of the Rings.*

Twain, Mark. *Adventures of Huckleberry Finn.* Mineola, N.Y.: Dover Publications, 1994.

Vaillant, George E. *The Natural History of Alcoholism Revisited.* Cambridge: Harvard University Press, 1995.

Veblen, Thorstein. *The Theory of the Leisure Class.* Montclair, N.J.: Dover Publications, 1994.

Wachtel, Paul L. *The Poverty of Affluence: A Psychological Portrait of the American Way of Life.* Philadelphia: New Society Publishers, 1989.

Walant, Karen B. *Creating the Capacity for Attachment: Treating Addictions and the Alienated Self.* Northvale, N.J.: Jason Aronson, 1995.

Watkins, Mary, and Helene Shulman. *Toward Psychologies of Liberation.* New York: Palgrave MacMillan, 2008.

Wood, Gordon S. *The American Revolution: A History.* New York: Modern Library, 2003.

——. *Revolutionary Characters: What Made the Founders Different.* New York: Penguin, 2006.

Woodman, Marion. *The Owl Was a Baker's Daughter: Obesity, Anorexia Nervosa and the Repressed Feminine.* Toronto: Inner City Books, 1980.

Zoja, Luigi. *Growth and Guilt: Psychology and the Limits of Development.* London: Routledge, 1995.

——. *La morte del prossimo* (*The Death of the Neighbor*). Torino: Giulio Einaudi editore, 2009.

——., ed. *Violence in History, Culture, and the Psyche: Essays* (translated by John Peck and Victor-Pierre Stirnimann). New Orleans: Spring Journal Books, 2009.

Film & Television

The African Queen, directed by John Huston (1951). Starring Humphrey Bogart and Katharine Hepburn.

Avatar, directed by James Cameron (2009). Starring Sam Worthington and Zoe Saldana.

Boyhood, directed by Richard Linklater (2014). Starring Ethan Hawke and Patricia Arquette.

Erin Brockovich, directed by Steven Soderbergh (2000). Starring Julia Roberts and Albert Finney.

Forrest Gump, directed by Robert Zemeckis (1994). Starring Tom Hanks and Sally Field.

The Good, The Bad and the Ugly, directed by Sergio Leone (1966). Starring Clint Eastwood and Lee Van Cleef.

The Great Gatsby, directed by Baz Luhrmann (2013). Starring Tobey McGuire and Leonardo DiCaprio.

Gunfight at the O.K. Corral, directed by John Sturges (1957). Starring Burt Lancaster and Kirk Douglas.

High Noon, directed by Fred Zinneman (1952). Starring Gary Cooper and Grace Kelly. A town marshal must face a gang of killers by himself when his town refuses to help him.

Kind of Blue: An Essay on Melancholia and Depression, directed by Mark Kidel (1994). A 52-minute documentary that was the Telluride Film Festival Selection, 1993.

Lincoln, directed by Steven Spielberg (2012). Starring Daniel Day Lewis and Sally Field.

Norma Rae, directed by Martin Ritt (1979). Starring Sally Field and Beau Bridges. A Southern textile worker tries to unionize her mill, despite dangers.

On the Waterfront, directed by Elia Kazan (1954). Starring Marlon Brando and Rod Steiger.

Pulp Fiction, directed by Quentin Tarantino (1994). Starring John Travolta and Uma Thurman. In 2013, the film was selected for the United States National Film Registry by the Library of Congress as being "culturally, historically, or aesthetically significant."

The Right Stuff, directed by Philip Kaufman (1983). Starring Sam Shepard and Ed Harris. It describes the Navy, Marine, and Air force pilots who pioneered the early days of space flight in the United States.

Rio Bravo, directed by Howard Hawks (1959). Starring John Wayne and Dean Martin.

Shane, directed by George Stevens (1953). Starring Alan Ladd and Jean Arthur.

The Simpsons (1989–). Animated sitcom depicting satirically a typical American middle-class family. Created by the cartoonist Matt Groening. Homer Simpson is the father.

About the Author

An author and journalist on psychology, spirituality and the American Psyche, Peay's work over the years has appeared in numerous magazines and newspapers, including *Utne* magazine, *Washingtonian*, Religion News Service, *The Washington Post*, *La Repubblica*, *The Cleveland Plain Dealer*, and past publications such as *George*, *New Woman*, and *Common Boundary*.

A regular contributor to *The Huffington Post*, she writes the America on the Couch blog for Psychology Today, and she has received awards for her work from The American Association of University Women and Women in the Media. Peay is also the author of a memoir of her father, *American Icarus: A Memoir of Father and Country*. In it she tells the iconic American story of Joe Carroll: The larger-than-life but troubled, alcoholic TWA airman and Missouri farmer she'd adored as a girl but had fled as an adult, his dramatic last days and redemptive death through the intervention of a quirky Hospice team, and her discovery of the larger American myths and narratives that shaped his life, and hers. She lives in Washington, D.C.

About the Publisher

✧✧✧

L ANTERN BOOKS was founded in 1999 on the principle of living with a greater depth and commitment to the preservation of the natural world. In addition to publishing books on animal advocacy, vegetarianism, religion, and environmentalism, Lantern is dedicated to printing books in the U.S. on recycled paper and saving resources in day-to-day operations. Lantern is honored to be a recipient of the highest standard in environmentally responsible publishing from the Green Press Initiative.

WWW.LANTERNBOOKS.COM